lonely planet

Thailand's Islands & Beaches

Bangkok p66

Ko Chang & the Eastern Seaboard p118

Hua Hin & the Upper Gulf p160

Ko Samui & the Lower Gulf p193

Phuket & the Andaman Coast p263

PLAN YOUR TRIP

ON THE ROAD

CATHERINE SUTHERLAND / LONELY PLANET ©

KO PHI-PHI DON P333

ANEKOHO / SHUTTERSTOCK ©

KAYAKING IN KO KUT P155

PANATFOTO / SHUTTERSTOCK ©

SNORKELLING IN KO CHANG P146

Contents

Welcome to Thailand's Islands & Beaches

With white-sand bays, technicolour coral reefs and jungle-covered karst formations emerging from turquoise seas, Thailand's islands and beaches are everyone's dream of a tropical paradise.

Best Beach Ever

Thailand's beaches are legendary. Palms angle over soft white sand, warm turquoise seas conceal colourful coral gardens, and beach parties beckon everyone to let their hair down. With two long coastlines and jungle-topped islands anchored in azure waters, Thailand embraces the hedonist and the hermit, the luxury lover and the budget backpacker. Scale Krabi's sheer sea cliffs, dive with whale sharks off Ko Tao and the Surin Islands, toe the curling tide alongside Trang's gypsy fishermen, stroll Ko Lipe's crescent beaches, feast at Hua Hin's sizzling seafood stalls or delight in luxury Phuket digs. The choice is yours.

Outdoor Adventures

Thailand's natural beauty is all the more intoxicating for the different ways it can be savoured. From white-knuckle jungle ziplines and river rafting, to seaside horse rides and stand-up paddleboarding, Thailand's activities menu is endlessly exhilarating. Outdoor lovers can hike sultry jungles in Ko Chang and Khao Sok National Parks, kitesurf off Phuket, Ko Lipe, Ko Samui and Hua Hin, practise yoga on Ko Lanta and Ko Samui, kayak past Ao Phang-Nga's limestone spires, rock climb Railay, and dive deep under the blue sea across the South.

Yummy Thailand

Beaches may bring you to Thailand, but it's often the food that lures you back and then sends you in search of it when you return home. Thai cuisine embodies the country's culture: generous and warm, outgoing and nuanced, refreshing and relaxed, delicate and surprising. With its tropical bounty, the varied national menu twirls around four fundamental flavours: spicy, sweet, salty and sour. And it's exquisitely hot and salty in the seafood-focused south. Dishes build on fresh, local ingredients, from pungent lemongrass, juicy yellow mangoes and searing chillies to just-caught seafood, plump tofu and crispy fried chicken.

Sun-Kissed Smiles

Whether it's the glimmering eye of the meditative *wâi* (the palms-together Thai greeting) or the joyful grin of passers-by, it's hard not to be charmed by the Land of Smiles. Thailand has long been Southeast Asia's most friendly country, inviting travellers from near and far to indulge in the kingdom's natural splendours. While development has had an impact on Thailand's beauty, the welcome is still as delightful as ever and on the islands and beaches you're still greeted by a heady mix of sparkling seascapes, limestone towers and equatorial sunshine.

Why I Love Thailand's Islands & Beaches

By David Eimer, Writer

It's obvious why Thailand's islands and beaches are superstars in the world of travel, but what I love best about this region is the welcome you get from the locals. Everyone is so quick to smile, and that unconditional delight means this is a place where everyone can fit in, whatever their tastes or personal travel style. I can also never get enough of floating in that turquoise sea, exulting in the tropical breezes and watching the sun go down, before enjoying a cold beer and some of the most delicious seafood you'll ever taste.

For more about our writers, see p448

Above: Ko Phing Kan (James Bond Island; p285)

Thailand's Islands & Beaches

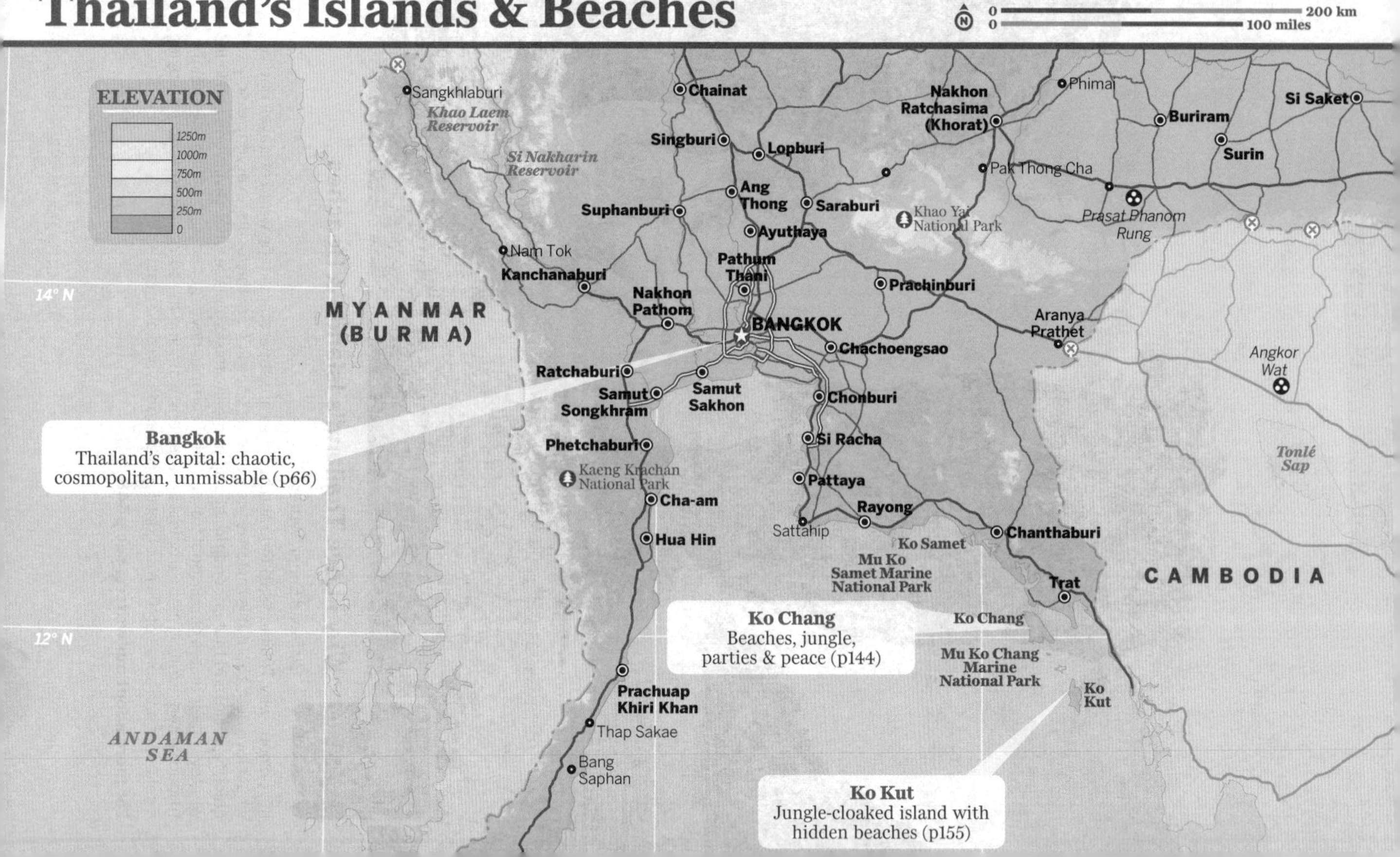

ELEVATION
1250m
1000m
750m
500m
250m
0

Sangkhlaburi
Khao Laem Reservoir
Si Nakharin Reservoir
Nam Tok
Kanchanaburi
Chainat
Singburi
Lopburi
Ang Thong
Suphanburi
Saraburi
Ayuthaya
Pathum Thani
Nakhon Pathom
BANGKOK
Nakhon Ratchasima (Khorat)
Phimai
Pak Thong Cha
Khao Yai National Park
Prasat Phanom Rung
Buriram
Surin
Si Saket
Prachinburi
Aranya Prathet
Chachoengsao
Angkor Wat
Tonlé Sap
14° N
MYANMAR (BURMA)
Ratchaburi
Samut Songkhram
Samut Sakhon
Chonburi
Si Racha
Pattaya
Phetchaburi
Kaeng Krachan National Park
Cha-am
Hua Hin
Sattahip
Rayong
Ko Samet
Mu Ko Samet Marine National Park
Chanthaburi
Trat
CAMBODIA
Ko Chang
Mu Ko Chang Marine National Park
Ko Kut
12° N
Prachuap Khiri Khan
Thap Sakae
Bang Saphan
ANDAMAN SEA

Bangkok
Thailand's capital: chaotic, cosmopolitan, unmissable (p66)

Ko Chang
Beaches, jungle, parties & peace (p144)

Ko Kut
Jungle-cloaked island with hidden beaches (p155)

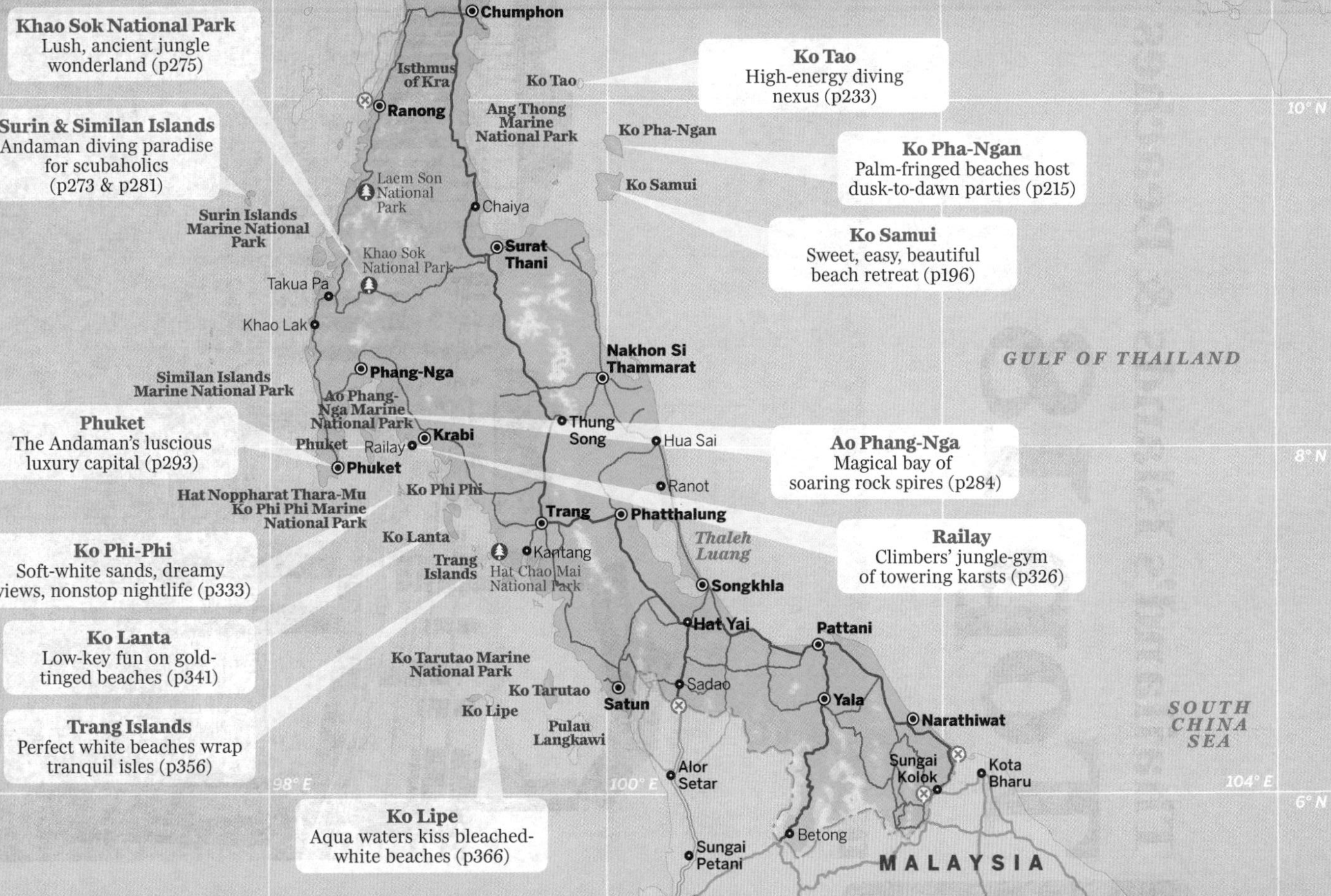

Khao Sok National Park
Lush, ancient jungle wonderland (p275)
Surin & Similan Islands
Andaman diving paradise for scubaholics (p273 & p281)
Phuket
The Andaman's luscious luxury capital (p293)
Ko Phi-Phi
Soft-white sands, dreamy views, nonstop nightlife (p333)
Ko Lanta
Low-key fun on gold-tinged beaches (p341)
Trang Islands
Perfect white beaches wrap tranquil isles (p356)
Ko Lipe
Aqua waters kiss bleached-white beaches (p366)
Ko Tao
High-energy diving nexus (p233)
Ko Pha-Ngan
Palm-fringed beaches host dusk-to-dawn parties (p215)
Ko Samui
Sweet, easy, beautiful beach retreat (p196)
Ao Phang-Nga
Magical bay of soaring rock spires (p284)
Railay
Climbers' jungle-gym of towering karsts (p326)
Chumphon
Isthmus of Kra
Ranong
Ko Tao
Ang Thong Marine National Park
Ko Pha-Ngan
Ko Samui
Laem Son National Park
Chaiya
Surin Islands Marine National Park
Surat Thani
Khao Sok National Park
Takua Pa
Khao Lak
Nakhon Si Thammarat
Phang-Nga
Similan Islands Marine National Park
Ao Phang-Nga Marine National Park
Thung Song
Krabi
Hua Sai
Phuket
Railay
Phuket
Ranot
Hat Noppharat Thara-Mu Ko Phi Phi Marine National Park
Ko Phi Phi
Trang
Phatthalung
Ko Lanta
Thaleh Luang
Kantang
Trang Islands
Hat Chao Mai National Park
Songkhla
Hat Yai
Pattani
Ko Tarutao Marine National Park
Ko Tarutao
Sadao
Satun
Yala
Ko Lipe
Narathiwat
Pulau Langkawi
Alor Setar
Sungai Kolok
Kota Bharu
Betong
Sungai Petani
MALAYSIA
GULF OF THAILAND
SOUTH CHINA SEA
10° N
8° N
6° N
98° E
100° E
104° E

Thailand's Islands & Beaches Top 18

1

Island-Hopping in Trang

1 The honeylike morning sun casts shadows across another green-cloaked isle rising out of the blue. All you can hear is the motor of the weather-beaten long-tail boat, adorned with multicoloured cloth bands that frame the scene. Your next island-hopping stop is that brilliantly white beach in the distance – one of many to explore, snorkel and hike from. It might be beach-chic Ko Ngai (pictured below; p356), shimmering Ko Kradan or popular Ko Muk, but the boat ride is so extraordinarily gorgeous that it's just as delightful as your dreamy Trang Islands (p354) destination.

Rock Climbing in Railay

2 Whether you're an expert or have never grabbed a notch hole in your life, the Railay (p326) rock-climbing world will have you scrambling skywards with excitement. Over 1000 routes on limestone walls deliver unbeatable vistas across some of the world's most spectacular scenery – vertical rock spires draped in greenery, surrounded by crystalline sea and luscious beaches – and even the shortest jaunt guarantees thrills. Seasoned climbers stay for months. For the ultimate adventure, try deep-water soloing: climbs ending with a splash into the water below. When you're done, mellow reggae bars await.

JAKGREE / GETTY IMAGES ©

2

SOMPORN SUEBHAIT / SHUTTERSTOCK ©

Solitude on Ko Kut

3 Thailand's fourth-largest island and eastern island frontier is an easygoing verdant canvas of dense jungle hemmed by silky pristine beaches – perfect for uninterrupted afternoons of sun worshipping or slow kayaking and snorkelling, and calm evenings blissfully free of throbbing sound systems. Although the topography of Ko Kut (p155) is similar to that of many other Thai islands, with rainforest and waterfalls hidden deep within, its location on the southern tip of the Ko Chang archipelago means that the coastal waters glimmer with a unique emerald tint.

Ko Pha-Ngan

4 World-famous for its debauched Full Moon Parties (pictured right) and all-night electronic madness, Ko Pha-Ngan (p215) long ago graduated from sleepy bohemian island to full-on attraction pulling in travellers of all types. The beach shanties are turning more boutique, so comfort seekers and families have an alternative to Ko Samui. And on the northern and eastern coasts, hammock hangers can still escape enough to feel like a modern-day castaway – but a well-fed one, of course. Just offshore is Sail Rock, one of the gulf's best dive sites, which is visited by elusive whale sharks.

3

Ang Thong Marine National Park

5 When Alex Garland wrote his novel *The Beach* (which later became a movie starring Leonardo DiCaprio), he must have been thinking about Ang Thong Marine National Park (p247). Known as Mu Ko Ang Thong in Thai, this stunning archipelago contains 42 small islands featuring sheer limestone cliffs, hidden lagoons, perfect peach-coloured beaches and an interesting menagerie of tropical creatures. You can dive, snorkel, kayak and hike on these pristine islands, which are best explored on a day trip from Ko Samui or Ko Pha-Ngan.

6

7

Beautiful Ko Phi-Phi

6 One of Thailand's most recognisable characters, Ko Phi-Phi (p333) deserves all the praise and criticism it receives. Stunning turquoise waters, salt-white beaches and soaring limestone cliffs make it ideal for diving, hiking, snorkelling or just soaking up the scenery while you roast on the beach. After dark, Phi-Phi morphs into a hedonistic party haven, with daredevil fire dancers and energetic revellers slugging super-sweet cocktail buckets. Hangovers are inevitable, but there are plenty of sandy stretches and island cruises to recover on until the next round.

Diving in Ko Tao

7 Thailand's diving headquarters, Ko Tao (p233) is still the cheapest and easiest spot in the region to learn how to strap on a tank and dive into the deep. The water is gentle and bathtub-warm, and the submarine visuals are not to be missed. Just offshore, scenic rocky coves and shallow coral reefs frequented by all manner of fish provide a snorkelling 'aperitif'. Ko Tao's small size means you can easily explore all of its jungly nooks and crannies when you need a break from diving.

Ko Lanta

8 Even a short wander off the gorgeous tourist beaches of Ko Lanta (p341) is a ticket to a wonderland of friendly Muslim fishing villages, unexplored coves and gentle jungle scenery. Don't miss Ban Si Raya, with its century-old stilted houses and artsy shops, on the still tranquil and authentic east coast. For natural beauty, Mu Ko Lanta National Park (pictured above) is hard to beat, and there are plenty of caves and lovely blonde beaches en route. Add to this good diving and snorkelling, yoga and a chilled-out nightlife scene.

Ko Lipe's Beaches

9 Ko Lipe (p366) beguiles with its fantastic beaches. On the south coast, Hat Pattaya is a perfect arc of alabaster sand with long-tail boats bobbing in its azure bay and busy seafood barbecues and laid-back beach bars dotted along the foreshore. Soft, blonde Hat Sunrise is equally exquisite, stretching along the east coast until it curves at the sight of majestic Ko Adang across the blue. If you tire of these fabulous but busy beaches, take jungle-shrouded trails to wilder Hat Sunset and hidden swaths of sand. Offshore, stellar dive sites shine in the early monsoon.

MATTHEW WAKEM / GETTY IMAGES ©

Ko Yao Islands

10 Shhh, it's only about an hour from Phuket Town to the serene banks of the low-key Ko Yao islands (p286) that float, like a silent neighbour, right in the heart of stunning Ao Phang-Nga. Swap bars and beach clubs for subdued Muslim fishing communities and quiet sunrises over outlying limestone isles. One of the region's most luxurious resorts is found here, but mostly the islands are a place for simpler, eco-friendly resorts where you can lay your head after days of diving, rock climbing and mountain biking. Yoga class on Ko Yao Noi (p286)

Luxury in Phuket

11 Loved for its luxury resorts, plush beach clubs, chic boutiques and Patong's after-hours nightlife, Phuket (p288) has many more attractions than the clichés suggest. Stroll past incense-cloaked shrines and beautiful restored Sino-Portugese buildings in Phuket Town (pictured above), dig in to local history in Thalang, hike the jungles of Khao Phra Thaew Royal Wildlife & Forest Reserve, join a cooking class, go diving, or try surfing or kitesurfing during low season. For beach lounging away from the buzz, head to northern beaches like Hat Nai Thon or south to Laem Phanwa.

Kayaking in Ao Phang-Nga

12 While other visitors squeeze onto speedboats for glimpses of the spectacular limestone-tower-studded bay of Ao Phang-Nga Marine National Park (p285), early-morning sea-kayakers enjoy it in slow silence. Glide past sea caves inscribed with prehistoric rock art, picnic on secluded beaches, swim in silky water and, if you like, stay overnight at the stilted Muslim village clinging to Ko Panyi. At nightfall, become enchanted with the bay's famed bioluminescence. Top right: Canoeing in Ao Phang-Nga near Tham Lod Cave (p284)

Khao Sok National Park

13 Escape inland to the jungle-coated hills and low-slung valleys of the South's most beloved national park (p275). Roam dirt trails below verdant canopies to multilevel waterfalls, sky-reaching limestone towers and explorable caves, your eyes peeled for local inhabitants that include bears, bats, gibbons, wild elephants, the odd tiger and the elusive Rafflesia kerrii, one of the planet's most pungent flowers. A one-of-a-kind Khao Sok highlight involves overnighting atop dramatic Chiaw Lan Lake in floating huts (pictured right).

Ko Chang

14 The rugged landscape of Ko Chang (p144) conceals some of Southeast Asia's best-preserved wilderness. Its mountainous interior holds a real-life Jurassic Park that stars exotic reptiles, colourful birds and lumbering elephants. The hills are cut by waterfalls, and plenty of guides are available to help you explore the abounding biodiversity on jungle hikes. Although developers have bagged all the beachfront real estate and there's a lively party scene, sand-fringed nooks in the east and south still feel decidedly off the beaten path. Top: Snorkelling off Ko Chang (p146)

Underwater in the Similan & Surin Islands

15 The marine national parks of the Similan and Surin Islands are two of Thailand's treasures. Largely untouched by development, they're home to white-sand beaches and rainforested interiors. But it's the offshore attractions that are the real draw here. Superbly clear water make these islands two of the best places in Thailand to delve into the underwater world. Divers will want to head to the Similans (p281), especially Ko Bon and Ko Tachai, while snorkellers will be in paradise off the Surin Islands. Bottom: Diving in the Similan Islands (p281)

14

15

ALEKSANDAR TODOROVIC / SHUTTERSTOCK ©

HAFIZ JOHARI / SHUTTERSTOCK ©

Live-Aboard Cruising to Richelieu Rock

16 The world-renowned dive sites dotting the crystal seas of the Surin and Similan Islands Marine National Parks are some of the best spots in the country to get underwater. The ultimate prize, however, is distant Richelieu Rock (pictured; p274), a citadel of limestone spires that jut up from 40m deep. About 200km northwest of Phuket and accessible only to those who venture north towards the so-called Burma Banks on a live-aboard diving trip, the unique outcrop acts as a feeding station luring manta rays and whale sharks.

Ko Samui

17 Eager to please Ko Samui (p196) is a civilised beach-resort island for the holidaying masses, many of whom fly in and out and rarely leave the confines of their resort to engage with the local culture. But peel yourself off your sun-lounger and venture away from your resort and you'll be rewarded with sleepier beaches and coves to the south and west, which recall Samui's old moniker, 'Coconut Island'. Swim in waterfalls, explore the thriving wellness scene with its myriad yoga, meditation and detox retreats, and stop by a temple or two. Top right: Wat Plai Laem (p196)

Bangkok

18 Setting aside a few days for Thailand's frenzied, cosmopolitan capital adds another dimension to your islands and beaches tour. Among its most atmospheric neighbourhoods, the artificial island of Ko Ratanakosin is the birthplace of modern Bangkok (p66) and home to the bulk of the city's must-see sights, such as Wat Pho and Wat Phra Kaew, with its stunning Emerald Buddha. And then there are the sweaty street-side food markets, sophisticated skyscraper bars, shiny mega-malls, a buzzing Chinatown and the seemingly endless Chatuchak Weekend Market to explore.

Need to Know

For more information, see Survival Guide (p411)

Currency
Thai baht (B)

Language
Thai

Visas
Thirty-day visas for international air arrivals; 15-day visas at land borders (30 days if you hold a passport from a G7 country).

Money
Most places in Thailand deal only with cash. Some foreign credit cards are accepted in high-end establishments.

Mobile Phones
Thailand is on a GSM network; inexpensive prepaid SIM cards are available. Bangkok, major cities and the more populated islands have 4G.

Time
GMT/UTC plus seven hours

When to Go

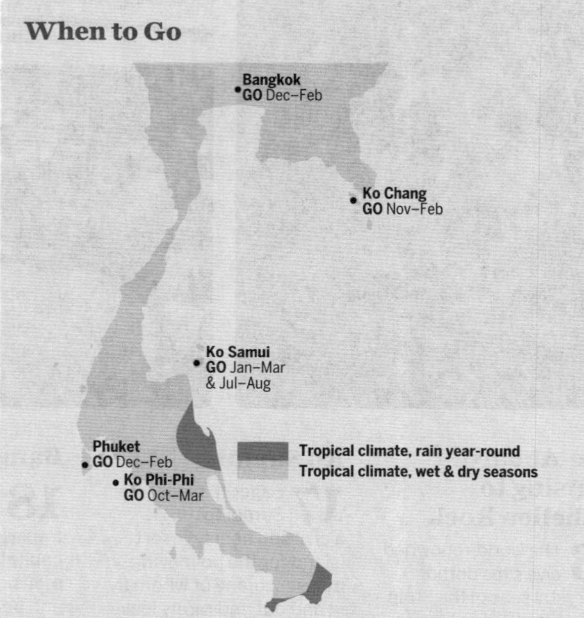

High Season (Nov–Mar)

➡ A cool, dry season follows the monsoon, meaning lush landscapes and comfortable temperatures.

➡ Christmas and both Western and Chinese New Year holidays bring crowds and inflated accommodation rates.

Shoulder Season (Apr–Jun)

➡ Generally very hot and dry, with an average temperature of 30°C (86°F), but the sea breeze provides plenty of natural air-con.

Low Season (Jul–Oct)

➡ The Andaman and gulf coasts take turns being pummelled by monsoon rains.

➡ Weather is generally favourable along the southern gulf in July and August.

➡ Some islands shut down and boats are limited during stormy weather.

Useful Websites

Tourism Authority of Thailand (TAT; www.tourismthailand.org) National tourism department covering info and special events.

Thaivisa (www.thaivisa.com) Expat site with useful forum.

Lonely Planet (www.lonelyplanet.com/thailand) Destination information, hotel bookings, traveller forum and more.

Thai Language (www.thai-language.com) Online dictionary and Thai tutorials.

Thai Travel Blogs (www.thaitravelblogs.com) Thailand-based travel blogger.

Important Numbers

Thailand's country code	66
Emergency	191
International access codes	001, 007, 008, 009 (different service providers)
Operator-assisted international calls	100
Tourist police	1155

Exchange Rates

Australia	A$1	24B
Canada	C$1	24B
China	Y10	49B
Euro	€1	38B
Japan	¥100	29B
New Zealand	NZ$1	23B
Russia	R10	5B
UK	£1	44B
USA	US$1	31B

For current exchange rates, visit www.xe.com.

Daily Costs

Budget: Less than 2000B

- Dorm bed or basic guesthouse room: 300–1000B
- Market and street-stall meals: 40–100B
- Small bottle of beer: 80B
- Motorcycle taxi or short long-tail boat ride: 40–200B

Midrange: 2000–5000B

- Flashpacker guesthouse or midrange hotel room: 1000–3000B
- Western lunches and seafood dinners: 250–500B
- Snorkelling tour: 1500–2000B
- Motorbike hire: 200–250B per day

Top end: More than 5000B

- Boutique hotel room: from 3000B
- Meal at fine-dining restaurant: from 500B
- Spa treatments: from 500B
- Car hire: from 1200B per day

Opening Hours

Banks 9.30am–3.30pm Monday–Friday; ATMs 24 hours

Bars 6pm–midnight or 1am

Clubs 8pm–2am

Government offices 8.30am–4.30pm Monday–Friday; some close for lunch (noon–1pm), while others are open Saturday (9am–3pm)

Restaurants 10am–10pm; some shops specialise in morning meals and close by 3pm

Shops Local shops 9am–6pm daily; department stores 10am–10pm daily. In some small towns, local stores close on Sunday. 7-Elevens stay open 24 hours.

Arriving in Thailand

Suvarnabhumi International Airport (p422) Metered taxis (220B to 380B) take about an hour to the city. Public buses run to central Bangkok (40B, frequent from 5am to 10pm). The airport rail link (45B, 30 minutes, 6am to midnight) local service runs to Phaya Thai station every 15 minutes; the express service runs to Makkasan or Phaya Thai stations.

Don Mueang International Airport (p422) Metered taxis (200B to 220B) take 30 minutes to one hour to the city. Air-conditioned buses take one to two hours to Th Khao San (150B, 10am to 1am); shuttles (30B, 8.30am to 11pm) run half-hourly between the airport and Mo Chit BTS station (20 minutes) and Victory Monument (30 minutes). Trains run to Hualamphong train station (5B to 20B, 45 minutes) every one to 1½ hours from 4am to 11.30am and then roughly every hour from 2pm to 9.30pm.

Getting Around

Planes, trains, buses and boats easily whisk you to the south. Or you can fly directly to Phuket or Ko Samui from abroad rather than connecting through Bangkok.

Air Increasing numbers of flights and destinations, but can be expensive.

Bus & minivan Lots of options; cheap and efficient.

Train Cheap and comfortable, but less reliable than buses.

Boat Everything from big, slow ferries to fast, private long-tails or flashy speedboats.

Rentals Vehicle hire is available in every town.

For much more on **getting around**, see p424

First Time Thailand's Islands & Beaches

For more information, see Survival Guide (p411)

Checklist

- Make sure your passport is valid for at least six months.
- Inform your debit/credit card company of your travels.
- Visit the Thai consulate for a tourist visa for stays of more than 30 days.
- Organise travel and diver's insurance.
- Check baggage restrictions.
- Go for a check-up and medical clearance if you want to go diving.

What to Pack

- Thai phrasebook
- power converter
- waterproof sunscreen
- mosquito repellent with DEET
- anti-itch cream (for sandfly bites)
- light, long-sleeve shirt
- breathable pants
- hat
- sunglasses
- comfortable sandals
- torch/headlamp

Top Tips for Your Trip

- If you rent a vehicle (especially a motorbike or jet ski), take pictures of it before use. This may shield you from the rife rental scam of accusing tourists of damaging already beaten-up vehicles.
- If booking accommodation online, make sure you know exactly where your hotel is located. Many 'great deals' end up being out in the middle of nowhere. Pay upfront for as few nights as possible so you can leave without having to haggle your money back.
- Don't lose your cool, even in the most difficult situations. Thais greatly respect a 'cool heart', and shouting or anger will only escalate a situation, never to your benefit.
- Avoid conversations that involve the monarchy or politics.

What to Wear

Light, loose-fitting clothes will prove the most comfortable in the tropical heat throughout the year. Bring one reasonably warm jacket for the odd cool evening (or the blasting air-con on the buses and planes). For visiting temples, you will need shirts or tops with long sleeves and full-length pants. While sandals or flip-flops are the way to go on the islands, you should bring one smarter pair of shoes for the occasional night out in the big cities (ordinary sandals are not permitted in many of Bangkok's sky bars, for example).

Sleeping

Resorts Range from villas with their own swimming pools and butlers, to bamboo shacks cooled by sea breezes.

Guesthouses These are still prevalent, despite the growing number of resorts. They may lack amenities but come with low price tags and helpful service.

Hostels Tend to be found on islands that attract backpackers.

Taxes & Refunds

Thailand has a 7% value-added tax (VAT) on many goods and services. Midrange and top-end hotels and restaurants might also add a 10% service tax. When the two are combined this becomes the 17% hit known as 'plus plus', or '++'.

You can get a refund on VAT paid on shopping, though not on food or hotels, as you leave the country. For how-to info, visit www.rd.go.th.

Bargaining

Bargaining forms the crux of almost any commercial interaction in Thailand.

- If you're purchasing something, it's best to buy in bulk – the more T-shirts you buy, the lower the price will go. Always keep it light-hearted.
- Don't bargain in restaurants, 7-Elevens and petrol stations.
- Don't haggle for a better price at high-end hotels, though bargaining is fair game at most beach establishments.

Tipping

Tipping is not generally expected in Thailand. The exception is loose change from a large restaurant bill; if a meal costs 488B and you pay with a 500B note, some Thais will leave the 12B change. It's a way of saying 'I'm not so money grubbing as to grab every last baht'. At many hotel restaurants and upmarket eateries, a 10% service charge will be added to your bill.

RMNUNES / GETTY IMAGES ©

Yaksha statue, Wat Phra Kaew (p68)

Etiquette

Thais are generally very understanding and hospitable, but there are some important taboos and social conventions.

Saving face The best way to win over the Thais is to smile (p392) – visible anger or arguing is embarrassing; the locals call this 'loss of face'.

Temples When visiting a temple, dress neatly and conservatively with shoulders to knees covered. Remove all footwear before entering. Sit with your feet tucked behind you, so they are not facing the Buddha image. Women may not touch monks or their belongings.

At the beach Avoid public nudity; in fact, many Thais swim fully clothed. Away from the sand, men should wear shirts and women should wear a cover-up over swimwear.

Royal respect It is a criminal offence to disrespect the royal family; treat objects depicting the king (like money) with respect.

Body language Avoid touching anyone on the head and be careful where you point your feet; they're the lowest part of the body literally and metaphorically.

Eating

There's seafood galore on Thailand's islands and beaches, as well as all your usual delicious Thai curries, salads and stir-fries, and an ever-increasing range of international food.

For more information, see p52.

What's New

Phuket Elephant Sanctuary

Phuket's excellent elephant sanctuary has quickly become one of the island's top destinations, offering the chance to feed the elephants and watch them bathe and hang out in their forest retirement home. (p322)

Pattaya–Hua Hin Catamaran

A new daily fast catamaran service connects Pattaya and Hua Hin. The service runs year-round, cutting the journey time between the two popular resort towns to a mere two hours.

Charming Chanthaburi

Sleepy Chanthaburi is transforming itself into a cool new destination, with the wooden shophouses in the charismatic riverfront area home to hip cafes and hotels. Nearby are still little-known beaches. (p137)

Freedive Ko Tao

Already the number one spot to learn how to dive in the islands, Ko Tao is fast becoming Thailand's freediving hub too, with schools galore to show you how to dive 20m down just by holding your breath. (p233)

Ko Lanta Bridge

The bridge linking Ko Lanta Noi with Ko Lanta Yai has finally opened, meaning no more queuing for ferries and cutting journey times from Krabi to lovely Lanta dramatically. (p341)

Still No Airport

Ko Pha-Ngan is still waiting for its partially completed airport to open, as new investors are sought for the project. If they get the extra cash, then it will take another year to finish construction. (p215)

On & Off the Grid

Twenty-four-hour electricity has reached Ko Phayam (p270), so there are no more reading-by-torchlight evenings when the power goes. But the climber/hippie beach of Hat Ton Sai (p326) on Railay is still without electricity much of the time.

Earlier to Bed Samui

Bars and clubs on Ko Samui are shutting by 1am as the police crack down on all-night partying, although the policy isn't being applied all the time. (p196)

Grab App on Phuket

The Grab App (www.grab.com/th/en) is available all over Thailand, but is especially useful on Phuket for beating the local taxi mafia. Now taxis can be ordered where and whenever you like, and they use their meters, resulting in much cheaper rides.

For more recommendations and reviews, see **lonelyplanet.com/thailand/thailand-s-islands-beaches**

If You Like...

Beaches

The days of having paradise to yourself may be gone, but Thailand's beaches remain some of the most stupendous on Earth.

Ko Kut Kilometres of unpopulated sand arc around lonely Ko Kut. Hat Khlong Chao is particularly dreamy. (p155)

Trang Islands Different shades of turquoise sea fringe bleach-blonde beaches and limestone karsts across this alluring archipelago. (p354)

Ko Pha-Ngan The original beach-bum island hosts wild Full Moon Parties, plus hammock-hanging on northern beaches. (p215)

Ko Lipe Crystal-white sand on Hat Pattaya and Hat Sunrise brings out the beach addict in everyone. (p366)

Great Food

Street stalls spring up out of nowhere, night markets serve up dinner, family restaurants offer traditional favourites and high-end fusion cuisine blends it all together.

Bangkok The entire spectrum of Thai eats, from street-side noodle soup to celebrity-chef-driven gastronomy. (p66)

Hua Hin Seafood meets a night market geared towards Thai tourists: crab curry, mussel omelettes and giant prawns. (p170)

Trang Famed for roast pork, dim sum, filtered-coffee shops and the Andaman Coast's star night market. (p352)

Phuket Town Classy, fantastic-value fusion Thai served in restored Sino-Portuguese buildings, plus sensational street and market food. (p293)

Diving & Snorkelling

The clear waters of the Gulf of Thailand and the Andaman Sea harbour a variety of underwater landscapes and marine species that rank Thailand among the world's top diving destinations.

Surin & Similan Islands Marine National Parks With some of the world's top diving and snorkelling spots, these Andaman islands have dramatic rocky gorges, hard and soft coral reefs and hordes of marine life. (p273; p281)

Ko Lanta Nearby feeding stations for manta rays, whale sharks and other large pelagic fish earn this Andaman island high diving marks. (p341)

Ko Tao Affordable dive schools, shallow waters and year-round conditions, Ko Tao is the kingdom's scuba-training island. (p233)

Adventure Sports

Thailand has plenty of diving sites, but you'll find just as many blood-pumping thrills without strapping on a tank.

Rock climbing, Railay The Andaman's signature limestone towers peak dramatically in Railay. Join hundreds of climbers dangling up high. (p326)

Kitesurfing off Phuket, Krabi, Ko Samui & Hua Hin Steady winds and shallow waters make these coasts ideal for tackling this increasingly popular sport. (p291; p322; p196; p170)

Hiking, Khao Sok National Park Wind through jungled hills to gushing waterfalls, keeping your eyes open for unique local wildlife. (p275)

Sea kayaking, Ao Phang-Nga Paddle through calm waters in kayak comfort, gazing up at jagged stone piercing the clouds above. (p285)

Surfing, Kata Yai The low-season waves at this Phuket beach are ideal for beginners. The break at Hat Bang Sak on the mainland Andaman Coast is also one to try. (p310)

Five-Star Pampering

Thailand's larger islands house some of the world's glitziest five-star properties (and a few are surprisingly affordable).

Point Yamu by Como A parade of upmarket accommodation graces Phuket's white-fringed coastline, such as this exclusive east-coast place. (p322)

Six Senses Samui No one does sustainable luxury like this exquisitely private Ko Samui resort. (p208)

Rayavadee A serene beachfront property on Railay where you're surrounded by nature. (p328)

Peninsula Hotel Intense competition keeps prices fairly low in Bangkok, so splurge on a capital luxury headliner like this one. (p93)

Back to Basics

Although numbers are dwindling, there are still cheap beachside bamboo bungalows in Thailand, with just a terrace, bed, cold shower and mosquito net.

Ko Phayam Despite some development, Ko Phayam revels in its barefoot-beach-shack vibe, embodied by Aow Yai Bungalows. (p270)

Ko Pha-Ngan There are still some nooks on Ko Pha-Ngan that are mostly development-free, including Chalok Lam. (p215)

Ko Wai Laze in Ko Wai Paradise bungalows on this fleck of white sand in the Ko Chang Archipelago. (p158)

Ko Chang (Ranong) This beachy slice of jungle-clad hippiedom near the Myanmar border is slow to change. (p269)

Top: Hiking in Khao Sok National Park (p275)

Bottom: Seafood dish with giant prawns, Hua Hin

Month by Month

TOP EVENTS

Songkran, April

King's Birthday, July

Vegetarian Festival, October

Loi Krathong, November

Full Moon Party, Monthly

January

The weather is cool and dry in Thailand, ushering in the peak tourist season when Europeans escape dreary winter weather.

Chinese New Year

Thais with Chinese ancestry celebrate the Chinese lunar new year (dates vary) with a week of house-cleaning and fireworks. Phuket, Bangkok and Pattaya all host citywide festivities, but in general Chinese New Year *(đrùt jeen)* is a family event. This is a peak time for Chinese tourists to come to Thailand.

February

Still in high-season swing, Thailand sees yet more escapees from the northern hemisphere chill arriving for sun and fun.

Flower Festival

Chiang Mai displays its floral beauty during a three-day period. The festival highlight is the flower-decorated floats that are paraded through town.

Makha Bucha

One of three holy days marking significant moments of Buddha's life, Makha Bucha *(mah·ká boo·chah)* commemorates the day when 1250 *arhats* (saints) assembled to visit Buddha and received the principles of Buddhism. The festival falls on the full moon of the third lunar month and is a public holiday.

March

The hot and dry season approaches, and the beaches start to empty. The winds kick up swells, ushering in the kiteboarding season. This is also Thailand's semester break, and students head out on sightseeing trips.

Golden Mango Season

Luscious, ripe mangoes come into season from March to June and are sliced before your eyes, packed in containers with sticky rice and accompanied with a sweet sauce.

Kite-Flying Festivals

During the windy season, colourful kites battle it out over the skies of Sanam Luang in Bangkok and elsewhere in the country.

Pattaya International Music Festival

Pattaya showcases pop and rock bands from across Asia at this free music event, attracting busloads of Bangkok university students.

April

Hot, dry weather sweeps in as the tourist season winds down, except for one last hurrah during Songkran, when the whole country is on the move.

Poi Sang Long

This colourful Buddhist novice ordination festival held in late March/early April in Mae Hong Son and Chiang Mai sees young Shan (Tai Yai) boys between the ages of seven and 14 parading in festive costumes, headdresses and make-up.

Songkran

Thailand's traditional new year (mid-April) starts with morning visits to the temple. Afterwards everyone loads up their water guns and heads out to the streets for battle: water is thrown and sprayed from roving commandos at targets both willing and unwilling.

May

Leading up to the rainy season, festivals encourage plentiful rains and bountiful harvests. Prices are lower and tourists are few, but there's still plenty of sun.

Rocket Festival

In the northeast, where rain can be scarce, villagers craft painted bamboo rockets *(bâng fai)* that are fired into the sky to encourage precipitation. This festival is celebrated in Yasothon, Ubon Ratchathani and Nong Khai.

Royal Ploughing Ceremony

This royal ceremony employs astrology and ancient Brahman rituals to kick off the rice-planting season. Sacred oxen are hitched to a wooden plough and part the ground of Sanam Luang in Bangkok. The ritual was revived by the late king in the 1960s.

Visakha Bucha

Visakha Bucha (on the full moon of the sixth lunar month in May or June) is considered the date of the Buddha's birth, enlightenment and *parinibbana* (passing away). Activities are centred on the local wát,

Top: Loi Krathong

Bottom: Songkran

with candlelit processions, chanting and sermonising.

June

In some parts of the region, the rainy season is merely an afternoon shower, leaving the rest of the day for music and merriment.

Hua Hin Jazz Festival

Jazz groups descend on this royal retreat for a musical homage to the late King Rama IX, who was an accomplished jazz saxophonist and composer. Sometimes held in May. (p173)

Phi Ta Khon

The Buddhist holy day of Bun Phra Wet is given a carnival makeover in Dan Sai village in northeast Thailand. Revellers disguise themselves in garish 'spirit' costumes and parade through the streets wielding wooden phalluses and downing rice whisky. Dates vary between June and July.

July

With the start of the rainy season, the religious community and attendant festivals prepare for Buddhist Lent, a period of reflection and meditation.

Asahna Bucha

The full moon of the eighth lunar month commemorates Buddha's first sermon. Khao Phansaa, also called Buddhist Lent, begins the day after.

Khao Phansaa

Buddhist Lent (the first day of the waning moon in the eighth lunar month) is the traditional time for men to enter the monkhood, and monks typically retreat inside the monastery for a period. During Khao Phansaa, worshippers make offerings to the temples and attend ordinations.

King's Birthday

The King's birthday on 28 July is a national holiday. Th Ratchadamnoen Klang in Bangkok is decorated with lights and regalia. Many Thais wear pink shirts: pink being the colour associated with the monarchy.

August

Overcast skies and daily showers mark the middle of the rainy season. The predictable rain just adds to the ever-present humidity.

Queen's Birthday

The birthday of Queen Sirikit, the consort of the late King Rama IX, on 12 August is a public holiday and national mother's day. In Bangkok the day is marked with cultural displays along Th Ratchadamnoen and Sanam Luang.

October

Religious preparations for the end of the rainy season and Buddhist Lent begin. The monsoons are reaching the finish line (in most of the country).

Ork Phasana

The end of Buddhist Lent (three lunar months after Khao Phansaa) is followed by the *gà·tǐn* ceremony, in which new robes are given to monks by merit-makers.

Vegetarian Festival

The Vegetarian Festival is a holiday from meat taken for nine days (during the ninth lunar month) in adherence with Chinese Buddhist beliefs of mind and body purification. In Phuket the festival can turn extreme, with entranced marchers transforming themselves into human shish kebabs.

November

The cool, dry season arrives and you'll beat the tourist crowds if you get here early. The landscape is lush: perfect for trekking and waterfall-spotting.

Loi Krathong

Loi Krathong is celebrated on the first full moon of the 12th lunar month. The festival thanks the river goddess for providing life to the fields and forests, and asks for forgiveness. Origami-like boats made from banana leaves are set adrift on the country's waterways.

December

The peak period of the tourist season with fair skies and a holiday mood.

King's Birthday

The birthday of the late King Rama IX on 5 December is commemorated by a public holiday. It is also national father's day.

Itineraries

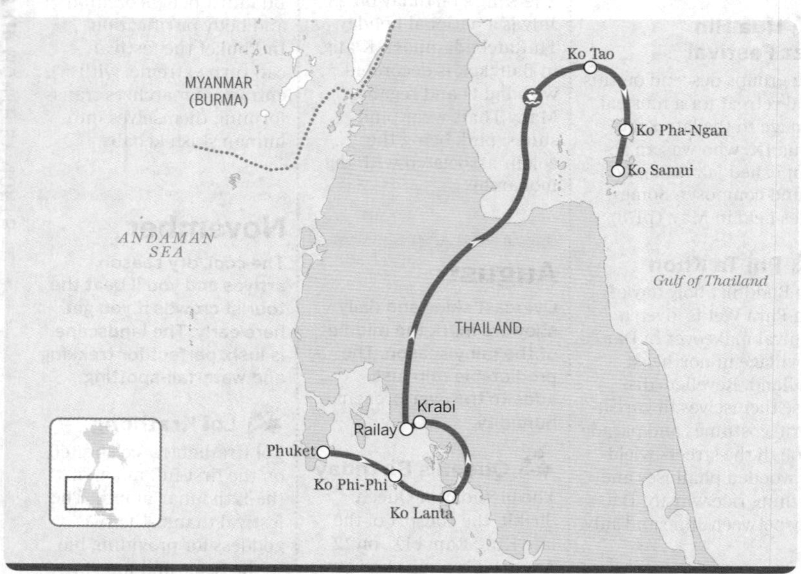

First-time Thailand

Head directly to **Phuket** and pick a beach where you can recover from jet lag for a day or two before starting your journey along one of the finest stretches of coastline in the world. Serious party-goers should base themselves in lively, if a little sleazy, Patong, while tranquility lovers can choose the quieter northern beaches.

Once you're properly unwinding, hop on a boat to **Ko Phi-Phi** and join the legions of whisky-bucket-wielding backpackers as they sit in the soft sands of the island's signature hourglass bays, or take a boat to the quieter eastern side of the island. Soak in the beauty of this place for a couple of days, before riding another boat to **Ko Lanta**, where flat vistas of tawny shoreline and lapping waves await. From there, head via **Krabi** to **Railay**, where craggy spires of limestone are a rock-climbing heaven and some of the most awesome beaches and sea views on the planet await.

Now it's time to switch coasts, an easy journey of a few hours by bus or minivan. Choose one or two of the gulf's triad of idyllic islands – dive-centric **Ko Tao**, lazy, lie-in-the-sun **Ko Pha-Ngan** or luxury-focused **Ko Samui** – for around five days before your flight out. If you're up for some serious partying, arrange your visit to coincide with Ko Pha-Ngan's notorious Full Moon Party, which comes roaring to life every month on the southeastern shore.

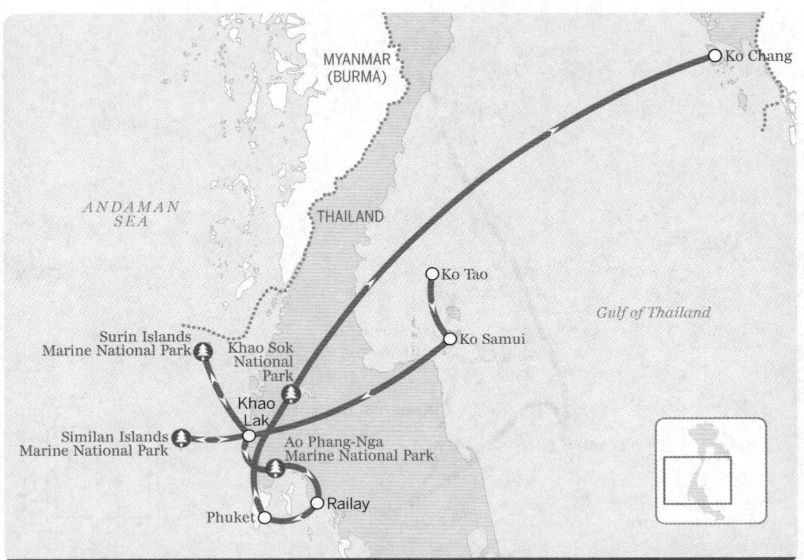

Outdoor Underwater Adventures

It's not just gorgeous beaches here: a whole different universe lies underwater, where world-renowned dive sites and super snorkelling await. Above the sea, you can kayak to hidden caves, climb karst formations, or go animal-spotting while trekking through some of the oldest rainforest on earth.

Novice divers should head first to **Ko Tao**, still the cheapest and easiest place to learn how to blow bubbles. But there are dive schools on many islands, including **Ko Samui,** where plenty of operators will take you to the same dive sites if you're short on time. More experienced divers will want to make for **Khao Lak**. Day trips and live-aboard cruises (ranging from three days to a week) depart here daily from mid-October to mid-May for the diver's dream destination of the **Similan Islands**. The ultimate dive sites here include Ko Bon, where manta rays circle healthy reefs that attract a myriad of smaller fish. Further north is Richelieu Rock, the number-one dive site in Thailand and sometimes home to elusive whale sharks, and the **Surin Islands**, with crystal-clear water and perhaps the finest snorkelling in the country.

Kayakers can cruise through the jaw-dropping limestone karsts of **Ao Phang-Nga Marine National Park** in search of part-underwater caves and ancient rock art, or simply paddle off the many islands that rent out kayaks. Rock climbers can make for **Railay**, where you can join the monkeys and dangle from jungly cliffs that look down on dreamy beaches. There are plenty of routes for beginners, and no shortage of operators to (literally) show you the ropes. Then there's deep-water soloing, where the climb ends with a plunge into the turquoise sea. If you're on the track of wildlife, the jungle interiors of northern **Phuket** and **Ko Chang** have wildlife sanctuaries and national parks. Or make for the prehistoric rainforest of the **Khao Sok National Park** on the mainland to hike to hidden waterfalls and spot rare flowers.

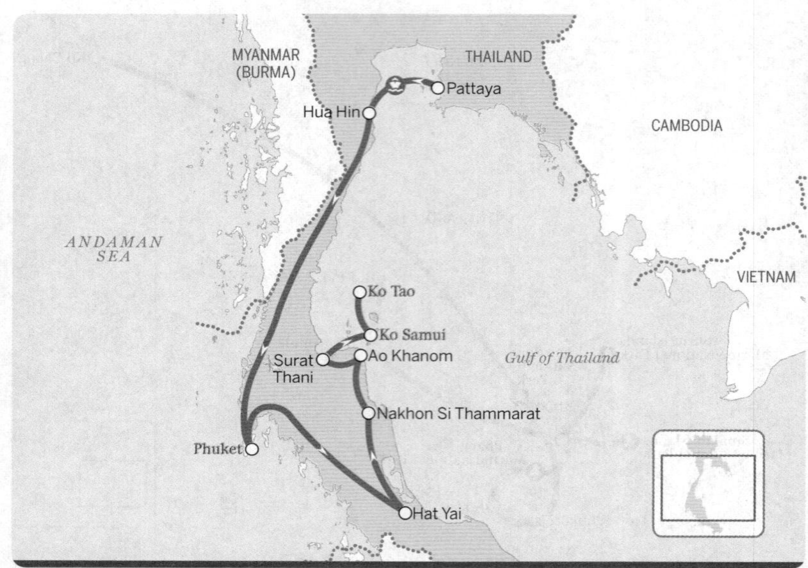

Eat Your Way Along the Coast

The lure of white-sand beaches and jade-green seas may have brought you here, but we're betting that the superb cuisine you'll encounter will stay in your memories for just as long.

A couple of hours' drive south of Bangkok, **Pattaya** offers excellent seafood and a wide variety of international choices. Ignore the go-go bars and tuck in. From Pattaya, take the two-hour catamaran ferry across the Gulf of Thailand to **Hua Hin**, where seafood markets and pier restaurants await. The dishes you'll experience here will be as Thai as they come – cooked with local taste buds in mind – as this is a key destination for domestic travellers from all over the country.

After gorging yourself for a couple of days, your next stop is **Phuket**. From Hua Hin, take a minivan directly to either of Bangkok's two airports and fly there, or alternatively catch the overnight bus. Thailand's largest island offers the most varied eating experiences of all the islands and beaches. There's brilliant street food and fantastic night markets in Phuket Town, and super seafood along every beach, as well as fusion eateries and an ever-increasing number of international restaurants, including exclusive fine-dining options hidden away in the high-end resorts. You'll also find top-rated Thai cooking schools here.

If you're still hungry after all that, consider continuing your gastronomic tour by taking the bus from Phuket to **Hat Yai** for some of the best and most authentic Chinese food in Thailand. From Hat Yai you can hop on a train north to sleepy **Nakhon Si Thammarat**, home to some superb restaurants, before jumping aboard a minivan to speed along the coast further north to **Ao Khanom** for lunch or dinner with gorgeous views over the Gulf of Thailand (keeping an eye out for the local pink dolphins). If your taste buds are still hopping, keep venturing to **Ko Samui** and the other islands of the Lower Gulf via **Surat Thani**, where a succession of outstanding restaurants leads all the way to **Ko Tao**.

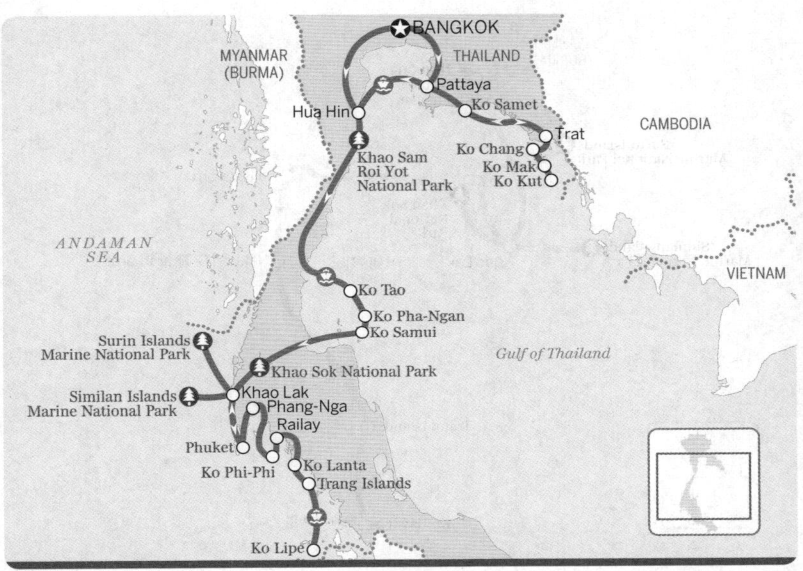

4 WEEKS The Full Monty

A month? This is not just any old beach trip; it allows enough time to sample the full range of southern Thailand's islands, beaches and jungle-clad national parks.

Start your journey in Thailand's capital, **Bangkok**, before heading south. Your first stop is beach-lined **Ko Samet**, where Bangkokians and expats let loose on weekends. Follow the coast to sleepy **Trat**, then hop on a boat for one of the Ko Chang archipelago's many islands. Hike the jungle interior of **Ko Chang**, the largest and most developed island in the region. Hop over to flat but beachy **Ko Mak** or rugged **Ko Kut**.

Next, backtrack to Trat and take a bus to **Pattaya**, from where it is a two-hour catamaran ride to **Hua Hin**, the preferred holiday destination of the Thai royals and upmarket locals. It's home to a thriving local and expat scene with seafood markets and charming shanty piers. Trek the craggy hills of quiet **Khao Sam Roi Yot National Park** before making your way out to **Ko Tao** (via Chumphon) where you can strap on your tank for an underwater adventure. Move over to **Ko Pha-Ngan** for subdued beachside relaxing. **Ko Samui**, next door, offers a bit more variety and has a magical stash of holiday fodder to suit every budget and desire.

From Ko Samui stop in at mainland **Khao Sok National Park** (via Surat Thani), known to be one of the oldest stretches of jungle in the world. After trekking in the rainforest, unwind on the beaches at **Khao Lak**, from where you can also take a day trip or live-aboard diving excursion to the world-famous dive sites of the **Surin Islands** and **Similan Islands Marine National Parks**. Travel down the coast to **Phuket** and sample Thailand's finest iteration of luxury hospitality. Paddle around the majestic limestone islets of quiet **Phang-Nga** then sleep beneath the ethereal crags of **Ko Phi-Phi** after a night of beach dancing and fire twirling. Scale the stone towers of **Railay** next door, zoom around the flat tracts of land on mellow **Ko Lanta**, then hop on a boat bound for the **Trang Islands** – paradise found. One last archipelago awaits those who travel further south towards the Malaysian border – **Ko Lipe** is the island of choice for those looking for stunning beaches with a fun, social vibe.

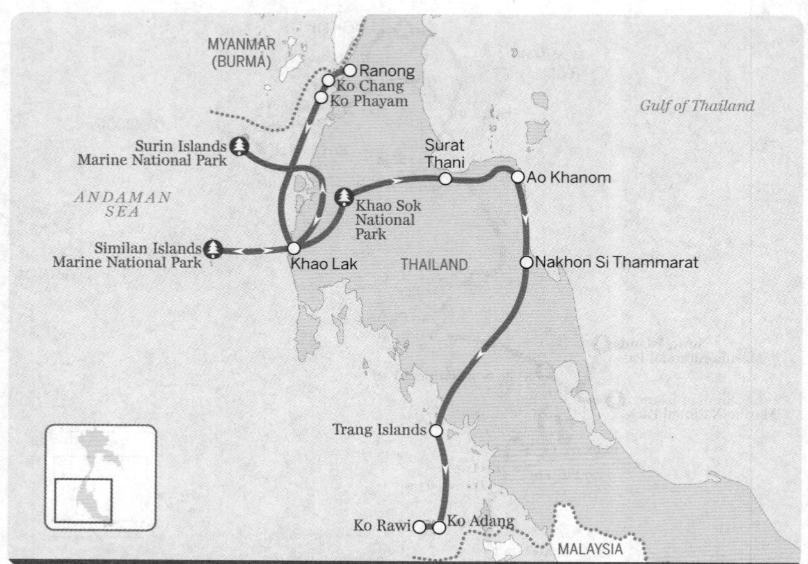

Lesser-Known Islands

Buck the travel trends and take the sea lanes less travelled through some of the least-known beaches and islands of southern Thailand, switching from west to east and back again.

Kick off in the bustling frontier town of **Ranong** on the eastern bank of the Sompaen River, a 45-minute boat ride from the Myanmar border, before sinking your tanned tootsies into the warm white sands of a beach on the nearby, sparsely populated island of **Ko Phayam**. Take more time out on no-frills 'Little' **Ko Chang** (not to be confused with the 'big' Ko Chang in Trat Province near Cambodia), a rustic getaway with an easygoing, almost horizontal vibe. You can trade some serious diver tips in **Khao Lak** further south and hop aboard a day-long diving and snorkelling excursion to the **Similan** and **Surin Islands,** or push the boat out on a live-aboard for three to five days.

Back on mainland terra firma, flip coasts and zip east, breaking the journey in **Khao Sok National Park** to immerse yourself in some of the oldest rainforest jungle on the planet and hunt out one of the world's largest flowers, or go hiking, kayaking, rafting or boating. Don't overlook **Surat Thani** – a traditional Thai town with a large Thai-Chinese population and a scattering of colourful Chinese temples – on your way east. You'll find lazy beach days waiting once you reach the gulf's **Ao Khanom**, minus the pockets of overdevelopment and crowds on Ko Samui, Ko Pha-Ngan and Ko Tao. Hopefully the local pink dolphins will muster an appearance.

Travel south to explore the rich, cultural centre of **Nakhon Si Thammarat**, a likeable and historic city that is home to one of Thailand's most significant and sacred Buddhist temples. Head back to the Andaman Coast to pick up where you left off: island-hopping. Take your pick from the lonely limestone specks of the **Trang Islands** – perhaps the allure of white sand-fringed Ko Kradan, sleepy Ko Sukorn or lush, wildlife rich Ko Libong – then wander south for a snorkelling excursion with the *chow lair* ('sea gypsies') on whisper-quiet **Ko Rawi** or **Ko Adang** north of Ko Lipe.

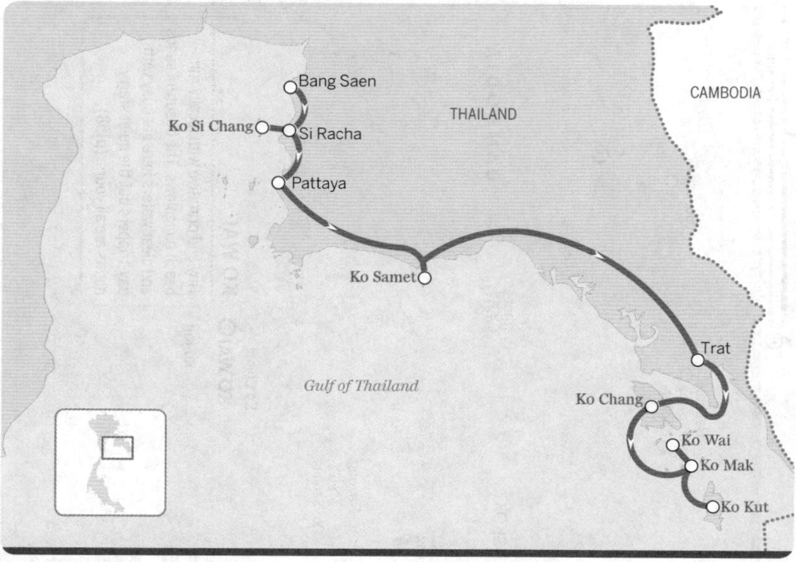

Exploring the Eastern Seaboard

Thailand's southern coast is undoubtedly home to the kingdom's true treasure islands, but there's plenty to enjoy on the eastern seaboard too. If you're pushed for time or Cambodia-bound, give these islands a go.

Once the least-visited coastal region of Thailand, the islands of the eastern gulf are easily accessible from Bangkok and are popular for beach-combing, diving, snorkelling, hiking and kayaking. The beach and long promenade at **Bang Saen**, the nearest stretch of sand to Bangkok, is a mere hour away from the capital (so gets busy at weekends). From here it's a short journey to the the seaside town of **Si Racha** and the nearby rocky island retreat of **Ko Si Chang**; the island isn't strong for beaches, but it's great to explore.

Skipping the supercharged beach scene and go-go bars of **Pattaya** is no great loss – but consider taking your pick of its excellent international restaurant scene and admiring its astonishing temple-like Sanctuary of Truth. Head further down the coast to join flashpackers on the gorgeous white-sand beaches and fire-juggling shows of slender and forested **Ko Samet**. Bangkokians let loose on big boisterous weekends, but there's more than enough room to escape, journeying from cove to cove along the lovely coastal footpath. Despite its fame, the island hasn't been overdeveloped yet and many of its sleeping options are still rustic and old-school.

Back on the mainland, follow the coast around to the traditional charms of sleepy **Trat**, then hop on a boat for one of the Ko Chang archipelago's myriad islands. Hike the lush interior of rugged, jungle-topped **Ko Chang**, the largest and most developed island in the region, or pop yourself into a kayak to size up the island from the waves. Some excellent dive sites await the underwater-inclined; choose between Ko Rang, Ko Yak, Ko Tong Lang and Ko Laun, all reachable from Ko Chang. If you want to get off the beaten track, spend a night on secluded, pint-sized **Ko Mak** or reef-fringed **Ko Wai**, where you can snorkel in crystal waters. Hardcore Robinson Crusoe types can go one step further on neighbouring, ultra-simple Ko Kham. Spend a few hours walking the talcum-powder-soft sands of nightlife-free **Ko Kut** to round off your journey.

Off the Beaten Track: Thailand's Islands & Beaches

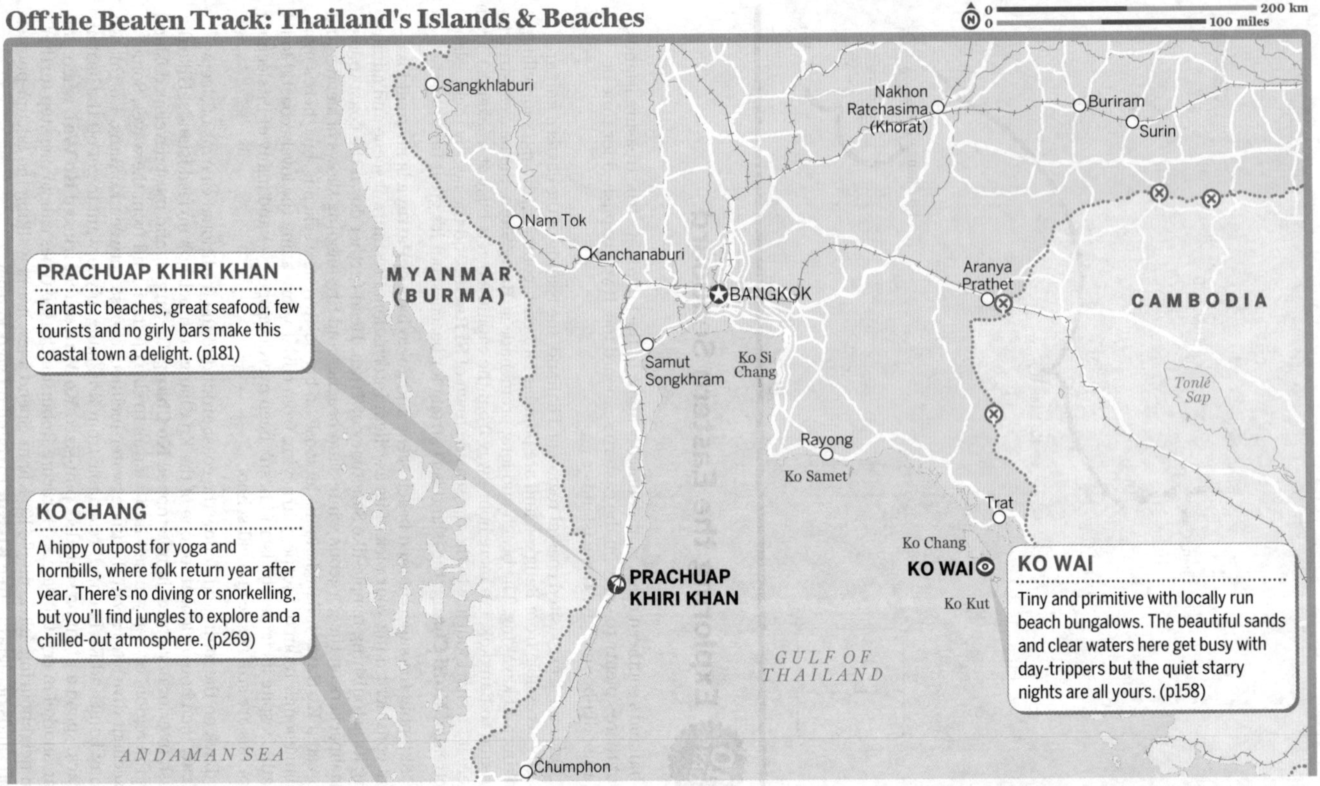

PRACHUAP KHIRI KHAN

Fantastic beaches, great seafood, few tourists and no girly bars make this coastal town a delight. (p181)

KO CHANG

A hippy outpost for yoga and hornbills, where folk return year after year. There's no diving or snorkelling, but you'll find jungles to explore and a chilled-out atmosphere. (p269)

KO WAI

Tiny and primitive with locally run beach bungalows. The beautiful sands and clear waters here get busy with day-trippers but the quiet starry nights are all yours. (p158)

0 200 km
0 100 miles
Sangkhlaburi
Nakhon Ratchasima (Khorat)
Buriram
Surin
Nam Tok
Kanchanaburi
MYANMAR (BURMA)
BANGKOK
Aranya Prathet
CAMBODIA
Samut Songkhram
Ko Si Chang
Tonlé Sap
Rayong
Ko Samet
Trat
Ko Chang
KO WAI
Ko Kut
PRACHUAP KHIRI KHAN
GULF OF THAILAND
ANDAMAN SEA
Chumphon

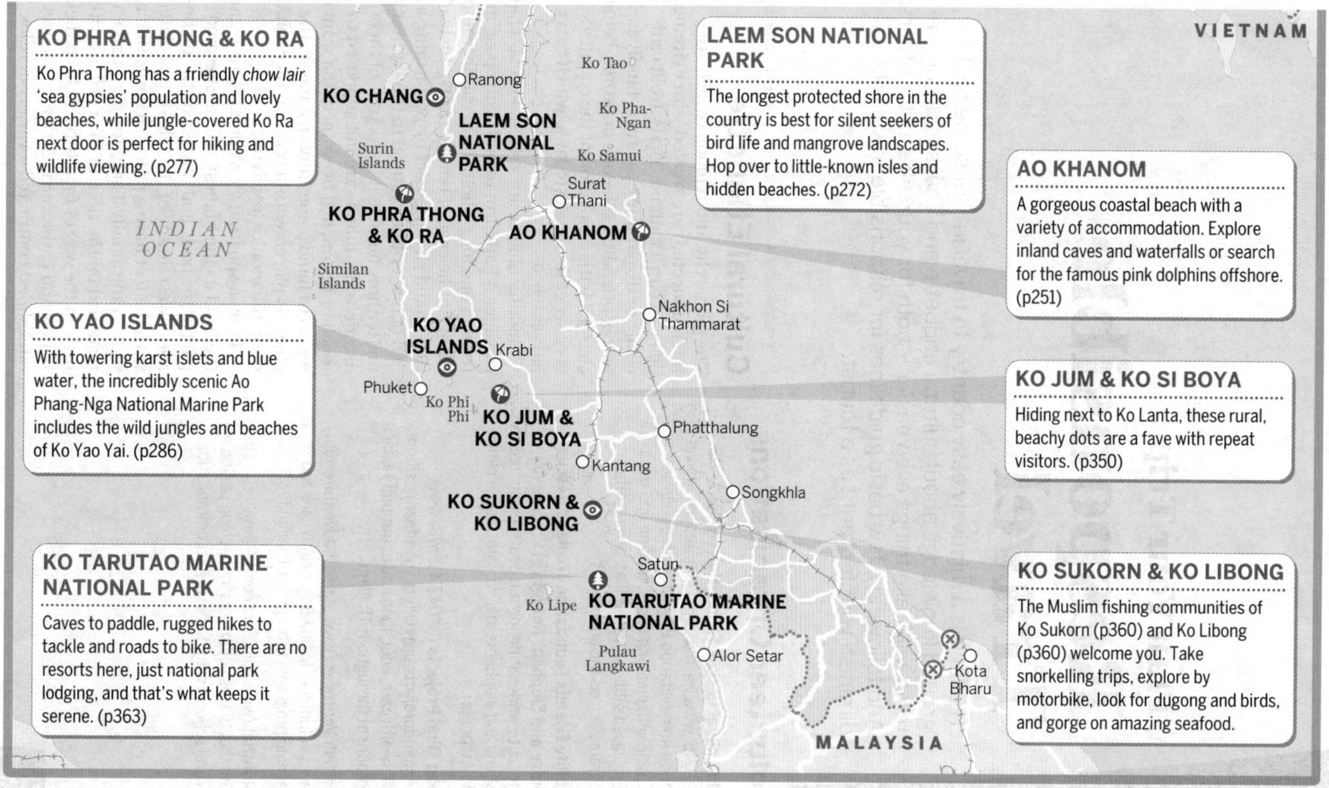

KO PHRA THONG & KO RA

Ko Phra Thong has a friendly *chow lair* 'sea gypsies' population and lovely beaches, while jungle-covered Ko Ra next door is perfect for hiking and wildlife viewing. (p277)

KO YAO ISLANDS

With towering karst islets and blue water, the incredibly scenic Ao Phang-Nga National Marine Park includes the wild jungles and beaches of Ko Yao Yai. (p286)

KO TARUTAO MARINE NATIONAL PARK

Caves to paddle, rugged hikes to tackle and roads to bike. There are no resorts here, just national park lodging, and that's what keeps it serene. (p363)

LAEM SON NATIONAL PARK

The longest protected shore in the country is best for silent seekers of bird life and mangrove landscapes. Hop over to little-known isles and hidden beaches. (p272)

AO KHANOM

A gorgeous coastal beach with a variety of accommodation. Explore inland caves and waterfalls or search for the famous pink dolphins offshore. (p251)

KO JUM & KO SI BOYA

Hiding next to Ko Lanta, these rural, beachy dots are a fave with repeat visitors. (p350)

KO SUKORN & KO LIBONG

The Muslim fishing communities of Ko Sukorn (p360) and Ko Libong (p360) welcome you. Take snorkelling trips, explore by motorbike, look for dugong and birds, and gorge on amazing seafood.

Plan Your Trip
Responsible Travel

Thailand is a relatively easy country to travel in. But some background knowledge about cultural etiquette and Thai social conventions will make things even easier – both for yourself and for others. And following a few basic guidelines for responsible travel will diminish your footprint as a tourist.

Volunteer Organisations

Wild Animal Rescue Foundation (WARF; ☎02 712 9715; www.warthai.org) Operates the Phuket Gibbon Rehabilitation Project (where volunteers can help with cleaning cages, feeding and tracking released gibbons), as well as several other programs across the country.

Wildlife Friends Foundation Thailand Rescue Centre and Elephant Refuge (p172) Puts volunteers to work caring for sun bears, macaques, gibbons and elephants at its animal rescue centre in Phetchaburi.

Open Mind Projects (☎042 413578; www.openmindprojects.org) Offers volunteer positions in IT, health care, education and community-based ecotourism throughout Thailand.

Starfish Ventures (www.starfish-adventure.com) Places volunteers in building, health care and teaching programs throughout Thailand.

Volunthai (www.volunthai.com) A family-run operation that places volunteers in teaching positions at rural schools with homestay accommodation.

Cultural Etiquette

The monarchy and religion (which are interconnected) are treated with extreme deference in Thailand. Thais avoid criticising or disparaging the royal family for fear of offending someone or, worse, being charged with a violation of the country's very strict lèse-majesté laws, which carry a jail sentence.

Buddha images are sacred objects. Thais consider it bad form to pull a silly pose in front of one for a photo, or to clamber upon them (in the case of temple ruins). Instead they would show respect by performing a *wâi* (a prayer-like gesture) to the figure no matter how humble it is. As part of their ascetic vows, monks are not supposed to touch or be touched by women. If a woman wants to hand something to a monk, the object is placed within reach of the monk or on the monk's 'receiving cloth'.

From a spiritual viewpoint, Thais regard the head as the highest and most sacred part of the body and the feet as the dirtiest and lowest. Many of the taboos associated with the feet have a practical derivation as well. Traditionally Thais ate, slept and entertained on the floor of their homes with little in the way of furniture. To keep their homes and eating surfaces clean, the feet (and shoes) contracted a variety of rules.

Shoes aren't worn inside private homes and temple buildings, both as a sign of respect and for sanitary reasons. Thais can kick off their shoes in one fluid step and many lace-up shoes are modified by the wearer to become slip-ons. Thais also step over – not on – the threshold, which is where the spirit of the house is believed to reside. On some buses and 3rd-class trains, you'll see Thais prop their feet up on the adjacent bench, and while this isn't the height of propriety, do notice that they always remove their shoes before doing so. Thais also take off their shoes if they need to climb onto a chair or seat.

Thais don't touch each others' heads or ruffle hair as a sign of affection. Occasionally you'll see young people touching each others' heads, which is a teasing gesture, maybe even a slight insult, between friends.

Social Conventions & Gestures

The traditional Thai greeting, known as *wâi,* is made with a prayer-like, palms-together gesture. The depth of the bow and the placement of the fingers in relation to the face is dependent on the status of the person receiving the *wâi*. Adults don't *wâi* children, and in most cases service people (when they are doing their jobs) aren't *wâi*-ed, though this is a matter of personal discretion.

In the more traditional parts of the country, it is not proper for members of the opposite sexes to touch one another, either as lovers or as friends. Hand-holding is not acceptable behaviour outside the major cities such as Bangkok. But same-sex touching is quite common and is typically

ESSENTIAL ETIQUETTE

Do

Stand respectfully for the royal and national anthem They are played on TV and radio stations as well as in public and government places.

Smile a lot It makes everything easier.

Bring a gift if you're invited to a Thai home Fruit, drinks or snacks are acceptable.

Take off your shoes When you enter a home or temple building.

Dress modestly for temple visits Cover to the elbows and ankles and always remove your shoes when entering any building containing a Buddha image.

Sit in the 'mermaid' position inside temples Tuck your feet beside and behind you.

Give and receive politely Extend the right hand out while the left hand gently grips the right elbow when handing an object to another person or receiving something.

Don't

Get a tattoo of the Buddha It is considered sacrilegious.

Criticise the monarchy The monarchy is revered and protected by defamation laws – more so now than ever.

Prop your feet on tables or chairs Feet are considered dirty and people have to sit on chairs.

Step on a dropped bill to prevent it from blowing away Thai money bears a picture of the king. Feet + monarchy = grave offence.

Step over someone or their personal belongings Aaah, attack of the feet.

Tie your shoes to the outside of your backpack They might accidentally brush against someone: gross.

Touch a Thai person on the head It is considered rude, not chummy.

Touch monks or their belongings (women) Step out of the way when passing one on the footpath and do not sit next to them on public transport.

a sign of friendship, not sexual attraction. Older Thai men might grab a younger man's thigh in the same way that buddies slap each other on the back. Thai women are especially affectionate with female friends, often sitting close to one another or linking arms.

Thais hold modesty in personal dress in high regard, though this is changing among the younger generation. The importance of modesty extends to the beach as well. Except for urbanites, most provincial Thais swim fully clothed. For this reason, sunbathing nude or topless is not acceptable and in some cases is even illegal. Remember that swimsuits are not proper attire off the beach; wear a cover-up in between the sand and your hotel.

Tourism

Elephant Encounters

Throughout Thai history, elephants have been revered for their strength, endurance and intelligence, working alongside their mahouts harvesting teak, transporting goods through mountainous terrain or fighting ancient wars.

Many of the elephants' traditional roles have either been outsourced to machines or outlawed, leaving the 'domesticated' animals and their mahouts without work. Some mahouts turned to begging on the streets in Bangkok and other tourist centres, but most elephants find work in Thailand's tourism industry. Their jobs vary from circus-like shows and elephant camps giving rides to tourists to 'mahout-training' schools, while sanctuaries and rescue centres provide modest retirement homes to animals that are no longer financially profitable to their owners.

It costs about 30,000B (US$1000) a month to provide a comfortable living for an elephant, an amount equivalent to the salary of Thailand's upper-middle class. Welfare standards within the tourism industry are not standardised or subject to government regulations, so it's up to the conscientious consumer to encourage the industry to ensure safe conditions for elephants.

With more evidence available than ever to support claims by animal welfare experts that elephant rides and shows are harmful to these gentle giants, who are often abused to force them to perform for humans, a small but growing number of sanctuaries offer more sustainable interactions, such as walking with and bathing retired and rescued elephants.

Lonely Planet does not recommend riding on elephants or viewing elephant performances. We also urge visitors to be wary of organisations that advertise as being a conservation centre but actually offer rides and performances.

Volunteering

Environmental & Animal Welfare Work

At centres and sanctuaries that rely on volunteer labour, your hard work is often rewarded with meaningful interactions with the animals.

Humanitarian & Educational Work

When looking for a volunteer placement, it is essential to investigate what your chosen organisation does and, more importantly, how it goes about it. For any organisation working with children, child protection is a serious concern, and organisations that do not conduct background checks on volunteers should be regarded with extreme caution.

Ko Chang (p144)

Plan Your Trip

Choose Your Beach

It's a terrible dilemma: Thailand has too many beaches to choose from. Choices can be daunting even for those visiting a second time, and development is so rapid that where you went five years ago may now be completely different. Here, we break it down for you so you can find your dream beach.

Best Beaches for...

Relaxation and Activities

Ko Mak Beach bar scene, explorably flat and vast expanses of sand.

Ko Phayam Bike back roads to empty beaches or to parties.

Hat Mae Nam Quiet Ko Samui beach close to lots of action.

Ko Bulon Leh Chilled-out vibe but lots to do.

Local Culture

Ko Yao Noi Thai-Muslim fishing island with beautiful karst scenery.

Ko Sukorn Agricultural and fishing gem filled with mangroves and water buffalo.

Ko Phra Thong Look for rare orchids with a *chow lair* (a Moken 'sea gypsy') guide.

Hua Hin Mingle with middle-class Thais in this urban beach getaway.

Easy Access from Bangkok

Nowadays the closest beaches to Bangkok aren't necessarily the quickest and easiest to get to. There are international flights direct to Phuket and Ko Samui that allow you to skip the big city altogether, and flights from Bangkok (and some other Southeast Asian countries) can shuttle you to several southern towns with ease.

If you don't want to fly but are still short on time, the nearest beach island to Bangkok is Ko Samet (count on around four hours' total travel time), while the closest beach resorts are Bang Saen (one hour by bus) and Pattaya (1½ hours). The next-closest stops by land are the beach towns of Cha-am (2½ hours) and Hua Hin (three hours). It takes around six hours to get to Ko Chang, which beats the minimum of 10 hours to reach the Lower Gulf islands. If you're in a hurry and want to take the bus, the Andaman Coast is not your best choice.

To Party or Not to Party

Where

A big percentage of travellers to southern Thailand aim to party, and the local tourism industry happily accommodates them, with an array of thumping beach bars lining many of the main beaches. Luckily, it's just as easy to escape the revelry as it is to join in. The main party zones are well known to be just that. Anywhere you go that's not a major tourist enclave will have peace and quiet on offer.

Girly Bars

Bangkok, Pattaya and Patong in Phuket are the capitals of push-up bras and short skirts, while Hat Lamai on Ko Samui is the centre of this small universe in the lower Gulf Islands. Islands like Ko Chang and mid-sized towns such as Hat Yai and Ao Nang have small enclaves of questionable massage parlours and bars, but it won't be in your face. Smaller islands will be clear of this sort of thing, as will most mainland towns.

Your Party Level

Level One: Dead Calm Surin and Similan Islands, Laem Son National Park, Hat Pak Meng, Hat Chang Lang

Level Two: A Flicker of Light Ko Tarutao, Ko Libong, Prachuap Khiri Khan

Level Three: There's a Bar Ko Yao Islands, Ao Khanom, Ko Kut

Level Four: Maybe a Few Bars Hat Khao Lak, Ko Muk, Ao Thong Nai Pan (Ko Pha-Ngan)

Level Five: Easy to Find a Drink Hua Hin, Bo Phut (Ko Samui), Ao Nang

Level Six: There's a Beach-Bar Scene Ko Mak, Ko Phayam, Railay

Level Seven: Magic Shake Anyone? Ko Lanta, Ko Chang, Ban Tai (Ko Pha-Ngan)

Level Eight: I Forget What Eight Was For Hat Lamai (Ko Samui), Ko Lipe, Ko Samet

Level Nine: What Happened Last Night? Hat Chaweng (Ko Samui), Pattaya, Ko Tao

Level Ten: Don't Tell Me What Happened Last Night Patong (Phuket), Ko Phi-Phi, Hat Rin (Ko Pha-Ngan)

OVERVIEW OF THAILAND'S ISLANDS & BEACHES

BEACHES	PACKAGE TOURISTS	BACK-PACKERS	FAMILIES	PARTIES	DIVE/ SNORKEL	PERSONALITY
Ko Chang & the Eastern Seaboard						
Ko Samet	✓	✓	✓	✓		pretty beaches, easy getaway from Bangkok
Ko Chang	✓	✓	✓	✓	✓	international resort, mediocre beaches, jungle
Ko Wai		✓	✓		✓	primitive; day-trippers, deserted in the evening
Ko Mak	✓	✓	✓			mediocre beaches, great island vibe
Ko Kut	✓	✓	✓			lovely semi-developed island, great for solitude
Hua Hin & the Upper Gulf						
Hua Hin	✓	✓	✓			international resort, easy access to Bangkok
Pranburi area	✓		✓			quiet & close to Bangkok
Ban Krut			✓			low-key, popular with Thais
Bang Saphan Yai		✓	✓			cheap mainland beach
Ko Samui & the Lower Gulf						
Ko Samui	✓	✓	✓	✓		international resort for social beach-goers
Ko Pha-Ngan	✓	✓	✓	✓	✓	popular beaches, some secluded; boozy Hat Rin
Ko Tao	✓	✓	✓	✓	✓	dive schools galore
Ang Thong		✓	✓			karst scenery, rustic
Ao Khanom		✓	✓			quiet, little-known
Phuket & the Andaman Coast						
Ko Chang (Ranong)		✓	✓		✓	rustic and secluded
Ko Phayam		✓	✓			quiet, getting more popular
Surin & Similan Islands			✓		✓	dive sites accessed by live-aboards
Ko Yao	✓	✓	✓			poor beaches but nice vibe, great scenery
Phuket	✓	✓	✓	✓	✓	international resort for social beach-goers
Ao Nang	✓	✓	✓		✓	touristy, close to Railay
Railay	✓	✓	✓			rock-climbing centre with some superb beaches
Ko Phi-Phi		✓		✓	✓	pretty party island
Ko Jum	✓	✓	✓			mediocre beach, nice vibe
Ko Lanta	✓	✓	✓		✓	reasonable beaches
Trang Islands	✓	✓	✓		✓	Ko Ngai is good for kids
Ko Bulon Leh		✓	✓		✓	pretty, little-known
Ko Tarutao		✓	✓			developing national park
Ko Lipe	✓	✓	✓	✓	✓	hotspot, good beaches, handy for visa runs
Ko Adang		✓			✓	popular with day-trippers

Choose your own Beach Adventure

How far will you travel to find your perfect beach? Pick a starting point based on your travel priorities, then fill in the blanks.

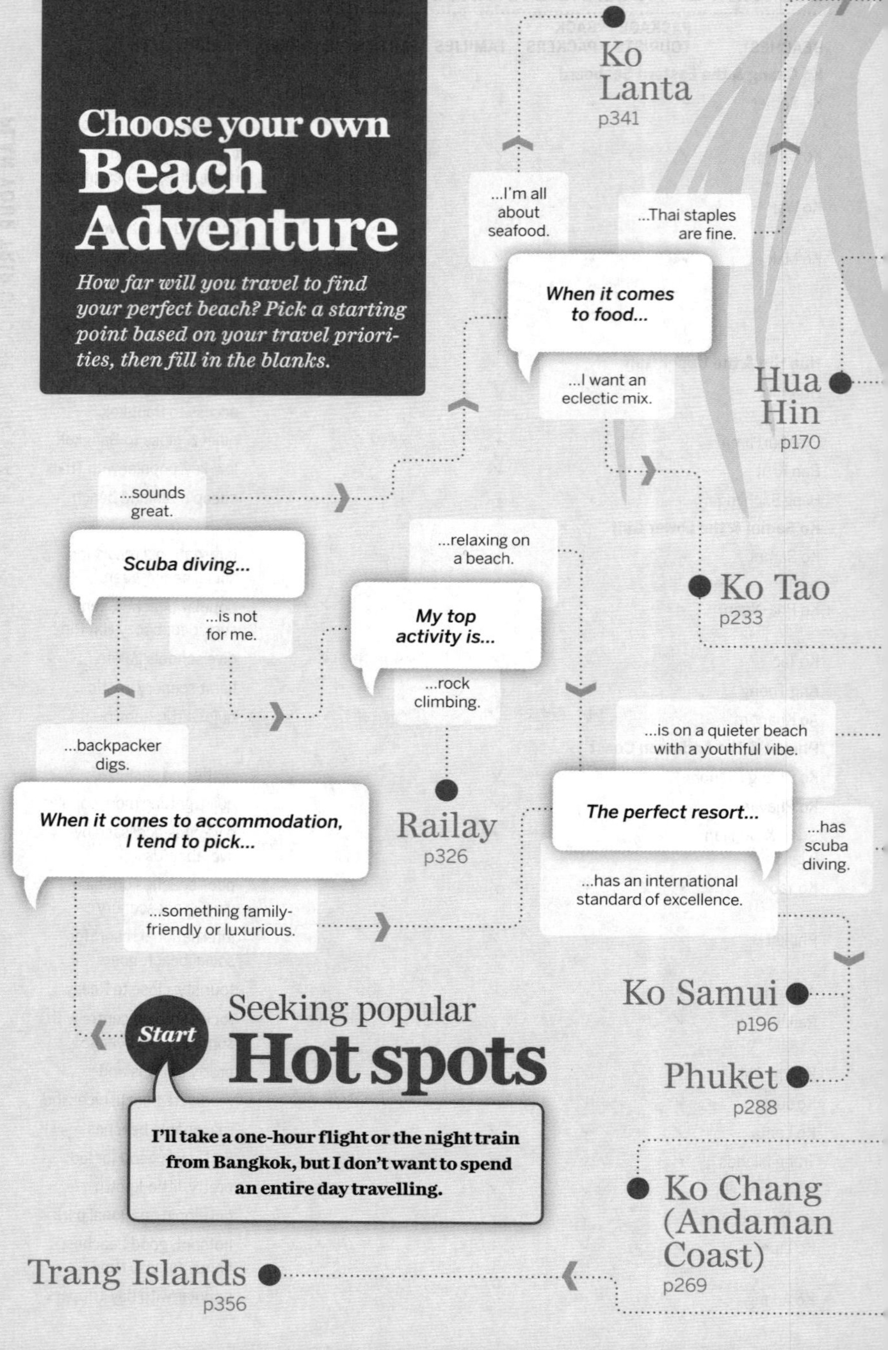

Start

Seeking popular Hot spots

I'll take a one-hour flight or the night train from Bangkok, but I don't want to spend an entire day travelling.

When it comes to accommodation, I tend to pick...

...backpacker digs.

...something family-friendly or luxurious.

Scuba diving...

...sounds great.

...is not for me.

My top activity is...

...relaxing on a beach.

...rock climbing.

When it comes to food...

...I'm all about seafood.

...Thai staples are fine.

...I want an eclectic mix.

The perfect resort...

...is on a quieter beach with a youthful vibe.

...has scuba diving.

...has an international standard of excellence.

Ko Lanta p341

Hua Hin p170

Ko Tao p233

Railay p326

Ko Samui p196

Phuket p288

Ko Chang (Andaman Coast) p269

Trang Islands p356

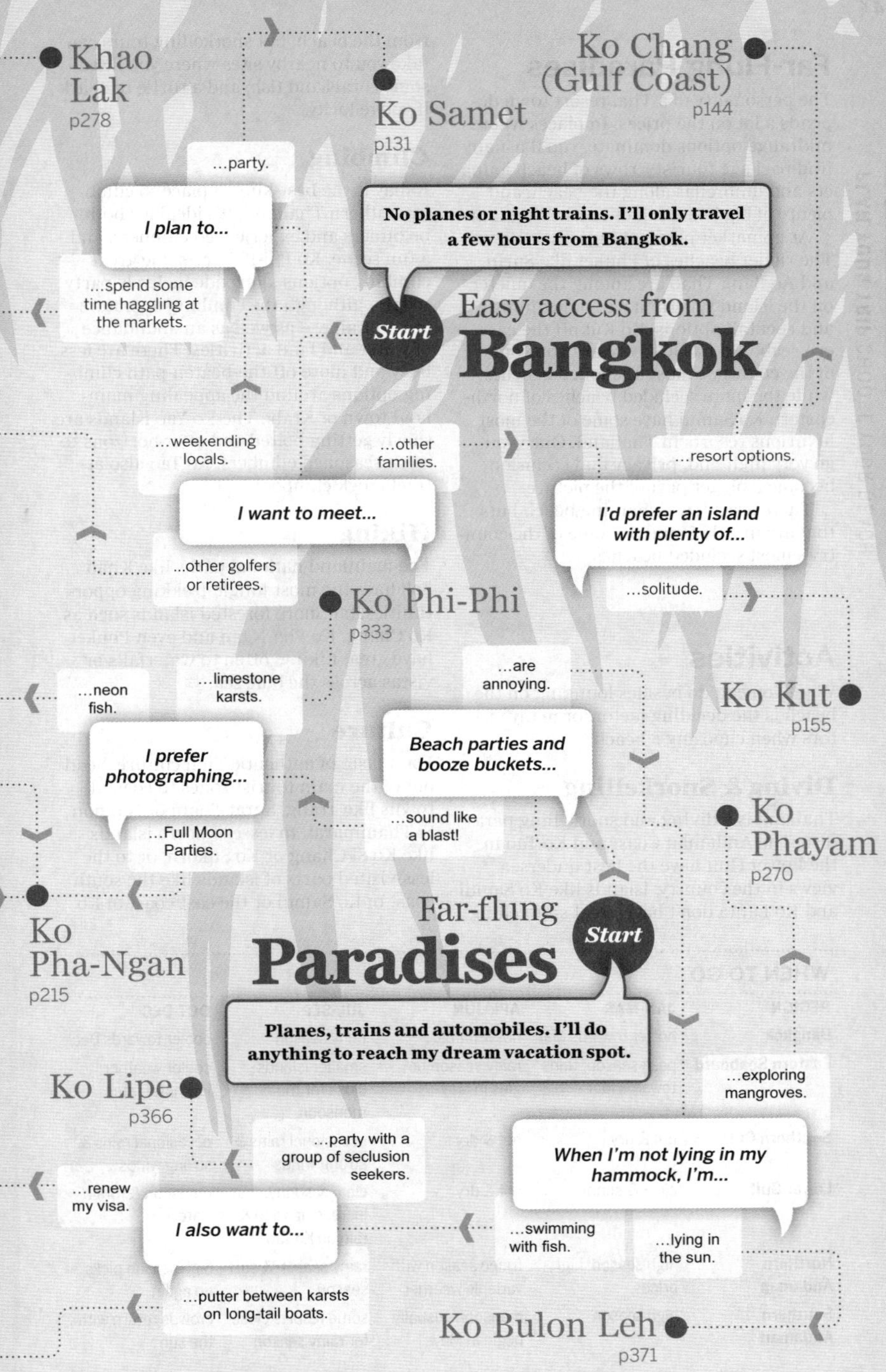

Khao Lak
p278
Ko Samet
p131
Ko Chang (Gulf Coast)
p144
...party.
I plan to...
...spend some time haggling at the markets.
No planes or night trains. I'll only travel a few hours from Bangkok.
Start
Easy access from
Bangkok
...weekending locals.
...other families.
...resort options.
I want to meet...
I'd prefer an island with plenty of...
...other golfers or retirees.
...solitude.
Ko Phi-Phi
p333
...neon fish.
...limestone karsts.
...are annoying.
Ko Kut
p155
I prefer photographing...
Beach parties and booze buckets...
...Full Moon Parties.
...sound like a blast!
Ko Phayam
p270
Ko Pha-Ngan
p215
Far-flung
Paradises
Start
Planes, trains and automobiles. I'll do anything to reach my dream vacation spot.
Ko Lipe
p366
...exploring mangroves.
...party with a group of seclusion seekers.
When I'm not lying in my hammock, I'm...
...renew my visa.
I also want to...
...swimming with fish.
...lying in the sun.
...putter between karsts on long-tail boats.
Ko Bulon Leh
p371

Far-Flung Paradises

The personality of a Thai resort town depends a lot on the prices. In places where midrange options dominate, you'll usually find package tourists, rows of beach loungers and umbrellas along the beach, and plenty of big boats full of snorkelling tours.

At upmarket places things settle down. The ritzier beaches of Phuket like Surin and Ao Bang Thao are among the quieter on the island yet still have some dining and cocktail options. Ko Kut off the eastern seaboard has lovely resorts on some of the country's most unspoiled beaches, while the more secluded beaches of northeastern Ko Samui have some of the most luxurious resorts in Thailand. Once you go very high-end, privacy and seclusion become a bigger part of the picture.

There are a few remaining beach huts that are mostly found on some of the country's most secluded beaches.

Activities

What you can do besides lounging on the beach is the deciding factor for many visitors when choosing a beach.

Diving & Snorkelling

Thailand is a diving and snorkelling paradise. The Andaman Coast and Ko Tao in the Lower Gulf have the best undersea views in the country. Islands like Ko Samui and Ko Lanta don't have great snorkelling from the beach, but snorkelling tours can take you to nearby sites where you'll see some corals and fish, and a turtle or shark if you're lucky.

Climbing

Railay is the best-known place to climb in southern Thailand; it's ideal for both beginners and experienced climbers, and a fun scene. Ko Phi-Phi has some great climbing options alongside its lively party scene – although the climbing operators are on Railay – as well as an abundance of water and land activities. There are less busy and more off-the-beaten-path climbing options around the appealing mainland town of Krabi. The Ko Yao islands are slowly getting bolted and offer horizons to more seasoned climbers. Ko Tao also attracts rock-climbers.

Hiking

The mainland national parks like Khao Sok have the most jungle-trekking opportunities, but more forested islands such as Ko Chang, Ko Pha-Ngan and even Phuket have great hiking, often to waterfalls or vistas across the blue sea.

Culture

For a taste of authentic Thai culture, head out of the main tourist zones to coastal towns like Trang, Surat Thani or Nakhon Si Thammarat, to lesser-known islands like Ko Si Chang or Ko Sukorn, or to the less-visited parts of islands like the south coast of Ko Samui or the east coast of Ko

WHEN TO GO

REGION	JAN-MAR	APR-JUN	JUL-SEP	OCT-DEC
Bangkok	hotter towards Mar	hot & humid	rainy season	cooler towards Dec
Eastern Seaboard	peak season; thins towards Mar	rainy season begins in May	smaller islands close for the monsoon	cooler weather; low hotel rates
Southern Gulf	hot & dry	hot & dry	occasional rains & strong winds	occasional rains & strong winds
Lower Gulf	clear & sunny	hot & dry	clear & sunny; increasing wind & rain on Ko Tao	monsoon & rough waters
Northern Andaman	high season; high prices	fringe season with variable weather	rainy season & surf season	high season picks up again
Southern Andaman	high season	monsoons usually begin in May	some resorts close for rainy season	crowds return with the sun

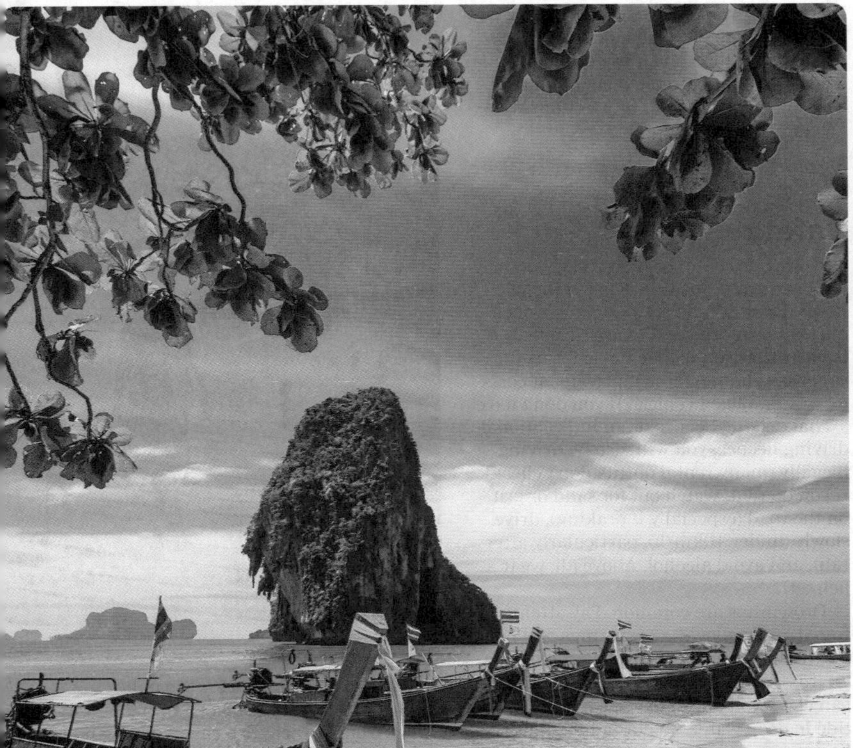

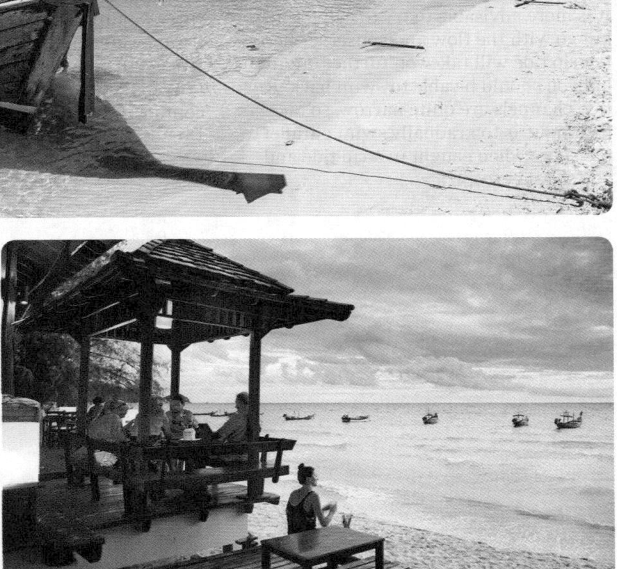

Top: Hat Tham Phra Nang, Railay (p326)

Bottom: Ko Tao (p233)

MATT MUNRO / LONELY PLANET ©

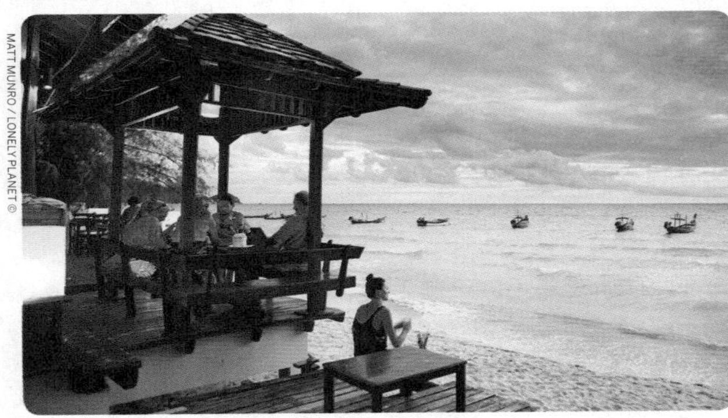

Lanta. But even tourist-central Patong or Ko Phi-Phi can give you a taste of what's beyond resort land, just by eating at food stalls and talking to the owners, smiling a lot and being open to interactions with locals.

Safety

If renting a scooter or motorbike, you may not be insured. Insurance is not included in most rentals and your own insurance may not cover the cost of any accident. It is likely that you will be liable for medical expenses and repair or replacement costs for any damaged vehicle. If you don't have a Thai driving licence or an international driving licence, you will also be driving illegally (many rental outfits don't check). If you do rent, watch out for sand or grit on the road (especially if braking), drive slowly (under 40km/h), particularly after rain, and avoid alcohol. Above all, wear a helmet.

Drownings are common. Pay attention to red- and yellow-flag warnings and be aware that many beaches do not have life guards. Also beware of rip tides, which can carry you out to sea. If caught in a rip tide in deep water, do not fight against it as you may rapidly, and dangerously, tire. It is more advisable to try to call for help, but go with the flow and conserve energy; the rip tide will take you further out to sea, but you should be able to swim back. Rip tide channels are quite narrow, so another technique is to gradually swim parallel to the shore when caught in a rip tide and you should escape it.

Ko Nang Yuan (p233)

Signs on some beaches warn of box jellyfish, so check before swimming. Stings from box jellyfish can be fatal, and although there are few deaths, there were three fatalities in Ko Pha-Ngan and Ko Samui waters in a 12-month period between 2014 and 2015.

Watch out for jet skis and long-tail boats coming in to the shore when swimming. Do not expect them to see you.

Snorkelling off Ko Rang (p146)

Plan Your Trip

Diving & Snorkelling

Whether it's your first plunge or your 100th, Thailand offers some of the world's leading underwater experiences, with warm, clear waters, abundant marine life and some of the planet's most beautiful dive sites. Reasonable prices mean it's also a great place to learn to dive.

Diving & Snorkelling Highlights

Best Places to Learn

Ko Tao Fantastic dive energy and scores of shallow dive sites sometimes visited by whale sharks. This is the best (and cheapest) place in Thailand to lose your diving virginity. Sail Rock (closer to Ko Pha-Ngan) and Chumphon Pinnacle are the star sites.

Best Live-Aboards

Khao Lak The gateway to the Surin and Similan Islands. Explore the myriad dive sites on a live-aboard trip and check out Richelieu Rock – a stunning dive spot discovered by Jacques Cousteau.

Best Marine Life

Ko Lanta and Ko Phi-Phi Don Top spots for plenty of fish, recurrent visits by manta rays and the odd whale shark. Try the submerged pinnacles at Hin Daeng and Hin Muang, which are accessible from both sites.

Best Snorkelling

Ko Phi-Phi Has made a triumphant comeback after the tsunami, with loads of shimmering reefs. Ko Mai Phai and Ko Nok are great snorkelling spots, while Hin Bida and Ko Bida Nok are the local diving faves.

Diving

For the beginner through to the pro, Thailand has some of the most affordable, easily accessible and stunning diving in the world.

Courses

Thailand is one of the best places in the world to learn how to dive. If you are looking for the best bang for your baht, we recommend getting certified on Ko Tao, where coursework starts at 9000B to 10,000B depending on the type of licence you receive. Beyond Ko Tao, there are plenty of places to get certified, though you're looking at an extra 3000B to 6000B for your Open Water Diver certificate. Ko Pha-Ngan, Ko Phi-Phi, Khao Lak and Ko Lanta round out Thailand's top five places to learn to dive.

Children are eligible to take a PADI Open Water Course from the age of 10. There are any number of reputable dive schools across the region offering introductory dive experiences.

Freediving

Freediving involves the diver submersing with a single breath hold (with no diving gear or snorkel). One of the top spots to try this sport is on Ko Tao in the southern gulf, but freediving schools have also appeared on Ko Pha-Ngan and Ko Lanta. Beginner courses (usually two days of diving) cost around 5000B.

For more information on freediving, check out AIDA International (www.aidainternational.org) and CMAS (www.cmas.org).

Live-Aboards

The live-aboard industry has been steadily growing in Thailand over the past 20-odd years. Most live-aboards are based out of Khao Lak, just north of Phuket on the Andaman Coast. These live-aboard excursions are all-inclusive (lodging on the boat, food, diving gear, guides), varying in length from two to five nights. When it's low season on the Similan Islands off the Andaman Coast, a few live-aboards head to the Gulf to operate on dive sites around Koh Tao, Ang Thong Marine National Park and Koh Pha-Ngan.

Technical Diving

Technical diving (often called tec diving) is an advanced type of scuba diving involving additional equipment and, most notably, a tank of mixed breathing gases to allow for deeper dives. Technical diving is often taken on as a recreational sport for those interested in exploring deep wrecks and caves.

Underwater caving has really taken off in recent years, and there are several operators on Ko Tao that offer one-day/one-night trips out to nearby submerged grottoes.

Planning Your Trip

The monsoon rains and peak tourist season are two factors determining when to go and which islands and beaches to pick. The severity of the rainy weather varies between seasons and coasts, and there are dry and wet microclimates as well.

Costs

Diving in Thailand is significantly cheaper than in most other nations. A 10-dive package goes for around 7000B to 12,000B on the more affordable beaches. Day-trip prices largely depend on how far the boat will travel, as petrol prices are at a premium. Figure on around 2250B for a day trip from Ko Pha-Ngan and up to 6000B for a trip out to Hin Daeng and Hin Muang from Ko Lanta.

Advance Booking

It is not normally necessary to pre-book diving excursions unless you plan on doing a live-aboard up to the Surin Islands and Similan Islands Marine National Parks, as places on these boats are limited. Note, however, that rooms on Ko Pha-Ngan in the week up to and including the Full Moon Party sell out and rooms in Ko Tao can be stuffed in the days after the monthly shenanigans, so book early if diving then, or simply go at another time.

Where to Dive

Thailand's coastal topography sits at the junction of two distinct oceanic zones – the Andaman waters wash in from the west, while the gulf coast draws its waters from the islands of Indonesia and the South China Sea.

The Andaman Sea When the weather is right, the Andaman Sea has some of the finest diving in Southeast Asia. Many would argue that the Andaman has better diving than the gulf, but this is mostly attributed to excellent visibility during the few months of favourable sea conditions. Over the last several years coral bleaching has been an issue; you'll encounter less of this around more remote sites like Richelieu Rock and Ko Bon.

The Gulf of Thailand Sea conditions in the Gulf of Thailand are generally favourable throughout the year. The southwestern gulf coast has the finest

PRESERVING THAILAND'S REEFS

Thailand's underwater kingdom is incredibly fragile and it's worth taking some time to educate yourself on responsible and sustainable practices while you're visiting. Here are a few of the more important things you can do, but this is by no means an exhaustive list.

- Whether on an island or in a boat, take all litter with you – even biodegradable material like apple cores – and dispose of it back on the mainland.
- Remember that it is an offence to damage or remove coral in marine parks.
- Don't touch or harass marine animals.
- Never rest or stand on coral because touching or walking on it will damage it. It can also cause some nasty cuts.
- Ensure that no equipment is dragging over the reef.
- If you're snorkelling (and especially if you are a beginner), practise your technique away from coral until you've mastered control in the water.
- Hire a wetsuit or rash vest rather than slathering on sunscreen, which can damage the reef.
- Watch where your fins are – try not to stir up sediment or disturb coral.
- Do not take any shells home with you – it's illegal.
- Snorkelling is the best way to see whale sharks; divers' bubbles can annoy or confuse them.
- Join a coral clean-up campaign that's sponsored by dive shops.
- Don't feed the fish or allow your dive operator to dispose of excess food in the water. The fish become dependent on this food source and don't tend to the algae on the coral, causing harm to the reef.

Scuba diving off the Andaman Coast

diving spots, near the islands of Ko Tao and Ko Pha-Ngan. Pattaya, a quick two-hour hop from the Bangkok bustle, offers a few memorable dives as well, including a couple of wrecks. On the far eastern side of the coast, the Ko Chang archipelago has some pleasant scuba possibilities including several dive wrecks, although choppy seas limit the season to between November and May.

When to Go

Generally speaking, the Gulf of Thailand has a year-round dive season, while the Andaman Coast has optimal diving conditions between December and April. In the Ko Chang archipelago, November to early May is the ideal season. Try to avoid the monsoon and rainy seasons.

Dec–Feb Days are mostly rain-free and under the waves you'll find a conglomeration of large pelagics at the feeding stations along the Andaman Coast.

Apr–Jun Things are pretty quiet along the gulf at this time, and the weather holds out nicely, allowing for good visibility underwater.

Jun–Sep The monsoon rains arrive on the Andaman Coast, some hotels shut down and boat travel can be interrupted by storms.

Oct–Dec The gulf coast bears the brunt of its rainy season.

Safe Diving

Before You Dive

Before embarking on a diving trip, carefully consider the following points to ensure a safe and enjoyable experience:

- Ensure you feel comfortable diving and that you are very hydrated on the days you dive.
- Remember that your last dive should be completed 24 hours before you fly. It is, however, fine to dive soon after arriving by air.
- Make sure your insurance policy covers diving injuries. If it doesn't, consider purchasing additional coverage via www.diversalertnetwork.org.
- Download and check through PADI's medical health, as there are some strict health requirements for diving.

Decompression Chambers

For the amount of diving occurring in Thailand, the kingdom has a surprisingly limited number of medical facilities dedicated to diving accidents.

Decompression (hyperbaric) chambers can be found at most major hubs, including Bangkok, Ko Samui, Pattaya and Phuket. Ko Tao does not have an emergency chamber – the nearest one is on Ko Samui, a 1½-hour speedboat journey away. Injured divers out of Khao Lak are generally rushed south to Phuket (about an hour away). We advise you to ask your dive operator about the nearest chamber. Also make sure there is an emergency supply of oxygen on your dive boat.

Snorkelling

Many islands, including the Trang island chain, Ko Tao, Ko Pha-Ngan, Ko Phi-Phi, Ko Lipe and the islands in the Ko Chang archipelago, have phenomenal snorkelling spots right offshore.

On Your Own

Orchestrating your own snorkelling adventure is easy – there are loads of resorts and dive shops spread throughout Thailand's islands and beaches that rent out gear for 100B to 200B per hour. If you plan on snorkelling under your own steam, follow the same simple rules that you would for diving:

- Take a buddy with you.
- Don't go without a guide if you're not a confident swimmer, or are unsure how to handle rips.
- Let someone on land know that you are going snorkelling, just in case something happens to you and your buddy.
- Keep an eye out above water to make sure you're not swimming too far out.
- Watch for boats: don't expect them to see you!

WHALE SHARKS

The elusive whale shark – the largest fish in the sea – has a giant mouth that can measure about 2m wide (so just imagine how big their bodies are!). Don't worry: they are filter feeders, which means they mostly eat plankton, krill and other tiny organisms. Usually these gentle creatures gravitate towards submerged pinnacles. They often hang out at a site for several days before continuing on, so if rumours are flying around about a recent sighting, grab your snorkel gear and hit the high seas.

Tours

Many tour offices and dive operators offer snorkelling trips from 600B and up; the price will depend on how far you travel. A snorkelling component is often tied into larger day trips that take in pristine islands and kayaking too.

High-end excursions usually use fancy speedboats and expensive equipment, while cheaper deals tend to focus more on the social aspect of the trip, taking customers to so-so reefs.

Night market in Hua Hin (p170)

Plan Your Trip

Eat & Drink Like a Local

Incendiary curries, oodles of noodles, fresh seafood and the tropical fruit you've been dreaming about – Thailand has it all. To experience the true flavours of Thailand, you need to familiarise yourself with the dishes of Thailand's various regions and ethnic groups.

GREGD / SHUTTERSTOCK ©

The Year in Food

Summer (March to June)

Thailand's hot season is the best time of year for fruit. Durian (pictured left), mangoes, mangosteen and lychees are all at their juicy peak during these months.

Rainy Season (July to October)

One event to look out for during the rainy season is Thailand's annual Vegetarian Festival, typically held in late September or early October. The festival is celebrated particularly in places with large Chinese populations, such as Bangkok, Phuket Town and Trang.

Winter (November to January)

During Thailand's brief cool season, open-air beer halls, many serving spicy Thai drinking snacks, spring up in the larger cities.

Food Experiences

Meals of a Lifetime

Krua Apsorn (p101), Bangkok This award-winning restaurant has a thick menu of decadent fare influenced by Bangkok and central Thailand.

One Chun (p297), Phuket Town Southern-style curries and seafood served in a Sino-Portuguese shophouse that looks like it hasn't been touched since the 1950s.

Chanthorn (p140), Chanthaburi Just up from the waterfront, this is a fine spot to try traditional flavours like pork with chamung leaves.

Koti (p175), Hua Hin You know a restaurant in Thailand is good when the queue for a table stretches around the corner.

In Town Seafood (p184), Prachuap Khiri Khan Fantastic seafood and views of the awesome bay at this locals' favourite.

Krua Thara (p333), Krabi One of Thailand's very best seafood kitchens attracts domestic tourists from around the country.

Cheap Eats

MBK Food Island (p83), Bangkok A cheap, clean and tasty introduction to Thai and Thai-Chinese staples.

Abdul's Roti Shop (p296), Phuket Town A local legend, friendly Abdul has been cooking delicious *roh·dee* (a fried 'pancake') at the front of his shop for years, served either sweet with sticky banana or savoury with spicy fish or meat curries.

Jek Pia (p174), Hua Hin Some of the city's best cooks work together at this culinary gem.

Krua Talay (p254), Nakhon Si Thammarat Simply superb Thai seafood in an alluring garden setting.

Blues Blues Restaurant (p153), Ko Chang This arty oasis does brilliant stir-fries and makes a great break from the brasher face of the island.

Cooking Courses

A standard one-day course usually features a shopping trip to a local market to choose ingredients, followed by preparation of curry pastes, soups, curries, salads and desserts.

Amita Thai Cooking Class (p86), Bangkok Learn to make Thai dishes at this canalside family compound.

Samui Institute of Thai Culinary Arts (p200), Ko Samui Courses in fruit-carving are also available here.

Hemingway's on the Beach (p210), Ko Samui Learn to cook Thai food at this beach-side restaurant.

Phuket Thai Cookery School (p301), Ko Sireh A menu of dishes that changes on a daily basis is taught here.

Local Specialities

Despite having evolved in a relatively small area, Thai cuisine is anything but a single entity and takes a slightly different form every time it crosses a provincial border.

Bangkok & Central Thai Cuisine

When foreigners think of Thai food, they're often thinking of the dishes of Bangkok and the central plains. A wealth of agriculture, access to the sea and the influence of foreign cuisines have come together in a cuisine that is both sophisticated and diverse.

The people of central Thailand are fond of sweet-savoury flavours, and many dishes include freshwater fish, pork, coconut milk and palm sugar – common ingredients in the central Thai plains. Because of the region's proximity to the Gulf of Thailand, central Thai eateries, particularly those in Bangkok, also serve a wide variety of seafood. Chinese labourers and vendors introduced a huge variety of noodle and wok-fried dishes to central Thailand as many as 200 years ago.

Must-eat central Thai and Bangkok dishes include the following:

Pàt tai Thin rice noodles stir-fried with dried and/or fresh shrimp, bean sprouts, tofu, egg and seasonings, traditionally served with lime halves and a few stalks of Chinese chives and a sliced banana flower.

Yam Ƅlah dùk foo Fried shredded catfish, chilli and peanuts served with a sweet/tart mango dressing.

Đôm yam Lemongrass, kaffir lime leaf and lime juice give this soup its characteristic tang; fresh chillies or an oily chilli paste provide it with its legendary sting. Available just about everywhere, but it's hard to beat the version at Krua Apsorn (p101).

Yen đah foh Combining a slightly sweet crimson-coloured broth with a variety of meatballs, cubes of blood and crispy greens, *yen đah foh* is probably both the most intimidating and popular noodle dish in Bangkok. Available at many street stalls.

Gaang sôm Central Thailand's famous 'sour soup' often includes freshwater fish, vegetables and/or herbs, and a thick, tart broth.

Gŏo•ay đĕe•o reua Known as boat noodles because they were previously served from small boats along the canals of central Thailand, these intense pork- or beef-based bowls are among the most full-flavoured of Thai noodle dishes.

Southern Thai Cuisine

Don't say we didn't warn you: southern Thai cooking is undoubtedly the spiciest regional cooking style in a land of spicy regional cuisines. The food of Thailand's southern provinces also tends to be very salty, and seafood, not surprisingly, plays an important role. Fresh fish is grilled, added to soups, dried, or pickled and fermented for sauces and condiments. Two of the principal crops in the south are coconuts and cashews, both of which find their way into a variety of dishes. Nearly every meal is accompanied by a platter of fresh herbs and vegetables, and a spicy 'dip' of shrimp paste, chillies, garlic and lime.

Dishes you are likely to come across in southern Thailand include the following:

Gaang đai Ƅlah An intensely spicy and salty curry that includes *đai Ƅlah* (salted fish kidney); much tastier than it sounds.

Gaang sôm Known as *gaang lĕu·ang* (yellow curry) in central Thailand, this sour/spicy soup gets its hue from the liberal use of turmeric, a root commonly used in southern Thai cooking.

Gài tôrt hàht yài The famous deep-fried chicken from the town of Hat Yai gets its rich flavour from a marinade containing dried spices.

Kà·nŏm jeen nám yah This dish of thin rice noodles served with a fiery curry-like sauce is always accompanied by a tray of fresh vegetables and herbs.

Kôo·a glîng Minced meat fried with a fiery curry paste is a southern staple.

Pàt sà·đor This popular stir-fry of 'stink beans' with shrimp, garlic, chillies and shrimp paste is both pungent and spicy.

Ethnic Specialities

In addition to geography, the country's predominant minorities – Muslims and the Chinese – have had different but profound influences on the local cuisine.

Thai-Chinese Cuisine

Immigrants from southern China have been influencing Thai cuisine for centuries, and it was most likely Chinese labourers and vendors who introduced the wok and several varieties of noodle dishes to Thailand. They also influenced Bangkok's

Pàt tai noodle dish

cuisine in other ways: beef is not widely eaten in Bangkok due to a Chinese-Buddhist teaching that forbids eating 'large' animals.

Thai-Chinese dishes you're likely to run across in Bangkok's Chinatown (and elsewhere) include the following:

Kôw kăh mŏo Braised pork leg served over rice, often with a side of greens and a hard-boiled egg, is the epitome of the Thai-Chinese one-dish meal. It's available at the **Soi 10 Food Centres** (Map p88; Soi 10, Th Silom; mains 20-60B; ⏰8am-3pm Mon-Fri; Ⓜ Si Lom exit 2, Ⓢ Sala Daeng exit 1) and other street markets.

Kôw man gài Chicken rice, originally from the Chinese island of Hainan, is now found in just about every corner of Bangkok. We particularly like the version served at **Boon Tong Kiat Singapore Chicken Rice** (Map p84; 440/5 Soi 55/Thong Lor, Th Sukhumvit; mains 65-300B; ⏰10am-10pm; ❄; Ⓢ Thong Lo exit 3 & taxi).

Bà·mèe Chinese-style wheat-and-egg noodles typically served with slices of barbecued pork, a handful of greens and/or wontons. **Mangkorn Khăo** (Map p92; cnr Th Yaowarat & Th Yaowaphanit; mains from 50B; ⏰6pm-midnight Tue-Sun; ⛴ Ratchawong Pier, Ⓜ Hualamphong exit 1), a street stall in Chinatown, does one of Bangkok's better bowls.

Săh·lah ƀow Chinese-style steamed buns, served with sweet or savoury fillings, are a favourite snack in Bangkok.

Gŏo·ay đěe·o kôoa gài Wide rice noodles fried with little more than egg, chicken, salted squid and garlic oil is a popular Thai-Chinese dish.

Hŏy tôrt Another Bangkok Chinatown staple, this dish combines a sticky, eggy batter topped with oysters. **Nai Mong Hoi Thod** (Map p70; 539 Th Phlap Phla Chai; mains 50-70B; ⏰5-10pm Tue-Sun; ⛴ Ratchawong Pier, Ⓜ Hua Lamphong exit 1) does what is arguably Bangkok's best take on this dish.

Gŏoay jáp This dish consists of an intensely peppery broth and pork offal.

Thai-Muslim Cuisine

When Muslims first visited Thailand during the late 14th century, they brought with them a meat- and dried-spice-based cuisine from their homelands in India and the Middle East. Nearly 700 years later, the impact of this culinary commerce can still be felt in Bangkok.

PAVARID / SHUTTERSTOCK ©

Gaang mát·sà·màn

While some Muslim dishes such as *roh·đee,* a fried bread similar to the Indian paratha, have changed little, if at all, others such as *gaang mát·sà·màn* are a unique blend of Thai and Indian–Middle Eastern cooking styles and ingredients.

Common Thai-Muslim dishes include the following:

Kôw mòk Biryani, a dish found across the Muslim world, also has a foothold in Bangkok. Here the dish is typically made with chicken and is served with a sweet-and-sour dipping sauce and a bowl of chicken broth.

Sà·dé (satay) These grilled skewers of meat probably came to Thailand via Malaysia. The savoury peanut-based dipping sauce is often mistakenly associated with Thai cooking.

Má·đà·bà Known as murtabak in Malaysia and Indonesia, these are *roh·đee* that have been stuffed with a savoury or sometimes sweet filling and fried until crispy. It's available at Karim Roti-Mataba (p101) in Bangkok.

Súp hăhng woo·a Oxtail soup, possibly another Malay contribution, is even richer and often more sour than the 'Buddhist' Thai *đôm yam*. Try the dish at Muslim Restaurant (p103) in Bangkok.

Sà·làt kàak Literally 'Muslim salad' (*kàak* is a somewhat derogatory word used to describe people or things of Indian and/or Muslim origin), this dish combines iceberg lettuce, chunks of firm tofu, cucumber, hard-boiled egg and tomato, all topped with a sweet peanut sauce.

Gaang mát·sà·màn 'Muslim curry' is a rich coconut-milk-based dish, which, unlike most Thai curries, gets much of its flavour from dried spices. As with many Thai-Muslim dishes, there is an emphasis on the sweet. A non-halal version is often served at upmarket restaurants such as nahm (p102) in Bangkok.

Roh·đee This crispy fried pancake, drizzled with condensed milk and sugar, is the perfect street dessert.

How Thais Eat

Aside from the occasional indulgence in deep-fried savouries, most Thais sustain themselves on a varied and relatively healthy diet of fruits, rice and vegetables mixed with smaller amounts of animal protein and fat. Satisfaction seems to come not from eating large amounts of food at any one meal but rather from nibbling at a variety of dishes with as many different flavours as possible throughout the day.

Nor are certain kinds of food restricted to certain times of day. Practically anything can be eaten first thing in the morning, whether it's sweet, salty or chilli-ridden. *Kôw gaang* (curry over rice) is a very popular breakfast, as are *kôw nĕe·o mŏo tôrt* (deep-fried pork with sticky rice) and *kôw man gài* (sliced chicken served over rice cooked in chicken broth). Lighter morning choices, especially for Thais of Chinese descent, include *bah·tôrng·gŏh* (deep-fried fingers of dough) dipped in warm *nám đow·hôo* (soy milk). Thais also eat noodles, whether fried or in soup, with great gusto in the morning, or as a substantial snack at any time of the day or night.

As the staple with which almost all Thai dishes are eaten (noodles are still seen as a Chinese import), *kôw* (rice) is considered an indispensable part of the daily diet. Most Bangkok families will put on a pot of rice, or start the rice cooker, just after rising in the morning to prepare a base for the day's menu.

Finding its way into almost every meal is *ƀlah* (fish), even if it's only in the form of *nám ƀlah* (a thin amber sauce made from fermented anchovies), which is used to salt Thai dishes, much as soy sauce is used in east Asia. Pork is undoubtedly the preferred protein, with chicken in second place and beef rarely consumed.

Thais are prodigious consumers of fruit. Vendors push glass-and-wood carts filled with a rainbow of fresh sliced papaya, pineapple, watermelon and mango, and a more muted palette of salt-pickled or candied seasonal fruits. These are usually served in a small plastic bag with a thin bamboo stick to use as an eating utensil.

Because many restaurants in Thailand are able to serve dishes at an only slightly higher price than they would cost to make at home, Thais dine out far more often than their Western counterparts. Dining with others is always preferred because it means everyone has a chance to sample several dishes. When forced to fly solo by circumstances – such as during lunch breaks at work – a single diner usually sticks to one-plate dishes such as fried rice or curry over rice.

Where to Eat

Prepared food is available just about everywhere in Thailand and it shouldn't come as a surprise that the locals do much of their eating outside the home. In this regard, as a visitor, you'll fit right in.

Open-air markets and food stalls are among the most popular places for Thais to eat. In the morning, stalls selling coffee and Chinese-style doughnuts spring up along busy commuter corridors. At lunchtime, midday eaters might grab a plastic chair at yet another stall for a simple stir-fry, or pick up a foam box of noodles to wolf down at the office. In most small towns, night markets often set up in the middle of town with a cluster of vendors, metal tables and chairs, and some shopping as an after-dinner mint.

There are, of course, restaurants *(ráhn ah·hăhn)* in Thailand that range from simple food stops to formal affairs. Lunch is the right time to point and eat at the *ráhn kôw gaang* (rice-and-curry shop), which sells a selection of pre-made curries and other dishes. Come dinner, the ubiquitous *ráhn ah·hăhn đahm sàng* (food-to-order shop) can often be recognised by a display of raw ingredients – Chinese kale, tomatoes, chopped pork, fresh or dried fish, noodles, eggplant, spring onions – and serves a standard repertoire of largely Chinese-influenced dishes. As the name implies, the cooks attempt to prepare any dish you can name, which is a slightly more difficult operation if you can't speak Thai.

Glossary

a·ròy – the Thai word for delicious

bà·mèe – wheat-and-egg noodles

đôm yam – Thailand's famous sour and spicy soup

gaang – curry

gài – chicken

gŏo·ay đĕe·o – the generic term for noodle soup

kà·nŏm – Thai-style sweet snacks

kôw – rice

kôw nĕe·o – sticky rice

lâhp – a 'salad' of minced meat

mŏo – pork

nám dèum – drinking water

nám ƀlah – fish sauce

nám prík – chilli-based dips

pàk – vegetables

pàt – fried

pàt see·éw – wide rice noodles fried with pork and greens

pàt tai – thin rice noodles fried with egg and seasonings

pèt – spicy

ƀèt – duck

ƀlah – fish

pŏn·lá·mái – fruit

prík – chilli

ráhn ah·hăhn – restaurant

tôrt – deep-fried

yam – a Thai-style salad

Food Spotter's Guide

Spanning four distinct regions, influences from China to the Middle East, a multitude of ingredients and a reputation for spice, Thai food can be more than a bit overwhelming. So to point you in the direction of the good stuff, we've put together a shortlist of the country's must-eat dishes.

1. Đôm yam

The 'sour Thai soup' moniker featured on many menus is a feeble description of this mouth-puckeringly tart and intensely spicy herbal broth.

2. Pàt tai

Thin rice noodles fried with egg, tofu and shrimp, and seasoned with fish sauce, tamarind and dried chilli, have emerged as the poster child for Thai food.

3. Gaang kĕe·o wăhn

Known outside of Thailand as green curry, this intersection of a piquant, herbal spice paste and rich coconut milk is single-handedly emblematic of Thai cuisine's unique flavours and ingredients.

4. Yam

This family of Thai 'salads' combines meat or seafood with a tart and spicy dressing and fresh herbs.

5. Lâhp

Minced meat seasoned with roasted rice powder, lime, fish sauce and fresh herbs is a one-dish crash course in the rustic flavours of Thailand's northeast.

6. Bà·mèe

Although Chinese in origin, these wheat-and-egg noodles, typically served with roast pork and/or crab, have become a Thai hawker-stall staple.

7. Kôw mòk

The Thai version of biryani couples golden rice and tender chicken with a sweet and sour dip and a savoury broth.

8. Sôm·đam

'Papaya salad' hardly does justice to this tear-inducingly spicy dish of strips of crunchy unripe papaya pounded in a mortar and pestle with tomato, long beans, chilli, lime and fish sauce.

9. Kôw soy

Even outside of its home in Thailand's north, there's a cult following for this soup that combines flat egg-and-wheat noodles in a rich, spice-laden, coconut-milk-based broth.

10. Pàt pàk bûng fai daang

Crunchy green vegetables, flash-fried with heaps of chilli and garlic, is Thai comfort food.

1

6

8

NARIN NONTHAMAND / SHUTTERSTOCK ©
NENEULTIMATE / SHUTTERSTOCK ©
CHOCKDEE ROMKAEW / SHUTTERSTOCK ©
PAUL_BRIGHTON / SHUTTERSTOCK ©
MOXUMBIC / SHUTTERSTOCK ©
CBENJASUWAN / SHUTTERSTOCK ©
PIYATO / SHUTTERSTOCK ©

Plan Your Trip

Travel with Children

Thais are serious 'cute' connoisseurs and exotic-looking foreign kids rank higher on their adorable meter than stuffed animals and fluffy dogs. Children are instant celebrities and attract a lot of attention. Older kids get less interest, but will revel in the sandy beaches, warm water and many activities on offer.

Best Regions for Kids

Ko Samui & the Lower Gulf

Ko Samui's northern beaches and Ko Pha-Ngan's northern and eastern beaches are popular with toddlers, while Hat Chaweng appeals to older kids. Older children can snorkel Ko Tao without worry.

Phuket & the Northern Andaman Coast

Phuket has amusements galore, as well as the beach, but steer clear of the Patong party scene. Ko Lanta's long beaches with mellow surf are good for kids, while the Trang islands offer shallow, easy swimming.

Ko Chang & the Eastern Seaboard

Shallow seas are kind to young swimmers and low evening tides make for good beachcombing. Older kids will like the interior jungle and mangrove kayaking.

Hua Hin & the Southern Gulf

Hua Hin has a long sandy coastline and hillside temples for monkey spotting. Phetchaburi's cave temples often deliver a bat sighting. Ban Krut and Bang Saphan Yai are casual and ideal for kids.

Thailand's Islands & Beaches for Kids

It's hard to beat this region for its kid-friendliness. Not only are the Thais genuinely enamoured of children – restaurants and resorts will welcome them with open arms – but this is a safe place to travel and everywhere you go kids will find sandy beaches, a warm, mostly placid sea to swim in and any number of amusements and activities to keep them entertained.

The larger islands – Phuket, Ko Samui and Ko Chang – are especially well set-up for children. Many resorts organise specific water sports for kids over six, while there are a big array of outdoor activities, as well as amusement parks and wildlife sanctuaries to visit.

Children's Highlights

Beaches

Swimming, Trang Islands & Ko Samui The shallow, gentle bays of the Trang Islands (p354) and the northern beaches of Ko Samui (p196) are perfect for beginner or younger swimmers.

Snorkelling, Ko Lipe & Ko Wai Older kids can strap on a mask and snorkel close to the beach on Ko Lipe (p366) and Ko Wai (p158).

Splash Jungle water park (p292)

Surfing (p310), Hat Kata Yai The gentle breaks at Hat Kata Yai on Phuket are ideal for beginners. Sign the older ones up for a day's surf school.

Diving (p233), Ko Tao Children are eligible to take an open-water course from the age of 10. With many reputable dive schools and shallow diving, Ko Tao is the ideal place to learn.

Kayaking (p285), Ao Phang-Nga Marine National Park Take a kayaking tour in this spectacular reserve.

Resorts, Phuket, Ko Chang & Ko Samui Many of the big resorts on Phuket (p288), Ko Samui (p196) and Ko Chang (p144) offer organised water sports ideal for children aged six years and older.

Outdoor Activities

Amusement parks, Phuket Plentiful on Phuket. Try Splash Jungle (p292) or Phuket Wake Park (p292).

Cycling, Hua Hin & Phuket Both Hua Hin Bike Tours (p172) and Amazing Bike Tours (p295) on Phuket offer great cycling tours.

Khao Sok National Park (p275) Trek through the rainforest and search for hidden waterfalls and caves.

Rock-climbing, Railay The region's best climbing, along with good instructors and many beginner routes suitable for children, can be found on stunning Railay (p326).

Ziplining, Ko Chang & Phuket Kids over the age of seven can whizz through the air on ziplines above the jungly interiors of Ko Chang (p144) and Phuket (p288).

Wildlife Encounters

Animal rescue, Ko Lanta & Ko Chang There are a few animal rescue organisations, including Lanta Animal Welfare (p342) and the Koh Chang Animal Project (p148), where you can see the animals and volunteer to walk the dogs or play with the kittens.

Phuket Aquarium (p300) Tonnes of colourful fish, and sharks and electric eels too at this impressive aquarium.

Phuket Elephant Sanctuary (p322) Children love to feed the retired elephants and watch them bathe and hang out.

Phuket Gibbon Rehabilitation Project (p321) Children can't get too close to the gibbons but they still like looking at them.

Monkeys, Ko Phi-Phi, Railay & Phetchaburi On the beach at Ko Phi-Phi (p333), dangling from limestone cliffs in Railay (p326) and hanging out at the temples of Phetchaburi (p162).

Unexpected Fun

Food markets, Phuket & Trang Outdoor eating is a lot of fun, and the Indy Market (p297) in Phuket Town and the Trang Night Market (p352) have gentle live music as well.

Malls, Hua Hin & Phuket Great air-con, shops, restaurants and cinemas in the malls at Hua Hin (p170), Phuket (p293) and the bigger towns. They make good rain shelters in the monsoon season.

Train Overnight journeys can be fun for kids. They can walk around on the train and they're assigned the lower sleeping berths with views of the stations. Some children like the dinky Hua Hin Train Station (p172).

Temples (p162), Phetchaburi The hilltop pagodas and cave temples here are fun and easy to explore and there are bats and monkeys to see too.

Planning

➡ Child-safety seats for cars, high chairs in restaurants and nappy-changing facilities in public restrooms are virtually nonexistent. Parents will have to be resourceful in seeking out substitutes, or follow the example of Thai families (holding smaller children on their laps).

➡ Baby formula and nappies (diapers) are available at mini-markets and 7-Elevens in larger towns and cities, but sizes are usually small, smaller and smallish. If your kid wears size three or larger, head to Tesco Lotus, Big C or Tops Market stores. Nappy-rash cream is sold at pharmacies.

➡ Thailand's footpaths are often too crowded to push a pram. Opt for a lightweight, compact umbrella stroller that can squeeze past the fire hydrant and the mango cart and that can be folded up and thrown in a túk-túk. A baby pack is also useful, but make sure that the child's head doesn't sit higher than yours: there are lots of hanging obstacles poised at forehead level.

➡ Avoid arriving in the rainy season if you can. Equally, you may want to avoid the hottest part of the year.

For all-round information and advice, check out Lonely Planet's *Travel with Children*.

Eating With Kids

Dining with children, particularly with infants, in Thailand is a liberating experience as the Thais are so fond of kids. Take it for granted that your babies will be fawned over, played with and, more often than not, carried around by restaurant waitstaff. Regard this as a much-deserved break, not to mention a bit of free cultural exposure.

Because much Thai food is so spicy, there is an entire art devoted to ordering 'safe' dishes for children, and the vast majority of Thai kitchens are more than willing to oblige. Many restaurants and resorts have specific kids' menus featuring Western kiddie favourites, which makes life much easier.

In general, Thai children don't start to eat spicy food until primary school. Before then they seemingly survive on rice and jelly snacks. Other kid-friendly meals include chicken in all its nonspicy permutations – *gài yâhng* (grilled chicken), *gài tôrt* (fried chicken) and *gài pàt mét má•môo•ang* (chicken stir-fried with cashew nuts) – as well as *kài jee•o* (Thai-style omelette). Mild options include *kôw man gài* (Hainanese chicken rice).

The Thais have a sweet tooth and there are many cake and dessert options, so if you are concerned about sugar consumption be watchful.

Health & Safety

For the most part parents needn't worry too much about health concerns, although a few ground rules (such as regular hand washing) can head off potential medical problems. In particular:

➡ Children should be warned not to play with animals (from dogs to monkeys), as bites can be nasty and rabies is relatively common in Thailand.

➡ Mosquito bites often leave big welts on children. If your child is bitten, there are a variety of locally produced balms that can reduce swelling and itching. All the usual health precautions apply.

➡ If kids do need medical treatment, then the hospitals in big towns, or on big islands like Phuket, Ko Samui and Ko Chang, offer international standards of care.

Regions at a Glance

Bangkok

Culture & History
Nightlife
Food

Buddhist Temples

Once a show of strength after the devastating 1765–67 war with Burma (now Myanmar), Bangkok's royal Buddhist temples are now both national pilgrimage sites and fabulous, intriguing displays of classical art and architecture.

Drinking Views

In Bangkok, it's common to slap a bar on top of a skyscraper. Indeed, the city has become associated with elegant open-air rooftop bars, with venues packing views that range from riverside to hyper-urban.

Street-Side Eats

For adventurous foodies who can live without white tablecloths, there's probably no better dining destination than Bangkok. And until you've eaten on the capital's streets, your just-sizzled noodles mingling with your sweat amid a cloud of exhaust fumes, you haven't actually eaten Thai food.

p66

Ko Chang & the Eastern Seaboard

Islands
Small Towns
Diving

Island Trifecta

Ko Chang has jungles and party animals, Ko Mak boasts a laid-back island vibe and Ko Kut has some of the prettiest views you'll ever see. There are easy transport connections between these three islands.

Provincial Towns

The eastern seaboard's small towns include trendy Bang Saen; charming and increasingly hip Chanthaburi, famous for a weekend gem market; and Trat, a transit link to Ko Chang. These provincial towns delight with their ordinariness and a middle-class prosperity not found on the islands.

Underwater Discoveries

It may not compare with those further south, but wrecks and coral banks make this a worthy region to blow bubbles. Finely preserved reefs cluster around uninhabited Ko Rang, while the purposely sunk *HTMS Chang* lies in wait off Ko Chang.

p118

Hua Hin & the Upper Gulf

Coastal Scenery
Culture & History
Food

Atmospheric Panoramas

Mellow Prachuap Khiri Khan has stunning karst panoramas dotted with bobbing fishing boats, while Hua Hin and Phetchaburi boast atmospheric shophouse districts dating from the time when parts of Thailand's coast were settled by Chinese merchants.

Capital Escape

Thai kings started the escape from Bangkok's stifling climate to Hua Hin, and modern Bangkokians follow in their footsteps. The region's coastline is long, inviting and not as crowded as Thailand's other resort areas.

Seafood Thai Style

For a taste of how the Thais like their seafood – think spicy – head to the upper gulf coast, which caters more to Thai tourists. Get ready for an explosion of tastes amid the affordable markets and seafood eateries of Prachuap Khiri Khan and Chumphon.

p160

Ko Samui & the Lower Gulf

Nightlife
Beaches
Diving

Beach Parties

The biggest and boldest of Thailand's beach parties bursts into action once a month on Hat Rin Nok on Ko Pha-Ngan. Prepare for fire twirling, thumping bass, neon body paint, sickly sweet booze buckets and absolutely no sleep.

Sand & Sun

On the classic gulf trail, Ko Pha-Ngan's beach layabout vibe stands strong, while professional Ko Samui caters to international tastes, high-end tendencies and active holidaymakers. Stunning limestone Ang Thong Marine National Park, a day-trip dreamboat, juts out of azure seas.

Underwater Fun

With warm gentle seas, shallow bays, year-round activity and wallet-friendly dive schools, Ko Tao remains one of the world's top places to master the art of scuba diving. Just offshore are snorkelling points that make fish-spotting easy and fun.

p193

Phuket & the Andaman Coast

Diving
Food
Spas

Market Fare

Fantastic night markets in Phuket Town, a growing number of excellent but affordable international eateries and many fine-dining options make Phuket and the Andaman Coast a foodie paradise. And did we mention the seafood?

Pampering

There's perhaps no better place in Thailand than Phuket for pampering. Some of the finest spas in the country can be found here. If the budget is tight, then there are many affordable massage options too.

World-Class Sites

Big fish, beautiful corals, great visibility – stellar diving and snorkelling sites orbit the renowned Similan and Surin Islands. Hop on a live-aboard to cavort with manta rays and the occasional whale shark at Richelieu Rock, Ko Bon and Ko Tachai.

p263

On the Road

Bangkok

☎ 02 / POP 9.27 MILLION

Includes ➡

Best Places to Eat

- nahm (p102)
- Eat Me (p103)
- Krua Apsorn (p101)
- Jay Fai (p102)
- MBK Food Island (p83)
- Soul Food Mahanakorn (p104)

Best Places to Stay

- AriyasomVilla (p98)
- Phra-Nakorn Norn-Len (p99)
- Siam Heritage (p97)
- Loy La Long (p91)
- Lamphu Treehouse (p91)

Why Go?

Same same, but different. This Thailish T-shirt philosophy sums up Bangkok, a city where the familiar and the exotic collide like the flavours on a plate of *pàt tai*.

Climate-controlled mega-malls sit side by side with 200-year-old village homes; gold-spired temples share space with neon-lit strips of sleaze; slow-moving traffic is bypassed by long-tail boats plying the royal river. For adventurous foodies who don't need white tablecloths, there's probably no better dining destination. And with immigration bringing every regional Thai and international cuisine to the capital, it's a truly diverse experience.

With so much daily life conducted on the street, exploring Bangkok is handsomely rewarded. Cap off a boat trip with a visit to a hidden market. Get lost in Chinatown's lanes and stumble upon a Chinese opera performance. And after dark let the Skytrain escort you to Sukhumvit, where the nightlife reveals a cosmopolitan and dynamic city.

When to Go

Bangkok

°C/°F **Temp** — **Rainfall** inches/mm

40/104 – 30/86 – 20/68 – 10/50 – 0/32

20/500 – 16/400 – 12/300 – 8/200 – 4/100 – 0

J F M A M J J A S O N D

Nov–Mar It's relatively cool and dry, but high-season crowds bring inflated rates.

May–Oct The city can receive more than 200mm of rain monthly.

Dec–Jan A couple of weeks of relative coolness provide a break from the heat.

Bangkok Highlights

1. **Wat Pho** (p72) Trying to stop your jaw from dropping to the floor upon encountering the enormous reclining Buddha.

2. **Wat Phra Kaew & Grand Palace** (p71) Basking in the glow of the Emerald Buddha.

3. **Chatuchak Weekend Market** (p110) Burning baht on colourful souvenirs, vintage gear and food galore.

4. **Jim Thompson House** (p79) Admiring the best of Thai architecture and artwork.

5. **Thai massage** (p83) Being blissfully pounded into submission at a terrific-value massage centre.

6. **Chinatown** (p77) Eating yourself into a stupor at Chinatown's street stalls.

7. **Rooftop Bars** (p142) Toasting the stars and the twinkling skyscraper lights from a lofty bar.

8. **Cooking Schools** (p86) Mastering spices and learning authentic recipes in a Thai cookery class.

9. **Thonburi's Canals** (p76) Gliding between sightseeing spots on a leisurely cruise.

10. **Amphawa** (p78) Exploring quaint wooden buildings in this canalside town outside Bangkok.

History

Now the centre of government and culture in Thailand, Bangkok's founding was a historical miracle during a time of turmoil. Following the fall of Ayuthaya in 1767, the kingdom fractured into competing forces, from which General Taksin emerged as a decisive unifier. He established his base in Thonburi, on the western bank of Mae Nam Chao Phraya (Chao Phraya River), a convenient location

Wat Phra Kaew & Grand Palace

EXPLORE BANGKOK'S PREMIER MONUMENTS TO RELIGION & REGENCY

The first area tourists enter is the Buddhist temple compound generally referred to as Wat Phra Kaew. A covered walkway surrounds the area, the inner walls of which are decorated with the ❶ ❷ **murals of the Ramakian**. Originally painted during the reign of Rama I (r 1782–1809), the murals, which depict the Hindu epic the *Ramayana*, span 178 panels that describe the struggles of Rama to rescue his kidnapped wife, Sita.

After taking in the story, pass through one of the gateways guarded by ❸ **yaksha** to the inner compound. The most important structure here is the ❹ **bòht, or ordination hall**, which houses the ❺ **Emerald Buddha**.

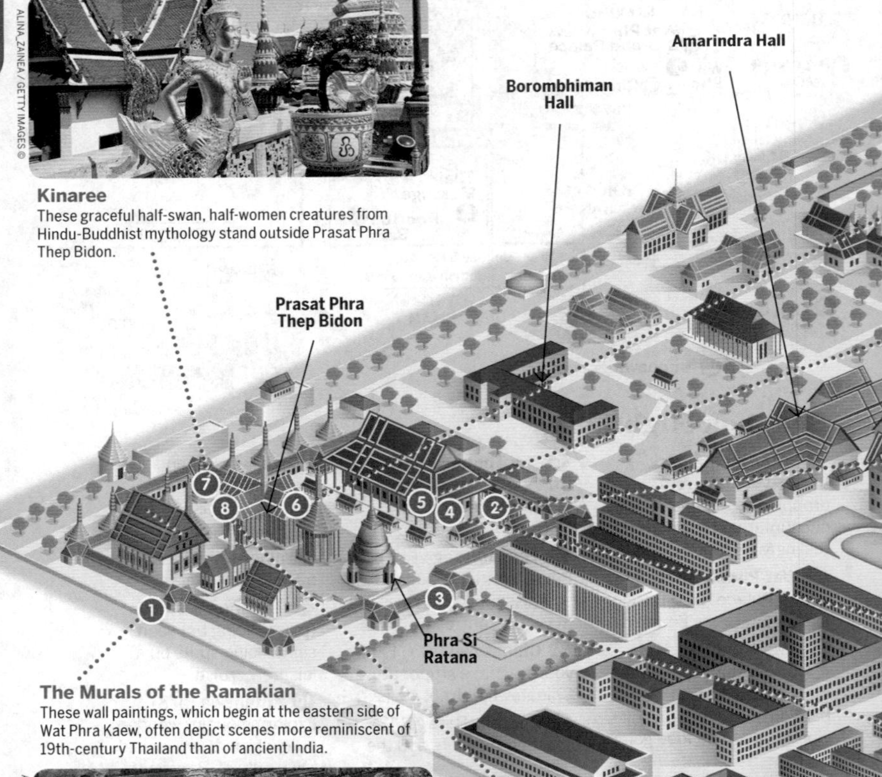

Kinaree

These graceful half-swan, half-women creatures from Hindu-Buddhist mythology stand outside Prasat Phra Thep Bidon.

The Murals of the Ramakian

These wall paintings, which begin at the eastern side of Wat Phra Kaew, often depict scenes more reminiscent of 19th-century Thailand than of ancient India.

ANTONIO D'ALBORE / GETTY IMAGES ©

Hanuman

Rows of these mischievous monkey deities from Hindu mythology appear to support the lower levels of two small *chedi* near Prasat Phra Thep Bidon.

Head east to the so-called Upper Terrace, an elevated area home to the 6 **spires of the three primary chedi**. The middle structure, Phra Mondop, is used to house Buddhist manuscripts. This area is also home to several of Wat Phra Kaew's noteworthy mythical beings, including beckoning 7 **kinaree** and several grimacing 8 **Hanuman**.

Proceed through the western gate to the compound known as the Grand Palace. Few of the buildings here are open to the public. The most noteworthy structure is 9 **Chakri Mahaprasat**. Built in 1882, the exterior of the hall is a unique blend of Western and traditional Thai architecture.

The Three Spires
The elaborate seven-tiered roof of Phra Mondop, the Khmer-style peak of Prasat Phra Thep Bidon, and the gilded Phra Si Ratana *chedi* are the tallest structures in the compound.

LEPNEVA IRINA / SHUTTERSTOCK ©

Emerald Buddha
Despite the name, this diminutive statue (it's only 66cm tall) is actually carved from nephrite, a type of jade.

ALEXEY STIOP / GETTY IMAGES ©

The Death of Thotsakan
The panels progress clockwise, culminating at the western edge of the compound with the death of Thotsakan, Sita's kidnapper, and his elaborate funeral procession.

Chakri Mahaprasat
This structure is sometimes referred to as *fa·ràng sài chá·dah* (Westerner in a Thai crown) because each wing is topped by a *mon·dòp*: a spire representing a Thai adaptation of a Hindu shrine.

DESIGN PICS / BLAKE KENT / GETTY IMAGES ©

9

Dusit Hall

Bòht (Ordination Hall)
This structure is an early example of the Ratanakosin school of architecture, which combines traditional stylistic holdovers from Ayuthaya along with more modern touches from China and the West.

Yaksha
Each entrance to the Wat Phra Kaew compound is watched over by a pair of vigilant and enormous *yaksha*, ogres or giants from Hindu mythology.

ZZVET / GETTY IMAGES ©

Ko Ratanakosin, Banglamphu & Thonburi

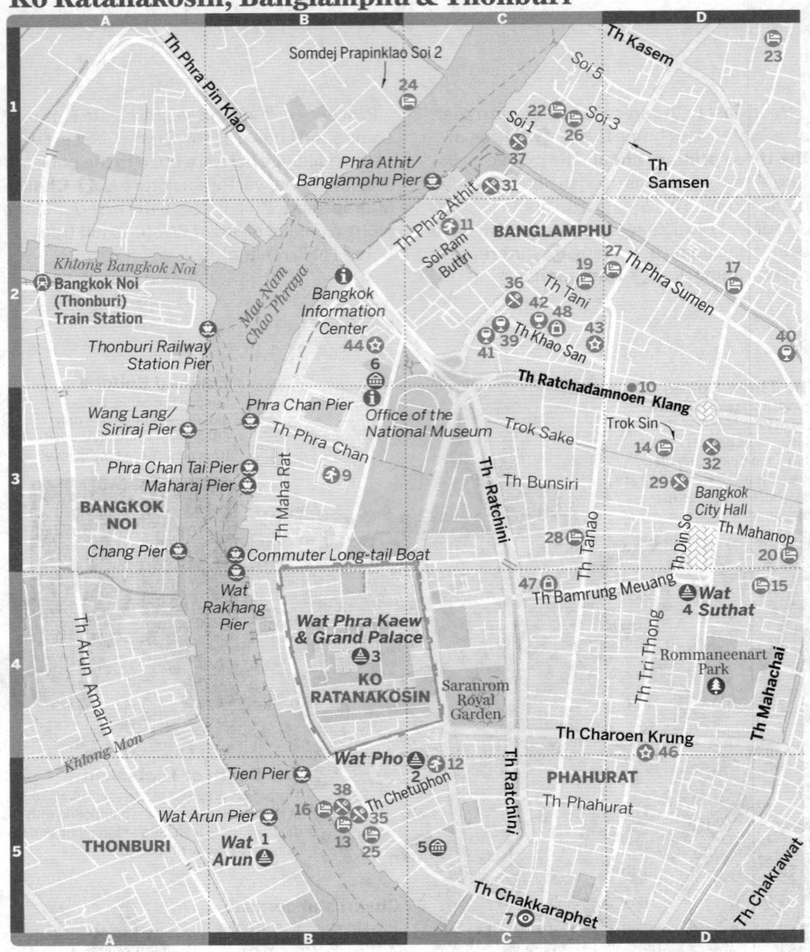

for sea trade from the Gulf of Thailand. Taksin proved more of a military strategist than a popular ruler. He was later deposed by another important military general, Chao Phraya Chakri, who in 1782 moved the capital across the river to a more defensible location in anticipation of a Burmese attack. The succession of his son in 1809 established the present-day royal dynasty, and Chao Phraya Chakri is referred to as Rama I.

Court officials envisioned the new capital as a resurrected Ayuthaya, complete with an island district (Ko Ratanakosin) carved out of the swampland and cradling the royal court (the Grand Palace) and a temple to the auspicious Emerald Buddha (Wat Phra Kaew). The emerging city, which was encircled by a thick wall, was filled with stilt and floating houses ideally adapted to seasonal flooding.

Modernity came to the capital in the late 19th century as European aesthetics and technologies filtered east. During the reigns of Rama IV (King Mongkut; r 1851–68) and Rama V (King Chulalongkorn; r 1868–1910), Bangkok received its first paved road (Th Charoen Krung, formerly known as New Road) and a new royal district (Dusit) styled after European palaces.

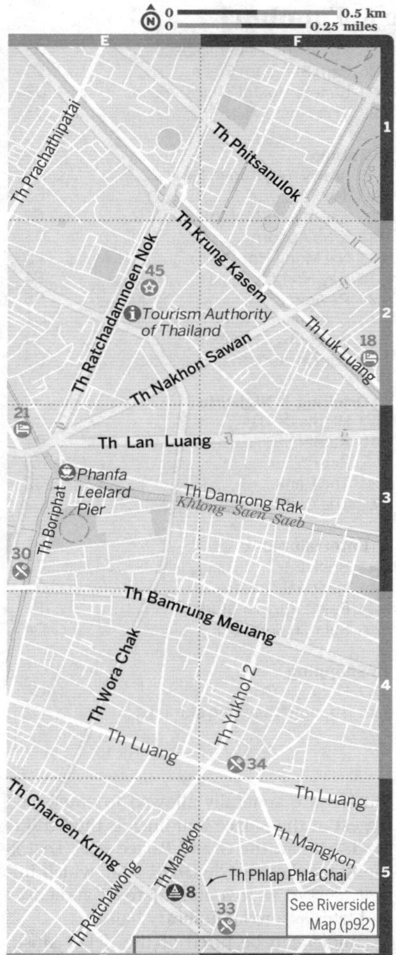

Bangkok was still a gangly town when soldiers from the American War in Vietnam came to rest and relax in the city's go-go bars and brothels. It wasn't until the boom years of the 1980s and 1990s that Bangkok exploded into a fully fledged metropolis crowded with hulking skyscrapers and an endless spill of concrete that gobbled up rice paddies and green space. The city's extravagant tastes were soon tamed by the 1997 economic meltdown, the effects of which can still be seen in the numerous half-built skyscrapers. Nearly two decades later, many of these still exist, but they are becoming increasingly obscured behind a modern public-transport system and the seemingly endless high-rise condos and vast glass-fronted mega-malls that have come to define the Bangkok of today.

In recent years the military junta has embarked on several policies and projects that have had a huge impact on the city. A ban on street vendors in certain neighbourhoods has already altered the city's footpaths. A plan to build a 14km promenade along Mae Nam Chao Praya has already resulted in the demolition of nearly 300 riverside structures, many of which were decades old. These forces, coupled with commercial interests, mean that Bangkok is changing at an astonishing rate.

Sights

Cultural and religious destinations form the bulk of Bangkok's most popular sights. If you're open to self-guided exploration, then you can add fresh markets and neighbourhoods to this list.

Ko Ratanakosin

The birthplace of Bangkok, the artificial island of Ko Ratanakosin is where it all started more than 200 years ago. The remnants of this history – today Bangkok's biggest sights – draw just about every visitor to the city. The big-hitters, Wat Phra Kaew: the Grand Palace and Wat Pho, are a short walk from the Chao Phraya Express Boat piers at Chang Pier, Maharaj Pier and Tien Pier, and are within walking distance of each other, although the hot sun may make doing this a more demanding task than it appears. Alternatively, túk-túks (pronounced *đúk đúk*) are a dime a dozen around here. If you're planning on visiting several sights, it's a good idea to arrive early in the morning for the cooler weather and to avoid the crowds. Evening is best for photography, particularly if you're hoping for the classic sunset shot of Wat Arun.

★Wat Phra Kaew & Grand Palace BUDDHIST TEMPLE

(วัดพระแก้ว, พระบรมมหาราชวัง; Map p70; Th Na Phra Lan; 500B; 8.30am-3.30pm; Chang Pier, Maharaj Pier, Phra Chan Tai Pier) Also known as the Temple of the Emerald Buddha, Wat Phra Kaew is the colloquial name of the vast, fairy-tale compound that also includes the former residence of the Thai monarch, the Grand Palace.

This ground was consecrated in 1782, the first year of Bangkok rule, and is today Bangkok's biggest tourist attraction and a

Ko Ratanakosin, Banglamphu & Thonburi

Top Sights
1 Wat Arun B5
2 Wat Pho C5
3 Wat Phra Kaew & Grand Palace B4
4 Wat Suthat D4

Sights
5 Museum of Siam C5
6 National Museum B2
7 Pak Khlong Talat C5
8 Wat Mangkon Kamalawat E5

Activities, Courses & Tours
9 Center Meditation Wat Mahadhatu B3
Chetawan Traditional Massage School .... (see 25)
10 Grasshopper Adventures D3
11 Jaroenthong Muay Thai Gym C2
12 Massage Pavilions C5
National Museum Tours .... (see 6)

Sleeping
13 Arun Residence B5
14 Baan Dinso D3
15 Chern D4
16 Inn a Day B5
17 Lamphu Treehouse D2
18 Loog Choob Homestay F2
19 NapPark Hostel C2
20 Niras Bangkoc D3
21 Old Capital Bike Inn E3
22 Penpark Place C1
23 Phra-Nakorn Norn-Len D1
24 Praya Palazzo C1
25 Royal Tha Tien Village B5
26 Sam Sen Sam Place C1
27 Suneta Hostel Khaosan D2
28 Vivit Hostel C3

Eating
29 Arawy Vegetarian Food D3
30 Jay Fai E3
31 Karim Roti-Mataba C1
32 Krua Apsorn D3
33 Nai Mong Hoi Thod F5
34 Nay Hong F4
35 Pa Aew B5
36 Shoshana C2
37 Somsong Phochana C1
38 Tonkin-Annam B5

Drinking & Nightlife
39 Hippie de Bar C2
40 Ku Bar D2
Roof .... (see 16)
41 The Bank C2
42 The Club C2

Entertainment
43 Brick Bar C2
44 National Theatre B2
45 Rajadamnern Stadium E2
46 Sala Chalermkrung D4

Shopping
47 Heritage Craft C4
48 Thanon Khao San Market C2

pilgrimage destination for devout Buddhists and nationalists. The 94.5-hectare grounds encompass more than 100 buildings that represent 200 years of royal history and architectural experimentation.

Housed in a fantastically decorated *bòht* (ordination hall), the **Emerald Buddha** is the temple's primary attraction.

Except for an anteroom here and there, the buildings of the Grand Palace are now put to use by the king only for certain ceremonial occasions, such as Coronation Day, and are largely off limits to visitors. Formerly, Thai kings housed their huge harems in the inner palace area, which was guarded by combat-trained female sentries. Outer palace buildings that visitors can view include **Borombhiman Hall**, a French-inspired structure that served as a residence for Rama VI (King Vajiravudh; r 1910–25). The building to the west is **Amarindra Hall** (open from Monday to Friday), originally a hall of justice, more recently used for coronation ceremonies, and the only palace building that tourists are generally allowed to enter. The largest of the palace buildings is the **Chakri Mahaprasat**, the Grand Palace Hall. Last is the Ratanakosin-style **Dusit Hall**, which initially served as a venue for royal audiences and later as a royal funerary hall.

Guides can be hired at the ticket kiosk; ignore offers from anyone outside. An audio guide can be rented for 200B for two hours.

Admission for the complex includes entrance to Dusit Palace Park (p82), which includes Vimanmek Teak Mansion and Abhisek Dusit Throne Hall.

★ Wat Pho — BUDDHIST TEMPLE

(วัดโพธิ์/วัดพระเชตุพน, Wat Phra Chetuphon; Map p70; Th Sanam Chai; 100B; ⌚8.30am-6.30pm; ⛴Tien Pier) You'll find (slightly) fewer tourists here than at Wat Phra Kaew, but Wat Pho is our favourite among Bangkok's biggest sights. In fact, the compound incorporates a host of superlatives: the city's largest reclining Buddha, the largest collection of Buddha images in Thailand and the country's earliest centre for public education. Almost too big for its shelter is Wat Pho's highlight, the genuinely impressive **Reclining Buddha**.

The rambling grounds of Wat Pho cover 8 hectares, with the major tourist sites occupying the northern side of Th Chetuphon and the monastic facilities found on the southern side. The temple compound is also the national headquarters for the teaching and preservation of traditional Thai medicine, including Thai massage, a mandate legislated by Rama III when the tradition was in danger of extinction. The famous massage school has two **massage pavilions** (Thai massage per hour 420B; 9am-4pm; T-ien Pier) located within the temple area and additional rooms within the training facility (p86) outside the temple.

Museum of Siam MUSEUM
(สถาบันพิพิธภัณฑ์การเรียนรู้แห่งชาติ; Map p70; www.museumsiam.org; Th Maha Rat; 300B; 10am-6pm Tue-Sun; ; Tien Pier) Although temporarily closed for renovation when we stopped by, this fun museum's collection employs a variety of media to explore the origins of the Thai people and their culture. Housed in a European-style; 19th-century building that was once the Ministry of Commerce, the exhibits are presented in a contemporary, engaging and interactive fashion not typically found in Thailand's museums. They are also refreshingly balanced and entertaining, with galleries dealing with a range of questions about the origins of the nation and its people.

National Museum MUSEUM
(พิพิธภัณฑสถานแห่งชาติ; Map p70; 4 Th Na Phra That; 200B; 9am-4pm Wed-Sun; Chang Pier, Maharaj Pier, Phra Chan Tai Pier) Often touted as Southeast Asia's biggest museum, Thailand's National Museum is home to an impressive, albeit occasionally dusty, collection of items, best appreciated on one of the museum's free twice-weekly guided **tours** (free with museum admission; 9.30am Wed & Thu).

Most of the museum's structures were built in 1782 as the palace of Rama I's viceroy, Prince Wang Na. Rama V turned it into a museum in 1874, and today there are three permanent exhibitions spread out over several buildings. When we stopped by, several of the exhibition halls were being renovated.

The recently renovated **Gallery of Thai History** is home to some of the country's most beautiful Buddha images.

The **history wing** has made impressive bounds towards contemporary curatorial aesthetics with a succinct chronology of prehistoric, Sukhothai-, Ayuthaya- and Bangkok-era events and figures. Gems include King Ramkhamhaeng's inscribed stone pillar, said to be the oldest record of Thai writing (although this has been contested); King Taksin's throne; the Rama V section; and the screening of a movie about Rama VII, *The Magic Ring*.

The **decorative arts and ethnology exhibit** covers seemingly every possible handicraft including traditional musical instruments, ceramics, clothing and textiles, woodcarving, regalia and weaponry. The **archaeology and art history wing** has exhibits ranging from prehistory to the Bangkok period.

In addition to the main exhibition halls, the **Bhuddhaisawan (Phutthaisawan) Chapel** includes some well-preserved murals and one of the country's most revered Buddha images, Phra Phuttha Sihing. Legend claims the image came from Sri Lanka, but art historians attribute it to the 13th-century Sukhothai period.

Banglamphu

Next to Ko Ratanakosin, leafy lanes, antique shophouses, buzzing wet markets and golden temples convene in Banglamphu – easily the city's most quintessentially 'Bangkok' neighbourhood. It's a quaint postcard picture of the city that used to be that is until you stumble upon Th Khao San, arguably the world's most famous backpacker enclave.

WAT PHRA KAEW DRESS CODE & TICKET TIPS

- Enter Wat Phra Kaew and the Grand Palace complex through the clearly marked third gate from the river pier. Tickets are purchased inside the complex; anyone telling you it's closed is a gem tout or a con artist.
- At Wat Phra Kaew and the Grand Palace grounds, dress rules are strictly enforced. If you're flashing a bit too much skin, expect to be shown into a dressing room and issued with a shirt or sarong (rental is free, but you must provide a refundable 200B deposit).
- Admission to the complex includes entrance to Dusit Palace Park (p82).

Wat Pho

A WALK THROUGH THE BIG BUDDHAS OF WAT PHO

The logical starting place is the main *wí·hăhn* (sanctuary), home to Wat Pho's centre piece, the immense ❶ **Reclining Buddha**. In addition to its enormous size, note the ❷ **mother-of-pearl inlay** on the soles of the statue's feet. The interior walls of the *wí·hăhn* are covered with murals that depict previous lives of the Buddha, and along the south side of the structure there are 108 bronze monk bowls; for 20B you can buy 108 coins, each of which is dropped in a bowl for good luck.

Exit the *wí·hăhn* and head east via the two ❸ **stone giants** who guard the gateway to the rest of the compound. Directly south of these are the four towering ❹ **royal chedi**.

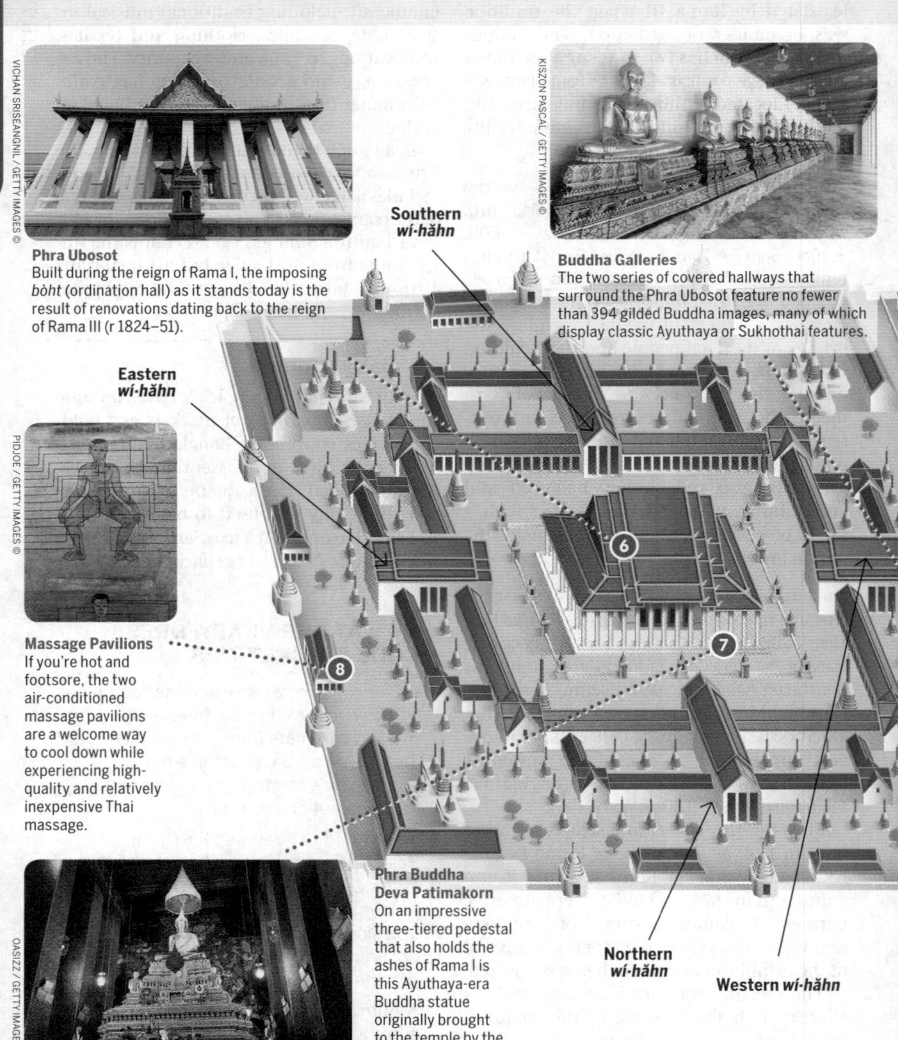

Phra Ubosot
Built during the reign of Rama I, the imposing *bòht* (ordination hall) as it stands today is the result of renovations dating back to the reign of Rama III (r 1824–51).

Buddha Galleries
The two series of covered hallways that surround the Phra Ubosot feature no fewer than 394 gilded Buddha images, many of which display classic Ayuthaya or Sukhothai features.

Massage Pavilions
If you're hot and footsore, the two air-conditioned massage pavilions are a welcome way to cool down while experiencing high-quality and relatively inexpensive Thai massage.

Phra Buddha Deva Patimakorn
On an impressive three-tiered pedestal that also holds the ashes of Rama I is this Ayuthaya-era Buddha statue originally brought to the temple by the monarch.

Continue east, passing through two consecutive **5 galleries of Buddha statues** linking four *wí·hăhn*, two of which contain notable Sukhothai-era Buddha statues; these comprise the exterior of **6 Phra Ubosot**, the immense ordination hall that is Wat Pho's second-most noteworthy structure. The base of the building is surrounded by bas-relief inscriptions, and inside is the notable Buddha statue, **7 Phra Buddha Deva Patimakorn**.

Wat Pho is often referred to as Thailand's first university, a tradition that continues today in an associated traditional Thai medicine school and, at the compound's eastern extent, two **8 massage pavilions**.

Interspersed throughout the eastern half of the compound are several additional minor *chedi* and rock gardens.

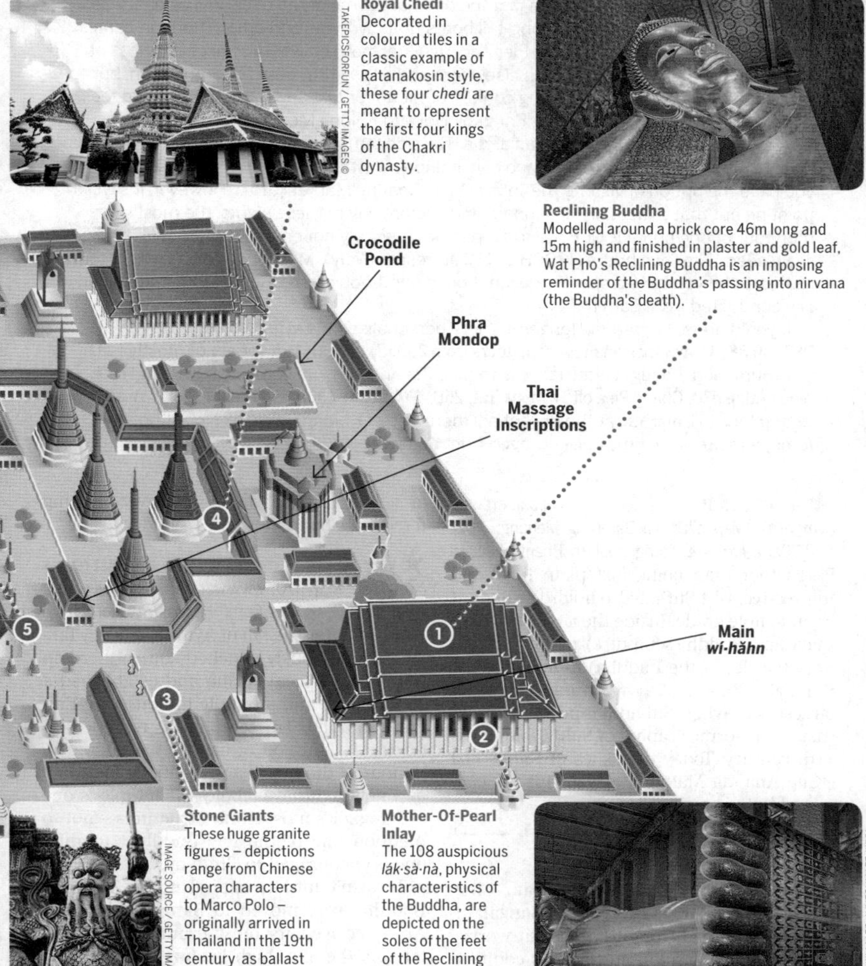

Royal Chedi
Decorated in coloured tiles in a classic example of Ratanakosin style, these four *chedi* are meant to represent the first four kings of the Chakri dynasty.

Reclining Buddha
Modelled around a brick core 46m long and 15m high and finished in plaster and gold leaf, Wat Pho's Reclining Buddha is an imposing reminder of the Buddha's passing into nirvana (the Buddha's death).

Stone Giants
These huge granite figures – depictions range from Chinese opera characters to Marco Polo – originally arrived in Thailand in the 19th century as ballast aboard Chinese junks.

Mother-Of-Pearl Inlay
The 108 auspicious *lák·sà·nà*, physical characteristics of the Buddha, are depicted on the soles of the feet of the Reclining Buddha.

WORTH A TRIP

THONBURI: CRUISING THE 'VENICE OF THE EAST'

Bangkok was formerly known as the Venice of the East, as the city used to be criss-crossed by an advanced network of *klorng* (also spelt *khlong*), artificial canals that inhabitants used both for transport and to ship goods. Today cars and motorcycles have superseded boats, and the majority of Bangkok's canals have been filled in and covered by roads, or are fetid and drying up. Yet a peek into the watery Bangkok of yesteryear can still be had west of Mae Nam Chao Phraya, in Thonburi.

Thonburi's network of canals and river tributaries still carries a motley fleet of watercraft, from paddle canoes to rice barges. Homes, trading houses and temples are built on stilts with front doors opening out to the water. According to residents, these waterways protect them from the seasonal flooding that plagues the capital. **Khlong Bangkok Noi** is lined with greenery and historic temples; smaller **Khlong Mon** is largely residential. **Khlong Bangkok Yai** was in fact the original course of the river until a canal was built to expedite transits. Today long-tail boats that ply these and other Thonburi canals are available for charter at Chang Pier and Tien Pier, both on Ko Ratanakosin. Prices at these piers are slightly higher than elsewhere and allow little room for negotiation, but you stand the least chance of being conned or hit up for tips and other unexpected fees.

Trips generally traverse Khlong Bangkok Noi and Khlong Mon, taking in the Royal Barges National Museum, Wat Arun and a riverside temple with fish feeding. Longer trips diverge into Khlong Bangkok Yai, and can include a visit to an orchid farm. On weekends, you have the option of visiting the Taling Chan Floating Market (p114). However, it's worth pointing out that to actually disembark and explore any of these sights, the most common tour of one hour (1000B, up to six people) is simply not enough time; you'll most likely need 1½ or two hours (1300B or 1500B respectively). Most operators have set tour routes, but if you have a specific destination in mind, you can request it. Tours are generally conducted from 8am to 5pm.

If you'd prefer something longer or more personalised, **Pandan Tour** (☎02 689 1232, 087 109 8873; www.thaicanaltour.com; tours from 2395B) conducts a variety of mostly full-day tours. And a budget alternative is to take the one-way-only **commuter long-tail boat** (Map p70; Chang Pier, off Th Maha Rat; 25B; ⌚4.30am-7.30pm; ⛴Chang Pier) from Chang Pier to Bang Yai, at the distant northern end of Khlong Bangkok Noi, although foreigners are sometimes discouraged from doing so.

★**Wat Suthat** BUDDHIST TEMPLE

(วัดสุทัศน์; Map p70; Th Bamrung Meuang; 20B; ⌚8.30am-9pm; ⛴klorng boat to Phanfa Leelard Pier) Other than being just plain huge and impressive, Wat Suthat also holds the highest royal temple grade. Inside the *wí·hăhn* (sanctuary for a Buddha sculpture) are intricate *Jataka* (stories of the Buddha) murals and the 8m-high **Phra Si Sakayamuni**, Thailand's largest surviving Sukhothai-period bronze, cast in the former capital of Sukhothai in the 14th century. Today the ashes of Rama VIII (King Ananda Mahidol; r 1935–46) are contained in the base of the image.

Thonburi

Thonburi, located across Mae Nam Chao Phraya (Chao Phraya River) from Banglamphu, is a seemingly forgotten yet visit-worthy zone of sleepy residential districts connected by *klorng* (canals; also spelt *khlong*). The area is accessible via the 3B river-crossing ferries at Chang Pier and Tien Pier.

★**Wat Arun** BUDDHIST TEMPLE

(วัดอรุณฯ; Map p70; www.watarun.net; off Th Arun Amarin; 50B; ⌚8am-6pm; ⛴cross-river ferry from Tien Pier) After the fall of Ayuthaya, King Taksin ceremoniously clinched control here on the site of a local shrine and established a royal palace and a temple to house the Emerald Buddha. The temple was renamed after the Indian god of dawn (Aruna) and in honour of the literal and symbolic founding of a new Ayuthaya. Today the temple is one of Bangkok's most iconic structures – not to mention one of the few Buddhist temples one is encouraged to climb on.

It wasn't until the capital and the Emerald Buddha were moved to Bangkok that Wat Arun received its most prominent characteristic: the 82m-high ***prahng*** (Khmer-style tower). The tower's construction was started during the first half of the 19th century by Rama II (King Phraphutthaloetla Naphalai; r 1809–24) and later completed by Rama III (King Phranangklao; r 1824–51). Steep stairs lead to the top, from where there's amazing views of Mae Nam Chao Phraya. Not apparent from a distance are the ornate floral **mosaics** made from broken, multihued Chinese porcelain, a common temple ornamentation in the early Ratanakosin period, when Chinese ships calling at the port of Bangkok discarded tonnes of old porcelain as ballast.

Also worth an inspection is the interior of the ***bòht*** (ordination hall). The main Buddha image is said to have been designed by Rama II himself. The **murals** date from the reign of Rama V (King Chulalongkorn; r 1868–1910); particularly impressive is one that depicts Prince Siddhartha encountering examples of birth, old age, sickness and death outside his palace walls, an experience that led him to abandon the worldly life. The ashes of Rama II are interred in the base of the presiding Buddha image.

Frequent cross-river ferries run over to Wat Arun from Tien Pier (3B).

Chinatown & Phahurat

Chinatown embodies everything that's hectic, noisy and polluted about Bangkok, but that's what makes it such a fascinating area to explore. The area's big sights – namely Wat Traimit (Golden Buddha) and the street markets – are worth hitting, but be sure to set aside enough time to do some map-free wandering among the neon-lit gold shops, hidden temples, crumbling shopfronts and pencil-thin alleys, especially the tiny winding lanes that extend from Soi Wanit 1 (aka Sampeng Lane).

For ages, Chinatown was home to Bangkok's most infamous traffic jams, but the arrival of the MRT (Metro) in 2005 finally made the area a sane place to visit. Still, the station is about a kilometre from many sights, so you'll have to take a longish walk or a short taxi ride. An alternative is to take the Chao Phraya Express Boat to the stop at Ratchawong Pier, from where it's a brief walk to most restaurants and a bit further to most sights.

At the western edge of Chinatown is a small but thriving Little India, Phahurat.

★ Wat Traimit (Golden Buddha) — BUDDHIST TEMPLE

(วัดไตรมิตร, Temple of the Golden Buddha; Map p92; Th Mittaphap Thai-China; 100B; 8am-5pm; Ratchawong Pier, M Hua Lamphong exit 1) The attraction at Wat Traimit is undoubtedly the impressive 3m-tall, 5.5-tonne, **solid-gold Buddha image**, which gleams like, well, gold. Sculpted in the graceful Sukhothai style, the image was 'discovered' some 60 years ago beneath a stucco/plaster exterior, when it fell from a crane while being moved to a new building within the temple compound.

It has been theorised that the covering was added to protect it from marauding hordes, either during the late Sukhothai period or later in the Ayuthaya period when the city was under siege by the Burmese. The temple itself is said to date from the early 13th century.

Donations and a constant flow of tourists have proven profitable, and the statue is now housed in an imposing four-storey marble structure.

The 2nd floor of the building is home to the **Phra Buddha Maha Suwanna Patimakorn Exhibition** (นิทรรศการพระพุทธมหาสุวรรณปฏิมากร; Map p92; 40B; 8am-5pm Tue-Sun), which has exhibits on how the statue was made, discovered and came to arrive at its current home, while the 3rd floor is home to the **Yaowarat Chinatown Heritage Center** (ศูนย์ประวัติศาสตร์เยาวราช; Map p92; 8am-5pm Tue-Sun), a small but engaging museum with multimedia exhibits on the history of Bangkok's Chinatown and its residents.

Talat Mai — MARKET

(ตลาดใหม่; Map p92; Soi Yaowarat 6/Charoen Krung 16; 6am-6pm; Ratchawong Pier, M Hua Lamphong exit 1 & taxi) With nearly two centuries of commerce under its belt, New Market is no longer an entirely accurate name for this strip of commerce. Regardless, this is Bangkok's, if not Thailand's, most Chinese market, and the dried goods, seasonings, spices and sauces will be familiar to anyone who's ever spent time in China. Even if you're not interested in food, the hectic atmosphere (be on guard for motorcycles squeezing between shoppers) and exotic sights and smells create something of a surreal sensory experience.

Wat Mangkon Kamalawat — BUDDHIST TEMPLE

(วัดมังกรกมลาวาส; Map p70; cnr Th Charoen Krung & Th Mangkon; 6am-6pm; Ratchawong Pier, M Hua Lamphong exit 1 & taxi) FREE Clouds of incense and the sounds of chanting form the backdrop at this Chinese-style Mahayana

WORTH A TRIP

JOURNEY TO AMPHAWA

Amphawa is only 80km from Bangkok, but if you play your cards right, you can reach the town via a long journey involving trains, boats, a motorcycle ride and a short jaunt in the back of a truck. Why? Because sometimes the journey is just as interesting as the destination. The adventure begins at Thonburi's Wong Wian Yai (p113) train station. Just past the Wong Wian Yai traffic circle is a fairly ordinary food market that camouflages the unspectacular terminus of this commuter line. Hop on one of the hourly trains (10B, one hour, 5.30am to 8.10pm) to Samut Sakhon.

After 15 minutes on the rattling train, the city density yields to squat villages. From the window you can peek into homes, temples and shops built a carefully considered arm's length from the passing trains. Further on, palm trees, patchwork rice fields and marshes filled with giant elephant ears and canna lilies line the route, punctuated by whistle-stop stations. The backwater farms evaporate quickly as you enter **Samut Sakhon**, popularly known as Mahachai because it straddles the confluence of Mae Nam Tha Chin and Khlong Mahachai. This is a bustling port town, several kilometres upriver from the Gulf of Thailand, and the end of the first rail segment. Before the 17th century it was called Tha Jiin (Chinese Pier) because of the large number of Chinese junks that called here.

After working your way through one of the most hectic fresh markets in the country, you'll come to a vast harbour clogged with water hyacinths and wooden fishing boats. A few rusty cannons pointing towards the river testify to the existence of the town's crumbling fort, built to protect the kingdom from sea invaders.

Take the ferry across to **Baan Laem** (3B to 5B), where you'll jockey for space with school teachers riding motorcycles and people running errands. If the infrequent 5B ferry hasn't already deposited you there, take a motorcycle taxi (10B) for the 2km ride to **Wat Chawng Lom** (วัดช่องลม; Ban Laem, Samut Sakhon; ⌚daylight hours) FREE, home to the **Jao Mae Kuan Im Shrine**, a 9m-high fountain in the shape of the Mahayana Buddhist Goddess of Mercy that is popular with regional tour groups. Beside the shrine is Tha Chalong, a train stop with three daily departures for Samut Songkhram at 8.10am, 12.05pm and 4.40pm (10B, one hour). The train rambles out of the city on tracks that the surrounding forest threatens to engulf, and this little stretch of line genuinely feels a world away from the big smoke of Bangkok.

The jungle doesn't last long, and any illusion that you've entered a parallel universe free of concrete is shattered as you enter **Samut Songkhram**. And to complete the seismic shift, you'll emerge directly into a hubbub of hectic market stalls. Between train arrivals and departures these stalls are set up directly on the tracks and must be hurriedly cleared away when the train arrives – it's quite an amazing scene.

Commonly known as Mae Klong, Samut Songkhram is a tidier version of Samut Sakhon and offers a great deal more as a destination. Owing to flat topography and abundant water sources, the area surrounding the provincial capital is well suited to the steady irrigation needed to grow guava, lychee and grapes. From Mae Klong Market pier *(tâh đà·làht mâa glorng)*, you can charter a boat (1000B) or hop in a *sŏrng·tăa·ou* (passenger pick-up truck; 8B) near the market for the 10-minute ride to Amphawa.

Buddhist temple. Surrounding the temple are vendors selling food for the gods – steamed lotus-shaped dumplings and oranges – which are donated to the temple in exchange for merit.

Dating back to 1871, it's the largest and most important religious structure in the area, and during the annual Vegetarian Festival (p90), religious and culinary activities are particularly active here.

Riverside

The Riverside area is great for an aimless wander among old buildings. This stretch of Mae Nam Chao Phraya was formerly Bangkok's international zone, and today retains a particularly Chinese and Muslim feel. Most of the sights in this area can be seen in a morning; the BTS stop at Saphan Taksin is a good starting point.

★**Bangkokian Museum** MUSEUM

(พิพิธภัณฑ์ชาวบางกอก; Map p92; 273 Soi 43, Th Charoen Krung; admission by donation; 10am-4pm Wed-Sun; Si Phraya/River City Pier) A collection of three antique structures built during the early 20th century, the Bangkokian Museum illustrates an often-overlooked period of the city's history, and functions as a peek into a Bangkok that, these days, is disappearing at a rapid pace.

The main building was built in 1937 as a home for the Surawadee family and, as the signs inform us, was finished by Chinese carpenters on time and for less than the budgeted 2400B (which would barely buy a door handle today). This building and the large wooden one to the right, which was added as a boarding house to help cover costs, are filled with the detritus of postwar family life and offer a fascinating window into the period. The third building, at the back of the block, was built in 1929 as a surgery for a British doctor, though he died soon after arriving in Thailand.

Lumphini Park & Rama IV

At 58 hectares, Lumphini is central Bangkok's largest and most popular park. The easiest ways to reach the area are via the BTS stop at Sala Daeng or the MRT stops at Si Lom and Lumphini.

★**Lumphini Park** PARK

(สวนลุมพินี; Map p88; bounded by Th Sarasin, Rama IV, Th Witthayu/Wireless Rd & Th Ratchadamri; 4.30am-9pm; ; M Lumphini exit 3, Si Lom exit 1, S Sala Daeng exit 3, Ratchadamri exit 2) Named after the Buddha's place of birth in Nepal, Lumphini Park is the best way to escape Bangkok without actually leaving town. Shady paths, a large artificial lake and swept lawns temporarily blot out the roaring traffic and hulking concrete towers.

Silom & Sathon

Th Silom, with its towering hotel and office buildings, is Bangkok's de facto financial district, while adjacent Th Sathon is home to many of the city's embassies. Incongruously, lower Th Silom functions as Bangkok's gaybourhood.

The BTS stop at Sala Daeng and the MRT stop at Si Lom put you at lower Th Silom, perfect jumping-off points for either Lumphini Park or the area's restaurants and sights.

Queen Saovabha Memorial Institute ZOO

(สถานเสาวภา, Snake Farm; Map p88; cnr Rama IV & Th Henri Dunant; adult/child 200/50B; 9.30am-3.30pm Mon-Fri, to 1pm Sat & Sun; ; M Si Lom exit 1, S Sala Daeng exit 3) Thailand's snake farms tend to gravitate towards carnivalesque rather than humanitarian, except at the Queen Saovabha Memorial Institute. Founded in 1923, the snake farm gathers antivenom by milking the snakes' venom, injecting it into horses, and harvesting and purifying the antivenom they produce. The antivenoms are then used to treat human victims of snake bites. Regular milkings (11am Monday to Friday) and snake-handling performances (2.30pm Monday to Friday and 11am Saturday and Sunday) are held at the outdoor amphitheatre.

MR Kukrit Pramoj House HISTORIC BUILDING

(บ้านหม่อมราชวงศ์คึกฤทธิ์ปราโมช; Map p88; 02 286 8185; Soi 7, Th Naradhiwas Rajanagarindra/Chong Nonsi; adult/child 50/20B; 10am-4pm; S Chong Nonsi exit 2) Author and statesman Mom Ratchawong Kukrit Pramoj (1911–95) once resided in this charming complex now open to the public. Surrounded by a manicured garden, the five teak buildings introduce visitors to traditional Thai architecture, arts and the former resident, who served as prime minister of Thailand in 1974 and '75, wrote more than 150 books and spent 20 years decorating the house.

Siam Square & Pratunam

Multistorey malls, outdoor shopping precincts and never-ending markets leave no doubt that this is Bangkok's commercial district. If you're serious about shopping, set aside the better part of a day to burn your baht here. Try to arrive around 11am, when the crowds are minimal. Likewise, try to avoid Sundays when half of Bangkok seems to flock to the area's air-conditioned malls.

Siam Sq is most easily accessed via the BTS (Skytrain)

★**Jim Thompson House** HISTORIC BUILDING

(เรือนไทยจิมทอมป์สัน; Map p80; www.jimthompsonhouse.com; 6 Soi Kasem San 2; adult/student 150/100B; 9am-6pm, compulsory tours every 20min; klorng boat to Sapan Hua Chang Pier, S National Stadium exit 1) This jungly compound is the former home of the eponymous American silk entrepreneur and art collector. Born in Delaware in 1906, Thompson briefly served in the Office of Strategic Services (the forerunner of the CIA) in Thailand

Siam Square

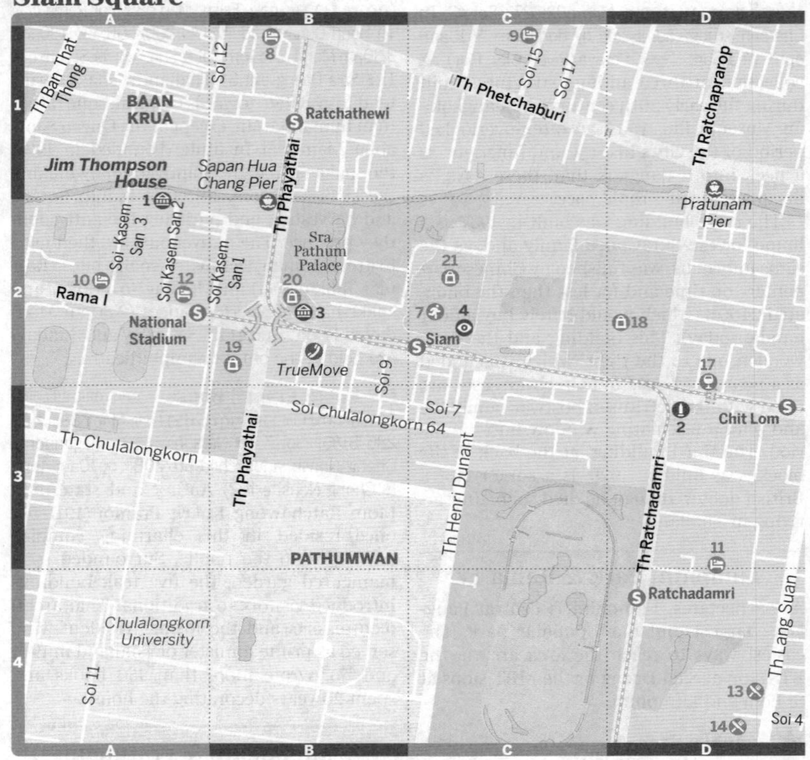

during WWII. He settled in Bangkok after the war, when his neighbours' handmade silk caught his eye and piqued his business sense; he sent samples to fashion houses in Milan, London and Paris, gradually building a steady worldwide clientele.

In addition to textiles, Thompson also collected parts of various derelict Thai homes and had them reassembled in their current location in 1959. Some of the homes were brought from the old royal capital of Ayuthaya; others were pulled down and floated across the *klorng* from Baan Khrua, including the first building you enter on the tour. One striking departure from tradition is the way each wall has its exterior side facing the house's interior, thus exposing the wall's bracing system. His small but splendid Asian art collection and his personal belongings are also on display in the main house. Thompson's story doesn't end with his informal reign as Bangkok's best-adapted foreigner, however. While out for an afternoon walk in the Cameron Highlands of western Malaysia in 1967, Thompson mysteriously disappeared. That same year his sister was murdered in the USA, fuelling various conspiracy theories. Was it communist spies? Business rivals? Or a man-eating tiger? Although the mystery has never been solved, evidence revealed by American journalist Joshua Kurlantzick in his profile of Thompson, *The Ideal Man,* suggests that the vocal anti-American stance Thompson took later in his life may have made him a potential target of suppression by the CIA.

Beware of well-dressed touts in soi (lanes) near the Thompson house who will tell you it is closed and try to haul you off on a dodgy buying spree.

Erawan Shrine MONUMENT

(ศาลพระพรหม; Map p80; cnr Th Ratchadamri & Th Phloen Chit; 6am-11pm; S Chit Lom exit 8) FREE The Erawan Shrine was originally

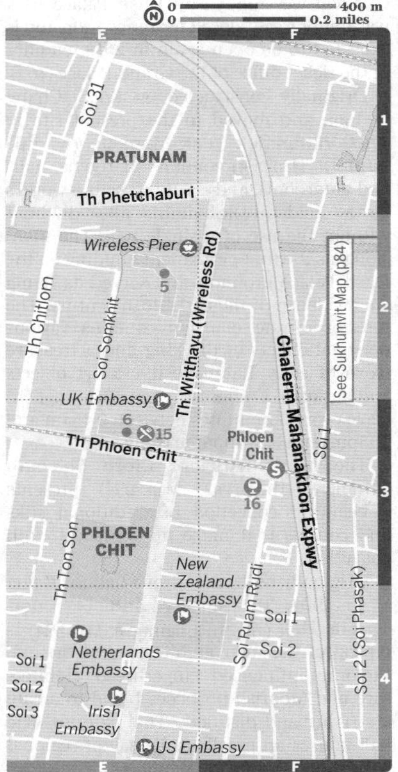

Siam Square

Top Sights

1 Jim Thompson House A2

Sights

2 Erawan Shrine D3
3 Madame Tussauds B2
4 Sea Life Ocean World C2

Activities, Courses & Tours

5 Asian Oasis E2
6 Issaya Cooking Studio E3
7 KidZania C2

Sleeping

8 Bed Station Hostel B1
9 Boxpackers Hostel C1
10 Chao Hostel A2
11 Hansar D3
12 Lub*d A2
Siam@Siam .... (see 10)

Eating

Din Tai Fung .... (see 18)
13 Gaa D4
14 Gaggan D4
MBK Food Island .... (see 19)
15 Open House E3

Drinking & Nightlife

16 Hair of the Dog F3
17 Mixx D2

Shopping

18 CentralWorld D2
19 MBK Center B2
20 Siam Discovery B2
21 Siam Paragon C2

built in 1956 as something of a last-ditch effort to end a string of misfortunes that occurred during the construction of a hotel, at that time known as the Erawan Hotel.

After several incidents ranging from injured construction workers to the sinking of a ship carrying marble for the hotel, a Brahman priest was consulted. Since the hotel was to be named after the elephant escort of Indra in Hindu mythology, the priest determined that Erawan required a passenger, and suggested it be Lord Brahma. A statue was built and, lo and behold, the misfortunes miraculously ended.

Although the original Erawan Hotel was demolished in 1987, the shrine still exists, and today remains an important place of pilgrimage for Thais, particularly those in need of some material assistance. Those making a wish at the statue should ideally come between 7am and 8am, or 7pm and 8pm, and should offer a specific list of items that includes candles, incense, sugar cane or bananas, all of which are almost exclusively given in multiples of seven. Particularly popular are teak elephants, with money from the sale of these items donated to a charity run by the current hotel, the Grand Hyatt Erawan. And as the tourist brochures depict, it is also possible to charter a classical Thai dance, often done as a way of giving thanks if a wish is granted.

A bomb exploded near the shrine in August 2015, killing 20 and slightly damaging the shrine. It was repaired and reopened just two days later.

Sukhumvit

Japanese enclaves, burger restaurants, Middle Eastern nightlife zones and tacky 'sexpat' haunts: it's all here along Th Sukhumvit, Bangkok's unofficial international district.

Where temples and suburban rice fields used to be, today you'll also find shopping centres, nightlife and a host of other amenities that cater to middle-class Thais and resident foreigners. The BTS (Skytrain) runs along the length of Th Sukhumvit, making it a snap to reach just about anywhere around here. BTS stops are also a convenient way to define the street's various vibes.

★Siam Society & Kamthieng House MUSEUM
(สยามสมาคม & บ้านคำเที่ยง; Map p84; www.siam-society.org; 131 Soi 21/Asoke, Th Sukhumvit; adult/child 100B/free; ⏲9am-5pm Tue-Sat; M Sukhumvit exit 1, S Asok exit 3 or 6) Kamthieng House transports visitors to a northern Thai village complete with informative displays of daily rituals, folk beliefs and everyday household chores, all within the setting of a traditional wooden house. This museum is operated by and shares space with the Siam Society, publisher of the renowned *Journal of the Siam Society* and a valiant preserver of traditional Thai culture.

Thewet & Dusit

Thewet, particularly the area near Th Samsen, has the hectic, buzzy feel often associated with Bangkok. The adjacent river is the only respite from the action, and it also functions as a good point from which to approach the area, as most sights and restaurants are a short walk from the river ferry pier.

Dusit, on the other hand, is possibly Bangkok's most orderly district, home to the kind of tree-lined avenues and regal monuments you'd expect to find in Paris. Dusit's sights are relatively far apart and are best approached by taxi or túk-túk.

★Dusit Palace Park MUSEUM, HISTORIC SITE
(วังสวนดุสิต; Map p94; bounded by Th Ratchawithi, Th U Thong Nai & Th Nakhon Ratchasima; adult/child 100/20B, with Grand Palace ticket free; ⏲9.30am-4pm Tue-Sun; Thewet Pier, S Phaya Thai exit 2 & taxi) Following his first European tour in 1897, Rama V (King Chulalongkorn; r 1868–1910) returned with visions of European castles and set about transforming these styles into a uniquely Thai expression, today's Dusit Palace Park. These days the king has yet another home and this complex now holds a house museum and other cultural collections.

When we stopped by, Dusit Palace Park was temporarily closed for renovation and is expected to be open again in 2018; enquire at the ticket office of the Grand Palace (p71).

Originally constructed on Ko Si Chang in 1868 and moved to the present site in 1910, **Vimanmek Teak Mansion** (พระที่นั่งวิมานเมฆ; Map p94) contains 81 rooms, halls and anterooms, and is said to be the world's largest golden-teak building, allegedly built without the use of a single nail. The mansion was the first permanent building on the Dusit Palace grounds, and served as Rama V's residence in the early 20th century. The interior of the mansion contains various personal effects of the king and a treasure trove of early Ratanakosin-era art objects and antiques. Compulsory tours (in English) leave every 30 minutes between 9.45am and 3.15pm, and last about an hour.

The nearby **Ancient Cloth Museum** (พิพิธภัณฑ์ผ้าไทยโบราณ; Map p94) presents a beautiful collection of traditional silks and cottons that make up the royal cloth collection.

Originally built as a throne hall for Rama V in 1904, the smaller **Abhisek Dusit Throne Hall** (พระที่นั่งอภิเศกดุสิต; Map p94) is typical of the finer architecture of the era. Victorian-influenced gingerbread architecture and Moorish porticoes blend to create a striking and distinctly Thai exterior. The hall houses an excellent display of regional handiwork crafted by members of the Promotion of Supplementary Occupations & Related Techniques (Support) foundation, a charity organisation sponsored by Queen Sirikit.

Near the Th U Thong Nai entrance, two large stables that once housed three white elephants – animals whose auspicious albinism automatically make them crown property – now form the **Royal Thai Elephant Museum** (พิพิธภัณฑ์ช้างต้น). One of the structures contains artefacts and photos outlining the importance of elephants in Thai history and explaining their various rankings according to physical characteristics. The second stable holds a life-sized model of the previous king's first royal white elephant. Draped in royal vestments, the statue is more or less treated as a shrine by the visiting Thai public.

Because this is royal property, visitors should wear shirts with sleeves and long pants (no cropped pants) or long skirts.

LOCAL KNOWLEDGE

BANGKOK LIKE A LOCAL

Don't want to feel like a sheltered package holidaymaker? Rest assured that it's a cinch to get local in Bangkok, a city where hectic tourist attractions often rub shoulders with classic local neighbourhoods. Often it takes little more than a tiny detour from the big-hitter sights.

The Banglamphu (p105) neighbourhood is home to heaps of bars frequented mostly by young locals, the dance clubs of Royal City Avenue (p112) pull the majority of local partiers and Silom (p106) is the magnet for the local LGBT crowd.

Come dinnertime, it doesn't get more local than the street stalls of Bangkok's Chinatown (p102). Alternatively, head the hoods north of Bangkok, such as the area surrounding the Victory Monument, for unpretentious street food. At some point during your stay, be sure to hit a food court, like **MBK Food Island** (Map p80; 6th fl, MBK Center, cnr Rama I & Th Phayathai; mains 35-150B; ⏲10am-9pm; ❄✍; S National Stadium exit 4), to see how the locals dine.

BK (www.bk.asia-city.com) is probably the best English-language guide to cover what the locals are up to.

Northern Bangkok

There are several reasons to visit greater Bangkok, but most people come for markets like Chatuchak Weekend Market (p110). For the day markets you'll want to arrive as early as possible. Most of the markets are located within easy access of the northern extents of the BTS (Skytrain) and/or MRT (Metro). Reaching other destinations in Bangkok's burbs often involves a taxi ride from BTS or MRT terminal stations and a bit of luck. A smartphone with a mapping function is an invaluable tool for helping you arrive at the right place and on time.

Chang Chui MARKET

(ช่างชุ่ย; Map p94; www.en.changchuibangkok.com; 460/8 Th Sirindhorn; 20-40B; ⏲11am-11pm Tue-Sun) An abandoned areoplane, craft-beer bars, a hipster barber shop, performance spaces, a skull-shaped florist, an insect-themed restaurant... This tough-to-pin-down marketplace is one of the most eclectic and exciting openings Bangkok has seen in years. Spanning 18 different structures (all of which are made from discarded objects), a handful of the outlets are open during the day, but the best time to go is during weekend evenings, when the place has the vibe of an artsy, more sophisticated Chatuchak Weekend Market.

Activities

Massage & Spas

Oriental Spa SPA

(Map p92; ☎02 659 9000; www.mandarinoriental.com; Mandarin Oriental, 48 Soi 40/Oriental, Th Charoen Krung; massage & spa packages from 2900B; ⏲9am-10pm; ⛴Oriental Pier or hotel shuttle boat from Sathon/Central Pier) Regarded as among the premier spas in the world, the Oriental Spa sets the standard for Asian-style spa treatment. Depending on where you flew in from, the jet-lag massage might be a good option, but all treatments require advance booking.

Health Land MASSAGE

(Map p84; ☎02 261 1110; www.healthlandspa.com; 55/5 Soi 21/Asoke, Th Sukhumvit; Thai massage 2hr 550B; ⏲9am-11pm; M Sukhumvit exit 1, S Asok exit 5) A winning formula of affordable prices, expert treatments and pleasant facilities has created a small empire of Health Land centres across Bangkok.

Asia Herb Association MASSAGE

(Map p84; ☎02 392 3631; www.asiaherbassociation.com; 58/19-25 Soi 55/Thong Lor, Th Sukhumvit; Thai massage 1hr 500B, with herbal compress 1½hr 1100B; ⏲9am-midnight; S Thong Lo exit 3) With multiple branches along Th Sukhumvit, this Japanese-owned chain specialises in massage using *prà·kóp* (traditional Thai herbal compresses) filled with 18 different herbs.

Meditation & Yoga

Center Meditation Wat Mahadhatu MEDITATION

(Map p70; ☎02 222 6011, 02 223 3813; Section 5, Wat Mahathat, Th Maha Rat; donations accepted; ⏲classes 7am, 1pm & 6pm; ⛴Chang Pier, Maharaj Pier, Phra Chan Tai Pier) Located within Wat Mahathat, this small centre offers informal daily meditation classes. Taught

Sukhumvit

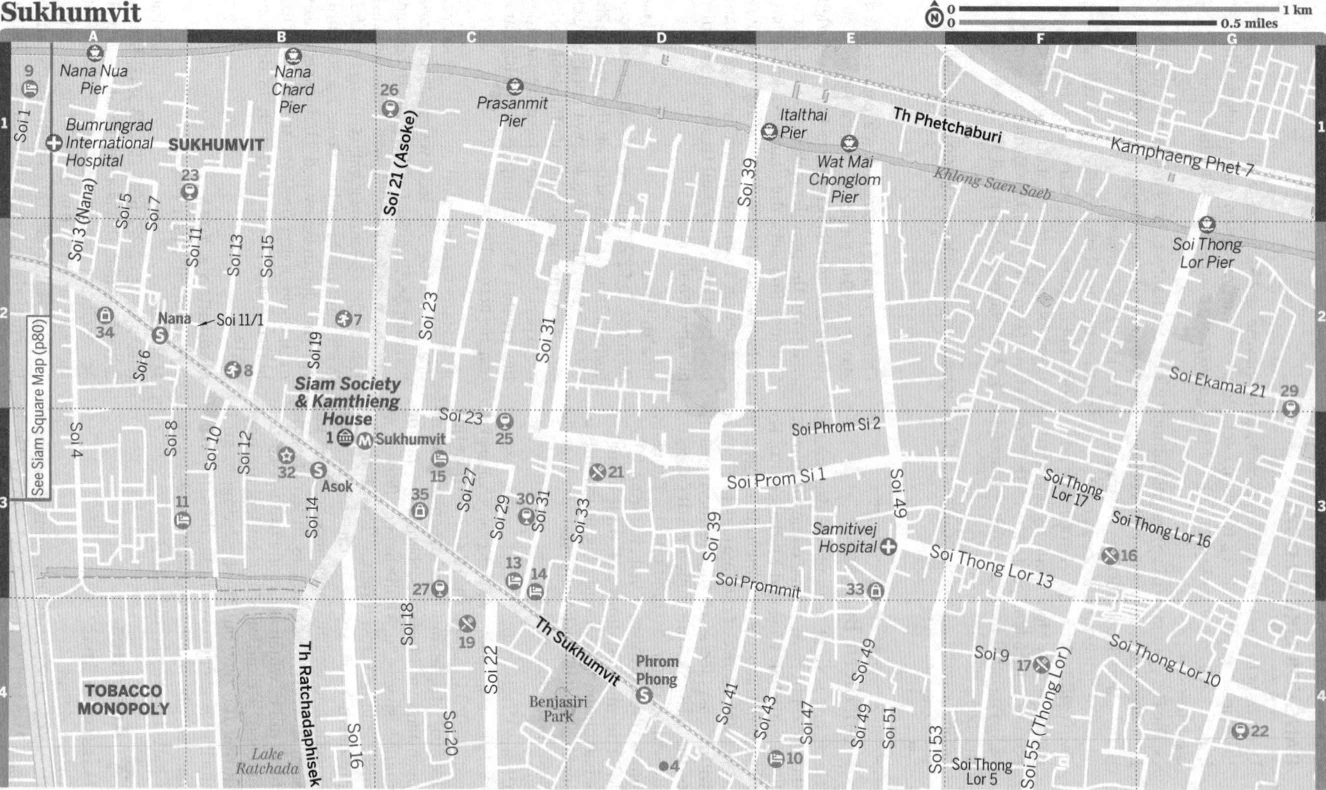
0
1 km
0
0.5 miles
A
B
C
D
E
F
G
1
2
3
4
Nana Nua Pier
Nana Chard Pier
Prasanmit Pier
Italthai Pier
Wat Mai Chonglom Pier
Soi Thong Lor Pier
Th Phetchaburi
Kamphaeng Phet 7
Khlong Saen Saeb
Soi 1
Bumrungrad International Hospital
SUKHUMVIT
Soi 3 (Nana)
Soi 5
Soi 7
Soi 11
Soi 13
Soi 15
Soi 21 (Asoke)
Soi 39
Nana
Soi 11/1
Soi 19
Soi 23
Soi 31
Soi 6
See Siam Square Map (p80)
Siam Society & Kamthieng House
Sukhumvit
Soi Ekamai 21
Soi Phrom Si 2
Soi Prom Si 1
Soi 4
Soi 8
Soi 10
Soi 12
Asok
Soi 14
Soi 27
Soi 29
Soi 33
Soi 49
Soi Thong Lor 17
Soi Thong Lor 16
Samitivej Hospital
Soi Thong Lor 13
Soi Prommit
Th Sukhumvit
Soi 18
Soi 22
Soi 9
Soi Thong Lor 10
Th Ratchadaphisek
Phrom Phong
Soi 41
Soi 43
Soi 47
Soi 51
Soi 53
Soi 55 (Thong Lor)
TOBACCO MONOPOLY
Benjasiri Park
Soi 16
Soi 20
Lake Ratchada
Soi Thong Lor 5

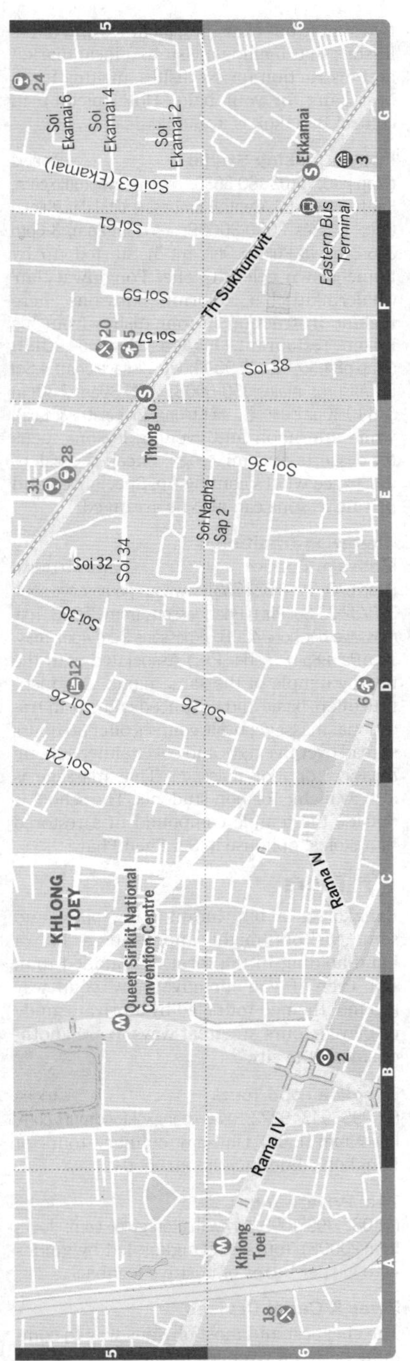

Sukhumvit

Top Sights
1 Siam Society & Kamthieng House.....B3

Sights
2 Khlong Toey Market.....B6
3 Stanley MiniVenture.....G6

Activities, Courses & Tours
4 ABC Amazing Bangkok Cyclists.....D4
5 Asia Herb Association.....F5
6 Fun-arium.....D6
7 Health Land.....B2
8 Yoga Elements Studio.....B2

Sleeping
9 AriyasomVilla.....A1
10 Cabochon Hotel.....E4
11 FU House Hostel.....A3
12 Pause Hostel.....D5
13 S31.....C3
14 S-Box.....C3
15 Tints of Blue.....C3

Eating
16 Boon Tong Kiat Singapore Chicken Rice.....F3
Gateway Ekamai.....(see 3)
17 Gokfayuen.....F4
18 Issaya Siamese Club.....A6
Jidori Cuisine Ken.....(see 4)
19 Saras.....C4
20 Soul Food Mahanakorn.....F5
21 Sri Trat.....D3

Drinking & Nightlife
22 Golden Coins Taproom.....G4
23 Levels.....B1
24 Mikkeller.....G5
25 Narz.....C3
26 Q&A Bar.....C1
27 Scratch Dog.....C3
28 Studio Lam.....E5
29 Tuba.....G2
30 Walden.....C3
31 WTF.....E5

Entertainment
32 The Living Room.....B3

Shopping
33 Duly.....E3
34 Rajawongse.....A2
35 ThaiCraft Fair.....C3

by English-speaking Prasuputh Chainikom (Kosalo), classes last three hours. Longer periods of study, which include accommodation and food, can be arranged, but students are expected to follow a strict regimen of conduct.

Yoga Elements Studio YOGA
(Map p84; 02 255 9552; www.yogaelements.com; 7th fl, 185 Dhammalert Bldg, Th Sukhumvit; classes from 600B; S Chit Lom exit 5) Run by American Adrian Cox, who trained at Om in New York and who teaches primarily *vinyasa* and *ashtanga*, this is the most respected yoga studio in town. The high-rise location helps you rise above it all, too.

Martial Arts

Jaroenthong Muay Thai Gym MARTIAL ARTS
(Map p70; 02 629 2313; www.jaroenthongmuaythaikhaosan.com; Th Phra Athit; lessons from 600B; drop-in hours 10-11.30am & 2-9pm; Phra Athit/Banglamphu Pier) With branches around the country, this lauded gym has opened up an outlet a short walk from Th Khao San. Beginners can drop in and train in air-conditioned comfort, or the more experienced can opt for longer training regimens.

Courses

Having consumed everything Bangkok has to offer is one thing, but imagine the points you'll rack up if you can make the same dishes for your friends back at home. A visit to a Thai cooking school has become a must-do on many Bangkok itineraries and for some visitors it's a highlight of their trip.

★ **Amita Thai Cooking Class** COOKING
(Map p94; 02 466 8966; www.amitathaicooking.com; 162/17 Soi 14, Th Wutthakat, Thonburi; classes 3000B; 9.30am-1pm Thu-Tue; klorng boat from Maharaj Pier) One of Bangkok's most charming cooking schools is held in this canalside house in Thonburi. Taught by the delightfully enthusiastic Piyawadi 'Tam' Jantrupon, a course here includes a romp through the garden and instruction in four dishes. The fee covers transport, which in this case takes the form of a boat ride from Maharaj Pier.

★ **Cooking with Poo & Friends** COOKING
(080 434 8686; www.cookingwithpoo.com; classes 1500B; 8.30am-1pm;) This popular cooking course was started by a native of Khlong Toey's slums and is held in her neighbourhood. Courses, which must be booked in advance, span three dishes and include a visit to Khlong Toey Market and transport to and from Emporium Shopping Centre.

Silom Thai Cooking School COOKING
(Map p88; 084 726 5669; www.bangkokthaicooking.com; 68 Soi 13, Th Silom; classes from 900B; 9am-12.20pm, 1.40-5pm & 6-9pm; S Chong Nonsi exit 3) This cooking school is spread over two simple but charming facilities and offers lessons that include a visit to a local market and instruction for six dishes, making it the best bang for your baht. Hotel pick-up in central Bangkok is available.

Issaya Cooking Studio COOKING
(Map p80; 02 160 5636; www.issayastudio.com; Eatthai, level LG, Central Embassy, 1031 Th Phloen Chit; classes 2000-3000B; 11am-2pm, 3-6pm & 6-8pm; S Phloen Chit exit 5) Started up by home-grown celebrity chef Pongtawat 'Ian' Chalermkittichai, morning lessons here include instruction in four dishes from his linked restaurant, **Issaya Siamese Club** (Map p84; 02 672 9040; www.issaya.com; 4 Soi Sri Aksorn; mains 150-600B; 11.30am-2.30pm & 6-10.30pm; ; M Khlong Toei exit 1 & taxi), while afternoon and evening lessons focus on desserts and mixology; check the calendar to see what's coming up. Specialised and private lessons can also be arranged.

Chetawan Traditional Massage School HEALTH & WELLBEING
(Map p70; 02 622 3551; www.watpomassage.com; 392/32-33 Soi Phen Phat; lessons from 2500B, Thai massage per hour 420B; lessons 9am-4pm, massage 9am-8pm; Tien Pier) Associated with the nearby temple of the same name, this institute offers basic and advanced courses in traditional massage; basic courses offer 30 hours spread over five days and cover either general massage or foot massage. Thai massage is also available for non-students. The school is outside the temple compound in a restored Bangkok shophouse in Soi Phen Phat.

Tours

Bangkok is a big, intimidating place and some visitors might appreciate a bit of hand-holding in the form of a guided tour. But even if you already know your way around, themed tours led by a private guide or bicycle tours are great ways to see another side of the city.

Bangkok Food Tours WALKING
(095 943 9222; www.bangkokfoodtours.com; tours from 1150B) Half-day culinary tours of Bangkok's older neighbourhoods.

Thai Private Tour Guide TOURS
(082 799 1099; www.thaitourguide.com; tours from 2000B) Tours of Bangkok led by guides who garner heaps of positive feedback.

River & Canal Cruises

The cheapest and most obvious way to commute between riverside attractions is on the

BANGKOK FOR KIDS

Kids are welcome almost anywhere and you'll rarely experience the sort of eye-rolling annoyance often seen in the West.

Kid-Friendly Museums

The **Children's Discovery Museum** (พิพิธภัณฑ์เด็ก; Map p94; Th Kamphaengphet 4, Queen Sirikit Park; 9am-5pm Tue-Fri, 10am-6pm Sat & Sun; ; M Chatuchak Park exit 1, S Mo Chit exit 1) FREE has interactive displays ranging in topic from construction to culture. Although not specifically targeted towards children, the Museum of Siam (p73) has lots of interactive exhibits that will appeal to kids. Siam Discovery has a branch of the famous **Madame Tussauds wax museum** (Map p80; www.madametussauds.com; 4th fl, Siam Discovery, cnr Rama I & Th Phayathai; adult/child 990/790B; 10am-9pm; S Siam exit 1).

Outside of town, the open-air **Ancient City** (เมืองโบราณ, Muang Boran; www.ancientcitygroup.net/ancientsiam; 296/1 Th Sukhumvit, Samut Prakan; adult/child 600/350B; 9am-7pm; S Bearing exit 1) re creates Thailand's most famous monuments. They're linked by bicycle paths and were practically built for being climbed on.

Parks, Playgrounds & Zoos

Lumphini Park (p79) is a trusty ally in the cool hours of the morning and afternoon for kite flying (February to April), swan-boat rentals and fish feeding. Nearby, kids can view lethal snakes becoming reluctant altruists at the antivenin-producing Queen Saovabha Memorial Institute (p79), aka the Snake Farm.

Dusit Zoo (สวนสัตว์ดุสิต/เขาดิน; Map p94; www.dusitzoo.org; Th Ratchawithi; adult/child 150/70B; 8am-6pm; Thewet Pier, S Phaya Thai exit 3 & taxi) has shady grounds, plus a lake with paddle boats for hire and a children's playground.

Kids can join the novice monks and Thai children at **Thewet Pier** (Map p94) as they throw food (bought on the pier) to thousands of flapping fish.

For kid-specific play centres, consider **Fun-arium** (Map p84; 02 665 6555; www.funarium.co.th; 111/1 Soi 26, Th Sukhumvit; 110-330B; 9am-6pm Mon-Thu, to 7pm Fri-Sun; ; S Phrom Phong exit 1 & taxi), central Bangkok's largest, or the impressive **KidZania** (Map p80; 02 683 1888; www.bangkok.kidzania.com; 5th fl, Siam Paragon, 991/1 Rama I; adult 425-500B, child 425-1000B; 10am-5pm Mon-Fri, 10.30am-8pm Sat & Sun; S Siam exits 3 & 5). Alternatively, **Siam Park City** (02 919 7200; www.siamparkcity.com; 203 Th Suansiam; adult/child US$30/25; 10am-6pm; M Chatuchak Park exit 2 & taxi, S Mo Chit exit 1 & taxi) and **Dream World** (02 577 8666; www.dreamworld.co.th; 62 Mu 1, Th Rangsit-Nakornnayok, Pathum Thani; from 1200B; 10am-5pm Mon-Fri, to 7pm Sat & Sun; M Chatuchak Park exit 2 & taxi, S Mo Chit exit 1 & taxi) are vast amusement parks found north of the city.

Rainy-Day Fun

If you're visiting during the rainy season (approximately from June to October), you'll need a few indoor options in your back pocket.

MBK Center (p110) and **Siam Paragon** (Map p80; www.siamparagon.co.th; 991/1 Rama I; 10am-10pm; S Siam exits 3 & 5) both have bowling alleys to keep the older ones occupied. The latter also has an IMAX theatre and **Sea Life Ocean World** (Map p80; www.sealifebangkok.com; basement, Siam Paragon, 991/1 Rama I; adult/child from 490/350B; 10am-9pm; S Siam exits 3 & 5), a basement-level aquarium. For those particularly hot days, **CentralWorld** (Map p80; www.centralworld.co.th; Th Ratchadamri; 10am-10pm; S Chit Lom exit 9 to Sky Walk, Siam exit 6 to Sky Walk) has an ice rink. Most malls have amusement centres with video games, small rides and playgrounds (often near the food courts). **Gateway Ekamai** (Map p84; www.gatewayekamai.com; 982/22 Th Sukhumvit; 10am-10pm; ; S Ekkamai exit 4) has an arcade and a branch of **Stanley MiniVenture** (Map p84; www.stanleyminiventure.com; 2nd fl, Gateway Ekamai, 982/22 Th Sukhumvit; adult/child 500/400B; 10am-8pm), a model-train-like miniature town.

Silom & Sathon

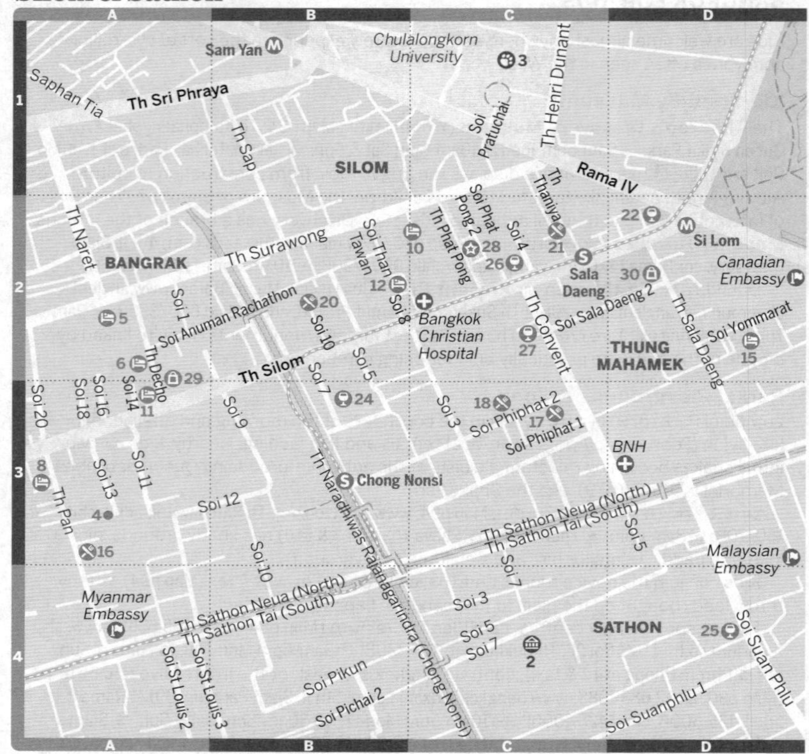

commuter boats run by **Chao Phraya Express Boat** (☎02 623 6001; www.chaophrayaexpressboat.com). The terminus for most northbound boats is Nonthaburi Pier, while for most southbound boats it's Sathon Pier (also called Central Pier), near the Saphan Taksin BTS station (although some boats run as far south as Wat Ratchasingkhon).

For a more personal view, you might consider chartering a long-tail boat along the city's canals. Alternatively, Pandan Tour (p76) offers 'small-boat', full-day private tours of Bangkok's canals. Another option is one of the dinner cruises that ply Mae Nam Chao Phraya at night.

A little faster than the days of sailing ships, river cruises from Bangkok north to the ruins of the former royal capital of Ayuthaya take in all the romance of the river. Normally only one leg of the journey between Bangkok and Ayuthaya is aboard a boat, while the return or departing trip is by bus. Recommended outfits include **Asian Oasis** (Map p80; ☎088 809 7047, 081 496 4516; www.asian-oasis.com; 7th fl, Nai Lert Tower, 2/4 Th Witthayu/Wireless Rd; 2-day trip 7850-16,100B; ⊙9am-5pm Mon-Fri; S Phloen Chit exit 1) and **Thanatharee** (Map p94; ☎02 440 1979; www.thanatharee.com; 21/8 Th Krung Thonburi; 2-day trip 11,900-16,200B; S Wongwian Yai exit 1).

Bicycle Tours

You might be wondering who would want to get on a bike in the notorious traffic jams and sauna-like conditions of Bangkok's streets. But these trips allow discovery of a whole side of the city that's virtually off limits to four-wheeled transport. Several companies run regular, well-received tours starting at about 1000B for a half-day.

Grasshopper Adventures CYCLING
(Map p70; ☎02 280 0832; www.grasshopperadventures.com; 57 Th Ratchadamnoen Klang; half-/

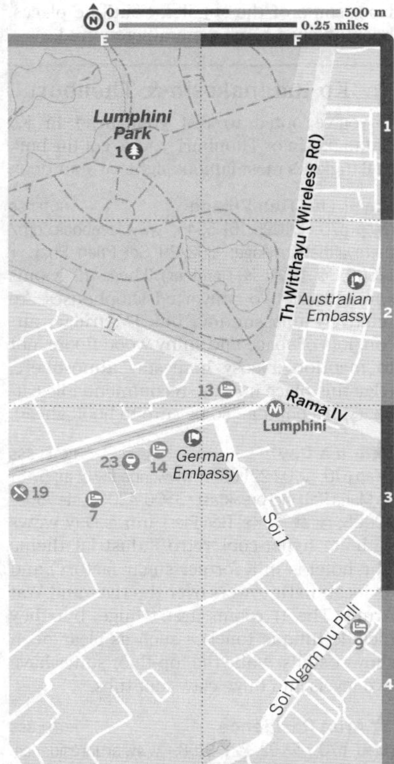

full-day tours from 1350/2400B; 8.30am-6.30pm; klorng boat to Phanfa Leelard Pier) This lauded outfit runs a variety of unique bicycle tours in and around Bangkok, including a night tour and a tour of the city's historic zone.

ABC Amazing Bangkok Cyclists CYCLING
(Map p84; 081 812 9641; www.realasia.net; 10/5-7 Soi Aree, Soi 26, Th Sukhumvit; tours from 1300B; daily tours at 8am, 10am, 1pm & 6pm; ; Phrom Phong exit 4) A long-running operation offering morning, afternoon and all-day bike tours of Bangkok and its suburbs.

Co van Kessel Bangkok Tours CYCLING
(Map p92; 02 639 7351; www.covankessel.com; ground fl, River City, 23 Th Yotha; tours from 950B; 6am-7pm; River City Pier) This originally Dutch-run outfit offers a variety of tours in Chinatown, Thonburi and Bangkok's green zones, many of which also involve boat rides. Tours depart from the company's office in the River City shopping centre.

Silom & Sathon

Top Sights
1 Lumphini Park........E1

Sights
2 MR Kukrit Pramoj House........C4
3 Queen Saovabha Memorial Institute........C1

Activities, Courses & Tours
4 Silom Thai Cooking School........A3

Sleeping
5 kokotel........A2
6 LUXX........A2
7 Metropolitan by COMO........E3
8 Mile Map Hostel........A3
9 S1 Hostel........F4
10 Siam Heritage........C2
11 Silom Art Hostel........A3
12 Smile Society........B2
13 Sofitel So........F2
14 Sukhothai Hotel........E3
15 Urban House........D2

Eating
16 Chennai Kitchen........A3
17 Eat Me........C3
18 Jay So........C3
19 nahm........E3
20 Soi 10 Food Centres........B2
21 Sushi Tsukiji........C2

Drinking & Nightlife
22 DJ Station........D2
23 Moon Bar........E3
24 Namsaah Bottling Trust........B3
Park Society........(see 13)
25 Smalls........D4
26 Telephone Pub........C2
27 Vesper........C2

Entertainment
28 Patpong........C2

Shopping
29 House of Chao........A2
30 July........D2

Festivals & Events

Many Thai festivals follow the lunar calendar (a complex system based on astrology) and therefore change annually relative to the Gregorian calendar. Contact local tourist offices for exact festival dates.

Chinese New Year CULTURAL
(Jan or Feb) Thai-Chinese celebrate the Lunar New Year with a week of house-cleaning, lion dances and fireworks. Most festivities centre on Chinatown. Dates vary.

Songkran CULTURAL

(mid-Apr) The celebration of the Thai New Year has morphed into a water war with high-powered water guns and water balloons being launched at suspecting and unsuspecting participants. The most intense water battles take place on Th Silom and Th Khao San.

Vegetarian Festival FOOD & DRINK

(Sep or Oct) This 10-day Chinese-Buddhist festival wheels out yellow-bannered streetside vendors serving meatless meals. The greatest concentration of vendors is found in Chinatown. Dates vary.

Loi Krathong CULTURAL

(early Nov) A beautiful festival where, on the night of the full moon, small lotus-shaped boats made of banana leaf and containing a lit candle are set adrift on Mae Nam Chao Phraya.

King Bhumibol's Birthday/Father's Day CULTURAL

(5 Dec) Locals celebrate the previous monarch's birthday with lots of parades and fireworks.

Sleeping

If your idea of the typical Bangkok hotel was influenced by *The Hangover Part II,* you'll be relieved to learn that the city is home to a variety of modern hostels, guesthouses and hotels. To further improve matters, much of Bangkok's accommodation offers excellent value and competition is so intense that fat discounts are almost always available. And the city is home to so many hotels that, apart from some of the smaller, boutique places, booking ahead isn't generally required.

ROOMS WITH VIEWS

Arun Residence Handsome rooms directly across from Wat Arun.

Millennium Hilton (p93) Tall riversider featuring some of Bangkok's best watery views.

Bangkok Tree House (Map p94; 082 995 1150; www.bangkoktreehouse.com/cozy-nests.html; near Wat Bang Na Nork, Phrapradaeng; bungalow incl breakfast 6000-10,000B; ; Bang Na exit 2 & taxi) Take in the greenery and river from these elevated bungalows in Bangkok's 'green lung'.

Sofitel So (p96) Rooms peering over the urban oasis that is Lumphini Park.

Ko Ratanakosin & Thonburi

If you've opted to rest your head in Ko Ratanakosin or Thonburi, you've got the bulk of Bangkok's most famous sights at your door.

Royal Tha Tien Village HOTEL $$

(Map p70; 095 151 5545; www.facebook.com/theroyalthatienvillage; 392/29 Soi Phen Phat; r 1200B; ; Tien Pier) These 12 rooms spread over two converted shophouses are relatively unassuming, but TV, fridge, air-con, lots of space and shiny wood floors, not to mention a cosy homestay atmosphere, edge this place into the recommendable category. It's popular, so be sure to book ahead.

★**Inn a Day** HOTEL $$$

(Map p70; 02 221 0577; www.innaday.com; 57-61 Th Maha Rat; incl breakfast r 3500-4200B, ste 7500-9000B; ; Tien Pier) Inn a Day wows with its hyper-cool retro/industrial theme (the hotel is in a former sugar factory) and its location (it towers over the river and Wat Arun). The 11 rooms aren't huge, but they include unique touches such as clear neon shower stalls, while the top-floor suites have two levels and huge claw-foot tubs.

★**Arun Residence** HOTEL $$$

(Map p70; 02 221 9158; www.arunresidence.com; 36-38 Soi Pratu Nokyung; incl breakfast r 3500-4200B, ste/villa 5800/12,000B; ; Tien Pier) Although strategically located on the river directly across from Wat Arun, this multilevel wooden house boasts much more than just great views. The seven rooms here manage to feel both homey and stylish (the best are the top-floor, balcony-equipped suites). There are also inviting communal areas, including a library, rooftop bar and restaurant. Reservations essential.

Banglamphu & Around

Banglamphu still holds the bulk of Bangkok's budget places, although nowadays it's also home to nearly the entire spectrum of accommodation in Bangkok. Lots of eating, drinking and shopping options are other clever reasons to stay in Banglamphu, although it can feel somewhat isolated from the rest of Bangkok.

Suneta Hostel Khaosan HOSTEL $

(Map p70; 02 629 0150; www.sunetahostel.com; 209-211 Th Kraisi; incl breakfast dm 470-570B, r

1180B; ❄@📶; ⛴Phra Athit/Banglamphu Pier) A pleasant, low-key atmosphere, a unique, retro-themed design (some of the dorm rooms resemble sleeping-car carriages), a location just off the main drag and friendly service are what make Suneta stand out.

Vivit Hostel HOSTEL $
(Map p70; ☎02 224 5888; www.vivithostel.com; 510 Th Tanao; dm/r incl breakfast 475/965B; ❄📶; ⛴klorng boat to Phanfa Leelard Pier) Flower-patterned curtains, framed portraits of flowers and grandfather clocks provide this hostel with an overwhelmingly mature feel, despite it having opened in 2017. Nonetheless the dorms represent excellent – if slightly bland – value.

★ **Lamphu Treehouse** HOTEL $$
(Map p70; ☎02 282 0991; www.lamphutreehotel.com; 155 Wanchat Bridge, off Th Prachathipatai; incl breakfast r 1650-2500B, ste 3500-4500B; ❄@📶🏊; ⛴klorng boat to Phanfa Leelard Pier) Despite the name, this attractive midranger has its feet firmly on land, and as such represents brilliant value. The wood-panelled rooms are attractive, inviting and well maintained, and the rooftop sun lounge, pool, internet cafe, restaurant and quiet canalside location ensure that you may never feel the need to leave. An annexe a few blocks away increases the odds of snagging an elusive reservation.

Baan Dinso HOSTEL $$
(Map p70; ☎02 621 2808; www.baandinso.com; 113 Trok Sin; r incl breakfast 900-2500B; ❄@📶; ⛴klorng boat to Phanfa Leelard Pier) This antique wooden villa may not represent the best value in Bangkok, but for accommodation with a nostalgic feel and palpable sense of place, it's almost impossible to beat. Of the 10 small yet spotless rooms, only five have en suite bathrooms, while all have access to functional and inviting communal areas.

Old Capital Bike Inn HOTEL $$$
(Map p70; ☎02 629 1787; www.oldcapitalbkk.com; 609 Th Phra Sumen; r incl breakfast 3200-7800B; ❄@📶; ⛴klorng boat to Phanfa Leelard Pier) The dictionary definition of a honeymoon hotel, this antique shophouse has 10 rooms that are decadent and sumptuous, blending rich colours and heavy wood furnishings. True to its name, the bicycle theme runs throughout, and bikes can be borrowed free.

Praya Palazzo HOTEL $$$
(Map p70; ☎02 883 2998; www.prayapalazzo.com; 757/1 Somdej Prapinklao Soi 2; incl breakfast r 6900-8900B, ste 11,900-18,900B; ❄📶🏊; ⛴hotel shuttle boat from Phra Athit/Banglamphu Pier) After lying dormant for nearly 30 years, this elegant 19th-century mansion in Thonburi has been reborn as an attractive riverside boutique hotel. The 17 rooms can seem rather tight, and river views can be elusive, but the meticulous renovation, handsome antique furnishings and bucolic atmosphere convene in a boutique hotel with authentic old-world charm.

Chinatown & Phahurat

Chinatown is home to some good-value budget and midrange accommodation options; access to some of the city's best street food and its main train station are additional pluses. Downsides include noise, pollution and the neighbourhood's relative distance from both public transport and 'new' Bangkok.

Wanderlust HOSTEL $
(Map p92; ☎083 046 8647; www.facebook.com/onederlust; 149-151 Rama IV; dm 450B, r 1300-1800B; ❄📶; ⛴, Ⓜ Hua Lamphong exit 1) An almost clinical-feeling industrial vibe rules at this new hostel. The dorms span four to eight beds, and the private rooms are on the tight side, with the cheapest sharing bathrooms. These are united by a hyper-chic ground-floor cafe-restaurant. Not the greatest value accommodation in Chinatown, but quite possibly the most image-conscious.

★ **Loy La Long** HOTEL $$
(Map p92; ☎02 639 1390; www.loylalong.com; 1620/2 Th Songwat; r incl breakfast 2700-4900B; ❄@📶; ⛴Ratchawong Pier, Ⓜ Hua Lamphong exit 1 & taxi) Rustic, retro, charming: the six rooms in this 100-year-old wooden house can lay claim to more than their fair share of personality. United by a unique location elevated over Mae Nam Chao Phraya, it's also privy to a hidden, almost secret, feel.

The only hitch is in finding it; to get here proceed to Th Songwat and cut through **Wat Patumkongka Rachaworawiharn** (วัดปทุมคงคาราชวรวิหาร; Map p92; off Th Songwat; ⏰daylight hours; ⛴Marine Department Pier, Ⓜ Hua Lamphong exit 1 & taxi) FREE to the river.

Shanghai Mansion HOTEL $$$
(Map p92; ☎02 221 2121; www.shanghaimansion.com; 479-481 Th Yaowarat; incl breakfast r 2500-4500B, ste 4500B; ❄@📶; ⛴Ratchawong Pier, Ⓜ Hua Lamphong exit 1 & taxi) Easily the most consciously stylish place to stay in Chinatown, if not in all of Bangkok; this award-winning

Riverside

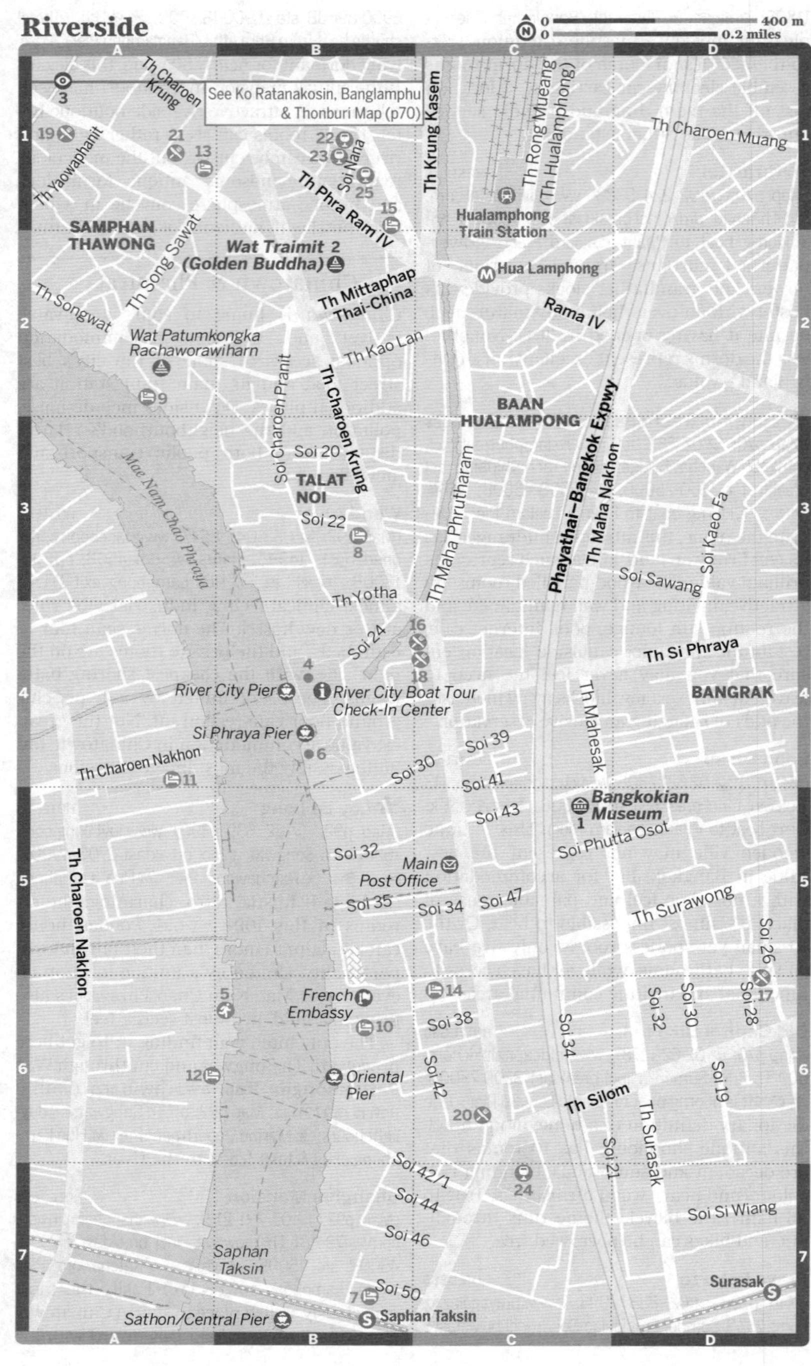

0 400 m
0 0.2 miles
See Ko Ratanakosin, Banglamphu & Thonburi Map (p70)
Th Charoen Krung
Th Yaowaphanit
Th Krung Kasem
Th Rong Mueang (Th Hualamphong)
Th Charoen Muang
Soi Nana
Th Phra Ram IV
Hualamphong Train Station
SAMPHAN THAWONG
Th Song Sawat
Wat Traimit (Golden Buddha)
Hua Lamphong
Th Mittaphap Thai-China
Rama IV
Th Songwat
Wat Patumkongka Rachaworawiharn
Th Kao Lan
Soi Charoen Pranit
Th Charoen Krung
BAAN HUALAMPONG
Phayathai–Bangkok Expwy
Soi 20
TALAT NOI
Mae Nam Chao Phraya
Th Maha Phrutharam
Th Maha Nakhon
Soi 22
Soi Kaeo Fa
Soi Sawang
Th Yotha
Soi 24
Th Si Phraya
River City Pier
River City Boat Tour Check-In Center
BANGRAK
Th Mahesak
Si Phraya Pier
Soi 39
Th Charoen Nakhon
Soi 30
Soi 41
Bangkokian Museum
Soi 43
Soi Phutta Osot
Soi 32
Main Post Office
Soi 35
Soi 34
Soi 47
Th Surawong
Th Charoen Nakhon
Soi 26
French Embassy
Soi 38
Soi 34
Soi 32
Soi 30
Soi 28
Oriental Pier
Soi 42
Soi 19
Th Silom
Th Surasak
Soi 21
Soi 42/1
Soi 44
Soi Si Wiang
Soi 46
Saphan Taksin
Soi 50
Surasak
Sathon/Central Pier
Saphan Taksin

Riverside

Top Sights
1 Bangkokian Museum........C5
2 Wat Traimit (Golden Buddha)........B2

Sights
Phra Buddha Maha Suwanna Patimakorn Exhibition........(see 2)
3 Talat Mai........A1
Yaowarat Chinatown Heritage Center........(see 2)

Activities, Courses & Tours
Chao Phraya Princess........(see 4)
4 Chaophraya Cruise........B4
Co van Kessel Bangkok Tours........(see 4)
Grand Pearl........(see 4)
5 Oriental Spa........B6
Supanniga Cruise........(see 4)
6 Wan Fah........B4
White Orchid........(see 4)

Sleeping
7 Glur Bangkok........B7
8 Loftel 22........B3
9 Loy La Long........A2
10 Mandarin Oriental........B6
11 Millennium Hilton........A4
12 Peninsula Hotel........A6
13 Shanghai Mansion........A1
14 Swan Hotel........C6
15 Wanderlust........B1

Eating
16 80/20........C4
17 Bonita Cafe & Social Club........D6
18 Little Market........C4
19 Mangkorn Khǎo........A1
20 Muslim Restaurant........C6
21 Thanon Phadungdao Seafood Stalls........A1

Drinking & Nightlife
22 Ba Hao........B1
23 Pijiu Bar........B1
24 Sky Bar........C7
25 Tep Bar........B1

boutique hotel screams Shanghai c1935 with stained glass, an abundance of lamps, bold colours and cheeky Chinatown kitsch. If you're willing to splurge, ask for one of the bigger streetside rooms with tall windows that allow more natural light.

Riverside

Glur Bangkok HOSTEL $
(Map p92; ☎02 630 5595; www.glurbangkok.com; 45 Soi 50, Th Charoen Krung; incl breakfast dm 285-720B, r 1300-1600B; ; Sathon/Central Pier, Saphan Taksin exit 1) A narrow shophouse with three attractive and comfy eight-bed dorms. Space is limited, but Glur makes the most of it with fun and functional communal areas, including a ground-floor cafe.

Swan Hotel HOTEL $$
(Map p92; ☎02 235 9271; www.swanhotelbkk.com; 31 Soi 36/Rue de Brest, Th Charoen Krung; r incl breakfast 1200-2000B; @; Oriental Pier) The 1960s-era furnishings date this classic Bangkok hotel, despite renovations. But the rooms are airy and virtually spotless, and the antiquated vibe provides the Swan, particularly its pool area, with a fun, groovy vibe.

Mandarin Oriental HOTEL $$$
(Map p92; ☎02 659 9000; www.mandarinoriental.com; 48 Soi 40/Oriental, Th Charoen Krung; incl breakfast r 14,000-30,000B, ste 26,700-160,000B; @; Oriental Pier, or hotel shuttle boat from Sathon/Central Pier) For the true Bangkok experience, a stay at this grand old riverside hotel is a must. The majority of rooms are in the modern and recently refurbished New Wing, but we prefer the old-world ambience of the Garden and Authors' Wings. The hotel is also home to one of the region's most acclaimed spas, a legendary fine-dining restaurant and a cooking school.

Peninsula Hotel HOTEL $$$
(Map p92; ☎02 861 2888; www.peninsula.com; 333 Th Charoen Nakhon; incl breakfast r 7500-8100B, ste 10,600-130,000B; @; hotel shuttle boat from Sathon/Central Pier) At the age of 20, the Pen still seems to have it all: the location (towering over the river), the rep (it's consistently one of the top-ranking luxury hotels in the world) and one of the highest levels of service in town. If money is no obstacle, stay on one of the upper floors where you literally have all of Bangkok at your feet.

Millennium Hilton HOTEL $$$
(Map p92; ☎02 442 2000; www.bangkok.hilton.com; 123 Th Charoen Nakhon; incl breakfast r 4000-5900B, ste 6500-7000B; @; hotel shuttle boat from Sathon/Central Pier) As soon as you enter the dramatic lobby, it's obvious that this is among Bangkok's youngest, most modern riverside hotels. Rooms, all of which boast widescreen river views, carry on the theme and are decked out with funky furniture and Thai-themed photos. A glass elevator and an artificial beach are just some of the fun touches.

Greater Bangkok

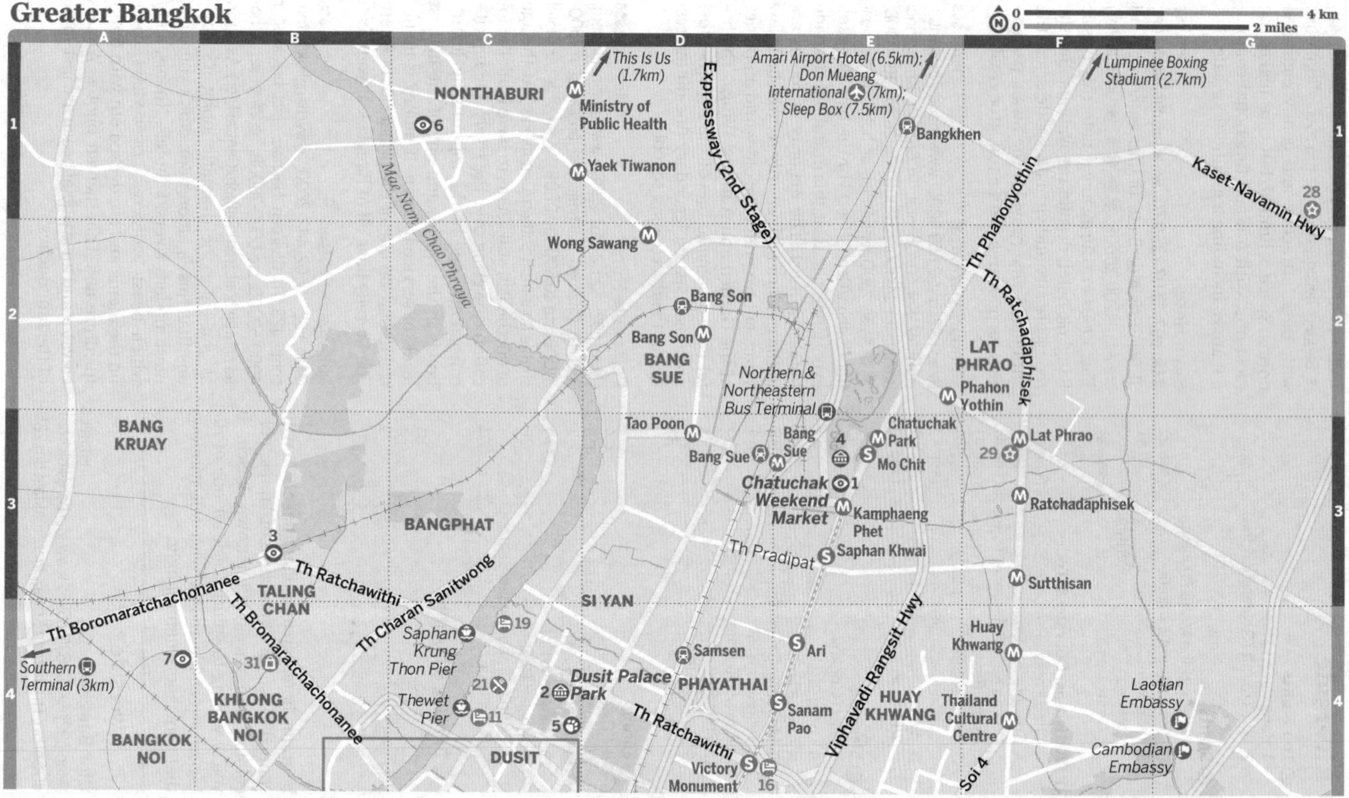

0 — 4 km
0 — 2 miles

A B C D E F G
1 2 3 4

This Is Us (1.7km)
Amari Airport Hotel (6.5km); Don Mueang International (7km); Sleep Box (7.5km)
Lumpinee Boxing Stadium (2.7km)
NONTHABURI
6
Ministry of Public Health
Yaek Tiwanon
Expressway (2nd Stage)
Bangkhen
Kaset-Navamin Hwy
28
Th Phahonyothin
Mae Nam Chao Phraya
Wong Sawang
Th Ratchadaphisek
Bang Son
Bang Son
BANG SUE
LAT PHRAO
Northern & Northeastern Bus Terminal
Phahon Yothin
BANG KRUAY
Tao Poon
Bang Sue
Bang Sue
4
Chatuchak Park
Mo Chit
Lat Phrao
29
Chatuchak Weekend Market
1
Kamphaeng Phet
Ratchadaphisek
BANGPHAT
3
Th Pradipat
Saphan Khwai
Sutthisan
Th Ratchawithi
Th Boromaratchachonanee
TALING CHAN
Th Charan Sanitwong
SI YAN
Th Bromaratchachonanee
19
Saphan Krung Thon Pier
Samsen
Ari
Viphavadi Rangsit Hwy
Huay Khwang
Southern Terminal (3km)
7
31
21
Dusit Palace Park
2
PHAYATHAI
Laotian Embassy
KHLONG BANGKOK NOI
Thewet Pier
11
5
Th Ratchawithi
Sanam Pao
HUAY KHWANG
Thailand Cultural Centre
BANGKOK NOI
DUSIT
Victory Monument
16
Soi 4
Cambodian Embassy

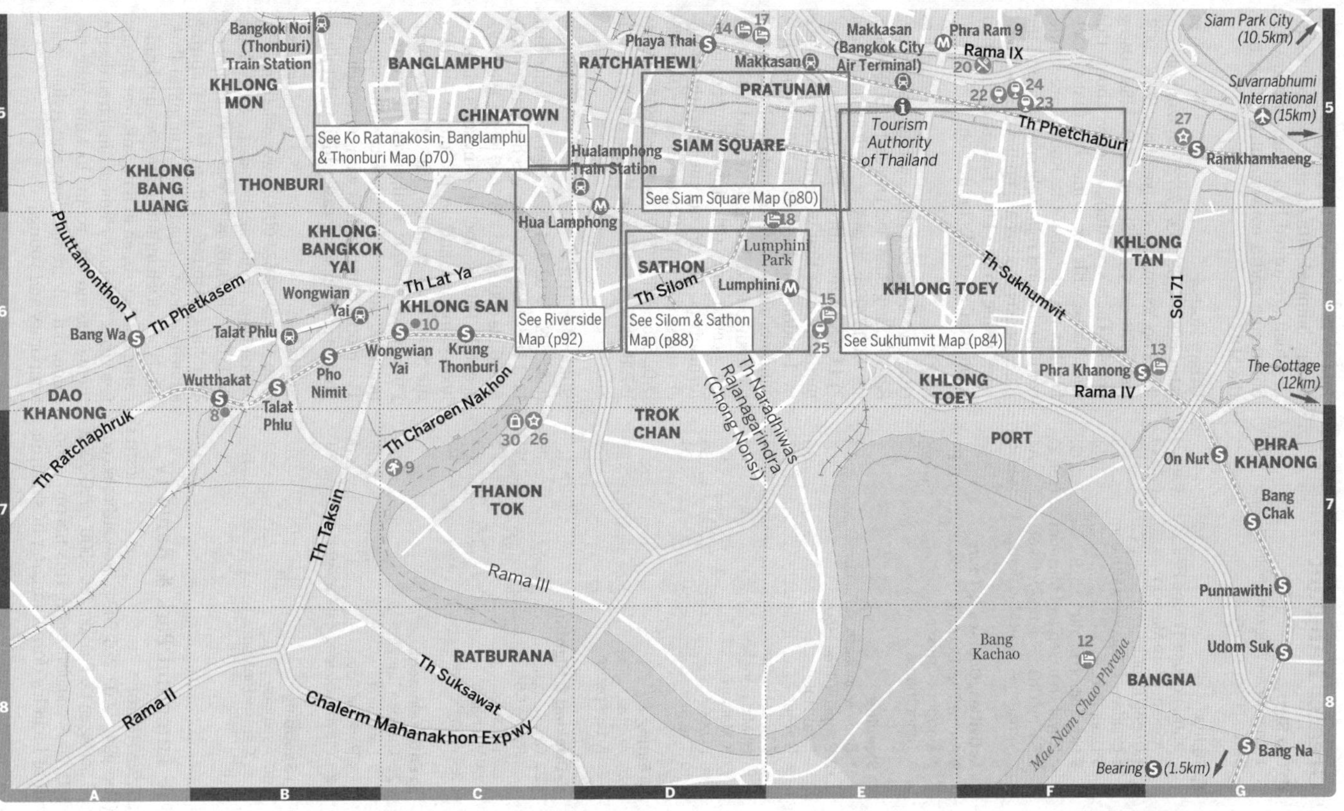
Bangkok Noi (Thonburi) Train Station
KHLONG MON
BANGLAMPHU
CHINATOWN
See Ko Ratanakosin, Banglamphu & Thonburi Map (p70)
RATCHATHEWI
Phaya Thai
Makkasan
Makkasan (Bangkok City Air Terminal)
Phra Ram 9
Rama IX
Siam Park City (10.5km)
Suvarnabhumi International (15km)
PRATUNAM
SIAM SQUARE
Hualamphong Train Station
Tourism Authority of Thailand
Th Phetchaburi
Ramkhamhaeng
See Siam Square Map (p80)
KHLONG BANG LUANG
THONBURI
Hua Lamphong
KHLONG BANGKOK YAI
Lumphini Park
SATHON
Th Silom
Lumphini
KHLONG TOEY
Th Sukhumvit
KHLONG TAN
Soi 71
Phuttamonthon 1
Th Phetkasem
Th Lat Ya
Wongwian Yai
KHLONG SAN
Bang Wa
Talat Phlu
Wongwian Yai
Krung Thonburi
See Riverside Map (p92)
See Silom & Sathon Map (p88)
See Sukhumvit Map (p84)
Pho Nimit
Wutthakat
Talat Phlu
Th Naradhiwas Rajanagarindra (Chong Nonsi)
Phra Khanong
The Cottage (12km)
Rama IV
DAO KHANONG
Th Charoen Nakhon
KHLONG TOEY
TROK CHAN
PORT
Th Ratchaphruk
On Nut
PHRA KHANONG
THANON TOK
Bang Chak
Th Taksin
Rama III
Punnawithi
Bang Kachao
RATBURANA
Udom Suk
BANGNA
Th Suksawat
Mae Nam Chao Phraya
Rama II
Chalerm Mahanakhon Expwy
Bang Na
Bearing (1.5km)

Greater Bangkok

Top Sights

1 Chatuchak Weekend Market.............E3
2 Dusit Palace Park.............C4

Sights

Abhisek Dusit Throne Hall.............(see 2)
Ancient Cloth Museum.............(see 2)
3 Chang Chui.............B3
4 Children's Discovery Museum.............E3
5 Dusit Zoo.............C4
6 Nonthaburi Market.............C1
Royal Thai Elephant Museum.............(see 2)
7 Taling Chan Floating Market.............A4
Vimanmek Teak Mansion.............(see 2)

Activities, Courses & Tours

8 Amita Thai Cooking Class.............B7
9 Manohra Cruises.............C7
10 Thanatharee.............C6

Sleeping

11 Baan Manusarn.............C4
12 Bangkok Tree House.............F8
13 Beat Hotel.............G6
14 Bizotel.............D5
15 ETZzz Hostel.............E6
16 HI Mid Bangkok.............D4
17 K Maison.............D5
18 LUXX XL.............E6
19 The Siam.............C4

Eating

20 Anotai.............F5
21 Krua Apsorn.............C4

Drinking & Nightlife

22 Onyx.............F5
Route 66.............(see 22)
23 Taksura.............F5
24 Vesbar.............F5
25 Wong's Place.............E6

Entertainment

26 Calypso Bangkok.............C7
27 Lam Sing.............G5
28 Parking Toys.............G1
29 Playhouse Magical Cabaret.............F3

Shopping

30 Asiatique.............C7
31 Central Pinklao.............B4

Lumphini Park & Rama IV

ETZzz Hostel HOSTEL $
(Map p94; 02 286 9424; www.etzhostel.com; 5/3 Soi Ngam Du Phli; dm 180-350B, r 750-900B; ; M Lumphini exit 1) This narrow shophouse includes dorms ranging in size from four to 12 beds, and two private rooms (the latter equipped with en suite bathroom), all of which are united by a neat, primary colour theme and a convenient location near the MRT.

Urban House HOTEL $$
(Map p88; 081 492 7778; www.urbanh.com; 35/13 Soi Yommarat; incl breakfast r 800-2300B, ste 1580B; ; M Si Lom exit 2, S Sala Daeng exit 4) There's nothing showy about this shophouse with six rooms, but that's exactly what we like about it. Rooms are subtle, comfortable and relatively spacious, and the place boasts a peaceful, homey atmosphere, largely due to the kind host and the quiet residential street it's located on.

LUXX XL HOTEL $$
(Map p94; 02 684 1111; www.staywithluxx.com; 82/8 Th Lang Suan; incl breakfast r 1500-2400B, ste 3700-7700B; ; S Ratchadamri exit 2) LUXX oozes with a contemporary, minimalist hipness that wouldn't be out of place in London or New York. Floor-to-ceiling windows allow heaps of natural light, suites have an added kitchenette, and all rooms are decked out with appropriately stylish furnishings. There's another slightly cheaper (and smaller) **Th Decho branch** (Map p88; 02 635 8844; 6/11 Th Decho; r 1060-1445B, ste 1570B; ; S Chong Nongsi exit 3), off Th Silom.

Sukhothai Hotel HOTEL $$$
(Map p88; 02 344 8888; www.sukhothai.com; 13/3 Th Sathon Tai/South; incl breakfast r 4000-5200B, ste 6000-80,000B; ; M Lumphini exit 2) This is one of Bangkok's classiest luxury options, and, as the name suggests, the Sukhothai employs brick stupas, courtyards and antique sculptures to create a peaceful, almost temple-like atmosphere. The rooms contrast this with high-tech TVs, phones and; in some cases, high-tech toilets.

Sofitel So HOTEL $$$
(Map p88; 02 624 0000; www.sofitel.com; 2 Th Sathon Neua/North; incl breakfast r 8100-9100B, ste 13,000-48,000B; ; M Lumphini exit 2) Taking inspiration from (and featuring amazing views of) adjacent Lumphini Park, this is one of a handful of large-yet-hip brand-name hotels to open in Bangkok over the last few years. The four-elements-inspired design theme has no two rooms looking quite the same, but all are spacious and stylish, contemporary and young.

Silom & Sathon

Mile Map Hostel HOSTEL $
(Map p88; ☎02 635 1212; 36/4 Th Pan; dm 250-285B, r 600-900B; ❄@🛜; Ⓢ Chong Nonsi exit 3) Despite the quasi-industrial theme, this hostel feels inviting, warm and fun. The 10-bed dorms are one of the best deals in town, and the private rooms have a funky, minimalist feel, although not much natural light.

★**Smile Society** HOTEL $$
(Map p88; ☎081 442 5800, 081 444 1596; www.smilesocietyhostel.com; 30/3-4 Soi 6, Th Silom; incl breakfast dm 450-600B, r 1100-2200B; ❄@🛜; Ⓜ Si Lom exit 2, Ⓢ Sala Daeng exit 1) Part boutique hotel, part hostel, this four-storey shophouse combines small but comfortable and well-equipped rooms, and dorms with spotless shared bathrooms. A central location, overwhelmingly positive guest feedback, and helpful, English-speaking staff are other perks. And a virtually identical annexe next door helps with spillover as Smile Society gains more fans.

★**kokotel** HOTEL $$
(Map p88; ☎02 235 7555; www.kokotel.com; 181/1-5 Th Surawong; r 1400-3400B; ❄@🛜; Ⓢ Chong Nonsi exit 3) Quite possibly the city's family-friendliest accommodation, kokotel unites big, sun-filled rooms with puffy beds, an expansive children's play area and a downstairs cafe (with, appropriately, a slide). Friendly rates also make it great value.

★**Siam Heritage** HOTEL $$$
(Map p88; ☎02 353 6101; www.thesiamheritage.com; 115/1 Th Surawong; incl breakfast r 3500-3800B, ste 5000-6500B; ❄@🛜🏊; Ⓜ Si Lom exit 2, Ⓢ Sala Daeng exit 1) Tucked off busy Th Surawong, this hotel overflows with homey Thai charm – probably because the owners also live in the same building. The 73 rooms are decked out in silk and dark woods with classy design touches and thoughtful amenities. There's an inviting rooftop garden/pool/spa, and it's all cared for by a team of professional, accommodating staff. Highly recommended.

★**Metropolitan by COMO** HOTEL $$$
(Map p88; ☎02 625 3333; www.comohotels.com; 27 Th Sathon Tai/South; incl breakfast r 3500-5300B, ste 6200-27,000B; ❄@🛜🏊; Ⓜ Lumphini exit 2) The exterior of Bangkok's former YMCA has changed relatively little, but a peek inside reveals one of the city's sleekest, sexiest hotels. The 171 rooms come in striking tones of black, white and yellow, though it's worth noting that the City rooms tend to feel a bit tight, while in contrast the two-storey penthouse suites are like small homes.

AIRPORT HOTELS

The vast majority of visitors to Bangkok need not consider the airport hotel rigmarole as taxis are cheap and plentiful, and early-morning traffic means the trip shouldn't take too long. That said, those worried about a super-early departure or late arrival may consider a stay at one of the following:

Novotel Suvarnabhumi Airport Hotel (☎02 131 1111; www.novotelairportbkk.com; Suvarnabhumi International Airport; incl breakfast r 4500-7300B, ste 9500-10,400B; ❄@🛜; Ⓢ Phra Khanong exit 3 & taxi, 🚌 Suvarnabhumi Airport & hotel shuttle bus) Has 600-plus luxurious rooms; located within the Suvarnabhumi International Airport compound.

The Cottage (☎02 727 5858; www.thecottagebangkokairport.com; 888/8 Th Lad Krabang; r incl breakfast 880-1379B; ❄@🛜🏊; Ⓢ Phra Khanong exit 3 & taxi, 🚌 Suvarnabhumi Airport & hotel shuttle bus) This solid midranger is near the Suvarnabhumi International Airport compound and within walking distance of food and shopping; has an airport shuttle.

Sleep Box (☎02 535 7555; Terminal 2, Don Mueang International Airport; r 1800B; ❄🛜) Finally, an alternative to snoozing on the chairs at Don Mueang International Airport. Rooms may induce claustrophobia, but include en suite bathrooms, water, wi-fi and even food coupons. Short stays (1000B for three hours) and showers (300B) are also available.

Amari Airport Hotel (☎02 566 1020; www.amari.com/donmueang; 333 Th Choet Wutthakat; r 1845-2205B, ste 2205-3105B; ❄@🛜🏊; Ⓜ Chatuchak Park exit 2 & taxi, Ⓢ Mo Chit exit 3 & taxi) International-standard hotel located directly opposite Don Mueang International Airport.

Siam Square & Pratunam

Boxpackers Hostel HOSTEL $

(Map p80; 02 656 2828; www.boxpackershostel.com; 39/3 Soi 15, Th Phetchaburi; incl breakfast dm 390-570B, r 1360-2000B; ; S Ratchathewi exit 1 & taxi) A contemporary, sparse hostel with dorms ranging in size from four to 12 double-decker pods – some of which are double beds. Communal areas are inviting, and include a ground-floor cafe and a lounge with pool table. A linked hotel also offers 14 small but similarly attractive private rooms.

★ **Siam@Siam** HOTEL $$$

(Map p80; 02 217 3000; www.siamatsiam.com; 865 Rama I; r incl breakfast 4500-7800B; ; S National Stadium exit 1) A seemingly random mishmash of colours and industrial/recycled materials in the lobby here result in a style one could only describe as 'junkyard chic' – but in a good way, of course. The rooms, which largely continue the theme, are found between the 14th and 24th floors, and offer terrific city views. There's a rooftop restaurant and an 11th-floor pool, and a recent renovation has it looking better than ever.

Hansar HOTEL $$$

(Map p80; 02 209 1234; www.hansarbangkok.com; 3 Soi Mahadlekluang 2; ste incl breakfast 5800-24,000B; ; S Ratchadamri exit 4) The Hansar can claim that elusive amalgam of style and value. All 94 rooms here are handsome and feature huge bathrooms and giant desks, but the smallest (and cheapest) studios are probably the best deal, as they have a kitchenette, washing machine, standalone tub, free wi-fi and in most, a balcony.

Sukhumvit

FU House Hostel HOSTEL $

(Map p84; 098 654 5505; www.facebook.com/fuhouseghostel; 77 Soi 8, Th Sukhumvit; dm/r incl breakfast 500/1650B; ; S Nana exit 4) Great for a quiet, low-key stay is this two-storey wooden villa on a residential street. Choose between attractive bunk beds in one of two spacious, private-feeling dorms, or rooms with en suite bathrooms.

★ **Tints of Blue** HOTEL $$

(Map p84; 099 289 7744; www.tintsofblue.com; 47 Soi 27, Th Sukhumvit; r incl breakfast 1800-2000B; ; M Sukhumvit exit 2, S Asok exit 6) The location in a leafy, quiet street is reflected in the rooms here, which manage to feel secluded, homey and warm. Equipped with kitchenettes, lots of space and natural light, and balconies, they're also a steal at this price.

S31 HOTEL $$

(Map p84; 02 260 1111; www.s31hotel.com; 545 Soi 31, Th Sukhumvit; incl breakfast r 3700B, ste 4200-25,000B; ; S Phrom Phong exit 5) The bold patterns and graphics of its interior and exterior make the S31 a fun, youthful choice. Thoughtful touches like kitchenettes with large fridge, super-huge beds and courses (Thai boxing and yoga) prove that the style also has substance. Significant discounts can be found online, and additional branches are located on Soi 15 and Soi 33.

Beat Hotel HOTEL $$

(Map p94; 02 178 0077; www.beathotelbangkok.com; 69/1 Th Sukhumvit; r incl breakfast 2000-2500B; ; S Phra Khanong exit 3) This art-themed hotel has a vibrant, youthful vibe that kicks off in the lobby. The 54 rooms continue this feeling, ranging in design from those with colourful floor-to-ceiling wall art to others painted in a monochromatic bold hue. It's worth shelling out for the super-huge Deluxe rooms.

S-Box HOTEL $$

(Map p84; 02 262 0991; www.sboxhotel.com; 4 Soi 31, Th Sukhumvit; r incl breakfast 1100-2200B; ; S Phrom Phong exit 5) The name says it all: the rooms here are little more than boxes – albeit attractive, modern boxes with stylish furniture and practical amenities. The cheapest are pod-like and lack natural light, while the more expensive have floor-to-ceiling windows.

★ **AriyasomVilla** HOTEL $$$

(Map p84; 02 254 8880; www.ariyasom.com; 65 Soi 1, Th Sukhumvit; r incl breakfast 6900-10,500B; ; S Phloen Chit exit 3) Located at the end of Soi 1 behind a wall of tropical greenery, this beautifully renovated 1940s-era villa is one of the worst-kept accommodation secrets in Bangkok. The 24 rooms are spacious and meticulously outfitted with thoughtful Thai design touches and sumptuous, beautiful antique furniture. There's also a spa and an inviting tropical pool. Book well in advance.

Breakfast is vegetarian and served in the villa's stunning glass-encased dining room.

Cabochon Hotel BOUTIQUE HOTEL $$$

(Map p84; 02 259 2871/3; www.cabochonhotel.com; 14/29 Soi 45, Th Sukhumvit; incl breakfast r 4900-6500B, ste 7200-13,000B; P ;

S Phrom Phong exit 3) The Cabochon, which means polished gem, is indeed a diamond in rowdy Bangkok. Rooms are light-filled and unfussy, and packed with thoughtful curiosities like antique telephones, typewriters, tortoise shells, model aeroplanes and vintage tea sets. Venture to the rooftop pool or nosh street-food style on mouthwatering Thai and Laotian dishes at the cosy Thai Lao Yeh Restaurant.

Ratchathewi

HI Mid Bangkok HOSTEL $$
(Map p94; 02 644 5744; www.midbangkok.com; 481/3 Th Ratchawithi; dm 390B, r 1000-2400B; ; S Victory Monument exit 4) Contemporary elements (industrial influences, smooth concrete) and old-school Bangkok touches (faux-antique tiles, wood furniture) mingle at this inviting hostel. Dorm rooms are cosy and share clean bathrooms, while private rooms are spacious, if somewhat bare (only the larger deluxe rooms have TV), with lots of natural light.

Bizotel HOTEL $$
(Map p94; 02 245 2424; www.bizotelbkk.com; 104/40 Th Rang Nam; r incl breakfast 1900-2100B; ; S Victory Monument exit 4) Attractive, bright and stuffed with useful amenities: you could be fooled into believing that the rooms at this hotel cost twice this much. A location in a relatively quiet part of town is another bonus, and helpful, friendly staff seal the deal.

K Maison BOUTIQUE HOTEL $$
(Map p94; 02 245 1953; www.kmaisonboutique.com; Soi Ruam Chit; incl breakfast r 2200-3500B, ste 6500B; ; S Victory Monument exit 4) The lobby, with its virginal white, swirling marble and streaks of blue, sets the tone of this boutique hotel. The 21 rooms follow suit, and are handsome in a delicate and attractively sparse way. Lest you think it's all about image, fear not: K Maison is also functional and comfortable.

Thewet & Dusit

Good budget options, a riverside village feel and proximity to visit-worthy sights are the benefits of staying in Thewet and Dusit.

Penpark Place HOTEL $
(Map p70; 02 628 8896; www.penparkplace.com; 22 Soi 3, Th Samsen; r 300-1700B, ste 2200B; ; Thewet Pier) This former factory has been turned into a good-value budget hotel. A room in the original building is little more than a bed and a fan, but an adjacent add-on sees a handful of well-equipped apartment-like rooms and suites.

★ **Sam Sen Sam Place** GUESTHOUSE $$
(Map p70; 02 628 7067; https://samsensam.com; 48 Soi 3, Th Samsen; r incl breakfast 600-2400B; ; Thewet Pier) One of the homiest places in this area, if not Bangkok, this colourful, refurbished antique villa gets glowing reports about its friendly service and quiet location. All the 18 rooms here are extremely tidy, and the cheapest are fan-cooled and share a bathroom.

★ **Phra-Nakorn Norn-Len** HOTEL $$
(Map p70; 02 628 8188; www.phranakorn-nornlen.com; 46 Soi Thewet 1; r incl breakfast 2200-4200B; ; Thewet Pier) Set in an enclosed garden compound decorated like a Bangkok neighbourhood of yesteryear, this bright and cheery hotel is a fun and atmospheric, if not necessarily stupendous-value, place to stay. Although the 31 rooms are attractively furnished with antiques and paintings, it's worth noting that they don't include TV, a fact made up for by daily activities, massage and endless opportunities for peaceful relaxing.

Baan Manusarn GUESTHOUSE $$
(Map p94; 02 281 2976; www.facebook.com/baanmanusarn; Th Krung Kasem; r incl breakfast 1400B; ; Thewet Pier) Steps from Thewet Pier is this inviting vintage shophouse with four rooms. All feature beautiful wood floors and lots of space – with the two family rooms being the most generous – and half boast balconies and en suite bathrooms.

Loog Choob Homestay GUESTHOUSE $$
(Map p70; 085 328 2475; www.loogchoob.com; 463/5-8 Th Luk Luang; incl breakfast r 2100B, ste 3800-4400B; ; Thewet Pier, S Phaya Thai exit 3 & taxi) Five rooms in a former gem factory outside the tourist zone might sound iffy, but the rooms here are stylish and inviting, and come supplemented by a huge array of thoughtful amenities and friendly, heartfelt service.

THE SINKING CITY

With much of the city around 1.5m above sea level, low-lying Bangkok has been sinking at a rate of 2cm per year. Some scientists estimate that the city may face submersion within approximately 15 years due to rising sea levels.

BANGKOK'S BEST HOSTELS

If you're on a shoestring budget, Bangkok has heaps of options for you, ranging from high-tech, pod-like dorm beds in a brand-new hostel to cosy bunk beds in a refurbished Chinatown shophouse. (And if you decide that you need a bit more privacy, nearly all of Bangkok's hostels also offer private rooms.)

Lub*d (Map p80; ☎02 612 4999; www.siamsquare.lubd.com; Rama I; dm 550B, r 1900-2500B; ❄@📶; Ⓢ National Stadium exit 1) The title is a play on the Thai *làp dee*, meaning 'sleep well', but the fun atmosphere at this modern-feeling hostel might make you want to stay up all night. Diversions include an inviting communal area stocked with games and a bar, and thoughtful facilities range from washing machines to a theatre room.

Chern (Map p70; ☎02 621 1133; www.chernbangkok.com; 17 Soi Ratchasak; dm 400B, r 1400-1900B; ❄@📶; ⛴klorng boat to Phanfa Leelard Pier) The vast, open spaces and white, over-exposed tones of this hostel converge in an almost afterlife-like feel.

Niras Bangkoc (Map p70; ☎02 221 4442; www.nirasbankoc.com; 204-206 Th Mahachai; dm 450-500B, r 1300-1500B; ❄📶; ⛴klorng boat to Phanfa Leelard Pier) Niras takes advantage of its location in an antique shophouse to arrive at a charmingly old-school feel. Both the four- and six-bed dorms here feature dark woods and vintage furniture, with friendly staff, a cosy ground-floor cafe and a location in an atmospheric corner of the city.

Silom Art Hostel (Map p88; ☎02 635 8070; www.silomarthostel.com; 198/19-22 Soi 14, Th Silom; dm 300-350B, r 1300-1500B; ❄@📶; Ⓢ Chong Nonsi exit 3) Quirky, artsy, bright and fun, Silom Art Hostel combines recycled materials, unconventional furnishings and colourful wall paintings to create a hostel that's quite unlike anywhere else in town. It's not all about style though: beds are functional and comfortable, with lots of appealing communal areas.

Loftel 22 (Map p92; www.loftel22bangkok.com; 952 Soi 22, Th Charoen Krung; dm 250-300B, r with shared bathroom 850-1300B; ❄@📶; ⛴Marine Department Pier, Ⓜ Hua Lamphong exit 1) Stylish, inviting dorms have been coaxed out of these two adjoining shophouses. Friendly service and a location in one of Chinatown's most atmospheric corners round out the package.

NapPark Hostel (Map p70; ☎02 282 2324; www.nappark.com; 5 Th Tani; dm 440-600B; ❄@📶; ⛴Phra Athit/Banglamphu Pier) This popular hostel features dorm rooms of various sizes, the smallest and most expensive of which boasts six pod-like beds outfitted with power points, mini-TV, reading lamp and wi-fi.

Chao Hostel (Map p80; ☎02 217 3083; www.chaohostel.com; 8th fl, 865 Rama I; incl breakfast dm 550B, r 1600-1800B; ❄@📶; Ⓢ National Stadium exit 1) Blending modern minimalist and Thai design elements, not to mention tonnes of open space, the new Chao is one of the most sophisticated hostels we've encountered in Bangkok.

Pause Hostel (Map p84; ☎02 108 8855; www.onedaybkk.com; Oneday, 51 Soi 26, Th Sukhumvit; incl breakfast dm 450-600B, r 1300-1500B; ❄@📶; Ⓢ Phrom Phong exit 4) Attached to a cafe/coworking space is this modern, open-feeling hostel. Dorms span four to eight beds and are united by a handsome industrial-design theme and inviting, sun-soaked communal areas.

S1 Hostel (Map p88; ☎02 679 7777; www.facebook.com/s1hostelbangkok; 35/1-4 Soi Ngam Du Phli; dm 330-380B, r 700-1300B; ❄@📶; Ⓜ Lumphini exit 1) A huge new hostel with dorm beds decked out in a simple yet attractive primary-colour scheme. A host of facilities (laundry, kitchen, rooftop garden) and a convenient location within walking distance of the MRT make it great value.

Bed Station Hostel (Map p80; ☎02 019 5477; www.bedstationhostel.com; 486/149-150 Soi 16, Th Phetchaburi; incl breakfast dm 500-650B, r 1350-1550B; ❄@📶; Ⓢ Ratchathewi exit 3) A handsome industrial-chic theme unites the dorms at this modern-feeling hostel. They range from four to eight beds and include access to tidy toilet facilities and a laundry room.

The Siam HOTEL $$$

(Map p94; ☎02 206 6999; www.thesiamhotel.com; 3/2 Th Khao; incl breakfast r 16,100-22,400B, villa 26,300-37,000B; ; Thewet Pier, or hotel shuttle boat from Sathon/Central Pier) Zoom back to the 1930s in this contemporary riverside hotel, where art deco influences, copious marble and beautiful antiques define the look. Rooms are spacious and well appointed, while villas up the ante with rooftop balcony and plunge pool. Yet it's not just about self-indulging, with activities ranging from Thai boxing lessons to a private theatre to keep you busy.

Eating

Nowhere else is the Thai reverence for food more evident than in Bangkok. To the outsider, the life of a Bangkokian appears to be a string of meals and snacks punctuated by the odd stab at work, not the other way around. If you can adjust your mental clock to this schedule, your visit will be a delicious one indeed.

Ko Ratanakosin

In stark contrast to the rest of Bangkok, there aren't many restaurants or stalls in Ko Ratanakosin, and those that are here predominantly serve Thai cuisine. For something more international, consider heading to Banglamphu, a short taxi ride away.

Pa Aew THAI $

(Map p70; Th Maha Rat; mains 20-60B; 10am-5pm Tue-Sat; Tien Pier) Pull up a plastic stool for some rich, seafood-heavy, Bangkok-style fare. It's a bare-bones, open-air curry stall, but for taste, Pa Aew is one of our favourite places to eat in this part of town.

There's no English-language sign; look for the exposed trays of food directly in front of the Krung Thai Bank near the corner with Soi Pratu Nokyung.

★**Tonkin-Annam** VIETNAMESE $$

(Map p70; ☎093 469 2969; www.facebook.com/tonkinannam; 69 Soi Tha Tien; mains 140-300B; 10am-10pm Wed-Mon; ; Tien Pier) The retro-minimalist interior here might be a red flag for hipster ethnic cuisine, but Tonkin-Annam serves some of the best Vietnamese food in Bangkok. Come for the deliciously tart and peppery banana blossom salad, or dishes you won't find elsewhere, such as *bánh bèo* (steamed cups of rice flour topped with pork), a speciality of Hue.

Banglamphu

Banglamphu is famous for its old-school central Thai food – the predominant cuisine in this part of town. For something more international, head to Th Khao San, where you'll find a few international fast-food franchises as well as foreign and vegetarian restaurants.

Somsong Phochana THAI $

(Map p70; off Th Lamphu; mains from 30B; 9.30am-4pm; Phra Athit/Banglamphu Pier) This is one of the few places in Bangkok that serves *gŏo·ay đĕe·o sù·kŏh·tai*, or Sukhothai-style noodles: barbecued pork and thin rice noodles in a clear broth seasoned with a little sugar, supplemented with sliced green beans, and garnished with ground peanuts. There's no English-language sign. To find Somsong, enter Th Lamphu, then take the first left, opposite Watsungwej School; the restaurant is on the right.

Karim Roti-Mataba THAI $

(Map p70; 136 Th Phra Athit; mains 40-130B; 9am-10pm Tue-Sun; ; Phra Athit/Banglamphu Pier) This classic Bangkok eatery may have grown a bit too big for its britches in recent years, but it still serves tasty Thai-Muslim dishes such as roti, *gaang mát·sà·màn* ('Muslim curry'), tart fish curry and *má·đà·bà* (something of a stuffed pancake).

An upstairs air-con dining area and a couple of outdoor tables provide barely enough seating for loyal fans and curious tourists alike.

★**Krua Apsorn** THAI $$

(Map p70; www.kruaapsorn.com; Th Din So; mains 100-450B; 10.30am-8pm Mon-Sat; ; klorng boat to Phanfa Leelard Pier) This cafeteria-like dining room is a favourite of members of the Thai royal family and restaurant critics alike. Just about all of the central and southern Thai dishes are tasty, but regulars never miss the chance to order the decadent stir-fried crab with yellow pepper chili or the *tortilla Española*–like fluffy crab omelette.

There's another **branch** (Map p94; 503-505 Th Samsen; mains 100-450B; 10.30am-7.30pm Mon-Fri, to 6pm Sat; ; Thewet Pier) on Th Samsen in Thewet and Dusit.

Shoshana ISRAELI $$

(Map p70; 88 Th Chakraphatdi Phong; mains 80-320B; 10am-midnight; ; Phra Athit/Banglamphu Pier) One of Khao San's longest-running Israeli restaurants, Shoshana resembles your grandparents' living room right down to the tacky wall art and plastic placemats. Feel safe in ordering anything deep-fried – staff do an excellent job of it – and don't miss the deliciously garlicky eggplant dip.

★ Jay Fai THAI $$$

(Map p70; 327 Th Mahachai; mains 180-1000B; ⌚3pm-2am Mon-Sat; klorng boat to Phanfa Leelard Pier) With its bare-bones dining room, it's hard to believe Jay Fai is renowned for serving Bangkok's most expensive *pàt kêe mow* ('drunkard's noodles': wide rice noodles fried with seafood and Thai herbs). The price, however, is justified by the copious fresh seafood, plus a distinct frying style resulting in an almost oil-free finished dish.

It's in a virtually unmarked shophouse, opposite a 7-Eleven.

Chinatown & Phahurat

When you mention Chinatown, most Bangkokians immediately dream of street food, the bulk of which is found just off Th Yaowarat.

On the western side of the neighbourhood is Phahurat, Bangkok's Little India, filled with small Indian and Nepali restaurants tucked into the tiny soi off Th Chakkaraphet.

Nay Hong STREET FOOD $

(Map p70; off Th Yukol 2; mains 35-50B; ⌚4-10pm; Ratchawong Pier, M Hua Lamphong exit 1 & taxi) The reward for locating this hole-in-the-wall is one of Bangkok's best fried noodle dishes – *gŏo·ay đĕe·o kôo·a gài* (flat rice noodles fried with garlic oil, chicken and egg). No English-language menu.

There's no English-language sign. To find Nay Hong, proceed north from the corner of Th Suapa and Th Luang, then turn right into the first side street; it's at the end of the narrow alleyway.

80/20 INTERNATIONAL $$

(Map p92; ☎02 639 1135; www.facebook.com/8020bkk; 1052-1054 Th Charoen Krung; mains from 240B; ⌚6pm-midnight Wed-Mon; ❄; Ratchawong Pier, M Hua Lamphong exit 1) Don't call it fusion; rather, 80/20 excels at taking and blending Thai and Western ingredients and dishes, arriving at something altogether unique. The often savoury-leaning desserts, overseen by a Japanese pastry chef, are especially worth the trip. A progressive breath of air in otherwise conservative Chinatown.

Little Market AMERICAN $$

(Map p92; www.facebook.com/littlemarketbkk; 1056/7 Soi 28, Th Charoen Krung; mains 100-180B; ⌚10am-10pm Tue-Sun; Ratchawong Pier, S Hua Lamphong exit 1) They may not look like much, but the sliders here are some of the best burgers in town. Throw into the mix the crispy tater tots, American-style breakfasts and a fun retro vibe with a classic rock soundtrack, and Little Market just might be the most authentically American eatery in Bangkok.

Thanon Phadungdao Seafood Stalls STREET FOOD $$

(Map p92; cnr Th Phadungdao & Th Yaowarat; mains 100-600B; ⌚4pm-midnight Tue-Sun; Ratchawong Pier, M Hua Lamphong exit 1 & taxi) After sunset, these two opposing open-air restaurants – each of which claims to be the original – become a culinary train wreck of outdoor barbecues, screaming staff, iced seafood trays and messy pavement seating. True, the vast majority of diners are foreign tourists, but this has little impact on the cheerful setting, the fun experience and the cheap bill.

Lumphini Park & Rama IV

★ nahm THAI $$$

(Map p88; ☎02 625 3388; www.comohotels.com; ground fl, Metropolitan Hotel, 27 Th Sathon Tai/South; set lunch 600-1600B, set dinner 2500B, mains 310-800B; ⌚noon-2pm Mon-Fri, 7-10.30pm daily; ❄; M Lumphini exit 2) Australian chef-author David Thompson is the man behind one of Bangkok's – and if you believe the critics, the world's – best Thai restaurants. Using ancient cookbooks as his inspiration, Thompson has given new life to previously extinct dishes with exotic descriptions such as 'smoked fish curry with prawns, chicken livers, cockles, chillies and black pepper'.

Silom & Sathon

Th Silom has a bit of everything, from old-school Thai to some of the city's best upmarket international dining.

Jay So THAI $

(Map p88; 146/1 Soi Phiphat 2; mains 45-80B; ⌚10am-4pm Mon-Sat; M Si Lom exit 2, S Sala Daeng exit 2) Jay So has no menu, but a mortar and pestle and a huge grill are the telltale signs of ballistically spicy *sôm·đam* (green papaya salad), sublime herb-stuffed, grilled catfish and other northeastern Thai specialities. There's no English signage (nor an English-language menu), so look for the ramshackle, white and green, Coke-decorated shack about halfway down Soi Phiphat 2.

Muslim Restaurant THAI $
(Map p92; 1354-6 Th Charoen Krung; mains 40-140B; 6.30am-5.30pm; Oriental Pier, S Saphan Taksin exit 1) Plant yourself in any random wooden booth of this ancient eatery for a glimpse into what restaurants in Bangkok used to be like. The menu, much like the interior design, doesn't appear to have changed much in the restaurant's 70-year history, and the biryanis, curries and samosas remain more Indian-influenced than Thai.

Sushi Tsukiji JAPANESE $$
(Map p88; 62/19-20 Th Thaniya; sushi per item 60-700B; 11.30am-2.30pm & 5.30-10.30pm; ; M Si Lom exit 2, S Sala Daeng exit 1) Our pick of the numerous Japanese joints along Th Thaniya is Tsukiji, named after Tokyo's famous seafood market. Dinner at this sleek sushi joint will leave a significant dent in the wallet, so instead come for lunch on a weekday, when Tsukiji does generous set meals for a paltry 300B.

★ **Eat Me** INTERNATIONAL $$$
(Map p88; 02 238 0931; www.eatmerestaurant.com; Soi Phiphat 2; mains 300-1400B; 3pm-1am; ; M Si Lom exit 2, S Sala Daeng exit 2) With descriptions like 'charred witlof and mozzarella salad with preserved lemon and dry-aged Cecina beef', the dishes may sound all over the map or perhaps somewhat pretentious, but they're actually just plain tasty. A casual yet sophisticated atmosphere, excellent cocktails, a handsome wine list and some of the city's best desserts also make this one of our favourite places in Bangkok to dine.

Siam Square, Pratunam & Around

If you find yourself hungry in this part of central Bangkok, you're largely at the mercy of shopping-mall food courts and chain restaurants. However, this is still Thailand, and if you can ignore the prefabricated atmosphere, the food can often be quite good.

Open House CAFE
(Map p80; 02 119 7777; www.centralembassy.com/anchor/open-house; 6th fl, Central Embassy, 1031 Th Phloen Chit; 10am-10pm; ; S Phloen Chit) Housed in posh Central Embassy mall, Open House is a chic, light-filled multi-use space from the same team who designed YouTube and Google's Tokyo headquarters. The open floor plan incorporates

DINNER CRUISES

A dinner cruise along Mae Nam Chao Phraya is touted as an iconic Bangkok experience, and several companies cater to this. Yet it's worth mentioning that, in general, the vibe can be somewhat cheesy, with loud live entertainment and mammoth boats so brightly lit inside you hardly know you're on the water. The food, typically served as a buffet, usually ranges from mediocre to forgettable. But the atmosphere of the river at night, bordered by illuminated temples and skyscrapers, and the cool breeze chasing the heat away, is usually enough to trump all of this.

A good one-stop centre for all your dinner cruise needs is the **River City Boat Tour Check-In Center** (Map p92; www.rivercity.co.th; ground fl, River City, 23 Th Yotha; 10am-10pm; Si Phraya/River City Pier, or shuttle boat from Sathon/Central Pier), where tickets can be purchased for **Grand Pearl** (Map p92; 02 861 0255; www.grandpearlcruise.com; cruises 2000B; cruise 7.30-9.30pm; Si Phraya/River City Pier), **Chaophraya Cruise** (Map p92; 02 541 5599; www.chaophrayacruise.com; cruises 1700B; cruise 7-9pm), **Wan Fah** (Map p92; 02 622 7657; www.wanfah.in.th; cruises 1500B; cruise 7-9pm), **Chao Phraya Princess** (Map p92; 02 860 3700; www.thaicruise.com; cruises 1500B; cruise 7-9.30pm) and **White Orchid** (Map p92; 02 438 8228; www.whiteorchidrivercruise.com; cruises 1400B; cruise 7.20-9.45pm). All cruises depart from River City Pier; take a look at the websites to see exactly what's on offer.

For something slightly more upmarket, consider **Manohra Cruises** (Map p94; 02 476 0022; www.manohracruises.com; cruises 2300B; hotel shuttle boat from Sathon/Central Pier) or **Supanniga Cruise** (Map p92; 02 714 7608; www.supannigacruise.com; cruises 1250-3250B; cruises 4.45-5.45pm & 6.15-8.30pm; Si Phraya/River City Pier), more intimate experiences that also get positive feedback for their food.

restaurants, galleries, a bookshop, a breezy balcony for lounging and 180-degree views of buzzy Th Sukhumvit. Pop in to recharge with an iced latte and connect to the fast wi-fi.

Gaa INTERNATIONAL $$$
(Map p80; ☎091 419 2424; www.gaabkk.com; 68/4 Soi Langsuan; set menu 1800-2400B; ⏲6-9.30pm; ❄; S Ratchadamri) A bright yellow and pink shophouse opposite **Gaggan** (Map p80; ☎02 652 1700; www.eatatgaggan.com; 68/1 Th Langsuan; set menu 5000B; ⏲6-11pm; ❄✎; S Ratchadamri exit 2) has been taken over by Gaggan's former sous chef, Garima Arora, who also honed her craft at Copenhagen's famed Noma. Classic Indian and Thai dishes are the specialities here, upgraded with modern cooking techniques and presented in artful 8-12-course tasting menus. Reservations are strongly recommended.

Din Tai Fung CHINESE $$
(Map p80; 7th fl, CentralWorld, Th Ratchadamri; mains 65-350B; ⏲11am-10pm; ❄✎; S Chit Lom exit 9 to Sky Walk, Siam exit 6 to Sky Walk) Most come to this lauded Taiwanese chain for the *xiao long bao* (broth-filled 'soup' dumplings). And so should you. But the other northern Chinese-style dishes are just as good, and justify exploring the more remote regions of the menu.

Sukhumvit

With the city's largest selection of international restaurants, this seemingly endless ribbon of a road is where to go if, for the duration of a meal, you wish to forget that you're in Thailand.

Gokfayuen CHINESE $
(Map p84; www.facebook.com/wuntunmeen; 161/7 Soi Thong Lor 9; mains 70-140B; ⏲11am-11.30pm; ❄; S Thong Lo exit 3 & taxi) Gokfayuen has gone to great lengths to re-create classic Hong Kong dishes in Bangkok. Couple your house-made wheat-and-egg noodles with roasted pork, steamed vegetables with oyster sauce, or the Hong Kong–style milk tea.

Saras INDIAN $
(Map p84; www.saras.co.th; Soi 20, Th Sukhumvit; mains 90-200B; ⏲9am-10.30pm; ❄✎; M Sukhumvit exit 2, S Asok exit 4) Describing your restaurant as a 'fast-food feast' may not be the cleverest PR strategy we've encountered, but it's a pretty spot-on description of this Indian restaurant. Order at the counter to be rewarded with *dosai* (crispy southern Indian bread), meat-free regional set meals or rich curries (dishes are brought to your table). We wish all fast food could be this satisfying.

BEST VEGETARIAN EATS

Bonita Cafe & Social Club (Map p92; www.bonitacafesocialclub.wordpress.com; 100 Soi 26, Th Silom; mains 100-300B; ⏲9.30am-9.30pm Wed-Mon; ❄📶✎; S Surasak exit 3) Foreign-influenced vegan dining.

Anotai (Map p94; www.facebook.com/anotaigo; 976/17 Soi Rama 9 Hospital, Rama IX; mains 150-300B; ⏲10am-9.30pm Thu-Tue; ❄✎; M Phra Ram 9 exit 3 & taxi) Sophisticated meat-free meals.

Saras (p104) Fast-food-feeling southern Indian.

Arawy Vegetarian Food (Map p70; 152 Th Din So; mains from 30B; ⏲7am-8pm; ✎; ⛴ klorng boat to Phanfa Leelard Pier) Long-standing Thai vegetarian.

Chennai Kitchen (Map p88; 107/4 Th Pan; mains 70-150B; ⏲10am-3pm & 6-9.30pm; ❄✎; S Surasak exit 3) Home-cooked southern Indian.

★**Soul Food Mahanakorn** THAI $$
(Map p84; ☎02 714 7708; www.soulfoodmahanakorn.com; 56/10 Soi 55/Thong Lor, Th Sukhumvit; mains 140-290B; ⏲5.30pm-midnight; ❄✎; S Thong Lo exit 3) This contemporary staple gets its interminable buzz from its dual nature as both an inviting restaurant – the menu spans tasty interpretations of rustic Thai dishes – and a bar serving deliciously boozy, Thai-influenced cocktails. Reservations recommended.

★**Sri Trat** THAI $$
(Map p84; www.facebook.com/sritrat; 90 Soi 33, Th Sukhumvit; mains 180-450B; ⏲noon-11pm Wed-Mon; ❄; S Phrom Phong exit 5) This new restaurant specialises in the unique fare of Thailand's eastern provinces, Trat and Chanthaburi. What this means is lots of rich, slightly sweet, herbal flavours, fresh seafood and dishes you won't find anywhere else in town. Highly recommended.

★**Jidori Cuisine Ken** JAPANESE $$
(Map p84; ☎02 661 3457; www.facebook.com/jidoriken; off Soi 26, Th Sukhumvit; mains 60-350B; ⏲5pm-midnight Mon-Sat, to 10pm Sun; ❄; S Phrom Phong exit 4) This cosy Japanese

restaurant does tasty tofu dishes, delicious salads and even excellent desserts; basically everything here is above average, but the highlight is the smoky, perfectly seasoned chicken skewers. Reservations recommended.

Drinking & Nightlife

Shame on you if you think Bangkok's only nightlife options include the word 'go-go'. As in any big international city, the drinking and partying scene in Bangkok ranges from trashy to classy and touches on just about everything in between. Way back in 2001, the Thaksin administration started enforcing closing times and curtailing other excesses that had previously made the city's nightlife famous. Since his 2006 ousting, the laws have been increasingly circumvented or inconsistently enforced. Post the 2014 coup, there are indications that Bangkok is seeing something of a return to the 2001-era; strictly enforced operating hours and zoning laws.

Ko Ratanakosin, Thonburi & Banglamphu

Rowdy Th Khao San is one of the city's best areas for a night out. If the main drag is too intense, consider the (sightly) quieter places along Soi Ram Buttri and Th Samsen. Bars are a rare sight in Ko Ratanakosin, although there is a growing number of hotel-based bars along the riverfront.

Roof BAR

(Map p70; www.salaresorts.com/rattanakosin; 5th fl, Sala Rattanakosin, 39 Th Maha Rat; 5pm-midnight Mon-Thu, to 1am Fri-Sun; Tien Pier) The open-air bar on top of the Sala Rattanakosin hotel has upped the stakes for sunset views of Wat Arun – if you can see the temple at all through the wall of selfie-snapping tourists. Be sure to get there early for a good seat.

Hippie de Bar BAR

(Map p70; www.facebook.com/hippie.debar; 46 Th Khao San; 3pm-2am; Phra Athit/Banglamphu Pier) Hippie boasts a funky retro vibe and indoor and outdoor seating, all set to the type of indie-pop soundtrack that you're unlikely to hear elsewhere in town. Despite being located on Th Khao San, there are surprisingly few foreign faces, and it's a great place to make some new Thai friends.

The Club CLUB

(Map p70; www.facebook.com/theclubkhaosanbkk; 123 Th Khao San; admission Fri & Sat 120B; 9pm-2am; Phra Athit/Banglamphu Pier) Located right in the middle of Th Khao San, this cavern-like dance hall hosts a good mix of locals and backpackers; check the Facebook page for upcoming events and guest DJs.

Ku Bar BAR

(Map p70; www.facebook.com/ku.bangkok; 3rd fl, 469 Th Phra Sumen; 7pm-midnight Thu-Sun) Tired of buckets and cocktails that revolve around Red Bull? Head to Ku Bar, in almost every way the polar opposite of the Khao San party scene. Climb three floors of stairs (look for the tiny sign) to emerge at an almost comically minimalist interior where sophisticated fruit- and food-heavy cocktails (sample names: Lychee, Tomato, Pineapple/Red Pepper) and obscure music augment the underground vibe.

Chinatown & Phahurat

A handful of new, artsy bars on Soi Nana and along Th Charoen Krung have finally made Chinatown an interesting nightlife destination.

★**Tep Bar** BAR

(Map p92; www.facebook.com/tepbar; 69-71 Soi Nana; 5pm-midnight Tue-Sun; M Hua Lamphong exit 1) We never expected to find a bar this sophisticated – yet this fun – in Chinatown. Tep does it with a Thai-tinged, contemporary interior, tasty signature cocktails, Thai drinking snacks, and raucous live Thai music performances from Thursday to Sunday.

Ba Hao BAR

(Map p92; www.ba-hao.com; 8 Soi Nana; 6pm-midnight Tue-Sun; Ratchawong Pier, M Hua Lamphong exit 1) At this point, there's little original about this retro Chinese-themed refurbished shophouse on Soi Nana, but potable craft beer, inventive cocktails and really excellent Chinese-style bar snacks (don't miss the Chinese pancake with braised pork belly, herbs and fried egg) make Ba Hao stand out.

Pijiu Bar BAR

(Map p92; www.facebook.com/pijiubar; 16 Soi Nana; 5pm-midnight Tue-Sun; Ratchawong Pier, M Hua Lamphong exit 1) Old West meets old Shanghai at this new yet classic-feeling bar. The emphasis here is on beer ('pijiu' is Chinese for beer), with four revolving craft brews on tap, but perhaps even more enticing are the charcuterie platters (300B) that unite a variety of smoked and preserved meats from some of the best vendors in Chinatown.

Silom & Sathon

Lower Silom is Bangkok's gaybourhood, but the area as a whole has several fun bars and dance clubs for all comers.

★ Smalls BAR

(Map p88; www.facebook.com/smallsbkk; 186/3 Soi Suan Phlu; 8.30pm-late; M Lumphini exit 2 & taxi) Even though it only opened its doors in 2014, Smalls is the kind of bar that feels like it's been here forever. Fixtures include a cheekily decadent interior, an inviting rooftop, food-themed nights (check the Facebook page) and live jazz on Wednesdays. The eclectic house cocktails are strong, if sweet, and bar snacks range from rillettes to quesadillas.

DJ Station CLUB

(Map p88; www.dj-station.com; 8/6-8 Soi 2, Th Silom; admission from 150B; 10pm-2am; M Si Lom exit 2, S Sala Daeng exit 1) One of Bangkok's and indeed Asia's most legendary gay dance clubs, here the crowd is a mix of Thai guppies (gay professionals), money boys and a few Westerners. There are several similar clubs in Soi 2.

Vesper BAR

(Map p88; www.vesperbar.co; 10/15 Th Convent; noon-2.30pm & 6pm-1am Mon-Fri, 6pm-midnight Sat, noon-2.30pm Sun; M Si Lom exit 2, S Sala Daeng exit 2) One of the freshest faces on Bangkok's drinking scene is this deceptively classic-feeling bar-restaurant. As the name suggests, the emphasis here is on cocktails, including several revived classics and mixed drinks mellowed by ageing for six weeks in white-oak barrels.

Namsaah Bottling Trust BAR

(Map p88; www.namsaah.com; 401 Soi 7, Th Silom; 5pm-2am; M Si Lom exit 2, S Sala Daeng exit 2) Namsaah is all about twists. From its home (a former mansion incongruously painted hot pink) to the cocktails (classics with a tweak or two) and the bar snacks and dishes (think *pàt tai* with foie gras), everything's a little bit off in just the right way.

Siam Square, Pratunam & Around

Bangkok's most central zone is home to a scant handful of bars.

Hair of the Dog BAR

(Map p80; www.hairofthedogbkk.com; 1st fl, Mahathun Plaza, 888/26 Th Phloen Chit; 5pm-midnight; S Phloen Chit exit 2) The craft-beer craze that has swept Bangkok over the last few years is epitomised at this semi-concealed bar. With a morgue theme, dozens of bottles and 13 rotating taps, it's a great place for a weird, hoppy night.

Sukhumvit

This long street is home to Bangkok's most sophisticated bars and clubs.

★ WTF BAR

(Map p84; www.wtfbangkok.com; 7 Soi 51, Th Sukhumvit; 6pm-1am Tue-Sun; ; S Thong Lo exit 3) Wonderful Thai Friendship (what did you think it stood for?) is a funky and friendly neighbourhood bar that also packs in a gallery space. Arty locals and resident foreigners come for the old-school cocktails, live music and DJ events, poetry readings, art exhibitions and tasty bar snacks. And we, like them, give WTF our vote for Bangkok's best bar.

★ Q&A Bar BAR

(Map p84; www.qnabar.com; 235/13 Soi 21/Asoke, Th Sukhumvit; 7pm-2am Mon-Sat) Imagine a mid-century modern dining car or airport lounge, and you're close to picturing the interior of Q&A. The short list of featured cocktails can appear to be a divergence from the classic vibe, but an old-world dress code and manners are encouraged.

★ Studio Lam BAR, CLUB

(Map p84; www.facebook.com/studiolambangkok; 3/1 Soi 51, Th Sukhumvit; 6pm-1am Tue-Sun; S Thong Lo exit 3) Studio Lam is an extension of uberhip record label ZudRangMa, and boasts a Jamaican-style sound system custom-built for world and retro-Thai DJ sets and the occasional live show. For a night of dancing in Bangkok that doesn't revolve around Top 40 cheese, this is the place.

★ Tuba BAR

(Map p84; www.facebook.com/tubabkk; 34 Room 11-12 A, Soi Thong Lor 20/Soi Ekamai 21; 11am-2am; S Ekkamai exit 1 & taxi) Part storage room for over-the-top vintage furniture, part restaurant and part friendly local boozer; this quirky bar certainly doesn't lack in diversity – nor fun. Indulge in a whole bottle (they'll hold onto it for your next visit if you don't finish it) and don't miss the moreish chicken wings or the delicious deep-fried *lâhp* (a tart/spicy salad of minced meat).

Mikkeller BAR
(Map p84; www.mikkellerbangkok.com; 26 Yaek 2, Soi Ekamai 10; ⌚5pm-midnight; Ⓢ Ekkamai exit 1 & taxi) These buzz-generating Danish 'gypsy' brewers have set up shop in Bangkok, granting us more than 30 beers on tap. Expect brews ranging from the local (Sukhumvit Brown Ale) to the insane (Beer Geek, a 13% alcohol oatmeal stout), as well as an inviting atmosphere and good bar snacks.

Golden Coins Taproom MICROBREWERY
(Map p84; ☎082 675 9673; www.facebook.com/goldencoinstaproom; Ekamai Mall, Ekkamai Soi 10; ⌚5pm-midnight; Ⓢ Ekkamai) Thailand's craft beer laws forced Golden Coins microbrewery to shut down their Chinatown outpost (RIP Let the Boy Die) and partner with local breweries in Vietnam to produce the ales that are on tap at their Ekkamai location. Six are on offer, including a dessert-style stout and a not-too-hoppy IPA that pairs perfectly with the American-style BBQ menu.

Walden BAR
(Map p84; 7/1 Soi 31, Th Sukhumvit; ⌚6.30pm-1am Mon-Sat; Ⓢ Phrom Phong exit 5) Get past the hyper-minimalist *Kinfolk* vibe, and the thoughtful Japanese touches of this bar make it one of the more welcoming places in town. The brief menu of drinks spans Japanese-style 'highballs', craft beers from the USA, and simple, delicious bar snacks.

☆ Entertainment

Shame on you if you find yourself bored in Bangkok. With traditional cultural performances, dance, art, live music and, yes, the infamous go-go bars, you have a city whose entertainment scene spans from – in local parlance – lo-so (low society) to hi-so (high society).

Gà·teu·i Cabaret

Over the last decade, choreographed stage shows featuring Broadway high kicks and lip-synched pop tunes performed by *gà·teu·i* (also spelt *kàthoey*) – Thai transgender and cross-dressing people – has become a 'must-do' fixture on the Bangkok tourist circuit. Playhouse Magical Cabaret (p105) caters to the trend, as does **Calypso Bangkok** (Map p94; ☎02 688 1415; www.calypsocabaret.com; Asiatique, Soi 72-76, Th Charoen Krung; adult/child 900/600B; ⌚show times 8.15pm & 9.45pm; ⛴ shuttle ferry from Sathon/Central Pier) , located in Asiatique market.

Live Music

★ **Parking Toys** LIVE MUSIC
(Map p94; ☎02 907 2228; 17/22 Soi Mayalap, off Kaset-Navamin Hwy; ⌚4pm-2am; Ⓜ Chatuchak Park exit 2 & taxi, Ⓢ Mo Chit exit 3 & taxi) One of Bangkok's best venues for live music, Parking Toys hosts an eclectic revolving cast of fun bands ranging in genre from rockabilly to electro-funk jam acts.

To get here, take a taxi heading north from BTS Mo Chit (or the MRT Chatuchak Park) and tell the driver to take you to the Kaset intersection and turn right on Th Kaset-Navamin; Parking Toys is just past the second stop light on this road.

LGBT BANGKOK

Bangkok has a notoriously pink vibe to it. From kinky male-underwear shops mushrooming at street corners to lesbian-only get-togethers, as a LGBT person you could eat, shop and play here for days without ever leaving the comfort of gay-friendly venues. Unlike elsewhere in Southeast Asia, homosexuality is not criminalised in Thailand and the general attitude remains extremely laissez-faire.

Bangkok Lesbian (www.bangkoklesbian.com) is the city's premier website for ladies who love ladies, while BK (www.bk.asia-city.com) and Siam2nite (www.siam2nite.com) are good sources for LGBT events in Bangkok. Noted pop parodists Trasher (www.facebook.com/trasherbangkok) organise gay-friendly parties – check the website to see if one's on when you're in town.

Don't miss DJ Station (p106) , one of the most iconic gay nightclubs in Asia. Other highlights are **Telephone Pub** (Map p88; www.telephonepub.com; 114/11-13 Soi 4, Th Silom; ⌚6pm-1am; 📶; Ⓜ Si Lom exit 2, Ⓢ Sala Daeng exit 1), a long-standing bar right in the middle of Bangkok's pinkest zone, and the city's premier drag show, **Playhouse Magical Cabaret** (Map p94; ☎02 024 5522; www.playhousethailand.com; 5 Th Ratchadapisek, Chompol Sub-District, Chatuchak; 960B; ⌚show times 8pm & 9.30pm; Ⓢ Lat Phrao exit 1).

DON'T MISS

ROOFTOP BARS

In Bangkok, nobody seems to mind if you slap the odd bar on top of a skyscraper. Indeed, the city has become associated with open-air rooftop bars, and the area around Th Sathon and Th Silom is home to some of its best, with locales boasting views that range from riverside to hyper-urban. Note that nearly all of Bangkok's hotel-based rooftop bars have strictly enforced dress codes barring access to those wearing shorts and/or sandals.

Moon Bar (Map p88; www.banyantree.com; 61st fl, Banyan Tree Hotel, 21/100 Th Sathon Tai/South; 5pm-1am; M Lumphini exit 2) An alarmingly low barrier at this rooftop bar is all that separates patrons from the street, 61 floors down. Located on top of the Banyan Tree Hotel, Moon Bar claims to be among the highest al fresco bars in the world. It's also a great place from which to see the Phrapradaeng Peninsula, the vast green area that's colloquially known as Bangkok's green lung.

Park Society (Map p88; 29th fl, Sofitel So, 2 Th Sathon Neua/North; 5pm-2am; M Lumphini exit 2) Gazing down at the green expanse of Lumphini Park, abruptly bordered by tall buildings on most sides, you can be excused for thinking that Bangkok almost, kinda, sorta feels like Manhattan. The drink prices at Park Society, 29 floors above the ground, may also remind you of New York City, although there are monthly promotions.

Sky Bar (Map p92; www.lebua.com; 63rd fl, State Tower, 1055 Th Silom; 6pm-1am; Sathon/Central Pier, S Saphan Taksin exit 3) Descend the Hollywood-like staircase to emerge at this bar that juts out over the city's skyline and Mae Nam Chao Phraya. This is the classic Bangkok rooftop bar – scenes from *The Hangover Part II* were filmed here – and the views are breathtaking, although the excessive drink prices and photo-snapping crowds have made it an increasingly hectic destination.

★ **Brick Bar** LIVE MUSIC
(Map p70; www.brickbarkhaosan.com; basement, Buddy Lodge, 265 Th Khao San; admission Sat & Sun 150B; 7pm-1.30am; Phra Athit/Banglamphu Pier) This basement pub, one of our favourite destinations in Bangkok for live music, hosts a nightly revolving cast of bands for an almost exclusively Thai crowd – many of whom will end the night dancing on the tables. Brick Bar can get infamously packed, so be sure to get there early.

★ **The Living Room** LIVE MUSIC
(Map p84; 02 649 8888; www.thelivingroomatbangkok.com; level 1, Sheraton Grande Sukhumvit, 250 Th Sukhumvit; 6pm-midnight; M Sukhumvit exit 3, S Asok exit 2) Don't let looks deceive you: every night this bland hotel lounge transforms into the city's best venue for live jazz. True to the name, there's comfy, sofa-based seating, all of it within earshot of the music. Enquire ahead of time to see which sax master or hide-hitter is in town. An entry fee of 300B is charged after 8.30pm.

Lam Sing LIVE MUSIC
(อีสานลำซิ่ง; Map p94; www.facebook.com/isanlamsing; 57/5 Th Phet Phra Ram; 9.30pm-4am; S Ekkamai exit 1 & taxi) Even Ziggy Stardust–era David Bowie has nothing on this dark, decadent, rhinestone-encrusted den, one of Bangkok's best venues for *mŏr lam* and *lôok tûng*, music with roots in Thailand's rural northeast. Come for raucous live-music performances accompanied by tightly choreographed, flagrantly costumed backup dancers. There's no English-language sign here, but most taxi drivers are familiar with the place.

Thai Boxing (Moo·ay tai)

★ **Rajadamnern Stadium** SPECTATOR SPORT
(สนามมวยราชดำเนิน; Map p70; www.rajadamnern.com; off Th Ratchadamnoen Nok; tickets 3rd class/2nd class/ringside 1000/1500/2500B; Matches Mon-Thur from 6.30-11pm, Sun 3pm & 6.30pm; Thewet Pier, S Phaya Thai exit 3 & taxi) Rajadamnern Stadium, Bangkok's oldest and most venerable venue for *moo·ay tai* (Thai boxing; also spelt *muay Thai*), hosts matches on Monday, Wednesday and Thursday from 6.30pm to around 11pm, and Sunday at 3pm and 6.30pm. Be sure to buy tickets from the official ticket counter or online, not from the touts and scalpers who hang around outside the entrance.

Lumpinee Boxing Stadium SPECTATOR SPORT
(02 282 3141; www.muaythailumpinee.net; 6 Th Ramintra; tickets 3rd class/2nd class/ringside 1000/1500/2500B; Matches Tue & Fri 6.30-11pm, Sat 2-8.30pm; M Chatuchak Park exit 2 & taxi, S Mo Chit exit 3 & taxi) The other of Bangkok's

two premier Thai boxing rings is located in a modern venue far north of town. Matches occur on Tuesdays and Fridays from 6.30pm to 11pm, and on Saturdays from 2pm to 8.30pm.

Go-Go Bars

Although technically illegal, prostitution is fully 'out' in Bangkok, and the influence of organised crime and lucrative kickbacks mean that it will be a long while before the existing laws are ever enforced. Yet despite the image presented by much of the Western media, the underlying atmosphere of Bangkok's red-light districts is not one of illicitness and exploitation (although these do inevitably exist), but rather an aura of tackiness and boredom. **Patpong** (Map p88; Th Phat Phong & Soi Phat Phong 2; ⌚4pm-2am; M Si Lom exit 2, S Sala Daeng exit 1) earned notoriety during the 1980s for its wild sex shows.

Theatre

Sala Chalermkrung THEATRE
(Map p70; ☎02 224 4499; www.salachalermkrung.com; 66 Th Charoen Krung; tickets 800-1200B; ⌚shows 7.30pm Thu & Fri; ⛴Saphan Phut/Memorial Bridge Pier, M Hua Lamphong exit 1 & taxi) This art deco Bangkok landmark, a former cinema dating to 1933, is one of the few remaining places *kŏhn* (masked dance-drama based on stories from the *Ramakian*, the Thai version of the Indian epic *Ramayana*) can be witnessed. The traditional dance-drama is enhanced here by laser graphics, high-tech audio and English subtitles. Concerts and other events are also held; check the website for details.

National Theatre THEATRE
(Map p70; ☎02 224 1342; 2 Th Ratchini; tickets 60-100B; ⛴Chang Pier, Maharaj Pier, Phra Chan Tai Pier) The National Theatre holds performances of *kŏhn* at 2pm on the first and second Sundays of the month from January to September, and *lá·kon* (classical dance-dramas) at 2pm on the first and second Sundays of the month from October to December. Tickets go on sale an hour before performances begin.

Shopping

Prime your credit card and shine your baht – shopping is serious business in Bangkok. Hardly a street corner in this city is free from a vendor, hawker or impromptu stall, and it doesn't stop there: Bangkok is also home to one of the world's largest outdoor markets, not to mention some of Southeast Asia's largest malls.

Banglamphu & Chinatown

Shopping in Banglamphu means street markets and traditional items, while Chinatown might be the city's most commerce-heavy hood, but bulk of wares are utilitarian and will hold little interest for travellers.

★ **Thanon Khao San Market** GIFTS & SOUVENIRS
(Map p70; Th Khao San; ⌚10am-midnight; ⛴Phra Athit/Banglamphu Pier) The main guesthouse strip in Banglamphu is a day-and-night shopping bazaar peddling all the backpacker 'essentials': profane T-shirts, bootleg MP3s, hemp clothing, fake student ID cards, knock-off designer wear, selfie sticks, orange juice and, of course, those croaking wooden frogs.

Heritage Craft ARTS & CRAFTS
(Map p70; 35 Th Bamrung Meuang; ⌚11am-6pm Mon-Fri; ⛴klorng boat to Phanfa Leelard Pier) Handicrafts with a conscience: this new boutique is an atmospheric showcase for the quality domestic wares of **ThaiCraft** (Map p84; www.thaicraft.org; L fl, Jasmine City Bldg, cnr Soi 23 & Th Sukhumvit; M Sukhumvit exit 2, S Asok exit 3), some of which are produced via fair-trade practices.

Items include silks from Thailand's northeast, baskets from the south and jewellery from the north, and there's also an inviting on-site cafe.

Riverside, Silom & Sathon

Asiatique MARKET
(Map p94; Soi 72-76, Th Charoen Krung; ⌚4-11pm; ⛴shuttle boat from Sathon/Central Pier) One of Bangkok's more popular night markets, Asiatique takes the form of warehouses of commerce next to Mae Nam Chao Phraya. Expect clothing, handicrafts, souvenirs and quite a few dining and drinking venues.

Frequent, free shuttle boats depart from Sathon/Central Pier from 4pm to 11.30pm.

House of Chao ANTIQUES
(Map p88; 9/1 Th Decho; ⌚9.30am-7pm; S Chong Nonsi exit 3) This three-storey antique shop, appropriately located in an antique shophouse, has everything necessary to deck out your fantasy colonial-era mansion. Particularly interesting are the various weather-worn doors, doorways, gateways and trellises

that can be found in the covered area behind the showroom.

Siam Square, Pratunam & Around

The area around Siam Sq is home to the city's greatest concentration of malls; if name brands are your thing, this is your place. Cheap clothing is found just north, in the Pratunam area.

★ **Siam Discovery** SHOPPING CENTRE
(Map p80; www.siamdiscovery.co.th; cnr Rama I & Th Phayathai; ⏲10am-10pm; S Siam exit 1) With an open, almost-market-like feel and an impressive variety of unique goods ranging from housewares to clothing (including lots of items by Thai designers), the recently renovated Siam Discovery is hands down the most design-conscious mall in town.

BEST AFTER-HOURS NIGHTLIFE

Wong's Place (Map p94; 27/3 Soi Si Bamphen; ⏲9pm-late Tue-Sun; M Lumphini exit 1) Open from midnight until the last punter crawls out.

The Bank (Map p70; 3rd fl, 44 Th Chakraphatdi Phong; ⏲6pm-late; ⛴ Phra Athit/Banglamphu Pier) Puff on *shisha* or dance into the wee hours on Th Khao San.

Narz (Map p84; www.narzclubbangkok.net; 112 Soi 23, Th Sukhumvit; from 400B; ⏲9pm-2am; M Sukhumvit exit 2, S Asok exit 3) With three vast zones to keep clubbers raving till dawn.

Levels (Map p84; www.levelsclub.com; 6th fl, Aloft, 35 Soi 11, Th Sukhumvit; 500B; ⏲9pm-late; S Nana exit 3) When most Soi 11 bars begin to close, this club heats up.

Mixx (Map p80; www.mixx-discotheque.com; basement, InterContinental Hotel, 973 Th Phloen Chit; 300B; ⏲10pm-2am; S Chit Lom exit 7) Basement-level late-night disco.

Scratch Dog (Map p84; basement, Windsor Suites Hotel, 8-10 Soi 20, Th Sukhumvit; 400B; ⏲midnight-late; M Sukhumvit exit 2, S Asok exit 4) For when closing times trump quality music.

★ **MBK Center** SHOPPING CENTRE
(Map p80; www.mbk-center.com; cnr Rama I & Th Phayathai; ⏲10am-10pm; S National Stadium exit 4) This eight-storey market in a mall has emerged as one of Bangkok's top attractions. On any given weekend half of Bangkok's residents (and most of its tourists) can be found here combing through a seemingly inexhaustible range of small stalls, shops and merchandise.

Northern Bangkok

★ **Chatuchak Weekend Market** MARKET
(ตลาดนัดจตุจักร, Talat Nat Jatujak; Map p94; www.chatuchakmarket.org; 587/10 Th Phahonyothin; ⏲7am-6pm Wed & Thu plants only, 6pm-midnight Fri wholesale only, 9am-6pm Sat & Sun; M Chatuchak Park exit 1, Kamphaeng Phet exits 1 & 2, S Mo Chit exit 1) Among the largest markets in the world, Chatuchak seems to unite everything buyable, from used vintage sneakers to baby squirrels. Plan to spend a full day here, as there's plenty to see, do and buy. But come early, ideally around 10am, to beat the crowds and the heat.

Information

DANGERS & ANNOYANCES

Bangkok is generally a safe city, but there are a few things to be aware of:

- In recent years, Bangkok has been the site of political protests that have occasionally turned violent; check your embassy's advisory travel warnings before leaving.
- Criticising the Thai monarchy in any way is a very serious social faux pas that carries potentially incriminating repercussions; don't do it.
- Avoid the common scams: one-day gem sales, suspiciously low transport prices, dodgy tailors.
- Bangkok's streets are extremely dangerous and its drivers rarely yield to pedestrians. Look in both directions before crossing any street (or footpath) and yield to anything with more metal than you.
- Most of Bangkok's street-food vendors close shop on Monday.
- Bangkok's rainy season is from May to October, when daily downpours – and occasional flooding – are the norm.

Thais are generally so friendly and laid-back that some visitors are lulled into a false sense of security. While your personal safety is rarely at risk in Thailand, you may be unwittingly charmed out of the contents of your wallet or fall prey to a scam (p112).

EMERGENCY & IMPORTANT NUMBERS

The police contact number functions as the de facto universal emergency number in Thailand and can also be used to call an ambulance or report a fire.

Bangkok area code	☎02
Country code	☎66
Directory assistance (free)	☎1133
International access code	☎001, 007
Operator-assisted international calls	☎100
Police	☎191
Tourist Police	☎1155

INTERNET & TELEPHONE

Wi-fi is standard in guesthouses and cafes. Signal strength deteriorates in the upper floors of multistorey buildings; you can always request a room near a router. Cellular data networks continue to expand and increase in capability.

The easiest phone option in Thailand is to acquire a mobile (cell) phone equipped with a local SIM card. Buying a prepaid SIM is as simple as finding a 7-Eleven. SIM cards include talk and data packages and you can add more funds with a prepaid reload card.

A convenient place to take care of your communication needs in the centre of Bangkok is **TrueMove** (Map p80; www.truemove.com; Soi 2, Siam Sq; ⏲7am-10pm; Ⓢ Siam exit 4), which has high-speed internet computers equipped with Skype, sells phones and mobile subscriptions, and can also provide information on citywide wi-fi access for computers and phones.

MEDIA

➡ Bangkok's predominant English-language newspapers are the *Bangkok Post* (www.bangkokpost.com) and the business-heavy *Nation* (www.nationmultimedia.com).

➡ *Bangkok 101* (www.bangkok101.com) is a tourist-friendly listings magazine; *BK* (www.bk.asia-city.com) is a slightly more in-depth listings mag; and *Coconuts Bangkok* (https://bangkok.coconuts.co) is where to go for listings and offbeat local 'news'.

➡ On Twitter, Richard Barrow (@RichardBarrow) is a great source of tourist information.

MEDICAL SERVICES

Bangkok is considered a centre of medical excellence in Southeast Asia. Private hospitals are more expensive than other medical facilities, but offer a superior standard of care and English-speaking staff. The cost of health care is relatively cheap in Thailand compared to most Western countries.

The following hospitals have English-speaking doctors:

Bangkok Christian Hospital (Map p88; ☎02 625 9000; www.bch.in.th; 124 Th Silom; Ⓜ Si Lom exit 2, Ⓢ Sala Daeng exit 1) Modern hospital in central Bangkok.

BNH (Map p88; ☎02 686 2700; www.bnhhospital.com; 9 Th Convent; Ⓜ Si Lom exit 2, Ⓢ Sala Daeng exit 2) Modern, centrally located hospital.

Bumrungrad International Hospital (Map p84; ☎02 667 1000; www.bumrungrad.com; 33 Soi 3, Th Sukhumvit; ⏲24hr; Ⓢ Phloen Chit exit 3) An internationally accredited hospital.

Samitivej Hospital (Map p84; ☎02 022 2222; www.samitivejhospitals.com; 133 Soi 49, Th Sukhumvit; Ⓢ Phrom Phong exit 3 & taxi) Modern hospital.

Pharmacies are plentiful, and in central areas most pharmacists will speak English. If you don't find what you need in a Boots, Watsons or a local pharmacy, try one of the hospitals.

MONEY

Banks generally open between 8.30am and 3.30pm, although branches in busy areas and shopping malls may open later. ATMs function round the clock and are common around Bangkok. The downside is that Thai ATMs charge a 200B foreign-transaction fee on top of whatever currency conversion and out-of-network fees your home bank charges.

Some foreign credit cards are accepted in high-end establishments; but most places deal only with cash. Go to 7-Eleven shops or other reputable places to break 1000B bills; don't expect a vendor or taxi to be able to change a bill 500B or larger.

POST

Main Post Office (Map p92; ☎02 233 1050; Th Charoen Krung; ⏲8am-8pm Mon-Fri, to 1pm Sat & Sun; ⛴ Oriental Pier)

TOILETS

Increasingly, the Asian-style squat toilet is less of the norm in Thailand and the Western-style toilet appears wherever foreign tourists can be found. However, even in places where sit-down toilets are installed, the septic system may not be designed to take toilet paper. In such cases there will be a waste basket where you're supposed to place used toilet paper and feminine hygiene products. For public toilets in Bangkok, your best bet is to head for a shopping centre or fast-food restaurant.

TOURIST INFORMATION

Bangkok Information Center (Map p70; ☎02 225 7612-4; www.bangkoktourist.com; 17/1 Th Phra Athit; ⏲8am-7pm Mon-Fri, 9am-5pm Sat & Sun; ⛴ Phra Athit/Banglamphu Pier) Handles city-specific tourism information.

Tourism Authority of Thailand (TAT; Map p94; ☎02 250 5500, nationwide 1672; www.tourismthailand.org; 1600 Th Phetchaburi;

WORTH A TRIP

LIVIN' IT UP ALONG ROYAL CITY AVENUE

By day a bland-looking strip of offices, come Friday and Saturday nights, Royal City Ave – known by everybody as RCA – transforms into one of Bangkok's most popular nightlife zones. Although some of the bigger clubs can draw thousands, keep in mind that they often require an ID check and also maintain a dress code (no shorts or sandals).

The easiest way to approach RCA is via taxi from the MRT stop at Phra Ram 9; taxis generally can't enter RCA itself, so you'll have to U-turn or cross busy Th Phet Uthai on foot. Approaching the strip from Th Phet Uthai, you'll find the following venues:

Onyx (Map p94; www.facebook.com/onyxbkk; RCA/Royal City Ave; 500B; ⌚8pm-2am; Ⓜ Phra Ram 9 exit 3 & taxi) Probably the most sophisticated club along RCA – evidenced by the hefty entry fee and the coiffed and coddled clientele. Check the Facebook page for upcoming DJ events.

Route 66 (Map p94; www.route66club.com; 29/33-48 RCA/Royal City Ave; 300B; ⌚8pm-2am; Ⓜ Phra Ram 9 exit 3 & taxi) This vast club has been around just about as long as RCA has, but frequent facelifts and expansions have kept it relevant. Top 40 hip-hop rules the main space here, although there are several different themed 'levels', featuring anything from Thai pop to live music.

Vesbar (Map p94; www.facebook.com/GoVesBar; 29/68 RCA/Royal City Ave; ⌚11am-midnight Mon-Sat; Ⓜ Phra Ram 9 exit 3 & taxi) This Vespa-themed bar-restaurant serves up international dishes, import beers and jazzy live music (Wednesday, Friday and Saturday).

Taksura (Map p94; 9 RCA/Royal City Avenue; ⌚6pm-2am; Ⓜ Phra Ram 9 exit 3 & taxi) Existing somewhere between restaurant and pub is retro-themed Taksura. If you're fuelling up for the clubs, the spicy *gàp glâam* (Thai drinking snacks) won't disappoint.

⌚8.30am-4.30pm; Ⓜ Phetchaburi exit 2) Government-operated tourist information and promotion service founded in 1960. Produces excellent pamphlets on sightseeing; check the website for contact information.

TRAVEL WITH CHILDREN

Bambi (www.bambiweb.org) A useful resource for parents in Bangkok.

Bangkok.com (www.bangkok.com/kids) This website lists a dizzying array of things to do with kids.

Thorn Tree Kids To Go forum (www.lonelyplanet.com/thorntree/forums/kids-to-go) Questions and answers from other travellers with children on Lonely Planet's community forum.

ℹ Getting There & Away

AIR

Located 30km east of central Bangkok is **Suvarnabhumi International Airport** (☎02 132 1888; www.suvarnabhumiairport.com), pronounced *sù·wan·ná·poom*. The airport website has real-time details of arrivals and departures.

Bangkok's other airport, **Don Mueang International Airport** (☎02 535 2111; www.donmueangairportthai.com), 25km north of central Bangkok, is the city's de facto budget hub. Terminal 1 handles international flights, while Terminal 2 is for domestic destinations.

BUS

Bangkok is the centre for bus services that fan out all over the kingdom. Buses using government bus stations are far more reliable and less prone to incidents of theft than those departing from Th Khao San or other tourist centres.

Allow an hour to reach all bus terminals from most parts of Bangkok.

The **Eastern Bus Terminal** (Map p84; ☎02 391 2504; Soi 40, Th Sukhumvit; Ⓢ Ekkamai exit 2) is the departure point for buses to Pattaya, Rayong, Chanthaburi and other points east, except for the border crossing at Aranya Prathet. Most people call it *sà·tǎh·nee èk·gà·mai* (Ekamai station). It's near the Ekkamai BTS station.

The **Northern & Northeastern Bus Terminal** (Mo Chit; Map p94; ☎northeastern routes 02 936 2852, ext 602/605, northern routes 02 936 2841, ext 325/614; Th Kamphaengphet; Ⓜ Kamphaeng Phet exit 1 & taxi, Ⓢ Mo Chit exit 3 & taxi) is located just north of Chatuchak Park. This hectic bus station is also commonly called *kǒn sòng mǒr chít* (Mo Chit station) – not to be confused with Mo Chit BTS station. Buses depart from here for all northern and northeastern destinations, as well as regional international destinations. To reach the bus station, take BTS to Mo Chit or MRT to Kamphaeng Phet and transfer onto city bus 3, 77 or 509, or hop on a taxi or motorcycle taxi.

A handful of buses bound for international destinations depart from Bangkok's Northern & Northeastern Bus Terminal.

DESTINATION	COST (B)	DURATION (HR)	DEPARTURE
Pakse (Laos)	900	12	8.30pm
Phnom Penh (Cambodia)	750	11	1.30am
Siem Reap (Cambodia)	750	7	9am
Vientiane (Laos)	900	10	8pm

The **Southern Bus Terminal** (Sai Tai Mai; ☎ 02 422 4444, call centre 1490; Th Boromaratchachonanee), commonly called *sǎi đâi mài*, lies a long way west of the centre of Bangkok. Besides serving as the departure point for all buses to destinations south of Bangkok, transport to Kanchanaburi and western Thailand also departs from here. The easiest way to reach the station is by taxi, or you can take bus 79, 159, 201 or 516 from Th Ratchadamnoen Klang.

Suvarnabhumi Public Transport Centre (☎ 02 132 1888; Suvarnabhumi Airport) Located 3km from Suvarnabhumi International Airport, this terminal has relatively frequent departures to points east and northeast including Aranya Prathet (for the Cambodian border), Chanthaburi, Ko Chang, Nong Khai (for the Lao border), Pattaya, Rayong, Trat and Udon Thani. It can be reached from the airport by a free shuttle bus.

TRAIN

The city's main train terminus is known as **Hualamphong** (☎ 02 220 4334, call centre 1690; www.railway.co.th; off Rama IV; Ⓜ Hua Lamphong exit 2). It's advisable to ignore all touts here and avoid the travel agencies. To check timetables and prices for destinations, check out the website of the State Railway of Thailand (www.railway.co.th/main/index_en.html).

Also known as Thonburi, **Bangkok Noi** (☎ 02 418 4310, call centre 1690; www.railway.co.th; off Th Itsaraphap; ⛴ Thonburi Railway Station, Wang Lang/Siriraj Pier, Ⓢ Wongwian Yai exit 4 & taxi) is a minuscule train station with (overpriced) departures for Kanchanaburi.

Wong Wian Yai (☎ 02 465 2017, call centre 1690; www.railway.co.th; off Th Phra Jao Taksin; Ⓢ Wongwian Yai exit 4 & taxi) is a tiny hidden station and the jumping-off point for the commuter line to Samut Sakhon (also known as Mahachai).

Getting Around

Bangkok may seem chaotic and impenetrable at first, but its transport system is gradually improving, and although you'll almost certainly find yourself stuck in traffic at some point, the traffic jams aren't as legendary as they used to be.

BTS The elevated Skytrain runs from 6am to midnight. Tickets 16B to 44B.

MRT The Metro runs from 6am to midnight. Tickets 16B to 42B.

Taxi Outside of rush hours, Bangkok taxis are a great bargain. Flagfall 35B.

Chao Phraya Express Boat Runs 6am to 8pm, charging 10B to 40B.

Klorng boat Bangkok's canal boats run from 5.30am to 8pm most days. Tickets 9B to 19B.

Bus Cheap but a slow and confusing way to get around Bangkok. Tickets 5B to 30B.

TO/FROM THE AIRPORTS

Suvarnabhumi International Airport

Train The **Airport Rail Link** (☎ call centre 1690; www.srtet.co.th) connects Suvarnabhumi International Airport with the BTS (Skytrain) stop at Phaya Thai (45B, 30 minutes, from 6am to midnight) and the MRT (Metro) stop at Phetchaburi (45B, 25 minutes, from 6am to midnight).

Bus & Minivan There is a public transport centre 3km from the airport that includes a bus terminal with buses to a handful of provinces and inner-city-bound buses and minivans. A free airport shuttle connects the transport centre with the passenger terminals. Bus lines that city-bound tourists are likely to use include line 551 to BTS Victory Monument station (40B, frequent from 5am to 10pm) and 552 to BTS On Nut (20B, frequent from 5am to 10pm).

DON'T MISS

BEST MARKET-BROWSING

Pak Khlong Talat (ปากคลองตลาด, Flower Market; Map p70; Th Chakkaraphet; ⏲ 24hr; ⛴ Pak Klong Taladd Pier, Saphan Phut/Memorial Bridge Pier) The capital's famous flower market; come late at night and don't forget your camera.

Talat Mai (p77) This frenetic fresh market is a slice of China in Bangkok.

Nonthaburi Market (ตลาดนนทบุรี; Map p94; Tha Nam Nonthaburi, Nonthaburi; ⏲ 5-9am; ⛴ Nonthaburi Pier) An authentic upcountry market only minutes from Bangkok.

Khlong Toey Market (ตลาดคลองเตย; Map p84; cnr Th Ratchadaphisek & Rama IV; ⏲ 5-10am; Ⓜ Khlong Toei exit 1) The city's largest fresh market.

WORTH A TRIP

FLOATING MARKETS

Pictures of *đà·làht nám* (floating markets) jammed full of wooden canoes pregnant with colourful exotic fruits have defined the official tourist profile of Thailand for decades. The idyllic scenes are as iconic as the Grand Palace or the Reclining Buddha, but they are also almost completely contrived for, and dependent upon, foreign and domestic tourists – roads and motorcycles moved Thais' daily errands onto dry ground long ago. That said, if you can see them for what they are, a few of Thailand's floating markets are worth a visit.

Tha Kha Floating Market (ตลาดน้ำท่าคา; Tha Kha, Samut Songkhram; ⏲7am-noon, 2nd, 7th & 12th day of waxing & waning moons plus Sat & Sun) The most real-feeling floating market is also the most difficult to reach. A handful of vendors coalesce along an open rural *klorng* (canal; also spelt *Khlang*) lined with coconut palms and old wooden houses. Boat rides (20B per person, 45 minutes) can be arranged along the canal and there are lots of tasty snacks and fruits for sale. Contact Amphawa's **tourist office** (☎034 752 847; 71 Th Prachasret; ⏲8.30am-4.30pm) to see when the next one is. To get here, take one of the morning *sŏrng·tăa·ou* (passenger pick-up trucks; 20B, 45 minutes) from Samut Songkhram's market area.

Amphawa Floating Market (ตลาดน้ำอัมพวา; Amphawa; dishes 20-40B; ⏲4-9pm Fri-Sun) The Amphawa Floating Market, located in Samut Songkhram Province, convenes near Wat Amphawa. The emphasis is on edibles and tourist knick-knacks; because the market is only there on weekends and is popular with tourists from Bangkok, things can get pretty hectic.

Taling Chan Floating Market (ตลาดน้ำตลิ่งชัน; Map p94; Khlong Bangkok Noi, Thonburi; ⏲7am-4pm Sat & Sun; Ⓢ Wongwian Yai exit 3 & taxi) Located just outside Bangkok on the access road to Khlong Bangkok Noi, Taling Chan looks like any other fresh-food market busy with produce vendors from nearby farms. But the twist emerges at the canal where several floating docks serve as informal dining rooms and the kitchens are canoes tethered to the docks. Taling Chan is in Thonburi and can be reached via taxi from Wongwian Yai BTS station or via air-con bus 79 (16B, 25 minutes), which makes stops on Th Ratchadamnoen Klang. Long-tail boats from any large Bangkok pier can also be hired for a trip to Taling Chan and the nearby Khlong Chak Phra.

Damnoen Saduak Floating Market (ตลาดน้ำดำเนินสะดวก; Damnoen Saduak, Ratchaburi; ⏲7am-noon) This 100-year-old floating market – the country's most famous – is now essentially a floating souvenir stand filled with package tourists. This in itself can be a fascinating insight into Thai culture, as the vast majority of tourists here are Thais and watching the approach to this cultural 'theme park' is instructive. But beyond the market, the residential canals are quite peaceful and can be explored by hiring a boat (100B per person) for a longer duration. Trips stop at small family businesses, including a Thai candy maker, a pomelo farm and a knife crafter. Minivans from the Southern Bus Terminal in Thonburi can link you with Damnoen Saduak (80B, two hours, frequent from 6am to 9pm).

Don Wai Market (ตลาดดอนหวาย; Don Wai, Nakhon Pathom; ⏲6am-6pm) Not technically a swimmer, this market claims a river bank location in Nakhon Pathom Province, having originally started out in the early 20th century as a floating market for pomelo and jackfruit growers and traders. As with many tourist attractions geared towards Thais, the main draw is food, including fruit, traditional sweets and *pèt pah·lóh* (five-spice stewed duck), which can be consumed aboard large boats that cruise Mae Nam Nakhorn Chaisi (60B, one hour). The easiest way to reach Don Wai Market is to take a minibus (45B, 35 minutes) from beside **Central Pinklao** (Map p94; Th Somdet Phra Pin Klao; ⏲10am-10pm; Ⓢ Talat Phlu exit 3 & taxi or Victory Monument exit 3 & taxi) in Thonburi.

From these points, you can continue by public transport or taxi to your hotel.

Taxi Metered taxis are available kerbside at Floor 1 – ignore the 'official airport taxi' touts who approach you inside the terminal. Typical metered fares from Suvarnabhumi include 200B to 250B to Th Sukhumvit; 250B to 300B to Th Khao San; and 400B to Mo Chit. Toll charges (paid by passengers) vary between 25B and 70B. Note that there's a 50B surcharge added to all fares departing from the airport, payable directly to the driver.

Don Mueang International Airport

Bus & Minivan From outside the arrivals hall, there are four bus lines: bus A1 stops at BTS Mo Chit (50B, frequent from 7.30am to 11.30pm); A2 stops at BTS Mo Chit and BTS Victory Monument (50B, every 30 minutes from 7.30am to 11.30pm); A3 stops at Pratunam and Lumphini Park (50B, every 30 minutes from 7.30am to 11.30pm); and A4 stops at Th Khao San and Sanam Luang (50B, every 30 minutes from 7.30am to 11.30pm). Public buses stop on the highway in front of the airport. Useful lines include 29, with a stop at Victory Monument BTS station, before terminating at Hualamphong Train Station (24 hours); line 59, with a stop near Th Khao San (24 hours); and line 538, stopping at Victory Monument BTS station (4am to 10pm); fares are approximately 20B.

Train The walkway that crosses from the airport to the Amari Airport Hotel also provides access to Don Muang Train Station, which has trains to Hualamphong Train Station every one to 1½ hours from 4am to 11.30am and then roughly hourly from 2pm to 9.30pm (from 5B to 10B).

Taxi As at Suvarnabhumi, public taxis leave from outside both arrival halls and there is a 50B airport charge added to the meter fare.

BICYCLE

Over the past few years, cycling has exploded in popularity in Bangkok. Bike sales are booming, the 23km bicycle track that circles Suvarnabhumi International Airport was being upgraded at the time of writing and a Bangkok cycling event in mid-2015 drew nearly 40,000 participants. There's even a bike-share initiative, although it appeared to be on its last legs at the time of writing. Yet despite all this, dangerous roads, traffic, heat, pollution and lack of bike lanes mean that Bangkok is still far from a safe or convenient place to use a bicycle as a means of transportation.

BOAT

A fleet of boats, both those that run along Mae Nam Chao Phraya and along the city's canals, serve Bangkok's commuters.

Canal Routes

Canal taxi boats run along Khlong Saen Saep (Banglamphu to Ramkhamhaeng) and are an easy way to get between Banglamphu and Jim Thompson House, the Siam Sq shopping centres (get off at Sapan Hua Chang Pier for both) and other points further east along Th Sukhumvit – after a mandatory change of boat at Pratunam Pier.

➡ These boats are mostly used by daily commuters and pull into the piers for just a few seconds – jump straight on or you'll be left behind.

➡ Fares range from 9B to 19B and boats run from 5.30am to 7.15pm from Monday to Friday, from 6am to 6.30pm on Saturday and from 6am to 6pm on Sunday.

River Routes

The Chao Phraya Express Boat (p88) operates the main ferry service along Mae Nam Chao Phraya. The central pier is known as Tha Sathon, Saphan Taksin or sometimes Sathon/Central Pier, and connects to the BTS at Saphan Taksin station.

➡ Boats run from 6am to 8pm. You can buy tickets (10B to 40B) at the pier or on board; hold on to your ticket as proof of purchase (an occasional formality).

➡ The most common boats are the orange-flagged express boats. These run between Wat

ONE NIGHT IN BANGKOK...ISN'T ENOUGH TO TAILOR A SUIT

Many tourists arrive in Bangkok with the notion of getting clothes custom-tailored at a bargain price. The golden rule is that you get what you pay for. Although an offer may seem great on the surface, the price may fluctuate significantly depending on the fabric you choose. Have a good idea of what you want before walking into a shop.

Set aside a week to get clothes tailored. Shirts and trousers can often be turned around in 48 hours or less with only one fitting, but no matter what a tailor may tell you, it takes more than one and often more than two fittings to create a good suit.

July (Map p88; ☎02 233 0171; www.julytailor.com; 30/6 Th Sala Daeng; ⏰9am-6pm Mon-Sat; M Si Lom exit 2, S Sala Daeng exit 4) Suits at this tailor to Thailand's royalty and elite don't come cheap and the cuts can be somewhat conservative, but the quality is unsurpassed.

Rajawongse (Map p84; ☎02 255 3714; www.dress-for-success.com; 130 Th Sukhumvit; ⏰10.30am-8pm Mon-Sat; S Nana exit 2) A legendary and long-standing Bangkok tailor; Jesse and Victor's creations are particularly renowned among American visitors and residents.

Duly (Map p84; ☎02 662 6647; www.laladuly.co.th; Soi 49, Th Sukhumvit; ⏰10am-7pm; S Phrom Phong exit 1) High-quality Italian fabrics and experienced tailors make Duly one of the best places in Bangkok to commission a sharp shirt.

Rajsingkorn, south of Bangkok, to Nonthaburi, north, stopping at most major piers (15B, frequent from 6am to 7pm).

➡ A blue-flagged tourist boat (40B, every 30 minutes from 9.30am to 5pm) runs from Sathon/Central Pier to Phra Athit/Banglamphu Pier, with stops at eight major sightseeing piers and a barely comprehensible English-language commentary. Vendors at Sathon/Central Pier tout a 150B all-day pass, but unless you plan on doing a lot of boat travel, it's not great value.

➡ There are also dozens of cross-river ferries, which charge 3B and run every few minutes until late at night.

➡ Private long-tail boats can be hired for sightseeing trips at Phra Athit/Banglamphu Pier, Chang Pier, Tien Pier and Oriental Pier.

BTS & MRT

The elevated **BTS** (Skytrain; ☎ 02 617 6000, tourist information 02 617 7341; www.bts.co.th), also known as the Skytrain *(rót fai fáa)*, whisks you through 'new' Bangkok (Silom, Sukhumvit and Siam Sq). The interchange between the two lines is at Siam station and trains run frequently from 6am to midnight. Fares range from 16B to 44B or 140B for a one-day pass. Most ticket machines only accept coins, but change is available at the information booths.

Bangkok's Metro, the **MRT** (☎ 02 354 2000; www.bangkokmetro.co.th) is most helpful for people staying in the Sukhumvit or Silom area to reach the train station at Hualamphong. Fares cost from 16B to 42B or 120B for a one-day pass. The trains run frequently from 6am to midnight.

BUS

Bangkok's public buses are run by the **Bangkok Mass Transit Authority** (☎ 02 246 0973, call centre 1348; www.bmta.co.th).

➡ As the routes are not always clear, and with Bangkok taxis being such a good deal, you'd really have to be pinching pennies to rely on buses as a way to get around Bangkok.

➡ Air-con bus fares range from 10B to 23B and fares for fan-cooled buses start at 6.50B.

➡ Most of the bus lines run between 5am and 10pm or 11pm, except for the 'all-night' buses, which run from 3am or 4am to mid-morning.

➡ You'll most likely require the help of thinknet's *Bangkok Bus Guide*.

CAR

For short-term visitors, you will find parking and driving a car in Bangkok more trouble than it is worth. If you need private transport, consider hiring a car and driver through your hotel or hire a taxi driver that you find trustworthy. One reputable operator is **Julie Taxi** (☎ 082 664 4789, 081 846 2014; www.facebook.com/tourwithjulietaxi), which offers a variety of vehicles and excellent service.

But if you still want to give it a go, all the big car-hire companies have offices in Bangkok, as well as counters at Suvarnabhumi and Don Mueang International airports. Rates start at around 1000B per day for a small car. A passport plus a valid licence from your home country (with English translation if necessary) or an International Driving Permit are required for all rentals.

MOTORCYCLE TAXI

Motorcycle taxis (known as *motorsai*) serve two purposes in Bangkok.

Most commonly and popularly they form an integral part of the public transport network, running from the corner of a main thoroughfare, such as Th Sukhumvit, to the far ends of sois that run off that thoroughfare. Riders wear coloured, numbered vests and gather at either

COMMON BANGKOK SCAMS

Commit these classic rip-offs to memory and join us in our ongoing crusade to outsmart Bangkok's crafty scam artists.

Gem scam We're begging you – if you aren't a gem trader, then don't buy unset stones in Thailand. Period.

Closed today Ignore any 'friendly' local who tells you that an attraction is closed for a Buddhist holiday or for cleaning.

Túk-túk rides for 20B These alleged 'tours' bypass the sights and instead cruise to all the fly-by-night gem and tailor shops that pay commissions.

Flat-fare taxi ride Flatly refuse any driver who quotes a flat fare, which will usually be three times more expensive than the reasonable meter rate.

Friendly strangers Be wary of smartly dressed men who approach you asking where you're from and where you're going.

BANGKOK TAXI TIPS

- Never agree to take a taxi that won't use the meter; usually these drivers park outside hotels and in tourist areas. Simply get one that's passing by instead.
- Bangkok taxi drivers will generally not try to 'take you for a ride' as happens in some other countries; they make more money from passenger turnover.
- It's worth keeping in mind that many Bangkok taxi drivers are in fact seasonal labourers fresh from the countryside and may not know their way around.
- If a driver refuses to take you somewhere, it's probably because they need to return the hired cab before a certain time, not because they don't like how you look.
- Very few Bangkok taxi drivers speak much English, so an address written in Thai can help immensely.
- Older cabs may be less comfortable but typically have more experienced drivers because they are driver-owned, as opposed to the new cabs, which are usually hired.

end of their soi, usually charging 10B to 20B for the trip (without a helmet unless you ask).

Their other purpose is as a means of beating the traffic. You tell your rider where you want to go, negotiate a price (from 20B for a short trip up to about 150B going across town), strap on the helmet (they will insist for longer trips) and say a prayer to any god you're into.

RIDE-SHARE APPS

App-based alternatives to the traditional taxis that operate in Bangkok:

All Thai Taxi (www.allthaitaxi.com)
GrabTaxi (www.grab.com/th)
Uber (www.uber.com/cities/bangkok)

TAXI

- Although many first-time visitors are hesitant to use them, in general Bangkok's taxis are new and comfortable and the drivers are courteous and helpful, making them an excellent way to get around.
- All taxis are required to use their meters, which start at 35B, and fares to most places within central Bangkok cost 60B to 90B. Freeway tolls – 25B to 70B depending on where you start – must be paid by the passenger.
- **Taxi Radio** (☎1681; www.taxiradio.co.th) and other 24-hour 'phone-a-cab' services are available for 20B above the metered fare.
- If you leave something in a taxi your best chance of getting it back (still pretty slim) is to call ☎1644.

TÚK-TÚK

- Bangkok's iconic túk-túk (pronounced *đúk đúk;* a type of motorised rickshaw) are used by Thais for short hops not worth paying the taxi flagfall for. For foreigners, however, these emphysema-inducing machines are part of the Bangkok experience, so despite the fact that they overcharge outrageously and you can't see anything due to the low roof, pretty much everyone takes a túk-túk at least once.
- Túk-túk are notorious for taking little 'detours' to commission-paying gem and silk shops and massage parlours. En route to 'special' temples, you'll meet 'helpful' locals who will steer you to even more rip-off opportunities. Ignore anyone offering too-good-to-be-true 20B trips.
- The vast majority of túk-túk drivers ask too much from tourists (expat *fa·ràng* never use them). Expect to be quoted a 100B fare, if not more, for even the shortest trip. Try bargaining them down to about 60B for a short trip, preferably at night when the pollution (hopefully) won't be quite so bad. Once you've done it, you'll find taxis are cheaper, cleaner, cooler and quieter.

WALKING

You'll notice very few Thais walking around in Bangkok, and it doesn't take long to see why: hot weather, pollution, uneven or nonexistent footpaths, footpaths clogged with vendors and motorcycles and the sheer expanse of the city make walking one of the least convenient ways to get around.

Ko Chang & the Eastern Seaboard

Includes ➡

Best Places to Eat

➡ Mantra (p129)

➡ Chanthorn (p140)

➡ Blues Blues Restaurant (p153)

➡ Namchok (p143)

➡ Pan & David Restaurant (p124)

Best Places to Stay

➡ Baan Luang Rajamaitri (p139)

➡ Baan Rim Nam (p150)

➡ Bann Makok (p156)

➡ Mangrove Hideaway (p152)

➡ Rabbit Resort (p128)

Why Go?

Two islands – Ko Samet and Ko Chang – are the magnets that draw travellers to the eastern seaboard. The mainland has plenty of its own attractions, particularly the charismatic, old-world charm of Trat and Chanthaburi.

Ko Samet, the nearest major island to Bangkok, is a flashpacker fave where visitors sip from vodka buckets and admire the fire jugglers or head for the quieter southern coves. Further down the coast is Ko Chang, Thailand's second-largest island. Spend your days diving, chilling on the west-coast beaches or hiking through dense jungle – then recover in time to experience the island's vibrant party scene.

Fewer travellers make it to Si Racha or Bang Saen, though their seafood restaurants and the latter's long beach make them worth a stopover. Less serene is the raucous resort of Pattaya, with its hedonistic nightlife and family-friendly attractions.

When to Go

➡ The best time to visit is the end of the rainy season (usually around November) but before the start of high season (December to March), when the weather is cool, the landscape green and rates reasonable. Peak season on Ko Chang is the Christmas and New Year holiday period. Crowds thin in March, the start of the hot season.

➡ The rainy season runs from May to October, though there are often days or weeks with no rain at all. A few businesses on Ko Chang and Ko Kut close, and Ko Mak and Ko Wai go into hibernation with many places shut. Your best bet during monsoon is Ko Samet, which enjoys its own microclimate and stays relatively dry.

Si Racha ศรีราชา

☎038 / POP 80,000

Si Racha (pronounced 'see-ra-cha') is the gateway to the worthwhile little island of Ko Si Chang. Colourful, creaking fishing boats and squid rigs are still moored in Si Racha, but these days they share the water with giant container ships. Similarly, a building boom is overshadowing the traditional low-rise centre.

Sushi restaurants and karaoke bars cater for the hundreds of Japanese employees who work at nearby industrial estates, giving the town centre a Little Tokyo vibe. The real heart of Si Racha, though, is the waterfront, with rickety stilt guesthouses, a peaceful health park and a busy pier.

Sights

Ko Loi ISLAND

(เกาะลอย) Attached to the mainland via a road, this rocky island hosts a **Thai-Chinese temple** (วัดเกาะลอย; daylight hours) FREE and a viewing area for the impressive sunsets. Below the temple is a giant pond, where behemoth turtles can be fed squid. At time of last research, the bridge to the island was under major renovation and everything was closed down until completion.

Sleeping

The most authentic places to stay are the wooden hotels on the piers, which offer plenty of character, though the cheaper ones are very basic.

Samchai Resort GUESTHOUSE, HOSTEL $

(☎081-963 1855; Soi 10, Th Jermjompol; dm 275B, r 350-900B;) There's plenty of character at this sprawling pier guesthouse that has a helpful English-speaking owner and a wide range of rooms, from functional windowless boxes to air-con sea-view suites. There's a great spot to sit at the end of the pier and gaze out across the water. Cheaper rooms are fan-only.

Triple B HOTEL $$

(☎092 897 7881; www.triplebhotel.com; 119/1 Mu 2, Surasak Subdistrict; d incl breakfast 700-1000B;) Handy if you're arriving by minibus, this hotel offers comfortable, spacious rooms with some attractive design features. A few things don't quite work as they should, but it's a good deal at this price. The breakfast room overlooks the small plunge pool; the best rooms are on the top floor, with more of an outlook.

Eating & Drinking

There's a lively knot of Thai bars along Th Thetsaban. Northwest of here is a solid grid of karaoke bars.

My One VIETNAMESE $

(☎089 693 3270; 14/10 Th Surasak 1; mains 50-160B; 9am-9pm) This simple Thai-Vietnamese restaurant has a variety of fresh, healthy dishes, including rice paper rolls and salads. Look for the coffee cart out front.

Labubon Sriracha THAI $

(☎087 748 1696; Th Si Racha Nakorn; mains 60-160B; 8.30am-10pm) This open-plan barn of a spot offers reliably good eating; it's an Isan place with yummy *nám đòk mŏo* (spicy pork salad) and some great fish dishes that would serve two.

Mum Aroi SEAFOOD $$

(☎038 771555; Soi 8, Th Jermjompol; mains 160-450B; 11am-10pm;) Mum Aroi delivers on its name, 'delicious corner'. This is *the* place to enjoy a seafood meal with views of the squid rigs, with its tiers of terraces giving most diners a shot at a water vista. It is north of the town: head for Samitivej Sriracha Hospital; look opposite it for the tank with the 2m fish out front.

Teab Ta CRAFT BEER

(www.facebook.com/teabtasriracha; Soi 16, Th Jermjompol; 5pm-midnight Mon-Fri, 4pm-midnight Sat & Sun;) On the long pier, Teab Ta has a

LOCAL KNOWLEDGE

HOT STUFF

Given that 'Sriracha' chilli sauce is hot stuff in the USA and elsewhere, you may expect it to be celebrated in its eponymous home town. But no. The sauce is thought to have been created in Si Racha decades ago, but it was a Vietnamese immigrant living in Los Angeles who launched the company with the rooster logo and made his sauce famous.

Thailand does have its own version *(nám prík sĕe rah·chah)*. It is usually eaten as a dip with *kài jee·o* (omelette) and *hŏy tôrt* (fried mussel omelette), and is sweeter than the more famous rooster brand.

Ko Chang & the Eastern Seaboard Highlights

1. **Ko Chang** (p144) Snorkelling and jungle trekking on this sizeable island that offers something for everyone.
2. **Ko Kut** (p155) Floating the day away at the marvellous beaches of this southeastern island.
3. **Ko Wai** (p158) Swimming with the fishes in gin-clear waters at this diminutive favourite near Ko Chang.
4. **Ko Samet** (p131) Walking between pretty coves on lovely Ko Samet.
5. **Chanthaburi** (p137) Strolling through the old waterfront community of this historic riverside town.
6. **Trat** (p141) Kicking back in the old-time atmosphere of this pleasing town's wooden shophouse quarter.
7. **Ko Si Chang** (p123) Taking a day trip on the ferry from pleasant Si Racha to peaceful Ko Si Chang.

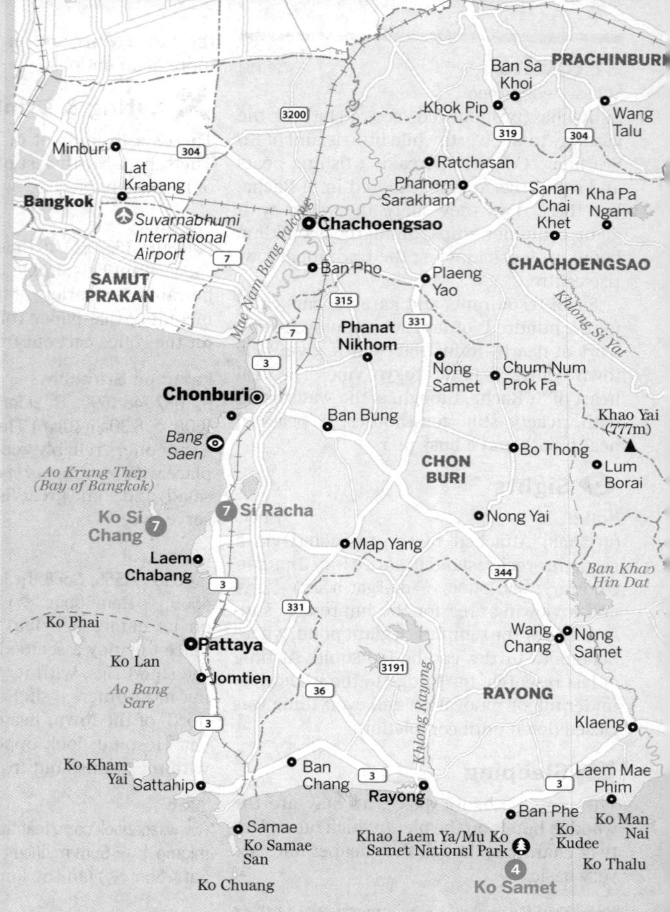

Kabin Buri
SA KAEO
Ta Phraya
33
Non Mak Mun
348
Sa Kaew
Lam Prachinburi
Ang Sila
Huay Jot
33
Aranya Prathet
Watthana Nakhon
Khao Chakan
Poipet
Sai Diaw
Sisophon
3395
Non Non Sao-Eh
317
Khao Takrup (660m)
Khlong Hat
Wang Mai
CAMBODIA
Khao Daeng
Thun Khanan
Khao Soi Dao Nua (1566m)
Tamun
Battambang
CHANTHABURI
Pung Ngon
Ban Pakard
Nong Chek Soi
Pong Nam Ron
Takra
Psar Pruhm
Nong Khla
Pailin
Khao Khitchakut National Park
317
Si Yaek Kong Din
3
Makham
Tha Mai
5 Chanthaburi
Chang Thun
Ban Pa-Ah
Laem Sadet
Nam Tok Phlio National Park
Chao Lao
Ta Chalap
Nong Sii
Chak Yai
Laem Sing
Khlung
3157
Pong
Dan Chumpon
Laem Ko Proet
Tha Chot
3271
3394
TRAT
Ban Noen Sung
Bang Kradan
6 Trat
3156
Laem Muang
Laem Ngop
318
Ao Trat
CAMBODIA
Tha Sen
1 Ko Chang
Laem Sok
Hat Mai Rut
Mu Ko Chang National Marine Park
Mai Rut
Ko Khlum
3 Ko Wai
Hat Ban Chun
Ko Kradat
Ko Ran
Ko Mak
Khlong Yai
Ko Mai Si
Ko Kut 2
Hat Lek
Koh Kong City

Si Racha

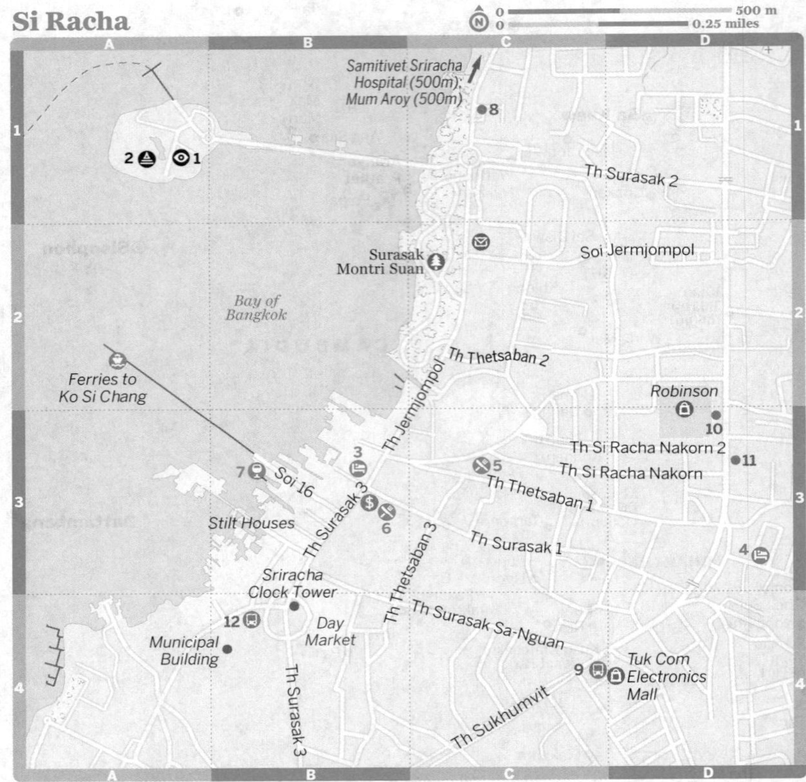

Si Racha

Sights
1 Ko Loi....A1
2 Wat Ko Loi....A1

Sleeping
3 Samchai Resort....B3
4 Triple B....D3

Eating
5 Labubon Sriracha....C3
6 My One....B3

Drinking & Nightlife
7 Teab Ta....B3

Information
8 Immigration Office....C1

Transport
9 Buses to Bangkok....C4
10 Minivans to Bangkok....D3
11 Minivans to Pattaya and Rayong....D3
12 Sŏrng·tăa·ou to Pattaya & Bang Saen....B4

fabulous selection of craft beer from around the world and various northern European brewing masterpieces, all at northern European prices. It's a great spot for a sundowner on the deck over the water: a lovely outlook. There's a reasonably priced menu of bar snacks and simple dishes plus a carefully curated modern indie soundtrack.

Information

Immigration Office (☎038 312571; www.immchonburi.go.th; 3/1 Th Jermjompol; ⊙8.30am-4.30pm Mon-Fri)

Krung Thai Bank (www.ktb.co.th; cnr Th Surasak 1 & Th Jermjompol; ⊙8.30am-4.30pm Mon-Fri) Has an ATM and exchange facilities.

Post Office (Th Jermjompol; ⌚8.30am-4.30pm Mon-Fri, to 12.30pm Sat) Opposite the municipal park.

Samitivej Sriracha Hospital (☎038 320300; www.samitivejhospitals.com; Soi 8, Th Jermjompol)

Getting There & Around

Minivans, including services to **Bangkok**, **Pattaya and Rayong**, leave from Th Sukhumvit (Hwy 3) near **Robinson department store** (☎037 771001; www.robinson.co.th; 90/1 Th Sukhumvit; ⌚10.30am-9pm Mon-Fri, 10am-9pm Sat & Sun), and both **buses** and minivans leave from the nearby IT mall, **Tuk Com** (☎038 773619; www.tukcom.com; Th Sukhumvit; ⌚10.30am-9pm Mon-Fri, 10am-9pm Sat & Sun).

White *sŏrng·tăa·ou* (passenger pick-up trucks) leave from near Si Racha's **clock tower** for Pattaya's Naklua market (40B, 45 minutes, 6am to 6pm); red *sŏrng·tăa·ou* go to Bang Saen (15B, 20 minutes, 6am to 6pm).

Motorbike taxis zip around town for 30B to 40B.

Ko Si Chang

เกาะสีชัง

☎038 / POP 5000

Once a royal beach retreat, Ko Si Chang has a fishing-village atmosphere and enough attractions to make it a decent day's excursion from Si Racha, or a fine overnight stop for those who want to chill out. It gets busier at weekends, when Thais come to eat seafood, snap selfies by the sea and make merit at the local temples.

The island's one small settlement faces the mainland and is the terminus for the ferry. A bumpy road network links the village with the other sights.

Sights & Activities

Several locals run **snorkelling** trips to nearby Ko Khang Khao (Bat Island), which has a good beach, or you can take a speedboat (400B) there from the main pier. **Kayaks** are available (200B per hour) on **Hat Tham Phang** (หาดถ้ำพัง, Fallen Cave Beach), the only sandy beach on the island. You can paddle to Ko Khang Khao in 45 minutes.

Phra Chudadhut Palace HISTORIC SITE

(พระจุฑาธุชราชฐาน; ⌚9am-5pm) FREE This former royal palace was used by Rama V (King Chulalongkorn) over the summer months, but was abandoned when the French briefly occupied the island in 1893. The main throne hall – a magnificent golden teak structure known as Vimanmek Teak Mansion – was moved to Bangkok in 1910. What's left are subdued Victorian-style buildings set in gardenlike grounds. It's a 15-minute stroll from the ferry. The museum buildings are closed Monday.

San Chao Pho Khao Yai BUDDHIST TEMPLE

(ศาลเจ้าพ่อเขาใหญ่) FREE The most imposing sight on the island, this ornate dragon-infested temple dates back to the days when Chinese traders anchored in the sheltered waters. During New Year in February, the island is overrun with Chinese tourists. There are shrine caves, multiple platforms and a good view of the island and sea. It's just north of the main town.

TRANSPORT TO/FROM SI RACHA

DESTINATION	BUS	MINIVAN	TRAIN
Bangkok's Eastern Bus Terminal (Ekamai)	103B, 1½hr, hourly 5am-8pm	N/A	N/A
Bangkok Hualamphong	N/A	N/A	from 28B, 3¼ hr, 1 daily Mon-Fri
Bangkok's Northern Bus Terminal (Mo Chit)	113B, 2hr, hourly 5am-7.30pm	N/A	N/A
Bangkok Suvarnabhumi International Airport	110B, 1hr, hourly 5.10am-8pm	N/A	N/A
Bangkok's Victory Monument	N/A	110B, 1½hr, every 30min 5am-8pm	N/A
Pattaya	N/A	40B, 30min, frequent	from 5B, 30 minutes, 1 daily Mon-Fri

Sichang Healing House MASSAGE
(081 572 7840; off Th Makham Thaew; 9am-4pm Thu-Tue) The charming, English-speaking owner of this leafy haven offers a range of excellent massages (300B to 600B). She also sells homemade health products and has modest bamboo rooms for rent (300B).

Sleeping & Eating

Charlie's Bungalows GUESTHOUSE $$
(061 749 4242; www.kosichang.net; Th Makham Thaew; r 1000-1100B; P ❄ 📶) Bright, fresh, all-white bungalows set around a garden. All come with TVs and DVD players. Friendly and helpful staff. Book ahead at weekends and public holidays.

Somewhere Ko Sichang BOUTIQUE HOTEL $$$
(038 109400; www.somewherehotel.com; 194/1 Mu 3, Th Thewawong; r incl breakfast 2600-3600B; P ❄ ≋) White, modern and charming, this place occupies a very central but secluded location. Rooms have loads of space and a breezy maritime feel to the decor; most have balconies and sea views. The restaurant area is handsome and staff are eager to please. A relaxing and stylish retreat.

FlowerBlue CAFE $
(081 305 5544; www.facebook.com/flowerblue.coffee; mains 70-190B; 7am-10pm; ❄ 📶) Popular with the Bangkok set, who appreciate the air-con and fair prices, this trendy cafe is always busy. It does breakfasts, burgers, speciality coffees and more in the attractive space, festooned with real plants and other botanical iconography.

★ **Pan & David Restaurant** INTERNATIONAL, THAI $$
(038 216629; www.ko-sichang.com; 167 Mu 3, Th Makham Thaew; mains 170-300B; 10am-10.30pm Mon-Fri, 8.30am-10pm Sat & Sun; 📶) With free-range chicken, homemade ice cream, a reasonable wine list, excellent Thai dishes and an Italian touch, you can't go wrong here. It also has a series of rooms and bungalows available in spacious grounds (750B to 1800B), which include characterful converted fishing boats in dry dock.

Pee Noi SEAFOOD $$
(Th Makham Thaew; mains 100-350B; 11am-9pm) This eat-on-the-street and takeaway restaurant is a favourite with locals thanks to its great seafood options. Look for the blue tables and umbrellas.

Information

Pan & David's website (www.ko-sichang.com) is an excellent source of local information.

Kasikornbank (99/12 Th Atsadang; 8.30am-3.30pm) Has an ATM and exchange facilities.

Post Office (Th Atsadang; 8.30am-4.30pm Mon-Fri, to 12.30pm Sat)

Getting There & Around

Boats to Ko Si Chang leave hourly from 7am to 8pm from the end of the main jetty in Si Racha (one way 50B, 45 minutes), dodging around the plethora of cargo ships unloading in the bay. From Ko Si Chang boats shuttle back hourly from 6am to 7pm. Outward ferries stop at little Ko Karm en route.

Motorbike taxis wait at the pier and will take you anywhere for 30B to 50B, and souped-up săhm·lór (three-wheel pedicabs; also spelt săamláw) do tours of the main spots for 250B.

Motorbikes are available to rent on the pier (80B hourly, 250B per day, 300B for 24 hours). **Bikes** (089 747 9097; per day/24hr 120/160B) are also available.

Bang Saen บางแสน

038 / POP 45,000

As the closest beach to Bangkok, Bang Saen is a weekend favourite for those wanting to escape city life. A handsome palm-lined beachfront and a huge quantity of accommodation have boosted its popularity. During the day, the 4km-long promenade is packed with tandem bicycles and seafood stalls. By night, the string of hip restaurants and bars facing the sea draws a studenty crowd. While there are cleaner strips of sand in Thailand,

OFF THE BEATEN TRACK

SECRET MANGROVE FOREST

The **Mangrove Forest Conservation Centre** (ศูนย์ศึกษาธรรมชาติและอนุรักษ์ป่าชายเลนเพื่อการท่องเที่ยว; 038 398268; Ang Sila; 8.30am-6.30pm) is such a well-kept secret, many locals don't even know it's here. A 2km-long wooden walkway runs a circuit around the mangrove forest. Look out for crabs, cockles and mudfish and enjoy the sounds and smells.

It's in Ang Sila, 6km north of Bang Saen.

if swimming isn't a priority, then this is a great spot to get a feel for a beach break, Thai style.

Sights

Nezha Sathaizhu Temple BUDDHIST TEMPLE
(ศาลเจ้าหน่าจาซาไท้จื้อ, Wihahn Tepsatit Pra Giti-chairloem; Ang Sila; 8am-5pm) FREE This opulent four-storey Chinese temple is fronted by an enormous heaven-earth pole and filled with intricate paintings and magnificent sculptures. Dragons and bats (which signify fortune) feature heavily in the decor. Locals regularly come to make merit, and temple volunteers are happy to explain the rituals if you want to make your own offerings. The temple is on the main road in Ang Sila, about 5km north of Bang Saen beach.

Khao Sam Muk HILL
(เขาสามมุข, Monkey Mountain; road open 5am-11pm) Hundreds of rhesus monkeys with greedy eyes and quick hands live on this small hill (avoid feeding them, as this just makes them more aggressive).

Sleeping & Eating

Running back from the beach, Soi 1 is wall-to-wall budget guesthouses, with rooms available from 200B upward. Some more upmarket choices are dotted northward along the coast. **KT Guesthouse** (096 747 6711; 197/10 Th Long Had Bang Saen; r without breakfast 500-600B;) is handy for the bar strip and close to the beach – all rooms have modern furnishings and some have balconies. **Song Row Guesthouse** (038 193545; Soi 1, Bang Saen Sai 1; r without/with bathroom 300/400B) offers spotless family-run rooms both with and without bathroom. Using hot water and air-con costs an extra 50B. There's no English sign, look for the red and white lozenge tiles.

Nibble lemon tart or waffles at **Summer's Corner** (090 970 6403; www.facebook.com/summerscorner193; 193/25 Th Long Had Bang Saen; mains 100-170B; 11am-10pm Thu-Tue;), or head to **Andy's Seafood** (Bang Saen Sai 1 near Soi 1; mains 120-350B; 5pm-midnight) to feast on steamed sea bass as you watch palms wave in the evening breeze. Th Long Had Bang Saen has a string of popular bars/nightclubs with boisterous student crowds, live music at deafening volumes and outdoor seating.

Getting There & Away

Minivans and buses leave from either side of Th Sukhumvit, close to the main turn-off into Bang Saen. Red *sŏrng·tăa·ou* go to Si Racha (15B, 20 minutes, 5.30am to 9pm), while blue ones on Line 1 connect Bang Saen with Ang Sila.

DESTINATION	BUS	MINIVAN
Bangkok's Eastern Bus Terminal (Ekamai)	86B; 1hr; hourly	N/A
Bangkok's Northern Bus Terminal (Mo Chit)	99B; 1½hr; hourly	120B; 1½hr; hourly; 5am-8.30pm
Bangkok Suvarnabhumi International Airport	110B; 1hr; hourly	N/A
Bangkok Victory Monument	110B; 1½ hr; hourly	N/A
Ban Phe (for Ko Samet)	N/A	190B; 2hr; 8am-5pm

Pattaya

เมืองพัทยา

038 / POP 300,000

Multicultural Pattaya boasts some excellent places to stay and eat, and the area is also a family-friendly resort coast. Nevertheless, the city itself is no tropical paradise; its reputation as a sex capital is totally deserved, with hundreds of beer bars, go-go clubs and massage parlours. Much of the rest is dedicated to mass-market sun-seeking tourism, with a huge retired expat population, and enormous tour groups hurried through town in an almost constant stream. For a relaxing stay in Pattaya, base yourself outside the central area.

The city is built around **Ao Pattaya**, a wide, crescent-shaped bay that was one of Thailand's first beach resorts in the 1960s when American GIs came for some R & R. North Pattaya (Pattaya Neua) is more upmarket while Pattaya South (Pattaya Tai) remains the nightlife hub. Further south **Jomtien** is a laid-back resort, while to the north **Naklua** is also quieter, with some top-end resorts at Wong Amat.

Sights & Activities

Rats on the beach and fuel from the numerous parked boats makes swimming in the centre of town a distinctly unappetising

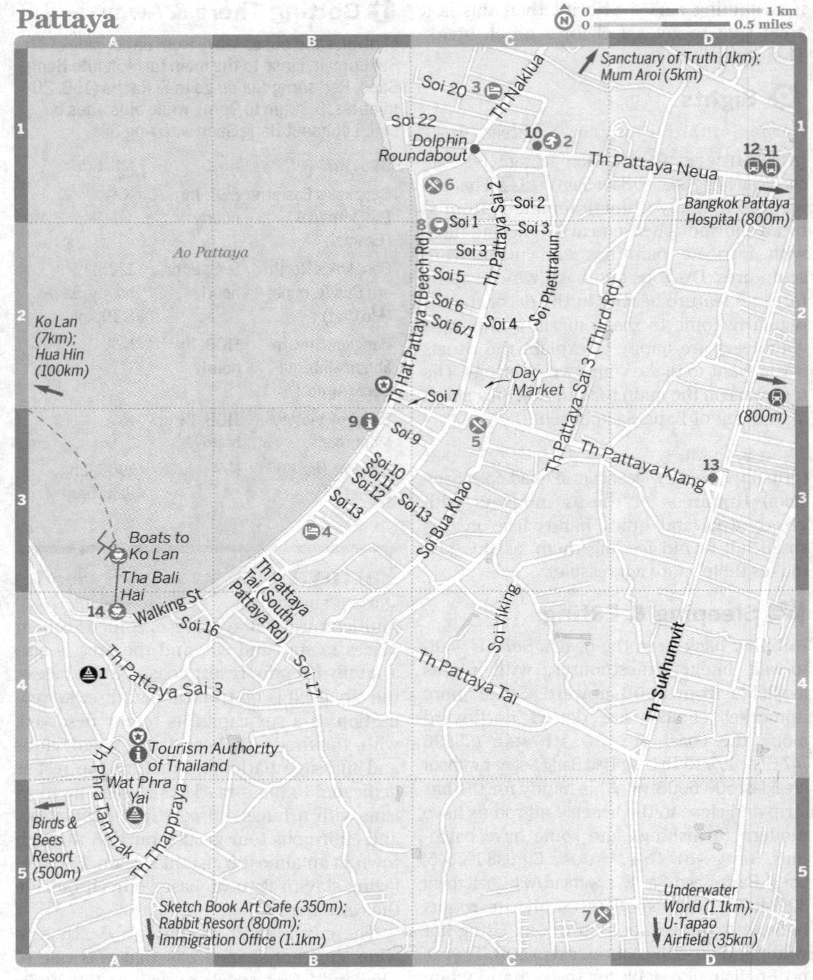

Pattaya

Sights
1 Khao Phra Tamnak A4

Activities, Courses & Tours
2 Fairtex Sports Club C1

Sleeping
3 Garden Lodge Hotel C1
4 Nonze Hostel B3

Eating
5 Leng Kee C3
6 Mantra C1
7 Thepprasit Market C5

Drinking & Nightlife
8 Gulliver's C2

Information
9 Tourist Information Kiosk B3

Transport
10 Bangkok Airways C1
11 Bell Travel Service D1
12 Bus Station D1
13 Minivans to Bangkok D3
14 Royal Ferry Group A4

prospect. Better is Jomtien, which has a gay-friendly beach at Hat Dongtan, while to the north Naklua is appealing.

Around 20km south of Pattaya, there's a good scene at Bang Sare, a resort area with a long, narrow beach.

The best beaches in the area are on Ko Samae San, a tiny island with good snorkelling, and the navy-run Hat Nahng Ram, both 35km south of Pattaya.

Sanctuary of Truth BUDDHIST MONUMENT

(ปราสาทสัจธรรม; ☎038 367229; www.sanctuaryoftruth.com; Soi Naklua 12; adult/child 500/250B; ⏲8am-6pm) Made entirely of wood (without any metal nails) and commanding a celestial view of the ocean, the Sanctuary of Truth is best described as a visionary environment: part art installation, religious shrine and cultural monument. Constructed in four wings dedicated to Thai, Khmer, Chinese and Indian religious iconography, its architecture and setting is impressive.

The ornate temple-like complex was conceived by Lek Viriyaphant, a Thai millionaire who spent his fortune on this and other heritage projects (such as Ancient City near Bangkok) that revived and preserved ancient building techniques and architecture in danger of extinction. In this case, the building continues to support hand-hewn woodworking skills as it's been under construction since 1981 and still isn't finished.

Every part of the 105m-tall building is covered with wood carvings of Hindu and Buddhist gods and goddesses – an artistic consolidation of centuries of religious myths under one unifying roof.

Compulsory tours are led through the building every 30 minutes. Thai dancing is at 11.30am and 3.30pm. The sanctuary is 1km down Soi 12 off Th Naklua, about 3km from the centre of town.

Anek Kusala Sala MUSEUM

(Viharn Sien; อเนกกุศลศาลา/วิหารเซียน; ☎038 235250; off Th Sukhumvit; 50B; ⏲8am-5.30pm) A popular stop for tour groups, this museum contains more than 300 impressive pieces of Chinese artwork, mainly bronze and brass statues depicting historical figures as well as Buddhist, Confucian and Taoist deities. Founded by Sa-nga Kulkobkiat, a Thai national who grew up in China, the museum was intended as a friendship-building project between the two countries.

The 1st floor is a crowded pavilion of Chinese immortals, from Pangu, the cosmic giant, to Guan Yin, the goddess of mercy. The 2nd-floor terrace is the museum's most dramatic, with larger-than-life-sized statues of Shaolin monks depicting different martial-arts poses. Nearby is a touching collection of daily life statues (a fortune teller, dress maker, liquor seller) that visitors place 1B coins on.

The museum is 16km south of central Pattaya; take a Pattaya–Sattahip *sŏrng·tăa·ou* (25B) to the Wat Yangsangwaram turn-off. Hire a passing motorbike to go the final 5km to the museum. Ask the driver to stick around, as a lift back is hard to find. Private transport is 1500B.

ISLAND DAY TRIP

The small island of **Ko Lan** (เกาะล้าน), 7km offshore from central Pattaya, is an easy day trip. On weekends, its five beaches entertain thousands of visitors and the aquamarine sea is busy with banana boats and other marine merriment. Ferries leave Pattaya's Bali Hai pier (30B, 45 minutes, 11 daily) at the southern end of Walking St. Some go to the main village, while others go to Tawaen beach. You can also charter speedboats from along Beach Rd (think 2500B). The last boat back is at 6pm.

Khao Phra Tamnak BUDDHIST TEMPLE

(เขาพระตำหนัก; ⏲4am-10pm) FREE This hill has a modest Buddhist temple as well as a much-revered memorial to the admiral who founded the modern Thai navy. There are marvellous views over the Pattaya bay and a little cafe terrace from which to enjoy them. Sunset is a particularly spectacular time to be here, but you won't be alone. You can walk here from the southern end of Walking St.

Underwater World Pattaya AQUARIUM

(อันเดอร์วอเตอร์เวิลด์ พัทยา; ☎038 756879; www.underwaterworldpattaya.com; 22/22 Mu 11, Th Sukhumvit; adult/child 500/300B; ⏲9am-6pm; 👪) The area's largest aquarium is particularly child-friendly, with touch pools and koi feeding sessions. The long viewing tunnel is the highlight. It's on the main road about 4km south of Pattaya.

Ramayana Water Park WATER PARK

(☎033 005929; www.ramayanawaterpark.com; adult/child 1190/890B; ⏲10am-6pm) This sizeable water park is excellent fun for the whole family, with a huge array of slides and pools. It's about 20km southeast of Pattaya, with packages that include transport available via the website. Towels and lockers are available there.

Flight of the Gibbon ADVENTURE SPORTS
(☎053 010 660; www.treetopasia.com; tours from 3600B) This zipline course extends 3km via 26 platforms through the forest canopy of Khao Kheow Open Zoo, between Pattaya and Bangkok. It is an all-day tour with additional add-on activities, like a jungle obstacle course and a visit to the neighbouring zoo. Children 1m tall and over can do the zipline independently, while nippers can ride tandem with adults.

Sleeping

Accommodation in Pattaya is pricey by Thai standards. Rooms around central or south Pattaya tend to be cheaper but closer to the noisy nightlife. North Pattaya and parts of Naklua host the signature hotels, while Soi Bua Khao and Jomtien have budget options.

Jomtien Hostel HOSTEL $
(☎038 233416; www.jomtienhostel.com; Soi Sarita Hotel, near Soi 12, Hat Jomtien; dm 300B, r 600-900B; ❄@🛜) A couple of kilometres south of the heart of Jomtien, this excellently maintained place has air-conditioned dorms with good bedding and privacy curtains. It's all spotless, and private rooms are a great deal. It's 300m from the beach; lockers are available. Rates drop in low season.

Nonze Hostel HOSTEL $
(☎038 711112; www.nonzehostel.com; Th Hat Pattaya; s/tw 650/1400B; ❄🛜) Very stylish industrial chic in a seafront building with views over the water makes this an appealing location. The rooms are capsules – tiny boxes stacked up like building blocks – but offer plenty of interest and are sweet if you're not a claustrophobe. Twin rooms give you a bit more breathing space. Bathrooms are shared but good.

Garden Lodge Hotel HOTEL $$
(☎038 429109; www.gardenlodgepattaya.net; cnr Soi 20 & Th Naklua; r/bungalow/ste 1200/1700/3000B; P❄🛜≋) A favourite among German tourists; the rooms here are old-fashioned but surrounded by landscaped gardens and a large swimming pool. It's in the salubrious end of Pattaya and a decent option for families.

★**Rabbit Resort** RESORT $$$
(☎038 251730; www.rabbitresort.com; Hat Dongtan, Jomtien; r incl breakfast 6800-9000B; P❄@🛜≋) On a different qualitative planet to most Pattaya accommodation, Rabbit Resort has stunning, stylish and secluded bungalows and villas that showcase Thai design and art, all set in peaceful beachfront greenery hidden between Jomtien and Pattaya Tai. With two pools (one designed for families) and superb service, the resort is an excellent option. The upstairs rooms are particularly luminous and appealing.

Birds & Bees Resort RESORT $$$
(☎038 250556; www.cabbagesandcondoms.com; Soi 4, Th Phra Tamnak; r 4500-11,000B; P❄@🛜≋) As well as being a tropical garden resort with two pools and good-sized rooms, this place helps fund the work of the PDA, a notable rural development charity. Cheaper rooms have no views. The complex itself is delightful, with meandering pathways signposted with quirky, thought-provoking comments about the state of things. There's direct beach access, with the restaurant overlooking it.

Eating & Drinking

It can be pretty hard to find a bad meal in much of Thailand, but it's very easy in

PATTAYA: EXPAT CENTRAL

Ever since the first US servicemen started arriving in the 1960s for some R & R, hedonism has been a permanent guest. But while Pattaya is known for sleaze, there is another side to the city. Thousands of expats live here, many attracted by the quality of life, relatively low cost of living and amenities – the area has some of Thailand's finest golf courses.

There's a large Russian population; many Brits have businesses here; there is a thriving Arab community centred on Soi 16 at the south end of Walking St; and Naklua is popular with the German crowd. Specialist shops offer everything from South American coffee to French cheese. An estimated 50,000 foreigners live in Pattaya, with many more spending part of the year here, and those numbers are likely to rise.

Pattaya, particularly in the overpriced nightlife area. Other parts of town and outside of the city, however, are a few excellent establishments. Bang Sare, busy at weekends, has a trendy international and Thai dining scene.

Walking St is a centre of sleaze but its profusion of bars are more fun for those just interested in a night out. The tawdrier red-light zone is a block back from the beach.

Leng Kee CHINESE **$**
(Th Pattaya Klang; mains 100-300B; ⏲24hr) Duck dishes rule the roost in this well-established Thai-Chinese restaurant, though the seafood dishes are also tasty. It's very reasonably priced for the quality, though the unromantic setting reminds you that you're not paying for the decor.

Thepprasit Market MARKET **$**
(cnr Th Thepprasit & Th Sukhumvit; snacks 30-80B; ⏲4-10pm Fri-Sun) As well as intriguing knick-knacks and endless clothes stalls, this thriving weekend market has a great range of smoothies, noodles and Thai snacks.

Mum Aroi SEAFOOD, THAI **$$**
(☎038 223252; 83/4 Soi 4, Th Naklua; mains 150-420B; ⏲11am-11pm) This long-established restaurant is perched beside the sea in the fishing-village end of Naklua. Old fishing boats sit marooned offshore and crisp sea breezes envelop diners as they devour fantastic Thai food. Try *sôm·đam poo* (spicy papaya salad with crab) and *plah mèuk nêung ma-now* (squid steamed in lime juice).

Sketch Book Art Cafe INTERNATIONAL, THAI **$$**
(☎038 251625; 478/938 Mu 12, Th Tha Phraya; mains 120-300B; ⏲8.30am-9pm) This gorgeous, leafy art cafe offers pleasant respite from the normal Pattaya vibe. It's surrounded by a sprawling garden, and the restaurant's walls are covered with the owner's artwork. Smoothies are lush and the Thai food, once you've selected from the telephone book of a menu, is fresh. Painting material is on sale if you feel inspired.

Glass House THAI **$$**
(☎081 266 6110; www.glasshouse-pattaya.com; Soi Najomtien 10, Hat Jomtien; mains 170-380B; ⏲11am-midnight; 📶) Diners at this all-white beachfront spot plunge their toes into the warm sand as waiters deliver seafood, pizza and steak. The quality of the Thai dishes in particular is excellent, and the atmosphere romantic. It's about 9km south of central Pattaya.

★ **Mantra** THAI, INTERNATIONAL **$$$**
(☎038 429591; www.mantra-pattaya.com; Th Hat Pattaya; mains 350-1100B; ⏲5pm-1am daily, plus 11am-3pm Sun; 📶) One of Pattaya's top restaurants, Mantra is fun even if you can only afford a classy cocktail (from 180B). The building and interior are sumptuous; try for a seat upstairs where you can overlook proceedings or nestle in a cosy booth. The menu has a range of international cuisines, but the Thai dishes are sensational, and beautifully presented.

Gulliver's BAR
(www.gulliverbangkok.com; Th Hat Pattaya; ⏲3pm-2am; 📶) The rather grand neo-colonial facade and mini Statue of Liberty belies the fairly standard sports bar inside this beach-road spot. Decent beer and service, air-conditioning and an absence of bar girls can make it an attractive option.

Information

DANGERS & ANNOYANCES

- Most problems in Pattaya are alcohol-induced, especially bad driving and fights.
- Leave valuables in your room to be on the safe side.
- Avoid renting jet skis as scams involving fictional damage are common.

EMERGENCY

The tourist police **head office** (☎emergency 1155; tourist@police.go.th) is beside the Tourism Authority of Thailand office on Th Phra Tamnak, with police boxes along **Pattaya** and Jomtien beaches.

IMMIGRATION

Immigration Office (☎038 252750; www.immigration.go.th; Soi 5, Hat Jomtien; ⏲8.30am-noon & 1-4.30pm Mon-Fri)

MEDICAL SERVICES

Bangkok Pattaya Hospital (☎038 259999; www.bangkokpattayahospital.com; 301 Mu 6, Th Sukhumvit, Naklua; ⏲24hr) For first-class health care.

MONEY

There are banks and ATMs throughout the city.

TOURIST INFORMATION

Tourism Authority of Thailand (TAT; ☎038 428750; www.tourismthailand.org; 609 Th Phra Tamnak; ⏲8.30am-4.30pm) Located at the northwestern edge of Rama IX Park. Helpful staff have brochures and maps.

Tourist Information Kiosk (⏰8am-6pm)

WEBSITES

Pattaya Mail (www.pattayamail.com) One of the city's English-language weekly newspapers.

Pattaya One (www.pattayaone.news) Offers an intriguing insight into the darker side of the city.

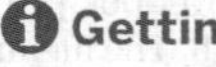

Getting There & Away

AIR

Pattaya's airport is **U-Tapao** (UTP; ☎038 245595; www.utapao.com), 33km south of town. Make sure taxi drivers know it's this airport you want, or they may assume you're going to Bangkok.

Destinations around Thailand are served from here daily by **Bangkok Airways** (☎038 412382; www.bangkokair.com; Fairtex Arcade, Th Pattaya Neua), **Air Asia** (www.airasia.com) and **Kan Airlines** (www.kanairlines.com).

Air Asia also has international flights, as do a couple of other airlines.

There are also regular charter flights here.

BOAT

A new fast catamaran service across the Gulf of Thailand between Pattaya and Hua Hin had recently launched at time of research. Despite some problems coping with choppy conditions, the service, run by **Royal Ferry Group** (☎038 488999; www.royalferrygroup.com), seemed to be established, charging 1250/1550B for standard/business class for the two-hour crossing, which slashes the normal travel time…for a price. At time of writing there was one service daily, but that was set to increase.

The same operator was mooting a service to Ko Chang from Sattahip, 30km south of Pattaya; don't bet on this getting off the ground.

BUS & MINIVAN

The main **bus station** is on Th Pattaya Neua. Services to Bangkok leave from here, as well as buses to Bangkok's Suvarnabhumi Airport (250B, 1½ to two hours, seven daily) run by **Bell Travel Service** (☎084 427 4608; www.belltravelservice.com; Th Pattaya Neua), which does hotel pick-ups if you prebook. **Roong Reuang Coaches** (www.airportpattayabus.com) run from Th Tha Phraya in Jomtien, near the corner of Th Thep Prasit, to Suvarnabhumi airport and vice versa for a much cheaper 120B.

Minivans heading north to Bangkok leave from the corner of Th Sukhumvit and Th Pattaya Klang. Minivans heading for the Cambodian border leave from the junction of Th Sukhumvit and Th Pattaya Tai. Downtown travel agents can book minivan services to Ko Chang (550B), Ko Mak (750B) and Ko Kut (800B).

TRAIN

Pattaya Train Station (☎038 429285) is off Th Sukhumvit east of town.

Getting Around

Locally known as 'baht buses', *sǒrng·tǎa·ou* do a loop along the major roads; just hop on and pay 10B when you get off. If you are going all the way to or from Naklua, you will have to change vehicles at the **Dolphin Roundabout** (Th Naklua & Th Pattaya Neua) in Pattaya Neua. Baht buses run to the bus station from the Dolphin

TRANSPORT TO/FROM PATTAYA

DESTINATION	BUS	MINIVAN	TRAIN
Aranya Prathet (for Cambodia)	N/A	260B, 5hr, hourly 4am-6pm	N/A
Bangkok's Eastern Bus Terminal (Ekamai)	108B, 2hr, every 30min 4.30am-11pm	130B, 2hr, frequent	N/A
Bangkok Hualamphong	N/A		from 31B, 4hr, 1 daily Mon-Fri
Bangkok's Northern Bus Terminal (Mo Chit)	117B, 2½hr, every 40min 4.30am-9pm	150B, 2½hr, frequent	N/A
Bangkok's Southern Bus Terminal	119B, 3hr, every 2hr 6am-6.30pm	150B, 2½hr, hourly	N/A
Hua Hin	389B, 6hr, 1 daily		N/A
Ko Samet	N/A	160B, 1hr, hourly	N/A
Rayong	N/A	100B, 1½hr, frequent	N/A
Si Racha	N/A	40B, 50min, frequent	from 5B, 30 minutes, 1 daily Mon-Fri

Roundabout as well. If you are going further afield, you can charter a baht bus; establish the price beforehand.

Motorbikes can be hired for 200B a day.

Rayong & Ban Phe ระยอง/บ้านเพ

038 / POP 70,000

You are most likely to transit through these towns en route to Ko Samet. Rayong is a sizeable, sprawling city with frequent bus connections to elsewhere. The little port of Ban Phe, 18km east, has ferry services to Ko Samet and quite a decent beach. Blue *sŏrng·tăa·ou* link the two towns (25B, 45 minutes, every 15 minutes). If you're spending time in Rayong, have a wander around its picturesque old town, south of the main road.

Sleeping & Eating

Rayong has a wide range of hotel accommodation, though most of it isn't particularly central. Ban Phe is well-stocked with mostly downmarket guesthouses and a string of eateries on its waterside road, including the impressive rainforest-style resort restaurant **Tamnanpar** (038 652884; www.tamnanpar-rayong.com; 167/6 Mu 7; mains 150-300B; 10am-10pm;).

La Paillote GUESTHOUSE **$$**
(038 651625; www.lapaillotebanphe.com; Ban Phe; r 700-900B;) A decent budget option in Ban Phe itself, handy for the piers and beach. It offers welcoming staff, simple but comfortable rooms with decent facilities and an on-site outdoor restaurant and bar. There are good family options.

Rayong President Hotel HOTEL **$$**
(038 622771; www.rayongpresidenthotel.com; Soi Klongkhud, off Th Sukhumvit, Rayong; r 700-850B; P) Rayong has better hotels than this, but they are all quite a way from the centre; this is one of the few within walking distance of the central bus station. Rooms have been somewhat renovated and offer OK value. Cheaper no-breakfast rates are also available.

Getting There & Around

Rayong has a central **bus station**, Number 1, and a **new one** 7km northwest of downtown (Number 2). All long-distance services now use the new one. The two are connected by very regular *sŏrng·tăa·ou* (15B, 20 minutes).

Minivans from Rayong's bus station 2 go to Bangkok's eastern (Ekamai) and northern (Mo Chit) bus terminals (both 160B, 3½ hours, hourly 4.40am to 8pm); these can also drop you off at the AirportLink station one stop away from Suvarnabhumi airport. There are also minivans to Pattaya (100B, 1½ hours, frequent), Chanthaburi (120B, two hours, frequent) and Trat (200B, three hours, frequent).

Ban Phe has regular boats and speedboats to Ko Samet. Buses opposite Ban Phe's Nuanthip pier go to/from Bangkok Ekamai (166B, four hours, every two hours, 7am to 6pm).

Ban Phe also has minivan services to Laem Ngop for boats to Ko Chang (250B, three hours, three daily) and overpriced services to Pattaya (200B, two hours, hourly) and Bangkok's Victory Monument (200B, four hours, every 40 minutes).

From Rayong's central bus station 1, there are frequent *sŏrng·tăa·ou* to Ban Phe (25B, 30 minutes).

From Ban Phe, catch them outside the main piers.

Ko Samet เกาะเสม็ด

Once the doyen of backpacker destinations, today Ko Samet shares its charms with a wider audience. The sandy shores, cosy coves and aquamarine waters attract ferryloads of Bangkokians looking to party each weekend, while tour groups pack out the main beach and many resorts. Fire-juggling shows and beach barbecues are nightly events on the northern beaches, but the southern parts of the island are far more secluded and sedate.

Despite being the closest major island to Bangkok, Ko Samet remains surprisingly underdeveloped, with a thick jungle interior crouching beside the low-rise hotels.

Sights & Activities

On some islands you beach-hop, but on Ko Samet you cove-hop. The coastal footpath traverses rocky headlands, cicada-serenaded forests and one stunning bay after another, where the mood becomes successively more mellow the further south you go.

Various activities like kayaking, parasailing, diving, snorkelling and stand-up paddleboarding (SUP) are available on the island. Squid-fishing and other angling trips are another option. **Seaddict** (085 397 2716; www.facebook.com/s3addict; Ao Hin Khok) on the main road, hires out SUPs, skimboards and windsurfing rigs, and offers lessons.

Ko Samet

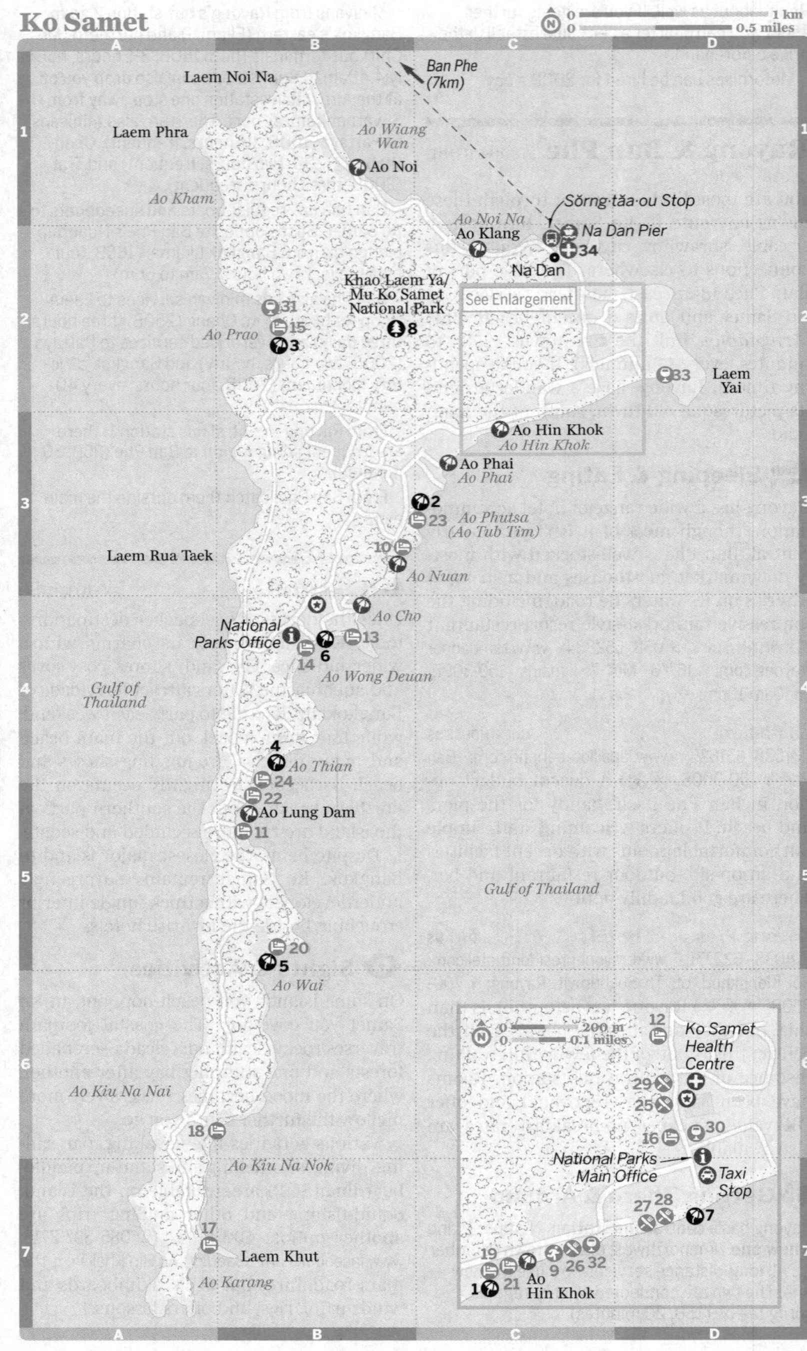
Ban Phe
(7km)
Laem Noi Na
Laem Phra
Ao Wiang Wan
Ao Noi
Ao Kham
Sŏrng·tăa·ou Stop
Ao Noi Na
Ao Klang
Na Dan Pier
34
Na Dan
Khao Laem Ya/
Mu Ko Samet
National Park
8
See Enlargement
31
15
Ao Prao
3
33
Laem Yai
Ao Hin Khok
Ao Hin Khok
Ao Phai
Ao Phai
2
23
Ao Phutsa
(Ao Tub Tim)
10
Laem Rua Taek
Ao Nuan
Ao Cho
National
Parks Office
13
14
6
Ao Wong Deuan
Gulf of
Thailand
4
Ao Thian
24
22
Ao Lung Dam
11
Gulf of Thailand
20
5
Ao Wai
Ao Kiu Na Nai
18
Ao Kiu Na Nok
17
Laem Khut
Ao Karang
200 m
0.1 miles
12
Ko Samet
Health
Centre
29
25
16
30
National Parks
Main Office
Taxi
Stop
27
28
7
19
9
26
32
1
21
Ao
Hin Khok
1 km
0.5 miles

Ko Samet

Sights

1 Ao Hin Khok & Ao Phai C7
2 Ao Phutsa C3
3 Ao Prao B2
4 Ao Thian B4
5 Ao Wai B5
6 Ao Wong Deuan B4
7 Hat Sai Kaew D7
8 Khao Laem Ya/Mu Ko Samet National Park B2

Activities, Courses & Tours

9 Seaddict C7

Sleeping

10 Ao Nuan Bungalows B3
11 Apaché B5
12 Baan Minnie D6
13 Blue Sky B4
14 La Lune Beach Resort B4
15 Lima Coco Resort B2
16 Mossman House D6
17 Nimmanoradee Resort A7
18 Paradee Resort A6
19 Samed Pavilion Resort C7
20 Samet Ville Resort B5
21 Silver Sand C7
22 Ton Had Bungalow B5
23 Tubtim Resort C3
24 Viking Holidays Resort B4

Eating

25 Banana Bar D6
26 Jep's Restaurant C7
27 Kitt & Food D7
28 Ploy Talay D7
29 Red Ginger D6

Drinking & Nightlife

30 Audi Bar D6
31 Breeze B2
32 Naga Bar C7
33 Talay Bar D2

Information

34 International Clinic Ko Samet C2

Tours

Ko Samet, along with nine neighbouring islands, is part of the **Khao Laem Ya/Mu Ko Samet National Park** (อุทยานแห่งชาติเขาแหลมหญ้า-หมู่เกาะเสม็ด; ☎038 653034; www.dnp.go.th; adult/child 200/100B). While there is some development on the other islands, most visitors come for day trips. **Ko Kudee** has a small, pretty sandy stretch, clear water for decent snorkelling and a nice little hiking trail. Ko Man Nai is home to the **Rayong Turtle Conservation Centre**, which is a breeding place for endangered sea turtles, and has a small visitor centre. Agents for boat tours can be found on the popular beaches and have a couple of different boat trips on offer (from 500B per person).

Sleeping

A word of caution to early risers: Hat Sai Kaew, Ao Hin Khok, Ao Phai and Ao Wong Deuan are the most popular beaches and host well-amplified night-time parties.

Hat Sai Kaew & Na Dan

In the island's northeastern corner near the ferry pier, Hat Sai Kaew (หาดทรายแก้ว), the 'town beach', is the island's widest, dirtiest and wildest stretch of sand. The beach can feel totally overrun and the scene is lively at night, too.

Mossman House GUESTHOUSE $
(☎038 644017; r 1200-1500B; ❄📶) On the main street, just before the national park ticket office, is this sound guesthouse, with large, comfortable rooms along a shared veranda and leafy grounds. Choose a spot at the back for some quiet as the bar opposite stays open late. Off-season rooms go for around 800B.

Baan Minnie GUESTHOUSE, APARTMENT $$
(☎086 691 9662; www.facebook.com/baanminnie; Silver Park Ave, Na Dan; d 1200-1700B; P❄📶) There are several places to stay in these rows of terraced accommodation behind the main strip in Ko Samet's capital village. Rooms have firm, comfortable mattresses and attractive modern decor; some have a patio seating area. There are also 'houses' which are well-kept apartments, some duplex, sleeping up to six. It's pretty casual; you're left to your own devices.

Ao Hin Khok & Ao Phai อ่าวหินโคก/อ่าวไผ่

Less frenetic than Hat Sai Kaew, Ao Hin Khok and Ao Phai are two gorgeous bays separated by rocky headlands. The crowd here tends to be younger than in Hat Sai Kaew; these two beaches are the island's traditional backpacker party centres.

Silver Sand RESORT $$
(☎038 644300; www.silversandsamed.com; Ao Phai; r incl breakfast 2500-2800B; P❄@📶) An ever-expanding empire, Silver Sand is

BEACH ADMISSION FEE

Ko Samet is part of the Khao Laem Ya/Mu Ko Samet National Park (p133) and charges all visitors an entrance fee (adult/child 200/100B) upon arrival. If you can prove that you live and work in Thailand, it will only cost you 40B, the price Thais pay. The fee is collected at the **National Parks Main Office** (www.dnp.go.th; Hat Sai Kaew; 8.30am-8pm); *sŏrng·tăa·ou* from the pier will stop at the gates for payment. Hold on to your ticket for later inspections. There's another **park office** (8.30am-4.30pm) at Ao Wong Deaun, and rangers elsewhere will charge you the fee if you arrive by speedboat. There is a 20B fee when using Na Dan pier.

a miniresort, complete with a restaurant, shops and a lively LGBT-friendly bar. It's a little impersonal but the rooms are decent quality and the place is set on a super strip of beach.

Samed Pavilion Resort RESORT $$$
(038 644420; www.samedpavilionresort.com; Ao Phai; d incl breakfast 3500-5500B; P) This handsome boutique resort has elegant, spacious rooms in an upstairs-downstairs configuration tightly set around a sociable pool. It's a good spot for families, with lots of dedicated rooms for them, beach access and removal from the road. Rates are usually best online, but it has off-season promotions for direct bookings. It's substantially cheaper midweek.

Ao Phutsa & Ao Nuan

South of Ao Hin Khok and Ao Phai is cute, sandy Ao Phutsa (อ่าวพุทรา), which strikes a good balance, being relatively accessible but generally not too crowded.

★ **Ao Nuan Bungalows** BUNGALOW $$
(081 781 4875; Ao Nuan; bungalows with fan 800-1200B, with air-con 1500-3000B;) Samet's one remaining bohemian bay is tucked off the main road down a dirt track. Running down a jungle hillside to the sea are cute wooden bungalows ranging from simple fan-cooled affairs with shared cold-water bathroom to romantic air-conditioned retreats with elegant deck furniture. There's a bar and simple restaurant; if you need more action, Tubtim beach is a few minutes' stroll.

Tubtim Resort RESORT $$
(038 644025; www.tubtimresort.com; Ao Phutsa/Ao Tub Tim; r incl breakfast fan 700-1400B, air-con 2200-3700B; P) A well-organised place with great, nightly barbecues and a range of solid, spacious bungalows of varying quality close to the beach. Confusingly, the best are in the 'N' zone, right by the sand with a great outlook from bed, desk and deck. 'A' zone sea-view rooms are older and set back a little, but still pleasant.

Ao Wong Deuan & Ao Thian อ่าววงเดือน/อ่าวเทียน

Ao Wong Deuan, meaning 'crescent moon bay', is Samet's second-busiest beach, with a range of resorts and more modest guesthouses. It's a wide, flat arc with a shallow gradient that's good for kids. Ao Thian (Candlelight Beach) is one of Samet's most easy-going beaches, punctuated by big boulders that shelter small sandy spots.

Apaché BUNGALOW $
(081 452 9472; Ao Thian; r 800-1500B;) Apaché's eclectic, quirky decorations and cheerfully random colour scheme add character to this super-chilled spot at the southern end of a tranquil strip. Bungalows are basic but adequate. The on-site restaurant on stilts is well worthwhile.

Blue Sky BUNGALOW $
(089 936 0842; Ao Wong Deuan; r 800-1200B;) A rare budget spot on Ao Wong Deuan, Blue Sky has beaten-up bungalows set on a rocky headland at the north end of the beach. It's run by a friendly couple but they are a bit cagey about advanced bookings, so you'll probably have to turn up and see.

★ **Viking Holidays Resort** BUNGALOW $$
(038 644354; www.vikingholidaysresort.com; Ao Thian; r incl breakfast 1500-1800B; P) One of a line of casual bungalow complexes on this tranquil beachside, Viking is well run and has pretty, compact rooms with carpet and strings of seashells for decoration. Staff are particularly helpful and friendly and good English is spoken. Unlike many Ko Samet bungalows, you can book online (and pick your bungalow location).

Ton Had Bungalow BUNGALOW **$$**
(☎081 435 8900; Ao Thian; r incl breakfast 1200-1800B) Simple bungalows decorated with seashells and offering both fan and air-con make for a peaceful sleep at this sweet family-run spot at Ao Thian. It's located on the short rocky shore between two beaches: views are great but you've got an almost two-minute stroll to the sand. Things are tough here.

La Lune Beach Resort HOTEL **$$$**
(☎Koh Samet 089 892 9690, reservations Bangkok 02 260 3592; www.lalunebeachresort.com; Ao Wong Deuan; r incl breakfast 3000-4500B; P ❄ 📶 🏊) Meet the new face of Samet. Stylish, chic resorts like this are becoming more common. The 40 rooms, all with stressed wood underfoot and a soft greeny-grey-and-white theme, are set around a central pool in a three-level U-shape that opens onto the beach. The three grades of room differ only by outlook, which isn't so different.

Ao Wai อ่าวหวาย

Ao Wai is a lovely beach far removed from everything else (though in reality it's only 1.5km from Ao Thian).

Samet Ville Resort RESORT **$$**
(☎038 651682; www.sametvilleresort.com; standard r incl breakfast fan/air-con 1400/2000B, superior r 2300-5000B; P ❄ 📶 🏊) Spread over two bays – Ao Wai and Ao Hin Kleang – this leafy, 4.5-hectare resort is secluded and soporific. The rooms, of which there are several types, are all a few steps from the excellent beach. For this price, though, they are badly in need of a touch-up and the lackadaisical management could do with the same sort of treatment.

Ao Prao อ่าวพร้าว

On the west coast, Ao Prao (Coconut Beach) is one of the island's prettiest beaches. It's secluded but backed by three high-end resorts, so it still gets quite busy.

Lima Coco Resort RESORT **$$$**
(☎Bangkok 02 129 1140; www.limaresort.co.th; r incl breakfast 3000-8900B; ❄ 📶 🏊) Ao Prao, on Samet's west coast, has three fancy resorts. Lima Coco, in the middle, is the cheapest of these, with compact whitewashed rooms in a variety of categories climbing up the hill behind the beach. It's a little down at heel but offers energetic staff, beachside massages and other facilities.

Ao Pakarang & Ao Kiu

The southernmost tip of the island has an exclusive, discreet feel.

Paradee Resort RESORT **$$$**
(☎038 644283; www.samedresorts.com/paradee; Ao Kiu; r incl breakfast 25,000-35,000B; P ❄ 📶 🏊) Exclusive and offering excellent privacy, this sleek resort near the southern end is one of the island's most luxurious. Golf carts hum about among discreetly screened thatched villas, most of which have their own jacuzzi. The lovely beach is effectively private and, across the road, a bar deck lets you appreciate the sunset views from the island's western shore.

Nimmanoradee Resort RESORT **$$$**
(☎038 644271; www.nimmanoradee.com; Ao Pakarang; r incl breakfast 3000-5800B; P ❄ 📶) The southernmost resort on the island, Nimmanoradee offers tranquillity, plenty of space and cheerfully coloured octagonal bungalows. There's good swimming here and a pretty little boutique promontory. Kayaks and snorkels are on hand to explore the area, staff are friendly and the very pleasant open-air restaurant serves decent food at fair prices.

Eating

Along the beaches are strung restaurant and bars, while many hotels and guesthouses have restaurants that do beach barbecues at night. There are cheapie Thai places along the main road in Na Dan.

GIGANTIC WELCOME

The imposing statue of a topless female giant at Na Dan pier is impossible to miss (although at time of last research she was modestly wearing a wrap). She is an allusion to Ko Samet's most famous son, the poet Sunthorn Phu, and his famous story *Phra Aphaimani*. In the tale, a prince is exiled to an undersea kingdom ruled by the lovesick female giant. A mermaid helps the prince escape to Ko Samet, where he defeats the giant by playing a magical flute. You can see mermaid and prince together at the western end of Hat Sai Kaew.

Banana Bar THAI $
(☎038 644033; Na Dan; mains 80-150B; ⊙11am-11.30pm) Casual and relaxed, this somewhat ramshackle yet oddly attractive main street spot is a good choice for well-priced Thai food. Run by a staunch motherly figure, it offers smallish portions of Thai curries, salads and Isan dishes; it's all very tasty.

Jep's Restaurant INTERNATIONAL $
(☎038 644 112; www.jepsbungalows.com; Ao Hin Khok; mains 70-200B; ⊙7am-11pm; ✎) Canopied by the branches of an arching tree decorated with pendant lights, this pretty place right on the sand does a wide range of international, and some Thai, dishes. Leave room for dessert.

Red Ginger INTERNATIONAL, THAI $$
(☎084 383 4917; www.redgingersamed.com; Na Dan; mains 120-565B; ⊙11am-10pm; 📶✎) An atmospheric main-street eatery that feels like an extension of this Canadian-Thai family's lounge room: expect cheery informality, quirks and chatting over a drink with the personable owner. The menu is short but tasty, with authentic, flavoursome Thai dishes complemented by a handful of international offerings. Excellent oven-baked ribs slathered in barbecue sauce are the highlight.

Kitt & Food SEAFOOD, THAI $$
(☎038 644087; Hat Sai Kaew; mains 120-400B; ⊙11am-10.30pm) Better than most of the beachfront restaurants, this is a romantic place for dinner, with tables almost lapped by the waves. Don't plough too deep into the phonebook of a menu – seafood is the speciality here. Various fresh fish (mostly farmed) are arrayed; pick one and decide how you want it done. Baked in salt takes a while but is great.

Ploy Talay SEAFOOD, THAI $$
(☎038 644212; Hat Sai Kaew; mains 110-400B; ⊙11am-11pm; 📶) The busiest of the string of mediocre beach restaurants on Hat Sai Kaew, this packs out for its nightly 8.30pm fire show, which is quite a sight (and smell). You can see it from the beach too, but people enjoy their leisurely (the service will ensure that) seafood dinners here. The location is better than the quality, but the food is OK.

Drinking & Nightlife

On weekends, Ko Samet is a boisterous night owl with tour groups crooning away on karaoke machines and the young ones slurping down beer and buckets to a techno beat. There is usually a crowd on Hat Sai Kaew, Ao Hin Khok, Ao Phai and Ao Wong Deuan.

Audi Bar BAR
(☎084 418 8213; Na Dan; ⊙4pm-4am; 📶) Sharing an upstairs main-street space with a gym, this bar offers good people-watching from its high vantage point, the Samet-standard Day-Glo graffiti and a couple of pool tables. It's notably welcoming – staff want you to enjoy yourself – and serves as a one-last-drink venue for those straggling back from the beach dance floors.

Talay Bar BAR
(☎083 887 1588; Hat Sai Kaew; ⊙2pm-midnight; 📶) Cheerily fronted by burning torches and Thai flags, this is at the eastern end of the island's busiest beach, away from the most crowded parts. It's an upbeat, enthusiastic spot with space to lounge on the sand and kick back with a cocktail or beer bomb from the unfeasibly large (size-wise) menu.

Naga Bar BAR
(Ao Hin Khok; ⊙3pm-late) This busy beachfront bar is covered in Day-Glo art and run by a friendly bunch of locals who offer good music, lots of whisky and vodka/Red Bull buckets. It gets lively later on, with dance-floor action.

Breeze BAR
(☎038 644100; www.samedresorts.com; Ao Prao Resort, Ao Prao; ⊙7am-10.30pm; 📶) On the sunset side of the island, this is a lovely sea-view restaurant perfect for a sundowner. You will need private transport to reach it, or it's a 2.5km walk from Hat Sai Kaew.

Information

There are plenty of ATMs on Ko Samet, including some near the Na Dan pier, outside the 7-Eleven behind Hat Sai Kaew, and at Ao Wong Deuan, Ao Thian and Ao Phutsa, as well as at several resorts.

There are tourist police points at both the **main village** (☎24hr 1155) and **Ao Wong Deuan** (☎24hr 1155).

The **Ko Samet Health Centre** (☎038 644123; ⊙24hr) and **International Clinic Ko Samet** (☎038 644414, emergency 086 094 0566; www.sametclinic.in.th; ⊙8am-6pm, emergencies until midnight), both in the village near Na Dan pier, offer health services. The nearest full-service hospital is in Rayong.

Getting There & Away

Ko Samet is accessed via the mainland piers in Ban Phe. There are many piers, each used by different ferry companies, all of which charge the same fares (one-way from mainland/return/one-way from island 70/100/50B, 40 minutes, hourly, 8am to 5pm) and dock at **Na Dan** (usage fee 20B), the main pier on Ko Samet. The last boat back to the mainland leaves at 6pm.

If you are staying at Ao Wong Deuan or further south, catch a ferry from the mainland directly to the beach (one-way/return 90/140B, one hour, two to three daily departures).

Speedboats charge 200B to 500B one-way and will drop you at the beach of your choice, but only leave when they have enough passengers. Otherwise, you can charter one for around 1500B.

Ticket agents at the Ban Phe piers will often try to rip you off on tickets for both ferries and speedboats and will try and pressure you to take a speedboat by saying that there are no slow boats for the next few hours etc.

From Bangkok, head to Rayong. You'll arrive at bus station 2; there are some minibuses from here to Ban Phe, but it'll usually be quicker to catch a *sŏrng·tăa·ou* to bus station 1, then another from there to Ban Phe. There is no Rayong service from Suvarnabhumi airport; either head to Pattaya and change there or head into Bangkok's Ekamai bus station and catch Rayong- or Ban Phe–bound transport from there.

From the island, it's easy to arrange minibus transfers to Bangkok (250B), Suvarnabhumi airport (500B), Ko Chang piers (250B) and elsewhere.

Getting Around

Ko Samet's small size makes it a great place to explore on foot. A network of roads connects most of the island.

Green sŏrng·tăa·ou meet boats at the pier and provide drop-offs at the various beaches (20B to 200B, depending on the beach and number of passengers). Chartering one ('taxi') costs 150B to 700B on the official rate sheet, but you can usually negotiate a discount. Taxis also congregate at a stop (Hat Sai Kaew) by the national park entrance.

You can rent motorcycles nearly everywhere along the northern half of the island for 100/300B per hour/day. The road is good, but be careful on steep descents. It's 7km by road from the ferry pier to the southern tip of the island. For those who prefer four wheels, golf carts are also available for hire.

Chanthaburi จันทบุรี

☎039 / POP 120,000

Chanthaburi is proof that all that glitters is not gold. Here, gems do the sparkling, with precious stones ranging from sapphires to emeralds traded every weekend in a bustling street market. Nearby, wonderfully restored waterfront buildings in a charming historic quarter are evidence of how the Chinese, French and Vietnamese have influenced life – and architecture – here.

Vietnamese Christians fled persecution from Cochin China (southern Vietnam) in the 19th century and came to Chanthaburi. The French occupied Chanthaburi from

OFF THE BEATEN TRACK

ROAD-TRIPPING THE CHANTHABURI COAST

Little visited by island-hungry foreigners, the coast near Chanthaburi is a rewarding day trip from the city or a scenic diversion en route to/from Rayong. It's within bicycle reach of the city and is a popular cycling circuit for Thais. All the beaches mentioned here offer places to stay and eat.

At **Laem Sing**, some 20km from Chanthaburi by road, the river estuary, spanned by a bridge, is wide and handsome. There's a fishing fleet here, an offshore island and a long beach backed by a park.

From here, Rte 4036 heads northwestish, passing turn-offs to a handful of quiet beach villages before reaching more developed **Hat Chao Lao**. Close by is **Hat Laem Sadet**, with medium-market resort hotels, a beach and a bay, Ao Khung Kraben. A mangrove reserve lets you explore the estuarine ecosystem on wooden boardwalks.

The last of the beaches on this stretch, some 15km beyond Chao Lao and Laem Sadet, is **Hat Khung Wiman**, with a nice narrow beach and pleasant westerly outlook. The road through the village loops round to a fishing village on the bay side; there are good places to snack on simple seafood here.

Chanthaburi

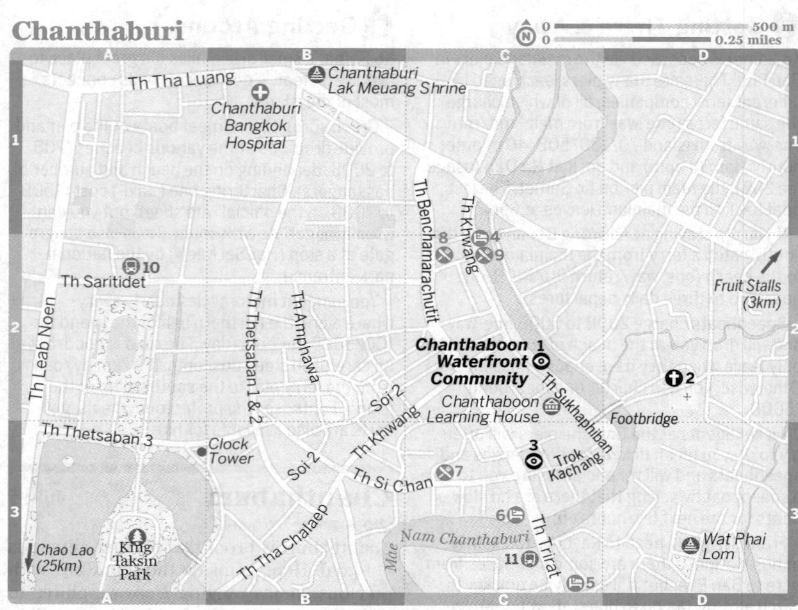

Chanthaburi

Top Sights

1 Chanthaboon Waterfront Community C2

Sights

2 Cathedral of the Immaculate Conception D2
3 Gem Market C3

Sleeping

4 Baan Luang Rajamaitri C2
5 Chernchan Hostel C3
6 River Guest House C3

Eating

7 786 Muslim Restaurant C3
8 Chanthorn C2
9 Tamajun Restaurant C2

Transport

10 Bus & Minivan Station A2
11 Minivans to Ban Pakard C3

1893 to 1905 due to a dispute over the border between Siam and Indochina. More Vietnamese arrived in the 1920s and 1940s as they fled French rule, then a third wave followed in 1975 after the communist takeover of southern Vietnam.

The surrounding area has waterfall-heavy national parks and charming beach villages to discover.

Sights

★ Chanthaboon Waterfront Community — HISTORIC SITE

(ชุมชนริมน้ำจันทบูร; Th Sukhaphiban) Hugging the banks of Mae Nam Chanthaburi is this charismatic part of town, filled with restored houses and elderly residents sitting around reminiscing with each other about their Chanthaburi tales. The **Learning House** (ศูนย์เรียนรู้ประจำชุมชนริมน้ำจันทบูร; ☎081 945 5761; 69 Th Sukhaphiban; ⏲10am-4pm) **FREE** displays neighbourhood photos, paintings and architectural designs, including upstairs drawings of intricate ventilation panels that feature Chinese characters and French fleurs-de-lis.

Gem Market — MARKET

(ตลาดพลอย; Th Si Chan & Trok Kachang; ⏲9am-6pm Fri-Sun) Every weekend, the normally quiet streets near Th Si Chan (or 'Gem Road') burst into life as gem traders arrive to bustle and bargain. It's incongruously humble considering the value of the commodities on offer, as people cluster around makeshift tables examining small piles of unset stones.

Cathedral of the Immaculate Conception CATHEDRAL
(อาสนวิหารพระนางมารีอาปฏิสนธินิรมล; ⏲8.30am-4.30pm) FREE Thailand's largest cathedral, on the east bank of Mae Nam Chanthaburi, started life as a modest chapel in 1711. Since then there have been four reconstructions and the current Gothic-style structure includes some impressive stained-glass windows and an upstairs gallery that gives the interior the feel of a medieval hall. The statue of the Virgin Mary at the front is bedecked with more than 200,000 sapphires – a fitting link between religion and the city's famous gem trade.

Sleeping

River Guest House GUESTHOUSE $
(☎092 717 1470; www.facebook.com/theriverguesthouse; 3/5-8 Th Si Chan; s 170-250B, d 300-350B; ❄📶) Right by the river, albeit next to a noisy bridge, is this friendly guesthouse with a range of simple rooms, some of which are tiny. Beds are basic but the riverside seating area compensates for this. The cheapest rooms have a shared bathroom; rooms with hot water and air-con cost a little more. It hires bikes and mopeds.

★ **Baan Luang Rajamaitri** HISTORIC HOTEL $$
(☎088 843 8516; www.baanluangrajamaitri.com; 252 Th Sukhaphiban; r incl breakfast 1250-1900B, ste 3100-3300B; ❄📶) 🍃 Community-owned and named after a local philanthropist, this expertly restored historic hotel has wonderfully characterful elegant rooms in the heart of the riverfront district. Dark wooden furniture, creaky floorboards and a great waterside deck make for excellent atmosphere. The cheapest rooms are small with a comfortable bunk bed and little terrace. Quirky antique touches abound; it's a top spot.

Chernchan Hostel HOSTEL $$
(☎065 573 8841; www.facebook.com/chernchan2017; 43/11-13 Th Tirat; dm 450B, r 900-1500B; ❄📶) On a quiet lane close to the river, this boutique hostel has eye-catching modern design and helpful staff. Dorms and rooms are compact but comfortable; downstairs in the cafe an abundant breakfast is

WORTH A TRIP

NATIONAL PARKS NEAR CHANTHABURI

Two small national parks are easily reached from Chanthaburi, and make good day trips. Both are malarial, so take the usual precautions.

Khao Khitchakut National Park (อุทยานแห่งชาติเขาคิชฌกูฏ; ☎039 452074; http://nps.dnp.go.th; 200B; ⏲8.30am-4.30pm) is 28km northeast of town. Though it's one of Thailand's smallest national parks (59 sq km), it's bordered by wildlife sanctuaries and harbours wild elephants. The cascade of Nam Tok Krathing is only impressive just after the rainy season. Another attraction atop a hill is a temple where, by an enormous boulder, Buddha is believed to have left a footprint. To get to Khao Khitchakut, take a *sŏrng·tăa·ou* (passenger pick-up truck) from next to the post office, near the northern side of the market in Chanthaburi (35B, 45 minutes). The *sŏrng·tăa·ou* stops 1km from the park headquarters on Rte 3249, from which point you will have to walk. Returning transport is scarce so expect to wait.

Namtok Phlio National Park (อุทยานแห่งชาติน้ำตกพลิ้ว; ☎039 434528; http://nps.dnp.go.th; 200B; ⏲8am-6pm), off Hwy 3, is 14km to the southeast of Chanthaburi and is much more popular. A pleasant short nature trail loops around the waterfalls, which writhe with soro brook carp; you can bathe here. Also on display are the strikingly mossy Phra Nang Ruar Lom stupa (c 1876) and Along Khon *chedi* (c 1881). To get to the park, catch a *sŏrng·tăa·ou* from the northern side of the market in Chanthaburi to the park entrance (50B, 30 minutes). You will get dropped off about 1km from the entrance. Private transport is 1500B.

Accommodation is available at both parks; book with the **park reservation system** (☎02 562 0760; www.dnp.go.th).

GETTING TO CAMBODIA: BAN PAKARD TO PAILIN

Getting to the border In Chanthaburi, **minivans** (092 037 6266) depart from a stop across the river from the River Guest House (p139), where you can book your spot, to Ban Pakard (180B, 1½ hours, 10am and noon). There are also *sŏrng·tăa·ou* from the bus station (100B, two hours) that tend to leave early.

At the border This is a far less busy and more pleasant crossing than Poipet further north. You need a passport photo and US$30 for the visa fee. Cambodian e-visas aren't officially accepted here, though some travellers have reported getting through. Demanding US$35 for the visa is standard practice here.

Moving on Hop on a motorbike taxi to Pailin in Cambodia. From there, you can catch frequent shared taxis (US$5 per person, 1½ hours) to scenic Battambang. After that, you can move on to Siem Reap by boat, or Phnom Penh by bus.

served (included in room but not dorm rates). It rents bikes.

Eating

Chanthaburi is famed for its fruit. You can taste why at the various **fruit stalls** (fruit 20-80B; 8am-9pm;) that line Th Sukhumvit, 8km northeast of the city (you pass them on the way into Chanthaburi), which sell a range of rambutans, bananas, mangosteens and more. The annual **Fruit Festival** (May or Jun) is an even better excuse to sink your teeth into the region's superbly sticky, juicy produce...including the ever-pungent durian.

Crab noodles and pork with *chamung* leaf are also local specialities. A string of eateries can be found on Th Sukhaphiban and there are lots of options around the centre in general. Across the other side of the river are some open-air spots that look across to Chanthaboon.

786 Muslim Restaurant INDIAN $
(081 353 5174; Th Si Chan; mains 50-80B; 9.30am-6pm) In among all the Chanthaburi gem dealers, this restaurant run by Thai Muslims is worth a stop for its excellent *paratha, biryani,* curries, meatballs and chai tea.

★ **Chanthorn** THAI $$
(102/5-8 Th Benchamarachutit; mains 120-250B; 9am-9pm;) This welcoming family-run restaurant in the centre near the waterfront is a great place to try local specialities; the *chamung* leaves with pork and Chanthaburi crab noodles are particularly good, but it's all really excellent quality. It's a fairly early closer at dinner time.

Tamajun Restaurant THAI $$
(039 311977; www.tamajunhotel.com; Th Sukhaphiban; mains 140-260B; food 4-11pm;) The most sophisticated of the riverside restaurants, Tamajun has elegant vintage-style decor and excellent tables hanging over the water. Live crooner bands operate at night, when tasty dishes that pack a serious spice punch cover prawn and pork specialities as well as other fare.

TRANSPORT TO/FROM CHANTHABURI

DESTINATION	BUS	MINIVAN
Bangkok's Eastern Bus Terminal (Ekamai)	184B, 4hr, 25 daily	210B, frequent
Bangkok's Northern Bus Terminal (Mo Chit)	187B, 4hr, 4 daily	215B, frequent
Nakhon Ratchasima (Khorat)	279B, 4hr, every 2 hours	
Rayong		120B, 2hr, hourly
Sa Kaew	145B, 2hr, every 2 hours	
Trat		52-70B, 1hr, frequent

Information

Banks with change facilities and ATMs can be found across town.

Chanthaburi Bangkok Hospital (☎ 039 319888; www.chanthaburihospital.com; Th Tha Luang; ⏲ 24hr) is central and has 24-hour emergency service.

Getting There & Around

Chanthaburi's bus station (Th Saritidet) is west of the river. Minivans also leave from the bus station. Motorbike taxis charge 20B to 40B for trips around town.

Trat ตราด

☎ 039 / POP 22,000

Trat is a major transit point for Ko Chang and coastal Cambodia, and worth a stop anyway for its underappreciated old-world charm. The guesthouse neighbourhood occupies an atmospheric wooden shophouse district, bisected by winding sois and filled with typical Thai street life: children riding bikes, homemakers running errands and small businesses selling trinkets and necessities.

Sights

Walk down Th Lak Meuang and you will see that the top floors of shophouses have been converted into **nesting sites** for birds that produce the edible nests considered a Chinese delicacy. Swiflets' nests were quite rare (and expensive) in the past because they were only harvested from precipitous sea caves.

In the 1990s entrepreneurs figured out how to replicate the cave atmosphere in multistorey shophouses.

Indoor Market MARKET

(ตลาดกลาง; Soi Sukhumvit; ⏲ 6am-5pm) The indoor market sprawls east from Th Sukhumvit to Th Tat Mai and has a little bit of everything, especially all the things that you forgot to pack. Without really noticing the difference you will stumble upon the day market (p143), selling fresh fruit, vegetables and takeaway food.

Sleeping

Trat has many budget hotels in traditional wooden houses on and around Th Thana Charoen.

Trat Province

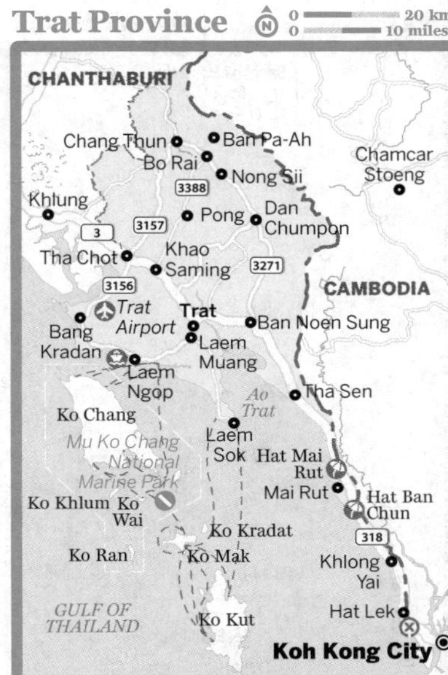

★ **Ban Jai Dee Guest House** GUESTHOUSE $

(☎ 039 520678, 083 589 0839; banjaideehouse@yahoo.com; 6 Th Chaimongkol; s/d 250/300B; 📶) This relaxed traditional wooden house has simple rooms with shared bathrooms (hot-water showers). Paintings and objets d'art made by the artistically inclined owners decorate the beautiful common spaces. There are only seven rooms and an addictively relaxing ambience so it can fill fast. The owners are full of helpful information and understand a budget traveller's needs.

Yotin Guest House GUESTHOUSE $

(☎ 089 224 7817; Th Thana Charoen; r 350-600B; ❄📶) Backing a typically venerable building in Trat's lovely old quarter are pretty, inviting refurbished rooms with colourful linen and comfortable mattresses. Cheaper rooms are compact and either share a bathroom or have a very tight en suite; higher grade rooms have more space. The couple that run the place are thoughtful and helpful: it's a very sound base. You can hire bikes here.

★ **Rimklong Boutique Hotel** BOUTIQUE HOTEL $$

(☎ 039 523388; www.facebook.com/Rimklong-Boutique-Hotel-trat-127177424027071/; 194 Th Lak

Trat

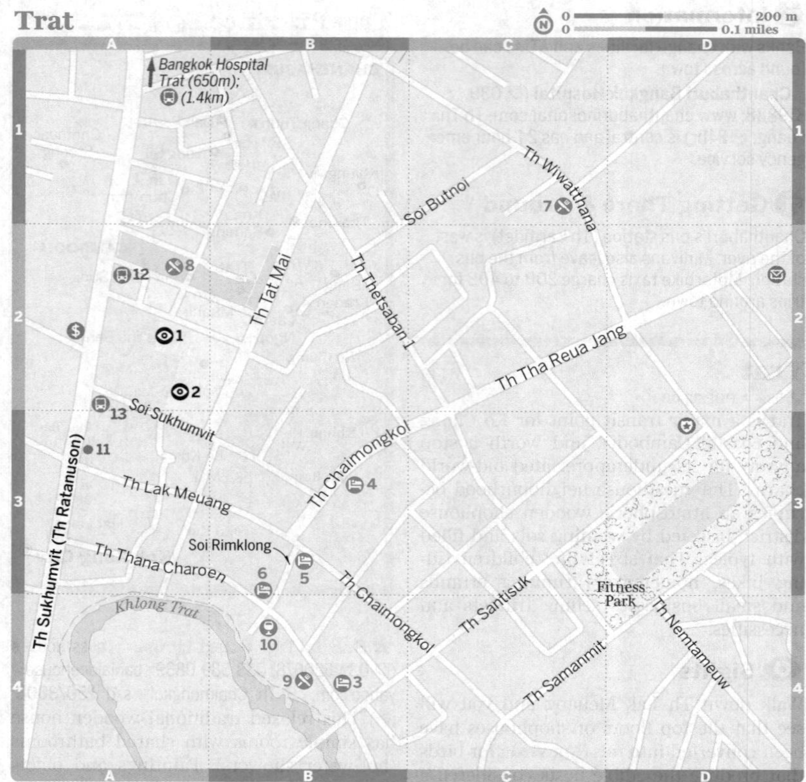

Trat

Sights
1 Day Market A2
2 Indoor Market A2

Sleeping
3 Artist's Place B4
4 Ban Jai Dee Guest House B3
5 Rimklong Boutique Hotel B3
6 Yotin Guest House B3

Eating
7 Namchok C1
8 Night Market A2
9 Pier 112 ...... B4

Drinking & Nightlife
10 Cafe Oscar B4

Transport
11 Family Tour A3
12 Sŏrng·tăa·ou to Bus Station & Laem Sok A2
13 Sŏrng·tăa·ou to Ko Chang ferries A2

Meuang; s 650B, d 950-1100B, ste 1300B; P ❄ ≋) Run by refined and helpful Mr Tuu, this hotel offers compact, sparkling rooms in the heart of the old part of town. It's well worth booking ahead, as it's often full, and understandably so. Prices are very reasonable for this quality of accommodation; some rooms are in an annexe a few paces down the soi. Out front it does real espresso and cocktails.

Artist's Place GUESTHOUSE $$
(☎082 469 1900; pier.112@hotmail.com; 132/1 Th Thana Charoen; r incl breakfast 300-1100B; P ❄ ≋) The individually decorated rooms, and pieces of art dotted around the adjoining garden,

come courtesy of the owner, Mr Phukhao. Cheaper rooms with fans share bathrooms, but are dark and lack the same character. Check in at Pier 112 restaurant opposite.

Eating & Drinking

Trat is all about market eating: head to the **day market** (ตลาด; Th Tat Mai; ⏲6am-5pm) for *gah·faa bohrahn* (ancient coffee), the **night market** (off Th Sukhumvit; mains from 30B; ⏲5-9pm), or the indoor market (p141) for lunch-time noodles. Food stalls line Th Sukhumvit come nightfall.

★Namchok THAI $$
(Th Wiwatthana; mains 100-250B; ⏲10am-10pm) This uncomplicated open-walled restaurant is deservedly a local favourite, with some excellent seafood dishes and well-meaning service from an army of young helpers. The unpriced English menu could be better translated, but they get ostrich right, and there are some other intriguing dishes: try the raw softshell crab salad. It's only sign-posted in Thai: look for the Coke and Chang logos.

Pier 112 THAI $$
(132/1 Th Thana Charoen; mains 80-250B; ⏲10.30am-9pm; 📶✍) In the old town by the river, Pier 112 has a large selection of vegetarian dishes, as well as reliable curries. You can eat outside in a plant-festooned garden. Service can be on the slow side, but what's the hurry?

Cafe Oscar BAR
(Th Thana Charoen; ⏲4.30pm-late) An eclectic crew of locals and expats gather at this cubbyhole corner bar, with wooden furniture and a retro 1970s and '80s soundtrack. In high season it opens during the day too.

Information

Th Sukhumvit runs through town, though it is often called Th Ratanuson. This is where you'll find the bulk of banks and ATMs.

Bangkok Hospital Trat (☎039 552777; www.bangkoktrathospital.com; 376 Mu 2, Th Sukhumvit; ⏲24hr) Located 400m north of the town centre, this hospital offers the best health care in the area.

Krung Thai Bank (Th Sukhumvit; ⏲8.30am-4.30pm Mon-Fri) Has an ATM and currency-exchange facilities.

Police Station (☎24hr 1155; cnr Th Santisuk & Th Wiwatthana) A short walk from Trat's centre.

Post Office (Th Tha Reua Jang; ⏲8.30am-4.30pm Mon-Fri, 9am-noon Sat & Sun) East of Trat's commercial centre.

Getting There & Away

AIR

Bangkok Airways (☎039 525767; www.bangkokair.com; Trat Airport; ⏲8.30am-6.30pm) operates three daily flights to/from Bangkok's Suvarnabhumi International Airport (one hour).

BUSES FROM TRAT

Trat's bus station is 2km out of town, and serves the following destinations:

DESTINATION	FARE (B)	DURATION (HR)	FREQUENCY
Bangkok Eastern (Ekamai) Bus Terminal	256	4½	hourly 6am-11.30pm
Bangkok Northern (Mo Chit) Bus Terminal	265	5½	4 daily
Bangkok Suvarnabhumi International Airport	245	4-4½	5 daily
Chanthaburi	70	1	every 2hr 8.15am-6pm

There are also minivans to the following destinations:

DESTINATION	FARE (B)	DURATION (HR)	FREQUENCY
Bangkok Eastern (Ekamai) Bus Terminal	280	4	every 2hr 8.30am-4.30pm
Bangkok Northern (Mo Chit) Bus Terminal	280	4	every 2hr 8.30am-4.30pm
Chanthaburi	70	50min	frequent 6am-6pm
Hat Lek (for the border with Cambodia)	120	1½	hourly 5am-6pm
Pattaya	300	3½	every 2hr 8am-6pm
Rayong/Ban Phe (for Ko Samet)	200	3½	every 2hr 8am-6pm

Trat's airport is 40km from town, and taxis into town cost 600B; try to hail a *sŏrng·tăa·ou*.

BOAT

To/from Ko Chang

The piers that handle boat traffic to/from Ko Chang are located west of Laem Ngop, about 30km southwest of Trat. There are three piers, each used by different boat companies, but the most convenient services are through **Koh Chang Ferry** (☎039 555188; Laem Ngop; adult/child/car one way 80/30/120B; ⌚6.30am-7pm), from Tha Thammachat, and **Centrepoint Ferry** (☎039 538196; Laem Ngop; adult one way/return 80/150B, child one way/return 40/70B, car one way/return 100/180B; ⌚hourly 6am-7.30pm, to 7pm May-Oct), from Tha Centrepoint.

Sŏrng·tăa·ou (Th Sukhumvit) to Laem Ngop and the piers (50B to 60B per person, 300B for the whole vehicle, 40 minutes) leave from Th Sukhumvit, just past the market. It should be the same charter price if you want to go directly from Trat's bus station to the pier.

From Bangkok, you can catch a bus from Bangkok's Eastern (Ekamai) station all the way to Tha Centrepoint (250B, five hours, three morning departures). This route includes a stop at Suvarnabhumi (airport) bus station as well as Trat's bus station. In the reverse direction, buses have two afternoon departures from Laem Ngop.

To/from Ko Kut

Ferries to Ko Kut run from the pier at **Laem Sok** (p157), 22km southeast of Trat, the nearest bus transfer point. If you prebook, the boat operators offer free transport from central Trat or its bus station (but not the airport) to the pier.

There's no public transport between Laem Ngop and Laem Sok piers; think 400B to 500B for a taxi. In high season, you won't need this option, as you can travel directly between Ko Chang and Ko Kut.

BUS

A useful minivan operator is **Family Tour** (☎081 940 7380; Th Sukhumvit), with services to Bangkok, as well as to Phnom Penh and Siem Reap.

Getting Around

Motorbike taxis charge 20B to 30B for local hops.

Local *sŏrng·tăa·ou* leave from **Th Sukhumvit** near the market for the bus station (20B to 60B, depending on the number of passengers). Chartering one to the airport costs 600B.

Motorbikes can be rented for 150B to 200B a day along Th Sukhumvit near the guesthouse area.

OFF THE BEATEN TRACK

HAT MAI RUT

The sliver of Trat Province that extends southeast towards Cambodia is fringed by sandy beaches. One of the easiest beaches to reach is Hat Mai Rut, roughly halfway between Trat and the border crossing of Hat Lek. Nearby is a traditional fishing village filled with colourful wooden boats and the sights and smells of a small-scale industry carried on by generations of families. **Mairood Resort** (☎089 841 4858; www.mairood-resort.com; 28 Mu 6, Khlong Yai; bungalows incl breakfast 1650B-2250B, huts 750B; P ❄ @ 📶 ≋ 🐾) is a lovely spot to stay overnight, with cottages by the sea and in the mangroves.

You can get to Hat Mai Rut from the Trat bus station via Hat Lek–bound *sŏrng·tăa·ou*. The resort is 3km from the Km 53 highway marker.

Around 7km beyond here, Hat Ban Chun has several resorts and hotels.

Ko Chang เกาะช้าง

☎039 / POP 10,000

With steep, jungle-covered peaks, picturesque Ko Chang (Elephant Island) retains its remote and rugged spirit – despite the transformation of parts of it into a package-tour destination. Sweeping bays are sprinkled along the west coast; most have superfine sand, some have pebbles. What it lacks in sand it makes up for in an unlikely combination: accessible wilderness with a thriving party scene.

Because of its relative remoteness, it is only in the last 20 years or so that tourists have arrived. Today, it is still a slog to get here, but the resorts are now busy with package tourists, Cambodia-bound backpackers and island-hopping couples funnelling through to more remote islands in the marine park. Along the populous west coast are sprawling minitowns that have outpaced the island's infrastructure. For a taste of old-school Chang, head to the southeastern villages and mangrove forests of Ban Salak Phet and Ban Salak Kok.

GETTING TO CAMBODIA: HAT LEK TO CHAM YEAM

Getting to the border From Trat, the closest Thai–Cambodia crossing is from Hat Lek to the Cambodian town of Cham Yeam, and then on to Ko Kong. Minivans run to Hat Lek hourly from 5am to 6pm (120B, 1½ hours) from Trat's bus station.

At the border Attempts to overcharge for the Cambodian visa (officially US$30) at this border are common; they may quote the e-visa rate (US$36) or demand payment in Thai baht at an unfavourable exchange rate. You will need a passport photo too. To avoid the hassle, you may feel that just getting an e-visa beforehand is worthwhile. Avoid anyone who says you require a 'medical certificate' or other paperwork. The border opens at 7am and closes at 8pm.

Thai visas can be renewed at this border, but note that visas at land borders are now limited to two a year. They'll give you 30 days.

Moving on Take a taxi (US$10), túk-túk (US$5) or *moto* (motorcycle taxi; US$3) to Ko Kong where you can catch onward transport to Sihanoukville (four hours, one or two departures per day) and Phnom Penh (five hours, two or three departures until 11.30am).

Sights

West Coast

The west coast is by far the most developed part of Ko Chang, thanks to its beaches and bays. Public *sŏrng·tăa·ou* (passenger pick-up trucks) make beach-hopping easy and affordable. Some beaches are rocky, so it's worth bringing swim booties for children. Most of the time the seas are shallow and gentle but be wary of rips during storms and the rainy season (May to October).

The longest, most luxurious stretch of sand on the island is **Hat Sai Khao** (หาดทรายขาว; White Sands Beach), packed with package-tour hotels and serious sunbathers. Head to the north section of the beach to find the more secluded backpacker spot. Meanwhile **Lonely Beach** (หาดท่าน้ำ) is anything but: this is Ko Chang's backpacker enclave and the liveliest place to be after dark when vodka buckets are passed around and speakers are turned up. **Hat Kai Mook** (หาดไข่มุก) means 'pearl beach', although the 'pearls' here are really just large pebbles that culminate in fish-friendly headlands. Swimming and sunbathing are out but there's good snorkelling.

Ao Khlong Prao (อ่าวคลองพร้าว; Khlong Prao) is a pretty sweep of sand pinned between hulking mountainous headlands and bisected by two estuaries. At low tide, beachcombers stroll the rippled sand eyeing the critters left naked by the receding water. Its companion beach is **Hat Kaibae** (หาดไก่แบ้), a slim strip of sand that unfurls around an island-dotted bay and is a good spot for families and thirty-something couples.

Ban Bang Bao VILLAGE
(บ้านบางเบ้า) At this former fishing community built in the traditional fashion of interconnected piers, the villagers have swapped their nets for renting out portions of their homes to souvenir shops and restaurants. Most visitors come for the excellent seafood and shopping.

East Coast

You will need private transport to explore the peaceful, undeveloped east coast.

Ban Salak Phet VILLAGE
(บ้านสลักเพชร) To discover what Ko Chang was like before the tourists came, visit Ban Salak Phet, in the far southeastern corner. This sleepy community is full of stilt houses, fishing boats and yawning dogs who stretch out on the roadside; it also provides access to some good treks.

Ao Salak Kok BAY
(อ่าวสลักคอก) The dense tangle of mangroves here is protected by a group of fisherfolk who recognise its ecological importance. Mangroves are the ocean's nurseries, fostering the next generation of marine species, as well as resident birds and crustaceans, and this bay is now Ko Chang's prime ecotourism site. Villagers operate an award-winning program to preserve the environment and traditional way of life. They rent kayaks through the Salak Kok Kayak Station (p148) and run an affiliated restaurant.

Ko Chang

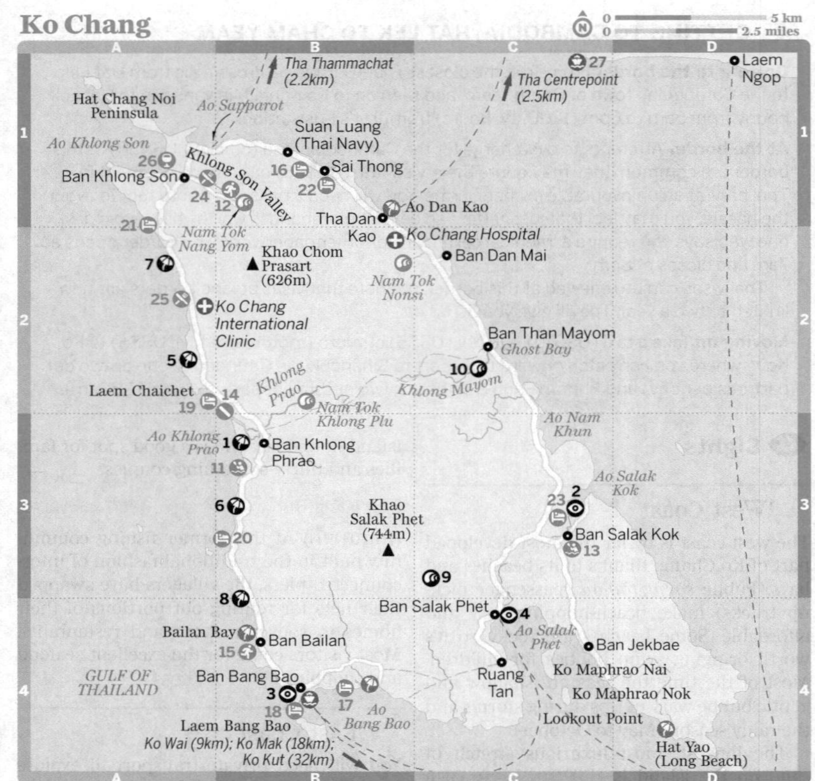

Nam Tok Khiri Phet WATERFALL
(น้ำตกคีรีเพชร) This small waterfall, 2km from Ban Salak Phet, is a 15-minute walk from the road and rewards you with a small, deep plunge pool. It is usually less crowded than many of the larger falls and is easily reached if you are in the neighbourhood of Ao Salak Phet.

Nam Tok Than Mayom WATERFALL
(น้ำตกธารมะยม; park fee 200B; ⏲8am-5pm) A series of three falls along the stream of Khlong Mayom can be reached via the park office near Nam Tha Than Mayom. The view from the top is superb and nearby there are inscribed stones bearing the initials of Rama V, Rama VI and Rama VII.

Activities

Numerous operators offer boat cruises, often with a glass-bottom option and snorkelling stops. Most of these leave from Bang Bao.

Diving & Snorkelling

The dive sites near Ko Chang offer a variety of coral, fish and beginner-friendly shallow waters.

The seamounts off the southern tip of the island within the Mu Ko Chang National Marine Park are reached within a 30-minute cruise. Popular spots include **Hin Luk Bat** and **Hin Rap**, rocky, coral-encrusted seamounts with depths of around 18m to 20m. These are havens for schooling fish and some turtles. In 2013, near Hin Rap, a 30m gunship was deliberately sunk and now lies on its side.

By far the most pristine diving in the area is around **Ko Rang**, an uninhabited island protected from fishing by its marine park status. Visibility here is much better than near Ko Chang and averages between 10m and 20m. Everyone's favourite dive is **Hin Gadeng** – spectacular rock pinnacles with coral visible to around 28m. On the eastern

Ko Chang

Sights

1 Ao Khlong Prao ... B3
2 Ao Salak Kok ... C3
3 Ban Bang Bao ... B4
4 Ban Salak Phet ... C4
5 Hat Kai Mook ... A2
6 Hat Kaibae ... B3
7 Hat Sai Khao ... A2
8 Lonely Beach ... B4
9 Nam Tok Khiri Phet ... C3
10 Nam Tok Than Mayom ... C2

Activities, Courses & Tours

BB Divers ... (see 3)
11 KayakChang ... B3
12 Koh Chang Animal Project ... B1
13 Salak Kok Kayak Station ... C3
14 Scandinavian Chang Diving Centre ... B2
Scubadawgs ... (see 3)
15 Tree Top Adventure Park ... B4

Sleeping

16 Amber Sands ... B1
Arunee Resort ... (see 7)
17 Bang Bao Beach Resort ... B4
BB Lonely Beach ... (see 8)
Buddha View ... (see 3)
Chill ... (see 6)
18 Cliff Cottage ... B4
El Greco ... (see 3)
Garden Resort ... (see 6)
Green Resort ... (see 6)
Independent Bo's ... (see 7)
Little Eden ... (see 8)
Mangrove Hideaway ... (see 4)
Oasis Koh Chang ... (see 8)
19 Pajamas Hostel ... A2
Paradise Cottage ... (see 8)
20 Porn's Bungalows ... B3
21 Rock Sand Resort ... A1
22 Serenity Resort ... B1
23 Spa Koh Chang Resort ... C3
Starbeach Bungalows ... (see 7)
Warapura Resort ... (see 8)

Eating

Barrio Bonito ... (see 6)
24 Blues Blues Restaurant ... A1
Oodie's Place ... (see 7)
25 Paul's Restaurant ... A2
Porn's Bungalows Restaurant ... (see 20)
Saffron on the Sea ... (see 5)

Drinking & Nightlife

26 Shambhala ... A1

Information

Bang Bao Health Centre ... (see 3)
Nuttakit Tour ... (see 3)

Transport

Sawadee Koh Chang Travel ... (see 6)
27 Speedboats to Ko Mak and Ko Wai ... C1

side of Ko Rang, **Hin Kuak Maa** (also known as Three Finger Reef) is another top dive spot and is home to a coral-encrusted wall sloping from 2m to 14m and attracting swarms of marine life.

Ko Yak, **Ko Tong Lang** and **Ko Laun** are shallow dives perfect for both beginners and advanced divers. These small rocky islands can be circumnavigated and have lots of coral, schooling fish, pufferfish, morays, barracuda, rays and the occasional turtle.

About 7km offshore from Ban Bang Bao there's a popular dive to the wreck of the **HTMS Chang**, a 100m-long former Thai naval vessel purposely sunk in 2012 to form an artificial reef that now sits 30m beneath the surface.

Reef-fringed Ko Wai (p158) features a good variety of colourful hard and soft corals and is great for snorkelling. It is a popular day-tripping island but has simple overnight accommodation for more alone time with the reef.

The snorkelling on **Ko Mak** is not as good, but the island offers some decent dives, even if the reefs don't see as many fish as elsewhere.

One-day diving trips typically start at 3000B. Think 15,000B per person for PADI or other certification. Many dive shops remain open during the rainy season (May to October) but visibility and sea conditions are generally poor.

BB Divers DIVING
(☎039 558040; www.bbdivers.com; Bang Bao; 2 boat dives 3000B) Based at Bang Bao, this well-run diving outfit has branches in Lonely Beach and Hat Sai Khao, as well as outposts on Ko Kut and Ko Mak (high season only).

Scubadawgs DIVING
(☎080 038 5166; www.scuba-dawgs.com; Bang Bao; 2 boat dives 3000B) This upbeat outfit is helpful and customer focused. It does PADI and RAID certification.

Scandinavian Chang Diving Centre DIVING
(☎039 619022; www.changdiving.com; Ban Khlong Prao) Professional diving set-up with excellent instructors and equipment, offering a

good range of excursions and courses, including some aimed at families and kids.

Kayaking

Ko Chang cuts an impressive and heroic profile when viewed from the sea aboard a kayak. The water is generally calm and offshore islands provide a paddling destination that is closer than the horizon. Many hotels rent open-top kayaks (from 300B per day) that are convenient for near-shore outings and noncommittal kayakers; some provide them for free. Contact **KayakChang** (☎097 182 8319; www.kayakchang.com; Emerald Cove Resort, Khlong Prao; kayaks per day from 1000B) for more serious apparatus.

Salak Kok Kayak Station KAYAKING
(Chang Spirit Club; ☎087 748 9497; Baan Salak Kok; kayak rental per hour 200B) On the east side of the island, explore the mangrove swamps of Ao Salak Kok while supporting an award-winning ecotour program. Salak Kok Kayak Station rents self-guided kayaks and is a village work project designed to promote tourism without affecting the traditional way of life. They can also help arrange wooden-boat trips with a guide (200B), village homestays and hiking tours.

Hiking & Ziplining

Ko Chang isn't just about the beaches. The island has a well-developed trekking scene, with inland routes that lead to lush forests filled with birds, monkeys and flora. A handful of English-speaking guides grew up near the jungle and are happy to share their secrets.

Though the inadequate national park map shows a walking trail traversing the island, this is long overgrown: don't try it without a guide.

Mr Tan HIKING
(☎089 645 2019; hikes 600-1400B) A hiking guide with good English, Mr Tan offers ascents of Khao Chom Prasart, full-day treks to and around the Khlong Prao waterfall and easier family-friendly routes.

Jungle Fever HIKING
(☎081 588 3324; www.junglefever.in.th) Jungle Fever offers half-day (700B) and full-day (1200B) treks, including the waterfall-to-waterfall island traverse. It also offers ascents of the island's principal mountains and has dedicated walks for birdwatchers.

Evolution Tour TREKKING
(☎039 557078; www.evolutiontour.com) If you're interested in hiking in the island's interior, you can arrange guides with this agency as the ranger stations around the island aren't very useful for solo trekkers.

Tree Top Adventure Park ADVENTURE SPORTS
(www.treetopadventurepark.com; Ao Bailan; 1100B; 9am-5pm) Swing through the jungle like Tarzan, walk the rope bridges, or ride the ziplines, flying skateboards and bicycles at this popular attraction. Close to Bailan Bay, this is a two-hour adventure. Add on 150B for transport there and back. All tour agencies around Ko Chang can book it. No flip-flops or under sevens.

Volunteering

Koh Chang Animal Project VOLUNTEERING
(☎089 042 2347; www.kohchanganimalproject.org; Ban Khlong Son) Abused, injured or abandoned animals receive medical care and refuge at this nonprofit centre. With local people it also works on general veterinarian services and spaying and neutering. Volunteers and donations are welcome. Travelling vets and vet nurses often drop by, while

HOW TO SPEND A WEEK ON KO CHANG

First day just lie on the beach, rotate your body and repeat, with occasional forays into the ocean. On day two, rouse yourself out of your sun-induced stupor to explore the island. Do a day hike through the jungle or view the island from aboard a kayak. Catch a *sŏrng·tăa·ou* (passenger pick-up truck) to Ban Bang Bao (p145) for lunch or an early dinner, followed by souvenir shopping. The next day rent a motorbike and explore the mangrove forest and fishing villages of the east coast (p145). On day four, hit the beach again or go diving (p146).

Head to Ko Mak (p157) for some snorkelling or across to Ko Wai (p158) for powder-soft sands, or devote a day or two to giving back to the island by lending a hand at the Koh Chang Animal Project.

nonvets are needed to help with numerous odd jobs. Call to make an appointment.

Most *sŏrng·tăa·ou* drivers know how to get here; tell them you are going to 'Ban Lisa' (Lisa's House) in Khlong Son. If you have a bike, turn off the main road in Ban Khlong Son at the 7-Eleven; the project is 1.5km down the road.

Massage

Sima Massage MASSAGE

(081 489 5171; Khlong Prao; massage per hour 250-400B; 8am-10pm) Sima is regarded by locals as the best massage on the island – quite an accolade in a place where a massage is easier to find than a 7-Eleven. It's on the main drag through Khlong Prao.

Courses

Koh Chang Thai Cookery School COOKING

(039 557243; www.kohchangcookery.com; Blue Lagoon Bungalows, Khlong Prao; courses 1500B) Break up your lazy days with classes designed to enhance mind and body. Classes are typically five hours and include a market tour; book ahead. Slices, dices and sautés are performed in a shady open-air kitchen beside the estuary.

Sleeping

In general, rates have risen while quality has not, partly because hotels catering to group tours are guaranteed occupancy and don't have to maintain standards to woo repeat visitors or walk-ins. There is also a lot of copy-cat pricing, giving value-oriented visitors little choice.

On the west coast, Lonely Beach is still the best budget option, Hat Kaibae is the best-value option and Hat Sai Khao is the most overpriced.

Lonely Beach

One of the cheapest places to sleep on the island, though budget spots smack on the beach are harder to find. Ignored by the flashy resorts, the streets are filled with grungy bars and cheap guesthouses.

★**Paradise Cottage** BUNGALOW $

(081 773 9337; www.paradisecottageresort.com; 104/1 Mu 1; r basic/fan/sea view 450/990/1700B; P ❄) With house music as a backdrop, hammock-clad pavilions facing the sea and compact, handsome rooms, well-run Paradise Cottage is a gloriously relaxing retreat. The sea-view rooms have air-con and a marvellous outlook, while the cheapest ones have fans but lack hot water and sockets. At low tide a sandbank just beyond the rocks can be reached. Off-season prices are great.

Little Eden BUNGALOW $

(084 867 7459; www.littleedenkohchang.com; Soi 3; r with fan/air-con 950/1500B; P ❄) On the quiet side of the main road, but still close to the beach, Little Eden has a series of wooden bungalows, all connected by an intricate lattice of wooden walkways. Rooms are comfortable with a terrace, wooden floors and mosquito nets: expect plenty of chirping noise from forest critters.

There are good breakfasts and other meals, a pleasant communal area and friendly staff.

BB Lonely Beach HOSTEL $

(089 504 0543; www.bblonelybeach.com; dm 250B, r with fan 500-700B;) One of the only dorms within reach of the beach, this has basic and stuffy – but decent – shared and private rooms at bargain rates. There's plenty to do here, with a dive school, a gym, Belgian beers and a pool: it's a great spot to meet fellow travellers.

It's surrounded by bars so this is definitely one for party folk.

Oasis Koh Chang BUNGALOW $$

(081 721 2547; www.oasis-kohchang.com; 4/28 Mu 1; r 550-1600B; P ❄) Literally the top place in Lonely Beach – largely due to its hillside location – Oasis has great sea views, and the scene from its 12m-tall tree house is even more impressive. Run by a friendly Dutch couple, it has roomy, midrange bungalows in four categories. Cheaper rooms are fan-only.

Warapura Resort HOTEL $$

(039 558123; www.warapuraresort.com; 4/3 Mu 1; r incl breakfast 1700-3300B; P ❄ @) Right by the sea, Warapura has a series of excellent rooms lightly decorated with rustic furniture and a white colour scheme with turquoise trim. Higher-priced rooms are larger and closer to the sea, with great balconies and huge bathrooms. Though the beach isn't really swimmable just here, the sound of the waves and the decent pool make up for it.

Hat Kaibae

Hat Kaibae has some of the island's best variety of accommodation, from boutique hotels to budget huts and midrange bungalows. The trade-off is that the beach is only sandy in parts.

Porn's Bungalows BUNGALOW $
(☎080 613 9266; www.pornsbungalows-kohchang.com; r 600-1600B; P) This is a very chilled spot at the far western end of Kaibae beach, with a popular on-site restaurant. All of the wooden bungalows are fan-only. The beachfront bungalows are larger, have a great outlook, and are a fab deal at around 1000B. They can't be booked ahead, so you might have to find somewhere else first in busy periods.

Garden Resort HOTEL $$
(☎039 557260; www.gardenresortkohchang.com; 98/22 Mu 4; r incl breakfast 2200-3500B; P@) Just off the main road and yet secluded, Garden Resort has large, rather charming bungalows dotted either side of a shady garden pathway that leads to a pleasant swimming pool area. The bar and restaurant at the front are popular hang-outs. It's a short stroll to a sandy stretch of beach.

Green Resort BUNGALOW $$
(☎097 110 7094; www.thegreen-kohchang.com; 51/3 Mu 4; r 1200B; P) Just off the strip in Hat Kaibae, this resort nevertheless achieves tranquillity with its pleasingly attractive, if darkish, modern rooms around a lawn. Staff are friendly and helpful and the rooms are well-equipped, with decent wi-fi, cable TV and fridges.

Chill RESORT $$$
(☎039 552555; www.thechillresort.com; r incl breakfast 5250-14,400B; P@) Cleverly designed, with all ground-floor rooms opening onto one of three pools, Chill has contemporary, bright rooms with loads of space and bags of facilities. It's right on the beach and has good family-friendly features and very helpful staff.

Khlong Prao

Ao Khlong Prao is dominated by high-end resorts, with a few budget spots peppered in between.

★ **Pajamas Hostel** HOSTEL $
(☎039 510789; www.pajamaskohchang.com; Khlong Prao; dm/r incl breakfast 570/2600B; P) A couple of kilometres north of the main Khlong Prao strip and by the beach, this superb hostel oozes relaxation, with an open-plan lounge and bar overlooking the swimming pool. Good modern air-con dorms are upstairs, while the private rooms are really excellent, with platform beds, a cool, light feel and your own terrace/balcony. It's all spotless, and exceedingly well run.

★ **Baan Rim Nam** GUESTHOUSE $$
(☎087 005 8575; www.iamkohchang.com; Khlong Prao; r 1000-1900B;) This marvellously converted fishers house is right over the mangrove-lined river estuary and makes a supremely peaceful place to stay. Cool, appealing rooms open onto a wonderful waterside deck. The owner is a mine of information and keen that visitors enjoy what the region has to offer. Free kayaks and canoes are provided – the beach is a three-minute paddle away.

Blue Lagoon Bungalows BUNGALOW $$
(☎089 515 4617; www.kohchang-bungalows-bluelagoon.com; Ban Khlong Phrao; bungalows 800-2000B; P) Set beside a scenic estuary, Blue Lagoon has an eclectic bunch of bungalows and rooms arrayed in a rustic manner across a riverside mangrove with a walkway to the beach. They all have different layouts and design schemes; check out the elephant dung family room.

Dewa RESORT $$$
(☎039 557341; www.thedewakohchang.com; Khlong Prao; r incl breakfast 5100-12000B; P@) The top luxury pad in these parts, everything about Dewa is chic, from the dark-bottomed 700-sq-metre pool to the contemporary Thai-style rooms that are a design dream. Expect big discounts if booking early.

Ban Bang Bao & Around

Accommodation options are mainly converted pier houses overlooking the sea, with easy access to departing interisland ferries and lovely Khlong Kloi beach just east. Night owls should hire a motorbike or stay elsewhere, as *sŏrng·tăa·ou* become rare and expensive after dinnertime.

DON'T FEED THE ANIMALS!

On many of the around-the-island boat tours, operators amaze their guests with a stop at a rocky cliff to feed the wild monkeys. It seems innocent enough, and even entertaining, but there's an unfortunate consequence. The animals become dependent on this food source and when the boats don't come as often during the low season the young and vulnerable ones are ill-equipped to forage in the forest.

The same goes for the dive or boat trips that feed the fish leftover lunches, or bread bought on the pier specifically for this purpose. It might be a fantastic way to see a school of brilliantly coloured fish, but they then forsake the coral reefs for an easier meal, and without the daily grooming efforts of the fish the coral is soon overgrown with algae and will eventually suffocate.

Cliff Cottage BUNGALOW $

(☎080 823 5495; www.cliff-cottage.com; Ban Bang Bao; bungalows 950-1100B; ❄📶) Partially hidden on a verdant hillside west of the pier are a few dozen simple, comfortable huts overlooking a rocky cove with water on both sides. Most have sea views and a couple offer spectacular vistas.

★**Buddha View** GUESTHOUSE $$

(☎039 558157; www.thebuddhaview.com; Ban Bang Bao; r 800-1400B; ❄📶) This swish pier guesthouse is very easy on the eye. There are just seven thoughtfully designed, all-wood rooms, four of which come with private bathrooms (the shared ones are excellent anyway). The restaurant is great too: sit at the cutaway tables and dangle your feet over the water and sculptures below.

★**Bang Bao Beach Resort** BUNGALOW $$

(☎093 327 2788; www.bangbaobeachresort.com; Hat Khlong Koi; r 1700-2500B) Very sprucely set along green lawn right on super Khlong Koi beach, just east of Bang Bao, this is a marvellous spot. Old and new bungalows are available; both are attractively wooden and air-conditioned. It's a very efficiently run spot with easy access to beach bars and restaurants alongside. Walk along the beach from the canal bridge or drive the long way round.

El Greco GUESTHOUSE $$

(☎086 843 8417; elgrecoloungebar@gmail.com; Ban Bang Bao; r 1400-1600B; ❄📶) Run by a genial family, this has an excellent location halfway along Bang Bao pier. Rooms are simple but attractive, with mosquito nets, balconies and slightly hard beds. The on-site Greek restaurant is worth a look.

Hat Sai Khao

The island's prettiest beach is also its most expensive. Close to the finest sand, the northern and southern extremities have some budget and midrange options. There's a groovy backpacker enclave north of KC Grande Resort, accessible only via the beach.

Independent Bo's GUESTHOUSE $

(☎039 551165; r 300-800B; 📶) Quirky and enchanting, this is an old-school bohemian budget place right on the sand. It's a striking sight and experience: a warren of driftwood cabins, common areas and quirky signs with a communal, hippie feel and the sea at your feet. The fan-only rooms are simple and mostly rather charming; bathrooms range from extremely basic to modernised. No reservations (and no children).

Starbeach Bungalows GUESTHOUSE $

(☎089 574 9486; www.starbeach-kohchang.com; bungalows 600-750B; 📶) Right on the prime part of the beach, this ramshackle-looking spot is a glorious place for no-frills sand-and-sea sleeping. Fan-cooled rooms are simple but decent and all look out towards the water. There's a friendly on-site bar and restaurant. No reservations: text to see if there's a vacancy. Head towards the beach down the side of the 7-Eleven and turn right.

Rock Sand Resort GUESTHOUSE $$

(☎084 781 0550; www.rocksand-resort.com; r incl breakfast with fan/air-con 1000/3500B; P❄📶) Touting itself as a flashpacker destination, this is the most upmarket of the knot of places at the north end of White Sand Beach, but feels overpriced in summer. The sea-view rooms are, however, decent and share a balcony. Cheaper rooms are plain. Waves

PEAK SEASON PRICES

During the wet season (May to October) rates drop precipitously, although many places close altogether. Consider booking ahead and shopping for online discounts during peak season (November to March), weekends and holidays.

beat against the foundations; be prepared to wade here at high tide. You can get a vehicle here via the scarily steep road to White Sand Beach Resort.

Arunee Resort GUESTHOUSE $$
(086 111 9600; aruneeresorttour@hotmail.com; r incl breakfast with fan/air-con 500/1500B;) Recent renovations mean the super-cheap rooms have been replaced by bright and breezy ones. Arunee is set back from the main road and is a 50m-walk to the beach. It's not flash, but the price is OK for this location.

Interior & East Coast

You will likely need your own transport to not feel lonely out in the less developed parts of the island, but you'll be rewarded with a quieter, calmer experience.

★ **Mangrove Hideaway** GUESTHOUSE $$
(080 133 6600; www.themangrovehideaway.com; Ban Salak Phet; r 1900-2700B;) Facing the mangrove forest, this environmentally friendly guesthouse is a fabulous spot. Crisp, attractive rooms face the verdant front garden, while the sumptuous superior suites have gorgeous wooden floors and overlook the dining area and mangroved river estuary. There's an open-air jacuzzi and massage area upstairs; the resort was made using locally sourced wood and employs local villagers.

Serenity Resort HOTEL $$
(088 092 4452; www.serenity-koh-chang.com; Ao Dan Kao; r 2800-3200B;) Not far from the ferries, on the peaceful east side of the island, this well-presented spot has serene, cool white rooms with impressive towel-folding skills on show, even by Thai standards. Friendly, modern and spotless, the complex is right on the beach, where there's a bar and pool. Kayaks and SUPs are on hand.

Amber Sands HOTEL $$$
(039 586177; www.ambersandsbeachresort.com; Ao Dan Kao; r 3250-5250B; mid-Oct–Aug;) Right on a quiet orangey-red sand beach, this is an impeccably run place set around a beautifully kept garden. Rooms have wonderful wooden floors, elegant furnishings and are very easy on the eye. The outlook is perfect for relaxation. The restaurant opens to nonguests at mealtimes. It feels a world away but is close to the ferries; they'll arrange pick-up for you.

Spa Koh Chang Resort RESORT $$$
(083 115 6566; www.thespakohchang.com; Ao Salak Kok; r incl breakfast 2150-4000B;) Specialising in health-care packages, including fasting, yoga and meditation, this resort has lush, peaceful surroundings that almost touch the bay's mangrove forests. Elegantly decorated bungalows scramble up a flower-filled hillside providing a peaceful getaway for some quality 'me' time. The restaurant has vegan and veggie options. The 'hill' options are far lighter than the 'oriental' rooms. There's no beach access.

Eating & Drinking

Virtually all of the island's accommodation choices have attached restaurants with adequate but not outstanding fare. It's usually worth seeking places outside; there's some very decent eating to be done on the island.

Parties abound on the beaches and range from the more mature, restrained scene on Hat Sai Khao, to the younger and more frenetic one on Lonely Beach.

West Coast

Porn's Bungalows Restaurant THAI $
(Hat Kaibae; mains 80-180B; 11am-11pm;) This laid-back, dark-wood restaurant is the quintessential beachside lounge. Great barbecue. Feel free to have your drinks out-size your meal and don't worry about dressing up for dinner.

★ **Phu-Talay** SEAFOOD $$
(039 551300; 4/2 Mu 4, Khlong Prao; mains 120-320B; 10am-10pm) A beautiful place right on the *klorng*, Phu-Talay has cute wooden-floored, blue-and-white decor, a picturesque deck and its own boat (for pick-up up from nearby accommodations). It specialises in seafood, with standout softshell crab,

prawns and other fish dishes. It's far more reasonably priced than many other seafood places.

★ **Barrio Bonito** MEXICAN $$
(☎080 092 8208; www.barriobonito.com; Hat Kaibae; mains 160-280B; ⏲5-10pm Jul-late May; 📶 ✎) Fab fajitas and cracking cocktails are served by a charming French-Mexican couple at this roadside spot in the middle of Kaibae. Offering authentic, delicious, beautifully presented food and stylish surroundings, this is one of the island's finest places to eat.

Saffron on the Sea THAI $$
(☎039 551253; Hat Kai Mook; mains 120-350B; ⏲8am-10pm; 📶) Owned by an arty escapee from Bangkok, this friendly little boutique bungalow complex has a beautiful seafront dining area and a relaxed, romantic atmosphere. All the Thai dishes are prepared in the island style, more sweet than spicy. The menu is somewhat reduced off-season. The rooms (1200B to 1500B in high season) are attractive too; all face the front.

Baanta THAI $$
(www.facebook.com/baantaorchidrestaurant; Khlong Prao; mains 120-320B; ⏲noon-10pm; 📶) Baanta is an attractive main-road spot offering personable service and a wide choice of dishes, from Thai classics to regional specialities, seafood blowouts and a range of Western dishes and Japanese-influenced salmon plates. It's a reliably pleasant spot.

Oodie's Place INTERNATIONAL, THAI $$
(☎039 551193; www.facebook.com/oodies.place; Hat Sai Khao; mains 80-390B; ⏲11am-midnight) Local musician Oodie runs a nicely diverse operation with excellent French food, tasty Thai specialities, pizzas and live blues music from 10pm. After all these years, it is still beloved by expats.

Paul's Restaurant GERMAN, THAI $$
(☎039 551499; www.topresort-kohchang.com; Hat Sai Khao; mains 140-330B; ⏲6am-10pm; 📶) Quality cooking in big portions is served up at this clifftop hotel restaurant, along with side orders of sarcasm from the entertaining owner. The menu covers both German and Thai bases. You'll need to book ahead in high season, as it's deservedly popular.

Ka-Ti Culinary THAI $$
(☎081 903 0408; www.facebook.com/katikhruathai; Khlong Prao; 160-510B; ⏲noon-10pm Mon-Sat, 5-10pm Sun; 📶) Seafood, a few Isan dishes and their famous, homemade curry sauce are the best bets here. The menu features creative smoothies, featuring lychee, lemon and peppermint, and there's a children's menu. Daily specials might feature whole steamed snapper and other fishy delights.

Up2You THAI $$
(Khlong Prao; mains 120-300B; ⏲10am-10pm; 📶) With a nice line in seafood, this main-road spot near the 7-Eleven offers solid value and a welcoming atmosphere. Tasty scallop stir-fries and prawn dishes are highlights, but it's all pretty flavourful. Portion sizes aren't huge.

Interior & East Coast

★ **Blues Blues Restaurant** THAI $
(☎087 144 6412; Ban Khlong Son; mains 80-170B; ⏲9am-9pm) Through the green screen of tropical plants is an arty stir-fry hut that is beloved for its expertise, efficiency and economy. The owner's delicate watercolour paintings are on display too. Take the road to Ban Kwan Chang; it's 600m ahead on the right.

★ **Shambhala** BAR
(☎098 579 4381; www.shambhalabeachbar.com; Siam Royal View, Ao Khlong Son; ⏲11am-10pm or later Thu-Tue) Perched at the top of the island, this poolside bar has some excellent, fairly priced cocktails and a magnificent outlook across green lawn to a secluded golden sweep of beach and forested peninsula. It's the perfect spot for a sundowner; there are also quality Thai and international dishes. Enter via the southernmost 'Marina' entrance to the Siam Royal View complex.

ℹ Information

DANGERS & ANNOYANCES

- Take extreme care when driving from Ban Khlong Son south to Hat Sai Khao, as the road is steep and treacherous, with several hairpin turns. There are mud slides and poor conditions during storms. If you do rent a motorbike, ride carefully between Hat Kaibae and Lonely Beach, especially in the rainy season. Wear protective clothing when riding on a motorcycle.
- The police conduct regular drug raids on the island's accommodation. If you get caught with narcotics, you could face heavy fines or imprisonment.
- Be aware of the cheap minibus tickets from Siem Reap to Ko Chang; these usually involve

some sort of time- and money-wasting commission scam.

➡ Ko Chang is considered a low-risk malarial zone, meaning that liberal use of mosquito repellent is probably an adequate precaution.

EMERGENCY

Head to the **tourist police station** (☎1155; Khlong Prao) in Khlong Prao for any need.

MEDICAL SERVICES

Bang Bao Health Centre (☎039 558086; Ban Bang Bao; ⏲8.30am-4pm) For the basics. On the pier.

Ko Chang Hospital (☎039 586131; Ban Dan Mai) Public hospital with a good reputation and affordably priced care; south of the ferry terminal.

Ko Chang International Clinic (☎039 551555; www.bangkoktrathospital.com; Hat Sai Khao; ⏲24hr) Related to the Bangkok Hospital Group; accepts most health insurance and has expensive rates.

MONEY

There are banks with ATMs and exchange facilities along all the west-coast beaches.

POST

Ko Chang Post Office (☎039 551240; Hat Sai Khao; ⏲9am-5pm) At the far southern end of Hat Sai Khao.

TRAVEL AGENCIES

Nuttakit Tour (☎092 647 3009; nuttakit tour@gmail.com; Bang Bao) The first agency on the right after entering Bang Bao's pier itself, this is a step ahead of the rest, with helpful English-speaking staff who can arrange tailored boat trips as well as the usual excursions.

TOURIST INFORMATION

➡ The free magazine *Koh Chang Guide* (www.koh-chang-guide.com) is widely available on the island and has handy beach maps.

➡ The comprehensive website I Am Koh Chang (www.iamkohchang.com) is a labour of love from an irreverent Brit living on the island. It's jam-packed with opinion and information.

ℹ Getting There & Away

Whether starting from Bangkok or Cambodia, it is an all-day haul to reach Ko Chang. Overnighting in Trat is a pleasant way to break the journey.

Ferries from the mainland (Laem Ngop) leave from either Tha Thammachat, operated by Koh Chang Ferry (p144), or Tha Centrepoint with Centrepoint Ferry (p144). Boats from Tha Thammachat arrive at Tha Sapparot, Centrepoint ferries at a pier 3km further south. The Koh Chang ferries are faster and a little better.

Bang Bao Boat (☎084 567 8765; www.kohchangbangbaoboat.com; Ban Bang Bao; ⏲Nov-Apr) runs an interisland ferry that connects Ko Chang with Ko Mak and Ko Wai (with a speedboat connection from there to Ko Kut) during the high season. Boats leave from Bang Bao in the southwest of the island.

Speedboats travel between the islands during high season from both Bang Bao and Hat Kaibae.

It is possible to go to and from Ko Chang from Bangkok's Eastern (Ekamai) bus terminal via Chanthaburi and Trat; there are also direct bus and minibus **services** (☎083-794 2122; www.

TRANSPORT TO/FROM KO CHANG

DEPARTS	DESTINATION	BOAT	BUS
Bangkok's Eastern Bus Terminal (Ekamai)	Tha Thammachat (Laem Ngop)	N/A	269B, 6hr, 2 daily
Ko Chang	Bangkok's Suvarnabhumi International Airport	N/A	single/return 600/900B, 6-7hr, 2-3 daily
Ko Chang	Ko Kut	speedboat 900B, 2½hr, 3 daily; wooden boat plus speedboat 700B, 5hr, 1 daily	N/A
Ko Chang	Ko Mak	speedboat 600B, 1hr, 3 daily; wooden boat 400B, 2hr, 1 daily	N/A
Ko Chang	Ko Wai	speedboat 400B, 30min, 3 daily; wooden boat 300B, 1hr, 1 daily	N/A
Tha Centrepoint (Laem Ngop)	Ko Chang	80B, 40min, hourly 6am-7.30pm	N/A
Tha Thammachat (Laem Ngop)	Ko Chang	80B, 30min, every 45min 6.30am-7pm	N/A

bussuvarnabhumikohchang.com) from Bangkok's Suvarnabhumi International Airport.

The closest airport is in Trat. **Ko Chang Minibus** (☎ 087 785 7695; www.kohchangminibus.com) offers a variety of transfer packages from airport to beach.

Getting Around

Shared *sŏrng·tăa·ou* meet arriving boats to shuttle passengers to the various beaches (Hat Sai Khao 100B, Khlong Prao 150B and Lonely Beach 200B). Hops between neighbouring beaches range from 50B to 200B but prices rise dramatically after dark, when it can cost 500B to travel from Bang Bao to Hat Sai Khao.

Motorbikes can be hired from 200B per day. Ko Chang's hilly and winding roads are dangerous; make sure the bike is in good working order.

Hiring a car is also a decent option. **Sawadee Koh Chang Travel** (☎ 086 712 6804; sawadeekohchang@hotmail.co.th; Hat Kaibae; car per day from 1200B; ⏰ 8am-8.30pm) is one of a couple of places on the island to do so.

Ko Kut

เกาะกูด

☎ 039 / POP 2100

Ko Kut is often feted as the perfect Thai island, and it is hard to argue with such an accolade. The supersoft sands are like talcum powder, the water lapping the bays is clear and there are more coconut palms than buildings.

Unlike its larger neighbour Ko Chang, here you can forget about any nightlife or noise – this is where you come to do almost nothing. If you can be roused from your hammock, kayaking and snorkelling are the main activities (nearby Ko Rang is particularly good for fish-gazing).

Half as big as Ko Chang and the fourth-largest island in Thailand, Ko Kut (also known as Koh Kood) has long been the domain of package-tour resorts and a seclusion-seeking elite. But the island is becoming more egalitarian, and independent travellers, especially families and couples, will find a base here.

Sights & Activities

With its quiet rocky coves and mangrove estuaries, Ko Kut is great for snorkelling and kayaking. Most resorts have equipment on offer.

White-sand beaches with gorgeous aquamarine water are strewn along the western side of the island. **Hat Khlong Chao** is the island's best and could easily compete with Samui's Hat Chaweng in a beach beauty contest. **Ao Noi** is a pretty boulder-strewn beach with a steep drop-off and steady waves for strong swimmers. **Ao Prao** is another lovely sweep of sand.

There is no public transport on Ko Kut, though taxi services exist and you can rent motorbikes for exploring the west-coast beaches. The road is mostly paved from Khlong Hin in the southwest to Ao Noi in the northeast.

Nam Tok Khlong Chao WATERFALL

(น้ำตกคลองเจ้า) Two waterfalls on the island make good destinations for a short hike. The larger and more popular Nam Tok Khlong Chao is wide and pretty with a massive plunge pool. It is a quick jungle walk to the base from the end of the road, or you can kayak up Khlong Chao. Further north is **Nam Tok Khlong Yai Ki**, which is smaller but also has a large pool to cool off in.

Sleeping & Eating

During low season many boats stop running and some bungalow operations close altogether. On weekends and holidays during the high season, holidaying Thais fill the resorts. Call ahead to book so you can be dropped off at the appropriate pier by the speedboat operators or transfer drivers.

Most guesthouses have on-site restaurants but there are also lots of independent places, mainly specialising in seafood.

Mangrove Bungalow BUNGALOW $

(☎ 089 936 2093; www.kohkood-mangrove.com; Hat Khlong Chao; r incl breakfast with fan 700-1000B, with air-con 1500B; ❄📶) With a mangrove forest on one side and the beach a short walk away, this collection of wooden bungalows is immersed in nature. Khlong Chao waterfall is in easy striking distance by kayak or on foot. Rooms are clean and neat and there's a restaurant.

Cozy House GUESTHOUSE $

(☎ 089 094 3650; www.kohkoodcozy.com; Hat Khlong Chao; r incl breakfast 600-1200B; ❄📶) The go-to place for backpackers, Cozy is a 10-minute walk from delightful Hat Khlong Chao. There are cheap and cheerful fan rooms and more comfortable wooden bungalows with air-con.

Ko Mak & Ko Kut

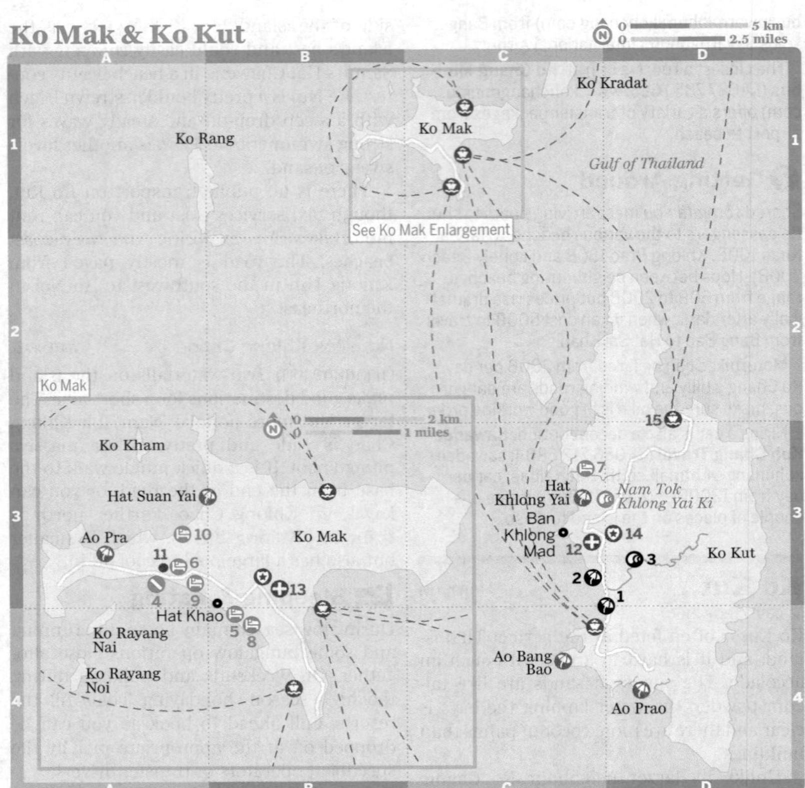

Ko Mak & Ko Kut

Sights
1 Ao Ngam Kho ... D3
2 Hat Khlong Chao ... C3
3 Nam Tok Khlong Chao ... D3

Activities, Courses & Tours
4 Koh Mak Divers ... A3

Sleeping
5 Ao Kao Resort ... B4
6 Baan Koh Mak ... A3
7 Bann Makok ... C3
Cozy House ... (see 2)
Kokut Coconut Garden Resort ... (see 1)
8 Lazy Day Resort ... B4
Mangrove Bungalow ... (see 2)
9 Monkey Island ... A3
10 Seavana ... A3
Tinkerbell Resort ... (see 2)

Eating
Ra Beang Mai ... (see 2)

Information
11 Ball Cafe ... A3
12 Hospital ... C3
13 Ko Mak Health Centre ... B3
14 Police Station ... D3

Transport
15 Ao Salad Pier ... D2

★ **Bann Makok** HOTEL $$
(☎088 203 0699; www.facebook.com/bannmakok; Khlong Yai Ki; r incl breakfast 3200-3800B; P ❄ @ 📶) This boutique hotel, tucked into the mangroves, uses recycled timbers painted in vintage colours to create a maze of eight rooms that resembles a traditional pier fishing village. Common decks and reading

nooks provide peaceful spaces to listen to birdsong or get lost in a book.

Kokut Coconut Garden Resort BUNGALOW $$
(Suan Maphrao; ☎086 833 7999; www.facebook.com/Suan-Maprao-Ko-Kut-Resort-1533121720312175; Ao Ngam Kho; r 1500B; P ❄ ⓦ) You'll get a genuine smile and welcome at this place just off the southern beach road (opposite the seaplane). Excellent modern huts are simple and stylish, with timber cladding and smoothed concrete interiors. They sit a short walk from the beach amid towering coconut palms. It's a lovely spot and is fronted by a decent restaurant.

Tinkerbell Resort RESORT $$$
(☎081 826 1188; www.tinkerbellresort.com; Hat Khlong Chao; r incl breakfast 9800-12,000B; P ❄ @ ⓦ ≈) Natural materials, like bamboo privacy fences and thatched-roof villas, sew this resort (one of a group of four Peter Pan–named ones) seamlessly into the landscape. The terracotta-coloured bungalows open right onto a postcard-perfect beach; the villas behind come with plunge pools. The bar is a great spot for a sundowner. Expect 40% discounts in low season.

Ra Beang Mai THAI $$
(Hat Khlong Chao; mains 100-180B; ⊙8am-10pm; ⓦ) Handy for the cluster of accommodation near Khlong Chao beach, this restaurant is cordially family-run and attractive, with a covered area plus pleasant outdoor seating on rustic wooden furniture. Dishes include plump prawn salads, seafood curries and international favourites and come bursting with flavour. It's a lovely spot.

ℹ Information

There is one ATM on Ko Kut but it's best not to rely on it. Major resorts can exchange money.

Almost all hotels and guesthouses have wi-fi.

A small **hospital** (☎039 525748; ⊙24hr) at Ban Khlong Mad can handle minor emergencies.

Police Station (☎039 525741; ⊙24hr) Near the hospital at Ban Khlong Dam.

ℹ Getting There & Away

Ko Kut is accessible from the mainland pier of **Laem Sok**, 22km southeast of Trat, the nearest bus transfer point. Three boat services as well as a speedboat service run from adjacent piers. Boat services offer free transport from Trat guesthouses and the bus station but not from the airport.

Speedboats will drop you off at your resort if possible; normal boats offer free land transfer on your arrival at **Ao Salad Pier** to your destination.

Koh Kood Princess (☎086 126 7860; www.kohkoodprincess.com) runs an air-con boat (350B, 1¾ hours, 12.30pm) that docks at Ao Salad, in the northeastern corner of the island.

Ko Kut Express (☎09-0506 0020; www.kokutexpress.in.th) runs an air-con fast ferry (350B, 1¼ hours, 1pm) to Ao Salad. It also runs a twice-daily speedboat service from November to April (600B, one hour, 10.30am and 2.30pm), dropping to weekends-only (and weather-permitting) off-season.

Boonsiri (☎085 921 0111; www.boonsiriferry.com) has a catamaran (500B, 1¼ to 1¾ hours, 10.45am and 2.20pm) that runs from Laem Sok to Ao Salad. The afternoon departure goes via Ko Mak. From mid-May to mid-October there's only one departure, at 1.30pm (and no Ko Mak link), with an extra 10.45am boat on Fridays. The company runs a direct bus service from Bangkok to meet the boats (850B including boat, five hours).

Two companies run speedboats from Ko Chang to Ko Kut (900B, 2½ hours) via Ko Wai and Ko Mak. The cheapest way to do this is to book a through-trip with Bang Bao Boat (p154) via Ko Mak, with the first section by wooden boat and the second by speedboat (700B).

ℹ Getting Around

Ko Kut's roads are steep, which rules out renting a push bike unless you are a champion cyclist.

Motorbikes can be rented for 200B to 300B per day.

Ko Mak เกาะหมาก

☎039 / POP 600

Little Ko Mak measures only 16 sq km and doesn't have any speeding traffic, wall-to-wall development, noisy beer bars or crowded beaches. The palm-fringed bays are bathed by gently lapping water and there's a relaxed vibe. It's a sweet place, despite sand flies and rubbish being a pain on some beaches, with a local movement that tries to keep the impact of tourism sustainable. The interior is a utilitarian but peaceful landscape of coconut and rubber plantations.

Visiting the island is easier in the high season (December to March); during the low season (May to September) many boats stop running.

WORTH A TRIP

KO WAI

Stunning Ko Wai (เกาะหวาย) is teensy and primitive, but endowed with gin-clear waters, excellent coral reefs for snorkelling and a handsome view across to Ko Chang. Expect to share the bulk of your afternoons with day trippers but have the remainder of your time in peace.

Overnight in simple wooden bungalows at **Ko Wai Paradise** (☎081 762 2548; r 300-500B; ⊙Oct–mid-May), on a postcard-perfect beach on the western side of the north coast. Equally good value is **Good Feeling** (☎081 850 3410; r 400-600B; ⊙Oct–mid-May), whose 12 wooden bungalows (all but one with private bathroom) are spread along a rocky headland with good snorkelling nearby. More upscale is **Koh Wai Beach Resort** (☎081 306 4053; www.kohwaibeachresort.com; r incl breakfast 2100-3400B; ⊙Oct–mid-May; ❄📶) on the southern side of the island, with all mod cons and just a few steps from the beach.

Note that all budget bungalows on Ko Wai close from May to September when seas are rough and flooding is common, and power is rationed and intermittent except at the resorts. There are no banks or ATMs, so stock up on cash before visiting the island.

Boat services run to Ko Wai from November to April; outside of this time (when most accommodation is closed anyway) you can ask for the reduced Ko Mak services to stop at Ko Wai. Speedboats (one-way 450B, 50 minutes) from Laem Ngop will drop you off at the nearest pier to your guesthouse; otherwise you'll have to walk 15 to 30 minutes along a narrow forest trail. From Ko Chang, speedboats (400B, 15 minutes, three daily) and the wooden Bang Bao (p154) ferry (300B, 45 minutes, one daily) head to Ko Wai, continuing to Ko Mak (wooden/speedboat 200/400B) and back. Speedboats head on to Ko Kut (700B).

Sights & Activities

The best beach on the island is **Ao Pra** in the west, but it is undeveloped and hard to reach. For now, swimming and beach strolling are best on the northwestern bay of **Ao Suan Yai**, which is a wide arc of sand and looking-glass-clear water that gets fewer sandflies than the southern beaches. It is easily accessible by bicycle or motorbike if you stay elsewhere.

Depending on winds, all beaches can suffer from quantities of rubbish washing up, much of it generated by the fishing boats.

Offshore is **Ko Kham**, a private island that was sold in 2008 for a reported 200 million baht. It used to be a popular day trippers' beach; today it's a resort island. You can still use the beach, but they'll ask you to pay a fee.

Koh Mak Divers DIVING
(☎083 297 7724; www.kohmakdivers.com; Ao Khao; 2-dive trips from 2500B) Runs dive trips to the Mu Ko Chang National Marine Park, about 45 minutes away. Its office is on the road near Baan Koh Mak.

Sleeping & Eating

Most budget guesthouses are on Ao Khao, a decent strip of sand on the southwestern side of the island, while the resorts sprawl out on the more scenic northwestern bay of Ao Suan Yai. Most bungalow operations and resorts open year-round, but a few still close from May to September. Beachside restaurants exist at nearly every guesthouse and resort, and there's a handful of family-run restaurants on the main road between Monkey Island and Makathanee Resort.

SPEEDBOATS TO/FROM KO MAK

DESTINATION	FARE (ONE WAY)	DURATION	FREQUENCY
Ko Chang	600B	1hr	3 daily
Ko Kut	400B	45min	3 daily
Ko Wai	400B	30min	3 daily
Laem Ngop (mainland pier)	450B	1hr	8 daily

Monkey Island BUNGALOW **$**

(☎085 389 0949; www.monkeyislandkohmak.com; Ao Khao; fan r with/without bathroom 600/400B, air-con r incl breakfast 1300-2000B; P ❄ @ 📶 ≋) Monkey Island has earthen or wooden bungalows in three creatively named models – Baboon, Chimpanzee and Gorilla – which range from very basic to beachfront villa chic. All have fun design touches and the hip restaurant does respectable Thai cuisine in a leisurely fashion. There's also a small children's pool.

Seavana RESORT **$$**

(☎090 864 5646; www.seavanakohmak.com; Ao Suan Yi; r 2900-5800B; P ❄ 📶 ≋) Stylish, wine-coloured buildings overlook garden, coconut palms and white sand at this top-drawer set-up near the northern pier. Staff are cordial and competent and the range of rooms is excellent. We especially like the upstairs ones with their own sea-view jacuzzi, perfect for quality time with someone special or stoking social media envy.

Lazy Day Resort BUNGALOW **$$**

(☎081 882 4002; www.kohmaklazyday.com; Ao Khao; r incl breakfast 2700-3000B; ⏲Oct-May; ❄ 📶) At the end of the sweep of Ao Khao, this professionally run operation has a dozen big white raised bungalows stationed around an attractive garden. The beach here is pretty but can suffer from plastic debris. Service is excellent, with a genuine welcome and relaxation guaranteed.

Baan Koh Mak BUNGALOW **$$**

(☎089 895 7592; www.baan-koh-mak.com; Ao Khao; r 1800-2600B; P ❄ 📶) Each of the slick bungalows here comes with heaps of natural light, arty features and a rakishly angled roof. The price goes up as you get closer to the beach. There's a decent restaurant and a beachside bar where fire twirlers heat up the revelry.

Ao Kao Resort BUNGALOW **$$$**

(☎080 567 0197; www.aokaoresort.com; Ao Khao; r 4500-5000B; P ❄ 📶) 🌿 In a pretty crook of the bay, Ao Kao has an assortment of stylish concrete bungalows with fab roof terraces offering thatched shade, hammocks and sea views. All have easy beach access. There are lots of amenities including sports options and a massage pavilion.

ℹ Information

There are no banks or ATMs on the island, so stock up on cash before visiting.

Ball Cafe (☎081 925 6591; Ao Khao; ⏲8am-9pm; 📶) Khun Ball runs his coffee shop and information centre in a spot just behind Baan Koh Mak; he's an active island promoter and runs www.kohmak.com as well as environmental initiatives. You can rent bikes (100B for 24 hours) and scooters (250B) here.

Ko Mak Health Centre (⏲8.30am-4.30pm) Can handle basic first-aid emergencies and illnesses. It is on the cross-island road near Ao Nid Pier.

Police Station (☎1155) Small station in the centre of the island.

ℹ Getting There & Around

Speedboats (450B one way, one hour) from Laem Ngop arrive at the pier on Ao Suan Yai, at Ao Nid or at Makathanee Resort on Ao Khao. The Ko Kut–bound Boonsiri (p157) ferry also stops in here once daily in high season (from mainland 400B).

In low season only one or two boats a day run from the mainland. Guesthouses and hotels pick people up free of charge.

From Ko Chang, speedboats (600B, one hour, three daily) and the wooden Bang Bao (p154) ferry (400B, two hours, one daily) head to Ko Mak via Ko Wai (wooden/speedboat 200/400B) and back. Speedboats head on to Ko Kut (400B).

Once on the island, you can pedal (40B per hour) or motorbike (200B per day) your way around.

Hua Hin & the Upper Gulf

Includes ➡

Best Places to Eat

- Cicada Market (p170)
- In Town Seafood (p184)
- Jek Pia (p174)
- Koti (p175)
- Sôm·đam Tanontok 51 (p174)

Best Places to Stay

- Baan Bayan (p174)
- Centara Grand Beach Resort & Villas (p174)
- La a natu Bed & Bakery (p179)
- Salsa Hostel (p188)
- The Theatre Villa (p187)

Why Go?

The upper gulf has long been the favoured playground of the Thai elite due to its proximity to Bangkok. Following in the footsteps of the royal family – every Thai king from Rama IV on has spent his summers at a variety of regal holiday homes here – they in turn have inspired countless domestic tourists to flock to this stretch of coast in pursuit of fun and fine seafood.

A winning combination of outdoor activities and culture is on offer here, with historic sites, national parks and long sandy beaches ideal for beachcombing (the swimming isn't all that great at most) also drawing an increasing number of expats for the twin delights of an unspoiled coastline and the relaxed pace of provincial life. There's not much diving or snorkelling, but kiteboarders will be in paradise as this part of the gulf is by far the best place in Thailand to ride the wind.

When to Go

- The best time to visit is during the hot and dry season (February to June).
- January through March is the best time to learn how to kiteboard, as the water is usually smooth.
- October is the rainiest month, but stays drier than rest of country so there's no need to stay away.
- November to March is the coolest time of year – visit to see the 'sea of fog' at Kaeng Krachan National Park.

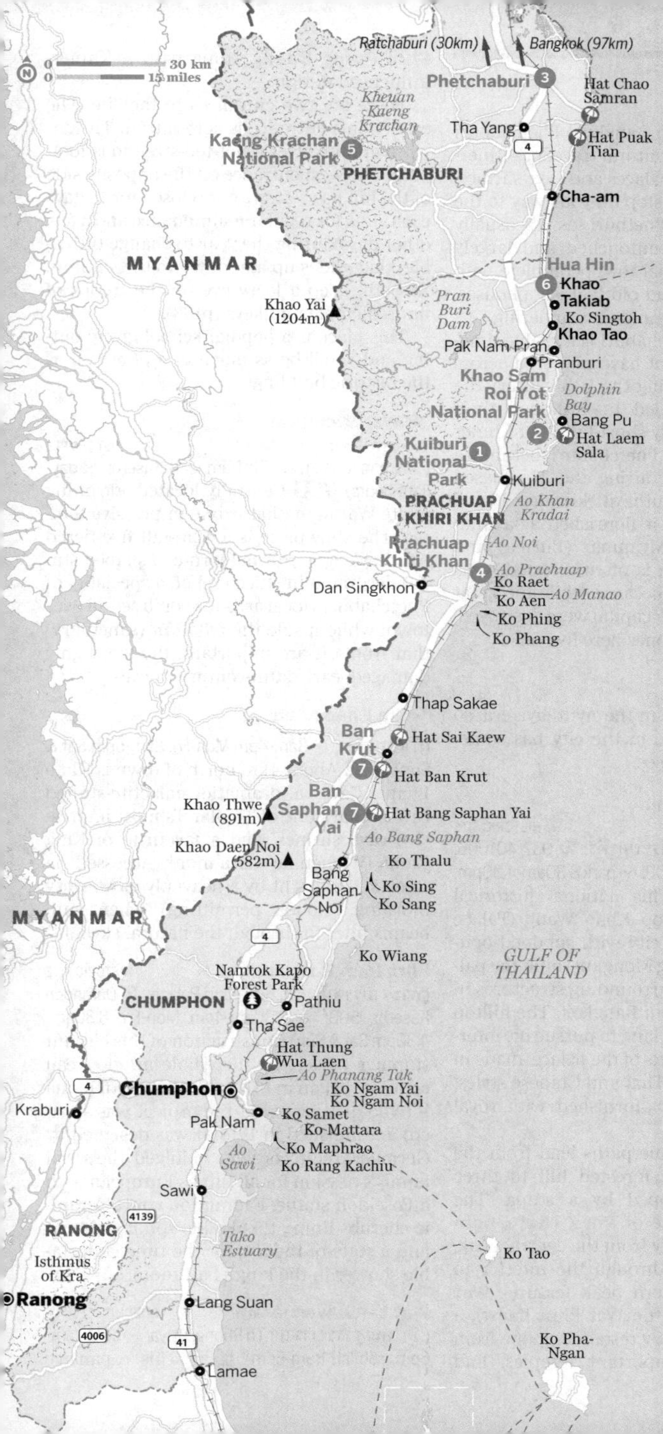

Hua Hin & the Upper Gulf Highlights

1 Kuiburi National Park (p178) Spotting wild elephants.

2 Khao Sam Roi Yot National Park (p180) Making the pilgrimage to see the illuminated cave shrine of Tham Phraya Nakhon.

3 Phetchaburi (p162) Exploring the hilltop palace and underground caves while dodging monkeys.

4 Prachuap Khiri Khan (p181) Motorcycling between curvaceous bays and limestone peaks.

5 Kaeng Krachan National Park (p166) Escaping into the depths of this national park, spotting tropical birds, swinging gibbons and the sea of fog.

6 Hua Hin (p170) Dining out in Hua Hin, home to countless good restaurants, both Thai and international.

7 Ban Krut & Bang Saphan Yai (p186) Stepping off the backpacker trail on your own secluded strip of sand.

Phetchaburi เพชรบุรี

032 / POP 23,200

An easy escape from Bangkok, Phetchaburi should be on every cultural traveller's itinerary. It has temples, palaces and cave shrines, and is a convenient stop on your way to the beach. Best of all, Phetburi, as it's usually called, remains an untouched and largely untouristed provincial town, complete with riverside markets and old teak shophouses. It's a great place for random wandering.

Historically, Phetchaburi is a visible timeline of kingdoms that have migrated across Southeast Asia. During the 11th century the Khmer empire settled in, although their control was relatively short-lived. As Khmer power diminished, Phetchaburi became a strategic royal fort during the Thai-based Sukhothai and Ayuthaya kingdoms and in the 17th century it flourished as a trading post between Myanmar (Burma) and Ayuthaya. The town is often referred to as a 'Living Ayuthaya' because while the great temples of the former capital were destroyed, smaller but similar ones here live on.

Sights

Phetchaburi thrived in the Ayuthaya era, so almost every temple in the city has something interesting to see.

★ Phra Nakhon Khiri Historical Park — HISTORIC SITE

(อุทยานประวัติศาสตร์พระนครคีรี; 032 401006; 150B, cable car return 50B; park 8.30am-4.30pm, museum 9am-4pm) This national historical park sits regally atop Khao Wang (Palace Hill), surveying the city with subdued opulence. Rama IV (King Mongkut) built the palace and dozens of surrounding structures in 1859 as a retreat from Bangkok. The hilltop location allowed the king to pursue his interest in astronomy. Parts of the palace, made in a mix of European, Thai and Chinese styles, are now a **museum** furnished with royal belongings.

Rolling cobblestone paths lead from the palace through the forested hill to three summits, each topped by a stupa. The 40m-tall white spire of **Phra That Chom Phet** skewers the sky from the central peak. You can climb up through the interior to its waist. The western peak features **Wat Phra Kaew Noi** (Little Wat Phra Kaew), a small building slightly resembling one from Bangkok's most important temples, and **Phra Prang Daeng** stupa with a Khmer-influenced design.

There are two entrances to the site. The east (front) entrance is across from Th Ratwithi and involves a not-too-strenuous footpath. The west entrance on the opposite side of the hill has a **cable car** (closed for 15 days each June for regular maintenance and a few other days during the year to change the cable) that glides up and down to the summit. At both, keep a leery eye on the troops of unpredictable monkeys (p163).

This place is a popular school-group outing and you'll be as much of a photo op as the historic buildings.

★ Wat Mahathat Worawihan — BUDDHIST TEMPLE

(วัดมหาธาตุวรวิหาร; Th Damnoen Kasem; daylight hours) FREE Centrally located, gleaming white Wat Mahathat is one impressive temple. The showpiece is a 42m-tall five-tiered Ayuthaya-style *prang* (corn-cob shaped stupa) decorated in stucco relief, a speciality of Phetchaburi's local artisans you'll see all over town, while inside the *wí·hăhn* (sanctuary) that fronts it are important, though highly damaged, early 20th-century murals.

Tham Khao Luang — CAVE

(ถ้ำเขาหลวง; 8am-4pm Mon-Fri, 8am-5pm Sat & Sun) FREE About 4km north of town is Khao Luang Cave, a dramatic stalactite-stuffed cavern that's one of Thailand's most impressive cave shrines, and a favourite of King Rama IV when he was a monk. Accessed via steep stairs, it's lit by a heavenly glow every morning (clouds permitting) when sunbeams filter in through the natural skylight.

Phra Ram Ratchaniwet — HISTORIC SITE

(พระรามราชนิเวศน์, Ban Peun Palace; Th Damnoen Kasem; 50B; 8.30am-4pm Mon-Fri, 8.30am-4.30pm Sat & Sun) Construction of this elegant summer palace, an incredible art nouveau creation, began in 1910 at the behest of Rama V (who died just after the project was started) and finished in 1916. It was designed by German architects who indulged the royal family's passion for all things European with a Poseidon statue, badminton court, ceramic cherubs lining the double spiral staircase and a state-of-the-art, for the time, adjustable shower in the king's bathroom.

Wat Yai Suwannaram — BUDDHIST TEMPLE

(วัดใหญ่สุวรรณาราม; Th Phongsuriya; bòht 7am-6pm, săh·lah 8am-5pm) FREE This expansive temple, founded in the late Ayuthaya era, holds quite a bit of history. Foremost are the faded murals inside the beautiful *bòht* (ordination hall), which date back to about 1700, making them some of the oldest Thai-temple murals still in existence. Mostly they're rows of various deities though the entrance wall vividly shows the demon Mara and his army trying to stop the Buddha from reaching enlightenment.

Shadow Puppet Museum MUSEUM
(พิพิธภัณฑ์หนังใหญ่ วัดพลับพลาชัย; Th Damnoen Kasem; 9am-5pm) FREE Not a fully fledged museum, rather there are 32 large *năng yài* shadow puppets, made by the former abbot, displayed on light boxes in Wat Plabplachai's old *bòht*. It's not kept open; you'll need to find a monk across the road to get a key. This temple also has a lot of masterful historic stucco work on the buildings.

Wat Phra Phuttaya Saiyat (Wat Phra Non) BUDDHIST TEMPLE
(วัดพระพุทธไสยาสน์/วัดพระนอน; Th Khiriataya; daylight hours) FREE The main attraction at this temple, also known as Wat Phra Non (the Reclining Buddha Temple), is 43m long. It's almost as big as the famous Wat Pho (p69) in Bangkok, but without the crowds.

Tham Khao Bandai-It CAVE
(ถ้ำเขาบันไดอิฐ; Rte 3171; 8am-5pm) FREE This hillside monastery, 2km west of town, sprawls through several large caverns converted into simple Buddha shrines and meditation rooms. There are some natural formations and skylights, and one chamber contains quite a few bats, but it's not nearly as beautiful as Tham Khao Luang (p162). It's well-lit and the floor is concrete throughout, so the kids who want to guide you aren't necessary; but if you do go with them, they expect a tip.

Festivals & Events

Phra Nakhon Khiri Fair CULTURAL
(งานพระนครคีรี-เมืองเพชร) Centred on Khao Wang hill, this provincial-style celebration lasts 10 days and usually takes place in February. Phra Nakhon Khiri Historical Park (p162) is festooned with lights, and there are traditional dance performances, craft and food displays, fireworks and a beauty contest.

Sleeping

★ 2N Guesthouse GUESTHOUSE $
(085 366 2451; two_nguesthouse@hotmail.com; 98/3 Mu 2, Tambol Bankoom; d & tw/q incl breakfast 580/850B; P) In a generally quiet neighbourhood 1.5km north of the city centre, the six rooms here are big and bright, and great for the price. The English-speaking owners do everything themselves and are really dedicated to pleasing their guests. They have free bicycles and can help with travel planning.

Ferngully Hostel HOSTEL $
(085 369 4692; www.ferngullyhostel.com; Th Chisa-In; dm incl breakfast 300B, q 700B;) Owner Fern has spruced up an older building with a few guest rooms and lots of social space. A traveller herself, she's a good source of advice about Phetchaburi. The hostel is right next to Phra Nakhon Khiri Historical Park (p162) and the caged rooftop lounge allows close encounters with monkeys and good views of Phra That Chom Phet stupa.

Sabaidee Resort GUESTHOUSE $
(086 344 4418; sabai2505@gmail.com; 65-67 Th Klongkrachang; r 350-500B;) It doesn't look like much at first, but step inside and you'll find good rooms around a little garden and shady terrace right on the river. There are modern concrete rooms and bamboo

MONKEY BUSINESS

Phetchaburi is full of macaque monkeys who know no shame or fear. Having once just congregated on Khao Wang hill (Phra Nakhon Khiri Historical Park; p162), they have now spread to the surrounding buildings, and there are additional troops at Tham Khao Luang (p162), Tham Khao Bandai-It and other forested places. There, they lurk by food stands, or eye-up passing pedestrians as potential mugging victims. These apes love plastic bags – regarding them as a signal that you're carrying food – and beverages, so be wary about displaying them. Keep a tight hold on camera bags, too. It's not just enough to heed the signs and don't feed or tease them, you should be on guard any time they are near. They do bite.

Phetchaburi (Phetburi)

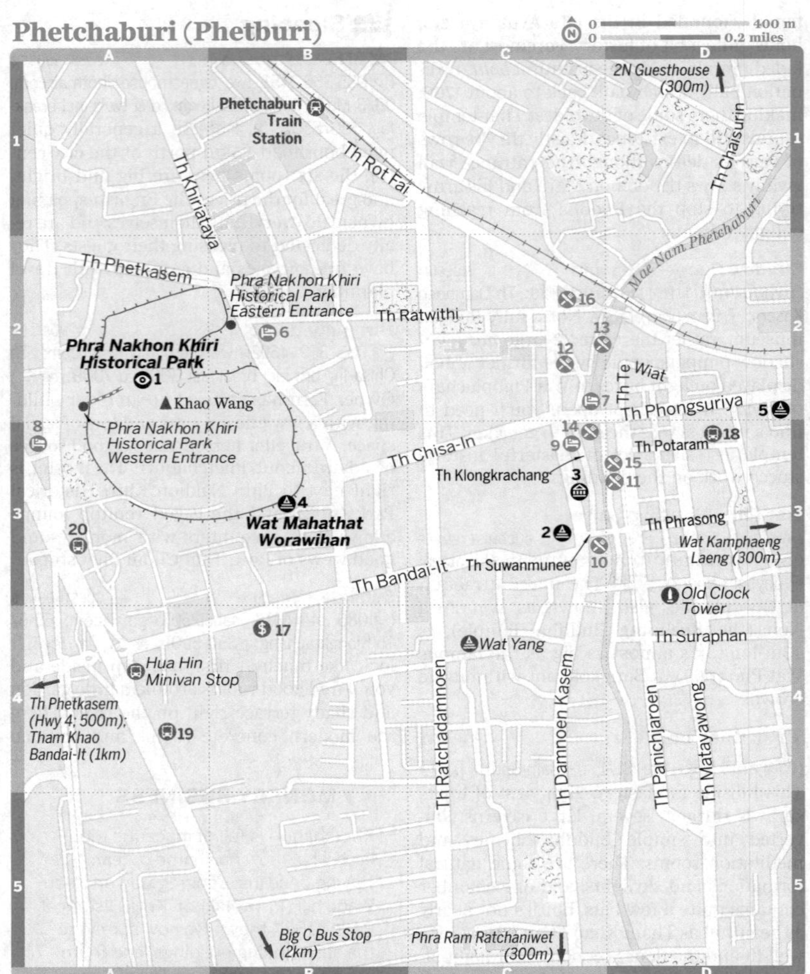

cottages, all with private bathrooms – the latter have cold showers. The pleasant owners can arrange Thai cooking classes, and bikes (50B) and scooters (300B) can be hired.

★White Monkey Guesthouse GUESTHOUSE $$

(☎092 840 1633; whitemonkey.guesthouse@gmail.com; 78/7 Th Klongkrachang; tw/d/f 500-650/900/1500; P ❄ @ ≋) Excellent guesthouse with bright, spacious, spick-and-span rooms (the cheapest with shared bathrooms and no air-con) and a great location. There's views of Phra Nakhon Khiri Historical Park (p162) and Wat Mahathat Worawihan (p162) from the rooftop terrace and helpful English-speaking staff who can organise trips in the area. Bikes are free.

Sun Hotel HOTEL $$

(☎032 401000; www.sunhotelthailand.com; Th Rim Khao Wang; r incl breakfast 850-950B; P ❄ @ ≋) Sitting opposite the cable car entrance to Phra Nakhon Khiri Historical Park (p162), the Sun Hotel has helpful staff and large, uninspiring rooms that are fine, but should be a little cheaper. There's a pleasant cafe downstairs and bikes are free.

Phetchaburi (Phetburi)

Top Sights
1 Phra Nakhon Khiri Historical Park........ A2
2 Wat Mahathat Worawihan...................... C3

Sights
3 Shadow Puppet Museum C3
4 Wat Phra Phuttaya Saiyat (Wat Phra Non)... B3
5 Wat Yai Suwannaram............................. D2

Sleeping
6 Ferngully Hostel.................................... B2
7 Sabaidee Resort..................................... C2
8 Sun Hotel A3
9 White Monkey Guesthouse C3

Eating
10 Cucina C3
11 Kow Chae Mae Awn D3
12 Ney & Neyn C2
13 Phetchaburi Walking Street.................C2
14 Rabieng Rimnam...................................C3
15 Rim Nam Market D3
16 Talat Taa Rot Tua C2

Information
17 Kasikorn Bank.......................................B4

Transport
18 Cha-am & Hua Hin Bus Stop.................D3
19 Southern Bus Stop................................A4
20 Wat Tham Kaew Minivan Station..........A3

While the location might sound good, it's actually pretty isolated from everything except the historical park.

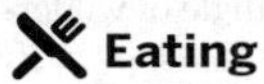

Eating

Surrounded by palm-sugar plantations, Phetchaburi is famous for its sweet concoctions, including *kà·nŏm môr gaang* (egg custard) and various 'golden' desserts made from egg yolks and sugar. They're sold in most markets, as is the raw sugar.

Nearby fruit orchards produce refreshingly aromatic *chom·pôo phet* (Phetchaburi rose apple – the fruit that adorns many street signs), pineapples and *nám wáh* bananas.

Rabieng Rimnam THAI, INTERNATIONAL $
(☎032 425707; rabieng@gmail.com; 1 Th Chisa-In; mains 50-120B; ⏲8am-midnight; 📶) This riverside restaurant serves up a real bygone-days atmosphere from an 1897 wooden home perched over the river and usually some good food, too – try the sugar palm tree fruit curry with prawn. English-speaking owners Nid and Tom will often join you for a chat about Thailand and share their decades of travel advice.

Talat Taa Rot Tua MARKET $
(Th Ratwithi; ⏲4-9pm) Big and bustling from the late afternoon, head to this covered night market for all the standard Thai favourites plus Phetchaburi's famous *kà·nŏm jeen tôrt man* (fresh rice noodles with curried deep-fried fishcake). There's lots of seating available.

Cucina THAI $
(Th Suwanmunee; mains 50-390B; ⏲10.30am-9pm; 📶✍) Hidden down a little passageway in front of Wat Mahathat (p162), this small restaurant has a big menu ranging from green curry fried rice to chicken teriyaki to waffle sandwiches. There's a few fun fusion foods like the *đôm yam* fish salad and 'cucina pizza', which is pizza with instant noodles as the crust.

Phetchaburi Walking Street MARKET $
(Th Chaisurin; ⏲4-9pm Sat) Unlike a typical walking street market, almost every vendor here is selling food and you can easily snack yourself full.

Kow Chae Mae Awn THAI $
(ข้าวแช่แม่อร; Th Panichjaroen; 15B; ⏲9am-4pm; ✍) Mae Awn sells her famous *kôw châe* (moist chilled rice) with a choice of fish, shrimp or pickled daikon radish along the walkway at the southeast corner of the **Rim Nam Market** (⏲5-11am). She has just two tables, but does a brisk take-away business.

Ney & Neyn THAI $
(Th Damnoen Kasem; mains 30-120B; ⏲8am-4pm) Great soups served in clay bowls are the signature dishes at this casual place. The *gŏo·ay đĕe·o gài* (chicken noodles) comes southern style with a whole chicken drumstick. There's no English sign, but just look for the stacks of clay bowls.

Information

There's no formal information source in town, but the guesthouses can provide up-to-date travel tips. The **Tourism Authority of Thailand's office in Cha-am** (TAT; ☎032 471005; tatphet@tat.or.th; Th Phetkasem; ⏲8.30am-4.30pm) handles all of Phetchaburi Province.

Kasikorn Bank (Th Bandai-It; ⏲11am-7pm) at Phetpaiboon Plaza shopping centre is the nearest extended hours bank to the city centre.

Getting There & Away

The train is usually the most convenient and comfortable way to travel, and Phetchaburi's **train station** (☎032 425211; Th Rot Fai) is within walking distance of most guesthouses.

There are no longer any buses to Bangkok originating or finishing in Phetchaburi, only minivans. These use the new **Wat Tham Kaew Minivan Station** (Th Bandai-It; *sà·tăh·nee bor kŏr sŏr wát tâm gâaou*), as do minibuses to Kaeng Krachan National Park. Most guesthouses can call to have the Kaeng Krachan minivans pick you up at their door for an extra 50B per person.

Minivans to Hua Hin, Cha-am and Prachuap Khiri Khan are 500m south of the minivan station on the side of the road next to Phetcharat Hospital and they also pick up further south in front of the Big C shopping centre. Some long-distance buses passing through town (going both north and south) will also stop by Big C, but if you want to try it, be prepared for a long wait. For Chumphon and southern cities, there's a small **southern bus stop** (Phetkasem Hwy) 300m south of the hospital. Another option to Hua Hin and Cha-am are the **ordinary buses** that depart from the town centre next to Wat Potaram.

Getting Around

Motorcycle taxis go anywhere in the town centre for 20B to 40B. Phetchaburi's four-wheel túk-túk (locally called *rót léng*) cost just a little more. You can also hire them for the day for about 700B to 800B.

All the guesthouses hire out bicycles (50B per day) and motorbikes (150B to 250B); Rabieng Rimnam (p165) charges the least. Reserve a motorcycle when you reserve a room because many guesthouses get them from outside sources and you may have to wait a while to get one if you just ask at the desk.

Kaeng Krachan National Park

อุทยานแห่งชาติแก่งกระจาน

Wake to an eerie symphony of gibbon calls as the early-morning mist floats through the forest canopy, and then hike through lush forests in search of elephant herds and other wildlife. Thailand's largest (2915 sq km) national park is surprisingly close to civilisation but shelters an intense tangle of wilderness that sees relatively few tourists.

Despite the park having a poaching problem, animal life includes wild elephants, tigers, leopards, tapir, gaur (wild cattle), white-handed gibbons, dusky langurs and black giant squirrels. This park also occupies an interesting, overlapping biozone for birds as the southernmost spot for northern species and the northernmost for southern species. The result is a bird list that exceeds 400 species, including blue pitta, ratchet-tailed

TRANSPORT TO/FROM PHETCHABURI

DESTINATION	BUS	MINIVAN	TRAIN
Bangkok Hualamphong	N/A	N/A	34-388B, 3-3½hr, 12 daily
Bangkok Southern & Northern (Mo Chit) Bus Terminals	N/A	100B, 2hr, frequent 3.30am-7.30pm	N/A
Bangkok Thonburi	N/A	N/A	31B, 4hr, 7.16am, 12.56pm
Cha-am	30B, 1hr, hourly 5.40am-4.30pm (from Wat Potaram)	50B, 45min, frequent 5am-6.20pm	8-38B, 40min, 5 daily
Chumphon	328-500B, 6hr, hourly 6.30am-8pm, frequent 8-10pm	N/A	58-455B, 5½-6½hr, 11 daily
Hua Hin	40B, 1½hr, hourly 5.40am-4.30pm (from Wat Potaram)	80B, 1hr, frequent 5am-6.20pm	14-341B, 1hr, 12 daily
Kaeng Krachan National Park	N/A	120B, 1hr, hourly 7.30am-6.30pm	N/A
Prachuap Khiri Khan	150-200B, 2½hr, hourly 6.30am-8pm, frequent 8-10pm	150B, 2½hr, every 40min 5am-6.20pm	31-382B, 2-3hr, 11 daily

treepie, banded broadbill, great slaty woodpecker and great hornbill.

The park, except for the scenic reservoir by the headquarters and **Pa La-U Waterfall** (น้ำตกป่าละอู; ⊙8am-5pm), closes to the public from August to October. The best, and also busiest, months to visit are between November and March, though only weekends and holidays see crowds. Independent visits without a vehicle are possible, though take some patience, and 4WD is required for some parts.

Sights & Activities

There are two main spots to visit in the heart of the park. The wildlife-rich **Ban Krang** area has a nice 2.5km nature trail and is really good for birdwatchers. It's another 15km up a 4WD-only road to Panoen Thung Viewpoint. The park's **visitor centre** (☎032 772311; Rte 3432; ⊙8am-4pm) at the main entrance, next to the photogenic **Kaeng Krachan Reservoir**, is a one-stop shop for park information and assistance.

In particular, this is where you hire drivers to go up into the park proper. Some staff speak English.

★**Panoen Thung Viewpoint** VIEWPOINT
(จุดชมวิวพะเนินทุ่ง) Up at the end of the 4WD-only road, Panoen Thung is refreshingly cool at 960m above sea level. Most visitors are here to see the fantastic mountain overlooks that are ideal for the early-morning 'sea of fog' *(tá·lair mòrk)* views. They can happen year-round, but are most common in the November to March cool season. If you're coming up in the morning, you'll need to leave headquarters at 5.30am to arrive in time to see it.

Also here is a 4km trail to **Nam Tok Tho Thip**, a nine-tiered waterfall, though you can only see five of them and you need to do the walk with a ranger.

Sleeping & Eating

There are simple **bungalows** (☎032 772311; http://nps.dnp.go.th/reservation.php; Kaeng Krachan National Park; bungalows 1200-3000B) and a **campsite** (per person with tent/tent hire 30/200-300B; Ⓟ) by the reservoir at the entrance to the park, though you won't see much wildlife here other than birds.

There are also campsites deep in the forest at **Ban Krang** (per person with tent/tent hire 30/200-300B; Ⓟ) and **Panoen Thung** (per person with tent/tent hire 30/200-300B; Ⓟ), and in the far south near **Pa La-U** (per person with tent/tent hire 30/200-300B; Ⓟ) waterfall. Camping equipment can be hired at each. The bungalows at Pa La-U are undergoing renovations.

There's a fast food noodle and rice restaurant at each of the campsites. Those up on the mountain (Ban Krang and Panoen Thung) generally serve from 8am to 6pm, though it will depend on the number of customers. Those at the headquarters and Pa La-U waterfall normally close at 4pm. There are also restaurants just outside the park entrance if you want a little more choice.

Getting There & Away

Kaeng Krachan is 52km southwest of Phetchaburi and 68km from Hua Hin. Tours are available from both towns, though they're pretty infrequent, especially from Phetchaburi, unless you pay for a private trip.

You can reach the headquarters by minivan from Phetchaburi and Bangkok, but in both cases be sure the driver knows you are going to Kaeng Krachan National Park and not just Kaeng Krachan town. In Petchaburi minivans leave hourly between 7.30am and 6.30pm and cost 120B; for an extra 50B per person, your guesthouse can have the van pick you up.

In Bangkok, minivans leave from the old Southern Bus Terminal *(sǎi đâi gòw)* hourly between 9am and 5pm for 250B and take 3½ hours hours. If you're travelling from Hua Hin, you can go to Tha Yang by a north-bound minivan and catch a Kaeng Krachan minivan (assuming seats are available) there instead of going all the way to Phetchaburi.

Getting Around

There's one road through the main section of the park. Regular cars can drive 35km up to the Ban Krang Campsite, but beyond this the road requires 4WD. There's no public transport and motorcycles and bicycles are not allowed (except for Pa La-U Waterfall) because of the danger of wild animals. Hitching requires patience.

There are drivers with 4WD trucks at headquarters and Bang Krang. The round-trip cost per truck (up to 10 people) per day from the visitor centre to Ban Krang Campsite is 1200B and it's 1600B to Panoen Thung Campsite; add 200B if you spend the night and come back the next morning. You can often, but not always, find other people at headquarters to share the costs. The road is so narrow that there are scheduled times for going up and going down. Vehicles can begin driving up from 5.30am to 7.30am and 1pm to 3pm, and begin the drive down from 9am to 10am and 4pm to 5pm.

Cha-am ชะอำ

032 / POP 35,600

Cheap and cheerful, Cha-am is a popular beach getaway for working-class families and Bangkok students. On weekends and public holidays, neon-painted buses (called *chìng·chàp tua*), their sound systems pumping, deliver groups of holidaymakers. It's a very Thai-style beach party, with eating and drinking marathons held around umbrella-shaded beach chairs and tables. Entertainment is provided by the banana boats that zip back and forth, eventually making a final jack-knife turn that throws the passengers into the sea.

Cha-am doesn't see many foreigners; visitors are usually older Europeans who winter here instead of more expensive Hua Hin. Like Hua Hin, the shallow sea is better for strolling and sunbathing than swimming, but unlike its southern neighbour, there isn't much else to do here beyond the beach and the gibbon-filled **forest park** (วนอุทยานชะอำ; Phetkasem Hwy; daylight hours). That said, the seafood is superb, the weekend people-watching entertaining and the prices are some of the most affordable anywhere on the coast.

Festivals & Events

Gin Hoy, Do Nok, Tak Meuk FOOD & DRINK

(Sep) You really can do it all at this annual festival held in September. The festival's English name is 'Shellfish Eating, Bird Watching & Squid Catching' and is a catchy slogan for some of Cha-am's local attractions and traditions. Mainly it's a food festival showcasing a variety of seafood, but there are also bird-watching events at nearby sanctuaries and nightly concerts.

Thailand International Kite Festival ART

(Mar) Most years, but not every, artistic kites from around the world take to the skies over the beach for a long weekend.

Sleeping

Cheap, charmless guesthouses in narrow concrete shophouses near the beach remain Cha-am's bread and butter. Avoid staying on seedy Soi Bus Station unless you're not planning to sleep much. Expect significant weekday discounts.

Pa Ka Ma GUESTHOUSE $$

(032 433504; Soi Cay-ben Tee-wee; r 1000B;) Probably the best low-cost guesthouse in Cha-am, and only a little more expensive than the average. It's attractively designed – each room has its own individual style and the rooms at the back have little balconies. The bathrooms are good too, though hot water can take a long time to arrive. Not much English is spoken.

It's on an unsigned soi between Sois 1 and 2 North. There are a few other good choices nearby if it's full.

Cha Inn @ Cha-Am HOTEL $$

(032 471879; www.chainn-chaam.com; 274/34 Th Ruamjit; r incl breakfast 1200-2000B;) The owners have creatively and beautifully adapted this old building into a stylish hotel that's refreshingly out of the ordinary for Cha-am. There's a restaurant on the ground floor and an airy lounge up above. And then there are the 17 rooms; large, comfortable and full of the same subtle design found in the public areas.

Dream Boutique Hotel HOTEL $$

(032 470896; 235/35 Soi Anatachai; d 800-1200, f 1800B; @) There's nothing boutique about it, but the misnomer is the only knock on a very well-run, impeccably clean hotel. Rooms aren't fancy, but they're fully kitted out and have balconies, plus guests can lounge on the roof. There's bike and motorcycle hire and you'll get picked up when you arrive in town.

It lies between Sois 1 and 2 South, which is actually the third soi south of Th Narathip.

Bann Pantai Resort HOTEL $$$

(032 470155; www.bannpantai.com; Th Ruamjit; r incl breakfast 4000-6000B;) Rather more upmarket than most hotels in Cha-am, this beautiful, family-friendly place has a huge pool and small fitness centre, and the beach is just across the road.

Rooms are big with great beds and terraces in front.

Eating & Drinking

From your deckchair you can wave down vendors selling plastic-wrapped meals, or order from the many nearby beachfront restaurants and they'll deliver.

The top seafood restaurants are found at the far northern end of the beach by the fishing pier.

The main expat enclave, full of cold beer, pool tables, TV sports, massage and *masaaaage,* is Soi Bus Station, the first street south of Th Narathip. You can also follow the lead of some Thai visitors and just stay in your beach chair with a bottle, even after the sun goes down.

Khrua Rua Makham THAI $$
(Th Ruamjit; mains 60-420B; ⏰7am-7pm Sun-Thu, 7am-8pm Fri & Sat; 📶) This alfresco restaurant serves mostly a regular Thai menu such as garlic fried chicken, green curry and the like. But there's also a good seafood selection, with grilled squid being a local speciality. The food probably won't wow you, but it won't let you down either.

Krua Medsai Seafood THAI $$
(Off Th Ruamjit; mains 40-450B; ⏰10am-10pm) Massive Medsai is one of dozens of seafood spots next to Cha-am's fishing port. While some of the smaller restaurants out here have more character, few others can offer this big a selection or provide a properly translated English menu.

ℹ Information

Phetkasem Hwy runs through Cha-am's busy town centre, which is about 1km away from the beach via Th Narathip. This is where you'll find banks, the fresh market, the train station and most bus stops.

There are plenty of ATMs and a few extended-hours exchange booths along Th Ruamjit.

ℹ Getting There & Away

There's a little minivan station for **Hua Hin-Pran Tour** (☎032 511654; Th Sasong) at the Soi Bus Station with departures to Bangkok (Southern and Mo Chit terminals) every half-hour from 7am to 5.30pm. All other public road transport stops on Phetkasem Hwy at the intersection with Th Narathip. Mostly it's minivans, since very few buses from Hua Hin or other southern towns stop to pick up passengers in Cha-am. The **Airport Hua Hin Bus** (☎084 697 3773; www.airporthuahinbus.com; Th Phetkasem, next to Hua Hin Airport) from Hua Hin to Bangkok's Suvarnabhumi Airport stops specifically in front of the Government Savings Bank while Shinnakeart Korat, with buses to Bangkok, Nakhon Ratchasim (328B, eight hours, 10.30am, 9.30pm) and Ubon Ratchathani (609B, 15 hours, 6.30pm), are also here.

The **train station** (☎032 471159; Th Narathip) is west of Phetkasem Hwy at the end of Th Narathip and is not served by any express trains. Note that Cha-am is listed in the timetable as 'Ban Cha-am'.

You can hire a taxi (any private car available for hire) along the beach. The fare is 500B to Hua Hin.

ℹ Getting Around

From the city centre to the beach it's a quick motorcycle (40B) or taxi (100B) ride.

You can hire bicycles (100B per day) and motorcycles (200B to 250B) all along Th Ruamjit.

TRANSPORT TO/FROM CHA-AM

DESTINATION	BUS	MINIVAN	TRAIN
Bangkok Don Mueang International Airport	N/A	180B, 4hr, every 40min 6.30am-6.30pm	N/A
Bangkok Hualamphong	N/A	N/A	40-143B, 4-4½hr, 1.40am, 4.55am, 2.33pm
Bangkok Southern and & Northern (Mo Chit) Bus Terminals	241B, 4½hr, 9.30am, 12.30pm, 2.40pm, 5.30pm	160B, 3½hr, frequent 4.30am-7.30pm	N/A
Bangkok Suvarnabhumi International Airport	269B, 4hr, every 90min 6.20am-6.20pm	N/A	N/A
Bangkok Thonburi	N/A	N/A	38B, 4hr, 6.41am, 12.13pm
Hua Hin	20B, 30min, hourly 6.30am-5.30pm	30B, 30min, frequent 6am-7.30pm	6-33B, 30min, 5 daily
Kanchanaburi	N/A	200B, 3½hr, hourly 6.40am-5.40pm	N/A
Phetchaburi	30B, 1hr, hourly 6.30am-4.30pm	50B, 45min, frequent 6am-7.30pm	8-38B, 40min, 5 daily

Hua Hin หัวหิน

☎032 / POP 59,369

Thailand's original beach resort is no palm-fringed castaway island and arguably is the better for it. Instead, it's a refreshing mix of city and sea with an almost cosmopolitan ambience, lively markets, good golf courses and water parks, international cuisine and excellent accommodation. In fact, many visitors never even step foot on the sand.

Hua Hin traces its aristocratic roots to 1911 when the railroad arrived from Bangkok and some in the royal family built vacation homes here. By the mid-1920s it was a full-fledged resort town for the Bangkok-based nobility with a golf course and a seaside hotel featuring a European restaurant manager. Even Kings Rama VI and VII built summer palaces here. The latter's **Phra Ratchawang Klai Kangwon** (พระราชวังไกลกังวล; Th Phetkasem; Far from Worries Palace) remains a royal residence today and was the full-time home of King Rama IX for many of his later years.

There's a lot of money swirling around Hua Hin, but it's still a good budget destination: seafood is plentiful and cheap, there's convenient public transport and it takes a lot less time and effort to get here from Bangkok than to the southern islands.

 Sights

A former fishing village, Hua Hin's old town retains links to its past with an old teak shophouse district bisected by narrow winding sois, fronted by pier houses that hold restaurants and guesthouses, and punctuated with a busy fishing pier still in use today. Along the shore beyond, especially to the north, there are still many historic wooden summer residences.

Hua Hin Beach (หาดหัวหิน) is a pleasant but not stunning stretch of fine white powder lapped by calm grey-green waves, made for strolling and sunbathing, not swimming. Watch out for jellyfish, especially in the wet season.

★Cicada Market MARKET

(ตลาดจั๊กจั่น; ☎080 650 4334; www.cicadamarket.com; Soi Hua Thanon 23, Th Phetkasem, South Hua Hin; ⏲4-11pm Fri-Sun) **FREE** Vastly better than the city-centre Hua Hin Night Market (p176), this popular place 3.5km to the south is a fun mix of food, shopping and performing arts. It's not a high-sell environment, rather it's a very relaxed shopping experience. Many artists come to sell their handmade home decor and clothes, and there's food from Thailand and beyond. Live entertainment hits the stage from 8.30pm and there are buskers all around.

The last green *sŏrng·tăa·ou* back to the city passes about 9pm.

Mrigadayavan Palace HISTORIC BUILDING

(พระราชนิเวศน์มฤคทายวัน; ☎032 508443; www.mrigadayavan.or.th; 30B; ⏲8.30am-4.30pm Thu-Tue, last tickets sold at 4pm) With a breezy seaside location 12km north of Hua Hin, this summer palace – Phra Ratchaniwet

WORTH A TRIP

BEACH-HOPPING NEAR HUA HIN

South of Hua Hin are a series of beaches framed by dramatic headlands that make great day trips when Hua Hin beach feels too urban.

Khao Tao (Turtle Mountain) protects an idyllic little cove where **Hat Sai Noi Beach** drops off quickly into the sea, providing a rare opportunity for deep-water swimming. A small resort (p174) and a couple of restaurants operate here and while weekends bring the expected crowds, it's quiet on weekdays – if you're lucky you could have it all to yourself.

Wat Tham Khao Tao, on the north side of the hill, has quite a bit of Buddhist and other statuary in a concrete 'cave' in front of a small real cave. Keep walking further back to see even more colourful shrines and climb stairs up to the Buddha on the hill. If you're walking or on a motorcycle just follow the base of the hill from the beach to the temple, but if you're driving a car you need to go the long way around the reservoir.

To get to the beach, take a Pranburi-bound bus from Hua Hin and ask to be dropped off at Ban Tao village (20B). From here a motorbike taxi (there aren't many, so you might have to wait a while) can take you to the beach (30B). Take the driver's phone number for getting back. Hitching would be very difficult.

Hua Hin

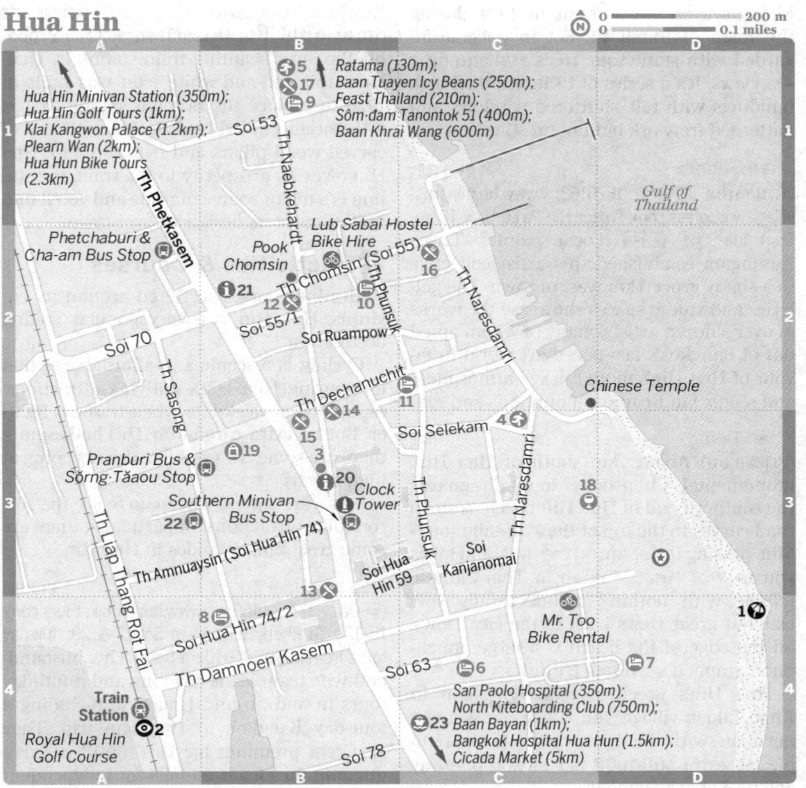

Hua Hin

Sights
- 1 Hat Hua Hin ... D4
- 2 Hua Hin Train Station ... A4

Activities, Courses & Tours
- 3 Hua Hin Adventure Tour ... B3
- 4 Hua Hin Golf Centre ... C3
- 5 Thai Massage by the Blind ... B1

Sleeping
- 6 Baan Somboon ... C4
- 7 Centara Grand Beach Resort & Villas ... D4
- 8 Chanchala Hostel ... B4
- 9 Hua Hin Place ... B1
- 10 King's Home ... B2
- 11 Love Sea House ... C2

Eating
- 12 Chomsin-Naebkehardt Junction Street Food ... B2
- 13 Hua Hin Vegan Cafe ... B3
- 14 Jek Pia ... B3
- 15 Koti ... B3
- 16 The Social Salad ... C2
- 17 Velo Cafe ... B1

Drinking & Nightlife
- 18 White Lotus Sky Bar ... C3

Shopping
- 19 Hua Hin Night Market ... B3

Information
- 20 Municipal Tourist Information Office ... B3
- 21 Tourism Authority of Thailand ... B2

Transport
- 22 Hua Hin-Pran Tour ... A3
- 23 Lomprayah ... C4

Mrigadayavan – was built in 1924 during the reign of Rama VI. Set in a beautiful garden with statuesque trees and stunning sea views, it's a series of 18 interlinked teak buildings with tall, shuttered windows and patterned fretwork built upon stilts.

Baan Silapin GALLERY
(บ้านศิลปิน; ☎086 1620162; www.huahinartistvillage.wordpress.com; Th Hua Hin-Pa Lu-U; ⏰10am-5pm Tue-Sun) FREE Local painter Tawee Kasangam established this artist collective in a shady grove 4km west of town. The galleries and studio spaces showcase the works of over a dozen artists, many of whom opted out of Bangkok's fast-paced art world in favour of Hua Hin's more relaxed atmosphere and scenic landscape of mountains and sea.

Khao Takiab HILL
(เขาตะเกียบ) About 7km south of Hua Hin, monumental Chopstick Mountain guards the southern end of Hua Hin beach. A steep road curves to the top of the 77m-tall mountain, passing the **seafood market**, and takes you to **Wat Khao Takiab**, a Thai-Chinese temple with nothing architecturally special, but great views back to the city. Down on the edge of the beach is a large, much-photographed **standing Buddha**.

Hua Hin's green *sŏrng·tăa·ou* stop in Khao Takiab village, 1km away, but you can negotiate with the drivers to go to the temple; an extra 50B-100B per person one-way will probably be enough.

Hua Hin Train Station HISTORIC SITE
(สถานีรถไฟหัวหิน; Th Liap Thang Rot Fai) Probably the most beautiful train station in Thailand, this red-and-white icon was built in 1926 to replace the original station. It has a Victorian gingerbread design with lots of carved wood pillars and trim. Because Hua Hin owes its prosperity to the train, the station is a major source of pride and you'll find imitations of its design all over town.

Activities & Courses

With nine courses scattered around its environs, Hua Hin is a very popular golfing destination.

Cycling is a scenic and affordable option for touring Hua Hin's outlying attractions, especially on weekdays when traffic is lighter. But be extra careful on Th Phetkasem – there are some truly terrible drivers going at high speeds.

Tours are a good way to go to see the surrounding attractions. In particular, there are some great biking guides in Hua Hin.

Hua Hin Bike Tours CYCLING
(☎081 173 4469; www.huahinbiketours.com; 15/120 Th Phetkasem, btwn Soi 27 & 29; full-day tours from 2950B; ⏰10am-8pm) This husband-and-wife team leads day-long and multi-day tours in and around Hua Hin, including a four-day Bangkok to Hua Hin trip. They also rent premium bicycles (500B per day, discount for longer rentals) for independent cyclists and can recommend routes.

DON'T MISS

ELEPHANT REFUGE

You don't have to spend long in Thailand to understand how little regard is given towards animal welfare. One of the most active groups trying to improve the situation, the Wildlife Friends Foundation Thailand, runs a **wildlife rescue centre** (มูลนิธิเพื่อนสัตว์ป่า; ☎032 458135; www.wfft.org; full-access tours incl lunch half-/full-day 1100/1800B), 45km west of Hua Hin, that adopts and cares for abused, injured and abandoned animals that cannot be released back into the wild.

The centre cares for over 500 animals, including bears, tigers, gibbons, macaques, loris and birds. There's also an affiliated elephant rescue program where the elephants live out their lives chain-free. A visit here is a great day out – far better than the elephant and tiger tourist traps featured on many tours out of Hua Hin. The centre offers full-access tours introducing animals and discussing rescue histories. The full-day option includes walking and bathing elephants. Drop-in visits are not allowed.

Hotel transfer from Hua Hin or Cha-am costs 200B per person and there's also a small lodge (4000B per night including meals) on-site. Those looking for a more in-depth experience can **volunteer** (☎032 458135; www.wildlifevolunteer.org) at the centre.

They also lead the long-distance **Tour de Thailand** (www.tourdethailand.com) charity bike tours across Thailand.

North Kiteboarding Club KITESURFING
(☎083 438 3833; www.northkiteboardingclub.com; 113/5 Th Phetkasem, at Soi 67, South Hua Hin; 3-day beginner course 11,000B; ⏲9am-9pm) Based in Hua Hin, but with outlets in Chumpon and Phuket, this is a well-established company offering lessons and a large store.

Hua Hin Golf Centre GOLF
(☎032 530476; www.huahingolf.com; Th Selakam; ⏲noon-8.30pm) The friendly staff at this pro shop run by **Hua Hin Golf Tours** (☎032 530119; Soi 41; ⏲6.30am-10pm), can steer you to the most affordable, well-maintained courses where the monkeys won't try to run off with your balls.

This company organises golf tours and rents sets of quality clubs (500B to 700B per day) to their customers.

Thai Massage by the Blind MASSAGE
(☎081 944 2174; The Naebkenhardt; Thai massage 200B; ⏲7am-9pm) Traditional head, foot and body massages by blind masseuses, plus some other treatments like herbal wraps. There are two other locations further out from the city centre.

Thai Cooking Course Hua Hin COOKING
(☎081 572 3805; www.thai-cookingcourse.com; Soi 19, Th Phetkasem; courses 1500B) Aspiring chefs should sign up for a one-day cooking class here that includes a market visit, making five dishes and a recipe book to take home. The course runs only if there are a minimum of three people and hotel pick-up is provided.

Tours

Feast Thailand FOOD
(☎095 461 0557, 032 510207; www.feastthailand.com; Th Naebkehardt, inside Raruk Hua Hin market; from 1350B; ⏲8.30am-4pm Mon-Sat) A small company with highly regarded half-day food tours. You pick your tour – either sample Thai cuisine basics or dive into some less-common foods – and they pick you up at your hotel. Join-in tours are sometimes available.

Hua Hin Adventure Tour ADVENTURE
(☎032 530314; www.huahinadventuretour.com; Th Naebkehardt; ⏲9am-6pm Mon-Sat) Hua Hin Adventure Tour offer active excursions, including kayaking trips in the Khao Sam Roi Yot National Park (p180) and wildlife watching in Kaeng Krachan National Park (p166).

Festivals & Events

Hua Hin Jazz Festival MUSIC
In honour of King Rama IX's personal interest in the genre, the city that hosts royal getaways also hosts an annual jazz festival featuring Thai and international performers. All events are free. It takes place in a new month each year and the dates are usually not announced very far in advance.

Sleeping

The city's character suddenly becomes more local and less boisterous north of Th Chomsin. Focused on Th Naebkehardt and Soi 51, this is the neighbourhood of choice for Bangkok's trendy youth.

If sun and surf are your main reasons for coming here, stay south where the beach is fairly quiet and mostly tout-free.

Chanchala Hostel HOSTEL $
(☎086 331 6763; www.chanchalahostelhuahin.com; 1/5 Th Sasong; dm incl breakfast 340B; ❄📶) This spick and span three-room dorm five minutes walk from the train station does things right. Each bed in the six- and eight-bed rooms (one for women only) comes with its own locker, reading light and power outlet. Guests mingle with the friendly staff in the coffee shop and with each other at the rooftop lounge.

★ **King's Home** GUESTHOUSE $$
(☎089 052 0490; www.huahinkingshome.blogspot.com; off Th Phunsuk; r 750-950B; ❄📶🏊) Family-run guesthouse with great prices and loads of character – you're greeted at the front door by a crystal chandelier and a statue of a German Shepherd wearing a floral lei on its head. The rest of the house, including the six small guestrooms, are also crammed with antiques and kitsch providing a real homey atmosphere.

Big Apple GUESTHOUSE $$
(☎089 686 1271; www.bigapplehuahin.com; Soi Hua Hin 83, Th Phetkasem, South Hua Hin; r/apt 1200/1800B; P❄📶🏊) This small, immaculate guesthouse (or Bed & Pool, as they call it) is in a soi between the beach and the massive Bluport shopping mall. There are five regular rooms and three apartments with small kitchens next to a playful garden with a big swimming pool. Book well in advance

during the high season. There's a two-night minimum stay.

Hua Hin Place GUESTHOUSE $$
(☎032 516640; www.huahin-place.com; 43/21 Th Naebkehardt; d & tw 400-1500 f 1200-1500B; ❄📶) Straddling a fine line between hotel and guesthouse, this fairly large place still falls into the latter thanks to the breezy ground-floor lounge – full of a museum's worth of shells, photos and other knick-knacks – where you can chat with the charming owner and other guests.

Love Sea House GUESTHOUSE $$
(☎080 079 0922; siamozohlie@hotmail.com; 35 Th Dechanuchit; r 700-800B; ❄📶) Pleasant, family-run guesthouse decked out in a blue-and-white nautical theme. The English-speaking elderly owners keep the good-sized rooms impressively clean. It's very near Hua Hin's party zone, but it's not an appropriate place for those planning to partake in it.

Baan Somboon GUESTHOUSE $$
(☎032 511538; 13/4 Soi Hua Hin 63, Th Damnoen Kasem; r 800B; ❄📶) With framed photos decorating the walls, polished wooden floors and a compact garden, this place on a very quiet centrally located soi is like staying at your favourite Thai auntie's house. Rooms are small and dated, but it's probably the homiest guesthouse in Hua Hin.

★ Centara Grand Beach Resort & Villas HOTEL $$$
(☎032 512021; www.centarahotelsresorts.com; 1 Th Damnoen Kasem; r incl breakfast 8700-14,000B; P❄@📶🏊) The historic Railway Hotel opened in 1922 and was Hua Hin's first hotel. It's been updated and expanded over the decades, but hasn't lost its genteel aura – no other local resort can match the ambience here. The rooms are large, the facilities fantastic and the staff on the ball, plus the vast gardens are full of frangipani and trimmed topiary.

★ Sanae Beach Club HOTEL $$$
(☎032 900971; www.sanaebeachclub.com; Hat Sai Noi; r incl breakfast 3700-4700B; P❄📶🏊🐾) The main thing about this small resort is that it's the only lodging right on gorgeous Hat Sai Noi (p170). The beach is nearly deserted on weekdays though it's very busy on weekends, and their 300B daily access pass means it's not just the beach that gets busy. Rooms are large and comfortable, although the all-white interior is a bit jarring.

★ Baan Bayan HOTEL $$$
(☎032 533540; www.beachfronthotelhuahin.com; Th Phetkasem, at Soi 69, South Hua Hin; r incl breakfast 4000-13,000B; P❄📶🏊) Centred on a beautiful teak house built in the early 20th century, Baan Bayan is perfect for travellers seeking a luxury experience without big resort overkill. The hotel is airy, with high-ceilinged rooms and attentive staff, and the location is absolute beachfront. Most of the rooms were added in modern times but share the same historic quality as the three originals.

Eating

Hua Hin is famous for its seafood, but locals prefer the simple restaurants in Ban Takiab south of the city, some of which do 400B buffets.

★ Baan Khrai Wang THAI, COFFEE $
(Th Naebkehardt; mains 65-285B; ⏲9am-6pm) The palm trees, flower garden, historic wooden beach homes and the sound of the surf make the setting at 'The House Near the Palace' pretty much perfect. For many, it's a place to lounge with coffee and coconut cake, but there's also a small menu of massaman curry, crab fried rice, *kôw châe* and Caesar salad wrap.

★ Jek Pia THAI $
(51/6 Th Dechanuchit; mains 35-150B; ⏲6.30am-12.30pm & 5.30-8pm) Once just a coffee shop, this 50-plus-year-old restaurant is one of Hua Hin's top culinary destinations. The late mother of the current owner invited her favourite cooks to come join her and it's now a gourmet food court of sorts, hence the stack of menus you get when you arrive.

★ Sôm·đam Tanontok 51 THAI $
(Th Damrongraj/Soi 51; mains 40-190B; ⏲10am-8pm; 📶) A stand-out restaurant in a great dining neighbourhood, this is real Isan food cooked by a family from Khorat. There's everything you'd expect to find including grilled catfish, *gaang orm* (coconut-milk-less herbal curry) and many versions of *sôm·đam* other than papaya, including cucumber and bamboo shoot. It also does a squid *lâhp*.

KITE CRAZY

Hua Hin is Thailand's kiteboarding capital, blessed with strong, gusty winds, shallow water and a long, long beach off which to practise your moves. Hua Hin even hosted the Kiteboarding World Cup in 2010.

From here down to Pranburi the winds blow from the northeast October to December, usually with lots of waves, and then from the southeast January to May usually with smooth water. Even during the rainy months in between there are plenty of days when the wind is fine for taking to the waves.

This is also one of the best places in Thailand to *learn* how to kiteboard, with a number of schools in Hua Hin offering lessons. Generally after three days with them you can be out on your own. January to March is the best time since the sea is less choppy. The schools also cater for more advanced students, and you can qualify as an instructor here.

Hua Hin Vegan Cafe VEGAN, THAI **$**
(Th Phetkasem; mains 100-250B; ⏲9.30am-9pm; 📶✍) 🍃 Except for the lack of animal products, this modern place has nothing in common with the typical Thai 'jae' vegan restaurant: there's wine, garlic, air-con, jazz, organic ingredients and creative cooking. There's lots of Thai – traditional and otherwise (quinoa *lâhp,* for example), but the menu knows no borders: pulled jackfruit teriyaki burgers, lentil tacos and West African peanut soup.

Chomsin-Naebkehardt Junction Street Food STREET FOOD **$**
(cnr Th Chomsin & Th Naebkehardt; ⏲6am-midnight) These noted street-food spots are a three-for-one deal and though the setting is humble, there's some excellent Thai food here. The action starts early each morning on Th Naebkehardt about 50m south of Chomsin and gradually more street carts start serving both here and across the road at the junction. Both spots sit under roofs for comfortable daytime dining.

At about 5pm the *dtôo rûng lék* (Little Night Market) takes over Soi 55/1 until late. It adds a little Isan food to the mix.

Baan Tuayen Icy Beans THAI **$**
(Th Naebkehardt; mains 55-145B; ⏲7am-10pm; 📶) A hipster hang-out that draws the crowds with three different menus for breakfast, lunch and dinner. There are dishes such as green curry with braised pork, but as the name suggests, desserts are the real stars; try the ice cream with red-bean sauce or red-bean smoothies.

Velo Cafe COFFEE **$**
(Th Naebkehardt; coffee from 50B; ⏲7.30am-5.30pm; 📶) Coffeeshops are everywhere in Hua Hin, but few are as serious as this little one, which roasts its own beans. It also makes very good sandwiches.

★ **Ratama** THAI **$$**
(12/10 Th Naebkehardt; mains 50-200B; ⏲8.30am-3.30pm) This restaurant's menu runs Thai omelettes to spicy seafood curries to a great panang curry, but it's famous for duck served in many forms including a bowl of *gŏo·ay đěe·o* noodle soup and a plate of fried beaks.

We also recommend trying the *súpêr đeen gài* (chicken-feet *đôm yam),* and if you ask they'll substitute duck feet.

The English-script sign is very hard to spot so look for the giant duck statue.

★ **Koti** CHINESE, THAI **$$**
(☎032 511252; 16/1 Th Dechanuchit; mains 40-400B; ⏲11am-10pm) This Thai-Chinese restaurant, opened in 1932, is a national culinary luminary. Thais adore the stir-fried oyster with flour and egg, while foreigners frequently aim for the *đôm yam gûng.* Everyone loves the *yam tá-lair* (spicy seafood salad) and classic green curry. Be prepared to wait for a table.

The Social Salad INTERNATIONAL **$$**
(1/8 Th Chomsin; mains 85-280B; ⏲8am-10pm; 📶✍) 🍃 This simple but nicely decorated place attracts many repeat customers for its 190B make-your-own salads – choose from a long checklist of fresh organic ingredients. Anti-salad folks can choose from a few pastas or fish and chips. Ten percent of proceeds go to tree-planting programs.

🍷 Drinking & Nightlife

Drinking destinations in Hua Hin's tourist zone are virtually all stuck in a time warp of sports bars or hostess bars. Try the posh hotels if you want something more sophisticated.

White Lotus Sky Bar BAR
(Th Naresdamri; beers from 200B; ⌚6pm-midnight; 📶) Up atop the Hilton Hotel, on the 17th floor, this classy lounge has inspiring views and refreshing breezes. And though it faces east, come early and you can watch an obstructed-view sunset. There's also a fancy Chinese restaurant here.

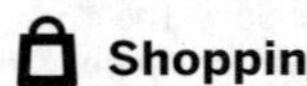

Shopping

Plearn Wan MARKET
(เพลินวาน; ☎032 520311; www.plearnwan.com; Th Phetkasem btwn Soi 38 & Soi 40; ⌚9am-9pm Sun-Thu, 9am-10pm Fri & Sat) One of Hua Hin's top destinations for Thai travellers, Plearn Wan ('Lose Yourself In The Past') is a retro-themed market with small stalls designed to resemble the old shophouses of Thai-Chinese neighbourhoods in Bangkok and Hua Hin. It's full of old photos, vintage furniture and Thais posing for photos.

Hua Hin Night Market MARKET
(Th Dechanuchit; ⌚5pm-midnight) An attraction that rivals the beach in popularity, Hua Hin's two-block-long night market is full of tourists every night. There's all the standard knock-off clothes and cheap souvenirs, plus dozens of very annoying restaurant hosts waving menus in your face from the middle of the road.

For what it's worth, Lung Ja seems to be the only restaurant here that Thai visitors eat at; locals don't eat here at all. The market's off-street section in the southeast, known as Chatsila, is mostly more of the same, but does has a few shops selling actual art.

Information

There are exchange booths open into the evening and ATMs all around the tourist centre, in particular on Th Naresdamri and Th Damnoen Kasen streets. For full service banking head to Th Phetkaksem and for banks open evenings and weekends head to a shopping mall.

Bangkok Hospital Hua Hin (☎032 616800; www.bangkokhospital.com/huahin; Th Phetkasem at Soi 94) An outpost of the well-regarded national hospital chain in south Hua Hin.

Immigration Office (☎032 905111; Th Phetkasem, at Soi 100, South Hua Hin; ⌚10am-6pm Mon-Fri) In the basement level of Bluport shopping mall. You can extend tourist visas here.

Municipal Tourist Information Office (☎032 611491; Th Naebkehardt; ⌚9am-4.30pm Mon-Fri, 9am-5pm Sat & Sun) Has a good free map of the city and surrounding area and can answer basic questions.

San Paolo Hospital (☎032 532576; www.sanpaulo.co.th; 222 Th Phetkasem, South Hua Hin) A small private hospital south of town at Soi 86; it's a good option for ordinary illnesses and injuries.

Tourism Authority of Thailand (TAT; ☎032 513854; www.tourismthailand.org/hua-hin; 39/4 Th Phetkasem, at Soi 55; ⌚8.30am-4.30pm) Staff here speak English and are quite helpful, though they rarely open on time.

Tourist Police (☎032 516219; Th Damnoen Kasem) At the eastern end of the street just before the beach.

HUA HIN ONLINE

Hua Hin Today (www.huahintoday.com) Expat-published newspaper. A paper version (50B) is printed monthly.

Tourism Hua Hin (www.tourismhuahin.com) Decent coverage of the city and the outlying area.

Getting There & Away

The train is the most pleasant way to get to or leave Hua Hin, but minivan is the most popular. If you prefer to get between Hua Hin and Bangkok as quickly (as little as three hours) and comfortably as possible, private cars start at 1600B.

BOAT

Lomprayah (☎032 532761; www.lomprayah.com; Th Phetkasem; ⌚8am-10pm) offers a bus-boat combination from Hua Hin to Ko Tao (1050B, six to nine hours), as well as to Ko Pha-Ngan (1300B, nine to 12 hours) and Ko Samui (1400B, 10 to 13 hours) with departures from its office at 8.30am and 11.30pm.

There's also now a **passenger ferry** (☎093 495 9499; www.royalferrygroup.com; Soi Ao Hua Don 3; economy/first-class/8-person VIP room 1250/1550/14,000B; ⌚departs Pattaya/Hua Hin 10am/1pm) between Hua Hin and Pattaya allowing you to skip Bangkok.

BUS & MINIVAN

Minivans going north (including Phetchaburi, Kanchanaburi and many destinations in Bangkok) use the new **Hua Hin Van Station** (Soi 51) while minivans (and the occasional bus) going south stop in the road next to the clock tower. Service runs frequently from about 6am to most places (4am for Bangkok and Phetchaburi) until the early evening.

The quiet little **Hua Hin Bus Station** (Th Phetkasem, at Soi 96) south of the city has a few buses (most going between Bangkok and the south don't come into town) to Bangkok, Chiang Mai, Nakhon Ratchasima (Khorat), Phuket and Ubon Ratchathani. Tickets should be bought a day in advance.

A more convenient place to get a bus to Bangkok (Southern Bus Terminal) is with Hua Hin-Pran Tour (p169) on Th Sasong near the night market, though the buses are old. Also, there's Airport Hua Hin Bus (p169) going from Hua Hin Airport to Bangkok's Suvarnabhumi International Airport and Pattaya. If you use this bus, they have a shuttle to your hotel for 100B, which is cheaper than what a túk-túk will charge to take you into town. The green *sŏrng·tăa·ou* don't go quite this far.

Ordinary (fan) buses go to Pranburi from Th Sasong by the night market and to Cha-am and Phetchaburi about hourly all day from Th Phetkasem across from the Esso petrol station.

Getting Around

Green *sŏrng·tăa·ou* (10B) depart from the corner of Th Sasong and Th Dechanuchit, by the night market. They travel from 6am to 9pm along Th Phetkasem south to Khao Takiab (turning east

TRANSPORT TO/FROM HUA HIN

DESTINATION	BUS	MINIVAN	TRAIN
Bangkok Don Mueang International Airport	N/A	200B, 4½hr, every 40min	N/A
Bangkok Ekkamai (Eastern Bus Station)	N/A	180B, 4½hr, hourly	N/A
Bangkok Hualamphong	N/A	N/A	44-402B, 3½-4½hr, 12 daily
Bangkok Northern (Mo Chit) Bus Terminal	241B, 4½hr, 9am, noon, 1.30pm, 3pm	180B, 4hr, frequent	N/A
Bangkok Southern Bus Terminal	155B, 4½hr, 3am, 10am, noon daily & 4pm, 9pm Fri-Sat	180B, 4hr, frequent	N/A
Bangkok Suvarnabhumi International Airport	269B, 4½hr, every 90min 6am-6pm	N/A	N/A
Bangkok Thonburi	N/A	N/A	42-96B, 4½hr, 2 daily
Cha-am	20-30B, 30-45min, hourly 6am-4pm	30B, 30min, frequent	6-33B, 30min, 5 daily
Chiang Mai	735-980B, 13hr, 5.30pm, 6pm, 6.15pm	N/A	N/A
Chumphon	328B, 5hr, noon	N/A	49-423B, 4-5hr, 12 daily
Kanchanaburi	N/A	220B, 4hr, hourly	N/A
Nakhon Ratchasima (Khorat)	347-518B, 6-7hr, 10am, 6pm, 9pm, 11pm	N/A	N/A
Pattaya	389B, 5hr, 11am	N/A	N/A
Phetchaburi	40B, 1½hr, hourly 6am-4pm	80B, 1hr, frequent	14-341B, 1hr, 12 daily
Phuket	587-913B, 10-11hr, 10am, 12,30pm, 7pm, 8.30pm, 9pm, 10.30pm, midnight	N/A	N/A
Prachuap Khiri Khan	N/A	80B, 1½hr, frequent	19-353B, 1-1½hr, 11 daily
Pranburi	20B, 30min, every 30min 7am-3pm	30B, 30min, frequent	5-31B, 30min, 3 daily
Ubon Ratchathani	628-868B, 12-13hr, 6pm, 9pm, 11pm	N/A	N/A

on Th Damnoen Kasem on the way) and north to the airport.

Four-wheeled túk-túk fares start at a whopping 100B for short trips. Motorcycle taxis are much more reasonable (30B to 50B) for short hops.

Many shops around town hire motorcycles (200B to 250B per day) and a few have bicycles (100B to 200B per day). Damnoen Kasem, Naebkehardt and Chomsin streets have several shops each. Hua Hin Bike Tours (p172) and **Velo Thailand** (032 900392; www.velothailand.com; Th Phetkasem; full-day tours from 3850B; 8am-6pm Sun-Thu, 8am-9pm Fri & Sat) rent top-of-the-line bikes.

There are roadside tables arranging taxis (any vehicle that you can charter, including pick-up trucks and túk-túk) all around the city centre. Prices are mostly fixed, but it's worth haggling. Don't agree to anything without knowing exactly what vehicle you are getting. Booking through your hotel or a tour company may cost a little more than doing it yourself.

Thai Rent A Car (083 887 5454; www.thairentacar.com; Th Phetkasem at Soi 84, South Hua Hin; 8.30am-6.30pm) is a professional Thailand-based car-rental agency with competitive prices, a well-maintained fleet, hotel drop-offs and one-way rentals.

Pranburi & Around ปราณบุรี

032 / POP 24,800

Half an hour south of Hua Hin is the country 'suburb' of Pranburi district, which serves as a quiet coastal alternative. There are many expensive boutique resorts ideal for anyone looking to escape the crowds without travelling too far from civilisation.

The core area is the small town of **Pak Nam Pran** (mouth of the Pranburi River), which has the biggest resorts but not much beach. Though tourism is growing here, fishing is still the key to the economy and most Thai visitors return home with some dried squid.

South of Pak Nam Pran there's a sandy shore and the coastal road provides a quick pleasant trip to **Khao Kalok** (Skull Mountain), a mammoth, oddly eroded headland that shelters the most, and pretty much only, attractive beach in the area. It's signed as Thao Kosa Forest Park, but locals and road signs all call it Khao Kalok.

Sights & Activities

Pak Nam Pran and points south have the same great kiteboarding winds as Hua Hin. For lessons and rentals there's **Yoda Kite School** (087 017 6428; www.pudla0.wixsite.com/yodakiteschool; Beach Rd, Pak Nam Pran; 10am-6pm) or talk to Karl Tindell at Beach House Bistro (p179) or at his new Beach House Bar, 250m south of Yoda.

★**Kuiburi National Park** NATIONAL PARK

(อุทยานแห่งชาติกุยบุรี; 085 266 1601; Rte 4024; adult/child 200/100B, wildlife-spotting trip per truck 850B; wildlife trips 2-6pm) Who doesn't want to see herds of wild elephants roaming through the forest or enjoying an evening bath? At Kuiburi National Park's *hôoay léuk* unit, up near the border with Myanmar, it's almost guaranteed. Wildlife-watching drives in the back of pick-up trucks (with bench seating for up to 10) go through forest and reclaimed farm fields where about 240 elephants live. They're used to seeing vehicles, so they pay them little mind, making this almost like an African safari experience.

There are also plenty of gaur (wild cattle) and they're seen fairly often. Most of the spotters don't speak English, but they know some relevant vocabulary. Avoid Saturdays if possible, as the park gets very busy. It's 45 minutes west of Khao Sam Roi Yot National Park (p180) – follow the national park signs for 'wildlife watching' – and the two make an ideal combo visit.

Pranburi Forest Park NATURE RESERVE

(วนอุทยานปราณบุรี, Wana-Utthayan Pranburi; 032 621608; 6am-6pm) Just north of the Pranburi River is an extensive natural mangrove forest. A 1km-long boardwalk with interpretive signs, some in English, lets you explore it from the perspective of a mud-dweller, while an observation tower gives you a bird's-eye view. At high tide fishermen will take visitors on 45-minute boat trips (500B) along the river and small canals.

You'll see hundreds of crabs, and usually a fair number of birds, mudskippers and water monitors. In some areas you'll hear snapping shrimp. There's quite a bit of variety within this forest – the ecosystem is different enough from the young, replanted mangrove across the river at **Sirinart Rajini Mangrove Ecosystem Learning Center** (ศูนย์ศึกษาเรียนรู้ระบบนิเวศป่าชายเลนสิรินาถราชินี; Pak Nam Pran; 8.30am-4.30pm) FREE that nature lovers will appreciate visiting both.

It's a 14km drive from Pak Nam Pran via Rte 1019, passing very near Hat Sai Noi (p170) on the way. A more direct route half this length is shown on many maps, but it's not passable any more.

Sleeping

Not all of the beach resorts earn the price tag so be discerning when making online reservations. As at Hua Hin, there are big weekday discounts.

Thongsuk Mini Resort HOTEL $$
(☎098 423 2661; jamsawang38@gmail.com; r 850B; P❄📶) Not the cheapest address in Pak Nam Pran, but for about 100B extra than most others, these nine white bungalows are a good budget option. There are free bikes and though the owners speak little English they're very eager to please. It's a two-minute walk from the squid roundabout where the minivans stop.

★**La a natu Bed & Bakery** BOUTIQUE HOTEL $$$
(☎032 689941; www.laanatu.com; south of Khao Kalok; r/fm incl breakfast & afternoon tea 5500-16,000/11,000B; P❄📶🏊) Turning the humble Thai rice village into a luxury living experience is what La a natu does and it does it with panache. The blissfully remote thatched-roof villas rising on stilts are full *Gilligan's Island* outside with a touch of luxury inside, and real rice paddies below.

Eating & Drinking

The obligatory seafood restaurants are up at the top of Pak Nam Pran town, near the river's mouth. The biggest **night market** (Beach Rd; ⊙5-9.30pm) takes place on the coastal road while there's also the much smaller 'Roundabout Market', **Talat Wong-Wian** (Th Pasukwanich at Soi 10; ⊙5-9pm), in the centre of town.

There are scattered bars, mostly occupied by expats and long-term guests, along the coastal road in Pak Nam Pran continuing down south to Khao Kalok.

★**Krua Renu** THAI $
(Th Pak Nam Pran; mains 40-120B; ⊙7am-10pm Thu-Tue) There are both budget and beautiful restaurants along the coastal road, but some of the best food in Pak Nam Pran is in the town at this tall restaurant 200m east of the squid roundabout. Go with the standard *đôm yam* or try the *gaang ɓàh hâang* (dried jungle curry).

Beach House Bistro INTERNATIONAL $$
(☎095 549 0206; Th Pak Nam Pran-Khao Kalok; mains 80-365B; ⊙9am-10pm; 📶) Though it's 1km from the sea, this small place does have a beach vibe. It does a little of everything – Italian, Mexican, baguette sandwiches, wine, Thai and a 265B Sunday roast – with all the quality of the four-star resorts, but at half the price.

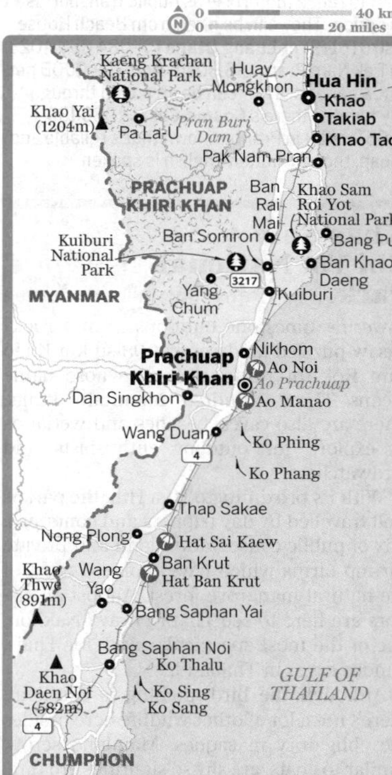

Getting There & Around

Pak Nam Pran is about 25km south of Hua Hin. Ordinary buses (20B, 30 minutes, every 30 minutes 7am to 3pm), minivans (30B, 30 minutes, frequent 6am to 7pm) and trains (5B to 31B, 30 minutes, 11.47am, 5.50pm, 8.10pm) will drop you off in Pranburi town, 10km from Pak Nam Pran and taxi drivers charge 200B between the two. There are also minivans (60B, one hour, frequent 5am to 6.40pm) and trains (14B to 62B, one hour, 4.51am, 10.03am, 2.26pm) from Prachuap Khiri Khan.

There's a direct minivan service from Pak Nam Pran (at the squid roundabout on the south side of town) every 30 minutes from early morning to late afternoon to Bangkok's Mo Chit and Southern bus terminals (200B, five hours). These vans also stop in Phetchaburi (140B, two hours), but do not stop in Hua Hin.

If you want to explore the area, you'll probably want to rent a motorbike as public transport isn't an option. They can be hired from Beach House Bistro (p179) or **Luang Utane** (☎ 084 080 4023; Th Pak Nam Pran; ⏱8.30am-5pm) for 200B per day. A car and driver can be arranged through any hotel or there's **Cosmo Car** (☎ 080 139 6665) rental in Pranburi town that's reliable and cheap, though limited English is spoken.

Khao Sam Roi Yot National Park

อุทยานแห่งชาติเขาสามร้อยยอด

Towering limestone outcrops form a rocky jigsaw-puzzled landscape at 98-sq-km Khao Sam Roi Yot National Park, whose name means Three Hundred Mountain Peaks. There are also caves, beaches and wetlands to explore for outdoor enthusiasts and birdwatchers.

With its proximity to Hua Hin, the park is well travelled by day trippers and contains a mix of public conservation land and private shrimp farms which have replaced most of the natural mangrove forest. Almost all visitors are here to see Tham Phraya Nakhon, one of the most spectacular and, for Thais, famous caves in Thailand.

Although the birdwatching is excellent, there's not a lot of other wildlife here besides the obligatory macaques. Mainland serow, similar to goats, are shy so sightings are rare. The adorable dusky langur is easy to find at Tham Phraya Nakhon and the visitor centre.

There's no park gate. Admission tickets are sold and checked, and maps provided at each of the park's attractions.

Sights & Activities

At the intersection of the East Asian and Australian migration routes, the national park hosts over 300 migratory and resident bird species, including yellow bitterns, purple swamphens, ruddy-breasted crakes, bronze-winged jacanas, black-headed ibises, great spotted eagles and oriental reed warblers. The park is one of the few places in Thailand where purple heron and Malaysian plover breed.

Most birders come here for waterbirds, which are most commonly seen in the cool season from November to March. The beach east of the headquarters and the marsh to the west are two hot spots. **Thai Birding** (www.thaibirding.com) provides in-depth information.

★ Tham Phraya Nakhon & Hat Laem Sala — CAVE

(ถ้ำพระยานคร/หาดแหลมศาลา; parking 30B; ⏱daylight hours) The park's most-visited attraction is this revered cave sheltering a royal *sǎh·lah* (often spelt *sala*) built for Rama V in 1890. Scenes of this **Khuha Kharuehat Pavilion** bathed in streams of morning light (usually starting at about 10.30am) are widespread making this place famous across the kingdom. Even more interesting is the cave itself. The roof has collapsed in both of the large chambers allowing small forests to grow, adding an otherworldly ambience.

The trail to the cave is a 430m-long, steep and rocky stairway built into the hill. You'll almost certainly meet macaques and dusky langur on the way up. The path begins at picturesque **Laem Sala Beach**, flanked on three sides by limestone hills and shaded by casuarina trees. It can get busy here on weekends, but it's always peaceful at night and in the early morning.

There's no road access to the beach. Most people ride a boat (200B one-way) from the fishing village of Bang Pu. Note that these are wet landings, but in shallow water. Alternatively, you can follow the steep footpath from Bang Pu for a 1km hike to the beach. A boat ride to Laem Sala from the Hat Sam Roi Yot resort area costs 1200B and for an extra 200B they throw in a 'monkey island'.

A leisurely visit to Tham Phraya Nakhon will take at least three hours, but it could easily be extended into a full day with time on the beach, or even an overnight if you camp (p181).

Khlong Khao Daeng — RIVER

(คลองเขาแดง; ☎ 062 479451; Rte 4020; up to 6 people 500B; ⏱8am-5.45pm) You can hire a covered boat at Wat Khao Daeng for a one-hour scenic cruise along this stream. There are great mountain views and you'll also see birds, macaques, water monitors and mudskippers. The guides don't speak much English, but they know some relevant vocabulary.

Tham Kaew — CAVE

(ถ้ำแก้ว; ⏱daylight hours, begin walk no later than 3.30pm) Though it's on the way to Tham Phraya Nakhon, few people visit this beautiful cave where the stalactites and flowstone glitter with calcite crystals; hence the name, 'Jewel Cave'. You enter the cavern down a ladder after a quite steep and rough 130m trail

DON'T MISS

DOLPHIN BAY

Hat Sam Roi Yot, aka Dolphin Bay as occasionally dolphins and porpoises can be spotted far offshore, is a 15-minute drive from Bang Pu, the primary entry point of Khao Sam Roi Yot National Park. Resorts are value-oriented, traffic is minimal and nightlife is nearly non-existent. The wide strip and powdery sand is not an inviting swimming beach, but it's a great place to sit and stare at the sculpted, jungle-covered islands to the south and the jagged coast to the north. There are kayaks for hire for 100B per hour, though some guesthouses have them free for guests.

Want to splash around for more than just a day? **Dolphin Bay Resort** (032 825190; www.dolphinbayresort.com; Th Liap Chai Tale, Hat Sam Roi Yot; r 4590-13,680B, f 1690-2790;) is a family-friendly retreat with a variety of standard-issue, value-oriented rooms and villas, plus two big pools, a playground and a toy room.

up the mountain. Inside you can walk pretty easily for about 200m to see the natural wonder and beyond that are more chambers that require getting dirty.

Sleeping & Eating

The **Laem Sala Beach Campground** (032 821568; per person with tent 30B, 2-person tent hire 150B), not accessible by road, is an attractive peaceful place to spend the night. **Thung Sam Roi Yot** (032 821568; per person with tent 30B) and **Sam Phraya Beach** (032 821568; per person with tent 30B, 3-person tent hire 150B) also have campgrounds. The bungalows at Khao Daeng aren't very pleasant. Many people stay just outside the park at Hat Sam Roi Yot beach.

There are restaurants, open 6am to 6pm, at Bang Pu where you start and end visits to Tham Phraya Nakhon. Restaurants at Laem Sala beach, Sam Phraya beach and Thung Sam Roi Yot generally open at 8am and close at 5.30pm, 8pm and 8pm, respectively.

Information

The Hat Sam Roi Yot tourist zone has ATMs and small shops.

Khao Sam Roi Yot Visitor Center (032 821568; Rte 4020; 8am-4.30pm) The park's main visitor centre has friendly, helpful staff, but there's generally no need to visit since tickets are sold and maps provided at all of the park attractions. There used to be a 900m boardwalk through the mangrove forest behind the visitor centre; it may reopen someday.

Getting There & Away

The park is around 50km from both Hua Hin and Prachuap Khiri Khan. There's no public transport to or within the park, so you need to come with your own wheels. Hiring a car and driver for the day from Hua Hin and Prachuap will cost about 1800B to 2000B including petrol while it's as little as 1200B from Hat Sam Roi Yot. Some people charge extra to include Thung Sam Roi Yot. Many people combine a morning visit to Khao Sam Roi Yot with afternoon elephant watching at Kuiburi National Park (p178). Most Hua Hin tour companies have day trips here, but they only visit Tham Phraya Nakhon.

Motorcycles (250B to 350B per day) and bikes (100B to 200B) can be hired at Dolphin Bay Resort and some other spots in Hat Sam Roi Yot.

A taxi from the train station or bus stop in Pranburi to Hat Sam Roi Yot is a fixed 400B. No public transport comes here any more.

Prachuap Khiri Khan ประจวบคีรีขันธ์

032 / POP 33,500

A sleepy seaside town, Prachuap Khiri Khan is a delightfully relaxed place; the antithesis of Hua Hin. The broad bay is a tropical turquoise punctuated by bobbing fishing boats and overlooked by honeycombed limestone mountains – scenery that you usually have to travel to the southern Andaman to find.

In recent years, foreigners have discovered Prachuap's charms and some Bangkokians drive past Hua Hin for their weekends away, but their numbers are still very small compared to better-known destinations.

Sights & Activities

Th Suseuk south of the Municipal Market 1 still has lots of old wooden houses and makes a great walk day and night. It hosts the **Suseuk Culture and Fun Street Market** with food, crafts, music and more food the first weekend of each month.

Prachuap Khiri Khan

0 500 m
0 0.25 miles
Rop Lom (620m); Golden Beach Hotel (900m)
Minivan Station (1.5km); (2.3km)
Th Prachuap Khiri Khan
Th Chai Thaleh
Th Phitak Chat
Th Salacheep
Ao Prachuap
Suan Saranrom Park
Th Thetsaban Bamrung
Pier
Th Kong Kiat
Tourist Office
Train Station
Th Maharat
Th Chai Thaleh
Th Suseuk
Th Maitri Ngam
Soi 5
Soi 6 (Th Rong Phayaban)
Ty I-House (270m); Khao Lammuak (2.3km)

Prachuap Khiri Khan

Sights

1	Ao Prachuap	B2
2	Khao Chong Krajok	B1

Activities, Courses & Tours

3	Sunset Cruise	B2

Sleeping

4	Grandma's House	B4
5	Maggie's Seaview Guesthouse	B4
6	Prachuap Beach Hotel	B4
7	Safehouse Hostel	A4
8	Yutichai Hotel	A3

Eating

9	Ciao Pizza	B4
	Grandma's House	(see 4)
10	In Town Seafood	B4
11	Krua Chaiwat	B4
12	Municipal Market 1	B3
13	Night Market	A2
14	Rim Taley Market	B2
15	Som Tam Baa Nook	B2

Drinking & Nightlife

16	Maggie's Wine Garden	B4
17	Top Deck	B4

Transport

18	Bangkok & Phetchaburi Bus Stop	A3

Ao Prachuap BAY

(อ่าวประจวบ) The town's crowning feature is Ao Prachuap (Prachuap Bay), a gracefully curving bay outlined by an oceanfront promenade and punctuated by dramatic headlands at both ends. The sunrise is superb and an evening stroll along the promenade and pier is a peaceful delight.

North of **Khao Chong Krajok** (เขาช่องกระจก), over the bridge, the bay stretches peacefully to a toothy mountain, part of **Khao Ta Mong Lai Forest Park** (วนอุทยานเขาตาม่องล่าย; 081 378 0026; daylight hours). The long sandy beach running parallel with the road before the forest park only sees people on weekends and even then not very many, making it a fine place to idle and beachcomb at any time. It's deep enough for swimming, but not very clean.

Wat Ao Noi BUDDHIST TEMPLE

(วัดอ่าวน้อย; daylight hours) FREE Leaving Ao Prachuap behind, turn north for 2.5km, passing the fishing village of **Ban Ao Noi**, where some of the larger boats dock and unload, to this large temple linking two bays: Ao Noi and Ao Khan Kradai. It features a lovely *bòht* constructed entirely of teak without nails, and the murals, mostly telling the Buddha's life story, are composed of framed painted wood carvings. The pond in front is filled with fish, eager to be fed by merit-makers.

Ao Manao BEACH

(อ่าวมะนาว; beach zone 5am-7pm, mountain zone 6am-6pm) On weekends, locals head to Ao Manao, an island-dotted bay ringed by a curving beach within Wing 5 Thai Air Force base – the only beach where locals go swimming as both the water and sand are clean. There are the usual seaside amenities: restaurants, beach chairs, umbrellas and inner tubes, plus some dry-land diversions including quad-bike rides and a petting zoo. It's packed on weekends but can be nearly deserted on weekdays.

You need to register at the base entrance, at the end of Th Salacheep. Normally no passport is necessary, but best to bring it in case you're asked. From here it's 2.5km to the beach. Across the bay from the public beach is Khao Lammuak.

Sunset Cruise CRUISE
(080 110 8272; www.samaowtour.com; Th Chai Thaleh; 300B) Sam Aow Princess Tour has a short sunset cruise in Prachuap Bay starting around 5.30pm or 6pm nightly, if there are enough passengers. Drinks are sold.

Sleeping

This is a town where you don't want to be far from the sea. The closest you can get to luxury are some decent midrange places. There are lots of small homestays and guesthouses in the city centre near the sea. Book ahead on high-season weekends.

In Town

Safehouse Hostel HOSTEL $
(087 909 4770; 28 Soi 6, Th Salacheep; dm 250, r 450-650B;) With fairly frumpy though very tidy rooms, the host Sherry is the real reason this small hostel has become popular. She goes out of her way to please guests and leads good tours to Kuiburi National Park (p178) and elsewhere. There's a communal kitchen.

Yutichai Hotel HOTEL $
(032 611055; yutichai_hotel@hotmail.com; 115 Th Kong Kiat; r with fan 220-450, air-con 500-550B;) A bit of history right near the train station, this old wooden hotel is properly maintained and the prices are right. Most rooms (including those with air-con, private bathrooms and hot water) are in a more modern, but still classic concrete building at the back. Light sleepers will want to stay at the back, or elsewhere.

★ **Prachuap Beach Hotel** HOTEL $$
(032 601288; www.prachuapbeach.com; 123 Th Suseuk; d & tw 800-900, tr 1200B;) The best located, and possibly quietest, hotel in the city is near lots of good restaurants, opens up to the promenade and has great views from upper floors. The 2nd-floor rooms are cheapest, but it's worth paying the extra 100B to be up higher – the 5th floor is the top.

The rooms are old-fashioned, though very good for the price.

★ **Grandma's House** BOUTIQUE HOTEL $$
(089 526 6896; grandmaprachuap@gmail.com; 238 Th Suseuk; r incl breakfast 700-900B;) Up above its popular vintage-themed **café** (mains 39-159B, coffee from 30B; 7.30am-6pm;), these three solid wooden rooms (two small and one large) are decorated with some actual antiques. They share two modern bathrooms.

You'll need to endure street noise, but there's normally not too much at night.

WORTH A TRIP

WORLD WAR II MONUMENTS

Prachuap was one of seven points on the gulf coast where Japanese troops landed on 8 December 1941 during their invasion of Thailand. The Air Force base at Ao Manao was the site of fierce skirmishes – the Japanese didn't fully capture the town until the next day after the Thai government ordered its soldiers to stop fighting since an armistice had been arranged.

Forty-one soldiers and civilians who died in the battle are memorialised at **Khao Lammuak** (เขาล้อมหมวก; 6am-6pm, museum 9am-3pm Sat & Sun), a soaring limestone mountain marking the southern end of Ao Prachuap. Several street names around town also refer to the battle such as Phitak Chat (Defend Country), Salacheep (Sacrifice Life) and Suseuk (Fight a Battle). About 400 Japanese also died.

About 400m in front of the mountain, three attractive monuments and the **Wing 5 Museum** commemorate the battle. You need to register at the Wing 5 Thai Air Force base entrance, at the end of Th Salacheep, and again at a second checkpoint. Bring your passport in case you're asked. It's 4.3km to the mountain from the entrance; follow the 'Historical Park' signs.

At the mountain's rocky summit are a Buddha footprint and fantastic views. However, because of many accidents, the climb, requiring pulling yourself up with ropes at some points, is now only allowed on long holiday weekends.

OFF THE BEATEN TRACK

MYANMAR (BURMA) BORDER MARKET

A mere 12km west of Prachuap Khiri Khan is the Myanmar border and for many years there has been talk of foreigners being able to cross 'in the near future'. Don't hold your breath. In the meantime, you can still visit the town of Dan Singkhon on the Thai side of the border, 20km drive from the city. There's a Saturday-morning border market for Burmese traders to come across and sell to Thais. Its former exotic appeal has been washed away by modern construction and few people now consider it worth the trip unless they're shopping for wooden furniture or orchids. Many of the people selling these products are here the rest of the week too. Minivans (100B, 30 minutes) make the trip from Prachuap Khiri Khan's minivan station (p186), but only depart when there are enough passengers.

Out of Town

★ Khao Ta Mong Lai Forest Park Campsite CAMPGROUND $
(☎081 378 0026; with tent 50B, 3-person tent hire 200B) There's a shady, seldom-used campground in this park (p182) with some of the cleanest facilities in Thailand. There are simple bungalows too, but they're intended for large groups. Since it's across the bay from the city centre, you get some great sunsets.

Golden Beach Hotel HOTEL $$
(☎032 601626; www.goldenbeachboutique.com; 113 Th Suanson; d & tw 1100-2500, f 1400-1800B; P ❄ 📶) After a full renovation, these large rooms are now some of Prachuap's best, if you don't mind being about 2km from the city centre. The higher prices get the biggest sea views, but the scenery is preferable from the cheapest rooms at the back, which has river and ocean views together. The beach is across the road.

Eating

Restaurants in Prachuap are known for cheap and excellent seafood, while Western options are easy to find. The **Municipal Market 1** (Th Maitri Ngam; ⏲4am-4pm) is the place to get pineapples fresh from the orchards; ask the vendor to cut it for you. There are a pair of small **night markets** (Th Kong Kiat; ⏲4.30pm-2am) in the city centre.

Krua Chaiwat THAI $
(Th Salacheep; mains 40-160B; ⏲9am-3pm & 4.30-8pm Mon-Sat; 📶 🖉) With good food at low prices, this small restaurant serves a mix of locals and expats. While Thai food is its strength – the *đôm yam* and *mêe·ang kam* (an assemble-it-yourself snack with wild pepper leaves) are quite good – there's also steaks and a few fusion foods like the stir-fried spaghetti with salted mackerel.

Ty I-House BAKERY $
(235 Th Suseuk; bakery 30B; ⏲8am-5pm Mon-Sat; 📶) Khun Suchada took an early retirement and has turned her hobby into a small business. She bakes what she feels like, only having a few things available at any one time, and sells it from a small table. Her chocolate brownie is excellent.

Som Tam Baa Nook THAI $
(Th Suseuk; mains 30-90B; ⏲7am-4pm) Baa Nook is a transplant from Isan and she serves real-deal northeastern fare from this rough-and-tumble street-food shop. The *sôm·đam* (spicy papaya salad) is excellent – she has the *bplah ráh* (fermented fish sauce) shipped down from her family back in Buriram – and there's chicken *lâhp*, grilled catfish and more.

Rim Taley Market MARKET $
(Th Chai Thaleh; ⏲4-8.30pm Mon-Thu, 4-9pm Fri & Sat) The 'Oceanside Market' isn't very large, but it makes an ideal dinner destination because you can eat your food on the promenade or pier. On Friday and Saturday the few dozen regular vendors are joined by about 200 more as the market morphs into **Walking Street**, though there's little in the way of artistic or handmade goods on sale.

★ In Town Seafood THAI $$
(Th Chai Thaleh; mains 50-350B; ⏲3-11pm) A go-to place for discerning locals, here you can eat streetside under a utilitarian tent while gazing at the squid boats in the bay. Great range of fresh seafood on display – barracuda, crab and shellfish – so you can point and pick if you don't recognise the names on the menu. Service can be slow.

Ciao Pizza ITALIAN $$
(Th Suseuk; mains 160-280B; ⏲11am-3pm & 4-10pm; 📶 🖉) Ciao Pizza is Italian-owned; come here for fine pizzas, pastas and gelato,

as well as fresh bread baked daily and a take-away selection of cheese and salami. There's a quiet dining area hidden at the back.

Rop Lom SEAFOOD $$

(Th Suanson; mains 70-190B; ⏲10am-9pm; wi-fi) Popular with the locals, the *pàt pŏng gà·rèe Ƃoo* (crab curry) comes with big chunks of sweet crab meat and the *yam tá-lair* (seafood salad) is spicy and zesty. On the non-oceanic side of things there's *yam dòk·kaa* (sesbania flower salad).

Drinking & Nightlife

The beach road is the place to be. There's a small bunch of low-key bars north of the Prachuap Beach Hotel; it's absolutely nothing like the loud sleazy bar scene in Hua Hin.

Maggie's Wine Garden BAR

(Th Chai Thaleh; slushy cocktails 200B; ⏲4-11pm Sat-Thu; wi-fi) Just a few doors down from her guesthouse (☎087 597 9720; Th Chai Thaleh; r 250-600B; air-con, internet, wi-fi), Maggie has a cosy bar with a big liquor list and a little food. The slushy margaritas and pineapple mojitos are more fitting of the vibe than the shiraz. There's a stage with instruments waiting for willing open-mike musicians.

Top Deck BAR

(53 Th Chai Thaleh; beers/cocktails from 65/130B; ⏲1.30-11pm Thu-Tue; wi-fi) At the Top Deck you can sip a libation until relatively late while gazing out at the winking lights of the fishing boats in the bay. Also does surprisingly good Thai plus a little Western food (80B to 300B).

Information

There are lots of banks and ATMs in the city centre. The nearest banks that are open evenings and weekends are in the Tesco-Lotus shopping mall out on the highway, 3km west of the city centre.

TRANSPORT TO/FROM PRACHUAP KHIRI KHAN

DESTINATION	BUS	MINIVAN	TRAIN
Ban Krut	70B, 1hr, 3 daily (to the town)	70-90B, 1hr, every 30min 5.40am-7pm (to the Hwy)	13-339B, 1hr, 8 daily
Bang Saphan Yai	80B, 1½hr, 10 daily (to the town)	80-100B, 1½hr, every 30min 5.40am-7pm (8 to the town, all others to the Hwy)	16-347B, 1¼hr, 9 daily
Bangkok Hualamphong	N/A	N/A	168-455B, 4½-5½hr, 9 daily
Bangkok Northern (Mo Chit) Bus Terminal	240B, 6-7hr, 3.30pm	220B, 5hr, every 45min 1.30am-7.30pm	N/A
Bangkok Southern Bus Terminal	200B, 6-7hr, every 90min 7.30am-9pm	200B, 5hr, every 45min 3am-7pm	N/A
Bangkok Thonburi	N/A		56-130B, 6hr, 1.05pm
Cha-am	N/A	120B, 2hr, frequent 5am-6.40pm	54-85B, 2hr, 4 daily
Chumphon	220B, 4hr, hourly 11am-midnight	180B, 3½hr, every 50min 6am-7pm	16-347B, 2½-3hr, 10 daily
Hua Hin	N/A	80B, 1½hr, frequent 5am-6.40pm	19-353B, 1-1½hr, 11 daily
Phetchaburi	150B, 2½hr, hourly 7.30am-9pm	150B, 2½hr, every 40 min 3am-7pm	31-382B, 2-2½hr, 11 daily
Phuket	587-913B, 9-10hr, 11am & every 30min 8pm-midnight	N/A	N/A
Pranburi	N/A	60B, 1hr, frequent 5am-6.40pm	14-62B, 1hr, 3 daily
Ranong	N/A	250B, 4½hr, 8am, 10am, 1pm, 3.30pm	N/A

Tourist Office (☎032 604143; Th Chai Taley; ⏲8.30am-noon & 1-4.30pm Mon-Fri) At the foot of the pier, has free city maps and the staff speak English.

Getting There & Around

Most buses do not come into town, they just park along the Phetkasem Hwy (Hwy 4) at an area known as 'sà·tăh·nee dern rót', 4km northwest of the city centre. Tickets are sold on the northbound side of the road; to be sure you get a seat, buy your ticket the day before because often buses are full when they pass Prachuap. The exception are the four daily air-conditioned buses to Bangkok's Southern Bus Terminal (200B, 9am, 11am, 1pm, 1am) and Phetchaburi (150B, two hours) from a small **bus stop** on Th Phitak Chat. Minivans form the backbone of Prachuap transportation and they all depart from **kew rót đôo** (Th Prachuap Khiri Khan/Rte 326) minivan station at the junction of Rte 326 and Hwy 4 near the main bus stop. The **train station** (☎032 611175; Th Maharat) is a 15-minute walk to the main accommodation area.

Prachuap is small enough to get around on foot, but you can hop on a motorcycle taxi to most places for 30B; 50B out to the bus stop and minivan station. Most hotels have motorcycle hire for 200B to 250B per day. A few also do bicycles for 50B.

Ban Krut & Bang Saphan Yai

☎032 / POP 4200 & 15,100

While calling Ban Krut and Bang Saphan Yai beaches idyllic is a bit of a stretch, they're no slouches in the beauty department. Around 65km and 90km south of Prachuap Khiri Khan, most people don't come here for the scenery, they come because so few others choose to come. There are no high-rises, no late-night bars and no speeding traffic to distract you from a serious regimen of reading, swimming, eating and biking. You'll often be all on your lonesome as you sit or stroll between the coconut trees and the crystalline blue sea that laps the long sandy coastline. There's a November to March high season, though it's a wonderfully meagre one.

Sights & Activities

Ban Krut has a string of resorts, restaurants and inner-tube rental shops sitting across the road from the sea. Families park their cars and spend the day eating, drinking and watching their kids splash around. That said, it's still much more subdued than a typical tourist beach as you don't need to go very far south to score a private patch of sand, even on holiday weekends.

Topping **Khao Thong Chai**, the headland north of Ban Krut beach, is a beautiful and unusually wide, 50m-tall stupa, **Phra Mahathat Chedi Phakdi Praka** (พระมหาธาตุเจดีย์ภักดีประกาศ; Rte 1029; ⏲8am-5pm) FREE. The main room has modern murals painted in traditional Thai style showing local festivals and ceremonies from around Thailand. Down below, beautiful coastal views form alongside the 10m-tall seated Buddha statue.

Bang Saphan Yai still clings to that famous beach cliché: Thailand 20 years ago before pool villas and package tourists pushed out all the beach bums. Much of the lodging is right on the beach itself (called Hat Suan Luang) and hawkers are rare. Islands off the coast, including **Ko Thalu** with its natural rock arch, offer good snorkelling and diving from March to October, with March and April being the best months. Although they're near Bang Saphan Yai, trips to these islands can also be arranged from Ban Krut.

Sleeping

Most places are pretty much empty on weekdays and are only really busy on holiday weekends when Bangkokians are willing to take the time to drive past Hua Hin.

Ban Krut บ้านกรูด

Most accommodation is in the busy core beach area that begins 1km from the tiny and timeless wooden shophouse-filled village. To the north of the temple-topped headland (this beach is called Hat Sai Kaew) and to the south it quickly turns remote and private with only a few scattered resorts in between coconut groves.

Siripong Guesthouse GUESTHOUSE $
(☎032 695464; Hat Ban Krut; r with fan 250-300, air-con 400B; P ❄ 📶) The region's cheapest lodging is pretty bare-bones, but the rooms are actually better than the dishevelled exterior would lead you to believe, and it's right at the junction, slightly away from the busiest parts of the beach. All showers are cold water and the fan rooms have either bucket-dump toilets in the rooms or shared bathrooms.

Proud Thai Beach Resort GUESTHOUSE **$$**
(☎089 682 4484; www.proudthairesort.com; Hat Ban Krut; r 800B; P ❄ 📶) Eight wooden bungalows, all with terraces, sit under the shade of trees across the road from the beach. They're old, but well-maintained by the English-speaking owner.

Bayview Beach Resort HOTEL **$$$**
(☎032 695566; www.bayviewbeachresort.com; Ban Krut; incl breakfast r 1900-2300, f 3500-4800B; P ❄ 📶 🏊) Bayview has handsome bungalows with large verandas, set amid shady grounds on a barely inhabited stretch of beach well north of the main tourist strip. There's a beachside pool with a kid-friendly wading pool, as well as a small playground. The resort also offers snorkelling and diving trips, and rents kayaks, motorcycles and bikes.

Bang Saphan Yai บางสะพานใหญ่

The beach is 6km south of Bang Saphan Yai town. There are a handful of small flash resorts here and also a row of basic, budget bungalows with direct beach access to the north of the Why Not Bar.

Ploy Bungalows BUNGALOW **$**
(☎032 817119; r 500-700B; P ❄ 📶) A quiet, casual place with brightly painted concrete bungalows. As a bonus to backpackers, all bungalows that are right up on the beach are the 500B fan variety. There are several other places of similar style along this road. There's no food here, so you'll have to walk a bit to eat.

★ **The Theatre Villa** HOTEL **$$**
(☎085 442 9150; www.thetheatrevilla.com; r incl breakfast 1350-2100B; P ❄ 📶) Quiet even by Bang Saphan standards, this small hotel sits on a great piece of beach and is meticulously cared for. Rooms are bright and very comfortable and come in three varieties: hotel-like rooms at the back, more expensive bungalows in the middle and two sea-view rooms at the front. It's west of the main road.

Coral Hotel HOTEL **$$$**
(☎032 817121; www.coral-hotel.com; incl breakfast r 3400, f 4940-6700B; P ❄ 📶 🏊) Catering mostly to French tourists – the restaurants are decent – this upmarket hotel is right on the beach and has all the resort amenities, including organised diving and snorkelling tours, trips to the national parks and Thai cooking classes. The tastefully decorated rooms are very comfortable and the pool is big.

Eating & Drinking

Locals eat almost exclusively along the road to town where there are a few regular restaurants, coffee shops and a mini night market (3pm to 9pm) next to Tesco-Lotus Express. Bang Saphan Yai has a few foreigner-focused restaurants.

There are bars in both towns. Ban Krut's cheapest beers are sold informally along the beach across from Siripong Guethouse – a mix of locals and expats lounge here. Kasama's has a good liquor list.

Bang Saphan Yai has a few popular expat watering holes. **Why Not Bar** is on the beach and **Blue Bar**, with pool table, is up almost at the highway junction. There's often live music at both.

Kasama's Pizza ITALIAN **$$**
(☎081 139 0220; www.kasamapizza.com; Rte 1029, Hat Ban Krut; mains 45-355B; ⊙10am-10pm, reduced hours in low season; 📶) A friendly spot and one of the longest-running restaurants in Ban Krut, Kasama's has substantial sandwiches, all-day breakfasts, pizzas and real chocolate milkshakes. And it delivers, even to the beach.

It's located off the access road, behind the 7-Eleven.

Information

Ban Krut Info (www.bankrutinfo.com) Local information on the area.

Bang Saphan Guide (www.bangsaphanguide.com) Local information on the area.

Bankrut Tour & Travel (☎081 736 3086; www.bankrut.co.th; Hat Ban Krut; ⊙8am-8pm) This is a friendly and reliable, full-service agency inside Na Nicha Bankrut Resort, just before the beach. Staff arrange day trips, including snorkelling at Ko Thalu, and onward travel, including ferry tickets for the southern islands.

Getting There & Away

Both towns have train stations. All 11 trains from Bangkok's Hualamphong to the far south stop at **Bang Saphan Yai Train Station** (☎032 691552; Soi Bang Saphan), 179B to 480B, five to seven hours, and seven of these also stop at **Ban Krut Train Station** (☎032 695004). Most of these trains arrive deep into the night. There's also a 7.30am ordinary train from Bangkok's Thonburi station (67B to 155B, 7½ hours). You can also get to both by rail from Prachuap Khiri Khan (16B to

347B, one hour), Chumphon (20B to 355B, 1½ to two hours) and Hua Hin (33B to 386B, two hours).

From Bangkok's southern terminal, buses go to Bang Saphan Yai (273B, six hours, hourly) about every two hours between 7.30am and midnight, and three of these stop in Ban Krut. Heading north, these buses will stop in Prachuap Khiri Khan (80B, one hour) and Phetchaburi (173B, 3½ hours), but not Hua Hin. Both bus stops are just a short distance south of the train stations. For a small fee you can get tickets through your resort or Bankrut Tour & Travel (p187).

Minivans (Rte 3169) from Bang Saphan Yai depart from the highway in front of Sweet Home Bakery in the heart of town. They go to Prachuap Khiri Khan (100B, one hour, eight daily from 6.20am to 4.50pm) and Chumphon (80B, two hours, 7am). The minivans to Prachuap pick up in Ban Krut. The Chumphon van normally doesn't pick up in Ban Krut, but Bankrut Tour & Travel can arrange it with the cost rising to 400B.

Other buses and minivans stop along the highway, about 10km west of both towns, rather than coming into town. Most buses that travel this route stop at Bang Saphan Yai, though few stop at Ban Krut and you risk waiting a long time if you try it there. In both cases, it's about a 100B motorcycle taxi ride to the town, more to the beach.

Getting Around

All but some of the cheapest resorts will pick you up in town and send you back for free, but all charge for going out to the Phetkasem Hwy.

The beach at Bang Saphan Yai is 6km south of the town via Rte 3374 – you can't miss the turn-off as there's a mass of resort signs. Ban Krut is 1km to the beach, though most of the accommodation is spread out far from the junction. Moto-taxis from Bang Saphan Yai to the beach cost 100B, from Ban Krut it's 20B to 30B.

In Ban Krut, Siripong Guesthouse (p186) and Bankrut Tour & Travel (p187) rent motorcycles for 200B per day, as do several other nearby shops around the junction. Several shops at Bang Saphan Yai's beach also hire motorcycles for 250B to 350B. Another option is to hire them in town at **Tae's Restaurant** (087 919 2910; Soi Bang Saphan; 2pm-1am), just down from the train station for 200B to 250B, though this is a very casual operation and they're often not available.

Chumphon ชุมพร

077 / POP 33,500

A transit town funnelling travellers to and from Ko Tao or southwards to Ranong or Phuket, Chumphon is where the south of Thailand starts proper; Muslim headscarves are a common sight here.

While there's not a lot to do in town while you wait for your ferry, it's not an unpleasant place and the surrounding beaches are alternative sun and sand stops far off the backpacker bandwagon. Beautiful **Hat Thung Wua Laen** (Fast Running Cow Beach), 15km northeast of town and full of traveller amenities, is the best known and during the week you'll have it mostly to yourself. On weekends it will be rocking.

Sights

It's not one of Thailand's biggest or best national museums, but the prehistoric pottery, axes and jewellery displayed in **Chumphon National Museum** (พิพิธภัณฑสถานแห่งชาติชุมพร; 077 504105; 100B; 9am-4pm Wed-Sun) will appeal to history buffs. Also worth a browse is Chumphon's main **fresh market** (ตลาดสดชุมพร; Th Pracha Uthit; midnight-3pm), the main source of meat, fruit and veggies for most of the city's restaurants. It's at its busiest very early in the morning.

Festivals & Events

Usually in mid-March, **Chumphon Marine Festival** (Mar) takes place at the seaside town of Paknam, 13km southeast of Chumphon city. There are four days of sea-related events, including boat trips, sand sculpture and underwater rubbish pick up.

To mark the end of Buddhist Lent (Ork Phansaa), which usually occurs in October, traditional long-tail boats race each other on the Lang Suan River about 60km south of Chumphon. Unlike long-tail boat races everywhere else in Thailand, here the winner must have someone hang on the bow of the boat and snatch a flag.

Sleeping

As most people overnighting in Chumphon are backpackers, there's a lot of accommodation serving them. **Th Tha Taphao** is the local Th Khao San, with cheap older guesthouses. Some newer flashier hostels are found east of the train station along Th Krumluang Chumphon. If you prefer sea to city, there's lodging up at **Hat Thung Wua Laen**, 15km northeast of town.

★ **Salsa Hostel** HOSTEL $

(077 505005; www.salsachumphon.com; 25/42 Th Krumluang Chumphon; incl breakfast dm 300-330, tw/d 650/750B;) East of the train

Chumphon

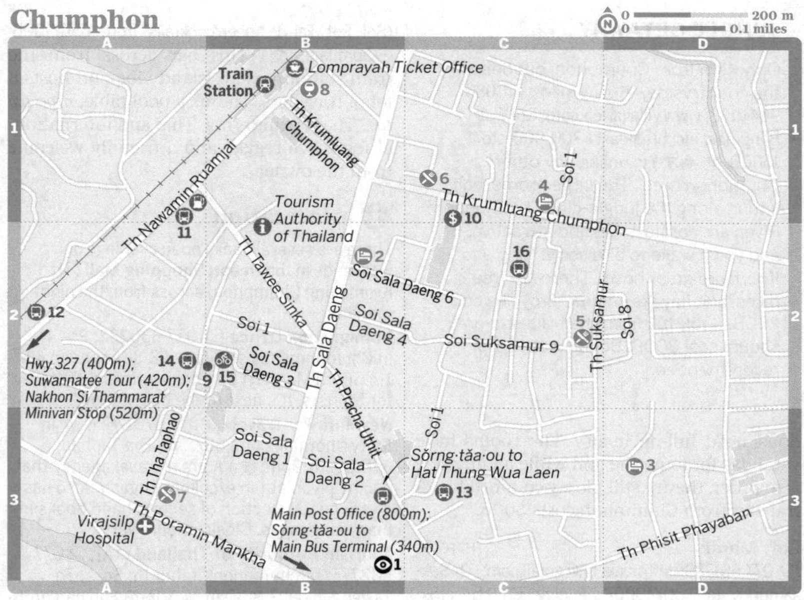

Chumphon

Sights
1 Chumphon Fresh Market B3

Sleeping
2 Fame Guesthouse B2
3 Loft Mania D3
4 Salsa Hostel C1

Eating
5 Kook Noy Kitchen C2
6 Night Market C1
7 Prikhorm A3

Drinking & Nightlife
8 Aeki's Bar B1

Information
9 New Infinity Travel B2
10 Ocean Shopping Mall C1

Transport
11 Affiliated Bus A1
12 Bang Saphan Yai Minivan Stop A2
13 Choke Anan Tour C3
14 Ranong Minivan Stop A2
15 San Tavee New Rest Home B2
16 Surat Thani & Prachuap Khiri Khan Minivan Stop C2

station near the night market, this is one of the best addresses in Chumphon. It's clean, friendly, not too big and a reliable source of local info in excellent English. The private rooms are some of the best in town, regardless of the price.

Fame Guesthouse GUESTHOUSE $
(077 571077; www.chumphon-kohtao.com; 188/20-21 Th Sala Daeng; r with shared/private bathroom 150-200/300B;) A *fa·ràng* depot, Fame does a little bit of everything, from providing clean basic rooms for people overnighting (or just resting during the day) to booking tickets and renting motorbikes. The attached restaurant is a key backpacker hang-out, and offers a wide range of Thai, Indian and Western food.

Chumphon Cabana Resort & Diving Centre HOTEL $$
(077 560245; www.chumphoncabanaresort.com; Hat Thung Wua Laen; r incl breakfast 1000-1500B;) Away from the road and on a great piece of beach, this is *the* place to stay at Hat Thung Wua Laen as long as you

JUNGLE GETAWAY

Only 4km from Chumphon, but deep in the countryside, **Villa Varich** (☎086 964 7123; www.villavarich.com; Soi Wat Bangmak; incl breakfast r 700-900, ste 1600B; P ❄ ☎) is unlike any other Chumphon hotel. The large rooms, half sitting along the jungle-clad Tha Taphao River, are comfortable and attractive, and you'll wake to bird song. Tang and Khom are great hosts. There are free bikes, and kayaks and motorcycles cost 200B. A túk-túk from the train station should cost 200B. Booking ahead is recommended.

don't need full-on luxury. The rooms have verandas for lounging and while an upgrade is in order, they're still plenty comfortable. A transfer from Chumphon costs 300B.

Loft Mania HOTEL **$$**
(☎077 501789; loftmania.bh@gmail.com; Th Suksamur; r/ste 1300/4000B; P ❄ ☎ ≈) The closest thing to luxury in Chumphon city, this popular hotel has quality rooms, industrial-chic design, helpful staff and a medieval coat of arms to greet you at the door. Guests get a pool, fitness centre and free bikes.

Eating & Drinking

Chumphon's main **night market** (Th Krumluang Chumphon; ⊙4pm-midnight) has a big variety of food options and good people-watching. There's more evening street food at the south end of Th Tha Taphao and south of the train station.

★**Kook Noy Kitchen** THAI **$**
(Th Suksamur; mains 40-180B; ⊙4pm-4am Mon-Sat; ☎) Just a concrete floor, a corrugated roof and a chaotic kitchen turning out central and southern Thai dishes you know like *đôm yam* with free-range chicken and crab fried rice, plus many you probably don't, including fried ducks beak and *pàt pèt gòp* (curry fried frog).

Prikhorm THAI **$$**
(32 Th Tha Taphao; mains 95-450B; ⊙11am-10pm; ☎ ✎) This wannabe fancy place has dishes from across the kingdom, from southern *gaang sôm* fish curry to northeastern mushroom *lâhp,* one of many vegetarian dishes.

Aeki's Bar BAR
(Soi Rot Fai 1; beer/cocktails from 65B/100B; ⊙3pm-late; ☎) This bar across from the train station has an island vibe and hosts a lot of travellers. There's a pool table, *moo·ay tai* (Thai boxing) ring, Thai and international food, live reggae and a friendly welcome from the owner.

Information

There are several banks open evenings and weekends in the **Ocean Shopping Mall** (Th Krumluang Chumphon) across from the night market.

Immigration Office (☎077 630282; Rte 41, in Chumphon bus station; ⊙8.30am-noon & 1-4.30pm Mon-Fri) Can do extensions of stays for tourists. It's next to the bus station.

New Infinity Travel (☎077 570176; new_infinity@hotmail.com; 68/2 Th Tha Taphao; ⊙8.30am-9pm; ☎) A great travel agency that can help you out in excellent English. Also has a very good selection of second-hand books in many languages. Closing hours vary.

Tourism Authority of Thailand (TAT; ☎077 502775; tatchumphon@tat.or.th; Soi 1, Th Tawee Sinka; ⊙8.30am-4.30pm) You can probably get all the information you need from your guesthouse, but if not, this office is helpful. And it gives out a good free map of Chumphon.

Virajsilp Hospital (☎077 542555; Th Poramin Mankha) Privately owned; handles emergencies.

Getting There & Away

For a transit hub, Chumphon is surprisingly unconsolidated – there's no single bus station and the ferry pier for boats to Ko Tao, Ko Pha-Ngan and Ko Samui are some distance from town. But travel agencies and guesthouses can point you to the right place, and sell tickets for all ferries, flights and many buses.

AIR

Chumphon's airport is nearly 40km from the centre of town and Nok Air, the only airline flying here, has one flight to Bangkok's Don Mueang Airport in the early morning and another in the late afternoon. Fame Guesthouse (p189) has an airport shuttle for 150B per person.

BOAT

There are essentially two options for getting to Ko Tao. **Lomprayah** (☎City 081 956 5644, Pier 077 558214; www.lomprayah.com; Th Krumluang Chumphon; ⊙4.30am-6pm) and **Songserm** (☎077 506205; www.songserm.com) have modern ferries sailing during the day. Lomprayah is the best and most popular; Songserm has a reputation for being poorly

TRANSPORT TO/FROM CHUMPHON

DESTINATION	BOAT	BUS	MINIVAN	TRAIN	AIR
Bang Saphan Yai			80B, 2hr, 2pm, 3.30pm	20-355B, 1½-2hr, 12 daily	
Bangkok Don Mueang International Airport					from 1200B, 1hr, 2 daily
Bangkok Hualamphong				seat/sleeper 192-510/620-1194B, 6½-8hr, 11 daily	
Bangkok Southern Bus Terminal		155-510B, 8hr, 11 daily 9am-10pm			
Bangkok Thonburi				80-383B, 9½hr, 7.30am	
Chiang Mai		1385B, 18hr, 6pm			
Hat Yai		328-355B, 7hr, 8 daily 7am-midnight		79-502B, 8-10½hr, 7 daily	
Hua Hin				49-423B, 4-5hr, 12 daily	
Ko Pha-Ngan (Lomprayah)	1000B, 3¼-3¾hr, 7am, 1pm				
Ko Pha-Ngan (Songserm)	900B, 4½hr, 7am				
Ko Samui (Lomprayah)	1100B, 3¾-4¼hr, 7am, 1pm				
Ko Samui (Songserm)	1000B, 6¼hr, 7am				
Ko Tao (car ferry)	400B, 6hr, 11pm Mon-Sat				
Ko Tao (Lomprayah)	600B, 1¾hr, 7am, 1pm				
Ko Tao (Songserm)	500B, 2¾hr, 7am				
Ko Tao (Sunday night boat)	450B, 6hr, midnight Sun				
Nakhon Si Thammarat			300B, 5½hr, every 2hr 8am-2pm		
Phetchaburi		328-500B, 6hr, hourly 7am-10pm		58-455B, 5½-6½hr, 11 daily	
Phuket		350-600B, 6-7hr, 7 daily 5am-2.30pm			
Prachuap Khiri Khan		220B, 4hr, hourly 7am-10pm	180B, 3½hr, every 50min 5.30am-6pm	16-347B, 2½-3hr, 10 daily	
Ranong		120B, 2½hr, 4 daily	120B, 2½hr, hourly 6am-5pm		
Surat Thani			170B, 3½hr, hourly, 6am-5.30pm	34-388B, 2-3hr, 12 daily	

organised and not providing promised transfers on its bus-boat combo tickets (though this isn't an issue when beginning in Chumphon). These boats also serve Ko Pha-Ngan and Ko Samui.

The other option is night boats operated by a variety of companies. From Monday to Saturday there are car ferries that have air-conditioned rooms with beds – essentially a dorm on the sea – while Sunday is a regular wooden boat with mattresses on the floor and only fans, no air-con.

Boats leave from different piers and transfer costs 50B to 100B. Sometimes tickets are sold that include the transfer, sometimes not – be sure you have a ticket for both the bus and the boat.

BUS

Chumphon's main **bus station** (☎ 077 576 796; Rte 41) is on the highway, an inconvenient 12km from Chumphon. It's not used much – many ticket offices are unstaffed for much of the day – since the main bus companies have their own stops in town.

Choke Anan Tour (☎ 077 511480; off Soi 1, Th Pracha Uthit), near the main market, has the most buses to Bangkok (via Phetchaburi and Prachuap Khiri Khan) and Phuket (via Ranong) plus one to Hat Yai. **Minivans to Ranong** leave from Th Tha Taphao across from New Infinity Travel and **minivans to Surat Thani and Prachuap Khiri Khan** (Th Krumluang Chumphon) leave from Chumphon Night Bazaar, 500m down Th Krumluang Chumphon from the train station near Salsa Hostel.

Other services are along Th Nawamin Ruamjai south of the train station. **Suwannatee Tour** (☎ 077 504901), running five buses to Bangkok including one cheap second-class bus, plus **minivans to Nakhon Si Thammarat** (☎ 077 506326) are across the river, about 1km away.

Affiliated Bus (☎ 082 284 6462) serves Hat Yai (plus a night bus to Bangkok) from its office next to the petrol station and **minivans to Bang Saphan Yai** are at the covered minivan stop that has a yellow sign, 400m south of the petrol station.

For the few services that do use the station, like Chiang Mai, you can buy tickets at guesthouses and travel agencies. Note that there's no scheduled direct service to Hua Hin, you'll need to change at Prachuap Khiri Khan.

TRAIN

There are frequent services between Bangkok and the far south stopping in Chumphon. Make reservations as far in advance as possible. Second-class sleepers are often available day of departure, but first-class rarely is.

Getting Around

Motorcycle taxis (20B to 30B per trip) are seemingly everywhere in town while the more expensive four-wheeled túk-túk are much less common, though there are always some parked at the train station.

Motorcycles can be rented through many guesthouses for 200B to 300B per day. Besides motorcycles, **San Tavee New Rest Home** (☎ 089 011 1749; Soi Sala Daeng 3) also hires bicycles for 100B.

Yellow *sŏrng·tăa·ou* to Hat Thung Wua Laen (30B, 30 minutes, frequent 5.30am to 6pm) leave from the Chumphon Fresh Market on Th Pracha Uthit and then follow Th Sala Daeng north. Little white *sŏrng·tăa·ou* to the main bus station and immigration (25B, 30 to 45 minutes, frequent 7am to 5pm) depart from Th Phinit Khadi next to the City Pillar Shrine. A túk-túk to the bus station will cost upwards of 300B from the city centre. There's an airport shuttle (150B per person) from Fame Guesthouse (p189).

Ko Samui & the Lower Gulf

Includes ➡

Best Places to Eat

- Dining On The Rocks (p208)
- Pepenero (p208)
- Fisherman's Restaurant (p228)
- Barracuda (p243; Ko Tao)
- Barracuda (p207; Ko Samui)

Best Places to Stay

- Six Senses Samui (p208)
- Four Seasons Koh Samui (p199)
- Kupu Kupu Phangan Beach Villas by l'Occitane (p223)
- Jamahkiri Resort & Spa (p242)

Why Go?

The Lower Gulf features Thailand's ultimate island trifecta: Ko Samui, Ko Pha-Ngan and Ko Tao. This family of spectacular islands lures millions of tourists every year with their powder-soft sands and emerald waters. Ko Samui is the oldest sibling who made it big, where high-class resorts operate with Swiss efficiency as uniformed butlers cater to every whim. Ko Pha-Ngan is the slacker middle child with tangled dreadlocks and a penchant for hammock-lazing and all-night parties. Meanwhile Ko Tao is the outdoorsy, fun-loving kid with plenty of spirit and energy – the island specialises in high-adrenalin activities, including world-class diving and snorkelling.

The mainland coast beyond the islands sees few foreign visitors, but is far more authentic Thailand. From the pink dolphins and waterfalls of sleepy Ao Khanom to the Thai Muslim flavours of beach-strolling Songkhla and the charm of Nakhon Si Thammarat, this region is stuffed with off-the-beaten-track wonders.

When to Go

- Visit from February to April to celebrate endless sunshine after the monsoon rains have cleared.
- June through August are the most inviting months, with relatively short drizzle spells, conveniently coinciding with the Northern Hemisphere's summer holidays.
- Expect torrential monsoon rains to rattle on hot tin roofs from October to December; room rates (excluding Christmas) drop significantly.

Ko Samui & the Lower Gulf Highlights

1. **Ko Tao** (p233) Finding Nemo in this technicolour dive kingdom.
2. **Ang Thong Marine National Park** (p247) Paddling to hidden bleach-blond beaches.
3. **Ko Pha-Ngan** (p215) Stringing up a cotton hammock and toeing the curling tide along a secluded beach on the east coast.
4. **Ko Samui** (p196) Enjoying five-star international cuisine and sipping fancy sunset cocktails.
5. **Full Moon Party** (p230) Joining the masses of party pilgrims and trancing the night away at Hat Rin on Ko Pha-Ngan.

6 Ao Khanom (p251) Spotting elusive pink dolphins gliding along the little-visited shores.

7 Domsila Viewpoint (p216) Trekking through jungle, past gushing waterfalls to this vantage point high above Ko Pha-Ngan.

GULF ISLANDS

Ko Samui เกาะสมุย

POP 62,000

Whether you're sun-seeking, dozing in a hammock, feasting on world-class cuisine, beach partying or discovering wellness in an exclusive spa, Ko Samui has it covered.

Ko Samui's beaches are a diverse bunch: roll up your beach towel and see what you can find. Make it Coco Tam's in Fisherman's Village for cocktails and serious relaxing, Chaweng Beach for sunrise and people-watching, lengthy Mae Nam Beach for peace, or napping under a coconut tree before giving in to a west-coast sunset across seas shimmering with bronze. Dining is Samui's other top indulgence. The island is stuffed with *kôw gang* (rice and curry) shops, often a flimsy wooden shack serving southern Thai-style curries. Follow locals to the food markets for pointers, but if you need atmosphere, seek out romantic, sunset-flecked dinners.

Add some full-on pampering to the leisurely mix. Cleansing fasts, yoga, tai-chi, herbal steam treatments and chakra-balancing restore equilibrium to out-of-kilter systems. And for those who just want to ease away the aches and pains of lying on the beach, Ko Samui's spas can ease them to the next level of serenity.

Sights

At 229 sq km, Ko Samui is pretty large – the island's main ring road is more than 50km total.

Wat Plai Laem BUDDHIST TEMPLE
(Map p198; dawn-dusk) FREE The most arresting statue on the island is the thousand-arm Kwan Im (the Buddhist bodhisattva of compassion), displayed here with 18 arms, in a fan arrangement at this recently built, stunning temple. Perched on an island in a lake, the colourful statue rises up next to a temple hall – similarly constructed above the water. To the north of the hall is a statue of the jovial Maitreya Buddha, or the Buddha to come. The setting is highly picturesque and photogenic.

Na Muang Waterfalls WATERFALL
(Map p198) Spilling down from the island's highest points, these two waterfalls – close to each other – are lovely when in full spate, pouring frigid water into rock pools and gushing down towards the blue sea. The larger of the two, at 30m, is the most famous waterfall on Samui and lies in the centre of the island about 12km from Na Thon. During the rainy season, the water cascades over ethereal purple rocks, and there's a superb, large pool for swimming at the base.

Na Muang Waterfall 2 (Map p198) FREE, the smaller of the two Na Muang falls, is accessed via the rather miserable Na Muang Safari Park, where you can pose for snaps with a tiger or leopard, or feed an elephant bananas (all for a fee, and not recommended).

Fisherman's Village VILLAGE
(Map p211; Bo Phut) This concentration of narrow Chinese shophouses in Bo Phut has been transformed into some trendy (and often midrange) boutique hotels, eateries, cafes and bars. The accompanying beach,

GULF ISLANDS IN...

One Week

After coming to terms with the fact that you only have a week to explore these idyllic islands, start on one of **Ko Pha-Ngan's** secluded western beaches or journey east to live out your ultimate castaway fantasies. For the second half of the week choose between partying in **Hat Rin**, pampering on **Ko Samui** or diving off little **Ko Tao**.

Two Weeks

Start on **Ko Tao** with a 3½-day Open Water certification course, or sign up for a few fun dives. Slide over to **Ko Pha-Ngan** and soak up the sociable vibe in party-central Hat Rin. Then, grab a long-tail and make your way to one of the island's hidden coves for a few days of detoxing and quiet contemplation. **Ko Samui** is next on the agenda. Try **Bo Phut** for boutique sleeps or live it up like a rock star on Chaweng or Choeng Mon beach. And, if you have time, do a day trip to **Ang Thong National Marine Park**.

particularly the eastern part, is slim and coarse but becomes whiter and lusher further west. The combination of pretty sands and gussied-up old village is a winner, but it can get busy during peak season. Off-season, it's lovely, quiet and elbow-free.

Ban Hua Thanon AREA
(Map p198; Ban Hua Thanon) Just south of Hat Lamai, Hua Thanon is full of photo ops and home to a vibrant Muslim community; its anchorage of high-bowed fishing vessels by the almost deserted beach through the palm trees at the end of the community is a veritable gallery of intricate designs, though it's a shame about all the rubbish on the sand. Look out for the green, gold and white **mosque** in the village, along the main drag.

Wat Racha Thammaram BUDDHIST TEMPLE
(Wat Sila Ngu; Map p206; off Rte 4169; ⌚dawn-dusk) This temple (the name means Snake Stone Temple) on the south side of Rte 4169 has a recently built red-clay temple hall, decorated with a fascinating display of bas-relief designs and statues. It's an astonishing sight against the blue sky. A golden pagoda contains relics of Sakyamuni, and a sacred bodhi tree also grows within the grounds. From the pagoda, steps head down to a collection of stupas, commemorating former monks.

Hainan Temple TEMPLE
(Hailam Nathon Shrine; 海南公所; Map p198; Na Thon; ⌚dawn-dusk) FREE Fronted by a pair of golden Chinese lions, adorned with coiling dragons and pretty much the most colourful Chinese temple (and guildhall) on the island, this shrine was set up by Thai-Chinese who originated from the island of Hǎinán in the far south of China. You can find signs to it pointing off Rte 4169.

Hin-Ta & Hin-Yai LANDMARK
(Map p206; Lamai) At the south end of Hat Lamai, you'll find these infamous genitalia-shaped stone formations (also known as Grandfather and Grandmother Rocks) that provide endless mirth for giggling Thai tourists.

Activities

Ko Samui offers many activities geared towards kids and teenagers. Be wary of 'ecotourism' tours on the island – many are just commercial operations with little concern for what they may appear to promote.

DON'T MISS

KO TAN

Tired of tours and busy beaches? For the intrepid DIY traveller there's no better way to spend a day on Ko Samui than with a trip to the white sands of Ko Tan. Hire a long-tail boat from the boatmen who beach their boats alongside the strip of seafood restaurants on Hat Thong Tanot on Ko Samui's south coast; a boat for up to six people should cost 1500B to 2000B for a four-hour trip. The island itself is only about 15 minutes from Ko Samui. While the snorkelling isn't that great, the white-sand beach is empty aside from the occasional visit by charter boats and local fishermen, and the views and swimming are sublime.

★ **Red Baron** CRUISE
(Map p211; contact@redbaron-samui.com; Hat Bang Rak; from 2500B) With day-long cruises around Ko Samui (9.30am Tuesday), brunch trips to Ko Pha-Ngan (11am Wednesday and Sunday), sunset dinner cruises to Ko Som (4.30pm, Monday and Friday) and journeys over the waves to Ang Thong Marine Park (8.30am, Thursday), Red Baron is a traditional and very popular sailing junk moored at Bangrak. Meals and drinks provided. Private charters also available.

Samui Dog & Cat Rescue Centre VOLUNTEERING
(Map p201; ☎081 893 9443; www.samuidog.org; Soi 3, Chaweng Beach Rd; ⌚9am-6pm) Donations of time and/or money are hugely appreciated at the aptly named Samui Dog & Cat Rescue Centre. Volunteers are always needed to take care of the animals at their kennel/clinic in Ban Taling Ngam (but not at the smaller Hat Chaweng branch). Call the centre for volunteering details or swing by for additional info. Check the website for directions.

Coco Splash Waterpark WATER PARK
(Map p206; ☎081 082 6035; www.samuiwaterpark.com; Ban Lamai; over/under 1.5m 349/329B, under 0.9m free; ⌚10.30am-5.30pm) Kids under 10 will love this small park of painted concrete water slides. Towel hire is 60B (200B deposit) and there's a restaurant (open till 10pm). Note that if you're planning on watching the kids and not going in the water yourself, you get in for free. Those under 1.5m get a T-shirt thrown in; if you're over 1.5m, it's a cocktail.

Ko Samui

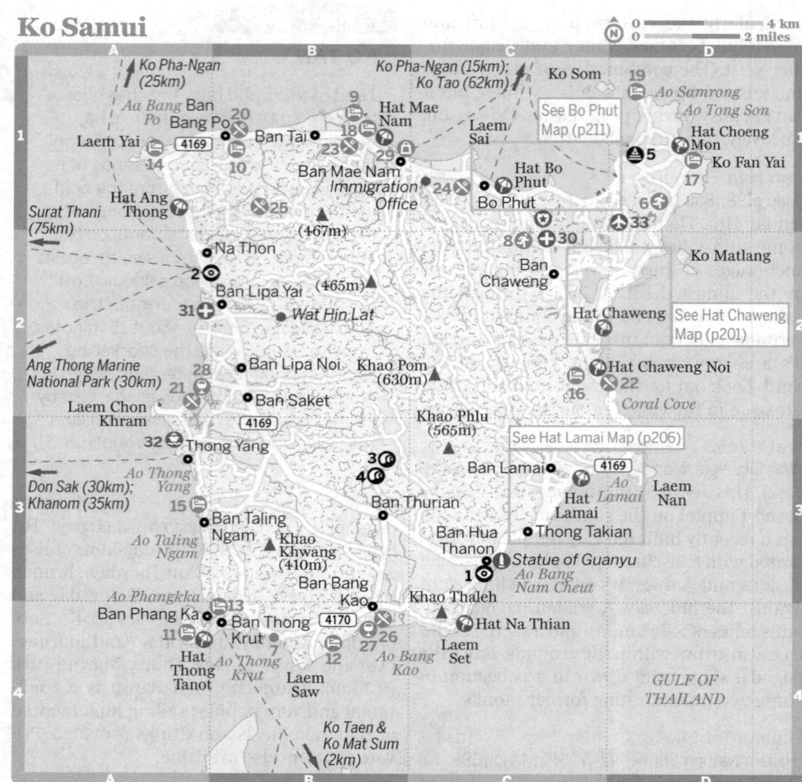

Koh Samui Rum DISTILLERY

(Map p198; ☎091 816 7416; www.rum-distillery.com; Ban Bang Kao; tasting shots 50-75B; ⏰9am-6pm) The only rum distillery in Thailand produces Caribbean agricole-style spirits (distilled from fresh, fermented sugarcane juice) in a variety of all natural flavours, including a delectable coconut rum obtained from soaking coconut meat in the rum for several months. There's a video about the production process, a tasting area, an excellent French-Thai restaurant and a shop in beautiful palm-shaded surrounds.

Kiteboarding Asia WATER SPORTS

(Map p198; ☎083 643 1627; www.kiteboardingasia.com; Na Thon; 1-/3-day course 4000/11,000B; ⏰9am-6pm) This pro place will get you kitesurfing on flat shallow water. The Na Thon location on the west side is for December to March winds (another in Hua Thanon in the south of the island is for April to October gusts).

Diving

If you're serious about diving, head to Ko Tao and base yourself there. If you're short on time and don't want to leave Samui, there are plenty of operators who will take you to the same dive sites (at a greater fee, of course). Try to book with a company that has its own boat (or leases a boat) – it's slightly more expensive, but you'll be glad you did it. Companies without boats often shuttle divers on the passenger catamaran to Ko Tao, where you board a second boat to reach your dive site. These trips are arduous, meal-less and rather impersonal.

Certification courses tend to be twice as expensive on Ko Samui as they are on Ko Tao, due largely to use of extra petrol, since Ko Tao is significantly closer to the preferred diving locations. You'll spend between 14,000B and 22,000B on an Open Water certification, and figure on between 4500B and 6200B for a

Ko Samui

Sights

1 Ban Hua Thanon C3
2 Hainan Temple ....
Ko Samui Central Mosque .... (see 1)
3 Na Muang Waterfall 2 .... B3
4 Na Muang Waterfalls B3
5 Wat Plai Laem D1

Activities, Courses & Tours

6 Absolute Sanctuary D1
7 Hemingway's on the Beach B4
Kiteboarding Asia .... (see 2)
Koh Samui Rum .... (see 26)
8 Mind Your Language C2
Samahita Retreat .... (see 12)
Spa at the Four Seasons .... (see 14)

Sleeping

Belmond Napasai .... (see 9)
Chytalay Palace Hotel .... (see 2)
9 Coco Palm Resort B1
10 Code B1
11 Conrad Koh Samui A4
12 Easy Time B4
13 Elements B4
14 Four Seasons Koh Samui A1
15 Intercontinental Samui Baan Taling Ngam Resort A3
16 Jungle Club C2
17 Samui Honey Cottages Resort D1
18 Shangri-la B1
19 Six Senses Samui D1

Eating

20 Bang Po Seafood B1
21 Big John's Seafood Restaurant A2
Dining On The Rocks .... (see 19)
22 Dr Frogs D2
23 Farmer B1
Fish Restaurant .... (see 29)
Gaon Korean Restaurant .... (see 29)
Hemingway's on the Beach .... (see 7)
Hua Thanon Market .... (see 1)
John's Garden Restaurant .... (see 18)
Lucky .... (see 2)
24 Pepenero C1
25 Phootawan Restaurant B1
26 Sweet Sisters Cafe B4

Drinking & Nightlife

Air Bar .... (see 15)
27 Buffalo Baby B4
Jungle Club .... (see 16)
Max Murphys .... (see 2)
28 Nikki Beach A2

Shopping

29 Mae Nam Walking Street B1
Thanon An Thong .... (see 2)

Information

30 Bandon International Hospital C2
31 Ko Samui Hospital A2

Transport

32 Raja A3
33 Samui International Airport D1

diving day trip including two dives, depending on the location of the site.

Ko Samui's **hyperbaric chamber** (Map p211; ☎077 427427, emergency 081 081 9555; www.sssnetwork.com/our-chambers-and-medical-clinics/koh-samui-thailand; Big Buddha Beach; ⊙24hr) is at Big Buddha Beach (Hat Bang Rak).

★100 Degrees East — DIVING

(Map p211; ☎077 423936; www.100degreeseast.com; Hat Bang Rak; ⊙9am-6.30pm Dec-Oct) Highly professional and recommended, with a dedicated team, for excellent and excellent diving and snorkelling expeditions to Ang Thong Marine National Park, Ko Tao, Sail Rock and other sites.

★The Life Aquatic — DIVING

(Map p211; ☎086 030 0286; www.thelifeaquatic.asia; The Wharf, Fisherman's Village) Overseen by friendly and very competent and experienced instructors, this first-rate dive operation offers a range of SSI & PADI dive courses, dive trips to Ko Tao as well as snorkelling trips and accommodation.

Spas & Yoga

Competition between Samui's five-star accommodation is fierce, meaning spas are of the highest calibre. The Spa Resort (p202) in Lamai is the island's original health destination, and is still known for its effective 'clean me out' fasting regime.

Yoga is offered at many hotels and is also big business. Ko Pha-Ngan is perhaps more the place for the hard-core, but you won't have a problem finding classes on Ko Samui – try Samahita Retreat (p200) or Absolute Sanctuary (p200).

★Spa at the Four Seasons — SPA

(Map p198; ☎077 243000; www.fourseasons.com/kohsamui/spa; Bang Po) The luxury **Four Seasons** on a rocky peninsula in the northwest corner of Ko Samui has one of the best spas around, with a heady range of therapies to pamper body and soul, from chakra-balancing to body-wraps and coconut pedicures. Emerge transformed.

★ Absolute Sanctuary YOGA, SPA
(Map p198; ☎077 601190; www.absolutesanctuary.com; Choeng Mon) Detox, spa, yoga, Pilates, fasting, lifestyle and nutrition packages, in an alluring Moroccan-inspired setting.

Samahita Retreat YOGA, SPA
(Map p198; ☎077 920090; www.samahitaretreat.com; Laem Sor Beach) Secreted away along the southern shores, Samahita Retreat has state-of-the-art facilities and a dedicated team of trainers for the growing band of therapeutic holidaymakers, wellness seekers and serious detoxers. Accommodation is in a comfy apartment block up the street, while yoga studios, wellness centres and a health-food restaurant sit calmly along the shore.

Tamarind Springs MASSAGE
(Map p206; ☎080 569 6654; www.tamarindsprings.com; off Rte 4169; spa packages from 1500B) Tucked far away from the beach within a silent coconut-palm plantation, Tamarind's small collection of villas and massage studios is seamlessly incorporated into nature: some have granite boulders built into walls and floors, while others offer private ponds or creative outdoor baths. There's also a superhealthy restaurant and packages for three-night or longer stays in the elegant villas and suites.

Courses

★ Samui Institute of Thai Culinary Arts COOKING
(SITCA; Map p201; ☎077 413172; http://sitca.com; Chaweng Beach Rd; courses 1850B) For Thai cooking skills, SITCA is the place to do it, with daily Thai cooking classes and courses in the aristocratic Thai art of carving fruits and vegetables into intricate floral designs. Lunchtime classes begin at 11am, while dinner starts at 4pm (both are three-hour courses with three or more dishes).

★ Lamai Muay Thai Camp HEALTH & WELLBEING
(Map p206; ☎087 082 6970; www.lamaimuaythaicamp.com; 82/2 Moo3, Lamai; day/week training sessions 300/1500B; ⏲7am-8pm) The island's best *moo·ay tai* (Thai boxing) training (for the seriously serious) is at this place, which caters to beginners as well as those wanting to hone their skills. There's also a well-equipped gym for boxers and nonboxers who want to up their fitness levels, plus accommodation and breakfast (and all-meals-included) packages.

Hemingway's on the Beach COOKING
(Map p198; ☎088 452 4433; off 4170, Ao Thong Krut; per person 1500B; ⏲10.30am-12.30pm) During the week, this restaurant on the southern sands of Thong Krut hosts a Thai cookery school – you get to select three dishes from the menu and learn how to cook it all up in a two-hour class. There's a minimum of two and a maximum of four people per class.

Mind Your Language LANGUAGE
(Map p198; ☎077 962088; www.mindyourlanguagethailand.com; 142/7 Mu 1, Bo Phut) With lessons from 600B per hour, this accessible and professional language school in Bo Phut can gear you up with classes in Thai, including intensive programs.

Sleeping

There is no shortage of top-end resorts sporting exclusive bungalows and pampering spas. Bo Phut, on the northern coast, has attractive boutique lodgings for midrange travellers. Backpack-lugging visitors may have to look harder, but budget digs pop up periodically along all beaches.

Hat Chaweng

Busy, throbbing, commercial Chaweng is packed with accommodation, from cheap backpackers to futuristic villas with swimming pools. The northern half of the beach is the biggest party zone, and nearby resorts are in ear-shot of Ark Bar at the centre of it all. If you're hoping for early nights, pick a resort to the south or bring earplugs.

Samui Hostel HOSTEL $
(Map p201; ☎089 874 3737; Chaweng Beach Rd; dm 200-300B, d 850B; ❄@) It doesn't look like much from the front, but this neat, tidy, friendly and popular place is very central, with clean fan and air-con dorm rooms and spruce air-con doubles on the nonbeach side of the road. Service is a cut above the rest and there's a popular room at the front with wooden tables for lounging and chatting.

Pott Guesthouse GUESTHOUSE $
(Map p201; Chaweng Beach Rd; r with fan/air con from 300/600B; ❄📶) The big, bright cement rooms all with attached hot-water bathrooms and balcony in this nondescript

Hat Chaweng

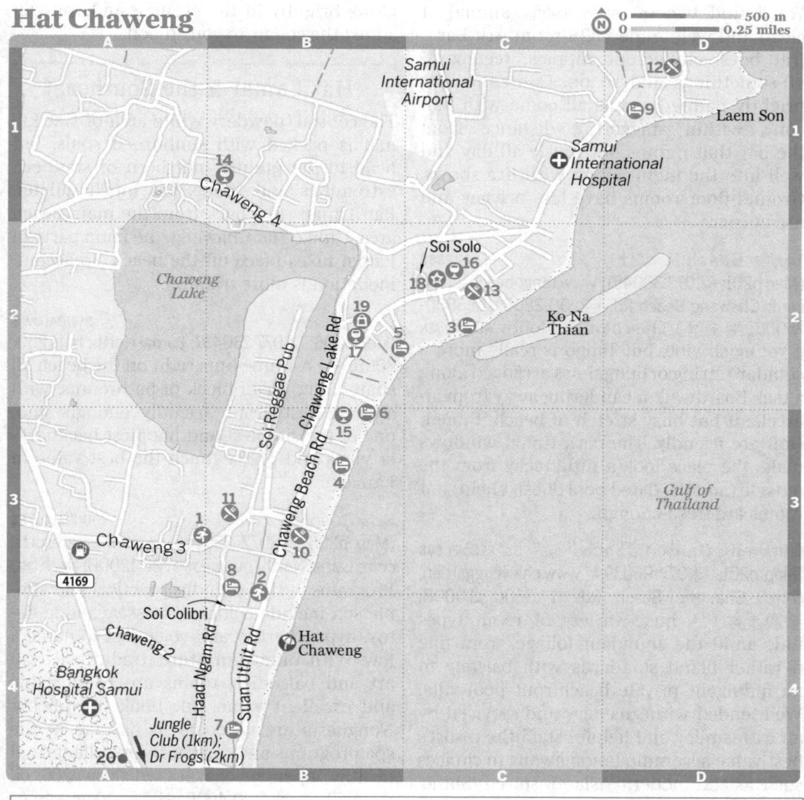

Hat Chaweng

Activities, Courses & Tours
1 Samui Dog & Cat Rescue Centre A3
2 Samui Institute of Thai Culinary Arts B3

Sleeping
3 Ark Bar Beach Resort C2
4 Buri Rasa Village B3
5 Chaweng Garden Beach B2
6 Library B3
7 Pott Guesthouse B4
8 Samui Hostel B3
9 Tango Beach Resort D1

Eating
10 Hungry Wolf B3
11 Laem Din Market B3
12 Larder D1
Page .... (see 6)
13 Tuk Tuk Backpackers C2

Drinking & Nightlife
Ark Bar .... (see 3)
14 Bees Knees Brewpub B1
15 Drink Gallery B3
16 Pride Bar C2
17 Sawasdee Bar B2

Entertainment
18 Paris Follies Cabaret C2

Shopping
19 Central Festival B2

Transport
20 Bangkok Airways A4

apartment block are a steal, but that's about it. Reception is at an unnamed restaurant on the main drag right opposite across the alley.

Ark Bar Beach Resort RESORT $$$
(Map p201; ☎077 961333; www.ark-bar.com; Chaweng Beach Rd; r from 2000B; ❄📶🏊)

You'll find two of every party animal at clean and well-tended 328-room Ark Bar – frat boys, chilled-out hippies, teenagers, 40-somethings and so on. Contemporary, brightly painted rooms all come with balcony, within staggering distance from the bar that pumps out music all day and well into the night, along with fire shows. Ground-floor rooms have less privacy and are noisier.

Tango Beach Resort RESORT **$$$**
(Map p201; ☎077 300451; www.tangobeachsamui.com; Chaweng Beach Rd; r 2200-2800, ste 3800-7500B; ❄📶🏊) The colourful lobby suggests a youngish vibe, but Tango is really more a standard string of bungalows arranged along a teak boardwalk meandering away from an excellent but busy stretch of beach, though staff are friendly. The dark tinted windows make the place look a little tacky from the outside (and the dated pool doesn't help) but rooms are fresh enough.

Chaweng Garden Beach RESORT **$$$**
(Map p201; ☎077 960394; www.chawenggarden.com; Chaweng Beach Rd; r 3600-33,000B; ❄@📶🏊) A huge variety of room types hide amid the abundant foliage, from fine if rather bland standards with balcony to an indulgent private beachfront pool villa. Well tended with greenery and serviced by an extrasmiley and helpful staff, the resort's best-value accommodation awaits in choices such as the modern Asian-inspired 'Shino' rooms and polished wood bungalows.

★**Buri Rasa Village** RESORT **$$$**
(Map p201; ☎077 956055; www.burirasa.com; Chaweng Beach Rd; r 4850-8900B; ❄📶🏊) This Zen-like place is beautifully landscaped with palms and frangipani. It's central, well priced and on a good stretch of busy beach, but the real reason to stay here is the bend-over-backwards friendly and helpful service, while Thai-style wooden doors lead to private villa patios and simple yet elegant rooms.

★**Library** RESORT **$$$**
(Map p201; ☎077 422767; www.thelibrary.co.th; Chaweng Beach Rd; studio/ste incl breakfast from 11,900/13,600B; ❄@📶🏊) This library is too cool for school. The entire resort is a sparkling white mirage accented with black trimming and slatted curtains. Besides the futuristic iMac computer in each page (rooms are 'pages' here), our favourite feature is the large monochromatic wall art – it glows brightly in the evening and you can adjust the colour to your mood.

Hat Lamai & the Southeast

The central, powdery white area of Hat Lamai is packed with sunburned souls, but head to the grainier northern or southern extremities and things get much quieter. Ban Lamai runs back from the main beach area. Unlike Hat Chaweng, the main party in Lamai takes place off the beach, so accommodation is more tranquil.

New Hut BUNGALOW **$**
(Map p206; ☎077 230437; Lamai North; huts 250-800B; 📶) A-frame huts right on the beach all share a big, clean block of bathrooms, with a lively restaurant, friendly enough staff, one of the simplest and happiest backpacker vibes and pretty much the best value in Lamai.

Spa Resort BUNGALOW **$$**
(Map p206; ☎077 230855; www.thesparesorts.com; Lamai North; bungalows 720-1200B; ❄📶🏊) Programs at this friendly, practical and simple spa include colonics, massage, aqua detox, hypnotherapy and yoga, just to name a few. With rattan furniture, traditional wall art and balconies, rooms are comfortable and excellent value, but book up quickly. Nonguests are welcome to partake in the spa programs and dine at the excellent (and healthy) open-air **restaurant** (Map p206; off Rte 4169; meals 100-400B; ⏰7am-10pm; 📶🌿) by the beach.

★**Rocky's Resort** RESORT **$$$**
(Map p206; ☎077 418367; www.rockyresort.com; off Rte 4169; r 8000-20,000B; ❄📶🏊) With a supremely calm reception area and two swimming pools, Rocky effortlessly finds the right balance between an upmarket ambience and an unpretentious, sociable vibe. During quieter months prices are a steal, since ocean views abound, and each room (some with pool) has been furnished with beautiful Thai-inspired furniture that seamlessly incorporates a modern twist.

Samui Jasmine Resort RESORT **$$$**
(Map p206; ☎077 232446; www.samuijasmineresort.com; 131/8 Moo 3, Lamai; r & bungalows 4600-12,000B; ❄📶🏊) Smack dab in the middle of Hat Lamai, varnished-teak yet frilly Samui Jasmine is a great deal. Go for the lower-priced rooms – most have excellent

views of the ocean and the crystal-coloured lap pool.

Bo Phut & the Northeast

The point of focus is Fisherman's Village, with a fine selection of accommodation. Things get very busy during peak season, but during the low season, prices are down and it can be particularly quiet and inviting.

Castaway Guesthouse GUESTHOUSE **$$**
(Map p211; 081 968 5811; www.castawaysamui.com; Fisherman's Village; r with fan/air-con 650-1500B;) A block away from the beach, Castaway's 15 rooms are all clean, bright and cheery.

Eden BUNGALOW **$$$**
(Map p211; 077 427645; www.edenbungalows.com; Fisherman's Village; bungalows 1500-2300B;) A short walk from the beach, the 10 bungalows and five rooms here are all tucked away in a lovely tangle of garden with a small pool at its centre. Cheaper options are rather shabby but an upgrade gets you a more stylish suite with yellow walls and naturalistic wood furniture; for families, there's a 100-sq-m apartment with kitchenette too.

Hacienda GUESTHOUSE **$$$**
(Map p211; 077 960827; www.samui-hacienda.com; Fisherman's Village; r 2500-4800B;) Polished terracotta and rounded archways lend the entrance a Spanish mission motif. Similar decor permeates the adorable rooms, which sport touches such as pebbled bathroom walls and translucent bamboo lamps. Hacienda Suites, the overflow property a few doors down, has the smaller and cheaper rooms which are mostly windowless, but still clean and comfortable. The tiny rooftop pool has gorgeous ocean views.

★ **Samui Honey Cottages Resort** RESORT **$$$**
(Map p198; 077 427093; www.samuihoney.com; Choeng Mon; r incl breakfast 3500-6500B;) At the quieter southern part of the beach, this small resort (with an equally small pool) isn't anything that special, but it's nicer than some of the other mediocre offerings in this price range on this beach. Expect attractive, classic Zen-style rooms.

★ **Scent** RESORT **$$$**
(Map p211; 077 960123; www.thescenthotel.com; Off Beach Rd; ste 8500-10,500B) Seek out the taste (and scent if you light your complimentary incense) of Indo-China at this tranquil gem that recreates the elegance of 1940s and '50s colonial Asia. The tall grey concrete structure is cut by elongated teak-framed windows and surrounds a courtyard swimming pool and ornamental trees and plants.

★ **W Retreat Koh Samui** RESORT **$$$**
(Map p211; 077 915999; www.wretreatkohsamui.com; Mae Nam; r from 20,000B;) A bejewelled 'W' welcomes guests on the curling road to the lobby, beyond which glittering infinity pools lead to an endless horizon. The trademark 'W glam' does its darnedest to fuse an urban vibe with tropical serenity throughout. Do note, though, that this hotel is on a hill and not on a beach, though it does have its own length of sand.

Mae Nam & the North Coast

Mae Nam has some excellent accommodation choices, especially in the top end, but budget-seekers can find some excellent value bungalows too.

Shangri-la BUNGALOW **$**
(Map p198; 077 425189; Mae Nam; bungalows with fan/air-con from 500/1300B;) A backpacker's Shangri La indeed – these are some of the cheapest huts around and they occupy a sublime stretch of the beach. Grounds are sparsely landscaped but the basic concrete bungalows, all with attached bathrooms (only air-con rooms have hot water), are well kept and the staff are pleasant.

★ **Code** HOTEL **$$$**
(Map p198; 077 602122; www.samuicode.com; Mae Nam; ste 3300-11,100B;) Sleek modern lines and dust-free white contrast against the turquoise sea and the hotel's large infinity pool, making for a stunning piece of architecture. The all-ocean-view suites are spacious and efficient, and the service is just as neat. Of course, everything you require is there at your fingertips, including a gym, spa, steam room, tennis court and restaurant.

Coco Palm Resort BUNGALOW **$$$**
(Map p198; 077 447211; www.cocopalmbeachresort.com; Mae Nam; bungalows 3000-9450B;) The huge array of bungalows at well-tended Coco Palm have been crafted with hardwood, bamboo and rattan touches, with a palm-fronted rectangular pool the centrepiece along the beach, facing the sea. The cheapest choices are the furthest

MOUNTAIN-TOP RETREAT

The perilous drive up the road from Chaweng is totally worthwhile once you take in the incredible views from **Jungle Club** (Map p198; ☎081 894 2327; www.jungleclubsamui.com; huts 800-1800B, houses 2700-4500B; ❄@📶🏊). With a relaxed back-to-nature vibe, this isolated mountain getaway is a huge hit among locals and tourists alike. Guests chill around the stunning horizon pool or catnap under the canopied roofs of an open-air *săh·lah*. Even if you don't stay here, it's worth a trip for a drink overlooking the views from the **bar** (⏰9am-9.30pm). Jungle Club can arrange pick up from Chaweng for 400B, or you can get a taxi for a similar fare.

from the sand, but even these are comfy. If you want to make a real splash, aim for the beachfront pool villas.

★**Belmond Napasai** RESORT **$$$**
(Map p198; ☎077 429200; www.napasai.com; Bang Po; r 15,800-80,800B; ❄@📶🏊) Gorgeously manicured grounds welcome weary travellers as they glide past grazing water buffalo and groundsmen donning cream-coloured pith helmets. A generous smattering of villas dot the expansive landscape – all sport traditional Thai-style decorations, from the intricately carved wooden ornamentation to streamers of luscious local silks and bamboo interiors, as well as sumptuous views over the Gulf of Thailand from the lovely balconies.

Na Thon & the West

Na Thon itself has few hotels of merit, though it's a handy hub for getting on or off the boat. Further south you'll find two of the island's best hotels: the Conrad Koh Samui and the Intercontinental Samui Baan Taling Ngam Resort.

Chytalay Palace Hotel HOTEL **$$**
(Map p198; ☎077 421079; 152 Nathon Moo 3; d 400-950B, tr 800-1000B; ❄📶) This quiet hotel on the beachfront road a short walk south from the pier has very good, spacious rooms with balcony overlooking the sea and some delightful sunsets. The lower-floor rooms have electricity cables partially blocking the view but are 400B less than the newer rooms upstairs. Cheaper doubles are fan only. All rooms have attached showers. Service is pleasant.

★**Conrad Koh Samui** RESORT **$$$**
(Map p198; ☎077 915888; www.conradkohsamui.com; villas 45,000-126,000B; ❄📶🏊) The 81 exceptionally neat-lined, contemporary and gorgeous villas of the sumptuous Conrad gaze out over an azure sea, by way of their very own infinity pools. Everything is simply state of the art, the bathrooms are marbled perfection and the full-on sunsets quite unforgettable. Four restaurants, a wine cellar and a superb spa round off a handsome and tempting picture.

★**Intercontinental Samui Baan Taling Ngam Resort** RESORT **$$$**
(Map p198; ☎077 429100; www.samui.intercontinental.com; Taling Ngam; r from 12,000B; ❄📶🏊) This 79-room resort on the west coast whisks you from the crowded east coast and ushers you into sunset-drenched luxury, with views out over to Ang Thong Marine National Park. Rooms are beautifully presented with darkwood furnishings, while the resort boasts seven swimming pools. The beachfront pool villas come with plunge pools, while dining and drinking choices are simply superb.

South Coast

Easy Time BUNGALOW **$$$**
(Map p198; ☎077 920111; www.easytimekohsamui.com; Bang Kao; villas 2300-4000B; ❄@📶🏊) Safely tucked away from the throngs of tourists, this little haven – nestled a few minutes' walk to the beach around a serene swimming pool – doesn't have well-oiled service so be prepared to be master of your own off-the-beaten-path getaway. Duplex villa units and a chic dining space create an elegant mood that is refreshingly unpretentious.

Elements RESORT **$$$**
(Map p198; ☎077 914678; www.kosamui.com/elements-boutique-resort; Ao Phang Ka; r incl breakfast 7400-24,000B; ❄@📶🏊) Peaceful Elements occupies a lonely strand of palm-studded sand with views of the stunning Five Islands, and is the perfect place for a meditative retreat or quiet couples' romantic getaway. Chic rooms are arranged in condo-like blocks, while hidden villas dot the path down to the oceanside lounge area. Free kayaks and bikes plus excellent service add to the calm.

Eating

The island enjoys an ample supply of fresh seafood as well as the various culinary influences of southern Thai cuisine: Malay, Indian, Chinese and Indonesian ingredients, flavours and dishes have found a place here. You'll find that curries are spicier than their central Thailand counterparts and are often seasoned with turmeric, which imparts a yellowish hue. Cloves, cinnamon and cardamom are some of the spices from Indonesia and India that are fed into the aromatic make-up of local dishes such as gang *mát·sà·mân* (Muslim curry) and *kôw mòk gài* (chicken biryani).

Hat Chaweng

Scores of restaurants on the 'strip' serve a mixed bag of local bites, international cuisine and fast food. Competition sees new arrivals all the time and a gradual raising of the bar. To escape the eardrum-piercing noise of the *moo·ay tai* (Thai boxing) vans at night, flee to the beach, where many bungalow operators set up tables on the sand.

Laem Din Market MARKET $
(Map p201; Chaweng; dishes from 35B; 4am-6pm, night market 6pm-2am) A busy day market, Laem Din is packed with stalls that sell fresh fruits, vegetables and meats and stock local Thai kitchens. Pick up a kilo of sweet green oranges or wander the stalls trying to spot the ingredients in last night's curry. For dinner, check out the adjacent night market to sample tasty southern-style fried chicken and curries.

Tuk Tuk Backpackers CAFE $
(Map p201; 087 268 2575; Chaweng Beach Rd; mains from 120B; 10am-2am) This full-on, no-holds-barred, high-impact, brazen and voluminous saloon-style Western cafe/restaurant/bar on Chaweng Beach Rd does good hangover-cure brekkies, with multiple TV screens, pool tables and all the usual trappings.

Hungry Wolf BURGERS $$
(Map p201; 094 408 2243; Chaweng Beach Rd; mains from 220B; 10am-10pm) With fun, vibrantly designed and catchy murals revolving around British culinary idioms, this neat Polish-run Chaweng restaurant does a good trade in juicy burgers, steaks, ribs, pizza and a whole variety of other delicious fare. It's not big, and attracts considerable custom, but the capable and enthusiastic owner makes everyone feel at home.

★ **Dr Frogs** STEAK $$$
(Map p198; 077 448505; www.drfrogssamui.com; Rte 4169; mains from 480B; 7am-11pm) Perched atop a rocky overlook, Dr Frogs combines beautiful ocean vistas with delicious international Italian grills, seafood, pasta, pizza and Thai favourites. Delectable steaks and crab cakes, and friendly owners, make it a winner. It's a romantic setting, and for harassed parents there's a kids' playground in the front garden. Live guitar music on Mondays and Wednesdays at 7.30pm.

★ **Page** FUSION $$$
(Map p201; 077 422767; www.thelibrarysamui.com/the-page; dishes 300-1650B; 7am-midnight;) If you can't afford to stay at the ultra-swanky Library (p202), have a meal at its beachside restaurant instead. It's not cheap, but lunch is a bit more casual and affordable, although you'll miss the designer lighting in the evening. Sunrise breakfasts are lovely.

★ **Larder** EUROPEAN $$$
(Map p201; 077 601259; www.thelardersamui.com; Chaweng Beach Rd; mains 300-820B; noon-11pm Mon-Sat;) This restaurant/bar/gastropub pulls out the stops in an invigorating menu of classic fare in a relaxing and tasteful setting, supported by a strong selection of wines and zesty cocktails. It's a winning formula, with dishes ranging from slow-cooked lamb spare ribs to fish and chips.

Hat Lamai & the Southeast

As Samui's second-most populated beach, Hat Lamai has a surprisingly limited assortment of decent eateries when compared to Hat Chaweng next door. The **Lamai Walking Street Night Market** (Map p206; Lamai; 4-10pm Sun) is excellent for street food, but turn on your pickpocket radar.

Hua Thanon Market MARKET $
(Map p198; Ban Hua Thanon; dishes from 30B; 6am-6pm) Slip into the rhythm of this village market slightly south of Lamai; it's a window into the food ways of southern Thailand. Vendors shoo away the flies from the freshly butchered meat, and housewives load bundles of vegetables into their baby-filled motorcycle baskets. Follow the market road to the row of food shops delivering edible Muslim culture: chicken biryani, fiery

Hat Lamai

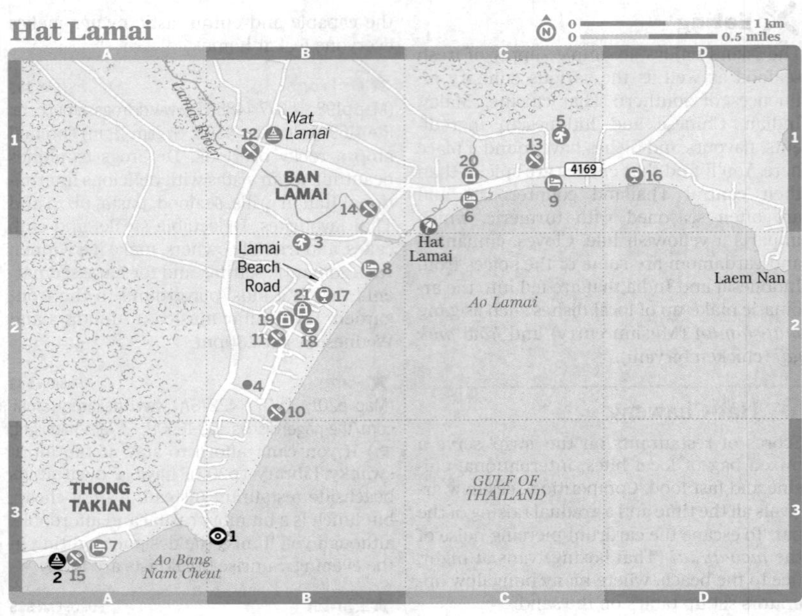

Hat Lamai

curries or toasted rice with coconut, bean sprouts, lemon grass and dried shrimp.

Pad Thai THAI $
(Map p206; ☎077 458560-4; www.manathai.com/samui/phad-thai; Rte 4169; mains from 70B; ⏱11am-9.30pm) On the corner of the huge Manathai hotel by the road, this highly affordable, semi-alfresco and smart restaurant is a fantastic choice for stir-fried and soup noodles, rounded off with a coconut ice cream.

Kangaroo THAI $
(Map p206; Lamai Beach Rd; mains from 120B; ⏱1-11pm) Colourful, efficient and friendly Kangaroo serves excellent Thai and Western dishes, and a wealth of succulent seafood, including shark steak, barracuda steak and blue crab as well as more standard chicken

curries, sizzling platters, fried rice dishes and pasta.

★ La Fabrique BAKERY $$
(Map p206; ☎077 961507; Rte 4169; set breakfasts from 120B; ⊙6.30am-10.30pm;) Ceiling fans chop the air and service is snappy and helpful at this roomy French-style boulangerie/patisserie away from the main drag, near Wat Lamai on Rte 4169. *The* place for brekkie, select from fresh bread, croissants, gratins, baguettes, meringues, yoghurts, pastries or unusually good set breakfasts that include fresh fruit. Wash down with a decent selection of coffees or teas.

★ Baobab FRENCH $$
(Map p206; ☎084 838 3040; Hat Lamai; mains 150-380B; ⊙8am-6pm) Grab a free beach towel and crash out on a sun lounger after a full meal at breezy Baobab, or have a massage next door, but seize one of the beach tables (if you can). You'll need two hands to turn over the hefty menu, with its all-day breakfasts, French/Thai dishes, grills, pastas and popular specials, including red tuna steak (350B).

Tandoori Nights INDIAN $$
(Map p206; ☎091 161 7026; Lamai; mains from 150B; ⊙11am-11pm) The set meals at this welcoming Indian restaurant will only set you back 190B for a vegetable curry, soft drink and a papadum; otherwise select your spice level from the à la carte menu or take a deep breath and order the eye-watering lamb vindaloo (290B), quenched with a chilled beer.

★ The Dining Room FRENCH $$$
(Map p206; www.rockyresort.com; off Rte 4169; dishes 300-950B; ⊙lunch & dinner) The signature beef Rossini at this fantastically positioned beachfront restaurant at Rocky's Resort (p202) is like sending your taste buds on a Parisian vacation as the views pop you into seventh heaven.

Bo Phut & the Northeast

Fisherman's Village has the nicest setting and a bounty of choice, including the busy Friday Walking Street market, plus heaps of well-priced options on the road leading inland towards the main road. Choeng Mon's lively main drag is well provided with eating options, although price tags are high and there's no beach view. There are several decent restaurants and cafes around Big Buddha Beach, west of Choeng Mon.

Ninja Crepes THAI $
(Map p211; 4171 Beach Rd, Bo Phut; mains from 80B; ⊙9am-9pm) The owners of this great place were recently turfed out of their lucrative Chaweng restaurant, but the pay-off is fine sea views; the location sees less custom, but that makes it quieter too. Expect Thai seafood, curries, crepes, soups and sticky desserts.

★ Salefino MEDITERRANEAN $$
(Map p211; ☎091 825 2190; www.salefinosamui.com; Hat Bang Rak; ⊙1-3pm & 5-9pm Mon-Fri, 5-10.30pm Sat) This new restaurant (sister establishment of Pepenero; p208) serves delightful seafood, pasta and tapas dishes with a strong tilt towards Italian, with a fine selection of wines and a lovely setting by the sea, all viewed from a rustic chic setting; dinner is particularly charming, with sunset.

Leonardo Gelateria Italiana GELATO $$
(Map p211; ☎092 847 7385; Wat Phra Yai; from 150B; ⊙9am-6pm) This small gelateria is not cheap – it's 150B for one cup of ice cream or sorbet – but there's a tempting range of 25 flavours and it stands out among the disappointing selection of eateries at Wat Phra Yai. Choose from lime, mango, tiramisu, pistachio, coconut, blackberry, passion fruit, black chocolate and more.

★ Barracuda MEDITERRANEAN $$$
(Map p211; ☎077 430003; www.barracuda-restaurant.com; The Wharf, Fisherman's Village; mains from 575B; ⊙6-11pm) Abounding in alluring Mediterranean culinary inflections, but only open come evening, Barracuda is one of the island's best dining options. The romantic and seductive night-time environment is almost as delightful as the menu: expect to be charmed and well fed on a diet of seared scallops, yellowfin tuna, rack of lamb, Norwegian salmon, delectable pasta dishes and fine service.

★ Chez François FRENCH $$$
(Map p211; ☎096 071 1800; www.facebook.com/chezporte; 33/2 Mu 1, Fisherman's Village; set meal 1700-1950B; ⊙6-11pm Tue-Sat) With no à la carte menu, but a reputation for outstanding cuisine that has sent waves across the culinary map of Ko Samui, Chez Francois serves a three-course surprise meal. Book ahead – and if you're only on Ko Samui for a few days, book early to get a table. It's tiny (and cash only).

CRAZY FOR COCONUTS

It's no surprise that Samui's most famous natural produce finds its way into a medley of dishes. There's sweet coconut jam to spread on your croissants in the morning. *Wai kôo·a* is a spicy and sour coconut-based curry featuring octopus. *Tom Kha* is a flavoursome chicken soup made with coconut milk, lemongrass, lime juice, ginger, fish sauce and chilli paste. Usually made with chicken, beef or lamb, Massaman curry also employs coconuts – the meat is simmered in spices and coconut milk to soften it up after frying. You'll also see seafood being barbecued over coals of coconut husks.

Chez Francois is hidden away behind a wooden door near a pharmacy.

★ **Zazen Restaurant** FUSION $$$
(Map p211; ☎077 425085, 098 015 8986; dishes 540-900B, set menu from 1300B; ⏲lunch & dinner) This superb romantic dining experience at the **Zazen Resort** (www.samuizazen.com) comes complete with ocean views, dim candle lighting and soft music. Thai dancers animate things on Thursday and Sunday nights from 8pm. Reservations recommended.

★ **Dining On The Rocks** FUSION $$$
(Map p198; ☎077 245678; www.sixsenses.com/resorts/samui/dining; Choeng Mon; set menus from 2800B; ⏲5-10pm) At the isolated **Six Senses Samui**, the island's ultimate dining experience takes place on nine cantilevered verandahs yawning over the gulf. After sunset (and wine), guests feel like they're dining on a barge set adrift on a starlit sea. Each dish on the set menu is the brainchild of cooks experimenting with taste, texture and temperature.

Mae Nam & the North Coast

Mae Nam has lots of eating options, from beachside, palm-thatch and driftwood affairs serving a mix of Thai, Western and seafood dishes to classier places tucked along the inland, lily-pad-pond-dotted tangle of roads. It's a lovely place to wander and find your own surprises. Don't overlook Mae Nam's **Walking Street** (Map p198; Mae Nam; ⏲from 5pm Thu), on Thursday evenings.

★ **Fish Restaurant** INTERNATIONAL $
(Map p198; ☎087 472 4097; Rte 4169, Mae Nam; mains from 50B; ⏲11am-11pm) With elegant Thai tablecloths and a well-priced, tasty menu of Thai seafood and pan-Asian dishes and international appetisers, this popular wood-floored eatery pulls in a regular stream of diners for its charming setting, winning spring rolls, gorgeous seafood curries, steamed sea bass and much more.

Bang Po Seafood SEAFOOD $$
(Map p198; Bang Po; dishes from 100B; ⏲dinner) A meal at Bang Po Seafood is a test for the taste buds. It's one of the only restaurants that serves traditional Ko Samui fare: recipes call for ingredients such as raw sea urchin roe, baby octopus, sea water, coconut and local turmeric.

★ **Pepenero** ITALIAN $$
(Map p198; ☎077 963353; www.pepenerosamui.com; Mae Nam; mains from 250B; ⏲6-10pm Mon-Sat) Pepenero continues to cause a stir on Ko Samui, moving to this more accessible Mae Nam location. What this excellent and neatly designed Italian restaurant lacks in views is more than made up for by a terrific menu (including cutting boards with cheese and cold cuts) and the care and attention displayed to customers by the very sociable, hard-working hosts. Put this one in your planner.

Gaon Korean Restaurant KOREAN $$
(Map p198; Mae Nam; mains from 180B; ⏲3-11pm) Right in China Town in Mae Nam, this excellent restaurant offers barbecued meat, grilled fish and steamed seafood sets, as well as Korean staples such as delicious *bulgogi* (marinated beef with mushroom and carrot on a hot plate), kimchi pancake, Korean ice cream, a kids' menu and a range of sizzling choices for vegetarians.

John's Garden Restaurant THAI $$
(Map p198; ☎077 247694; www.johnsgardensamui.com; Mae Nam; mains from 160B; ⏲1-10pm) This delightful garden restaurant is a picture, with tables slung out beneath bamboo and palms and carefully cropped hedges. It's particularly romantic when lantern-lit at night, so reserve ahead, but pack some mosquito repellent (which is generally provided, but it's good to have backup). The signature dish on the Thai and European menu is the excellent massaman chicken.

★ **Farmer** INTERNATIONAL $$$
(Map p198; ☎077 447222; www.farmersboutique resort.com/restaurant; Mae Nam; mains 300-1500B, set lunch 250-340B; ⏲7am-10.30pm) Magically set in front of a photogenic rice field with green hills in the distance, fantastic Farmer – within the boutique resort of the same name – is a choice selection, especially when the candlelight flickers on a starry night. The mostly European-inspired food is lovely and well-presented, there's a free pick-up for nearby beaches, and service is attentive.

Na Thon & the West

The quiet west coast features some of the best seafood on Samui as well as some of the best views, especially come sunset. Na Thon has a lot of choice, but the restaurants don't really stand out, although there's a giant day market on Th Thawi Ratchaphakdi.

Lucky INTERNATIONAL $$
(Map p198; ☎077 420392; Na Thon; 100-250B; ⏲8am-9pm Mon-Sat, noon-9pm Sun; 📶) This restaurant facing the sea serves tasty and filling enough Western and Thai food, and it's convenient if you're off the boat or travelling up the west coast, but it's the sunset views and friendly service that nudge it into the recommended bracket. Good choice of vegetarian dishes too.

Big John's Seafood Restaurant SEAFOOD $$
(Map p198; ☎077 485775; Lipa Noi; mains 150-300B; 📶) This friendly restaurant is a popular west-coast seafood choice for sunset dining, with live evening entertainment.

Phootawan Restaurant THAI $$
(Map p198; ☎081 978 9241; mains from 150B; ⏲9am-8.30pm) Getting up the hill to this restaurant is a struggle on a scooter, but it's worth the effort to be rewarded with ranging, glorious views over the trees, rather than just for the serviceable food. To enjoy the visuals at their best, sunset is the time to arrive.

South Coast

Sweet Sisters Cafe CAFE $
(Map p198; Bang Kao; ⏲11am-9pm; 📶) Charming, cosy and with an enticing interior, this roadside cafe down in the quiet south of Ko Samui, just before the turn off for Ao Bang Kao, is a welcoming place for shots of caffeine, juices and snacks as you explore the beaches, bays and pagodas of the southern shore.

SALT & SPICE IN SOUTHERN THAI CUISINE

Southern Thai cooking is undoubtedly the spiciest regional style in a land of spicy regional cuisines. The food also tends to be very salty, and seafood, not surprisingly, plays an important role, ranging from fresh fish that is grilled or added to soups, to pickled or fermented fish, and fish served as sauces or condiments.

Two of the principal crops are coconuts and cashews, both of which find their way into a variety of dishes. Nearly every meal is accompanied by a platter of fresh herbs and vegies, and a spicy 'dip' of shrimp paste, chillies, garlic and lime.

Dishes you are likely to come across in southern Thailand include the following:

Gaang đai þlah An intensely spicy and salty curry that includes *đai þlah* (salted fish stomach) – much tastier than it sounds.

Gaang sôm Known as *gaang lĕu·ang* (yellow curry), this sour/spicy soup gets its hue from turmeric.

Gài tôrt hàht yài The famous deep-fried chicken from the town of Hat Yai gets its rich flavour from a marinade containing dried spices.

Kà·nŏm jeen nám yah This dish of thin rice noodles served with fiery curry-like sauce is accompanied by fresh vegetables and herbs.

Kôo·a glîng Minced meat fried with curry paste is a southern staple.

Kôw yam A popular breakfast, this dish includes rice topped with sliced herbs, bean sprouts, dried prawns, toasted coconut and powdered red chilli, served with a sour/sweet fish-based sauce.

Pàt sà·đor This stir-fry of 'stink beans' with shrimp, garlic, chillies and shrimp paste is pungent and spicy.

★ **Hemingway's on the Beach** THAI $$
(Map p198; ☎088 452 4433; off Rte 4170, Ao Thong Krut; mains from 175B; ⏲10am-8pm Sat, Mon, Tue & Thu, 10am-6pm Sun) With appetising Thai dishes – and popular cookery courses too – this beachside choice on Rte 4170 as it loops into Thong Krut is an excellent reason to escape to the southwest corner of Ko Samui; tuck into fresh seafood and bask in the views, especially come sundown. Hemingway's also arranges long-tail and speedboat island tours, while massage is at hand for post-meal relaxation.

Drinking & Nightlife

A recent ruling that all bars need to close by 1am means the island is quieter at night than it once was. Samui's biggest party spot is brash and noisy Hat Chaweng. Lamai and Bo Phut come in second and third respectively, while the rest of the island is generally quiet, with drinking usually focused on resort bars. For sunset cocktails, hit the west coast, or parts of the north coast.

Hat Chaweng

★ **Drink Gallery** COCKTAIL BAR
(Chaweng Beach Rd; Map p201; ⏲4pm-1am) Part of the Library hotel (p202), this highly stylish bar along Chaweng Beach Rd has top design and some excellent cocktails. It's a place to be seen in, and a place to people-watch from or just admire the interior artwork, while nibbling on tapas-style Thai bites.

Bees Knees Brewpub BREWERY
(Map p201; ☎085 537 2498; www.samuibrew.pub; Chaweng Lake Rd; ⏲3pm-1am) The rather charmless interior decor and downcast service wins no prizes, but the beer (from 120B) – brewed on-site – gets serious accolades and big thumbs-up. Choose from five beers (wheaty bee, summer bee, black bee, bitter bee or black-and-tan) and enjoy some deeply rich and thorough flavours. The brewery is right next to the bar, visible through glass.

Sawasdee Bar BAR
(Map p201; Chaweng Beach Rd; ⏲5pm-midnight Mon-Fri) This bright-blue converted Volkswagen camper van sets up five days a week, serving outdoor cocktails (99B), beers (80B), cocktail buckets (450B) and spirits (140B) with servings of fun live music.

Ark Bar BAR
(Map p201; ☎7am-1am; www.ark-bar.com; Hat Chaweng) Drinks are dispensed from the multicoloured bar to an effusive crowd, guests recline on loungers on the beach, and the party is on day and night, with fire shows lighting up the sands after sundown and DJs providing house music from the afternoon onwards.

Pride Bar GAY & LESBIAN
(Map p201; ☎088 753 2921; Chaweng Beach Rd; ⏲5pm-2am) At the heart of Chaweng, this easygoing place attracts a mixed crowd of Thais and foreigners.

Hat Lamai & the Southeast

Lamai doesn't have the same range of bars or quality as nearby Chaweng, but it's a much more pleasant place for a drink for those who want more peace. There are far fewer girlie bars as well, and prices are a little lower, but overall, the bars have less character.

Bear Cocktails BAR
(Map p206; Lamai Beach Rd; ⏲5pm-2am) It's not a traditional bar, but a fun, open-air cocktail stall on the road run by some friendly girls (Bear and Lek); buy a strawberry daiquiri, grab a plastic seat and chat to whoever's at hand. It's not far from the McDonald's; cocktails are 79B.

Lava Lounge BAR
(Map p206; ☎080 886 5035; Hat Lamai; ⏲4pm-2am) One of the better bars in Hat Lamai, Lava Lounge is a chilled-out spot with an

DON'T MISS

'WALKING STREET' NIGHT MARKETS

These food-filled markets occur at least weekly, offering you the chance to sample local delicacies, shop for gifts and mingle with tourists and locals. They start at around 4pm and run until around midnight. To avoid the crowds arrive before 6pm or after 10pm. Pickpockets can be prevalent.

This was the schedule at the time of research, but some are considering opening more frequently:

Ban Chaweng Monday to Thursday and Saturday

Ban Lamai Sunday

Ban Meanam Thursday

Bo Phut (Fisherman's Village) Friday

Ban Choeng Mon Friday

Bo Phut

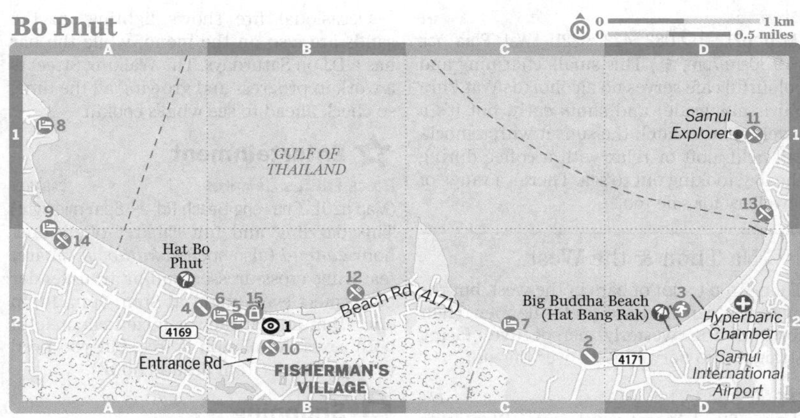

Bo Phut

invigorating menu of cocktails (99B to 150B), and a happy hour that runs from 4pm to 9pm, which includes a spirit with mixer for 79B.

Beach Republic BAR

(Map p206; ☎077 458100; www.beachrepublic.com; 176/34 Mu 4, Hat Lamai; ⏲7am-11pm) Recognised by its yawning thatch-patched awnings, Beach Republic could be the poster child of a made-for-TV, beachside, booze-swilling holiday. There's a wading pool, comfy lounge chairs, an endless cocktail list and even a hotel if you never, ever want to leave the party. The Sunday brunches (11.30am to 3.30pm) here are legendary.

Bo Phut & the Northeast

★Woobar BAR

(Map p211; ☎077 915999; Bo Phut; ⏲11am-midnight; 📶) With serious wow factor and 270-degree panoramas, the W Retreat's signature lobby bar gives the word 'swish' a whole new meaning, with cushion-clad pods of seating plonked in the middle of an expansive infinity pool that stretches out over the infinite horizon. This is, without a doubt, the best place on Samui for sunset cocktails blended with cool music mixes.

★Coco Tam's BAR

(Map p211; Fisherman's Village; ⏲1pm-1am) Grab a swing at the bar or plop yourself on a beanbag on the sand, order a giant cocktail served in a jar and take a toke on a shisha (water pipe; 500B). It's a bit pricey, but this boho, beach-bum-chic spot oozes relaxation, it's lovely when the sun goes down and the coconut milkshakes are to die for. Fire dancers perform most nights.

Chez Isa CAFE

(Map p211; ☎082 423 9221; Wat Phra Yai; ⏰9.30am-7pm; 📶) This small, charming and colourful cafe serves no alcohol (as Wat Phra Yai is alongside) and shuts early, but it's a lovely spot to catch the sunset with a mocktail held aloft or relax with a coffee during the day, looking out to sea. There's a range of jewellery for sale too.

Na Thon & the West

There aren't a lot of bars in the west, but the ones you can find are pretty dapper. Their forte is the westerly perspective, facing straight into fiery sunsets over the gulf.

★ **Air Bar** BAR

(Map p198; Intercontinental Samui Baan Taling Ngam Resort, Taling Ngam; ⏰5pm-midnight) Toast the setting sun as it sinks into the golden gulf from this magnificent outside bar perched above a cliff at this swanky resort (p204). There's an excellent menu of tapas and snacks if you simply can't pull yourself away and want to make a meal of it. This is pretty much the top romantic choice on the island.

Nikki Beach BAR

(Map p198; ☎077 914500; www.nikkibeach.com/kohsamui; Lipa Noi; ⏰11am-11pm; 📶) The acclaimed luxury brand brings international flair to the secluded west coast of Ko Samui. Think haute cuisine, chic decor, gaggles of jet-setters and killer sunsets. Themed brunch and dinner specials keep the masses coming throughout the week, and sleek villa accommodation is also on offer.

Max Murphys BAR

(Map p198; Na Thon) This fun Irish pub offers all the usual ingredients of a fun night: Premier League fixtures, Western and Thai pub grub, draught beer (Guinness, Kilkenny, Hoegaarden), a few craft beers, cocktails and obliging staff. It's as Irish as a bowl of tom yam soup, but after a few pints, you won't care.

South Coast

Buffalo Baby BAR

(Map p198; Bang Kao) Way down on the south shore at Ao Bang Kao, this fun beachside bar (run by the affable Maurice) really comes alive on Saturdays at 5pm when the Bang Kao Walking Street, a buzzing market set to live music on a stage right on the sand, takes off.

Occasional fire shows lighting up the sands are also on the menu, while the bar has a DJ on Saturdays. The Walking Street is a work in progress and growing all the time, so check ahead to see what's cookin'.

☆ Entertainment

Paris Follies Cabaret CABARET

(Map p201; Chaweng Beach Rd; ⏰8pm-midnight) This dazzling and fun cabaret offers one-hour *gà·teu·i* (also spelled *kàthoey*) cabaret featuring cross-dresser and/or transgender performers every night at 8pm, 9pm, 10pm and 11pm and attracts a mixed clientele of both sexes. Admission is free, but you need to buy a drink (from around 300B).

Shopping

★ **Central Festival** SHOPPING CENTRE

(Map p201; Chaweng Beach Rd; ⏰11am-11pm) This bright, shiny and huge monster-mall is stuffed with shops, cafes and restaurants and legions of Chinese shoppers. There's a terrific range of shopping options, and some of the dining choices are excellent too. There's a bouncy slide for kids.

Fisherman's Village Walking Street MARKET

(Map p211; Fisherman's Village; ⏰5-11pm Fri) Every Friday night, this busy and colourful Walking Street transforms Fisherman's Village into a forest of sharp elbows, market stalls, street food, handicrafts, T-shirts and cheap cocktails.

Thanon An Thong STREET

(Map p198; Na Thon) Just a block inland from the pier, this pretty street is lined with wooden shophouses, Chinese lanterns and caged singing birds, with souvenir shops plying goods and gifts you can pick up more cheaply and with less pushing and shoving than in Chaweng.

Island Books BOOKS

(Map p206; ☎061 193 2132; www.island-books-samui.com; off Rte 4169; ⏰9am-7pm) Tucked away on a lane off the 4169 and run by Liverpudlian Paul, Island Books on the main drag past Lamai has the largest selection of used books – in pretty much every language – on the island. There's another **smaller branch** (⏰9am-7pm) in Lamai village itself.

Information

DANGERS & ANNOYANCES

The repetitive scream of ambulances racing up and down the island's roads is a sure sign that the road accident fatality rate on Ko Samui is high. This is largely due to the significant number of (inexperienced) tourists who rent motorcycles and scooters only to find out that the winding roads, sudden tropical rains, frenzied traffic and sand on the roads can be lethal.

Look out for glass on less-visited beaches – it's incomprehensible how much broken glass can just lie on the sands. Parts of the beach in Na Thon have a lot of broken glass on them, but you'll also find potentially dangerous shards on lengths of sand such as the sandbar leading to Ko Ma in the northwest of the island. Tread carefully and keep a look-out at all times.

The seas of Samui can be rough, even for strong swimmers, and drownings do occur, especially in Chaweng and Lamai, which experience strong currents and rip tides. Hotels will usually post warnings of swimming hazards and conditions on a beach board or warning flags. If you are caught in a rip tide (a strong surface current heading seaward), swim parallel to the shore to exit the current or float along with it until it dissipates in deeper water and you are deposited.

Beach vendors are registered with the government and should all be wearing a numbered jacket. No peddler should cause an incessant disturbance – seek assistance if this occurs.

EMERGENCY

Tourist Police (Map p198; ☎077 430018; www.samui-tourist-police.com) Useful for contacting either for advice or if you are arrested.

INTERNET ACCESS

Wi-fi is widespread at effectively all accommodation choices, restaurants and bars. You may have to pay for wi-fi access at some high-end hotels, but it is generally provided free at most midrange and budget places.

LEGAL MATTERS

The Thai police tend to leave foreigners alone, but the laws regarding drugs can be rigidly enforced and the penalties for possession of drugs can be severe.

If arrested for any offence, the police will allow you to make one phone call. If arrested, being confrontational will make things worse for you.

Make sure you carry a copy of your passport or ID as the police can ask to see it. While you will see many drivers not wearing one, a helmet is required by law if you are driving a motorbike or scooter.

The Tourist Police can be of great help in any situation regarding the law.

MEDICAL SERVICES

Ko Samui has four private hospitals, located near Chaweng's Tesco Lotus supermarket on the east coast (where most of the tourists tend to gather). The government hospital (Samui Hospital) in Na Thon has seen significant improvements in the past couple of years but the service is still a bit grim because funding is based on the number of Samui's legal residents (which doesn't take into account the many illegal Myanmar workers).

Bangkok Hospital Samui (Map p201; ☎077 429500, emergency 077 429555; www.bangkokhospitalsamui.com) Centrally located, internationally accredited hospital in Chaweng. Your best bet for just about any medical problem.

Bandon International Hospital (Map p198; ☎077 245236; www.bandonhospitalsamui.com; off route 4169) A private hospital offering international standards of healthcare.

Ko Samui Hospital (Map p198; ☎077 913200; www.samuihospital.go.th/weben; Na Thon; 24hr) Public, government hospital located in the south of Na Thon.

Samui International Hospital (Map p201; ☎077 300394; www.sih.co.th; Chaweng Beach Rd; 24hr) International hospital in Chaweng. Emergency ambulance service is available 24 hours and credit cards are accepted.

MONEY

ATMs are widely available. Credit cards are accepted in most hotels and restaurants.

POST

In several parts of the island there are privately run post-office branches charging a small commission. You can almost always leave your stamped mail with your accommodation.

TOURIST INFORMATION

There is no official tourist office on the island. Tourist information is largely provided by hotels and travel agents.

Siam Map Company (www.siammap.com) Puts out quarterly booklets including a Spa Guide, Dining Guide and an annual directory, which

DOG WARNING

Dogs are everywhere on the island – they breed like rabbits and may bite. The Samui Dog & Cat Rescue Centre (p197) has the job of looking after and neutering/spaying stray dogs and controlling rabies (largely under control, but check with a health professional if bitten), and they have their work cut out for them. You may find menacing dogs at temples or sitting around the beaches in packs; exercise caution and don't stroke them.

lists thousands of companies and hotels on the island. Its *Samui Guide Map* is fantastic, free and easily found throughout the island.

VISA EXTENSIONS

The new **Immigration Office** (Map p198; ☎077 423440; Soi 1 Mu 1, Mae Nam; ⊙8.30am-4.30pm Mon-Fri) is located south of Rte 4169 in Mae Nam. Officials here tend to issue the minimum rather than maximum visa extensions. It's better located and bigger than the former offices in Na Thon, but you may still be denied an extension for no particular reason.

Don't overlook the option to join a three-month to one-year Thai language course with a school on the island, which would qualify you for a student visa to cover the length of the course.

Getting There & Away

AIR

Ko Samui Airport (www.samuiairportonline.com) is in the northeast of the island near Big Buddha Beach.

Bangkok Airways (www.bangkokair.com) operates flights roughly every 30 minutes between Samui and Bangkok's Suvarnabhumi International Airport (65 minutes). Bangkok Airways also flies direct from Samui to Phuket, Pattaya, Chiang Mai, Singapore, Kuala Lumpur, Hong Kong and other cities in Southeast Asia. Bangkok Airways also flies to Chéngdū and Guǎngzhōu in China. There is a **Bangkok Airways Office** (Map p201; ☎077 420512, 077 420519; www.bangkokair.com) in Hat Chaweng and another at the airport. The first (at 6am) and last (10pm) flights of the day are always the cheapest.

During the high season, make your flight reservations far in advance as seats often sell out.

MOTORBIKE RENTAL SCAMS

Even if you escape unscathed from a motorbike riding experience, some shops will claim that you damaged your rental and will try to extort some serious cash. The best way to avoid this is to take copious photos of your vehicle (cars included) at the time of rental, making sure the person renting you the vehicle sees you do it (they will be less likely to make false claims against you if they know you have photos).

If they still make a claim against you, keep your cool. Losing your temper won't help you win the argument and could significantly escalate the problem.

If things get really bad call the tourist police (p213), not the regular police.

If the Samui flights are full, try flying into Surat Thani from Bangkok and taking the short ferry ride to Samui instead. Flights to Surat Thani are generally cheaper than a direct flight to the island, although they involve much more hassle.

BOAT

To reach Samui, the main piers on the mainland are Ao Ban Don, Tha Thong, Don Sak and Chumphon – Tha Thong (in central Surat) and Don Sak being the most common. On Samui, the three most used ports are Na Thon, Mae Nam and Big Buddha Beach. Expect complimentary taxi transfers with high-speed ferry services.

To The Mainland

There are regular boat departures between Samui and Don Sak on the mainland.

High-speed **Lomprayah** (☎077 4277 656; www.lomprayah.com) departs from Na Thon (400B; 8am, 9.45am, 12.45pm & 3.30pm) and takes just 45 minutes; some departures can connect with the train station in Phun Phin (600B) for Surat Thani.

There's also the slower but regular **Raja** (Map p198; ☎022 768211-2, 092 274 3423-5; www.rajaferryport.com; adult 130B) car ferry (130B; 90 minutes) to Don Sak, which departs from Thong Yang. The slow night boat to Samui (300B) leaves from central Surat Thani each night at 11pm, reaching Na Thon around 5am. It returns from Na Thon at 9pm, arriving at around 3am. Watch your bags on this boat.

Lomprayah ferries also depart from Pralarn Pier in Mae Nam for Chumphon (1100B; 8am and 12.30pm; 3¾ hours).

To Ko Pha-Ngan & Ko Tao

There are almost a dozen daily departures between Ko Samui and Thong Sala on the west coast of Ko Pha-Ngan, and many of these continue on to Ko Tao. These leave from Na Thon, Pralarn Pier in Mae Nam or Big Buddha Beach pier, take from 20 minutes to one hour and cost 200B to 300B to Ko Pha-Ngan, depending on the boat.

To go directly to Hat Rin, the *Haad Rin Queen* goes back and forth between Hat Rin and Big Buddha Beach four times a day (the first boat leaves Hat Rin at 9.30am and departs Big Buddha Beach at 10.30am), with double the number of sailings the day after the Full Moon Party and an extra trip laid on at 7.30am the same day. The voyage takes 50 minutes, costs 200B and the last boat leaves Big Buddha Beach at 6.30pm.

Also for Hat Rin and the more remote east coast beaches of Ko Pha-Ngan, the small and rickety *Thong Nai Pan Express* runs once a day at noon from Mae Hat on Ko Samui to Hat Rin and then up the east coast, stopping at all the beaches as far as Thong Nai Pan Noi. Prices range from 200B to 400B, depending on the destination. The boat won't run in bad weather.

BUS & TRAIN

A bus-ferry combo is more convenient than a train-ferry package for getting to Ko Samui because you don't have to switch transportation in Phun Phin. However, the trains are much more comfortable and spacious – especially at night. If you prefer the train, you can get off at Chumphon and catch the Lomprayah catamaran service the rest of the way.

Several services offer these bus-boat combo tickets, the fastest and most comfortable being the Lomprayah, which has two daily departures from Bangkok, at 6am and 9pm, and two from Samui to Bangkok, at 8am and 12.30pm. The total voyage takes between 11 and 14 hours and costs between 1400B and 1450B.

Getting Around

Note that once you're in the Ko Samui sticks, you'll see signs everywhere for this or that bar, this or that restaurant or hotel, with a distance inscribed. As a rough guide, 300m on these signs equals 1km.

CAR & MOTORBIKE

You can rent motorcycles and scooters from almost every resort on the island. The going rate for a scooter is 150B to 200B per day, but for longer periods try to negotiate a better rate. You'll generally need to hand over your passport as a deposit (but you may need it if moving hotel, so plan ahead). You'll see petrol for sale in bottles at 40B at litre, but it's much cheaper at petrol stations.

If you decide to rent a motorcycle, protect yourself by wearing a helmet, and ask for one with a plastic visor; keep to driving slowly. If you rent a motorbike or scooter, be warned that if you don't have an international driving licence, you may have problems in the event of an accident and your insurer might not cover you.

MINIBUSES

Drivers of *sŏrng·tăa·ou* (pick-up minibuses) love to try to overcharge you, so it's always best to ask a third party for current rates, as they can change with the season. These vehicles run regularly during daylight hours. It's about 50B to travel between beaches, and no more than 100B to travel halfway across the island. Figure about 20B for a five-minute ride on a motorcycle taxi.

TAXIS

Taxi service is quite chaotic due to the plethora of cabs, and fares are ridiculously inflated compared to Bangkok. Taxis typically charge around 500B for an airport transfer. Some Hat Chaweng travel agencies can arrange minibus taxis for less.

Ko Pha-Ngan เกาะพงัน

POP 12,500

In the late 1970s, Ko Pha-Ngan was a pristine paradise that beckoned the intrepid. Its innocent days may be long gone, but don't let that deter you: this gulf isle offers much more than the Full Moon parties that made it famous.

Choose quieter days in the lunar calendar, or the smaller but still-raucous half-moon party periods, and the island's charms are brought to the fore. It's easier to get a room, prices are more reasonable and far fewer people are on the island, meaning more solitude and tranquillity. Even Hat Rin – party central when the moon is round – is quiet and relaxing during other periods, and the beaches are kept clean.

The quietest months are April to June, when the island is in low gear – an ideal time to visit for low accommodation prices, fewer elbows per square kilometre and safer roads.

Sights

Beyond Full Moon wild partying, this large jungle island boasts many overlooked, spectacular natural features to explore, including tree-clad mountains, waterfalls, unspoiled forest and national park land as well as some of the most spectacular beaches in all of Thailand. Also remember that, outside the Full Moon, the island is a largely peaceful and serene place.

Remember to change out of your beach clothes when visiting one of the 20 wát on Ko Pha-Ngan. Most temples are open during daylight hours.

Hat Than Sadet BEACH

(Map p216) Fronted by a fringe of coconut trees, the lovely beach of Hat Than Sadet rewards the scooter journey from Thong Sala, Ao Thong Nai Pan or Ban Tai. Explore up and down the delightful beach, and consider crossing the bridge at the south end to the Mai Pen Rai bungalows and following the rocks around the headland to the beach at Hat Thong Reng. The swimming is good at both beaches.

Hat Thong Reng BEACH

(Map p216) The smaller, very secluded sibling of Hat Than Sadet, Hat Thong Reng on Ao Thong Reng is located around the headland to the south of its big brother. It is a lovely beach, with good swimming. Follow the huge

Ko Pha-Ngan

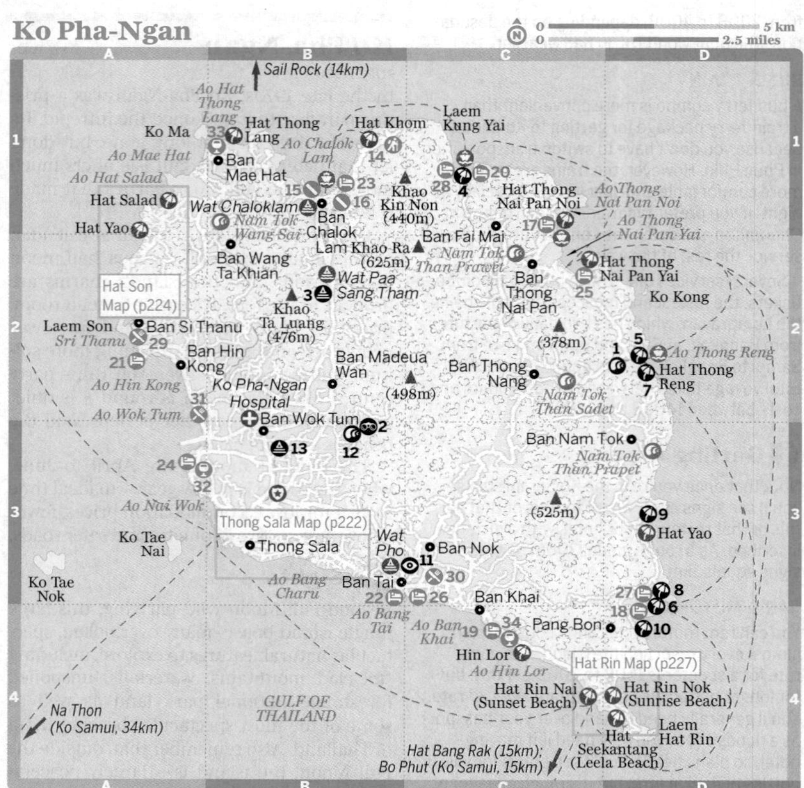

rocks around the south of Hat Than Sadet to reach the beach, but watch your step.

Nam Tok Phaeng WATERFALL
(Map p216) Nam Tok Phaeng is protected by a national park; this waterfall is a pleasant reward after a short but rough hike. After the waterfall (dry out of season), it's a further exhilarating 15-minute climb up a root-choked path (along the Phaeng-Domsila Nature Trail) to the fantastic **Domsila Viewpoint** (Map p216), with superb, ranging views. The two- to three-hour trail then continues on through the jungle in a loop, past other waterfalls before bringing you back. Take water and good shoes.

Ko Pha-Ngan's Tallest Yang Na Yai Tree LANDMARK
(Map p216) Thrusting into the heavens near Wat Pho, Ko Pha-Ngan's tallest Yang Na Yai (dipterocarpus alatus; ยางนา) is an astonishing sight as you veer round the bend for the diminutive Wat Nok temple, a small shrine tucked away in the greenery beyond. These giants grow to over 50m in height and, for tree lovers, are real beauties. This imposing specimen is often garlanded with colourful ribbons.

Hat Khuat BEACH
(Bottle Beach; Map p216) This lovely stretch of sand overlooked by green hills is a superb choice for a relaxing day of swimming and snorkelling, and the bungalow operations along the beach beckon would-be overnighters. There's a great hike from Ban Chalok Lam, the fishing village in the island's north, but take enough water and follow the bottles on poles that should mark the way; the usual way to the beach is by beach taxi from Ban Chalok Lam or Thong Nai Pan.

Deang Waterfall WATERFALL
(Map p216) Than Sadet has a string of waterfalls down to the beach at Ao Thong Reng,

Ko Pha-Ngan

Sights

1 Deang Waterfall ... D2
2 Domsila Viewpoint ... B3
3 Guanyin Temple ... B2
4 Hat Khuat ... C1
5 Hat Than Sadet ... D2
6 Hat Thian ... D4
7 Hat Thong Reng ... D2
8 Hat Wai Nam ... D3
9 Hat Yao (East) ... D3
10 Hat Yuan ... D4
11 Ko Pha-Ngan's Tallest Yang Na Yai Tree ... C3
12 Nam Tok Phaeng ... B3
13 Wat Phu Khao Noi ... B3

Activities, Courses & Tours

Apnea Koh Pha Ngan ... (see 15)
14 Chalok Lam to Bottle Beach Trek ... B1
15 Chaloklum Diving ... B1
16 Sail Rock Divers ... B1

Sleeping

17 Anantara Rasananda ... C1
18 Bamboo Hut ... D4
Barcelona ... (see 18)
19 Bay Lounge & Resort ... C4
Boom's Cafe Bungalows ... (see 19)
20 Bottle Beach II ... C1
21 Chills Resort ... A2
22 Divine Comedie ... B3
23 Fantasea ... B1
24 Kupu Kupu Phangan Beach Villas & Spa by l'Occitane ... A3
25 Longtail Beach Resort ... C2
Loyfa Natural Resort ... (see 21)
26 Mac Bay ... C3
Mai Pen Rai ... (see 5)
Mandalai ... (see 15)
Pariya Resort & Villas ... (see 18)
27 Sanctuary ... D3
28 Smile Bungalows ... C1

Eating

Bamboo Hut ... (see 18)
Bubba's Coffee Bar ... (see 22)
29 Crave ... A2
30 Fabio's ... C3
Fisherman's Restaurant ... (see 22)
31 JJ's Restaurant ... A2
Sanctuary ... (see 27)

Drinking & Nightlife

32 Amsterdam ... A3
Flip Flop Pharmacy ... (see 25)
33 Three Sixty Bar ... B1
34 Viewpoint Bar ... C4

and this is the best. Deang features a sequence of falls, a pool for swimming in and lots of rock-clambering opportunities. You may even find someone slumped in the main flow, cooling off on the rocks in the gush of the water. Look for the signs.

Secret Beach BEACH

(Hat Son; Map p224) Not so secret, this palm-fringed, soft-sand cove (aka Hat Son) down a steep road in the northwest of the island is a gorgeous choice for sunset, but any time of day will do. To fully get in the mood, check into the Haad Son Resort (p223), or sink a twilight cocktail at the Secret Beach Bar (p230). Swimming here is generally very good.

Hat Wai Nam BEACH

(Map p216) A small white-sand beach slung out between Hat Thian and Hat Yao on the more remote east coast, titchy Hat Wai Nam can be reached on foot from Hat Rin along the path up the mountain, but that's the long way round (you'll need four hours or more), and getting here by long-tail boat is advised. Expect a secluded beach with ravishing waters.

Hat Thian BEACH

(Map p216) Hat Thian is a pretty, relatively empty, back-to-nature beach on the east of the island, accessible either by boat or on foot trekking from Hat Rin (p218). You can walk here from **Hat Yuan** (Map p216) in under 10 minutes via the rocky outcrop. The longer trek from Hat Rin (the mountain path leading here goes from north of Hat Rin Nok) takes just over two hours, but it can be hot going so load up on fluids.

Hat Yao (East) BEACH

(Map p216) This lovely white-sand beach can only be reached on foot or by boat, lending it a gorgeous sense of seclusion. Most visitors arrive by boat, as the walk is a good four- to five-hour hike along the 7km-long mountain path from Hat Rin, which shouldn't be attempted if it's getting dark.

Guanyin Temple BUDDHIST TEMPLE

(Map p216; 40B; 7am-6pm) Signposted as the 'Goddess of Mercy Shrine Joss House', this fascinating Chinese temple is dedicated to Guanyin, the Buddhist Goddess of Mercy. The temple's Chinese name (普岳山) on the entrance gate refers to the island in China that is the legendary home of the goddess. The main hall – the Great Treasure Hall – is a highly colourful confection, containing several bodhisattvas, including Puxian (seated on an elephant) and Wenshu (sitting on a lion).

Hat Rin Nok BEACH

(Sunrise Beach; Map p227) Aka Sunrise Beach, aka Full Moon Party Beach, this is astonishingly (you may think) one of Ko Pha-Ngan's cleanest and most pleasant beaches. This is where much of the money goes from the monthly partying admission charge – to cleaning the sand and returning it to an attractive state. Its reputation as party central keeps many people away, so it can be surprisingly crowd-free at times.

Wat Phu Khao Noi BUDDHIST TEMPLE

(Map p216; dawn-dusk) FREE The oldest temple on the island is Wat Phu Khao Noi, near the hospital in Thong Sala. While the site is open to visitors throughout the day, the monks are only around in the morning.

Activities

Ko Pha-Ngan is stuffed with activities, from diving to trekking, kayaking, snorkelling, swimming and beyond.

Hiking and snorkelling day trips to Ang Thong Marine National Park generally depart from Ko Samui, but tour operators shuttle tourists from here too.

Many larger accommodation options can sort out jet skis and kayaks.

Diving & Water Sports

There's a more laid-back diving scene on Ko Pha-Ngan than on nearby Ko Tao, but there's no shortage of professional, competitively priced dive operations with courses from novice to instructor level as well as free-diving.

A drop in Open Water certification prices has also made local rates competitive with Ko Tao. Group sizes tend to be smaller on Ko Pha-Ngan since the island has fewer divers in general. Recommended dive outfits include **Haad Yao Divers**, **Lotus Diving**, **Chaloklum Diving**, and **Apnea Koh Pha Ngan** for free-diving.

Like the other islands in the Samui Archipelago, Pha-Ngan has several small reefs dispersed around the island. The clear favourite snorkelling spot is **Ko Ma**, a small island in the northwest connected to Ko Pha-Ngan by a charming sandbar. There are also some rock reefs of interest on the eastern side of the island.

A major perk of diving from Ko Pha-Ngan is the proximity to **Sail Rock** (Hin Bai), the best dive site in the Gulf of Thailand and a veritable beacon for whale sharks. This large pinnacle lies about 14km north of the island. An abundance of corals and large tropical fish can be seen at depths of 10m to 30m, and there's a rocky vertical swim-through called **The Chimney**.

Dive shops on Ko Tao also visit Sail Rock; however, the focus tends to be more on shallow reefs (for newbie divers) and the deep-dive waters at Chumphon Pinnacle. The most popular trips departing from Ko Pha-Ngan are three-site day trips which stop at Chumphon Pinnacle, Sail Rock and one of the other premier sites in the area. These three-stop trips cost from around 3650B to 4000B and include a full lunch. Two-dive trips to Sail Rock will set you back around 2500B to 2800B.

Apnea Koh Pha Ngan DIVING

(Map p216; 092 380 1494; www.apneakohphangan.com; Chalok Lam; from 1600B) Free-diving has taken off on Ko Pha-Ngan and this is the best-known operator on the island, with courses run on Sail Rock. A one-day intro course costs 4000B (taking you down to a maximum 12m), while the standard two-day course is 7000B (taking you down to a maximum 20m). The instructor-level course is 35,000B.

Sail Rock Divers DIVING

(Map p216; 077 374321; www.sailrockdiversresort.com; Ban Chalok Lam; from 3500B) Equipped with its own lovely 3m-deep pool, bungalow accommodation (900B to 1600B) and restaurant in Chalok Lam, Sail Rock Divers is a very popular and professional choice, with courses from beginner to advanced.

Chaloklum Diving DIVING

(Map p216; 077 374025; www.chaloklum-diving.com; from 1000B; 6am-8pm) One of the longer-established dive shops on the island, these guys (based on the main drag in Ban Chalok Lam) have quality equipment and provide high standards in all that they do, whether scuba-diving, free-diving, night diving or snorkelling trips.

Haad Yao Divers DIVING

(086 279 3085; www.haadyaodivers.com; from 1400B) Established in 1997, this dive operator has garnered a strong reputation by

maintaining European standards of safety and customer service. Prices start at 1400B for a beach dive at Hat Yao, but there's a huge selection of courses and options.

Wake Up WATER SPORTS
(☎087 283 6755; www.wakeupwakeboarding.com; from 1200B; ⊙Jan-Oct) Jamie passes along his infinite wakeboarding wisdom to eager wannabes at his small water sports school in Chalok Lam. Fifteen minutes of 'air time' will set you back 1200B, which is excellent value considering you get one-on-one instruction. Kneeboarding, wakeskating, wakesurfing and waterskiing sessions are also available.

Trekking

Almost 90% of Ko Pha-Ngan is made up of unspoiled tropical forest, with a whopping 40% protected national park land harbouring an abundance of wildlife. If trekking along more isolated areas, make sure you take loads of sunscreen and water.

Popular hikes include the Chalok Lam to Bottle Beach Trek, and the hilly hike from Hat Rin to Hat Yuan, Hat Thian and on to Hat Yao (east). The hike up to the Domsila Viewpoint, and beyond, above Nam Tok Phaeng is another excellent hike, don't miss it. From here it's also possible to continue up to Khao Ra, the highest mountain on the island at 625m. Switch your flip-flops for decent walking shoes.

Chalok Lam to Bottle Beach Trek HIKING
(Map p216) Long-tail boats run east from Chalok Lam to Bottle Beach, but you can also hike the 5km distance, though it's advisable to go early in the morning to avoid the midday sun. Look for the trail marked with bottles, just beyond the end of the road from Chalok Lam, which heads up the hill. The trek takes around an hour, but avoid the hike in wet weather, when things can get slippery.

Check on conditions at shops in Chalok Lam before setting out. At the other end, long-tail boats return to Chalok Lam, or you can continue by boat to Thong Nai Pan.

Courses

The Phangan Thai Cooking Class COOKING
(Map p222; ☎087 278 8898; Thong Sala; 1200-1500B) Located along the main road in Thong Sala, this fun school – run by likeable chef Oy – takes you to a market for supplies before knuckling down to the serious business in the kitchen.

C&M Vocational School LANGUAGE, HEALTH & WELLBEING
(Map p224; ☎077 349233; http://thaiculture.education; Ban Sri Thanu) Bridging the yawning experiential gulf between yelping at the full Ko Pha-Ngan moon and Thai culture, this large vocational school runs classes and courses in Thai language, cuisine, yoga and massage.

Sleeping

Ko Pha-Ngan's legendary history of laid-back revelry solidified its reputation as *the* stomping ground for the gritty backpacker lifestyle, even though many local mainstays have collapsed their bamboo huts in favour of newer, sleeker accommodation.

But backpackers fear not – it will still be a while before the castaway lifestyle vanishes.

Many operations have a minimum three-, four- or five-night stay during the Full Moon, Christmas and New Year periods.

Hat Rin

The thin peninsula of Hat Rin features three separate beaches: beautiful blond Hat Rin Nok (Sunrise Beach) is the epicentre of Full Moon tomfoolery; Hat Rin Nai (Sunset Beach) is the much less impressive stretch of sand on the far side of the tiny promontory; and Hat Seekantang (also known as Hat Leela), just south of Hat Rin Nai, is a smaller, lovely white and more private beach. The three beaches are linked by Ban Hat Rin (Hat Rin Town) – an inland collection of restaurants, hotels and bars. It takes only a few minutes to walk from one beach to another.

Hat Rin sees Thailand's greatest accommodation crunch during the Full Moon festivities. At this time, bungalow operations expect you to stay for a minimum number of days (usually five). If you plan to arrive the day of the party (or even the day before), we strongly suggest booking a room in advance, or else you'll probably have to sleep on the beach (which you might end up doing anyway, either intentionally or not). Some cattle-car-style dorms stack and cram a seemingly impossible number of beds into dark small rooms, and shared toilets are few.

Full Mooners can also stay on Ko Samui or other beaches on Ko Pha-Ngan and take speedboat shuttles to access the festivities – prices will depend on how far away you're staying, but the money you'll save on staying anywhere besides Hat Rin itself will probably make it worth it. With gory and often fatal accidents on a monthly basis, driving on Ko Pha-Ngan during the festivities is an absolutely terrible idea.

Expect room rates to increase by 20% to 300% during Full Moon.

Seaview Sunrise BUNGALOW $
(Map p227; ☎077 375160; www.seaviewsunrise.com; Hat Rin Nok; r 500-1400B; ❄📶) Budget Full Moon revellers who want to sleep inches from the tide should apply here (but note the minimum five-day policy during the lunar lunacy). Some of the options back in the jungle are sombre and musty, but the solid beachfront models have bright, polished wooden interiors facing onto a line of coconut trees and the sea.

Same Same GUESTHOUSE $
(Map p227; ☎077 375200; www.same-same.com; Ban Hat Rin; dm 400B, r 650B; ❄📶) Run by two Danish backpackers (Christina and Heidi), this sociable spot offers simple but bright rooms and plenty of party preparation fun for the Full Moon beach shenanigans; it's very lethargic outside lunar-lunacy periods, but that's a good time to pitch up. The restaurant and bar is a solid choice.

Lighthouse Bungalows BUNGALOW $
(Map p227; ☎077 375075; www.lighthousebungalows.com; Hat Seekantang; bungalows 400-1000B; ❄📶) This remote outpost perched on the rocks south of Hat Rin has simple, good-value fan options and air-con bungalows with sweeping views of the sea; plus there's a cushion-clad restaurant/common area and high-season yoga classes. To get there, follow the wooden boardwalk southeast from Hat Leela. Beware the monthly techno parties, unless that's on your wishlist.

Tommy Resort RESORT $$
(Map p227; ☎077 375215; www.tommyresort.com; Hat Rin Nok; r incl breakfast 2200-8500B; ❄📶🏊) This trendy address at the heart of Hat Rin strikes a balance between chic boutique and carefree flashpacker hang-out, with standard rooms, bungalows and pool villas. Wander down to a lovely strip of white sand, past flowering trees, to a resort with an azure slab of a pool at the heart of things and helpful, obliging staff. Rooms come with air-con, fridge and safe.

Delight GUESTHOUSE $$
(Map p227; ☎077 375527; www.delightresort.com; Ban Hat Rin; r 800-6400B; ❄📶🏊) Slap bang in the centre of Hat Rin, friendly Delight offers decent lodging in a Thai-style building that comes with subtle designer details (such as peacock murals), sandwiched between an inviting swimming pool and a lazy lagoon peppered with lily pads.

Pha-Ngan Bayshore Resort RESORT $$$
(Map p227; ☎077 375224; Hat Rin Nok; r 2300-6000B; ❄@📶🏊) This neat and well-maintained hotel-style operation soaks up an ever-increasing influx of Hat Rin flashpackers. Staff are on the ball and welcoming, while sweeping beach views and a giant swimming pool nudge it into one of the top addresses on Sunrise Beach, especially if you can nab one of the special promotions.

Sarikantang Resort & Spa RESORT $$$
(Map p227; ☎077 375055; www.sarikantang.com; Hat Seekantang; bungalows incl breakfast from 2400B; ❄📶🏊) Cream-coloured cabins, framed with teak posts and lintels, are sprinkled among swaying palms and crumbling winged statuettes on one of Hat Rin's best stretches of beach, with a spa at hand for some sunset pampering.

BOX JELLYFISH

There are several species of venomous jellyfish in the waters off Ko Pha-Ngan, Ko Samui and Ko Tao, including scyphozoans, hydrozoans and box jellyfish. The most notorious is the box jellyfish, a cnidarian invertebrate whose sting – which contains a potent venom that attacks the nervous system, heart and skin cells – can result in death. Growing up to 3m in length and named after the box-like appearance of its bell, the box jellyfish's sting can be so painful the swimmer can enter a state of shock and drown before reaching the shore. The jellyfish is more prolific in sea waters after heavy rain.

Ko Pha-Ngan and Ko Samui have the highest incidence of fatal and near-fatal box jellyfish stings in the whole of Thailand. Some beaches, such as Hat Rin Nok, are equipped with stations warning of the danger of jellyfish, as well providing a cylinder containing standard household vinegar, which should be poured onto the area affected by the sting for 30 seconds. Avoid the inclination to rub or scratch the stung area.

The Coast RESORT $$$
(Map p227; 077 951567; www.thecoastphangan.com; Hat Rin Nai; 3700-10,800B;) This dark grey, sharp-angled and stylish resort leads to a slim but OK stretch of beach away from the party hub. Swanky room interiors feature polished cement and beds topped with white duvets, while an infinity pool overlooks the sea, and service pulls out the stops. Hip, cool and minimalist, but comfy.

Ban Khai to Ban Tai

The waters at Ban Tai tend to be shallow and opaque, especially during low season, but lodging options are well priced compared to other parts of the island, and you're close to Thong Sala and not too far from Hat Rin.

As with Ban Tai, Ban Khai's beaches aren't the most stunning, but the accommodation is cheap and there are beautiful views of Ang Thong Marine National Park (p247) in the distance.

These beaches are where many of the moon-but-not-full-moon parties happen so even if your resort seems quiet, there's probably some boozed-up action nearby.

Boom's Cafe Bungalows BUNGALOW $
(Map p216; 081 979 3814; www.boomscafe.com; Ban Khai; bungalows 600-1000B;) Staying at Boom's is like visiting the Thai family you never knew you had. Superfriendly and helpful owner Nok takes care of all her guests and keeps things looking good. No one seems to mind that there's no swimming pool, since the curling tide rolls right up to your doorstep. At the far eastern corner of Ban Khai, near Hat Rin.

V-View Beach Resort BUNGALOW $$
(Map p222; 077 377436; Bantai Rd; r 600-2100B;) An effortless air of seclusion settles over this quiet beach resort, and although the sea can be a bit swampy, there are hammocks galore and a fine pool, decent bungalows and a helpful owner.

★**Divine Comedie** RESORT $$$
(Map p216; 077 377869, 080 885 8789; www.divinecomedyhotel.com; Ban Tai; r 2700-4300B, ste 4500-5600B;) A stunning mix of 1920s Chinese and perhaps Mexican hacienda architecture with a colour palette that shifts from mint to ochre, this 15-room (10 bungalows and five bedrooms) boutique oasis not only works, it's beguiling. Junior suites have rooftop terraces, while standard rooms have modest balconies, and the elongated infinity pool runs to the slim beach. No kids under 12.

Bay Lounge & Resort RESORT $$$
(Map p216; 077 377892; www.thebayphangan.com; Ban Khai; bungalows incl breakfast 1800-3200B;) On a private white nugget of beach sandwiched by jungle-topped boulders, this intimate, chic choice has bungalows that mingle with the natural surroundings, while inside it's all urban, with distressed concrete and bright modern art. It's midway between Hat Rin's Full Moon Party and the Half Moon Party in Ban Khai – the resort offers transport to each. Check-out time is late at 1pm.

Milky Bay Resort RESORT $$$
(Map p222; 077 332762; www.milkybaythailand.com; Ban Tai; bungalows 1800-13,200B;) A delightful picture in Ban Tai, with covered swimming pool, a sauna, gym, table tennis and comfy tree-bark and wood-chip shavings along the paths, accommodation at this tempting choice is a variety of minimalist-chic bungalows with dark tinted glass hidden in the shade of tall stands of bamboo.

Mac Bay BUNGALOW $$$
(Map p216; 077 238443; Ban Khai; bungalows 1200-8500B;) Home to the Black Moon Party (another lunar excuse for Ko Pha-Ngan to go wild), pleasant Mac Bay is a sandy slice of Ban Khai where even the cheaper bungalows are spic and span. At beer o'clock, grab a shaded spot on the sand and watch the sun dance amorphous shadows over the distant islands of Ang Thong Marine National Park.

Thong Sala

Thong Sala's beach is really just an extension of Ban Tai but the beaches are a bit wider up this way and have the advantage of being walking distance to Ko Pha-Ngan's main town, its restaurants and services.

★**Coco Garden** BUNGALOW $
(Map p222; 077 377721, 086 073 1147; www.cocogardens.com; Thong Sala; bungalows 450-1100B;) One of the best budget hang-outs along the southern coast and superpopular with the backpacker set, fantastic Coco Garden one-ups the nearby resorts with well-manicured grounds and 25 neat bungalows plus a funtastic beach bar, where hammocks await and a beachfront restaurant supplies breakfast, lunch and dinner with views.

Thong Sala

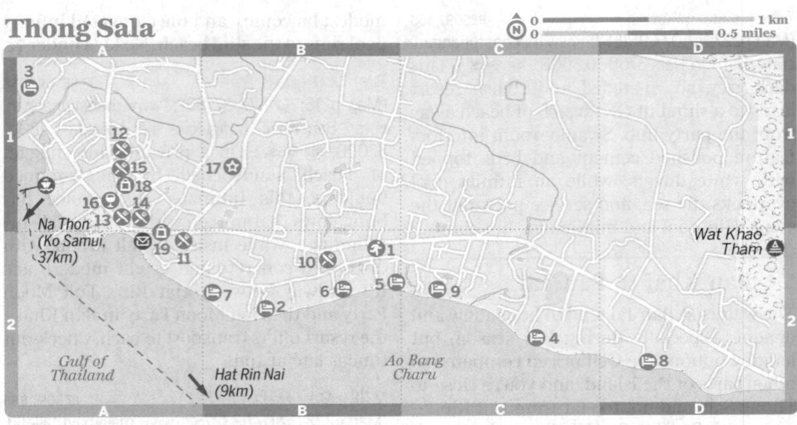

Thong Sala

Activities, Courses & Tours
1 The Phangan Thai Cooking Class B2

Sleeping
2 B52 Beach Resort B2
3 Baan Manali Resort A1
4 Charu Bay Villas C2
5 Coco Garden B2
6 Hacienda Resort B2
7 Lime n Soda B2
8 Milky Bay Resort D2
9 V-View Beach Resort C2

Eating
10 Ando Loco B2
Dots .... (see 12)
11 Fat Cat A2
12 Food Market A1
13 Nira's A1
14 Satimi A1
15 SOHO A1

Drinking & Nightlife
16 Hub A1

Entertainment
17 Moonlight Cinema B1

Shopping
18 Lilawadee A1
19 Thong Sala Walking Street A2

Hacienda Resort BUNGALOW $
(Map p222; ☎077 238825; www.beachresorthacienda.com; Thong Sala; dm 300B, r 500-1500B; ❄📶🏊) With good-looking blue-and-white painted bungalows, rooms in two-storey blocks further down and beachfront air-con dorms, the Hacienda is a spruce and efficient outfit, although the poolside bar can get noisy at night. There's a Phangan International Diving School office and an open-air gym.

Lime n Soda RESORT $$
(Map p222; ☎077 332721; www.limesodathailand.com; Thong Sala; bungalows 700-2300B; ❄📶🏊) This solid and decent Thong Sala choice offers clean and simple tiled bungalows in the shade of bamboo and coconut palms along a breakwater above the beach.

Baan Manali Resort BUNGALOW $$$
(Map p222; ☎077 377917; www.baan-manali.com; Thong Sala; bungalows 2000-3300B; ❄📶🏊) Quiet, clean and attractively laid out among the coconut trees, 14-bungalow Baan Manali is a convenient, relaxing and well-run choice with infinity pool and excellent restaurant, close to the action at Thong Sala, with a variety of room and bungalow choices.

Charu Bay Villas VILLA $$$
(Map p222; ☎084 242 2299; www.charubayvillas.com; Ao Bang Charu; villas & studios 1490-9900B; ❄📶) These fully equipped villas on the bay of Ao Bang Charu, just southeast of Thong Sala, are good value (especially if you're a group), and there's a modern garden self-catering seaside studio too, plus a two-bedroom garden-view villa with rooftop terrace. The

Beachfront Villa is a three-bed with large jacuzzi, big enough to sleep up to 10.

B52 Beach Resort BUNGALOW $$$

(Map p222; www.b52-beach-resort-phangan.info; Thong Sala; bungalows 1500-5000B;) B52's campus of Thai-styled bungalows sports plenty of thatch, polished concrete floors and rustic tropical tree trunks that lead down to the sea. It's all a bit Flintstones, staff are pleasant to boot and there's a pool.

Ao Nai Wok to Ao Sri Thanu

Close to Thong Sala, the resorts peppered along this breezy west-coast strip mingle with small beaches between patches of gnarled mangroves. There is a lack of sand, but the prices are cheap and the sunsets can be fantastic.

Loyfa Natural Resort BUNGALOW $$

(Map p216; 077 349022; www.loyfanaturalresort.com; Ao Sri Thanu; r 750B, bungalows 1300-3100B, villas from 3825B;) Loyfa scores high marks for its friendly, congenial French-speaking Thai staff, charming gardens, sturdy huts guarding sweeping ocean views and two pools (one for sunrise, the other for sunset). Modern bungalows tumble down the promontory onto an exclusively private sliver of ash-coloured sand. Cheapest rooms are in a hotel block.

Chills Resort RESORT $$

(Map p216; 089 875 2100; www.chillsresort.hotel.phanganbungalows.com; Ao Sri Thanu; r 1000-2300B;) Set along a stunning and secluded stretch of stony outcrops north of Ao Hin Kong, Chills' cluster of delightfully simple but modern rooms all have peaceful ocean views letting in plenty of sunlight, sea breezes and gorgeous sunset views.

★ **Kupu Kupu Phangan Beach Villas & Spa by l'Occitane** RESORT $$$

(Map p216; 077 377384; www.kupuphangan.com; Ao Nai Wok; villas from 8500B;) This supreme Balinese-style resort is one of the island's most swoon-worthy, with lily ponds, tall palms, a swimming pool straight from a luxury magazine centrefold, spa, rocky boulders that meet the sea and glorious west-coast sunsets. The delightful wooden villas boast dipping pools and spacious, elegant interiors.

Paragon Spa Resort BUNGALOW $$$

(Map p224; 090 982 5276; www.paragonsparesort.com; Ban Sri Thanu; bungalows 1750-12,000B;) A tiny hideaway with just seven rooms – each one different – the Paragon has decor that incorporates stylistic elements from ancient Khmer, India and Thailand, without forfeiting any modern amenities. Rooms upstairs have balconies.

Hat Yao & Hat Son

One of the busier beaches along the west coast, Hat Yao sports a swimmable beach, numerous resorts and a few extra services such as ATMs and convenience stores. With a delightful sense of seclusion, Hat Son is a quiet, much smaller beach that feels like a big secret.

Shiralea BUNGALOW $

(Map p224; 080 719 9256; www.shiralea.com; Hat Yao; dm 275B, bungalows 645-1400B;) The fresh-faced poolside bungalows are simple but the air-con dorms are great, and the ambience, with an on-site bar with draught beer, is fun and convivial. It's about 100m away from the beach and it fills up every few weeks with Contiki student tour groups.

Haad Son Resort & Restaurant RESORT $$

(Map p224; 077 349104; www.haadsonresort.net; Hat Son; bungalows 1875-6750B;) There's a mixed bag of rooms here, from big, older wooden bungalows with terraces on the hillside to polished-cement suites and rooms along the beachfront. The secluded beach setting is spectacular and is highlighted by one of the most beachy-chic restaurants on the island on a jungle- and boulder-clad peninsula overlooking the sea. During Full Moon, it's a three-night minimum stay.

Tantawan Bungalows BUNGALOW $$

(Map p224; 077 349108; www.tantawanbungalow.com; Hat Son; bungalows 600-2500B;) This relaxed, chilled-out 11-bungalow (fan and air-con) teak nest, tucked among jungle foliage, is attractive, with fantastic views and a fine pool, but it's a bit of a steep climb with luggage.

Haad Yao High Life BUNGALOW $$$

(Map p224; 077 349114; www.haadyaohighlife.com; Hat Yao; air-con bungalows 1500-3200B;) With dramatic ocean views from the infinity-edged swimming pool, High Life has 25 bungalows, of various shapes and sizes, on a palmed outcropping of granite soaring high above the cerulean sea. Staff are polite and responsive.

Hat Son

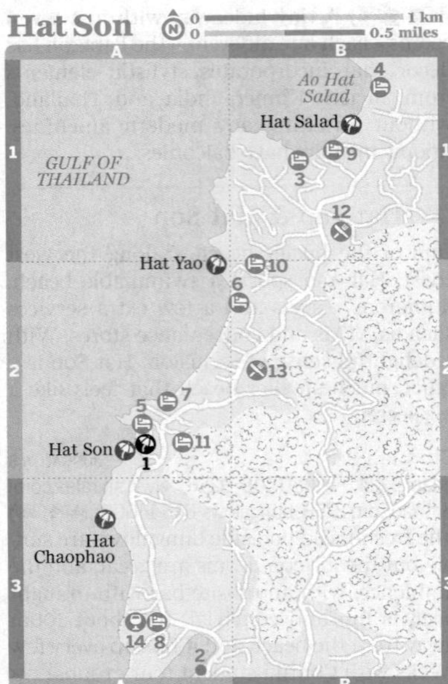

Hat Son

Sights
1 Secret Beach A2

Activities, Courses & Tours
2 C&M Vocational School A3

Sleeping
3 Cookies Salad B1
4 Green Papaya B1
5 Haad Son Resort & Restaurant A2
6 Haad Yao Bay View Resort B2
7 Haad Yao High Life A2
8 Paragon Spa Resort A3
9 Salad Hut B1
10 Shiralea B2
11 Tantawan Bungalows A2

Eating
12 Peppercorn B1
13 Pura Vida B2

Drinking & Nightlife
14 Belgian Beer Bar A3
Secret Beach Bar .... (see 1)

Haad Yao Bay View Resort RESORT **$$$**
(Map p224; ☎077 349141; www.haadyao-bayviewresort.com; Hat Yao; r & bungalows incl breakfast from 1500-4000B; ❄@🛜🏊) This blend of bungalows and hotel-style accommodation looks like a tropical mirage on Hat Yao's northern headland. There's a huge array of options, but we recommend the tiny but good-value rooms that hover right over the sea. For more luxe head up to the hillside sea-view bungalows.

Hat Salad

This slim, pretty beach on the northwest coast is fronted by shallow blue water – a clutch of photogenic long-tail boats tend to park at the southern end. It's slightly rustic, with local Thai fishermen coming out to throw their nets out at sunset, yet with plenty of amenities and comfortable accommodation.

Cookies Salad RESORT **$$$**
(Map p224; ☎083 181 7125, 077 349125; www.cookies-phangan.com; Hat Salad; bungalows 1700-3300B; 🛜🏊) Sling out on a hammock at this resort with private Balinese-style bungalows on a steep hill, orbiting a two-tiered lap pool tiled in various shades of blue. Shaggy thatching and dense tropical foliage give the place a certain rustic quality, although you won't want for creature comforts. It's super-friendly and books up fast.

Salad Hut BUNGALOW **$$$**
(Map p224; ☎077 349246; www.saladhut.com; Hat Salad; bungalows 2200-5000B; ❄@🛜🏊) Totally unpretentious despite sharing a beach with some distinctly upscale options, this small clutch of a dozen Thai-style bungalows sits a stone's throw from the rolling tide, though the pool is rather small. The perspective on the sun dipping below the golden seas from your lacquered teak porch or the beach bar is a major pull.

Green Papaya BUNGALOW **$$$**
(Map p224; ☎077 374230; www.greenpapayaresort.com; Hat Salad; bungalows 4100-10,400B; ❄@🛜🏊) With its tranquil, elegant setting, Green Papaya and its polished wooden bungalows are a clear, albeit pricey, standout along the lovely beach at Hat Salad.

Ban Chalok Lam (Chaloklum) & Hat Khom

In the north of the island, the small and quiet fishing village at Ban Chalok Lam is a conglomeration of teak shanties and huts, slowly being infiltrated by the occasional European-style bakery, authentic Italian restaurant or Russian-owned cafe. *Sŏrng·tăa·ou* ply the route from here to Thong Sala for around 150B per person.

Fantasea BUNGALOW $

(Map p216; ☎089 443 0785; www.fantasea-resort-phangan.info; Chalok Lam; bungalows with fan/air-con from 600/1200B;) This friendly place far from the Full Moon mayhem on the other side of the island is one of the better of a string of family-run bungalow operations along the quiet eastern part of Chalok Lam, with a thin beach out front, OK swimming and an elevated Thai-style restaurant area to chill out in.

Mandalai HOTEL $$$

(Map p216; ☎077 374316; www.mandalaihotel.com/web2014; Chalok Lam; r 2000-3000B;) This lovely small 'room-only' boutique hotel (with spa) quietly towers over the low-lying form of Chalok Lam, with floor-to-ceiling windows commanding views of tangerine-coloured fishing boats in the bay, and a small but inviting pool in the main courtyard, mere steps from the sand.

Hat Khuat (Bottle Beach)

This isolated dune in the north of the island has garnered a reputation as a low-key get-away, so it's pretty popular. Grab a long-tail taxi boat from Chalok Lam for 100B to 150B (depending on the boat's occupancy), or tackle the hike (but stay on the path and avoid the midday sun). The trek takes around two hours; follow the bottles on trees marking the way, take water and insect repellent and ensure you don't end up trekking back in darkness.

Smile Bungalows BUNGALOW $

(Map p216; ☎085 429 4995; www.smilebungalows.com; Hat Khuat; bungalows 520-920B; closed Nov) For real remoteness and seclusion, it's hard to beat this place at the far western corner of Bottle Beach. Family-run Smile features an assortment of all-fan wooden huts climbing up a forested hill: the two-storey bungalows (920B) are our favourite.

Bottle Beach II BUNGALOW $

(Map p216; ☎081 537 3833; Bottle Beach/Hat Khuat; bungalows 500-1500B; closed Nov;) At the far eastern corner of the beach, this double string of very basic, turquoise bungalows is the ideal place to chill out – for as long as you can – if you don't need many creature comforts, though there are some new modern family bungalows too, and the restaurant is a decent choice.

Thong Nai Pan

The pair of rounded bays in the northeast are some of the most remote yet busy beaches on the island. Ao Thong Nai Pan Yai (*yai* means 'big') is the southern half that has some excellent budget and midrange options, and Ao Thong Nai Pan Noi (*noi* means 'little') is Ko Pha-Ngan's most upscale beach, curving just above. Both bays are great for swimming and hiking. A taxi between the two is around 100B. The road from Thong Sala to Thong Nai Pan is now excellent.

Longtail Beach Resort BUNGALOW $

(Map p216; ☎077 445018; www.longtailbeachresort.com; Thong Nai Pan; bungalows with fan/air-con from 690/990B;) Tucked away by the forest at the lovely southern end of Thong Nai Pan – and a long way from Full Moon Ko Pha-Ngan madness – Longtail offers backpackers charming thatch-and-bamboo abodes that wind up a lush garden path; there's plenty of choice, too, for larger groups and families. The sand is fantastic and the lush, green setting is adorable.

Anantara Rasananda RESORT $$$

(Map p216; ☎077 956660; http://phangan-rasananda.anantara.com; Ao Thong Nai Pan Noi; villas from 11,000B;) Blink and you'll think you've been transported to Ko Samui. This five-star luxury resort is a sweeping sand-side property with a smattering of semi-detached villas – many bedecked with private plunge pools. A savvy mix of modern and traditional styling prevails, and superb Anantara management assures service is polished.

East Coast

Both Hat Thian and Hat Yuan, near the southeastern tip of the island, have a few bungalow operations, and are quite secluded. You can walk between the two in less than 10 minutes via the rocky outcrop that separates them.

To get here hire a long-tail from Hat Rin (300B to 400B) or organise a boat pick-up from your resort. A dirt road to Hat Yuan has been cleared for 4WDs, but is only passable in the dry season; even then the voyage by sea is much easier.

Bamboo Hut BUNGALOW $
(Map p216; ☎087 888 8592; Hat Yuan; bungalows 400-1000B;) Beautifully lodged up on the bouldery outcrops that overlook Hat Yuan and the jungle, groovy, friendly, hippie-village Bamboo Hut is a favourite for yoga retreats, meditative relaxation and some serious chilling out. The dark wood bungalows are small, with terraces, while the restaurant serves up superb views and reasonable food.

Barcelona BUNGALOW $
(Map p216; ☎077 375113; Hat Yuan; bungalows 400-700B) At the south end of Hat Yuan, these old, rickety wood fan bungalows with balconies – some with hammocks – climb up the hill on stilts behind a palm garden, looking onto decent vistas. Price depends on the view, but there's not a huge amount of variation between bungalows apart from size, so grab a cheap one.

Mai Pen Rai BUNGALOW $$
(Map p216; ☎093 959 8073; www.thansadet.com; Than Sadet; bungalows 683-1365B;) By the river at the south end of leisurely Than Sadet, this lovely, secluded retreat elicits sedate smiles. Bungalows – some temptingly right on the rocks by the sea – also mingle with Plaa's next door on the hilly headland, and sport panels of straw weaving with gabled roofs. Family bungalows are available and a friendly on-site restaurant rounds out an appealing choice.

★**Sanctuary** BUNGALOW $$$
(Map p216; ☎081 271 3614; www.thesanctuarythailand.com; Hat Thian; 2000-7300B) A friendly, forested enclave of relaxed smiles, the Sanctuary is a haven of splendid lodgings, yoga classes and detox sessions. Accommodation, in various manifestations of twigs, is scattered along a tangle of hillside jungle paths, while Hat Thian is wonderfully quiet and is great for swimming. Note that payment is cash only.

Pariya Resort & Villas RESORT $$$
(Map p216; ☎087 623 6678; www.pariyahaadyuan.com; Hat Yuan; villas 8000-17,000B;) The smartest option on gloriously soft sands of Hat Yuan has a large choice of very spacious and comfortable villas, but they're not cheap. It's remote and quiet, but getting about is hard and you're pretty isolated, which is perfect for some, but not for others.

Eating

Most visitors quickly adopt the lazy lifestyle and wind up eating at their accommodation, which is a shame as Ko Pha-Ngan has some excellent restaurants scattered around the island; at the very least, it's another reason to get exploring.

Hat Rin

Hat Rin has a large conglomeration of restaurants and bars on the island, yet many of them are pretty average so it's not worth coming here for the food alone.

Palita Lodge SEAFOOD $
(Map p227; Hat Rin Nok; mains from 100B) The front restaurant of the Sunrise Beach bungalows outfit of the same name offers up tasty Thai seafood and set meals with views overlooking a beach that's pretty serene outside of the Full Moon period.

Lazy House INTERNATIONAL $$
(Map p227; Hat Rin Nai; dishes 90-270B; ⏲lunch & dinner) Back in the day, this joint was the owner's apartment – everyone liked his cooking so much that he decided to turn the place into a restaurant and hang-out spot. Today, Lazy House is one of Hat Rin's best places to veg out in front of a movie with a scrumptious shepherd's pie.

Monna Lisa ITALIAN $$
(Map p227; ☎084 441 5871; Hat Rin Nai; pizza & pasta from 200B; ⏲3-11pm) Travellers still rave about the pizza here, and the pasta gets a thumbs-up as well. It's run by a team of friendly Italians and has a basic, open-air atmosphere. There's another branch in Thong Sala too.

Om Ganesh INDIAN $$
(Map p227; Hat Rin Nai; mains from 100B; ⏲9am-11pm;) Seasoned old-timer Om Ganesh sees a regular flow of customers for its north Indian curries, biryani rice, roti and lassis, with a token spread of Chinese dishes for good measure. Set meals start at 300B.

Southern Beaches

In recent years Thong Sala has attracted many new excellent restaurants, so spend some time dining here. There are also some well-established cafes that do excellent business and are among the best places on the island for breakfast. There are some superb restaurants and cafes dotted along the road between Thong Sala and Hat Rin.

On Saturday evenings from 4pm to 10pm, a side street in the eastern part of Thong

Hat Rin

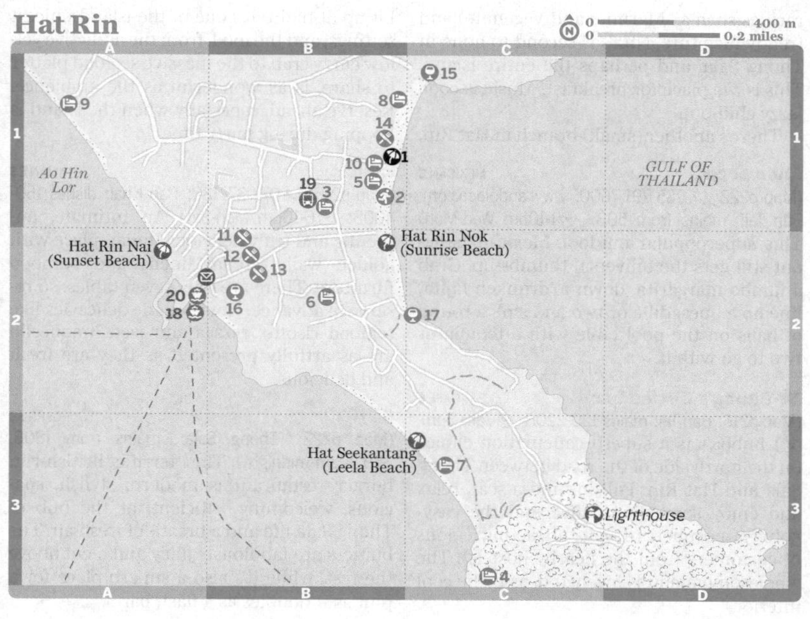

Hat Rin

Sights
1 Hat Rin Nok B1

Activities, Courses & Tours
2 Full Moon Party B1

Sleeping
3 Delight B1
4 Lighthouse Bungalows C3
5 Pha-Ngan Bayshore Resort B1
6 Same Same B2
7 Sarikantang Resort & Spa C3
8 Seaview Sunrise B1
9 The Coast A1
10 Tommy Resort B1

Eating
11 Lazy House B2
12 Monna Lisa B2
13 Om Ganesh B2
14 Palita Lodge B1

Drinking & Nightlife
15 Mellow Mountain C1
16 Palms Cafe B2
17 Rock C2
Sunrise .... (see 5)
Tommy .... (see 10)

Transport
18 Haad Rin Queen A2
19 Sŏrng•tăa•ou to Thong Sala B1
20 Thong Nai Pan Express A2

Sala becomes a fun **Walking Street** – a bustling pedestrian zone mostly filled with locals hawking their wares to other islanders. There's plenty on offer, from clothing to food.

★ **Food Market** MARKET $
(Map p222; Thong Sala; dishes 25-180B; 1-11pm) A heady mix of steam and snacking locals, Thong Sala's terrific food market is a must for those looking for doses of culture while nibbling on low-priced snacks. Wander the stalls for a galaxy of Thai street food, from vegetable curry puffs to corn on the cob, spicy sausages, kebabs, spring rolls, Hainanese chicken rice or coconut ice cream.

★ **Nira's** BAKERY $
(Map p222; Thong Sala; snacks from 80B; 7am-7pm;) With lots of busy staff offering outstanding service, a big and bright interconnected two-room interior, scrummy baked goodies, tip-top coffee (and exotic

rarities such as Marmite and Vegemite) and trendy furniture, Nira's is second to none in Thong Sala, and perhaps the entire island. This is *the* place for breakfast. Music is cool, jazzy chill-out.

There's another (small) branch in Hat Rin.

Ando Loco MEXICAN $
(Map p222; ☎085 791 7600; www.andoloco.com; Ban Tai; mains from 50B; ⊙1-10pm Wed-Mon) This superpopular outdoor Mexican hangout still gets the universal thumbs-up. Grab a jumbo margarita, down a 'drunken fajita', line up a quesadilla or two and sink a round of balls on the pool table with a tequila or two to go with it.

★**Bubba's Coffee Bar** CAFE $
(Map p216; Ban Tai; mains 120-220B; ⊙7am-5pm;) Bubba's is a superb caffeination choice on the north side of the road between Thong Sala and Hat Rin. Pull in, find a seat, relax and enjoy some fine coffee and the easy-going atmosphere (despite attracting legions of customers from the nearby hostels). The wholesome menu is lovely too, as is the cool interior.

★**Fat Cat** CAFE $
(Map p222; Thong Sala; breakfast from 70B, mains 90-195B; ⊙9am-3pm Mon-Sat;) This small, charming, colourful and busy – with staff rather run off their feet – Portuguese-run cafe does wholesome breakfasts and lovely coffees through the day. It's a very enjoyable place for a wake-up meal first thing in the morning, or any other time.

★**Dots** CAFE $
(Map p222; Thong Sala; snacks from 60B; ⊙8.30am-9pm Mon-Sat, 9am-6pm Sun;) Light, bright and spacious, Dots is a welcome addition to Thong Sala's cafe culture, with a modern and chilled vibe. Pretty much right next to the Food Market, it's a sharp-looking spot for a slice of carrot cake, frappé, full-flavoured coffee, hot choc or a croissant for brekkie.

Satimi ICE CREAM $
(Map p222; Thong Sala; per scoop 30-40B; ⊙10.30am-6.30pm Tue-Sun) The small and enterprising back-street gelateria sells home-made ice-cream and sorbets, using natural and locally sourced ingredients.

★**Fisherman's Restaurant** SEAFOOD $$
(Map p216; ☎084 454 7240; Ban Tai; dishes 50-600B; ⊙1.30-10pm) Sit in a long-tail boat looking out over the sunset and a rocky pier. Lit up at night, it's one of the island's nicest settings, and the food, from the addictive yellow curry crab to the massive seafood platter to share, is as wonderful as the ambience. Reserve ahead, especially when the island is hopping during party time.

Fabio's ITALIAN $$
(Map p216; ☎077 377180; Ban Khai; dishes 150-400B; ⊙6-10pm Mon-Sat) An intimate, authentic and truly delicious Italian place with golden walls, cream linens and bamboo furniture. There are only seven tables, so reserve in advance. House-made delicacies like seafood risotto, pizzas and iced limoncello are as artfully presented as they are fresh and delicious.

SOHO BURGERS $$
(Map p222; Thong Sala; mains from 180B; ⊙9.30am-midnight) This terrific British-run burger restaurant is modern, stylish, spacious, welcoming, efficient, at the hub of Thong Sala life and a breath of fresh air. The burgers are fabulously juicy and a cut above the rest, while it's also a superb place for a pint as it doubles as a flash bar.

Other Beaches

JJ's Restaurant THAI $
(Map p216; Ao Wok Tum; mains from 80B; ⊙9am-9pm) Drop off at scenically situated JJ's come sunset to swoon in front of stirring visuals over the young, replanted mangrove trees at Ao Wok Tum while devouring tasty treats from the kitchen and toasting it all with a chilled beer.

Pura Vida CAFE $
(Map p224; ☎095 034 9372; Hat Yao; mains from 120B; ⊙8.30am-3pm Mon-Sat) Hobbled only by short opening hours, this charming and bright Portuguese cafe is an alluring choice as you head up the west coast. Breakfasts are excellent, especially the pancakes and natural yoghurt, but you can go the whole hog with a full brekkie, and delicious burgers, sandwiches and paninis are also served. Love the 'Eat Well, Travel Often' campervan painting.

Bamboo Hut WESTERN, THAI $
(Map p216; Hat Yuan; dishes 100-300B; ⊙breakfast, lunch & dinner;) Lounge on a Thai-style cushion or sit at a teak table that catches sea breezes and looks over infinite blue. There are plenty of options, from vegetarian specialities and fresh juices for those coming off a

fast or cleanse, to classic, very well-prepared Thai dishes with all assortments of beef, chicken and prawns.

★ **Peppercorn** STEAK $$

(Map p224; ☎087 896 4363; www.peppercornphangan.com; Hat Salad; mains 160-400B; ⏲4-10pm Mon-Sat; ✎) Escargot, succulent steaks and schnitzel in a rickety jungle cottage? You bet! Peppercorn may be tucked in the brush away from the sea, but that shouldn't dissuade foodies from seeking out some of Ko Pha-Ngan's best international cuisine, with a fine selection of good vegetarian dishes to boot, and mango cake for dessert. No MSG or artificial ingredients.

★ **Crave** BURGERS $$

(Map p216; ☎098 838 7268; www.cravekohphangan.com; Sri Thanu; mains from 200B; ⏲6-10pm Wed-Mon; 📶) Attractively bedecked with glowing lanterns at night, this excellent, very popular and atmospheric choice in Sri Thanu puts together some fine burgers in a cosy and charming setting. Cocktails are great too, starting at 170B. Shame it's only open evenings.

Sanctuary HEALTH FOOD $$

(Map p216; www.thesanctuarythailand.com; Hat Thian; mains from 130B; 📶) The restaurant at the Sanctuary resort (p226) proves that wholesome food (vegetarian and seafood) can also be delicious. Enjoy a tasty parade of plates – from massaman curry to crunchy Vietnamese spring rolls. Don't forget to wash it all down with a blackberry, soya milk and honey immune booster. No credit cards.

Drinking & Nightlife

Every month, on the night of the full moon, pilgrims pay lunar tribute to the party gods with trance-like dancing, wild screaming and glow-in-the-dark body paint. For something mellower, the west coast has several excellent bars, where you can raise a loaded cocktail glass to a blood-orange sunset from a hilltop or over mangrove trees at the water's edge. Thong Sala has as a couple of decent bars too.

Hat Rin

Hat Rin is the beating heart of the legendary Full Moon fun. When the moon isn't lighting up the night sky, party-goers flock to other spots on the island's south side. Most party venues flank Hat Rin's Sunrise Beach from south to north.

Rock BAR, CLUB

(Map p227; ☎093 725 7989; Hat Rin Nok; ⏲8am-late) The superb views of the party from the elevated terrace – and excellent panoramas at all other times – on the far south side of the beach are matched by super cocktails and a mixed menu of plates for just about all palates.

Tommy BAR, CLUB

(Map p227; Hat Rin Nok) One of Hat Rin's largest venues lures the masses with loungers, low tables, black lights and blaring Full Moon trance music. Drinks are dispensed from a large ark-like bar.

Palms Cafe BAR

(Map p227; Hat Rin; ⏲10am-late; 📶) This smart cafe/bar and environmentally inclined restaurant near Hat Rin Nai is a good-looker – with its lovely poolside location – and provides a perfect escape from Hat Rin's noisier, rougher and busier backstreets. There's a good choice of cocktails and an experimental approach to all manner of protein shakes and health drinks.

Sunrise BAR, CLUB

(Map p227; ☎077 375144; Hat Rin Nok) A spot on the sand where trance beats shake the graffitied walls, with drum 'n bass coming into its own at Full Moon.

Mellow Mountain BAR

(Map p227; Hat Rin Nok; ⏲24hr; 📶) Also called 'Mushy Mountain' (you'll know when you get there), this trippy hang-out sits at the northern end of Hat Rin Nok, delivering stellar views of the shenanigans below.

Southern Beaches

Hub PUB

(Map p222; ☎088 825 4158; Thong Sala; ⏲8am-midnight; 📶) With chatty staff and a prime location on the corner straight down from the pier, cavernous wood-floored Hub is the sports bar of choice for those crucial Premier League fixtures, draft beer, cider and excellent pub fare. They also rent out scooters and motorbikes.

Viewpoint Bar BAR

(Map p216; Ban Khai; 📶) If you're heading back from Hat Rin to Thong Sala or Ban Tai, park up your scooter and head into this bar at the Viewpoint Hotel, with a terrific perch over the gulf from a high spot off this side of the road. The views are simply fantastic.

DON'T MISS

FULL MOON PARTIES

No one knows exactly when or how the wild **full-moon parties** (Map p227; Hat Rin Nok; 100B; ⌚ full moon, dusk till dawn) started – most believe they began in 1988, but accounts of the first party range from an Australian backpacker's going-away bash in August to a group of hippies escaping Samui's 'electric parties' in October. None of that is relevant now: today, thousands of bodies converge monthly on the kerosene-soaked sands of **Hat Rin Nok** (aka Sunrise Beach; p218) for an epic dusk-until-dawn trance-a-thon.

The pounding heart of the Full Moon action, Sunrise Beach sees crowds swell to an outrageous 40,000 party-goers during high season, while the low season still sees a respectable 8000 wide-eyed pilgrims. To take a break, head to the Rock (p229) bar at the south end or Mellow Mountain (p229) at the north end and chill out. You'll be knocking into stalls selling buckets of alcohol – vodka, gin, rum, whisky, mixed with coke and red bull – all along the beach, but go easy, you can quickly end up downing more than you think. Try to leave them until late.

Flaming among the thumping bass-lines and flashing neon are the petrol-drenched fire ropes where dancers are invited to hop over a swinging line of fire (burns are generally the order of the day on that one). Some critics claim the party is starting to lose its carefree flavour, especially given increasing violence and the fact that the island's government now charges a 100B entrance fee to party-goers (the money goes towards much-needed beach cleaning and security).

Have your accommodation sorted way in advance – if you turn up on the day, you won't find a bed for the night in Hat Rin, though you can always do an in-and-out from Ko Samui.

Other Beaches

★ **Belgian Beer Bar** BAR

(Map p224; www.seetanu.com; Ban Sri Thanu; ⌚ 8am-10pm) Run by the affable Quentin, this enjoyable bar defies Surat Thani's appropriation by yogis and the chakra-balancing crowd with a heady range of Belgian beer, the most potent of which (Amber Bush) delivers a dizzying 12.5% punch. If the yogic flying doesn't give you wings, this might.

★ **Secret Beach Bar** BAR

(Map p224; Hat Son; ⌚ 9am-7pm) There are few ways better to unwind at the end of a Ko Pha-Ngan day than watching the sun slide into an azure sea from this bar on the northwest sands of the island. Grab a table, order up a mojito and take in the sunset through the palm fronds.

Amsterdam BAR

(Map p216; ☎ 089 072 2233; Ao Plaay Laem; ⌚ noon-midnight) Near Ao Wok Tum on the west coast, hillside Amsterdam attracts tourists and locals from all over the island, seeking a superchilled spot to catch a Ko Pha-Ngan sunset and totally zone out.

Flip Flop Pharmacy BAR

(Map p216; Thong Nai Pan; ⌚ noon-1am; 📶) With flip-flops on the wall, this popular beach bar on the sands of Thong Nai Pan has a fine beach perspective (and a pool table) and a terrific setting.

Three Sixty Bar BAR

(Map p216; Ban Mae Hat; ⌚ 8am-midnight) High up a road east of Ko Ma, the Three Sixty Bar does what it says on the packet, with splendid, wide-angle views – sunset time is killer.

Shopping

★ **Thong Sala Walking Street** MARKET

(Map p222; Taladkao Rd, Thong Sala; ⌚ 4-10pm Sat) Thong Sala's Walking Street market kicks off every Saturday from around 4pm, with a terrific choice of street food, souvenirs, gifts, handicrafts and clothes. It's the best time to see Thong Sala at its liveliest.

★ **Lilawadee** CLOTHING

(Map p222; ☎ 630 920327; Thong Sala; ⌚ 10.30am-1.30pm & 5-9pm Fri-Wed) This neat and idiosyncratic shop stocks a sparkling range of customised, head-turning glitter motorbike helmets, stacked temptingly on shelves at the rear, fashion, art and clothing. If it's raining, expect hours to be reduced to noon to 8pm.

Information

DANGERS & ANNOYANCES

Some of your fondest holiday memories can hatch on Ko Pha-Ngan; just be mindful of the following situations where things can go pear-shaped:

Drugs There have been instances of locals approaching tourists and attempting to sell them drugs at a low, seemingly enticing, price. Upon refusing the offer, the vendor may drop the price even more. Once purchased, the seller informs the police, which lands said tourist in the local prison to pay a wallet-busting fine. If you're solicited to buy drugs, stand your ground and maintain refusal. This may happen frequently on Ko Pha-Ngan, so be aware and avoid the scenario if you suspect it happening. Another important thing to remember: your travel insurance does not cover drug-related injuries or treatment. Drug-related freak-outs *do* happen – we've heard first-hand accounts of party-goers slipping into extended periods of delirium. Suan Saranrom (Garden of Joys) Psychiatric Hospital in Surat Thani has to take on extra staff during Full Moon to handle the number of *fa·ràng* (Westerners) who freak out on magic mushrooms, acid or other abundantly available hallucinogens.

Women Travellers Female travellers should be particularly careful when partying on the island. We've received numerous reports about drug- and alcohol-related rape (and these situations are not limited to Full Moon parties). Women should also take care when accepting rides with local motorcycle taxi drivers. Several complaints have been filed about drivers groping female passengers; there are even reports of severe sexual assaults.

Motorcycles & Scooters Ko Pha-Ngan has more motorcycle accidents than injuries incurred from Full Moon tomfoolery, although bad motorcycle driving coincides with the Full Moon revelries. Nowadays there's a decent system of paved roads (extended to Than Sadet), but some tracks remain rutted dirt-and-mud paths and the island is also hilly, with some steep inclines. The island has a special ambulance that trawls the island helping injured bikers. If you don't have an international driving licence, you will also be driving illegally and your insurance may not cover you in the event of an accident, so costs could pile up fast.

Drowning Rip currents and alcohol don't mix well. Drownings are frequent; if swimming, it's advisable to be clear-headed rather than plunging into the sea on a Full Moon bender.

Dodgy Alcohol This is a common scam during the Full Moon mania at the bucket stalls on the beach and along the road. Buckets may be filled with low-grade moonshine rice whisky, or old bottles filled with homemade alcohol. Apart from obvious health risks, dodgy alcohol is also a prime mover in incidents from motorcycle accidents to drownings, fights and burns from jumping fire ropes.

Glass on the Beach Beware nasty cuts from broken glass in the sand – wear good footwear. The last time we visited, the southern reaches of the beach at Thong Sala (and other beaches) were full of broken bottles, just left there.

EMERGENCY

Main Police Station (Map p216; ☎191, 077 377114; Thong Sala) Located about 2km north of Thong Sala. Come here to file a report. You might be charged between 110B and 200B to file the report, which is for insurance, and refusing to pay may lead to complications. If you are arrested you have the right to an embassy phone call; you don't have to accept the 'interpreter' you are offered. If you have been accused of committing serious offence, do not sign anything written only in Thai, or write on the document that you do not understand the language and are signing under duress.

LAUNDRY

If you get fluorescent body paint on your clothes during your Full Moon revelry, don't bother sending them to the cleaners – it will never come out. Trust us, we've tried. For your other laundry needs, there are heaps of places that will gladly wash your clothes. Prices hover around 40B per kilo, and express cleanings shouldn't be more than 60B per kilo.

MEDICAL SERVICES

Be wary of private medical services in Ko Pha-Ngan, and expect unstable prices. Many clinics charge a 3000B entrance fee before treatment. Serious medical issues should be dealt with on nearby Ko Samui, which has superior facilities.

Ko Pha-Ngan Hospital (Map p216; ☎077 377034; ⏲24hr), about 2.5km north of Thong Sala, is a government hospital that offers 24-hour emergency services.

MONEY

Thong Sala, Ko Pha-Ngan's financial 'capital', has plenty of banks, currency converters and several Western Union offices. Hat Rin also has numerous ATMs and a couple of banks at the pier. There are also ATMs in Hat Yao, Chalok Lum and Thong Nai Pan.

WORTH A TRIP

CINEMA ESCAPISM

Set in a seductive garden-meets-jungle setting, the **Moonlight Cinema** (Map p222; ☎093 638 5051; www.moonlight-phangan.com; Thong Sala; 150B; ⏲3pm-1am Tue-Fri, 1pm-1am Sat & Sun; 📶) has a huge screen, great smoothies, a bar, fantastic vegan food and some excellent films (with headphones provided). It's fun, atmospheric and highly relaxing.

POST

Main Post Office (Map p222; Thong Sala; ⏲8.30am-4.30pm Mon-Fri, 9am-noon Sat)

Post Office (Map p227; Hat Rin)

TOURIST INFORMATION

There are no government-run Tourist Authority of Thailand (TAT) offices on Ko Pha-Ngan; instead tourists get their information from local travel agencies and brochures. Most agencies are clustered around Hat Rin and Thong Sala. Agents take a small commission on each sale, but their presence helps to keep prices relatively stable and standardised. Choose an agent you trust if you are spending a lot of money – faulty bookings do happen on Ko Pha-Ngan, especially since the island does not have tourist police.

Several mini-magazines also offer comprehensive information about the island's accommodation, restaurants, activities and Full Moon parties. Our favourite option is the pocket-sized quarterly Phangan Info (www.phangan.info), also available as a handy app.

Phanganist (www.phanganist.com) is an online resource that's full of insider tips for all things Ko Pha-Ngan.

At the time of writing, the enterprising Backpackers Information Centre (www.backpackersthailand.com) had shut, but may have reopened by the time you read this.

ℹ Getting There & Away

As always, the cost and departure times for ferries are subject to change. Rough waves are sometimes known to cancel ferries between November and December.

AIR

Ko Pha-Ngan's airport plans are on hold, so watch this space. At the time of writing, there were issues relating to the airport encroaching on land belonging to Than Sadet-Koh Phangan National Park, so everything was still in the air, so to speak.

BOAT

To Bangkok, Hua Hin & Chumphon

The **Lomprayah** (Map p222; www.lomprayah.com) and **Seatran Discovery** (www.seatrandiscovery.com) services have bus-boat combination packages (Lomprayah from around 1300B, Seatran from 1000B) that depart from the Th Khao San area in Bangkok and pass through Hua Hin and Chumphon. The whole voyage takes between 10 and 17½ hours.

It is also quite hassle-free (unless your train breaks down, which happens a lot) to take the train from Bangkok or Hua Hin to Chumphon and switch to a ferry service. In this case expect to pay 300B for a second-class seat on a train from Bangkok to Chumphon (about 8½ hours); Lomprayah boats from Chumphon to Ko Pha-Ngan take around 3 to 3¾ hours and costs 1000B.

To Ko Samui

There are around a dozen daily departures between Thong Sala on Ko Pha-Ngan and Ko Samui. These boats leave throughout the day from 7am to 6pm, take from 20 minutes to an hour and cost 200B to 300B depending on the boat.

The **Haad Rin Queen** (Map p227; ☎077 484668) goes back and forth between Hat Rin and Big Buddha Beach four times a day (the first boat leaves Hat Rin at 9.30am and departs Big Buddha Beach at 10.30am), with double the number of sailings the day after the Full Moon Party and an extra trip laid on at 7.30am the same day. The voyage takes 50 minutes, costs 200B and the last boat leaves Big Buddha Beach at 6.30pm.

The **Thong Nai Pan Express** (Map p227) is a wobbly old fishing boat (not for the faint-hearted) that runs once a day from Mae Nam on Ko Samui to Hat Rin on Ko Pha-Ngan and then up the east coast, stopping at all the beaches as far as the **pier** (Map p216) at Thong Nai Pan Noi. Prices range from 200B to 400B depending on the destination. The boat won't run in bad weather.

To Ko Tao

Ko Tao-bound **Lomprayah** ferries (500B to 600B) depart from Thong Sala on Ko Pha-Ngan at 8.30am, 1pm and 5.30pm and arrive at 9.30am, 2.15pm and 6.30pm. The **Seatran** service (450B, 90 mins) departs from Thong Sala at 8.30am, 1.30pm and 5pm daily. Taxis depart Hat Rin for Thong Sala one hour before the boat departure. The cheaper but slower **Songserm** (350B) leaves Ko Pha-Ngan at 12.30pm and alights at 2pm, before continuing to Chumphon.

To Surat Thani & The Andaman Coast

There are four daily **Lomprayah** (550B, 2¾ hours) services to Don Sak (for Surat Thani), both travelling via Ko Samui. These boats leave from Thong Sala from 7.20am to 2.30pm. One **Seatran** (www.seatrandiscovery.com) boat (700B) also leaves daily from Thong Sala for Surat Thani at 10.30am, with a bus connection to Phun Phin train station outside the city. Every night, depending on the weather, a night boat runs from Surat Thani (400B, seven hours), departing at 11pm. Boats in the opposite direction leave Ko Pha-Ngan at 10pm.

Combination boat-bus tickets are available at any travel agency. Simply tell them your desired destination and they will sell you the necessary links in the transport chain. Most travellers will pass through Surat Thani as they swap coasts.

Getting Around

Bicycle rentals are not such a great idea unless you're fit enough to take on the Tour de France.

Pick-up trucks and *sŏrng·tăa·ou* chug along the island's major roads, and the riding rates double after sunset. Ask your accommodation about free or discount transfers when you leave the island. The trip from Thong Sala to Hat Rin is 100B; further beaches will set you back around 150B to 200B. From Hat Rin, **sŏrng·tăa·ou** (Map p227) bound for Thong Sala depart from west of Hat Rin Nok.

Long-tail boats depart from Thong Sala, **Chalok Lam** (Map p216) and Hat Rin, heading to far-flung destinations such as **Hat Khuat** (Map p216; Bottle Beach) and **Hat Than Sadet** (Map p216). Expect to pay anywhere from 50B for a short trip, and up to 300B for a lengthier journey. You can charter a private boat ride from beach to beach for about 150B per 15 minutes of travel.

You can rent motorcycles all over the island for 200B to 250B per day; it's cheaper if you book for several days. Always wear a helmet – it's the law on Ko Pha-Ngan, and local policemen are starting to enforce it. But whatever the law, without a helmet, if you come off even at quite a low speed and hit your head, you can sustain serious injuries. Check that the motorcycle has enough space in the under-seat compartment to store your helmet. If you plan on riding over dirt tracks it is imperative that you rent a bike comparable to a Honda MTX125 – gearless scooters cannot make the journey. Avoid driving on the roads during any Full Moon.

Ko Tao เกาะเต่า

POP 2032

The baby of the Samui–Pha-Ngan–Tao trio, Ko Tao may still be the smallest in size but in many other ways it's all grown up. The island is consistently gaining in popularity and going more upscale, but for now this jungle-topped cutie has the busy vibe of Samui mixed with the laid-back nature of Pha-Ngan.

But Tao also has its wild card, something the others don't: easy-to-get-to, diverse diving right off its shores. Cavort with sharks and rays in a playground of tangled neon coral, toast the day with sunset cocktails on a white beach, then get up and do it all over again.

But even though the island is synonymous with diving, there is much more to the place. Hikers and hermits can re-enact an episode from *Lost* in the dripping coastal jungles. And when you're Robinson Crusoe-ed out, hit the pumpin' bar scene that rages on until dawn.

Sights

★ Ao Tanot BEACH

(Map p234) With crystal-clear waters and superb snorkelling, pretty Ao Tanot on the east coast also affords excellent rock-jumping opportunities from the huge rock in the bay. If diving or snorkelling, look out for angelfish, coral trout and bannerfish. There's a sunken catamaran in the bay. There are five resort and bungalow operations here if you want to overnight and catch the splendid sunrise.

★ Laem Thian Beach BEACH

(Map p234) In the lee of the headland, this secluded and sheltered little white-sand beach in the middle of the east coast, north of Ao Tanot, is a delightful place with excellent snorkelling, excellent rock jumping and very clear waters. It's quite a hike to get here along a dirt track; otherwise it's reachable by long-tail boat. There's the shell of an old resort here, crumbling away and covered in graffiti. If you hike, take loads of water and sunscreen.

Ko Nang Yuan ISLAND

(Map p234; 100B; ⏲10am-5pm) These three lovely islands off the northwest coast of Ko Tao are linked together by a sandbar, with superb view from the island highpoints. Boats run from the Lomprayah pier in Mae Hat.

Activities

Diving

If you've never been diving before, Ko Tao is *the* place in Thailand to lose your scuba virginity. The shallow bays scalloping the island are perfect for newbie divers to take their first stab at scuba; the waters are crystal clear, there are loads of neon reefs and the temperatures are bathwater warm. With many sheltered dive sites, waters around Ko Tao can be dived all year round; it's only during the monsoon months that diving may stop for a day or two if the waters are too choppy, but this is actually quite rare.

The best dive sites are found at offshore pinnacles within a 20km radius of the island, but seasoned scubaholics almost always prefer the top-notch sites along the Andaman coast. The local marine wildlife includes groupers, moray eels, batfish, bannerfish, barracudas, titan triggerfish, angelfish, clownfish (Nemos), stingrays, reef sharks and frequent visits by mighty whale sharks.

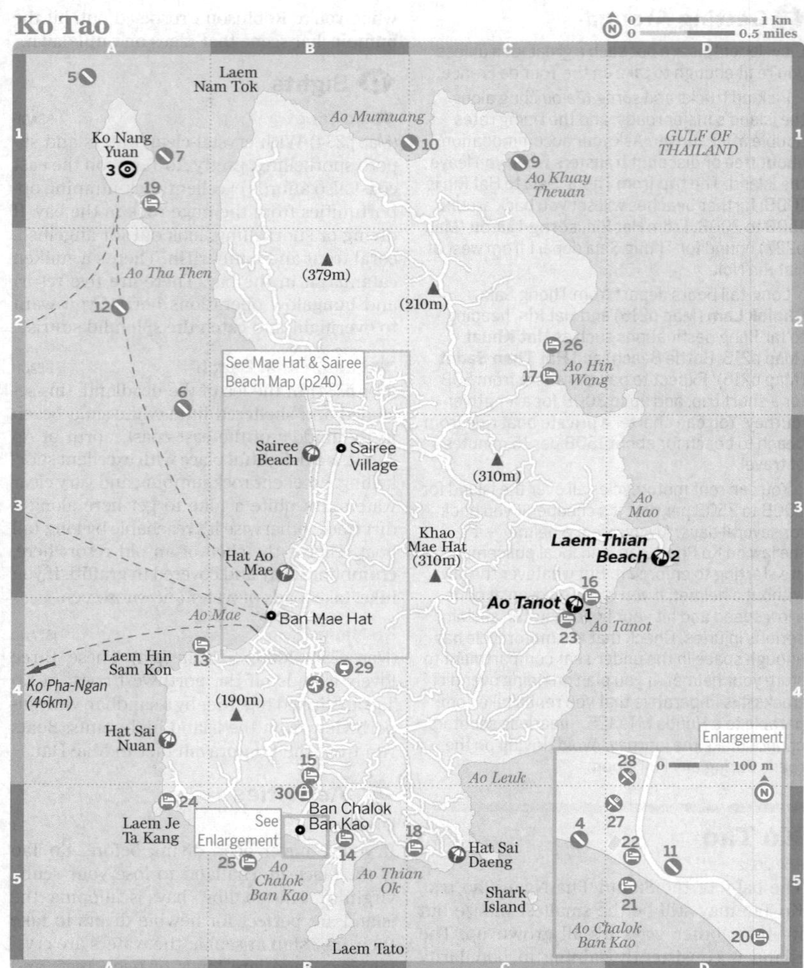

Onshore, scores of dive centres are ready to saddle you up with gear and teach you the ropes in a 3½-day Open Water certification course. The intense competition among scuba schools means that certification prices are unbeatably low and the standards of service top-notch; dozens of dive shops vie for your baht, so be sure to shop around. The island issues more scuba certifications than anywhere else in the world.

★Apnea Total DIVING
(Map p240; ☎081 956 5430, 081 956 5720; www.apneatotal.com; Sairee Beach; one-/two-day course 3500/5500B) The capable, outgoing and enthusiastic staff at Apnea Total, which has earned several awards in the free-diving world, possess a special knack for easing newbies into this awe-inspiring sport. The student-teacher ratio of three to one also ensures plenty of attention to safety. The standard intro course is over two days, getting you (potentially) down to 20m.

★Crystal Dive DIVING
(Map p240; ☎077 456106; www.crystaldive.com; Mae Hat) This award-winning school (and resort) is one of the largest operators on the

Ko Tao

Top Sights

1 Ao Tanot C4
2 Laem Thian Beach D3

Sights

3 Ko Nang Yuan A1

Activities, Courses & Tours

4 Buddha View C5
5 Green Rock Dive Site A1
6 HTMS Sattakut A2
7 Japanese Gardens Dive Site A1
8 Ko Tao Leisure Park B4
9 Lighthouse Bay C1
10 Mango Bay C1
11 New Heaven D5
12 White Rock Dive Site A2

Sleeping

13 Charm Churee Villa A4
14 Chintakiri Resort B5
15 Dearly Koh Tao Hostel B4
16 Family Tanote C3
17 Hin Wong Bungalows C2
18 Jamahkiri Resort & Spa C5
19 Ko Nangyuan Dive Resort A1
20 Ko Tao Resort D5
21 Koh Tao Tropicana Resort D5
22 New Heaven Resort D5
23 Poseidon C4
24 Tao Thong Villa A5
25 View Point Resort B5
26 View Rock C2

Eating

27 I (Heart) Salad D5
28 South Beach Cafe D4
Viewpoint Restaurant .... (see 25)

Drinking & Nightlife

29 Earth House B4

Shopping

30 Hammock Cafe Plaeyuan B5

island (and around the world), but high-quality instructors and intimate classes keep the school feeling quite personal. Multilingual staff members, air-conditioned classes and two on-site swimming pools sweeten the deal. Crystal also puts considerable energy into marine conservation projects on Ko Tao. Highly recommended.

New Heaven DIVING

(Map p234; ☎077 457045; www.newheavendiveschool.com; Chalok Ban Kao) The owners of this diving operation dedicate considerable time to preserving the natural beauty of Ko Tao's underwater sites with regular reef checks, and also contribute to reef restoration efforts. A special CPAD research diver certification program is available in addition to the regular programs and fun dives, as well as free-diving. Instructors are friendly, reassuring and encouraging.

ACE Marine Expeditions DIVING

(Map p240; ☎077 456547; www.divephotothai.com; Sairee Village) The luxe choice: entry level to advanced, plus courses for kids. Zip out on the James Bond–worthy speedboat and reach sites in a fraction of the time. Sunset cruises also offered to add a further golden sheen to your holiday.

Big Blue Diving DIVING

(Map p240; ☎077 456050; www.bigbluediving.com; Sairee Beach) If Goldilocks were picking a dive school, she'd probably go for Big Blue – this midsize operation (not too big, not too small) is popular for fostering a sociable vibe while maintaining high standards of service. Divers of every ilk can score accommodation across the budget ranges, from backpacker dorms up to top-notch family villas at their resort.

Ban's Diving School DIVING

(Map p240; ☎077 456466; www.bansdivingresort.com; Sairee Beach) A well-oiled diving machine that's relentlessly expanding, Ban's is one of the world's most prolific diver certification schools yet it retains a five-star feel. Classroom sessions tend to be conducted in large groups, but there's a reasonable amount of individual attention in the water. A breadth of international instructors means that students can learn to dive in their native tongue.

Buddha View DIVING

(Map p234; ☎077 456074; www.buddhaview-diving.com; Chalok Ban Kao; from 1000B; ⏲7am-6.30pm) One of several of the big dive operations on Ko Tao, Buddha View offers the standard fare of certification for around 2000B and special programs for technical diving (venturing beyond the usual parameters of recreational underwater exploration). Discounted accommodation is available at its friendly resort.

Snorkelling

Snorkelling is a popular alternative to diving, and orchestrating your own snorkelling adventure here is simple, since the bays on the east coast have small bungalow operations offering equipment rental for between 100B and 200B per day.

Most snorkel enthusiasts opt for the do-it-yourself approach on Ko Tao, which involves swimming out into the offshore bays or hiring a long-tail boat to putter around further out. Guided tours are also available and can be booked at any local travel agency. Tours range from 500B to 800B (usually including gear, lunch and a guide/boat captain) and stop at various snorkelling hotspots around the island.

Laem Thian is popular for its small sharks, **Shark Island** has loads of fish (but ironically no sharks), **Ao Hin Wong** is known for its crystalline waters, and Lighthouse Bay (p237), in the north, offers a dazzling array of colourful sea anemones. Ao Tanot (p233) is also a popular snorkelling spot.

Dive schools will usually allow snorkellers on their vessels for a comparable price – but it's only worth snorkelling at the shallower sites such as Japanese Gardens (p237). Note that dive boats visit the shallower sites in the afternoons.

Free-Diving

With a large number of fully qualified free-divers on the island, many traditional dive operators now offer free-diving (exploring the sea using breath-holding techniques rather than scuba gear). Apnea Total (p234) has earned several awards in the free-diving world and possesses a special knack for easing newbies into this heart-pounding sport. The student-teacher ratio of three to one also ensures plenty of attention to safety. Also worth a special mention is the highly capable **Blue Immersion** (Map p240; ☎081 188 8488; www.blue-immersion.com; Sairee Beach; from 3000B). Free-diving prices are pretty much standardised across the island – a 2½-day SSI beginner course will set you back 5500B.

Technical Diving & Cave Diving

Well-seasoned divers and hardcore Jacques Cousteaus should contact **Tech Dive Thailand** (www.techdivethailand.com) or one of a handful of other tech-diving schools if they want to take their underwater exploration to the next level and try a technical dive. Technical diving exceeds depths of 40m and requires stage decompressions, and a variety of gas mixtures are often used in a single dive. You must be a certified tech diver to undertake tech dives; training courses are available at many schools on the island, offering various tech-diving certifications.

For wreck exploration, the gulf has long been an important trading route, and new wrecks are being discovered all the time, from old Chinese pottery wrecks to Japanese *marus* (merchant ships). The HTMS *Sattakut* wreck and deeper pinnacle dive sites are also good for tech diving, and Tech Dive Thailand has a complete online database of dozens of wrecks.

Cave diving has taken Ko Tao by storm, and the most intrepid scuba buffs are lining up to make the half-day trek over to Khao Sok National Park. Beneath the park's main lake lurks an astonishing submarine world filled with hidden grottos, limestone crags and skulking catfish. In certain areas divers can swim near submerged villages that were flooded in order to create a reservoir and dam. Most cave-diving trips depart from Ko Tao on the afternoon boat service and return to the island on the afternoon boat service of the following day. Overnight stays are arranged in or near the park.

Underwater Photography & Videography

If your wallet is already full of diving certification cards, consider renting an underwater camera or enrolling in a marine videography course. Many scuba schools hire professional videographers to film Open Water Diver certifications, and if this piques your interest, you could potentially earn some money after completing a video internship. Your dive operator can put you in touch with any of the half-dozen videography crews on the island. We recommend **ACE Marine Images** (Map p240; ☎077 457054; www.acemarineimages.com; Sairee Beach), one of Thailand's leading underwater videography studios. An introductory course including camera, diving and instruction is 4500B and can also be used towards an Advanced PADI certification. **Crystal Images** (Map p240; ☎092 476 4110; www.crystalimageskohtao.com; Mae Hat) and **Oceans Below** (Map p240; ☎086 060 1863; www.oceansbelow.net; Sairee Village) offer videography courses and internships; each have their own special options.

Other Activities

★**Flying Trapeze Adventures** ACROBATICS
(FTA; Map p240; ☎080 696 9269; www.goodtimethailand.com; Sairee Beach; ⏲4-8pm, lessons 3.30-5.30pm) Test your vertigo and find if you're a great catch with a fun 90-minute

small-group beginner trapeze lesson (1500B). Courses are taught by a superfriendly posse of limber sidekicks, who take you from circus neophyte to soaring savant in four jumps or fewer. There are occasional nightly shows, involving audience participation. Class times vary depending on sundown; reserve ahead.

★ **Goodtime Adventures** HIKING, ADVENTURE SPORTS
(Map p240; ☎087 275 3604; www.gtadventures.com; Sairee Beach; ⏲noon-late) Dive, hike through the island's jungle interior, swing from rock to rock during a climbing and abseiling session, or unleash your inner daredevil cliff-jumping or throw yourself into multisport or powerboat handling. Alternatively, take a shot at all of them on the full-day Koh Tao Adventure (3300B).

★ **Shambhala** YOGA
(Map p240; ☎084 440 6755; www.shambhalayogakohtao.com; Sairee Beach; ⏲10am-noon & 6-7.30pm Mon-Sat, 10am-noon Sun) Ko Tao's leading yoga centre – making students supple for two decades – is housed in beautiful wooden

DIVE SITES AT A GLANCE

In general, divers don't have much of a choice as to which sites they explore. Each dive school chooses a smattering of sites for the day depending on weather and ocean conditions.

Deeper dive sites such as Chumphon Pinnacle are usually visited in the morning. Afternoon boats tour the shallower sites such as Japanese Gardens. There are two large sunken vessels off the coast, providing scubaphiles with wreck dives.

Divers hoping to spend some quality time searching for whale sharks at Sail Rock should join one of the dive trips departing daily from Ko Pha-Ngan.

Chumphon Pinnacle (36m maximum depth), 11km northwest of Ko Tao, has a colourful assortment of sea anemones along the four interconnected pinnacles. The site plays host to schools of giant trevally, tuna and large grey reef sharks. Whale sharks are known to pop up once in a while.

Green Rock (Map p234; 25m maximum depth) is an underwater jungle gym featuring caverns, caves and small swim-throughs. Rays, grouper and triggerfish hang around. It's a great place for a night dive.

Japanese Gardens (Map p234; 12m maximum depth) between Ko Tao and Ko Nang Yuan, is a low-stress dive site perfect for beginners. There's plenty of colourful coral, and turtles, stingray and pufferfish often pass by.

Mango Bay (Map p234; 16m maximum depth) might be your first dive site if you are putting on a tank for the first time. Lazy reef fish swim around as newbies practise their skills on the sandy bottom.

Lighthouse Bay (Gluay Teun Bay; Map p234; 14m maximum depth), also excellent for snorkelling, this shallow dive site on the northeastern tip of the island sports some superb coral. Look out or yellowtail barracuda, parrotfish and bannerfish.

Sail Rock (40m maximum depth), best accessed from Ko Pha-Ngan, features a massive rock chimney with a vertical swim-through, and large pelagics like barracuda and kingfish. This is one of the top spots in Southeast Asia to see whale sharks; in the past few years they have been seen year-round, so there's no clear season.

Southwest Pinnacle (28m maximum depth) offers divers a small collection of pinnacles that are home to giant groupers and barracudas, and whale sharks are sometimes spotted.

Tanot Bay (p233; 18m maximum depth) is suitable for every level of diver. It's pretty shallow and a superb snorkelling site. Look out for angelfish, coral trout, bannerfish and the sunken catamaran.

White Rock (Map p234; 29m maximum depth) is home to colourful corals, angelfish, clownfish and territorial triggerfish, and is a popular spot for night divers.

HTMS Sattakut (Map p234) In 2011, HTMS *Sattakut* was sunk southeast of Hin Pee Wee at a depth of 30m and has become one of the most popular wreck-diving sites.

TAKING THE PLUNGE: CHOOSING YOUR KO TAO DIVE SCHOOL

When you alight at the pier in Mae Hat, swarms of touts will try to coax you into staying at their dive resort. But there are dozens of dive centres on Ko Tao, so it's best to arrive armed with the names of a few reputable schools and go from there. If you're not in a rush, consider relaxing on the island for a couple of days before making any decisions – you will undoubtedly bump into swarms of scubaphiles and instructors who will offer their advice and opinions.

Remember: the success of your diving experience will largely depend on how much you like your instructor. Other factors to consider are the size of your diving group, the condition of your equipment and the condition of the dive sites, to name a few.

For the most part, diving prices are standardised across the island, so there's no need to spend your time hunting around for the best deal. A **PADI** (www.padi.com) Open Water Diver (OWD) certification course costs 9800B; an **SSI** (www.ssithailand.com) OWD certificate is slightly less (9000B) as the PADI teaching materials, which include the certification, command a higher price, which is passed on to students. Increasingly popular across the island, a **RAID** (www.diveraid.com) OWD course is 8500B. An **Advanced Open Water Diver** (AOWD) certification course will set you back 8500B, a rescue course is 9500B and the Divemaster program costs a cool 35,000B (which includes the divemaster pack which everyone requires). Fun divers should expect to pay roughly 1000B per dive, or around 7000B for a 10-dive package. These rates include all dive gear, boat, instructors/guides and snacks. Discounts are usually given if you bring your own equipment. Be wary of dive centres that offer too many price cuts – safety is paramount, and a shop giving out unusually good deals is probably cutting too many corners. The market is easy to enter as there are no barriers to access, meaning cheap and poorly run places pop up offering superb deals.

Most dive schools will hook you up with cheap or even free accommodation. Almost all scuba centres offer gratis fan rooms for anyone doing beginner coursework. Expect large crowds and booked-out beds throughout December, January, June, July and August, and a monthly glut of wannabe divers after every Full Moon Party on Ko Pha-Ngan.

săh·lah on the forested grounds of Blue Wind Resort. Led by experienced teachers, the two-hour classes cost 300B (10 classes 2500B). No need to book ahead, just drop by.

★Monsoon Gym & Fight Club MARTIAL ARTS
(Map p240; ☎086 271 2212; www.monsoongym.com; Sairee Beach) This popular club combines *moo·ay tai* (Thai boxing) programs and air-con dorm accommodation (300B) for students signed up to get to grips with the fighting art. It's an excellent and exhilarating way to spend time in Ko Tao, if diving isn't your scene. The well-equipped concrete gym is right alongside the Thai boxing ring. Drop-in fight training costs 300B, six sessions is 1500B and monthly unlimited use is 7000B.

Ko Tao Leisure Park BOWLING, MINIGOLF
(Map p234; ☎077 456316; ⊙noon-midnight) On the main road between Mae Hat and Chalok Ban Kao, this place has homemade bowling lanes where the employees reset the pins after every frame (300B per hour). The 18-hole minigolf course has a landmark theme – putt your ball through Stonehenge or across the Golden Gate Bridge. There are also *pétanque* courts, table tennis and a big outdoor screen.

Sleeping

If you are planning to dive while visiting Ko Tao, your scuba operator will probably offer you free or discounted accommodation to sweeten the deal. Some schools have on-site lodging, while others have deals with nearby bungalows. It's important to note that you only receive your scuba-related discount on the days you dive.

Sairee Beach

Giant Sairee is the longest and most developed strip on the island, with a string of dive operations, bungalows, travel agencies, minimarkets and internet cafes. The northern end is the prettiest and quietest, while there's more of a party scene and noise from the bars to the south. For most people, this is the choice beach to stay since it has a great blend of scenery and action and the sunsets are serene.

Spicytao Backpackers HOSTEL $

(Map p240; ☎082 278 7115; www.spicyhostels.com/Home.html; Sairee Village; dm 230-280B; ❄ 📶) With bargain prices, no-frills Spicytao is like your own supersocial country hangout; it is hidden off the main drag in a rustic garden setting. Backpackers rave about the ambience and staff who are always organising activities. Book in advance!

★ **Ban's Diving Resort** RESORT $$

(Map p240; ☎077 456466; www.bansdivingresort.com; Sairee Beach; r 700-10,000B; ❄ @ 📶 🏊) This dive-centric party palace offers a wide range of quality accommodation, from basic backpacker digs to sleek hillside villas, and it's growing all the time. Post-scuba chill sessions take place on Ban's prime slice of beach or at one of the two swimming pools tucked within the strip of jungle between the two-storey, pillared and terraced white hotel blocks.

Big Blue Resort BUNGALOW $$

(Map p240; ☎077 456050; www.bigbluediving.com; Sairee Beach; dm 400B, r 1500-10,000B; ❄ @) This scuba-centric resort has a summer-camp vibe – diving classes dominate the daytime, while evenings are spent en masse, grabbing dinner or watching fire twirling. There are basic six-bed fan dorms, air-con bungalows and villas as well as luxury family villas. Some rooms and accommodation options are only available if you are diving with Big Blue (p235).

★ **Place** RESORT $$$

(Map p240; www.theplacekohtao.com; villas 8000-9000B; ❄ 📶) About a 15-minute walk or five-minute taxi ride from its hilltop location to Sairee Beach, this romantic boutique choice has nine private luxury villas nestled in leaf-clad hills with sweeping ocean views. Honeymooners will rejoice: a private plunge pool is standard, and private chef services satisfy those who choose to remain in their nuptial nest instead of venturing out for sustenance.

Seashell Resort BUNGALOW $$$

(Map p240; ☎077 456271; www.seashell-kohtao.com; Sairee Beach; r 1950-4500B, villa 2680-12,500; ❄ 📶 🏊) A huge mix of lodging, from simple wood fan bungalows to hotel-style rooms in a block and plush villas, this is a busy resort with nicely tended grounds, but prices are rather out of whack with what you can find elsewhere. It's a good backup, however, that welcomes divers and nondivers.

Palm Leaf Resort BUNGALOW $$$

(Map p240; ☎077 456731; www.kohtaopalmleaf.com; Sairee Beach; bungalows 2000-4500B; ❄ 📶 🏊) Palm Leaf bungalows and villa rooms are good though nothing spectacular, but the location, at the quieter northern section of silky Sairee Beach simply can't be beaten.

Mae Hat

All ferry arrivals pull into the pier at the busy village of Mae Hat. As such this isn't the best beach for a tranquil getaway, although it's a good hub if your main goal is diving. The more charming options extend in both directions along the sandy beach, both north and south of the pier.

Ko Tao Central Hostel HOSTEL $

(Map p240; ☎077 456925; www.kohtaohostel.com; Mae Hat; dm 310B; ❄ 📶) Identified by its London Underground–style logo and decorated with Banksy murals and Tube-line stripes, this clean, central and friendly hostel has good 14-bed dorms, if all you need is a handy bed near to the pier. Check out is at 11am. Reception is in Island Travel next door; no towel service, so bring your own.

Captain Nemo Guesthouse GUESTHOUSE $$

(Map p240; www.captainnemo-kohtao.com; Mae Hat; d 890-2850B; ❄ 📶) With only five rooms, this popular, small choice a short walk from the pier is nearly always full, so book upfront. The owners are responsive, friendly and helpful, and everything is kept clean.

Ananda Villa HOTEL $$

(Map p240; ☎077 456478; www.anandavilla.com; Mae Hat; r 600-1800B; ❄ 📶) This friendly, two-storey cream-and-white hotel with verandahs and lined with decorative palms and plumeria has a colonial feel, a short walk north of the jetty. The cheapest bungalows are fan only, with hot water, in the garden on the far side of the road.

Nadapa Resort RESORT $$

(Map p240; ☎077 456495; www.nadaparesort.com; Mae Hat; tw & d 1500B; ❄ 📶) It's not really a resort and it's not the choice if what you want is a pool and a beach front, but reliable Nadapa is bright, clean and comfortable, with colour-coded rooms in a block with balcony and bungalows, amid a riot of fun, cartoonish statuettes. Away from, but not far from, the action and close to the pier.

Mae Hat & Sairee Beach

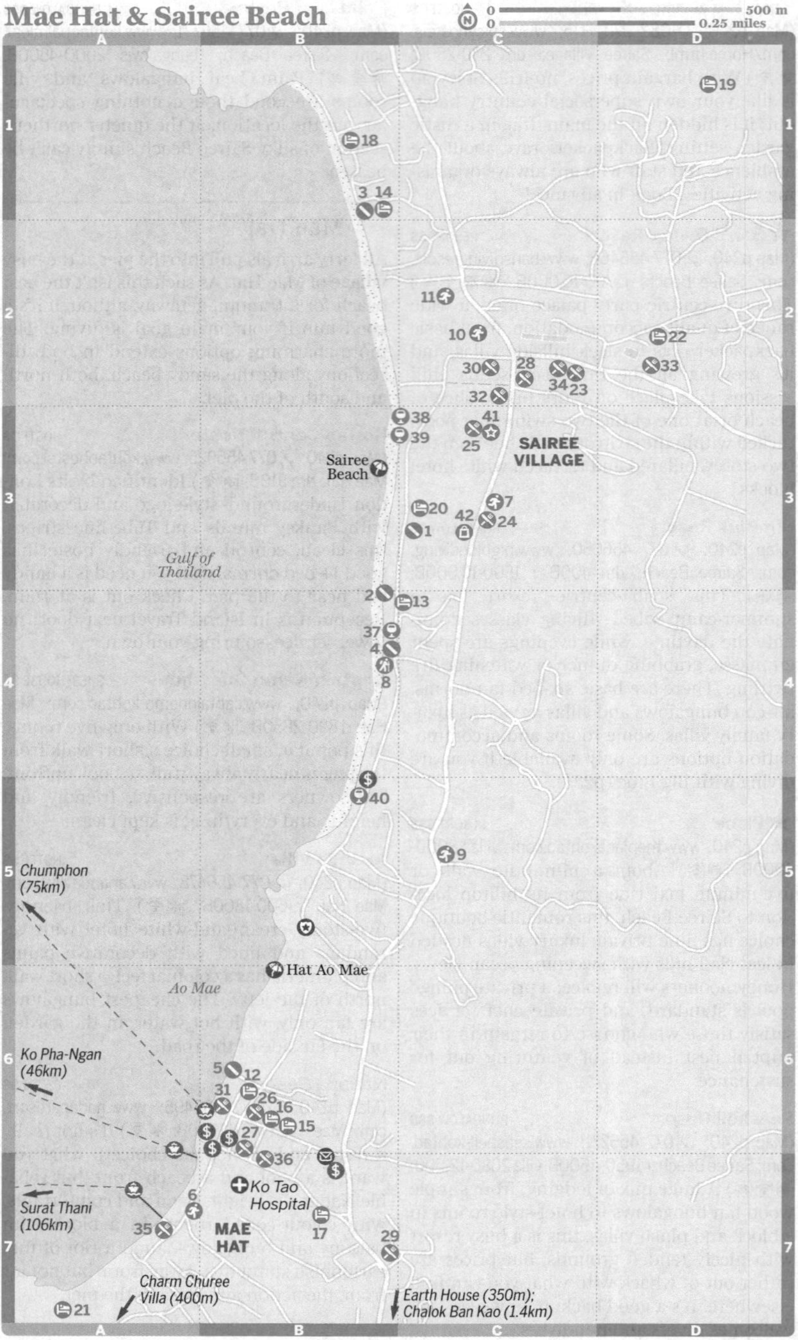

Mae Hat & Sairee Beach

Activities, Courses & Tours
ACE Marine Expeditions .... (see 34)
ACE Marine Images .... (see 34)
1 Apnea Total C3
2 Ban's Diving School B4
3 Big Blue Diving B1
4 Blue Immersion B4
5 Crystal Dive B6
6 Crystal Images A7
7 Flying Trapeze Adventures C3
8 Goodtime Adventures B4
9 Monsoon Gym & Fight Club C5
10 Oceans Below C2
11 Shambhala C2

Sleeping
12 Ananda Villa B6
13 Ban's Diving Resort C4
14 Big Blue Resort B1
15 Captain Nemo Guesthouse B6
16 Ko Tao Central Hostel B6
17 Nadapa Resort B7
18 Palm Leaf Resort B1
19 Place D1
20 Seashell Resort C3
21 Sensi Paradise Resort A7
22 Spicytao Backpackers D2

Eating
23 995 Roasted Duck C2
24 Bang Burgers C3
25 Barracuda Restaurant & Bar C3
26 Café del Sol B6
27 Cappuccino B6
28 Farango's C2
29 Greasy Spoon B7
30 Oishi Kaiso C2
Pranee's Kitchen .... (see 12)
31 Safety Stop Pub B6
32 Su Chili C2
33 Taste of Home D2
34 The Gallery C2
35 Whitening A7
36 Zest Coffee Lounge B7

Drinking & Nightlife
37 Fishbowl Beach Bar B4
38 Fizz C3
39 Lotus Bar C3
40 Maya Beach Club B5

Entertainment
41 Queen's Cabaret C3

Shopping
42 Chez Albert C3

Charm Churee Villa RESORT **$$$**
(Map p234; ☎077 456393; www.charmchureevilla.com; Mae Hat; bungalows 3600-39,100B;) Tucked under sky-scraping palms on a 48-hectare jungle plot away from the bustle of the pier, the luxuriant villas of Charm Churee are dedicated to the flamboyant spoils of the Far East. Staircases, chiselled into the rock face, wind their way down a palmed slope revealing teak huts strewn across smoky boulders. The villas' unobstructed views of the swishing waters are beguiling.

Sensi Paradise Resort RESORT **$$$**
(Map p240; ☎077 456244; www.sensiparadiseresort.com; Mae Hat; r 3300-15,000B;) 'Natural chic' on the prettiest stretch of Mae Hat proper, right up against some boulder outcrops. You won't escape the noise of the pier, however, and rooms on the hillside are rather worn (and not worth the price), while newer models closer to the beach are attractive and comfy. Friendly caretakers and several airy teak *săh·lah* add an extra element of charm.

Chalok Ban Kao

Ao Chalok Ban Ko, about 1.7km south of Mae Hat by road, has one of the largest concentrations of accommodation on Ko Tao. This is a slim stretch of sand in a scenic half-circle bay framed by boulders at either end. The milky-blue water here is quite shallow and at low tide a sandbar is exposed that's fun to wade out to for prime sunbathing.

Tao Thong Villa BUNGALOW **$**
(Map p234; ☎077 456078; Ao Sai Nuan; bungalows 500-2000B;) Popular with long-termers seeking peace and quiet, these no-frills bungalows have killer views. Tao Thong straddles two tiny beaches on a craggy cape about halfway between Mae Hat and Chalok Ban Kao. To reach it, grab a boat taxi for a short ride from the Mae Hat pier.

★ **Dearly Koh Tao Hostel** HOSTEL **$$**
(Map p234; ☎077 332494; www.thedearlykohtaohostel.com; 14/55 Mu 3, Chalok Ban Kao; dm 600-700B, d 1700-3000B, tr 2400B;) Located on the road that leads inland from Chalok Ban Kao, this new hostel has all the right ingredients: clean, comfortable, contemporary (but also traditional) rooms, bubbly and friendly staff, rattan furniture and a rooftop terrace. There's a mix of dorms and private rooms, and a swimming pool was going in when we visited. Breakfast is included.

Koh Tao Tropicana Resort GUESTHOUSE $$
(Map p234; ☎077 456167; www.koh-tao-tropicana-resort.com; Chalok Ban Kao; r 820-2500B) This friendly place offers basic, low-rise units peppered across a sandy, shady garden campus with fleeting glimpses of the blue ocean between fanned fronds and spiky palms.

New Heaven Resort BUNGALOW $$
(Map p234; ☎077 456422; www.newheavendiveschool.com; Chalok Ban Kao; dm 300B, r & bungalows 800-3500B; ❄📶) New Heaven – part of the diving operation of the same name – delivers colourful huts perched on a hill over impossibly clear waters, air-con beachfront rooms, family sea-view bungalows and budget dorm beds.

★ **View Point Resort** RESORT $$$
(Map p234; ☎091 823 3444; www.viewpointresortkohtao.com; Chalok Ban Kao; bungalows incl breakfast 2700-18,000B; ❄📶≋) Near Saan Jao beach, lush grounds of ferns and palms meander across a boulder-studded hillside offering stunning views over the sea and the bay. All options – from the exquisite private suites that feel like Tarzan and Jane's love nest gone luxury to the huge, view-filled bungalows – use boulders, wood and concrete to create comfortable, naturalistic abodes. Rates include taxi transfer.

Ko Tao Resort RESORT $$$
(Map p234; ☎077 456133; www.kotaoresort.com; Chalok Ban Kao; r & bungalows 2100-9500B; ❄@📶≋) Rooms at this resort are split between 'pool side' and 'paradise zone' – all are well furnished, water-sports equipment is on offer, and there are several bars primed to serve an assortment of fruity cocktails. Views of the milky-blue waters are gorgeous.

Chintakiri Resort RESORT $$$
(Map p234; ☎077 456133; Chalok Ban Kao; r & bungalows 3200-6200B; ❄@📶≋) Perched high over the gulf waters overlooking Chalok Ban Kao, Chintakiri is one of Ko Tao's more luxurious properties. Rooms are spread around the inland jungle and boast crisp white walls with lacquered finishing.

Hin Wong

This boulder-strewn bay on the serene east side of the island has crystal-clear waters and it's a picture. The road to Hin Wong is paved in parts, but sudden sand pits and steep hills can toss you off your motorbike, so take it easy. The walk is a steep but enjoyable workout.

Hin Wong Bungalows BUNGALOW $
(Map p234; ☎077 456006; Hin Wong; bungalows 400-700B; 📶) Above boulders strewn to the sea, these decent enough but basic corrugated roof huts are scattered across a lot of untamed tropical terrain. A rickety dock, jutting out just beyond the breezy restaurant, is the perfect place to dangle your legs and watch schools of black sardines slide through the cerulean water; or why not hop in with a snorkel?

View Rock BUNGALOW $
(Map p234; ☎077 456549, 077 456548; viewrock@hotmail.com; Hin Wong; bungalows 500-2000B; ❄📶) Coming down the dirt road into Hin Wong, follow the signs north past Hin Wong Bungalows. View Rock is precisely that: views and rocks; the hodgepodge of wooden huts, which resembles a secluded fishing village, is built into the steep crags, offering stunning views of the bay. Bungalows are simple and modest, but clean enough. Wi-fi in the restaurant only.

Ao Tanot (Tanote Bay)

Boulder-strewn Ao Tanot is more populated than some of the other eastern coves, but it's still rather quiet and picturesque and has some great rocks in the sapphire water for leaping from. This is also excellent snorkelling and shallow-diving territory.

Poseidon BUNGALOW $
(Map p234; ☎077 456735; poseidonkohtao@hotmail.com; Ao Tanot; bungalows 800-1500B; 📶) Poseidon keeps the tradition of the budget bamboo bungalow alive with basic but sleepable fan huts scattered near the sand. There's a reasonable restaurant here which is also a good spot for a drink.

Family Tanote BUNGALOW $$
(Map p234; ☎077 456757; Ao Tanot; bungalows 1000-3800B; ❄@📶) This family-run scatter of hillside bungalows is a so-so choice for solitude-seekers. Strap on a snorkel mask and swim around with the fish at your doorstep, or climb up to the restaurant for a tasty meal and beautiful views of the bay.

Ao Leuk & Ao Thian Ok

★ **Jamahkiri Resort & Spa** RESORT $$$
(Map p234; ☎077 456400; www.jamahkiri.com; Ao Thian Ok; bungalows incl breakfast 8400-30,000B; ❄@📶≋) Wooden gargoyle masks and stone fertility goddesses abound amid

swirling mosaics and multi-armed statues at this whitewashed estate. Hoots from distant monkeys confirm the jungle theme, as do the thatched roofs and tiki-torched soirees. There are lots of steps, but views are drop-dead gorgeous, the spa is top of the range and the dive centre is excellent.

Ko Nang Yuan

Photogenic Ko Nang Yuan, just off the northwest coast of Ko Tao, is easily accessible by the Lomprayah catamaran, and by water taxis that depart from Mae Hat and Sairee (100B each way). There's a 100B tax for all visitors to the island.

Ko Nangyuan Dive Resort BUNGALOW $$$
(Map p234; 077 456088; www.nangyuan.com; Ko Nangyuan; bungalows incl breakfast 1500-9000B;) The rugged collection of wood and aluminium bungalows winds its way across three coolie-hat-like conical islands connected by an idyllic beige sandbar. Yes, this is a private-island paradise but note it gets busy with day-trippers. The resort also boasts the best restaurant on the island (more precisely, the only place to eat). Prices include round-trip to Ko Tao.

Eating

With supersized Ko Samui lurking on the horizon, it's hard to believe that quaint little Ko Tao holds its own in the gastronomy category. Most resorts and dive operators offer on-site dining, and stand-alone establishments are multiplying at lightning speed in Sairee Beach and Mae Hat. The diverse population of divers has spawned a broad range of international cuisine dining options, including Mexican, French, Italian, Chinese, Indian and Japanese.

Sairee Beach

★**995 Roasted Duck** CHINESE $
(Map p240; Sairee Village; mains from 70B; 9am-9pm) You may have to queue a while to get a seat at this glorified shack and wonder what all the fuss is about. The fuss is excellent roast duck, from 70B for a steaming bowl of roasted waterfowl with noodles to 700B for a whole bird, served in a jiffy. You'd be quackers to miss out.

Su Chili THAI $
(Map p240; Sairee Village; dishes 85-225B; 10am-10.30pm) Inviting and bustling, Su Chili serves fresh and tasty Thai dishes, with friendly staff always asking how spicy you want your food and somehow getting it right. Try the delicious northern Thai specialities or Penang curries. There's a smattering of Western comfort food for homesick diners.

Oishi Kaiso JAPANESE $
(Map p240; 080 041 7263; Sairee Village; mains from 90B; 11.30am-10.30pm;) This neat and very slim establishment the size of a *gyoza* (Japanese dumpling) is often full, doing a brisk trade in *nigiri, sashimi* and *maki,* while maintaining a poised equilibrium, but it's a great bolthole if you miss rush hour. A couple of Thai dishes are thrown in for good measure, but you can find them elsewhere and the *gyoza* are very tempting indeed.

Bang Burgers BURGERS $
(Map p240; 081 136 6576; Sairee Village; mains from 130B; 10am-10pm) You may have to dig your heels in and wait in line at this terrific burger bar that does a roaring trade in Sairee. There's around a half-dozen burgers (cheese, double cheese, red chilli cheese) on the menu, including a vegie choice for meat-free diners; chips are 50B.

★**Barracuda Restaurant & Bar** FUSION $$
(Map p240; 080 146 3267; www.barracudakohtao.com; Sairee Village; mains 240-380B; 6-10.30pm;) Sociable chef Ed Jones caters for the Thai princess when she's in town, but you can sample his exquisite cuisine for mere pennies in comparison to her budget. Locally sourced ingredients are turned into creative, fresh, fusion masterpieces. Try the seafood platter, pan-fried barracuda fillet or vegetarian falafel platter – then wash it down with a passionfruit mojito.

★**The Gallery** THAI $$
(Map p240; 077 456547; www.thegallerykohtao.com; Sairee Village; mains 120-420B; noon-10pm) One of the most pleasant settings in town, the food here is equally special. The signature dish is *hor mok maprao on* (chicken, shrimp and fish curry served in a young coconut; 420B) but the white snapper fillet in creamy red curry sauce is also excellent and there's a choice of vegetarian dishes.

Taste of Home INTERNATIONAL $$
(Map p240; 086 012 0727; Sairee Village; mains 120-250B; 10am-1pm & 5-10pm;) German-run and serving a bit of everything (Swedish meatballs, Turkish kofta, Hungarian goulash and Wiener schnitzel to name a few), but

it is all delicious and prepared with heart. It's a small, simple setting popular with expats. Don't forget to finish your meal with the owner's homemade whiskey-and-cream liqueur!

Farango's PIZZA $$
(Map p240; ☎077 456205; www.farangopizzeria.com; Sairee Village; dishes 80-230B; ⊙11am-midnight; 📶) Things are cookin' at this busy pizzeria doing a fine trade in Sairee Village, with decent pizzas and other signature Italian fare. Payment is cash only.

Mae Hat

Zest Coffee Lounge CAFE $
(Map p240; Mae Hat; dishes 70-200B; ⊙6am-4pm; 📶) All brick and wood with a scuffed floor, Zest pulls out the stops to brew up some excellent coffee and wake up sleepyheads at brekkie time. Eggs Benedict gets the morning off on the right foot, while idlers and snackers can nibble on ciabatta sandwiches or sticky confections while nursing their creamy caffe latte. There's a second branch in Sairee (8am to 5pm), although we prefer this location.

Pranee's Kitchen THAI $
(Map p240; Mae Hat; dishes 50-150B; ⊙7am-10pm; 📶) An old Mae Hat fave, Pranee's serves scrumptious curries and other Thai treats in an open-air pavilion sprinkled with lounging pillows, wooden tables and TVs. English-language movies are shown nightly at 6pm.

Safety Stop Pub INTERNATIONAL $
(Map p240; ☎077 456209; Mae Hat; mains 60-250B; ⊙7am-11pm; 📶) A haven for homesick Brits, this pier-side restaurant and bar feels like a tropical beer garden. Stop by on Sundays to stuff your face with an endless supply of barbecued goodness; and the Thai dishes also aren't half bad.

Cappuccino CAFE $
(Map p240; ☎077 456870; Mae Hat; dishes from 30B; ⊙7am-6pm; 📶) With marble tabletops, wall mirrors and good grooves, chirpy Cappuccino's decor falls somewhere between the New York deli on *Seinfeld* and a French brasserie – it's a fine place to grab some caffeine and prepare for your Ko Tao day over croissants and cappuccino foam.

Greasy Spoon BREAKFAST $
(Map p240; Mae Hat; breakfast 140B; ⊙6.30am-3pm; 📶) Bringing a tear to the eyes of homesick Brits, Greasy Spoon stays true to its name by offering a variety of heart-clogging English breakfast fare: black pudding, eggs, sausage, hash browns, chips (and vegie options). The only thing missing is the free copies of the *Sun* and the *Daily Mirror*.

★ **Whitening** INTERNATIONAL $$
(Map p240; ☎077 456199; Mae Hat; dishes 160-480B; ⊙1pm-1am; 📶) This starched, white, beachy spot falls somewhere between being a restaurant and a chic seaside bar – foodies will appreciate the tasty twists on indigenous and international dishes. Dine amid dangling white Christmas lights while keeping your bare feet tucked into the sand. And the best part? It's comparatively easy on the wallet.

Café del Sol INTERNATIONAL $$
(Map p240; ☎077 456578; www.cafedelsol.ws; Mae Hat; mains from 100B; ⊙8am-10.30pm; 📶) This corner cafe a few steps away from the pier is an excellent choice to down a French, full English or diver's breakfast and watch the morning Ko Tao world go by. Lunch and dinner dishes range from hearty pepper hamburgers to homemade pasta, though prices can be quite inflated.

The cafe also has rooms from 1200B.

Chalok Ban Kao

South Beach Cafe CAFE $
(Map p234; ☎094 369 1979; Chalok Ban Kao; mains from 100B; ⊙6am-10pm) Service is rather slack, but the coffee is good, as are the breakfasts at this fresh, spruce and handsome addition to Chalok Ban Kao. The menu spans paninis, salads, pizzas, burgers, vegan dishes, cheesecake and glasses of house wine (99B), plus the obligatory full English breakfast (plus a full vegan), an early kick-off and a long day.

I (Heart) Salad CAFE $$
(Map p234; Chalok Ban Kao; mains from 120B; ⊙8am-9pm; 📶) This rustic choice offers a healthy array of salads using fresh ingredients, with a good supply of vegetarian and vegan dishes and sticky desserts to follow. There are also real fruit juices and healthy egg-white-only breakfasts.

Viewpoint Restaurant INTERNATIONAL $$$
(Map p234; ☎077 456444; Chalok Ban Kao; 250-1100B; ⊙7.30am-10pm) On a beautiful wood deck overlooking Ao Chalok Ban Kao, this is one of the most romantic settings on the island. The food is also the most upscale and holds its own against Ko Samui's best – try

the braised pork belly or the whole tuna from the oven. Apart from the Australian beef dishes, prices are reasonable.

Drinking & Nightlife

★Lotus Bar BAR
(Map p240; ☎087 069 6078; Sairee Beach) Lotus is the leading late-night hang-out spot along the northern end of Sairee; it also affords front-row seats to some spectacular sunsets. Muscular fire-twirlers toss around flaming batons, and the drinks are so large there should be a lifeguard on duty.

★Fizz BAR
(Map p240; Sairee Beach; ⌚8am-1am) Come sunset, sink into a green beanbag, order up a designer cocktail and let the hypnotic surf roll in amid a symphony of ambient sounds. Fantastic.

★Earth House BEER GARDEN
(Map p234; www.theearthhousekohtao.com; ⌚noon-midnight Mon-Sat) This relaxing, secluded and rustic spot serves up a global selection of 40 beers, craft labels and ciders in a dreamy garden setting. With its own relaxing treehouse, there's also a restaurant for bites (9am to noon and 1pm to 6pm Monday to Saturday) – and there are bungalows alongside for going prone if you overdo it on the Green Goblin (cider).

Earth House is on the road to Ao Tanot, just before the turn-off for Ao Leuk.

Fishbowl Beach Bar BAR
(Map p240; ☎062 046 8996; Sairee Beach; ⌚noon-2am) This buzzin' and hoppin' bar gazes out at sunset onto killer views; with fire shows, live music kicking off from 8pm and DJs casting their spell.

Maya Beach Club BAR
(Map p240; ☎080 578 2225; www.mayabeachclubkohtao.com; Sairee Beach; ⌚noon-9pm Sat-Thu, to 2am Fri) Rivalling Fizz for its entrancing sunset visuals and relaxing mood, Maya has nightly DJs and party nights. Make a move for a beach lounger and stay put.

Entertainment

★Queen's Cabaret CABARET
(Map p240; ☎087 677 6168; Sairee Village) Every night is different at this intimate bar where acts range from your standard sparkling Abba to steamy topless croons. If you're male, note you may get 'dragged' into the performance if you're sitting near the front. The show is free but it's expected that you will purchase a (pricey) drink – which is totally worth it. Show starts at 10.15pm.

Shopping

Although most items are cheap when compared to prices back home, diving equipment is a big exception to the rule. On Ko Tao you'll be paying Western prices plus shipping plus commission on each item so it's better to shop at home or online.

Pharmacies charge unnaturally high prices for imported sunscreen, shampoos, mosquito repellent and other items, including paracetamol and aspirin; check branches of 7-Eleven for better-priced equivalents.

★Hammock Cafe Plaeyuan HOMEWARES
(Map p234; ☎082 811 4312; ⌚9am-6pm Sun-Fri) This small French- and Thai-run cafe with tables out front on the road to Chalok Ban Kao doubles as a hammock shop, selling a fantastic selection of brightly coloured Mlabri hand-woven hammocks, some with up to 3km of fabric. Prices start at around 1700B for a sitting hammock, up to 5000B for the most elaborate. Attractive handmade jewellery is also for sale.

Chez Albert FOOD & DRINKS
(Map p240; ☎077 332577; Sairee Village; ⌚1.30pm-late Mon-Sat) Principally selling wine, this enterprising shop feeds expat palates with coffee, cheese, cold cuts and other imported desirables and gastronomic necessities.

Information

DANGERS & ANNOYANCES

While hiring a scooter is extremely convenient, this is really not the place to learn how to drive: the roads on Ko Tao are being paved but some remain treacherous. The island is rife with abrupt hills and sudden sand pits along gravel trails as well as trenches in the road; if driving a scooter, stick to good roads and if you are unsure, turn back. Wear a helmet at all times.

EMERGENCY

Police Station (Map p240; ☎077 456631) Between Mae Hat and Sairee Beach along the rutted portion of the beachside road.

INTERNET ACCESS

Wi-fi is widely available at resorts, bars and restaurants.

MEDICAL SERVICES

There are several walk-in clinics and mini-hospitals scattered around Mae Hat and Sairee,

DENGUE FEVER

Be aware that mosquito-borne dengue fever is a real and serious threat. The virus can spread quickly due to tightly packed tourist areas and the small size of the island.

There is currently no widely available vaccine for dengue; the best precaution is to avoid being bitten by mosquitoes: use insect repellent and wear loose but protective clothing.

but all serious medical needs should be dealt with on Ko Samui.

Ko Tao Hospital (Map p240; 077 456490; 24hr) For general medical and dental treatment.

MONEY

There are several **banks** (Map p240) in Mae Hat, at the far end of town along the island's main inland road. Most dive schools accept credit cards for a 3% handling fee.

There is a money exchange window at Mae Hat's pier and a second location near Chopper's in Sairee Beach.

There are 24-hour ATMs at the island's 7-Elevens and also a cluster orbiting the ferry docks at Mae Hat. Most will will charge you a 200B or so fee for withdrawing money, so figure than into your calculations.

ATMS (Map p240) are located near the pier in Mae Hat and by Sairee Beach.

POST

Post Office (Map p240; 077 456170; Mae Hat; 9am-5pm Mon-Fri, 9am-noon Sat) A 10- to 15-minute walk from the pier; at the corner of Ko Tao's main inner-island road and Mae Hat's 'down road'.

TOURIST INFORMATION

There's no government-run TAT office on Ko Tao. Transportation and accommodation bookings can be made at most dive shops or at any of the numerous travel agencies, all of which take a small commission on services rendered.

WEBSITES

Koh Tao Complete Guide (www.kohtaocompleteguide.com) Handy website and an excellent quarterly free hard copy guide in book form.

Koh Tao Online (www.kohtaoonline.com) An online version of the Koh Tao Info booklet.

Getting There & Away

Costs and departure times are subject to change. Rough waves are known to cancel ferries between October and December. When the waters are choppy we recommend taking the Seatran rather than the Lomprayah catamaran if you are prone to seasickness. The catamarans ride the swell, whereas the Seatran cuts through the currents as it crosses the sea. Note that we highly advise purchasing your boat tickets *several* days in advance if you are accessing Ko Tao from Ko Pha-Ngan after the Full Moon Party.

AIR

Nok Air (www.nokair.com) jets passengers from Bangkok's Don Mueng airport to Chumphon once or twice daily in each direction. Flights to/from Bangkok are usually around 3000B. Upon arriving in Chumphon, travellers can make a seamless transfer to the catamaran service bound for Ko Tao.

BOAT

Boat services are rarely disrupted by the weather, but you may get some days of cancellations during the monsoon months, if waves are too high.

To Ko Pha-Ngan

The **Lomprayah** (Map p240) catamaran offers a thrice-daily service (500B to 600B), leaving Ko Tao at 6am, 9.30am and 3pm and arriving on Ko Pha-Ngan around 7am, 10.45am and 4pm. The **Seatran** (Map p240) Discovery Ferry (430B) offers a similar service, but its earliest boat departs at 6.30am. The **Songserm** (Map p240) express boat (350B) departs daily at 10am and arrives on Ko Pan-Ngan at 11.30am. Hotel pick-ups are included in the price.

To Ko Samui

The Lomprayah catamaran offers a twice-daily service (600B), leaving Ko Tao at 9.30am and 3pm and arriving at Mae Nam on Ko Samui via Ko Pha-Ngan, around 11.20am and 4.40pm. An earlier boat (700B) at 6am goes to Na Thon on Ko Samui, arriving at 7.50am. The Seatran Discovery Ferry (600B) offers a similar service, with departures at 6.30am, 9am and 3pm. The Songserm express boat (500B) departs daily at 10am and arrives on Samui (again via Ko Pha-Ngan) at 1.15pm. Hotel pick-ups are included in the price.

To Surat Thani & the Andaman Coast

Many travellers head to Surat Thani via Ko Pha-Ngan or Ko Samui. Otherwise, board a Surat Thani-bound Lomprayah catamaran (800 to 1000B), then transfer to a bus upon arrival.

To Chumphon

Songserm boats leave for Chumphon (500B) at 2.30pm, arriving at 5.30pm. Lomprayah catamarans (600B) leave for Chumphon at 10.15am and 2.45pm, arriving at 11.45am and 4.15pm.

BUS

Bus-boat package tickets to/from Bangkok are available from travel agencies all over Bangkok and the south; tickets cost around 1000B and the whole voyage takes around 12 hours. Buses switch to boats in Chumphon, and Bangkok-bound passengers can choose to disembark in Hua Hin (for the same price as the Ko Tao–Bangkok ticket).

TRAIN

Travellers can plan their own journey by taking a boat to Chumphon, then making their way to Chumphon's town centre to catch a train up to Bangkok (or any town along the upper southern gulf); likewise in the opposite direction. A 2nd-class ticket to Bangkok will cost around 300B and the trip takes around 8½ hours.

From Ko Tao, the high-speed Lomprayah catamaran departs for Chumphon at 10.15am and 2.45pm (600B, 1½ hours), and a Songserm express boat makes the same journey at 2.30pm (500B) arriving at 5pm. There may be fewer departures if the swells are high.

Getting Around

If you know where you intend to stay, we highly recommend calling ahead to arrange a pick-up. Many dive schools offer free pick-ups and transfers as well.

MOTORBIKE

Renting a motorcycle can be a dangerous endeavour if you're not sticking to the main, well-paved roads. Daily rental rates begin at 150B for a scooter, with larger bikes starting at 350B. Discounts are available for weekly and monthly rentals. Be wary of renting all-terrain vehicles (ATVs) or jet skis – accidents are not uncommon. Most of the bottles of petrol on sale by the wayside cost 50B (on Ko Samui they are 40B).

SŎRNG·TĂA·OU

In Mae Hat *sŏrng·tăa·ou* (pick-up minibuses and motorbikes) crowd around the pier as passengers alight. If you're a solo traveller, you will pay 200B to get to Sairee Beach or Chalok Ban Kao. Groups of two or more will pay 100B each. Rides from Sairee to Chalok Ban Kao cost 150B per person, or 300B for solo tourists. These prices are rarely negotiable, and passengers will be expected to wait until their taxi is full unless they want to pay an additional 200B to 300B. Prices double for trips to the east coast, and the drivers will raise the prices when rain makes the roads harder to negotiate.

WATER TAXI

Boat taxis depart from Mae Hat, Chalok Ban Kao and the northern part of Sairee Beach (near Vibe Bar). Boat rides to Ko Nang Yuan will set you back at least 100B. Long-tail boats can be chartered for around 1500B per day, depending on the number of passengers carried.

Ang Thong Marine National Park

อุทยานแห่งชาติหมู่เกาะอ่างทอง

The 40-something jagged jungle islands of **Ang Thong Marine National Park** (adult/child 300/150B) stretch across the cerulean sea like a shattered emerald necklace – each piece a virgin realm featuring sheer limestone cliffs, hidden lagoons and perfect peach-coloured sands. These dream-inducing islets inspired Alex Garland's cult classic novel *The Beach*.

February, March and April are the best months to visit this ethereal preserve of greens and blues; crashing monsoon waves mean that the park is almost always closed during November and December.

Sights

Every tour stops at the park's head office on **Ko Wua Talap**, the largest island in the archipelago. The naturally occurring stone arches on **Ko Samsao** and **Ko Tai Plao** are visible during seasonal tides and in certain weather conditions. Because the sea is quite shallow around the island chain, reaching a maximum depth of 10m, extensive coral reefs have not developed, except in a few protected pockets on the southwest and northeast sides.

There's a shallow coral reef near Ko Tai Plao and Ko Samsao that has decent but not excellent snorkelling. There are also several novice dives for exploring shallow caves and colourful coral gardens, and spotting banded sea snakes and turtles. Soft powder beaches line **Ko Tai Plao**, **Ko Wuakantang** and **Ko Hintap**.

Viewpoint VIEWPOINT

(Ko Wua Talap) This viewpoint might just be the most stunning vista in all of Thailand. From the top, visitors will have sweeping views of the jagged islands nearby as they burst through the placid turquoise water in easily anthropomorphised formations. The trek to the lookout is an arduous 450m trail that takes roughly an hour to complete. Hikers should wear sturdy shoes and walk slowly on the sharp outcrops of limestone.

A second trail leads to **Tham Bua Bok**, a cavern with lotus-shaped stalagmites and stalactites.

Emerald Lagoon LAKE
(Ko Mae Ko) With an ethereal minty tint, the Emerald Sea (also called the Inner Sea) on Ko Mae Ko is a large lake in the middle of the island that spans an impressive 250m by 350m. You can look but you can't touch: the lagoon is strictly off limits to the unclean human body. A dramatic **viewpoint** can be found at the top of a series of staircases nearby.

Tours

The best way to experience Ang Thong is by taking one of the many guided tours departing Ko Samui and Ko Pha-Ngan. The tours usually include lunch, snorkelling equipment, hotel transfers and (fingers crossed) a knowledgeable guide. If you're staying in luxury accommodation, there's a good chance that your resort has a private boat for providing group tours. Some midrange and budget places also have their own boats, and if not, they can easily set you up with a general tour operator. Dive centres on Ko Samui and Ko Pha-Ngan offer scuba trips to the park, although Ang Thong doesn't offer the world-class diving that can be found around Ko Tao and Ko Pha-Ngan.

Tour companies tend to come and go like the wind. Ask at your accommodation for a list of current operators.

Sleeping & Eating

Ang Thong does not have any resorts; however, on Ko Wua Talap the national park has set up five bungalows, each housing between two and eight guests (500B to 1400B). Campers are also allowed to pitch a tent in certain designated zones. Online bookings are possible, although customers must forward a bank deposit within two days of making the reservation. For advance reservations contact the National Parks Services.

Food is generally provided by tours whisking visitors to and from the Marine National Park. A restaurant can be found at the park head office.

Information

National Parks Services (☎077 286025; www.dnp.go.th)

Getting There & Around

The best way to reach the park is to take a private day tour from Ko Samui or Ko Pha-Ngan (28km and 32km away, respectively). The islands sit between Samui and the main pier at Don Sak; however, there are no ferries that stop off along the way.

SURAT THANI PROVINCE

Surat Thani อำเภอเมืองสุราษฎร์ธานี

☎077 / POP 128,990

Known in Thai as 'City of Good People', Surat Thani was once the seat of the ancient Srivijaya empire. Today, this typical Thai town is a busy transport hub moving cargo and people around the country. Travellers rarely linger here as they make their way to the popular islands of Ko Samui, Ko Pha-Ngan and Ko Tao, but it's a great stop if you enjoy real Thai working cities, good southern-style street food and nosing around colourful Chinese temples and Chinese shopfronts.

Looking down from its elevated position is a vast **Statue of Guanyin** (Kwan Im; Th Na Muang), the Buddhist bodhisattva of compassion (more associated with the Mahayana tradition). It stands next to a temple and charity dedicated to the goddess, equipped with its own ambulance that runs the streets.

Sleeping

Prices are low – you get a lot for relatively few baht. If you're on a very tight budget, consider zipping straight through town and taking the night ferry to reach your island destination.

My Place @ Surat Hotel HOTEL $
(☎077 272288; 247/5 Th Na Muang; d 490-590B, f 620B; ❄📶) All smiles and nary a speck of dust, this excellent central hotel offers spacious, clean rooms, bright paint, colourful throw cushions, modern art on the walls, power showers and value for money. It may be budget, but it doesn't seem that way and will suit almost anyone. Breakfast is served in the so-so cafe next door.

Wangtai Hotel HOTEL $$
(☎077 283020; 1 Th Talad Mai; r 800-2000B; ❄@📶🏊) Across the river from the TAT office (p250), the 230-room Wangtai is a smart, marbled choice in the centre of town, offering pleasant and comfortable, if rather generic, rooms with good views of the city.

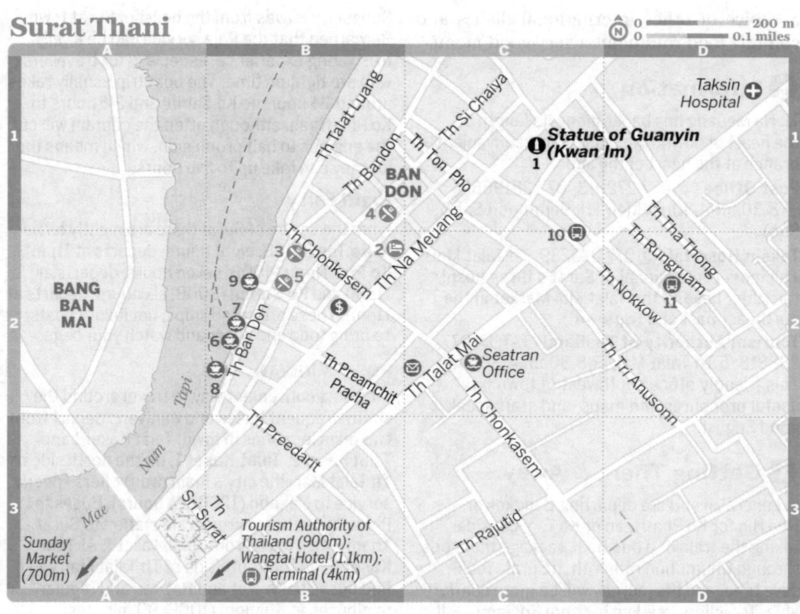

Surat Thani

Top Sights
1 Statue of Guanyin (Kwan Im)........C1

Sleeping
2 My Place @ Surat Hotel........B2

Eating
3 Milano........B2
4 Night Market........B1
5 Sweet Kitchen........B2

Transport
6 Ferry to Ko Samui........B2
7 Ko Tao Night Ferry Pier........B2
Lomprayah........(see 9)
8 Night Boat to Ko Pha-Ngan........B2
9 Seatran Discovery........B2
Songserm........(see 9)
10 Talat Kaset 1 Bus Terminal........C2
11 Talat Kaset 2 Bus Terminal........D2

Eating & Drinking

Surat Thani is packed with delicious street food for lunch and dinner. Aside from the central night market, stalls near the departure docks open for the daily night boats to the islands, and there's an afternoon **Sunday market** (⏲4-9pm) near the TAT office. During the day, many food stalls near the downtown bus terminal sell *kôw gài òp* (marinated baked chicken on rice).

Surat Thani doesn't have a great choice of bars and is rather a quiet city come sundown.

Sweet Kitchen INTERNATIONAL $
(mains from 80B) With easy-going music and a charming, unhurried interior, this restaurant also tempts with a fine menu and polite service. Dishes range from excellent seafood chowder through pasta to beef stroganoff and pages of Thai staples, with a decent selection of vegetarian choices too.

Night Market MARKET $
(Sarn Chao Ma; Th Ton Pho; dishes from 35B; ⏲6-11pm) A smorgasbord of food including masses of melt-in-your-mouth marinated meats on sticks, fresh fruit juices, noodle dishes and desserts.

Milano PIZZA $$
(☎084 011 2709; Th Bandon; pizza from 190B; ⏲noon-10pm) Often surprisingly busy, this Italian restaurant near the pier bakes up a tasty selection of pizza, while pasta and

a choice of other international dishes and comfort food round out a very good menu.

Information

Th Na Meuang has banks along its length in the heart of downtown, including a convenient branch at the heart of the action.

Post Office (☎077 272013, 077 281966; ⊗8.30am-4.30pm Mon-Fri, 9am-noon Sat & Sun)

Taksin Hospital (☎077 273239; Th Talat Mai) The most professional of Surat's three hospitals. Just beyond the Talat Mai Market in the northeast part of downtown.

Tourism Authority of Thailand (TAT; ☎077 288818; 5 Th Talat Mai; ⊗8.30am-4.30pm) This friendly office southwest of town has useful brochures and maps, and staff speak good English.

Getting There & Away

In general, if you are departing Bangkok or Hua Hin for Ko Pha-Ngan or Ko Tao, consider taking the train or a bus-boat package that goes through Chumphon rather than Surat. You'll save time, and the journey will be more comfortable. Travellers heading to/from Ko Samui will most likely pass through town.

AIR

Around 18km due west of the centre of town, Surat Thani International Airport has daily shuttles to Bangkok on Thai Air Asia (www.airasia.com), Thai Smile, Thai Lion Air and Nok Air (www.nokair.com). Although flights from Bangkok to Surat Thani are cheaper than the flights to Samui, it takes quite a bit of time to reach the gulf islands from the airport. Air Asia offers a convenient bus and boat shuttle with their flights that can alleviate some of the stress.

BOAT

Various ferry companies offer services to the islands. Try **Lomprayah** (p214), **Seatran Discovery** (☎077 275063; www.seatrandiscovery.com) or **Songserm** (☎077 377704; www.songserm-expressboat.com).

Bus-Boat Combination Tickets

In the high season travellers can usually find bus-boat services to Ko Samui and Ko Pha-Ngan directly from the Phun Phin train station (14km west of Surat). These services don't cost any more than those booked in Surat Thani and can save you some serious waiting time.

There are also several ferry and speedboat operators that connect Surat Thani to Ko Tao, Ko Pha-Ngan and Ko Samui. Most boats – such as the Raja and Seatran services – leave from Don Sak (about one hour from Surat; bus transfers are included in the ferry ticket) although the Songserm leaves from the heart of Surat town. Be warned that the Raja service can be a very frustrating experience, especially for travellers who are tight on time. The boat trip usually takes around 1½ hours to Ko Samui and 2½ hours to Ko Pha-Ngan, although often the captain will cut the engines to half propulsion, which means the journey can take up to five hours.

Night Ferry

From the centre of Surat there are nightly ferries to **Ko Tao** (600B, eight hours, departs at 11pm), **Ko Pha-Ngan** (400B, seven hours, departs at 11pm) and **Ko Samui** (300B, six hours, departs at 11pm). These are cargo ships, not luxury boats, so bring food and water and watch your bags.

BUS & MINIVAN

The most convenient way to travel around the south, frequent buses and minivans depart from two main locations in town: Talat Kaset 1 and Talat Kaset 2. **Talat Kaset 1**, on the north side of Th Talat Mai (the city's main drag) offers speedy service to Nakhon (120B, 1½ hours). Buses to Phun Phin – the nearest train station to Surat Thani – also leave from Talat Kaset 1. At **Talat Kaset 2**, on the south side of Th Talat Mai, you'll find buses to Phuket and Hat Yai, and regular minibuses to Khanom (100B, 90 minutes, hourly).

The 'new' bus terminal (actually quite a few years old now, but still referred to as new by the locals) is 7km south of town on the way to Phun Phin. This hub services traffic to and from Bangkok (380B to 800B, 11 to 14 hours).

Buses & Minivans From Surat Thani

DESTINATION	FARE	DURATION
Bangkok	425–860B	10hr
Hat Yai	165–300B	5hr
Khanom	100B	1hr
Krabi	170B	2½hr
Phuket	270B	6hr
Trang	180B	2hr 10min

TRAIN

When arriving by train you'll actually pull into Phun Phin, a nondescript town 14km west of Surat. From Phun Phin, there are buses to Phuket, Phang-Nga and Krabi – some via Takua Pa, a junction for Khao Sok National Park. Transport from Surat moves with greater frequency, but it's worth checking the schedule in Phun Phin first – you might be lucky and save yourself a slow ride between towns.

If you plan on travelling during the day, go for the express train. Night travellers should opt for the air-con couchettes. Trains passing through Surat stop in Chumphon and Hua Hin on their way up to the capital, and in the other direction you'll call at Trang, Hat Yai and Sungai Kolok before hopping across the border into Malaysia. The train station at Phun Phin has a 24-hour left-luggage room that charges around 20B a day. The advance ticket office is open from 6am to 6pm daily (with a nebulous one-hour lunch break somewhere between 11am and 1.30pm). The trip to Bangkok takes more than 8½ hours and costs 297B to 1379B depending on class.

Getting Around

Air-conditioned vans to/from Surat Thani airport cost around 100B per person and they'll drop you off at your hotel.

To travel around town, a *sŏrng·tăa·ou* will cost 10B to 30B (it's around 30B to reach Tesco Lotus from the city centre).

Fan-cooled orange buses run from Phun Phin train station to Surat Thani every 10 minutes (15B, 25 minutes). For this ride, taxis charge a cool 200B for a maximum of four people, while share taxis charge 100B per person. Other taxi rates are posted just north of the train station (at the metal pedestrian bridge).

NAKHON SI THAMMARAT PROVINCE

Home to south Thailand's highest peak – Khao Luang (1835m), surrounded by the majestic forests of Khao Luang National Park – Nakhon Si Thammarat Province is best known to travellers for stunning Wat Phra Mahathat Woramahawihaan in the province's namesake main town. More than the sum of its parts, the provincial capital is a likeable place, especially if you have recently pitched up from Ko Samui, Ko Pha-Ngan or Ko Tao in search of some genuine Thai flavour.

Ao Khanom อ่าวขนอม

Pretty and placid Ao Khanom, halfway between Surat Thani and Nakhon Si Thammarat, quietly sits along the blue gulf waters. Overlooked by tourists who flock to the jungle islands nearby, this pristine region, simply called Khanom, is a worthy choice for those seeking a serene beach setting unmarred by enterprising corporations. The waters are free of jet skis to protect the local pink dolphins, making the region quiet and undisturbed. Tours whisk visitors off to view the dolphins in their natural environment.

The beach area is long and comprises two beaches: the main, long Hat Nadan and the smaller and more remote Hat Nai Plao beyond. Beyond Hat Nai Plao is very quiet Hat Thong Yi at the end of the road, which is well worth a journey for its castaway feel. This area is also home to a variety of pristine geological features, including waterfalls and caves.

Sights

Pink Dolphins

The most special feature of Khanom is the pink dolphins – a rare albino breed with a stunning pink hue. They are regularly seen from the old ferry pier and the electric plant pier around dawn and dusk, and resorts are now offering full-day tours (from 1700B) that include viewing the dolphins by boat and a car tour to the area's caves and waterfalls.

If you just want to see the dolphins you can hire a boat for a few hours (for up to six people) for 1200B. Enquire at your hotel.

Caves

There are two beautiful caves along the main road (Hwy 4014) between Khanom and Don Sak. **Khao Wang Thong** has a string of lights guiding visitors through the network of caverns and narrow passages. A metal gate covers the entrance; stop at the house at the base of the hill to retrieve the key (and leave a small donation). Turn right off the main highway at Rd 4142 to find **Khao Krot**, with two large caverns (bring a torch).

Other Sights

★Hat Thong Yi BEACH

For a real escape, head as far down the main beach road as you can, till it joins the 4073, and turn left to follow the coast further south past Hat Nai Plao. Keep going as far as you can and the road will end at lovely and often deserted Hat Thong Yi, with its splendid views back down the bay. A beachside restaurant can get you a drink and food.

Dat Fa Mountain MOUNTAIN

(Khao Dat Fa) For splendid postcard-worthy vistas of the undulating coastline, head to Dat Fa Mountain (Khao Dat Fa; 732m), about 5km west of the coast along Hwy 4014 (look out for the sign). The area has not been developed for tourism and the hillside is usually deserted, making it easy to stop along the way to snap some photos.

Samet Chun Waterfall WATERFALL

This is the largest waterfall in the area, with tepid pools for cooling off, and superb views of the coast. To reach the falls, head south from Ban Khanom and turn left at the blue Samet Chun sign. Follow the road for about 2km and, after crossing a small stream, take the next right and hike up into the mountain following the dirt road. After about a 15-minute walk, listen for the waterfall and look for a small trail on the right.

Hin Lat Falls WATERFALL
The scenic Hin Lat Falls south of Hat Nai Plao is the smallest of the cascades in the area, but the easiest to reach. There are pools for swimming and several huts providing shade.

Sleeping

Khanom's beaches remain a very low-key and quiet retreat. Many resorts see very few customers, and irregular use may mean that some rooms can be a bit dank. In general, it's advisable to stay away from the large hotels and stick to beachside bungalow operations. It's not like Ko Samui: options are spaced far apart so you'll need wheels to get about.

Suchada Villa BUNGALOW $
(075 528459; Hat Naiplau; bungalows incl breakfast 800-1000B;) Right off the main road and a five-minute walk to the beach, Suchada offers a cache of brightly coloured, quite cute bungalows.

Sea Breeze House BUNGALOW $$
(081 276 1457; www.naiplao.com; Hat Nai Plao; r 850-1650B;) With a very secluded location, this lovely Swiss-owned choice has excellent beach-front rooms, including a large suite. If you seek peace and tranquillity, plus splendid views of the sunrise and a chance to see pink dolphins, it's excellent, but you'll need wheels to get about to find places to dine.

Talkoo Beach Resort BUNGALOW $$
(089 871 4442; www.talkoobeachresortkhanom.com; Hat Nadan; bungalows 1000-1500B;) Talkoo has a range of beachfront bungalows in a garden by the sand and cheaper ones across the main road in a more dry, sparse area. All are in good shape, spacious, comfortable and include charming touches like naturalistic bathrooms and traditional art.

Racha Kiri RESORT $$$
(075 300245; www.rachakiri.com; bungalows 3550-7150B;) With spa, pool and elegant rooms, Khanom's upscale retreat is a beautiful campus of rambling villas. The big price tag deters the crowds and the location is serene. Rooms come with terrace.

Khanom Hill Resort BUNGALOW $$$
(081 956 3101; www.khanom.info; Hat Naiplau; bungalows incl breakfast 2900-3900B;) Travellers love this spot on a small hill leading to a half-circle of dreamy white beach. Choose from modern, concrete villas with thatched roofs, cheaper models with Thai-style architecture or big family-sized apartments; all are clean and comfy.

Eating & Drinking

For cheap eats, head to Hat Kho Khao at the end of Rte 4232 where you'll find a steamy jumble of barbecue stands offering tasty favourites such as *mŏo nám đòk* (spicy pork salad) and *sôm·đam* (spicy green papaya salad). There are markets further inland on Wednesday and Sunday; and the coast road is dotted with a variety of Thai and Western restaurants, all looking out on to the sea.

Many of the restaurants down the beach double as bars come evening.

★Le Petit Saint-Tropez INTERNATIONAL $$
(093 727 0063; mains from 300B; 8am-9.30pm) With an open and breezy setting, this charming restaurant faces out onto the sea, serving delightful French and Thai fare.

CC Beach Bar & Bungalows INTERNATIONAL $$
(087 893 8745; www.ccbeachbarthai.wordpress.com; mains 100-300B; 9am-midnight) With a splendid perspective onto the bay over the sands, this beach bar and restaurant is a good choice for its mixed menu of Thai and Western food. English breakfasts, fish and chips, vegetable curry, pizza and fried catfish salad are all on the menu. It doubles as a bar in the evening.

Information

There's a 7-Eleven with an ATM in the heart of Khanom town.

The police station is just south of Ban Khanom at the junction leading to Hat Kho Khao.

The hospital is just south of Ban Khanom at the junction leading to Hat Kho Khao.

Getting There & Away

Minivans from both Surat Thani and Nakhon leave every hour on the hour from 5am to 5pm daily and drop passengers off in Khanom town, which is several kilometres from the beach.

A taxi to/from Don Sak pier for the gulf islands is 1000B and a motorcycle taxi is around 300B.

Getting Around

From Khanom town you can hire motorcycle taxis out to the beaches for about 25B to 100B depending on the distance you're going. If you've booked in advance your hosts may offer to pick you up in Khanom town for free.

Once at your lodging you'll be stranded unless you hire your own transport or take a tour with your hotel, so the best approach is to hire a scooter. There's a rental operator at the bus drop off from Surat Thani who charges around 150B a day.

Nakhon Si Thammarat

อำเภอเมืองนครศรีธรรมราช

075 / POP 120,836

With one of the most significant temples in the kingdom, the historic city of Nakhon Si Thammarat (usually shortened to 'Nakhon') is a natural and rewarding stop between Hat Yai and Surat Thani.

Hundreds of years ago, an overland route between the western port of Trang and the eastern port of Nakhon Si Thammarat functioned as a major trade link between Thailand and the rest of the world. This ancient influx of cosmopolitan conceits is still evident today in the local cuisine, and housed in the city's temples and museums.

Sights

South of the clock tower is the city's magnificent Wat Mahathat, while tantalising remains of the historic red-brick city walls stand near the park and public square of Sanam Na Muang. Note also the gold-coloured statues of the 12 animals of the Thai zodiac atop lamp-posts along Th Ratchadamnoen, each representing one of the 12 city states that were tributary to the Nakhon Si Thammarat kingdom.

★Wat Phra Mahathat Woramahawihaan TEMPLE

(Th Si Thamasok; 8.30am-4.30pm) FREE The most important wát in southern Thailand, stunning Wat Phra Mahathat Woramahawihaan (simply known as Mahathat) boasts an imposing 77m white *chedi* (stupa) crowned by a gold spire piercing the sky. According to legend, Queen Hem Chala and Prince Thanakuman brought relics to Nakhon more than 1000 years ago, and built a small pagoda to house the precious icons. The temple has since grown into a huge site, and today crowds gather daily to purchase the popular Jatukham amulets.

Shadow Puppet Museum MUSEUM

(Th Si Thamasok Soi 3; 9am-4.30pm) FREE There are two styles of local shadow puppets: *năng đà·lung* and *năng yài*. At just under 1m tall, the former feature movable appendages and parts; the latter are nearly life-sized, and lack moving parts. Both are intricately carved from cow hide. Suchart Subsin's puppet house has a small museum where staff can demonstrate the cutting process and put on performances for visitors (50B).

National Museum MUSEUM

(075 341075; Th Ratchadamnoen; 150B; 9am-4pm Wed-Sun) When the Tampaling (also known as Tambralinga) kingdom traded with merchants from Indian, Arabic, Dvaravati and Champa states, the region around Nakhon became a melting pot of crafts and art. Today, many of these relics are on display in this absorbing national museum.

Old City Walls RUINS

The intriguing and well-kept remains of the historic red-brick city walls can be seen in several sections close to one another along the Khlong Na Meuang canal near the park and public square of Sanam Na Muang on either side of Th Ratchadamnoen.

Sleeping

As an authentic Thai city, Nakhon has a particular and genuine charm about it, although accommodation diversity is not a forte. Nonetheless, you can find several decent enough options not far from the train station – just don't expect your hotel to be the highlight of your stay.

Thai Hotel HOTEL $

(075 341509; fax 075 344858; 1375 Th Ratchadamnoen; r with fan/air-con 350/450B;) The most central sleeping spot in town, not far from the train station, the Thai Hotel is a semi-smart bargain and is perfectly acceptable. Walls may be a bit thin and the wi-fi twitchy, but rooms are clean and a good deal, each with a TV – and the higher floors have good views of the urban bustle – while staff are lovely.

Nakorn Garden Inn HOTEL $

(075 323777; 1/4 Th Pak Nakhon; r 445B;) There's a lovely forested setting here that's more like a shady jungle than the centre of town, but sadly most of the bare-brick rooms

DON'T MISS

KHAO LUANG NATIONAL PARK

Known for its beautiful mountain and forest walks, cool streams, waterfalls and orchards, **Khao Luang National Park** (อุทยานแห่งชาติเขาหลวง; ☎075 300494; www.dnp.go.th; adult/child 400/200B) surrounds the 1835m peak of Khao Luang. A soaring mountain range covered in virgin forest and a habitat for a plethora of bird species, it's a good spot for any ornithologist. There are more than 300 species of orchid in the park, some of which are found nowhere else on earth. Camping is permitted, and there are **bungalows** (☎075 300494; www.dnp.go.th; per night 600-2000B) (from 600B). There's also a restaurant at park HQ.

To reach the park, take a *sŏrng·tăa·ou* (pick-up minibus) for around 40B from Nakhon Si Thammarat to Lan Saka; drivers will usually take you the extra way to park headquarters. The entrance to the park and the offices of the Royal Forest Department are 33km from the centre of Nakhon on Rte 4015, an asphalt road that climbs almost 400m in 2.5km to the office and a further 450m to the car park. Plenty of up-to-date details are available on the park's website.

are rather gloomy, although they come with air-con, TV, hot water and fridge. It's a nice rustic change from a cement block, though, and prices are a steal, although English is not spoken.

Twin Lotus Hotel HOTEL $$$
(☎075 323777; www.twinlotushotel.net; 97/8 Th Phattanakan Khukhwang; r 1500-2500B;) The 401-room, 16-storey Twin Lotus is still a good choice to go a little more upscale when in Nakhon; rooms are OK, but it's ageing. It's 2km southeast of the city centre, with a Tesco right across the road.

Eating

Nakhon is a great place to sample cuisine with a distinctive southern twist. In the evening, Muslim food stands sell delicious *kôw mòk gài* (chicken biryani), *má·đà·bà* (*murdabag;* Indian pancake stuffed with chicken or vegetables) and roti. A good hunting ground is along Th Neramit, which turns into Th Pak Nakhon – the street bustles with food stalls every night.

★**Krua Talay** THAI $
(1204/29-30 Th Pak Nakhon; dishes 50-300B; 4-10pm) Opposite the Nakorn Garden Inn (p253) and overseen by an all-seeing, all-knowing matriarch, this restaurant serves simply awesome seafood dishes. Take a seat in the lovely rear garden area and order up fried prawn cake, crispy catfish with hot & spicy salad or stir-fried vegetables in oyster sauce, and make a meal of it.

Hao Coffee CAFE $
(☎075 346563; Bovorn Bazaar; dishes 30-60B; 7am-4pm) This charming, shuttered and well-staffed cafe is always stuffed with talkative locals and decorated with an eclectic array of collectibles and knick-knacks, from pith helmets to hunting rifles, ancient ceramics and wall clocks. It's a great place for a scrambled-eggs breakfast, a larger meal or a caffeine fix, either inside or out front.

★**Pixzel Caffe** CAFE $$
(☎086 682 5471; pizza from 120B; 9am-7pm) The blurb says open 'eight days a week', pointing to a Beatles leaning at this arty, thin-crust pizza-serving, coffee-brewing place in a traditional-style wooden house just across the way from Wat Phra Mahathat. It's a popular and very cosy spot and makes an excellent break if you're templed out.

Glur House CAFE $$
(Th Ratchadamnoen; mains 60-260B; 8am-7pm;) A neat addition to town and decorated with smashed skateboards, this cool rough-concrete cafe is a decent place to hang out with a mocha latte, a mint latte, a caramel macchiato, an Italian soda, a hot dog, banana waffle, a brownie or even a waffle pizza (why not?).

Information

Several banks and ATMs hug Th Ratchadamnoen in the northern end of downtown.

Police Station (☎1155; Th Ratchadamnoen)

Post Office (Th Ratchadamnoen; 8.30am-4.30pm Mon-Fri, 9am-noon Sat & Sun)

Tourism Authority of Thailand (TAT; ☎075 346515; 8.30am-4.30pm) Housed in a fine 1926-vintage building in the northern end of the Sanam Na Muang (City Park), this office has some useful brochures, but spoken English is limited.

Getting There & Away

AIR

Several carriers such as Nok Air, Air Asia and Thai Lion Air fly from Bangkok Don Mueang International Airport to Nakhon every day. There are about six daily one-hour flights, with one-way fares around 1500B.

BUS

Ordinary buses to Bangkok leave from the main **bus station** off Rte 4016 in the west of town, a good 25-minute walk from the centre. The journey takes 12 hours and costs 426B to 851B depending on the class of bus. Minibuses also run from the station to Hat Yai (140B), Surat Thani (120B) and Khanom (80B), and buses run to Phuket (350B).

When looking for minivan stops to leave Nakhon, keep an eye out for small desks along the side of the downtown roads (minivans and waiting passengers may or may not be present nearby). It's best to ask around as each destination has a different departure point. Krabi and Don Sak minivans are grouped together – just make sure you don't get on the wrong one. Stops are scattered around Th Jamroenwithi, Th Wakhit and Th Yommarat.

TRAIN

There are two daily train departures (1pm and 3pm) to Bangkok from Nakhon (133B to 652B; stopping at Hua Hin, Chumphon and Surat Thani along the way). In the other direction, trains leave Bangkok at 5.35pm and 7.30pm. It's 15 hours in either direction, so they are night trains. These trains continue on to Hat Yai and Sungai Kolok.

Getting Around

Sŏrng·tăa·ou run north–south along Th Ratchadamnoen and Th Si Thammasok for 10B (a bit more at night). Motorcycle-taxi rides start at 30B and cost up to 50B for longer distances. A motorbike from the centre of town to the bus station is 40B.

SONGKHLA PROVINCE

Songkhla Province's two main commercial centres, Hat Yai and Songkhla, are less affected by the political turmoil plaguing the cities further south, although some state travel advisories warn against travel here. You won't be tripping over foreign backpackers, but you'll see a fair number of tourists drawn to wandering through local markets, savouring Muslim-Thai fusion cuisine, relaxing on breezy beaches and tapping into Hat Yai's fun and eclectic urban vibe.

Songkhla & Around สงขลา

074 / POP 90,780

'The great city on two seas' is photogenic in parts; however, slow-paced Songkhla doesn't see much in the way of foreign tourist traffic. Although the town hasn't experienced any of the Muslim separatist violence plaguing the provinces further south, it's still catching the same bad press.

The population is a mix of Thais, Chinese and Malays, and the local architecture and cuisine reflect this fusion at every turn.

Sights & Activities

★National Museum MUSEUM

(พิพิธภัณฑสถานแห่งชาติสงขลา; Th Wichianchom; 150B; 9am-4pm Wed-Sun, closed public holidays) This 1878 building was originally built in a Chinese architectural style as the residence of a luminary. This is easily the most picturesque national museum in Thailand and contains exhibits from all Thai art-style periods, particularly the Srivijaya. Walk barefoot on the wood floors to view elaborate wood carvings, historical photos and pottery salvaged from a shipwreck.

Hat Samila BEACH

(หาดสมิหลา) Stroll this beautiful strip of white sand and enjoy the kite-flying (a local obsession); it's a gorgeous spot for a wander at sundown. A bronze **Mermaid sculpture**, in tribute to Mae Thorani (the Hindu-Buddhist earth goddess), sits atop some rocks at the northern end of the beach. Locals treat the figure like a shrine, tying the waist with coloured cloth and rubbing the breasts for good luck.

Don't expect to sunbathe here – the local dress code is too modest – but it's a wholesome spot to meet locals and enjoy a distinctly Thai beach scene.

Songkhla Aquarium AQUARIUM

(สงขลาอะควาเรี่ยม; 088 788 1456; www.songkhlaaquarium.com; adult/child 300/200B; 9.30am-4pm) Children will love seeking out the clownfish at this fun aquarium and watching the feeding show, performed by divers; there's also a go-kart track (from 400B). Adults can have their feet nibbled clean by garaa rufa fish (200B).

Singora Tram Tour ACTIVITY
(9am-3pm) FREE These free 40-minute tours (six daily) in an open-air tram leave from next to the National Museum. You'll be lucky if you get any English narration but you will get a drive through the old part of town past the Songkhla mosque, a Thai temple, Chinese shrine and then out to Hat Samila.

Sleeping & Eating

Hotels in and around Songkhla tend to be lower-priced than other areas in the gulf, which makes going up a budget level a relatively cheap splurge.

For quality seafood, head to the street in front of the BP Samila Beach Hotel – the best spot is the restaurant directly in the roundabout. If market munching is your game, you'll find a place to sample street food most days of the week. The best cafe in town is the excellent Blue Smile Cafe.

Sook Soom Boon 2 HOTEL $
(074 323809; 14 Th Saiburi; d 550-650B;) The owner speaks good English and rooms are really decent value at this centrally located choice. It's nothing special, but it's serviceable, especially when compared to some less salubrious nearby choices.

BP Samila Beach Hotel HOTEL $$
(074 440222; 8 Th Ratchadamnoen; r 1600-2500B;) This landmark hotel is a great deal – you'd pay nearly double for the same amenities on the islands. The beachfront establishment offers large rooms with fridges, satellite TVs and a choice of sea or mountain views (both are pretty darn good), although it's rather set in its ways and checking on wi-fi reception in your room first is prudent.

DON'T MISS

SONGKHLA LAKE ISLAND

A popular day trip from Songkhla is **Ko Yo** (เกาะยอ) island in the middle of Songkhla Lake, which is actually connected to the mainland by bridges and is famous for its cotton-weaving industry; a roadside market sells cloth and ready-made clothes at excellent prices.

If you visit Ko Yo, don't miss **Wat Phrahon Laem Pho**, with its giant reclining Buddha, and check out the **Thaksin Folklore Museum** (074 591618; 100B; 8.30am-4.30pm), which actively aims to promote and preserve the culture of the region. The pavilions here are reproductions of southern Thai–style houses and contain folk art, handicrafts and traditional household implements.

★ **Blue Smile Cafe** CAFE $
(061 230 5147; 254 Th Nakhonnai; mains from 100B; 3-11pm Mon, Tue, Thu & Fri, from 10am Sat & Sun) A fine place for a snack, coffee, some alcohol or cool beats, we're not sure what we like best at this Canadian-owned place: the excellent roof garden – fantastic at sunset – *The Blues Brothers* poster, the B52s and Bob Dylan pics, the live jazz (from 7.15pm Friday and Saturday) or the baked goodies.

Ong Heap Huad CAFE
(081 690 6640; Th Nakhonnai; 10am-6pm) This family-run curiosity shop-slash-cafe has a mesmerising museum-like collection of ancient Chinese and Thai shop signs, antiques, statuette, lamps, stuffed animal heads and more. It's an enchanting place for a glass of tea. Look for the shop with the urns and bric-a-brac outside and the Chinese shop sign saying 黄協發, opposite No 239.

Information

Banks can be found all over town.

Indonesian Consulate (074 311544; www.kemlu.go.id/songkhla; 19 Th Sadao)

Malaysian Consulate (074 311062; 4 Th Sukhum, Songkhla; 8.15am-noon & 1-4pm Mon-Fri)

Police Station (074 321868; Th Laeng Phra Ram)

Post Office (Th Wichianchom)

Getting There & Away

BUS

The bus and minibus station is on Songkhla Plaza Alley (off Nakhonnok St) around 1km south of the **Blue Smile Cafe**. Three 2nd-class buses go daily to Bangkok (693B to 1080B), stopping in Nakhon Si Thammarat and Surat Thani, among other places. For Hat Yai, buses (21B) and minivans (30B to 40B) take around 40 minutes, and leave from Th Ramwithi. *Sŏrng·tăa·ou* also leave from here for Ko Yo.

TRAIN

From Songkhla you'll have to go to Hat Yai to reach most long-distance destinations in the south (trains no longer pass through town).

Hat Yai

หาดใหญ่

074 / POP 191,696

Welcome to the urban hub of southern Thailand, where Western-style shopping malls mingle with wafts from busy street-food stalls as old Chinese men watch the world go by on rickety chairs outside junk shops. You'll notice that the town's tourism scene is still predominantly Malaysian mixed with a few Western expats. Hat Yai has a seamy side, popular with Malaysian men on weekend visits.

Those who explore will be rewarded with some of the region's best food and the dynamic flavour of southern Thailand's big smoke.

Sleeping

Hat Yai has dozens of business-style hotels in the town centre, within walking distance of the train station, as well as a hostel and several cheap options.

Hat Yai Backpackers HOSTEL $

(www.hatyaibackpackershostel.com; 226 Th Niphat Uthit 1; dm 240B;) With four-bed female dorms and eight-bed mixed dorms, this central choice is a decent bet, and there are helpful staff at hand for Hat Yai pointers.

Red Planet HOTEL $

(074 261011; www.redplanethotels.com; 152-156 Th Niphat Uthit 2; r from 900B;) In a very central location, this hotel offers cleanliness, affordability and decent service, with uncluttered, but modern, functional rooms. The atmosphere and theme are generically chain charmless; prices depend a lot on how far in advance you book.

Centara HOTEL $$$

(074 352222; www.centarahotelsresorts.com; 3 Th Sanehanusorn; r/apt from 4000/5300B, ste 8500B;) The centrally located, 244-room Centara is a particularly smart choice, with pool, excellent rooms, terrific service and some fine views from the upper floors. Evening live jazz in the foyer bar brings some style.

Eating & Drinking

The city is the unofficial capital of southern Thailand's cuisine, offering Muslim roti and curries, Chinese noodles, duck rice and dim sum, and fresh Thai-style seafood from both the gulf and Andaman coasts. Hawker stalls are everywhere, but a particularly good hunting ground is along Th Supasarnrangsan. Meals here cost between 25B to 80B.

As you'd expect from a city with a commercial sex side, Hat Yai's nightlife is rather tacky.

Night Market MARKET $

(Th Montri 1) The night market boasts heaps of local eats including several stalls selling the famous Hat Yai-style deep-fried chicken and *kà·nŏm jeen* (fresh rice noodles served with curry), as well as a couple of stalls peddling grilled seafood.

Daothiam CAFE $

(79/3 Thammanoonvithi Rd; mains from 60B; 7am-7pm;) Serving Hat Yai patrons since 1959, this traditional Chinese cafe has framed banknotes on its walls, friendly staff, a reliable menu of Thai/Chinese dishes and fine breakfasts. Curiously, its name means 'Satellite'. It's opposite the Odean Shopping Mall.

Gedi Chadian CHINESE $

(Ko Ti Ocha; 134-136 Th Niphat Uthit 3; mains from 50B) This big, open, spacious and very busy restaurant serves steaming bowls of scrumptious wonton noodles, chicken rice, *chā shāo* pork and other filling Chinese staples. The name in Chinese means 'Brothers Tea Shop'.

Information

DANGERS & ANNOYANCES

The town is often said to be safe from the violent hullabaloo of the far south; however, it hasn't been ignored. The Lee Gardens Plaza Hotel was bombed in 2012, killing four people in a subsequent fire and injuring 400. Three bombs exploded in Hat Yai in 2014, injuring eight. In previous years pubs, malls, department stores and hotels have been targeted in other bombings.

It's up to you if you want to stop here, but changing transport shouldn't be too risky.

EMERGENCY

Tourist Police (Th Niphat Uthit 3; 24hr)

TOURIST INFORMATION

Tourism Authority of Thailand (TAT; www.tourismthailand.org/hatyai; 1/1 Soi 2, Th Niphat Uthit 3; 8.30am-4.30pm) The very helpful staff here speak excellent English and have loads of info on the entire region.

TRAVEL AGENCIES

Cathay Tour (086 488 0086; 93/1 Th Niphat Uthit 2; 8am-6pm) Superfriendly staff and full range of services, from tickets to tours to visa runs.

THAILAND'S FORGOTTEN WAR

Just 300km or so south of the party islands of Ko Samui and Ko Pha-Ngan, a guerrilla war between ethnic Malay Muslims and the overwhelmingly Buddhist Thai state has claimed almost 6000 lives since 2004. Military convoys rumble through the villages and towns, checkpoints dominate the roads and residents are subject to compulsory DNA tests designed to make identifying suspected insurgents easier.

Around 80% of the 1.8 million people who live in Thailand's three southernmost provinces of Pattani, Narathiwat and Yala are ethnic Malay Muslims. They speak a Malay dialect and many want their own independent state, as the region once was hundreds of years ago.

For the estimated 12,500 to 15,000 separatist fighters here, the Deep South is 'Patani': the name given to the Qatar-sized sultanate during its glory days in the 14th and 15th centuries. The insurgents view the Thai government as a colonial power and Thai Buddhists as interlopers in their land.

Ranged against the separatists are around 150,000 soldiers, police and militias. Targeted in ambushes along the coconut-tree-lined roads of the region, or by increasingly sophisticated IEDs (improvised explosive devices), barely a week goes by without a member of the Thai security forces being killed or wounded.

At the same time, the insurgency has set neighbours against each other. Gruesome tit-for-tat killings occur, with both Buddhist and Muslim civilians being gunned down as they ride home on their motorbikes or beheaded in the rubber plantations that are the mainstay of the local economy. Bombs are planted outside shops and in the markets of the towns, claiming random victims.

The few remaining Buddhist monks in the region have to be escorted by the army when they collect alms every morning for fear they will be assassinated, while mosques are riddled with bullet holes.

The insurgents have resisted attacking targets outside the Deep South, a tactic that would do huge damage to the Thai psyche and would garner them far more attention around the world. Nor do they appear to be connected to the more extreme Islamic militants of Indonesia and the Philippines. There seems to be no common leader of the insurgent groups, which renders the sporadic peace talks with the Thai government meaningless.

While the insurgency kicked into life in earnest in 2004, after 32 suspected Muslim rebels were cornered in an ancient mosque in Pattani Town and brutally killed by the Thai army, its roots go back hundreds of years. From the 16th century on, the sultanate of Patani was unwillingly under Thai rule for brief periods. But it wasn't until the Anglo-Siamese Treaty of 1909 that the Deep South was absorbed into Thailand proper. Britain recognised Thai sovereignty over the region, in return for Bangkok abandoning its claims to other parts of what were then the British-ruled Malay states.

Since then, Thailand, the most populous Buddhist country in the world, has set about attempting to remake the Deep South in its own image. Muslim schools have been shut down and all children made to study in Thai, even though most of them speak it only as a second language. They are also forced to learn about Buddhism, a part of the Thai national curriculum, despite following Islam. Officials from other parts of the country are imported to run the region.

With the insurgency mostly confined to just three provinces, and a small part of neighbouring Songkhla Province, few Thais are even aware of why the fighting is taking place. Nor are they willing to contemplate giving in to the separatists' demands. Imbued with the nationalism taught in their schools, the idea that the Deep South should want to secede from Thailand is unthinkable, both to ordinary Thais and the authorities.

Yet, some form of autonomy for the region is likely the only way to end the violence. Until that happens, Thailand's forgotten war will carry on and the grim list of casualties will continue to grow.

VISA EXTENSIONS

Immigration Office (Th Phetkasem) Near the railway bridge, it handles visa extensions.

Getting There & Away

AIR

Hat Yai International Airport (☎074 227131; www.hatyaiairportthai.com) is around 14km southwest of town. Air Asia (www.airasia.com), Nok Air (www.nokair.com), Thai Lion Air (www.lionairthai.com) and **Thai Airways** (THAI; www.thaiairways.com; 182 Th Niphat Uthit 1) have daily flights to and from Bangkok. Thai Smile (www.thaismileair.com) flies to Bangkok Suvarnabhumi International Airport.

There's an **airport taxi service** (182 Th Niphat Uthit 1; 100B per person; ⏲6.30am-6.45pm) that runs to the airport six times daily (6.45am, 10am, 12.15pm, 1.45pm, 3pm and 6.15pm). A private taxi for this run costs 320B.

BUS

Most interprovincial buses and southbound minivans leave from the bus terminal 2km southeast of the town centre, while most northbound minivans now leave from a minivan terminal 5km west of town at Talat Kaset, a 60B túk-túk ride from the centre of town. Buses link Hat Yai to almost any location in southern Thailand.

Cathay Tour (p257) can also arrange minivans to many destinations in the south.

Buses From Hat Yai

DESTINATION	FARE (B)	DURATION (HR)
Bangkok	688–1130B	15hr
Krabi	182–540B	5hr
Nakhon Si Thammarat	140B	4hr
Pak Bara	130B	2hr
Phuket	370B	7hr
Songkhla	40B	1½hr
Sungai Kolok	220B	4hr
Surat Thani	240B	5hr
Trang	110B	2hr

TRAIN

Four overnight trains run to/from Bangkok each day (259B to 945B, 16 hours); trains go via Surat Thani (105B). There are also seven trains daily that run along the east coast to Sungai Kolok (92B) and two daily trains running west to Butterworth (332B) and Padang Besar (57B), both in Malaysia.

There is an advance booking office and left-luggage office at the train station; both are open 7am to 5pm daily.

Getting Around

Sŏrng·tăa·ou run along Th Phetkasem (10B per person). Túk-túk and motorcycle taxis around town cost 20B to 40B per person.

DEEP SOUTH

In the deep southern Thai provinces, the culture, language, religion and historical influences of Malaysia penetrate and a regional identity that traces itself back to the Malay sultanate of Patani asserts itself. Most inhabitants of the region speak a dialect of Malay, being ethnically closer to their Malay cousins over the border.

The tourist potential in this fascinating region is largely unexploited, put on the back foot by a long-simmering insurgency that pits Muslim separatists against the Thai state, with just a small trickle of visitors and consequently a paucity of infrastructure to cater to them.

Yala ยะลา

☎073 / POP 61,250

Landlocked Yala wiggles its way south to the Malaysian border, making it Thailand's southernmost province. Its eponymous capital appears very different from other Thai metropolises and feels distinctly Western, with big boulevards and a well-organised street grid set around a huge circular park. Around three-quarters of the population is Muslim and it is a university town, the educational centre of the Deep South.

Sights

Yala's biggest attraction is **Wat Kuha Pi Muk** (Wat Khuhapimuk), one of the most important pilgrimage points in southern Thailand. Located 8km west of town on the road connecting Yala to Hat Yai (Rte 409), this Srivijaya-period cave temple (also called Wat Na Tham or Cave-front Temple) features a reclining Buddha that dates back to AD 757.

Further south, Betong is home to the largest **mail box** in Thailand, first built in 1924.

Sleeping & Eating

Yala is a pleasant place, but many of the city's cheapest lodgings double as unofficial brothels. There's not a great selection of places in town but the Yala Rama is a good choice.

TRAVEL IN THE DEEP SOUTH: SHOULD YOU GO?

No tourists, or indeed any Westerners, have been targeted by the insurgents. Yet, by nature insurgencies are unpredictable, and bombs kill indiscriminately. Explosive devices planted on parked motorbikes outside shops, or in markets, are a common tactic of the separatists and are frequently used in the city centres of Yala, Pattani, Narathiwat and Sungai Kolok.

It's best not to linger on the streets for too long; you could be in the wrong place at the wrong time. Nor is travel in the countryside in the early morning or after dark advisable. This isn't an area to be driving a motorbike in if you can't be identified as a foreigner.

The insurgency has stifled tourism to the extent that there is very little infrastructure for visitors. Travel between the major centres apart, you'll need private transport to get around. There are few hotels and restaurants, and almost no nightlife, while those beautiful beaches have absolutely no facilities.

If you do want to travel here, research the current situation carefully and take advice from your embassy.

There are excellent restaurants scattered around the park's perimeter.

Yala Rama HOTEL $
(☎ 073 212815; 21 Th Sri Bumrung; r 600B; ❄ 📶) Like most hotels in the region, this central and reputable nine-floor place, a short walk from the train station, would be more expensive if it weren't located in the Deep South. Clean, comfortable rooms and an OK attached restaurant.

 Information

Betong functions as a legal, but inconvenient, border crossing to Malaysia; contact Yala's **immigration office** (☎ 073 231292; Betong; ⏰ 8.30am-4.30pm).

 Getting There & Away

Yala's bus station is south of the city centre. There are three daily buses to and from Bangkok's southern bus terminal (783B to 1422B, 15 hours). The 4pm bus from Bangkok carries onto Betong.

Four trains a day run between Bangkok and Yala (18 hours). Two trains travel daily between Yala and Sungai Kolok (three to four hours). The train station is just north of the city centre.

Buses to Hat Yai (160B, 2½ hours) stop several times a day on Th Sirirot, outside the Prudential TS Life office.

Minivans to Betong and Sungai Kolok (100B, two hours) depart hourly from opposite the train station.

Pattani ปัตตานี

☎ 073 / POP 44,234

Once the heart of a large Muslim principality that included the neighbouring provinces of Yala and Narathiwat, Pattani Province has never adjusted to Thai rule. Although today's political situation has stunted the area's development, Pattani Town has a 500-year history of trading with the world's most notorious imperial powerhouses. The Portuguese established a trading post here in 1516, the Japanese passed through in 1605, the Dutch in 1609 and the British flexed their colonial muscles in 1612.

Yet despite the city's fascinating past, there's little of interest in Pattani. There are some decent beaches nearby, but the ongoing insurgency has made most of these sandy destinations unsafe for the independent traveller.

Sights

The Mae Nam Pattani (Pattani River) divides the older town to the east and the newer town to the west. Along Th Ruedi you can see what is left of old Pattani architecture – the Sino-Portuguese style that was once so prevalent in this part of southern Thailand. On Th Arnoaru there are several ancient but still quite intact Chinese-style homes.

Pattani could be one of the better beach destinations in the region. The coastline between Pattani Town and Narathiwat Province is stunning: untouched and deserted apart from fishing villages. But exploring much of this area independently is not a safe option at this time.

Matsayit Klang MOSQUE
(Th Naklua Yarang) One of Thailand's largest mosques, the Matsayit Klang is a traditional structure with a green hue and is probably still the south's most important mosque, dating to the 1960s. Non-Muslims can enter outside of prayer times.

Sleeping & Eating

Palace Hotel HOTEL $
(☎ 073 349171; 10-12 Pipit Soi Talattewiwat 2; r 180-350B; ❄) There's not a lot palatial about this place, but it's the only budget option in town for foreigners and close to the night market. Go for the air-con rooms with hot water.

CS Pattani Hotel HOTEL $$
(☎ 073 335093; www.cspattanihotel.com; 299 Moo 4, Th Nong Jik; r from 1400B; ❄@☎≋) The safest and best hotel in town, with soldiers outside and a metal detector in the lobby, this is where Thai politicians stay on their rare visits to the Deep South. The paucity of tourists means you get great rooms and facilities for a bargain price.

Night Market THAI $
(Soi Talattewiwat; dishes from 25B; ⏲4-9pm) Pattani shuts down far earlier than most Thai towns, but the night market offers solid seafood, as well as southern Thai-style curries and the usual noodle and fried-rice options.

Information

There are several banks along the southeastern end of Th Pipit, near the Th Naklua Yarang intersection.

Pattani Hospital (☎ 073 335135, 073 335134, 073 711010; Th Nong Jik)

Police Station (☎ 073 349018; Th Pattani Phirom)

Getting There & Away

Minivans and buses depart from Pattani's bus station on the western fringes of town, with frequent daytime departures to Hat Yai (110B, 1½ hours), Narathiwat (110B, 1½ hours) and Sungai Kolok (150B, 2½ hours).

There are two daily buses to and from Bangkok's southern bus terminal (765B to 1250B, 14 hours).

Getting Around

Motorbike taxis charge 30B for hops around town, but they become very scarce after dark.

Narathiwat นราธิวาส

☎ 073 / POP 41,342

Sitting on the banks of the Bang Nara River, Narathiwat is probably the most Muslim city in Thailand, with mosques scattered around town. A few old Sino-Portuguese buildings line the riverfront (although blink and you'll miss them), and there some excellent beaches just outside town, but few tourists pass through, due to the security situation.

OFF THE BEATEN TRACK

GATEWAY TO MALAYSIA: SUNGAI KOLOK

It's not the most prepossessing place to enter or exit the 'Land of Smiles', but Sungai Kolok is the main gateway between Thailand and Malaysia. As such, it's a scuzzy border town best known for smuggling and prostitution. Less of a target than the other major towns in the region, the unstable situation in the Deep South has nevertheless severely diminished its 'sin city' reputation, with the Malaysian men who once came here for wild weekends now favouring safer Hat Yai. Fewer travellers, too, leave Thailand here now; more come in the opposite direction and immediately hop on a train heading north.

If you do pass through, **Merlin Hotel** (☎ 073 611003; 68 Th Charoenkhet; r 600B; ❄☎) is clean and handy for the train station while **Genting Hotel** (☎ 073 613231; 250 Th Asia 18; r 700B; ❄@☎≋) has efficient security, though its midrange rooms are rather scuffed for the price; it's a few hundred metres east of the train station on the far side of the road. Reliable, Muslim-run **Kakyah Restaurant** (43/11 Th Charoenkhet; dishes from 30B; ⏲10am-10pm) offers decent Malaysian food. The long-distance **bus station** (Th Asia 18) is 2km west of the centre on Th Asia 18. There are four buses daily to and from Bangkok's southern bus terminal (707B to 1414B, 17 to 20 hours). Minivans to Hat Yai (200B, four hours) leave from here too.

There is an **immigration office** (☎ 073 614114; Th Charoenkhet; ⏲8am-5pm Mon-Fri) opposite the Merlin Hotel with helpful, English-speaking staff. The Thai border (open 5am to 9pm) is about 1.5km from the centre of Sungai Kolok. Motorbike taxis charge around 30B. After completing formalities, walk across the Harmony Bridge to the Malaysian border post. Two-hundred metres beyond the post, you can catch shared taxis and buses to Kota Bharu, the capital of Malaysia's Kelantan State.

Sights & Activities

Just 2km north of town is **Hat Narathat**, a 5km-long sandy beach fronted by towering pines, which serves as a public park for locals. Five kilometres south of town, **Ao Manao** is a superb strip of palm tree-fringed sand.

Wat Khao Kong BUDDHIST TEMPLE
(9am-5pm) FREE The tallest seated-Buddha image in southern Thailand is at Wat Khao Kong, 6km southwest of town on the way to the train station in Tanyongmat. Located in a park, the image is 17m long and 24m high, and made of reinforced concrete covered with tiny gold-coloured mosaic tiles that glint magically in the sun.

Matsayit Klang MOSQUE
(Yum lyah Mosque) Towards the southern end of Th Pichitbumrung stands Matsayit Klang, a wooden mosque built in the Sumatran style and known locally as the 'old central mosque'. It was reputedly built by a prince of the former kingdom of Pattani more than a hundred years ago. Non-Muslims can enter outside of prayer times.

Sleeping & Eating

Most of the town's accommodation is located on and around Th Puphapugdee along the Bang Nara River.

The centre of town, near the river, is well provided with restaurants and cafes.

Ocean Blue Mansion HOTEL $
(073 511109; 297 Th Puphapugdee; r 400-500B;) Decent-sized rooms have seen better days, but some have fine river views and this remains the best budget choice.

Tanyong Hotel HOTEL $$
(073 511477; 16/1 Th Sophaphisai; r 690-890B;) This respectable, welcoming hotel has big, comfortable rooms and an OK attached restaurant, while staff speak some English.

Mangkorntong THAI $
(073 511835; 433 Th Puphapugdee; dishes 55-200B; 10am-10pm) Perched over the river, you have a choice of two terraces to dine on here, with a wide selection of seafood dishes available, as well as vegie options; alcohol is served.

Information

The **Tourism Authority of Thailand** (TAT; Narathiwat 073 522411, nationwide call centre 1672) is located a few kilometres south of town, just across the bridge on the road to Tak Bai.

Getting There & Away

Air Asia (www.airasia.com) flies daily to and from Bangkok (from 1783B, 1½ hours), as does Thai Smile (www.thaismileair.com; from 1730B, 1½ hours).

Minivans and buses leave from Narathiwat's **bus terminal** (073 511552), 2km south of town on Th Rangae Munka. There are two daily buses to and from Bangkok's southern bus terminal (860B to 1350B, 15 to 17 hours).

Frequent minivans head to Hat Yai (170B, three hours), Pattani (100B, two hours), Sungai Kolok (70B, one hour) and Yala (100B, 1½ hours).

Getting Around

Narathiwat is small enough to navigate by foot. Motorcycle taxis charge 30B to get around.

Phuket & the Andaman Coast

Includes ➡

Best Places to Eat

- Eat Bar & Grill (p314)
- Efe (p340)
- Krua Thara (p333)
- One Chun (p297)
- Pad Thai Shop (p314)

Best Places to Stay

- Rayavadee (p328)
- Castaway Resort (p369)
- Iniala Beach House (p283)
- Fin Hostel (p311)
- Amanpuri Resort (p317)

Why Go?

The Andaman is Thailand's dream coast: one of those places that you see on a postcard which make you want to quit your job and live in flip-flops...forever. And it is stunning. Pure-white beaches of soft sand, a turquoise sea, towering limestone cliffs and jungle-covered isles extend down the Andaman Sea from the border of Myanmar to Malaysia. Phuket is the glitzy show-stealer, but head north and you'll uncover world-class dive sites, little-visited islands, and the waterfalls and caves of Phang-Nga's national parks. To the south, you can lazily island-hop down to the Malaysian border.

The catch? The Andaman Coast is no secret and its beaches are increasingly crowded with backpackers, package tourists, high-end jet-setters and everyone in between. Flashy resorts are pushing out the bamboo shacks and Thai-Rasta bars and authenticity hides largely in the backwaters now. But if you're willing to search hard, your postcard dream is still here.

When to Go

- May is the start of the five-month-long rainy season. Some resorts close, others slash their prices.
- The Vegetarian Festival is held in Phuket and Trang in September. Expect pierced-faced worshippers and fantastic food.
- December is the beginning of peak tourist season and conditions are ideal for diving and snorkelling.

Phuket & the Andaman Coast Highlights

1 **Trang Islands** (p355) Buzzing across jade-green waters between white-sand beaches.

2 **Ko Lipe** (p367) Snorkelling over colourful corals and explore the untouched nearby islands.

3 **Phuket** (p288) Experiencing the heady mix of luxury lodgings, super spas and street-food treats.

4 **Khao Sok National Park** (p275) Hiking through a real-life Jurassic Park.

5 **Railay** (p326) Scaling limestone cliffs above blissful beaches.

6 **Ko Phi-Phi** (p334) Floating in a

cerulean sea by day, then dance the night away.

7 **Similan** (p281) & **Surin Islands** (p273) Diving with manta rays and whale sharks.

8 **Ko Lanta** (p342) Exploring the culturally rich old town or laze on the laid-back beaches.

9 **Ao Phang-Nga** (p285) Marvelling as you kayak into spectacular, semi-submerged caves.

10 **Ko Phayam** (p270) Embracing the mellow beach-bar vibe.

RANONG PROVINCE

The Andaman's northernmost province is a whole different package to the white-sand, turquoise-sea paradise that is used to sell the Andamans on tourist brochures. Thailand's least populated and wettest region gets up to eight months of rain a year, so it's soggy, while beaches along the coast are scarce.

The upside is that Ranong's forests are lush and its smattering of beautiful islands – Ko Chang (p269) and Ko Phayam (p270) especially – remain *relatively* under the radar. Most visitors, though, come here to cross the border to Myanmar.

Ranong Town ระนอง

077 / POP 17,500

On the eastern bank of Mae Nam Pak Chan's turbid, tea-brown estuary, Ranong lies just a 45-minute boat ride from Myanmar. This border town par excellence (shabby, frenetic, slightly seedy) has a thriving population from Myanmar, bubbling hot springs, crumbling historical buildings and some sensational street food.

Once a backwater, Ranong is increasingly busy with cross-border business and visitors heading to nearby Ko Phayam and Ko Chang, and has clearly benefitted from Myanmar's more stable political situation. Now, there are quirky boutique hotels and a style-conscious local scene (relatively speaking).

Activities

Diving

Liveaboard dive trips from Ranong to world-class bubble-blowing destinations, particularly the Burma Banks and the Surin and Similan Islands, are deservedly popular.

Andaman International Dive Center DIVING
(089 814 1092; www.aidcdive.com; Bus Terminal, Th Phetkasem; Oct-Apr) Mainly focused on extensive excursions (six to 14 days) to the Mergui Archipelago in Myanmar, but also does a few trips to the Surin Islands. Four-day liveaboards 20,000B.

A-One-Diving DIVING
(077 832984; www.a-one-diving.com; 256 Th Ruangrat; Oct-Apr) Specialises in liveaboards to the Surin Islands and Myanmar's Mergui Archipelago (from 34,900B), plus PADI diving certification courses.

Spas & Hot Springs

★ **Siam Hot Spa** SPA
(077 813551; 73/3 Th Phetkasem; treatments 300-750B; 11am-8pm) This is a highly recommended mineral bath experience, classier than the public hot springs opposite in Ranong Town. Soak in a private hot tub, then add a salt scrub or a classic Thai massage.

Rakswarin Hot Springs HOT SPRINGS
(Th Phetkasem; 40B; 5am-9pm) Ranong's healing waters bubble from a sacred spring hot enough to boil eggs (65°C), on the south-eastern side of town. The riverside pools are blessed with chequered mosaic tiles, showers, towels and sunbeds. Just stretch out and let the heat work its natural magic.

Sleeping

Rueangrat Hotel HOTEL $
(092 279 9919; rueangratranong@gmail.com; 240/10 Th Ruangrat; r 690B;) Bright, shiny rooms set back from the road at this new place close to restaurants and shops. All come with fridges, TVs and decent bathrooms. There's free coffee in the lobby area, friendly staff and good wi-fi.

Ranong Backpacker's Hostel HOSTEL $
(091 041 7555, 077 983978; backpackers.rn@gmail.com; 240/9 Th Ruangrat; dm 320B;) Two eight-bed dorms here – one male, one female – with bunk beds and proper lockers. There's no real communal area, but it works if you're looking for a cheap and clean place to crash before or after crossing the border to/from Myanmar.

Luang Poj GUESTHOUSE $
(077 833377, 087 266 6333; www.facebook.com/luangpojhostel; 225 Th Ruangrat; r 600B;) This self-styled 'boutique guesthouse' is a cool remodel of a 1920s-era building that was Ranong's first hotel, decorated with mod-meets-vintage flair: Indian art, wall murals, one-of-a-kind light fixtures and retro photography. Rooms are spotless, comfy and cosy in signature colours (we like the hot orange). The drawback is that many rooms lack windows, while all share (clean) bathrooms.

The B BOUTIQUE HOTEL $$
(077 823111; Br.ranong@gmail.com; 295/1-2 Th Ruangrat; r 1300-2000B;) This good-value chunk of polished-concrete modernism is evidence of Ranong's rising fortunes. Stylish, comfy rooms have floating

Ranong

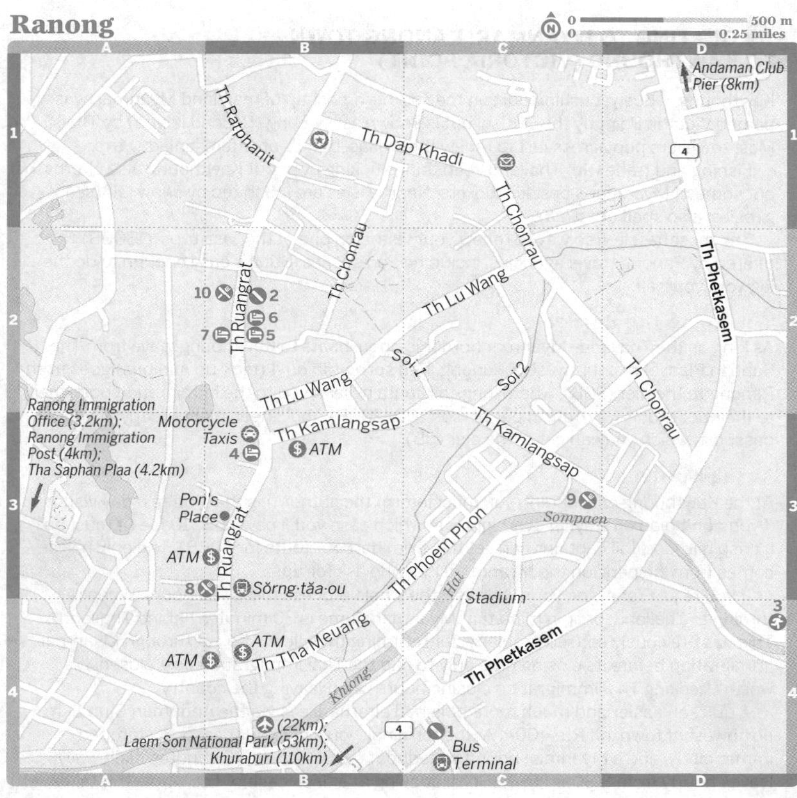

Ranong

Activities, Courses & Tours

1 Andaman International Dive Center C4
2 A-One-Diving B2
3 Rakswarin Hot Springs D4

Sleeping

4 Luang Poj B3
5 Ranong Backpacker's Hostel B2
6 Rueangrat Hotel B2
7 The B B2

Eating

8 Day Market B3
9 Night Market C3
10 Ranong Hideaway B2
The B Restaurant .... (see 7)

beds, rain showers and tasteful, bright decor. Extra points for the snooker bar, the B restaurant and, particularly, the rooftop infinity pool overlooking Ranong and the surrounding green hills.

Eating & Drinking

Ranong's food markets are excellent value. The bubbly **day market** (Th Ruangrat; mains 40-70B; ⏲5am-midnight) offers delicious, inexpensive Thai and Burmese meals, while the **night market** (Th Kamlangsap, off Hwy 4; mains 30-70B; ⏲2-7pm), just northwest off the highway, sizzles up brilliant Thai dishes at killer prices. There are restaurants along Th Ruangrat.

After dark, Ranong has a lively, very local drinking scene involving lots of karaoke.

Ranong Hideaway THAI, INTERNATIONAL **$$**
(☎077 832730; 323/7 Th Ruangrat; mains 110-480B; ⏲10am-11pm; ☎) A long-time favourite of expats and border businessmen, this small international eatery unfurls beneath a stilted bamboo roof, offering decent pastas,

GETTING TO MYANMAR: RANONG TOWN TO KAWTHOUNG (VICTORIA POINT)

Kawthoung, a dusty, bustling port on the southernmost tip of mainland Myanmar, was named Victoria Point by the British, but is known as Ko Song (Second Island) by Thais. Most travellers pop across just to renew their visas, but it's an interesting day trip.

Fishing and trade with Thailand keep things ticking over, but Kawthoung also churns out some of Myanmar's best kickboxers. Nearby isles are inhabited by *chow lair* (sea gypsies, also spelt *chao leh*).

The most hassle-free way to renew your visa is on one of the 'visa trips' (1300B) offered by Ranong travel agencies, including Pon's Place. But it's easy enough to do the legwork yourself.

Getting to the Border

As long as the Thailand–Myanmar border is open, boats to Kawthoung leave from Tha Saphan Plaa, 5km southwest of Ranong. Red *sŏrng·tăa·ou* 4 (pick-up minibus) goes from Ranong to the pier (20B), where long-tail captains lead you to the immigration post, then to their boat (one-way/return per person 100/200B). You'll need a photocopy of your passport, which you can get at the pier (5B).

At the Border

At the Kawthoung checkpoint, you must inform the authorities that you're a day visitor if you don't plan on staying overnight – in which case you'll pay a US$10 fee (it must be a crisp bill; long-tail captains can get this from harbour touts for 500B). The only hassle comes from 'helpers' on the Myanmar side, who ask for tips.

If you're just renewing your Thai visa, the whole process takes two hours. When returning to Thailand, bear in mind that Myanmar's time is 30 minutes behind Thailand's. This has previously caused problems for returning travellers who got through Myanmar Immigration before its closing time only to find the Thai immigration post closed. It's worth checking Thai immigration closing hours when leaving the country.

A quicker, easier and much more polished alternative is via the Andaman Club 8km northwest of town, off Rte 4004. At the terminal, you'll get your passport stamped immediately, and a Myanmar-bound speedboat (950B return, 15 minutes each way) leaves hourly from 8.30am to 3.30pm, docking at a flash casino. The whole trip takes one hour.

Moving On

It's possible to stay overnight in one of Kawthoung's overpriced hotels, but you'd probably rather not. If you have a valid Myanmar visa, which you'll have to apply for in advance at the Myanmar Embassy in Bangkok (or a third country), you'll be permitted to stay for up to 28 days and can exit anywhere you like. There are daily flights from Kawthoung to Yangon.

pizzas, meaty mains, Thai curries and international breakfasts, along with beers and foreign liquor.

The B Restaurant THAI, INTERNATIONAL **$$**
(Th Ruangrat; mains 120-390B; ⏰7am-1am; 📶) The B now has two restaurants: an open-air rooftop restaurant in the hotel itself (p266) and this new place on the street which attracts upmarket locals. There's a good choice of Thai food, as well Western classics such as steaks, pizzas, pastas and sandwiches. Live music most nights and a well-stocked bar.

Information

ATMs are clustered around the intersection of Th Ruangrat and Th Tha Meuang.

EMERGENCY

Police Station (Th Dap Khadi) Ranong's main police station.

IMMIGRATION

Andaman Club Immigration Office (Off Rte 4004; ⏰7am-5pm) The Thai immigration office at the Andaman Club, 8km northwest of town.

Ranong Immigration Office (Th Chalermprakiat; ⏰8.30am-5pm) Main immigration office, 4km southwest of town; handles visa extensions.

Ranong Immigration Post (Tha Saphan Plaa; ⏲8am-5pm) If you're just popping in and out of Myanmar's Kawthoung, visiting this small immigration post, 5km southwest of town, is sufficient.

POST

Post Office (Th Chonrau; ⏲8.30am-4.30pm Mon-Fri, 9am-noon Sat & Sun) You can send mail overseas from here.

TRAVEL AGENCY

Pon's Place (☎081 597 4549; www.ponplace-ranong.com; Th Ruangrat; ⏲8am-7.30pm; 📶) Friendly Pon's is Ranong's go-to spot for everything from wi-fi and European breakfasts to motorbike rental (200B to 250B), flight bookings, visa runs (1300B), airport pick-ups and bus schedules. You can also arrange a car for day trips to Laem Son National Park (2000B return).

Getting There & Away

Ranong Airport is 22km south of town. Nok Air (www.nokair.com) flies twice daily to Bangkok (Don Mueang).

The **bus terminal** (Th Phetkasem) is 1km southeast of the centre. The blue *sŏrng·tăa·ou* 2 (passenger pick-up truck) passes the terminal. From here, minivans head to Surat Thani (200B, 3½ hours, 6am and 2pm) and Chumphon (160B, two hours, hourly 7am to 5pm).

Getting Around

Motorcycle taxis (Th Ruangrat) cluster along Th Ruangrat and take you almost anywhere in town for 50B, including **Tha Saphan Plaa**, 5km southwest of the centre, for boats to Myanmar, and **Tha Ko Phayam**, 6km southwest of the centre, for Ko Chang and Ko Phayam. The red **sŏrng·tăa·ou 4** stops near the piers (20B).

Pon's Place helps with motorcycle and car rentals and offers shuttle vans from its office/the airport to the piers (70/200B).

Ko Chang

เกาะช้าง

The little-visited, rustic isle of Ko Chang is a long way (in every respect) from its much more popular Trat Province namesake. The speciality here is no-frills living, and electricity and wi-fi are still scarce. An all-pervading quiet lies over the island, with the hum of modern life replaced by the sound of the sea. Between May and October (low season) it's beyond mellow and many places shut down.

Wide west-coast **Ao Yai** has gorgeous marbled white-and-black sand in the south, which obscures the otherwise clear sea. White-sand snobs will be happiest on Ao Yai's north end. A short trail leads south over the bluff to **Ao Tadaeng**, a boulder-strewn beach and the island's best sunset spot.

Inland is the tiny village capital, cashew orchards and rubber plantations. Dirt trails wind around and across the island and if you're lucky, you'll spot sea eagles, Andaman kites and hornbills floating above the mangroves.

Activities

Aladdin Dive Safari DIVING

(☎087 274 7601; www.aladdindivesafari.com; Cashew Resort, Ao Yai; 2 dives 5800B; ⏲10am-6pm Nov-May) A relatively flash, long-established liveaboard operation that runs day trips to the Surin and Similan Islands, Open Water Dive courses (18,700B to 19,800B) and liveaboards to Myanmar's Mergui Archipelago, the Surins, the Similans, Ko Phi-Phi, Hin Daeng and Hin Muang (15,800B to 19,800B).

BUSES FROM RANONG

DESTINATION	FARE (B)	DURATION (HR)	FREQUENCY
Bangkok	403-627	9-10	7.30am, 8.10am, 10.30am, 1.30pm, 3.30pm, 7.30pm, 8pm (VIP), 8.30pm (VIP)
Chumphon	150	2	hourly 7am-5pm
Hat Yai	380	7	6am, 10am, 8pm
Khao Lak	165	3½	hourly 6.30am-5.45pm
Krabi	210	6	7am, 10am, 2pm
Phang-Nga	180	5	7am, 10am, 2pm
Phuket	225	5-6	hourly 6.30am-5.45pm
Surat Thani	190	4-5	hourly 6am-4pm

Om Tao YOGA
(☎ 085 470 9312; www.omtao.net; Ao Yai; classes 300B) German-run studio with daily yoga (8.30am) November to April. Classes are by request at other times.

Sleeping & Eating

Simple bamboo huts are the norm. Expect a bed, mosquito net, basic bathroom, hammock, small balcony and little else. Most are only open from November to April. Electricity is limited; some places have solar and wind power.

Most lodgings are in Ao Yai or tucked away on Ao Tadaeng, immediately south. To really get away from it all, head to the northwest coast. The only restaurants are inside the resorts.

★ **Crocodile Rock** GUESTHOUSE $
(☎ 080 533 4138; tonn1970@yahoo.com; Ao Yai; bungalows 400-700B; ⊙ Oct-Apr; Wi-fi) Simple metal-roofed bamboo bungalows with hammocks perched on Ao Yai's serene southern headland with superb bay views. The classy kitchen turns out homemade yoghurt, breads, cookies, good espresso, and a variety of veggie and seafood dishes. It's popular, so book ahead.

Sangsuree Bungalows BUNGALOW $
(☎ 081 2511 7726; bungalow.sangsuree@gmail.com; Ao Takien; bungalows 300-500B; Wi-fi) Ko Chang's northwest coast is dotted with hidden bays and Sangsuree's seven basic bungalows are positioned just above one of them commanding fine sea views. Run by a charming husband-and-wife team, this is a classic, old-school Thai island chill-out spot, with communal meals and much lazing around. It's a 10 minute walk to a sandy swimming beach.

Little Italy BUNGALOW $
(☎ 084 851 2760; daniel060863@yahoo.it; Ao Yai; r 400-500B; Wi-fi) Just three immaculate bungalows attached to a Thai-Italian restaurant amid the trees towards the southern end of Ao Yai. Two are stilted split-level concrete-and-wood jobs encircled by wraparound verandahs. The third concrete bungalow is back on earth, with a tiled bathroom. Book ahead in high season.

Sunset Bungalows BUNGALOW $
(☎ 084 339 5224; Ao Yai; bungalows 300-600B; ⊙ Oct–mid-Apr) Sweet wooden bungalows with bamboo decks and attached Thai-style bathrooms sit back in the trees along Ao Yai's finest (northern) patch of beach. Staff are as friendly as they come.

Information

Wi-fi has arrived at a few places, including Koh Chang Resort (southern Ao Yai). Connections are weak.

There are no ATMs.

Getting There & Around

From the centre of Ranong, *sŏrng·tăa·ou* (20B) and motorcycle taxis (50B) go from Th Ruangrat to Tha Ko Phayam pier near Saphan Plaa, from where two daily long-tail boats (200B, two hours) leave for Ko Chang at 9.30am and 2pm. In high season, they stop at the west-coast beaches, returning at approximately 8.30am and 1pm. During the monsoon, only one long-tail runs, at 2pm, docking at the main pier on the northeast coast.

During the November–April high season, two daily speedboats (350B, 30 minutes, 8.30am and 10.30am) travel between Ranong's Tha Ko Phayam and Ko Chang's northeast-coast pier. In low season, only the 8.30am speedboat runs.

High-season Ko Phayam–Ranong speedboats often drop off and pick up passengers in Ko Chang (350B) on request, though they're unreliable; get your resort to make (and confirm) the booking. You can charter long-tails to Ko Phayam (2000B) through Koh Chang Resort.

Motorcycle taxis meet boats, charging 100B between the northeast-coast pier and Ao Yai.

Ko Phayam เกาะพยาม

Technically part of Laem Son National Park (p272), Ko Phayam is fringed with beautiful soft-white beaches and is becoming increasingly popular as a family destination. If you're coming from Phuket or Ko Phi-Phi, it'll feel refreshingly wild and dozy. The spectacular northwest and southwest coasts are dotted with rustic bungalows, small-scale resorts, breezy sand-side restaurants and barefoot beach bars. Fauna includes wild pigs, monkeys and tremendous bird life (sea eagles, herons, hornbills).

The island's one 'village' (on the east coast, beside the main pier) caters mostly to tourists. But hit it during a festival (say the February Cashew Festival) and you'll see that the locals still have a firm grip on their island.

Narrow motorcycle pathways, concrete roadways and dirt trails run across the island's wooded interior; some are rutted to the point of hazardous – drive slowly.

Sights & Activities

Ko Phayam is dotted with gorgeous blonde sands, but don't expect to have them to yourself between November and April.

The most impressive beaches are **Ao Yai** (Long Beach), to the southwest, where you can rent boogie boards and surfboards (150B per hour), and **Ao Khao Kwai** (Buffalo Bay) to the northwest, a golden cove with jungle-clad bluffs. **Ao Mea Mai**, south of the pier on the east coast, is OK for swimming and popular with families.

Ko Phayam's main drawback is that the snorkelling isn't great; high sea temperatures have killed off all the coral. But the Surin Islands are close, and you can hop on liveaboard dive expeditions or speedboat transfers. **Phayam Divers** (☎086 995 2598; www.phayamlodge.com; Ao Yai; 2 dives 4900B; ⏲Nov-Apr) offers dive trips to the Surins, plus multiday liveaboards to the Surins, Ko Tachai and Ko Bon, as well as PADI Open Water courses (14,900B). Snorkellers are welcome too.

Wat Phayam BUDDHIST TEMPLE
(วัดเกาะพยาม; ⏲dawn-dusk) FREE Shrouded in jungle just north of the main pier, on Ko Phayam's east coast, you'll find a majestic golden Buddha flanked by a three-headed *naga* (serpent).

Sleeping & Eating

Many resorts stay open year-round. It's now more or less standard to have 24-hour power. The west-coast beaches are the most popular places to stay. The east coast is quieter and you're close to the village, but the beaches are not as good.

Ao Yai อ่าวใหญ่

Frog Beach House HOTEL $
(☎083 542 7559; www.frogbeachhouse.com; bungalows 500-1400B; 📶) Well-kept, traditional Thai-style hardwood chalets at the north end of Ao Yai, with wooden floors, outdoor bathrooms, glass-bowl sinks and mosquito nets, line up behind a nice slab of sand beside a small stream.

Bamboo Bungalows BUNGALOW $$
(☎077 820012; www.bamboo-bungalows.com; bungalows 750-2600B; 📶) Smart, rustic bungalows come with indoor/outdoor bathrooms, some decoration and balconies with hammocks. All are scattered throughout a leafy garden set just back from the middle of lovely Ao Yai. The beachfront restaurant is pretty good and kayaks and boogie boards can be hired. It has 24-hour electricity in high season.

Aow Yai Bungalows BUNGALOW $$
(☎098 313 1777; www.aowyaibungalows.com; bungalows 700-4000B; ❄📶) This French-Thai operation is the thatched bamboo bungalow pioneer that kicked it all off two decades ago. Choose between decent, rustic small wooden-and-bamboo bungalows amid towering palms and pines, and larger beachfront wood models that sleep three or concrete bungalows. Only the most expensive have air-con. Located at the southeast end of Ao Yai.

Ban Nam Cha INTERNATIONAL $$
(Ao Yai; mains 100-250B; ⏲9am-6.30pm) Twinkling lights, prayer flags and driftwood signs adorn this artsy, easygoing food shack. Tuck into fantastic homemade panini (garlic mushroom, cashew-nut pesto), sandwiches, cakes and a range of Burmese, European and vegetarian treats, and peruse a paperback from the lending library. It's 500m inland from central Ao Yai. Note that hours can vary.

Ao Khao Kwai อ่าวเขาควาย

Mr Gao BUNGALOW $$
(☎077 870222; www.mr-gao-phayam.com; bungalows 1000-1800B; @📶) These sturdy, varnished wood-and-brick or bamboo bungalows are popular with activity-oriented couples and families and are decent-sized coming with mosquito nets, tiled bathrooms and front decks. The owner arranges kayak rental, snorkelling and multiday trips to the Surin Islands. Now has 24-hour electricity, while the most expensive rooms have air-con (you'll pay a hefty surcharge if you want to use it).

Baan Klong Kleng BUNGALOW $$
(☎089 772 5090; www.baanklongkleng.com; r 1300-2000B; ⏲mid-Oct–Apr; 📶) Simple,

clean wooden bungalows cascade through trees to a luscious chunk of beach. They're comfy, if not overly exciting, with stylish ceramic-bowl sinks and semi-open bathrooms. The fabulous open-walled beachside **restaurant** (Ao Khao Kwai; mains 150-300B; ⌚8am-10pm mid-Oct-Apr;) has a fun vibe, dishing up fragrant Thai curries (veg versions available), delicious breakfasts and fusion specials like green-curry pasta.

Ao Hin Khow อ่าวหินขาว

PP Land BUNGALOW $$

(☎082 806 0413; www.ppland-heavenbeach.com; bungalows 900-1400B;) The concrete bungalows at this Thai-Belgian–owned ecolodge are powered by wind and sun, with 24-hour electricity and hammocks on terraces overlooking the sea. The owners bake cakes, run an organic garden, treat sewage and make their own all-natural laundry detergent.

The drawback is that you're on the least impressive beach on Ko Phayam. The resort is also adults only.

Information

Most resorts have wi-fi, but signals are often weak. There are no ATMs; bring cash with you.

Getting There & Away

Two daily ferries at 9.30am and 2pm travel from Ranong's Tha Ko Phayam (p269), 6km southwest of town, to Ko Phayam (200B, two hours), returning at 8.30am and 3pm. During the November–April high season, speedboats (350B, 35 minutes) make the run almost hourly from 7.30am to 5.30pm, returning to the mainland at 8am, 9am, 9.30am, 11.30am, noon, 3.30pm, 4pm and 4.30pm.

High-season speedboats go from Ko Phayam to Ko Chang (350B, 20 minutes) en route to Ranong at 8.30am, 9am, noon, 12.30pm, 3pm and 3.30pm, though they aren't completely reliable.

Getting Around

Motorcycle taxis from the pier to Ao Khao Kwai/Ao Yai cost 50/70B. Walking distances are long; it's about 45 minutes from the pier to Ao Khao Kwai, the nearest bay. You can rent motorbikes (around 250B) in the village (best) and from larger resorts; you'll need one to explore properly.

Laem Son National Park อุทยานแห่งชาติแหลมสน

This serene 315-sq-km **national park** (☎077 861431; www.dnp.go.th; adult/child 200/100B; ⌚8am-4.30pm) covers 60km of Andaman coastline (Thailand's longest protected shore) and over 20 islands, including increasingly popular Ko Phayam. It's 85% open sea. Much of the coast is fringed by mangroves and laced with tidal channels, home to fish, deer, macaques, civets, giant squirrels and over 100 bird species, including white-bellied sea eagles.

The most accessible beach is lovely, casuarina-backed 3km **Hat Bang Ben**, home to the park headquarters and accommodation. To the south, peninsulas jut out into the ocean concealing isolated coves accessible only by long-tail. All these beaches are allegedly safe for swimming year-round. From Hat Bang Ben you can see Ko Kam Yai, Ko Kam Noi, Mu Ko Yipun, Ko Khang Khao and, to the north, Ko Phayam. If there's a prettier sunset picnic spot in the northern Andaman, we missed it.

Hat Praphat, 56km south of Hat Bang Ben, is a turtle nesting ground.

Nature trails wind off from the park headquarters, where you can arrange one-day boat trips (2500B, maximum 10 people) to nearby islands. Turn left (south) towards the pier just before park headquarters to access the beach without paying park fees.

At **Wasana Resort** (☎077 861434; www.wasanaresort.org; Hat Bang Ben; bungalow fan/air-con 450/800B;), the welcoming Dutch-Thai owners make a gloriously authentic gado-gado, organise Laem Son day trips, lend bicycles and are full of fantastic ideas for exploring the park (ask about the stunning 10km trek around the headland). The national park offers simple air-conditioned concrete **bungalows and camping** (☎077 861431, in Bangkok 02 562 0760; www.dnp.go.th; Hat Bang Ben; r 1000-1800B, campsite per person 30B, with tent hire 270B;).

Getting There & Away

The Laem Son National Park turn-off is 44km south of Ranong on the west side of Hwy 4, between the Km 657 and Km 658 markers. Buses heading south from Ranong will drop you here (ask for Hat Bang Ben; 50B, one hour). You'll have to flag down a vehicle going towards the park or grab a taxi (200B) at the roadside agency. It's 10km from Hwy 4 to the park entrance.

A return taxi from Ranong is 2000B. Pon's Place (p269) in Ranong can arrange one.

PHANG-NGA PROVINCE

Jungle-shrouded mountains carved up by thick rivers leading to aqua bays sprinkled with sheer limestone karsts and, below, some of Thailand's finest underwater treasures. This is national park territory, with four of Thailand's finest conservation areas in fairly close proximity.

Phang-Nga is very seasonal. From mid-October to mid-April, visitors flood in for the clear waters, snow-white beaches and colourful reefs. But far fewer arrive during the May–October monsoon, leaving you plenty of space.

Khuraburi คุระบุรี

Blink and you'll miss it. But, if you keep your eyes wide open, you'll enjoy this soulful, dusty, roadside gateway to the Surin Islands. For local inhabitants, Khuraburi is a tiny market town relied on by hundreds of squid fishers. Until the Thai government started cracking down on people smuggling, the surrounding area had an unsavoury reputation as being a key entry point for people being trafficked or smuggled into Thailand from Myanmar.

Andaman Discoveries (☎087 917 7165; www.andamandiscoveries.com; 120/2 Mu 1, Th Phetkasem; 3-day trip per person 6000B; ⌚8.30am-5.30pm Mon-Fri) runs award-winning, community-based tours, snorkelling trips to the Surin Islands with the *chow lair* ('sea gypsies'; also spelt *chao leh*), village homestays and ecotours to Khao Sok National Park (p275). It also manages community projects that take volunteers, and can rent bicycles for 150B per day.

If you're sticking around, **Boon Piya Resort** (☎081 752 5457; 175/1 Th Phetkasem; bungalows 650B; ❄📶) offers spacious, sparkling-clean, modern concrete bungalows with tiled floors, hot-water bathrooms and little balconies. The helpful owner can book transport to/from the Surin Islands and Ko Phra Thong, as can **Tom & Am Tour** (☎086 272 0588; 298/3 Mu 1, Th Phetkasem; ⌚24hr).

Don't miss the **morning market** (Th Phetkasem; mains 20-40B; ⌚6-10am) at the north end of town: stallholders fry chicken, grill coconut waffles, and bubble kettles with Thai doughnuts to be dipped in thick, sugary green curry.

The small **night market** (Th Phetkasem; mains from 30B; ⌚3pm-7.30pm), actually at its peak in the late afternoon, offers noodle dishes and good fried chicken. It's just to the side of the Chinese temple, a 10 minute walk south of town along the highway.

Getting There & Away

Most buses running between Ranong (105B, two hours) and Phuket (150B, four hours) stop in Khuraburi. Take a Phuket-bound bus to Takua Pa (50B, 1¼ hours), 55km south, to transfer to further destinations including Khao Sok National Park.

The pier for the Surin Islands and Ko Phra Thong is 9km northwest of town. Whoever books your boat to the islands will arrange free pier transfer.

Surin Islands Marine National Park

อุทยานแห่งชาติหมู่เกาะสุรินทร์

The five gorgeous isles of the **Surin Islands Marine National Park** (☎076 491378; www.dnp.go.th; adult/child 500/300B; ⌚mid-Oct–mid-May) sit 60km offshore, 5km from the Thailand–Myanmar marine border. Healthy rainforest, spectacular white-sand beaches in sparkling, sheltered bays, and rocky headlands that jut into the ocean characterise these granite-outcrop islands.

Superbly clear water in never-ending shades of jade and turquoise makes for easy marine-life spotting, with underwater visibility of up to 30m outside monsoon. These shielded waters attract *chow lair,* an ethnic group of Malay origin who live on Ko Surin Tai during the May–November monsoon. Here they're known as Moken, from the local word *oken* ('salt water').

Ko Surin Tai (south) and Ko Surin Neua (north) are the two largest islands. Park headquarters, an information office (p275) and all visitor facilities are at Ao Chong Khad on southwest Ko Surin Neua. Khuraburi is the park's jumping-off point.

Sights & Activities

Ban Moken VILLAGE

(Ao Bon, Ko Surin Tai) Ban Moken on east Ko Surin Tai welcomes visitors. Post-tsunami, the Moken (from the Sea Gypsy ethnic group) have re-settled in this sheltered bay, where a major ancestral worship ceremony, **Loi Reua**, takes place each April. The colourfully carved bamboo poles dotted around embody Moken ancestors. This population experienced no casualties during the 2004 Boxing Day tsunami that wiped out the village, because they understood nature's signs and evacuated to the hilltop.

The Surin Islands Marine National Park runs two-hour trips from Ko Surin Neua to Ban Moken (150B per person, minimum five people). You'll stroll through the stilted village, where you can ask permission/guidance for hiking the 800m **Chok Madah trail** over the jungle-clad hills to an empty beach. Handicrafts for sale help support the local economy and clothing donations are accepted. Please refrain from bringing along alcohol and sweets; alcoholism is a growing problem among Moken.

Diving & Snorkelling

The park's dive sites include **Ko Surin Tai**, **Ko Torinla** (south) and **HQ Channel** between the two main islands. **Richelieu Rock**, a seamount 14km southeast, is also technically in the park and happens to be one of the Andaman's premier dive sites (if not the best). Manta rays pay visits and whale sharks are sometimes spotted here during March and April.

There's no dive facility inside the park, so dive trips (four-day liveaboards from 20,000B) must be booked through centres in Khao Lak, Phuket and Ranong. Transfers are usually included. There's a 200B park diving fee per day, plus the national park fee (adult/child 500/300B), which is valid for five days.

Though recent bleaching of hard corals means snorkelling isn't quite as fantastic as it once was, you'll still see plenty of colourful fish and soft corals. The most vibrant soft corals we saw were at **Ao Mai Yai**, off southwest Ko Surin Neua. There's good snorkelling at **Ao Sabparod** and **Ao Pak Kaad**, where you might spot turtles, off east and south Ko Surin Tai. More fish swim off tiny Ko Pajumba, but the coral isn't great. Ao Suthep, off north Ko Surin Tai, has hundreds of colourful fish.

The nearest decompression chamber is in Phuket. In the case of an accident, dive operators will contact the chamber's Khao Lak–based SSS Ambulance (p281), which meets boats and rushes injured divers south to Phuket.

Half-day snorkelling trips (150B per person, snorkel hire 160B) leave the island headquarters at 9am and 2pm. You'll be mostly in the company of Thais, who generally splash around semi-clothed in life jackets. For more serene snorkelling, charter a long-tail from the national park (3000B per day) or, better yet, directly from the Moken in Ban Moken.

Tour operators in Khuraburi and Khao Lak organise snorkelling day trips to the park (adult/child 3700/2450B).

Greenview Tour OUTDOORS

(☎ 076 472070; www.toursurinislands.com; 140/89 Mu 3, Khuraburi; ⏱ 7.30am-9pm) Impressive in safety, service and value, Greenview runs excellent Surin Islands snorkelling day trips (adult/child 3500/2100B) with knowledgeable guides. Rates include transfers, snacks, equipment and a delicious lunch. Also organises multi-night stays in the Surins.

Wildlife-Watching & Hiking

Around park headquarters, you can explore the forest fringes and spot crab-eating macaques and some of the 57 resident bird species, including the beautiful Nicobar pigeon, endemic to the Andaman islands, and the elusive beach thick-knee. Along the coast you're likely to see Brahminy kites and reef herons. Twelve species of bat live here, most noticeably the tree-dwelling fruit bat (flying fox).

Sleeping & Eating

Ko Surin Neua is the only island it is possible to stay on. The **bungalows** (☎ 076 472145; www.dnp.go.th; Ko Surin Neua; r 2000-3000B, campsite per person 80B, with tent hire 300B; ⏱ mid-Oct–mid-May; ❄) are good enough, if over-priced for what you get, although it can feel seriously crowded when full (around 300 people). The clientele is mostly Thai, giving the place a lively holiday-camp vibe. You can also camp here (tents can be hired). Book well in advance.

The two park restaurants, where the accommodation is, serve reasonable Thai food; try **Ao Mai Ngam Restaurant** (Ko Surin

Neua; mains 80-180B, set menu 120-280B; ⌚7.30-9am, noon-2pm & 6.30-8pm).

Information

Surin Islands Marine National Park Office (Ko Surin Neua; ⌚7.30am-8.30pm mid-Oct–mid-May) Offers information on the islands and accommodation bookings.

Getting There & Away

If you're not visiting on an organised tour, tour operator speedboats (return 1800B, 1¼ hours one-way) leave around 9am, return between 1pm and 4pm and honour open tickets. Return whenever you please, but confirm your ticket with Ko Surin Neua's park office the night before.

Khao Sok National Park

อุทยานแห่งชาติเขาสก

If you've had enough of beach-bumming, venture inland to the wondrous 738-sq-km **Khao Sok National Park** (077 395154; www.khaosok.com; Khao Sok; adult/child 300/150B; ⌚6am-6pm). Many believe this lowland jungle (Thailand's rainiest spot) dates back 160 million years, making it one of the world's oldest rainforests, and it's interspersed by hidden waterfalls and caves.

Khao Sok's vast terrain makes it one of the last viable habitats for large mammals. During rainy months you may spot bears, boars, gaurs, tapirs, gibbons, deer, marbled cats, wild elephants and perhaps even a tiger. And you'll find more than 300 bird species, 38 bat varieties and one of the world's largest (and smelliest) flowers, the increasingly rare *Rafflesia kerrii*, which, in Thailand, grows only in Khao Sok.

Animal-spotting aside, the best time to visit is the December–April dry season. During the June–October monsoon, trails get slippery and leeches come out in force. The upside is that the waterfalls are in full flow.

Sights & Activities

Kayaking (800B) and tubing (500B; rainy season) are popular activities. We strongly suggest avoiding the elephant tour.

The road leading 1.8km northeast from Rte 401 to park headquarters (p277) is lined with guesthouses and travel agents offering park tours and guide services. We recommend a two-day, one-night canoeing and hiking trip (2500B; per person) to Chiaw Lan, where you sleep on the lake in floating huts. Book through the park headquarters or any tour agency: the price is the same everywhere.

Chiaw Lan Lake LAKE

(เขื่อนเชี่ยวหลาน; day/overnight trip 1500/2500B) This stunning 165-sq-km lake sits 65km (an hour's drive) east of park headquarters (p277). It was created in 1982 by an enormous shale-clay dam called Ratchaprapha (Kheuan Ratchaprapha or Chiaw Lan). Limestone outcrops protruding from the lake reach up to 960m, over three times higher than Phang-Nga's formations. Most lake visits involve a day or overnight tour (including transfers, boats and guides).

Charter boats (2000B per day) from local fisherfolk at the dam's entrance to explore the coves, canals, caves and cul-de-sacs along the lakeshore.

Two caves can be accessed by foot from the southwestern shore. **Tham Nam Thalu** contains striking limestone formations and subterranean streams. Visiting during the rainy season isn't recommended; there have been fatalities. **Tham Si Ru** features four converging passageways used as a hideout by communist insurgents between 1975 and 1982.

Hiking

Khao Sok hiking is excellent. Most guesthouses and agencies arrange hiking tours (full day 1200B to 2000B); just ensure you find a certified guide (they wear official

VILLAGE OF THE DEAD

Ban Sok, the village on the banks of Mae Nam Sok, near the entrance to Khao Sok National Park, has a past so dark it had to rename itself. In the 1940s a vicious wave of smallpox swept through Takua Pa and Phuket, decimating populations. People escaped high into these limestone mountains. Sadly, death followed in such numbers that the village they settled in in 1944 became known as Ban Sop, Village of the Dead. By 1961, when Rte 401 was built to connect Surat Thani with Phang-Nga, the villagers had rebranded, naming their village Ban Sok, which technically means nothing at all.

badges). The park headquarters can also line you up with a reliable guide (1200B per day).

The park headquarters hands out basic hiking maps. You can hike independently from the headquarters to the waterfall at **Wing Hin** (2.8km); hikes to the waterfalls at **Bang Hua Rad** (3km), the 11-tiered waterfall at **Sip-Et Chan** (4km), **Than Sawan** (6km), the most impressive and least-visited waterfall, and **Than Kloy** (7km) require a guide.

Sleeping

All guesthouses have wi-fi, although connections aren't always great.

Jungle Huts BUNGALOW **$**
(☎077 395160; www.khaosokjunglehuts.com; 242 Mu 6, Khao Sok; r fan/air-con 400/1200B; ❄📶) This popular hang-out contains a collection of decent, individually styled bungalows, all with bathrooms and porches. Choose from plain stilted bamboo huts, bigger wooden editions, pink-washed concrete bungalows, or rooms along vertiginous walkways.

Tree Tops River Huts BUNGALOW **$$**
(☎081 747 3030; www.treetopsriverhuts.com; 54 Mu 6, Khao Sok; r 500-1200B; ❄📶) Clean and sturdy, if ageing, simply furnished pebble-dashed bungalows with porches and small bathrooms sit high on stilts in the trees at this riverside spot near the park headquarters. The cheapest are fan-only and more basic, but they do have hot water. The pleasant, semi-open restaurant overlooks the river.

Art's Riverview Jungle Lodge GUESTHOUSE **$$**
(☎090 167 6818; www.info@artsriverviewlodge.com; 54/3 Mu 6, Khao Sok; r 1200-2400B; 📶) In a monkey-filled jungle bordering a rushing river with a limestone cliff-framed swimming hole, Art's enjoys Khao Sok's prettiest setting. Stilted brick, shingled and all-wood bungalows are spacious and comfy and come with balconies, many offering river views. There's a host of family-friendly activities. It's signposted 1.5km northeast off Rte 401.

Nonguests can visit the swimming hole here, which is also popular with locals and monkeys.

Jasmine Garden RESORT **$$$**
(☎082 282 3209; www.khaosokjasmine.com; 35/6 Mu 6, Khao Sok; d 3800B; ❄📶🏊) Family-run Jasmine hosts some of Khao Sok's classiest non-luxury lodgings, plus cooking classes (800B). Five orange-toned concrete bungalows open onto roomy terraces overlooking a warm-blue pool with sensational cliff vistas. Delicate interiors involve wood-carved beds, Buddha paintings, tiled floors and plenty of teak. Book ahead.

★ **Elephant Hills** RESORT **$$$**
(☎076 381703; www.elephanthills.com; 170 Mu 7, Tambon Klong Sok; 3 days all-inclusive from 20,300B; 📶🏊) 🍃 Whether you're a five-strong family, honeymooning backpacker couple or a soloist, this resort makes everyone smile. Above Mae Nam Sok, at the foot of stunning limestone mountains draped in misty jungle, Khao Sok's only top-end tented camp offers rootsy Serengeti-style luxury. It's real glamping: the luxury tents have wood furnishings, full, big bathrooms, skylights and hammocks on porches.

All-inclusive prices cover meals, guided hikes and canoe trips downriver for a night at its elephant camp, where 12 lovely ladies (rescued from other camps where they were forced to carry tourists around) are treated kindly. You get to feed, bathe and spend quality time with them. It's a special experience. Another option is a night at their floating **Rainforest Camp** (Chiaw Lan Lake). Reservations only.

Eating

★ **Pawn's Restaurant** THAI **$$**
(Khao Sok; mains 110-250B; ⌚9am-10pm; 🌿) A friendly all-female team runs this humble but deservedly popular open-sided eatery: your go-to spot for deliciously spiced curries, from searing red pumpkin-and-veg to beautifully creamy tofu or chicken massaman, and huge hearty breakfasts. It's 500m southwest of the national park headquarters.

Chao Italian Restaurant ITALIAN **$$**
(☎087 264 2106; Khao Sok; mains 100-320B; ⌚noon-10pm; 📶) The go-to spot for fine,

KHAO SOK TOURS

Tours in and around Khao Sok can be up to 50% cheaper when booked through guesthouses or travel agents around the park itself. Tours booked from destinations further afield (Phuket or Khao Lak) include higher-priced transport and tour-agent commissions.

wood-fired pizzas, cooked by a veteran of Italian restaurants on Phuket, as well pasta, salads and your usual Thai curries, all served by smiley staff underneath a high thatched roof. It's a couple of minutes south of the national park headquarters.

Information

Khao Sok National Park Headquarters (077 395154; www.khaosok.com; 6am-6pm) About 1.8km northeast off Rte 401, exiting near the Km 109 marker; helpful maps and information.

There are several ATMS along the road leading to the park headquarters.

Getting There & Away

From Surat catch a bus going towards Takua Pa; from the Andaman Coast, take a Surat Thani–bound bus. Buses stop on Rte 401, 1.8km southwest of the visitors centre. If touts don't meet you, you'll have to walk to your chosen guesthouse (50m to 2km). Most minivans will drop you at your accommodation.

There is a daily bus to Bangkok (1000B, 11 hours) at 6pm.

Daily minivan departures include the following:

DESTINATION	FARE (B)	DURATION (HR)
Khao Lak	200	1¼
Ko Lanta	800	5
Ko Tao	1000	8
Krabi	350	3
Phang-Nga	250	2
Surat Thani	200	1

Ko Phra Thong & Ko Ra

เกาะพระทอง/เกาะระ

According to legend, pirates buried a golden Buddha beneath the sands at Ko Phra Thong (Golden Buddha Island) many centuries ago. The statue was never found, but the island's modern-day treasures are its endless sandy beaches, mangroves, vast bird life and rare orchids.

Home to around 300 people, this long, slender, wooded island is as quiet as a night on the open ocean. Fishing (squid, prawns, jellyfish) remains its main industry; the local delicacy is pungent *gà·pì* (fermented prawn paste). On the southern west coast lies 10km of virgin golden-sand beach kissed by blue sea.

Immediately north is barely inhabited Ko Ra, encircled by golden beaches and mangroves. This small isle is a mountainous jungle slab with impressive wildlife, including over 100 bird species, leopard cats, flying lemurs, wild pigs, monitor lizards, scaly anteaters and slow lorises.

Sleeping & Eating

Mr Chuoi's BUNGALOW $

(087 898 4636, 084 855 9886; www.mrchuoibarandhut.com; Ko Phra Thong; bungalows 500-750B;) Simple, attractive, artsy wood-and-bamboo bungalows, on the island's northwest coast, with evening electricity. You'll also find a tame deer, a fun bar and a decent restaurant, enlivened by Mr Chuoi himself. Call ahead and he'll arrange transport to Ko Phra Thong.

Golden Buddha Beach Resort BUNGALOW $$$

(081 892 2208, 081 895 2242; www.goldenbuddharesort.com; Ko Phra Thong; bungalows 3500-8500B; Oct-May;) The area's poshest resort attracts yogis, couples and families keen for a secluded getaway. Accommodation is in uniquely designed, naturalistic-chic, privately owned wooden houses, short- or long-term; there are big family-sized house options too. Rooms have open-air bathrooms, wood-carved interiors and glimpses of the fabulous 10km beach through surrounding forest and gardens. Everyone congregates at the mosaic-floored club house **restaurant-bar** (mains 220-400B; 7.30am-9.30pm;).

Horizon BUNGALOW $$$

(081 894 7195; www.horizonecoresort.com; Ko Phra Thong; bungalows 1300-1900B) This northwest-beach ecolodge has seven roomy, shaggy-haired, wood-and-bamboo bungalows made from natural local products from renewable sources (wherever possible) and only use fans; they sleep two or four. Horizon organises hiking tours to neighbouring Ko Ra (1600B, minimum three people) and has the island's only dive school, **Blue Guru** (096 284 8740; www.blue-guru.org; Ko Phra Thong; 2 dives 4500-6500B; Oct-May), ideally positioned for underwater explorations of the nearby Surin Islands.

Getting There & Away

You could theoretically charter a long-tail from the Khuraburi pier to Ko Phra Thong (return 1500B), but boatmen can be hard to find. For the same price, your accommodation on Ko Phra Thong, or tour operators and guesthouses in Khuraburi, will arrange your transport.

Khao Lak & Around เขาหลัก

When people refer to Khao Lak, they're usually talking about a series of beaches hugging Phang-Nga's west coastline, about 70km north of Phuket. With easy day trips to the Similan and Surin Islands, Khao Sok and Khao Lak/Lam Ru National Parks, or even Phuket, the area makes a central base for exploring the northern Andaman.

Southernmost **Hat Khao Lak** gives way to **Hat Nang Thong**, both within walking distance of Khao Lak proper (Khao Lak Town), a bland but convenient jumble of low-rise hotels, restaurants, bars, shops and tour and dive operators sited along grey Hwy 4.

About 2.5km north, **Hat Bang Niang** is a quieter version of sandy bliss with skinnier beaches. **Hat Pakarang** and **Hat Bang Sak**, 12km to 13km north of Hat Khao Lak, are a sleepy, unbroken sandy stretch surrounded by thick mangroves and rubber-tree plantations. You'll feel like you've really escaped it all there.

Sights

Khao Lak/Lam Ru National Park NATIONAL PARK
(อุทยานแห่งชาติเขาหลัก-ลำรู่; ☎076 485243; www.dnp.go.th; adult/child 200/100B; ⊙8am-4.30pm) Immediately south of Hat Khao Lak, this vast 125-sq-km park is a collage of sea cliffs, 1000m-high hills, beaches, estuaries, waterfalls, forested valleys and mangroves. Wildlife includes hornbills, drongos, tapirs, serows, monkeys, Bengal monitor lizards and Asiatic black bears.

The park office and visitors centre, 3km south of Khao Lak proper off Hwy 4, has little printed information, but there's a scenic open-air **restaurant** (off Hwy 4, Khao Lak; mains 130-250B; ⊙8.30am-7pm) perched on a shady slope overlooking the sea. From here, there's a fairly easy 3km (one-hour) round-trip nature trail south along the cape to often-deserted **Hat Lek**.

Activities & Tours

Diving and snorkelling day excursions to the Similan and Surin Islands are immensely popular but, if you can, go for a liveaboard. The islands are around 70km from the mainland (1½ hours by speedboat), so liveaboards allow you a more relaxing trip sans masses of day trippers. Dive shops offer liveaboard package trips from around 19,000B for three days and 35,000B for six days, and day trips for 5000B to 6000B.

Day trips normally involve two dives. On the multiday trips, you'll sink below the sea's surface up to four times daily. While both the Similan and Surin Islands have experienced vast coral bleaching in recent years, Richelieu Rock (p274), just north of the Surin Islands, is still the crème de la crème of the region's dive sites, frequented by whale sharks from March to April. **Ko Bon** and **Ko Tachai** are rewarding Similan sites due to the traffic of giant manta rays. Most dive shops welcome snorkellers, and tour operators offer day trips from 3700B.

Open Water certification costs between 10,500B and 16,650B. Beginners can join one-day Similans Discover Scuba trips for around 6000B. Rates exclude the 700B national park diving fee.

The Similan and Surin dive seasons run from mid-October to mid-May, when the national parks are open. Trips in April and May are weather dependent.

★**Fantastic** SNORKELLING
(☎076 485998; www.fantasticsimilan.com; adult/child 3200/2200B; ⊙mid-Oct–mid-May) Fantastic is an over-the-top frolic of a Similans snorkelling tour featuring players from the local cross-dressing cabaret as guides. It's a trip duplicated nowhere else on earth; they get you to the prime snorkel sites too. Prices include hotel pick-ups from Phuket or Khao Lak. Bookings essential online or by phone.

★**Wicked Diving** DIVING
(☎085 795 2221; www.wickeddiving.com; Th Nangthong, Khao Lak; 2 dives 5700B; ⊙Oct-May) Out to change the world 'one dive at a time', Wicked is an exceptionally well-run, environmentally conscious outfit. It offers diving and snorkelling day and overnight trips (three-day Surin Islands snorkelling trip 12,300B), a range of liveaboards (three-day

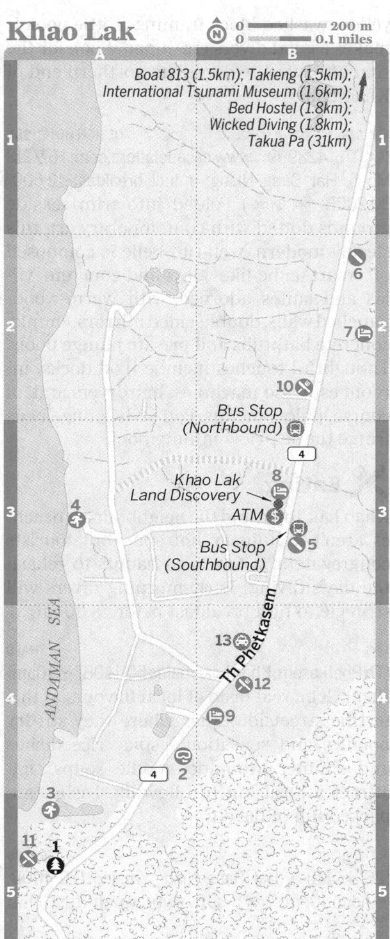

Khao Lak

Sights

1 Khao Lak/Lam Ru National Park........A5

Activities, Courses & Tours

2 Fantastic........A4
3 Hat Khao Lak........A5
4 Hat Nang Thong........A3
5 Sea Bees........B3
6 Sea Dragon Dive Centre........B2

Sleeping

7 Fasai House........B2
8 To Zleep........B3
9 Walker's Inn........B4

Eating

10 Go Pong........B2
11 Khao Lak/Lam Ru National Park Restaurant........A5
12 PhuKhaoLak........B4

Transport

13 Cheaper Than Hotel........B4

Similans trip from 19,400B), conservation trips and a range of dive courses (PADI Open Water certification costs 16,500B).

Sea Bees DIVING
(076 485174; www.sea-bees.com; Th Phetkasem, Khao Lak; 2 dives 2900-4900B; 11am-7pm) Well-organised German-run dive operation that offers two-dive Similan day trips, one-day tasters (8500B), Open Water courses (16,650B) and advanced diver courses, plus Similans liveaboards (two day trip from 17,500B). Snorkellers can join day trips (2900B).

Sea Dragon Dive Centre DIVING
(076 485420; www.seadragondivecenter.com; Th Phetkasem, Khao Lak; 2 dives 6000B; 9am-9pm) Khao Lak's oldest dive centre, super-efficient Sea Dragon maintains high standards, running snorkelling day trips (3500B), wreck dives (2600B), Open Water Diver certification (10,500B to 15,000B) and an array of Similan and Surin Islands liveaboards (three-day trip from 10,500B). Look for the small swimming pool outside its office.

Khao Lak Land Discovery ADVENTURE
(076 485411; www.khaolaklanddiscovery.com; 21/5 Mu 7, Th Phetkasem, Khao Lak; 8am-8.30pm) This multilingual agency, one of Khao Lak's most reliable, runs adventure-activity day trips (adult/child 2200/1600B) to Khao Lak/Lam Ru National Park, and day and overnight excursions into Khao Sok National Park (two-day trip adult/child 6700/4700B). It can also organise snorkelling trips to the Similan Islands (adult/child 3700/2450B).

Sleeping

Cheaper accommodation dominates Khao Lak Town's congested centre, while three- and four-star resorts line the coast. High-end hotels dot Hat Pakarang and Hat Bang Sak. Book ahead if you're planning to be here in the November–April period.

Walker's Inn GUESTHOUSE $
(084 840 2689; www.walkersinn.com; 26/61 Mu 7, Th Phetkasem, Khao Lak; dm/r 250/600B;) A long-running backpacker fave, Walker's is looking its age these days. Rooms are old-fashioned and plain, if big, while the dorm is fan-only. But the price is right. The downstairs pub dishes up hearty breakfasts and Thai and Western classics. It rents motorbikes (200B per day).

Bed Hostel HOSTEL $
(087 387 4050; krittayakorn.d@gmail.com; 6/3 Mu 5, Hat Bang Niang; dm fan/air-con 370/450B, r 1600B;) This modest, family-run hostel lacks a communal area, but the compact dorms are clean and come with lockers and it's fine if you just want a place to lay your head, after a day's diving or lazing on the sand. It's a 15-minute walk to the beach.

To Zleep GUESTHOUSE $$
(076 485899; www.tozleep.com; Th Phetkasem, Khao Lak; r 700-1200B;) This chequered roadside block is a tasteful, hostel-feel guesthouse full of colourful wall murals and small, spotlessly smart rooms. Some have bunks, others doubles. All come coolly kitted out with minimalist furnishings, concrete floors and colour-on-white themes. It is worth spending more for the biggest and brightest rooms, which are corner mountain-view doubles.

Fasai House GUESTHOUSE $$
(076 485867; www.fasaihouse.com; 5/54 Mu 7, Khao Lak; r 950B;) One of Khao Lak's best budget choices, Fasai wins us over with its delightful staff and simple but immaculate, motel-style air-con rooms set in a warm yellow-washed block framing a little pool. It makes a good divers crash-pad. Look for the sign off Hwy 4 towards the northern end of Khao Lak.

Casa de La Flora DESIGN HOTEL $$$
(076 428999; www.casadelaflora.com; 67/213 Mu 5, Hat Bang Niang; r incl breakfast 12,600-30,200B;) Folded into trim seaside grounds dotted with contemporary art, this sleekly modern, well-run belle is composed of smart cube-like glass-and-concrete villas and suites adorned with warm-wood-panelled walls, double-sided mirrors, chunky concrete bathtubs and private plunge pools. Thoughtful touches include iPod docks, in-room espresso machines, hairdryers and, of course, pillow menus. Pod-style lounge beds fringe the sea-view infinity pool.

Eating

Khao Lak Town and the neighbouring beaches aren't a culinary hot spot, but tourists congregate at a few local haunts to rehash the day's diving. Early-morning divers will struggle to find breakfast before 8.30am.

Go Pong THAI $
(Th Phetkasem, Khao Lak; mains 50-140B; 10am-11pm) Get a real taste of local flavours at this terrific streetside diner where they stir-fry noodles and sensational spicy rice dishes and simmer aromatic noodle soups that attract a loyal lunch following. Dishes are packed full of flavour.

Takieng THAI $$
(26/43 Mu 5, Hat Bang Niang; mains 120-400B; noon-10pm;) Of two open-air Thai

THE 2004 TSUNAMI

On 26 December 2004, an earthquake off the Sumatran coast sent enormous waves crashing into Thailand's Andaman Coast, claiming almost 5400 lives (some estimates have it much higher) and causing millions of dollars of damage.

In 2005, Thailand officially inaugurated a national disaster warning system. The public will be warned via the nationwide radio network, dozens of TV channels and SMS messages. For non-Thai speakers, there are warning towers along high-risk beachfront areas that will broadcast announcements in various languages, accompanied by flashing lights.

The wave-shaped **Tsunami Memorial Park** (Ban Nam Khem; 24hr) FREE in Ban Nam Khem, a squid-fishing village 26km north of Hat Khao Lak that was nearly wiped out, was built to memorialise those who lost their lives. **Boat 813** (Bang Niang) lies 1km inland from Hat Bang Niang where it was deposited by the wave, just around the corner from the **International Tsunami Museum** (พิพิธภัณฑ์สึนามิระหว่างประเทศ; Hwy 4, Bang Niang; adult/child 200/100B; 9am-9pm). The moving memorials augment what, for years, were unofficial pilgrimage sites for those who came to pay their respects.

restaurants beneath stilted tin roofs on Hwy 4, 2.5km north of Khao Lak Town, Takieng is the most popular and attractive. It steams fresh fish in sweet green curry, does a scintillating chicken or pork *lâhp*, bubbles up beautifully spiced curries, and fries squid in a delicious chilli paste. Service is impeccable.

Jumbo Steak & Pasta ITALIAN $$
(☎098 059 8293; Th Phetkasem, Ban Khukkhuk; mains 80-280B; ⊙10am-10pm) A hole-in-the-wall joint on the west side of Hwy 4, 6km north of Khao Lak proper, launched by a former Le Meridien line chef who does beautiful pasta dishes in all kinds of flavours, plus a host of pizzas and terrific steaks. Dishes are great value in terms of quality, though portions aren't huge.

PhuKhaoLak INTERNATIONAL, THAI $$
(☎076 485141; www.phukhaolak.com; Mu 7, Th Phetkasem, Khao Lak; mains 100-350B; ⊙7am-10pm Oct-May; 📶 🌿) With cloth tables spilling to the lawn edge at the south end of Khao Lak's highway strip, this place is hard to miss. And you shouldn't, because there's a never-ending, well-prepared Thai-European menu of fried/grilled/steamed fish, sirloin steaks, pastas and sandwiches, and a dedicated veg section featuring such delights as spicy tofu with peanut sauce.

ℹ Information

Wi-fi is widely available.

ATMs are spread along the coast, along with banks and money-change offices. There is an ATM in the centre of **Khao Lak Town**.

SSS Ambulance (☎076 209347, emergency 081 081 9000; ⊙24hr) For diving-related emergencies, the SSS Ambulance rushes injured persons down to **Phuket International Hospital** (Map p290; ☎076 361818, 076 249400; www.phuketinternationalhospital.com; 44 Th Chalermprakiat), and can also be used for car or motorcycle accidents.

ℹ Getting There & Around

Any bus between Takua Pa (60B, 45 minutes) and Phuket (100B, two hours) will stop at Hat Khao Lak if you ask. Both **northbound** and **southbound** buses stop and pick up on Hwy 4.

Minivans run daily to Ko Samui (850B, eight hours) at 9am. There are also hourly minivans to Krabi (350B, 3½ hours) from 8am to 4pm. They'll pick you up at your accommodation.

Khao Lak Land Discovery (p279) runs shared minibuses to Phuket International Airport (600B, 1¼ hours). Alternatively, you can take **Cheaper Than Hotel** (☎085 786 1378, 086 276 6479; cheaperkhaolak1@gmail.com; Hwy 4) taxis to Phuket airport (1000B) and points south. Otherwise, taxis cost 1200B from Khao Lak to the airport. Or tell a Phuket-bound bus driver to drop you at the 'airport'; you'll be let off at an intersection from which motorcycle taxis usually take you to the airport (10 minutes, 100B).

Numerous travel agencies and guesthouses rent motorbikes by the day (200B to 250B).

Similan Islands Marine National Park

อุทยานแห่งชาติหมู่เกาะสิมิลัน

Known to divers the world over, the beautiful 70-sq-km **Similan Islands Marine National Park** (☎076 453272; www.dnp.go.th; adult/child 500/300B; ⊙mid-Oct–mid-May) lies 70km offshore from Phang-Nga Province. Its smooth granite islands are as impressive above the bright-aqua water as below, topped with rainforest, edged with blindingly white beaches and fringed by coral reefs. Coral bleaching has killed off many hard corals, but soft corals are still intact and the fauna and fish are still there. However, the Similans are now on the tourist trail and many beaches and snorkel sites get packed out with day trippers.

You can stay on Ko Miang (Island 4) and Ko Similan. The park visitors centre (p283) and most facilities are on Ko Miang. The islands all have names, but are more commonly known by their numbers.

Hat Khao Lak is the park's jumping-off point. The pier and mainland national park headquarters (p283) are at Thap Lamu, 12km south (Hwy 4, then Rte 4147).

Activities

Diving & Snorkelling

The Similans offer diving for all levels, at depths from 2m to 30m. There are rock reefs at **Ko Hin Pousar** (Island 7) and dive-throughs at **Hin Pousar** (Elephant Head Rock), with marine life ranging from tiny plume worms and soft corals to schooling fish, manta rays and rare whale sharks. **Ko Bon** and **Ko Tachai** are two of the better diving and snorkelling areas. There are dive sites at each of the six islands north of **Ko Miang**. The park's southern section (Islands 1, 2 and 3) is an off-limits turtle nesting ground.

Similan Islands Marine National Park

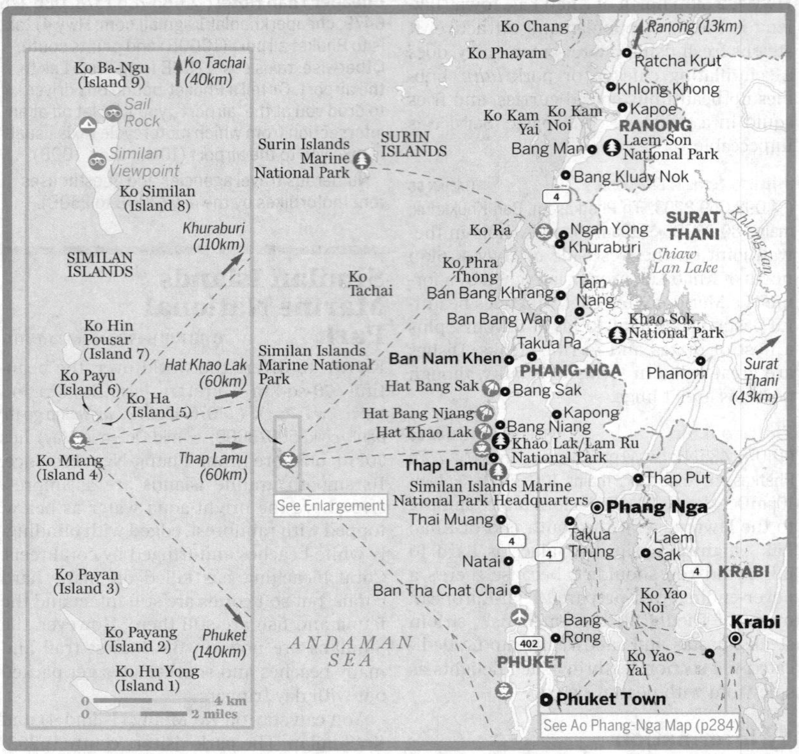

No facilities for divers exist in the national park, so you'll be taking a dive tour. Dive schools in Hat Khao Lak book day trips (two dives 6000B) and liveaboards (three-/six-day trip from around 19,000/35,000B), as do Phuket dive centres (two-dive day trip from 5600B, three-day liveaboard from 18,900B).

Agencies in Khao Lak offer snorkelling-only day trips that visit three or four sites from 3200B.

Wildlife-Watching & Hiking

The forest around Ko Miang's visitors centre has some walking trails and great wildlife. The fabulous Nicobar pigeon, with its wild mane of grey-green feathers, is common here. It's one of the park's 39 bird species. Hairy-legged land crabs and fruit bats (flying foxes) are relatively easy to spot in the forest, as are flying squirrels.

A small beach track, with information panels, leads 400m east from the visitors centre to a tiny snorkelling bay. Detouring from the track, the **Viewpoint Trail**, about 500m or 30 minutes of steep scrambling, has panoramic vistas from the top. A 500m (20-minute) walk west from the visitors centre leads through forest to smooth west-facing granite platform **Sunset Point**.

On Ko Similan, there's a 2.5km forest hike to a **viewpoint**, and a shorter, steep scramble off the north-coast beach to **Sail Rock** (Balance Rock), during daylight it's clogged with visitors.

Sleeping & Eating

You will need to book at least two to three months ahead to guarantee a bed or a tent.

A **restaurant** (Ko Miang (Island 4); mains 120-150B, lunch buffet 230B; 7.30am-8.30pm) beside the park office on Ko Miang serves simple Thai food. There's another one on Ko Similan for those staying the night.

Similan Islands Marine National Park Accommodation BUNGALOW $$

(☎076 453272, in Bangkok 02 562 0760; www.dnp.go.th; Ko Miang (Island 4); r fan/air-con 1000/2000B, campsite with tent hire 570B; ⏰mid-Oct–mid-May; ❄) On Ko Miang, there are 20 bungalows, the best with balconies, or tents. You are paying for the location: the bungalows are simple. During the day, many tour groups will drop by. Electricity operates 6pm to 6am.

Book ahead online, by phone or through the mainland park headquarters at Thap Lamu. If you are camping, bring repellent: the mosquitoes are ferocious.

Information

Similan Islands Marine National Park Headquarters (☎076 453272; www.dnp.go.th; 93 Mu 5, Thap Lamu; ⏰8am-5pm mid-Oct–mid-May) You can book accommodation on the Similan Islands well in advance with this office south of Khao Lak.

Similan Islands Marine National Park Visitors Centre (Ko Miang (Island 4); ⏰7.30am-8pm mid-Oct–mid-May) Visitors centre on Ko Miang.

Getting There & Away

There's no official public transport to the Similans. Theoretically, independent travellers can book return speedboat transfers (2000B, 1½ hours each way) with a Khao Lak day-trip operator, though they discourage independent travel. Most will collect you from Hat Khao Lak, but if you book through the national park you'll have to find your own way to the office in Thap Lamu and wait for a pier transfer.

Dive centres and tour agents in Hat Khao Lak and Phuket book day/overnight tours (from 4900/8500B), dive trips (three-day liveaboards from 10,500B to 19,000B) and multiday trips including park transport, food and lodging, which cost little more than what you'd pay getting to and staying on the islands independently.

Natai นาใต้

☎076

Officially in Phang-Nga Province, Natai's spiritual home is high-end Phuket, but reality it's even more flash and fabulous. Just 26km north of Phuket International Airport, this luxury bolt-hole lies within easier reach of Phuket than parts of Phuket itself. There's little else out here yet, apart from a delicious broad blonde beach that disappears into turquoise waters and which some of southern Thailand's most exclusive restaurants and lodgings gaze out upon. Don't bother turning up unless your pockets are very deep.

Sleeping & Eating

★**Iniala Beach House** DESIGN HOTEL $$$

(☎076 451456; www.iniala.com; 40/14 Mu 6, Ban Natai; d full-board US$2200-3100; ❄📶🏊) From expertly concocted passion-fruit welcome drinks to highly personal service, in-house dining and bold, one-of-a-kind futuristic design, Iniala oozes cool, creativity and sophistication. This is southern Thailand's most luscious design property. It took 10 designers to create the 10 uniquely fashioned rooms, tucked into three self-contained three-suite villas and a penthouse, with skinny dark-tiled infinity pools meandering to Natai's beautiful beach.

Aleenta BOUTIQUE HOTEL $$$

(☎in Bangkok 02 514 8112; www.aleenta.com; 33 Mu 5, Ban Natai; r incl breakfast 24,900-77,100B; ❄📶🏊) Sleek loft-style rooms spill out into shared infinity pools through floor-to-ceiling windows. Boardwalks criss-cross lily ponds to secluded, uber-chic villas and suites, where private pools reflect soaring palms. Split-level quadruples with kitchenettes are ideal for families. Swish cabanas dot the black-tiled seafront infinity pool and there's an elegant spa.

Esenzi SEAFOOD $$$

(☎076 451456; www.esenzirestaurant.com; 40/14 Mu 6, Ban Natai; mains 700-2000B; ⏰6pm-11pm Tue-Sat; 📶) Seafood from around the world is the theme at Esenzi, the latest incarnation of the acclaimed restaurant at Iniala Beach House. The menu moves between Europe, Japan and the US, as well as Thailand. If you're feeling flush, the eight-course tasting menu (8000B) is the way to go. Super service and wine list.

Getting There & Away

Taxis to/from Phuket airport cost 700B. Alternatively, you can rent a car at the airport (from 1454B per day) and drive here yourself.

Ao Phang-Nga

Ao Phang-Nga อ่าวพังงา

Between turquoise bays peppered with craggy limestone towers, brilliant-white beaches and tumbledown fishing villages, Ao Phang-Nga is one of the Andaman's most spectacular landscapes. Little wonder then that it was here, among looming cliffs and swifts' nests, that James Bond's nemesis, Scaramanga (*The Man with the Golden Gun*), chose to build his lair. Modern-day wanted assassins with world-domination goals would doubtless skip the place, as it's swarming with tourists, motorboats and sea kayaks year-round.

Phang-Nga พังงา

☎076 / POP 10,800

Phang-Nga is an unremarkable small town set against sublime limestone cliffs. There isn't much to see or do unless you're here during the annual **Vegetarian Festival** (late September or October), and it's very much a staging post for people heading further north to Khao Lak (p278) or Khao Sok National Park (p277). Hotels and amenities are mostly on Th Phetkasem.

Tours

Although it's fun to create your own Ao Phang-Nga itinerary by chartering a boat, it's easier (and cheaper) to join a tour with one of Phang-Nga's agencies, most of which are at the bus station. Quality varies, but all offer near-identical itineraries and prices.

Sayan Tours BOATING
(☎090 708 3211, 076 430348; www.sayantour.com; Old Bus Station, off Th Phetkasem; half/full day 800/1100B; ⊙7am-9pm) A long-standing Ao Phang-Nga tour company offering day trips to Ko Panyi, Ko Phing Kan and Tham Lod (covered in stalactites), and overnight stays on Ko Panyi (1950B).

Mr Kean Tour BOATING
(☎089 871 6092; Old Bus Station, off Th Phetkasem; half/full day 800/1100B; ⊙7am-6pm) Mr Kean has been running tours of Ao Phang-Nga for over 25 years. Half- and full-day tours include Tham Lod, Ko Phing Kan and Ko Panyi. You can add kayaking (300B per person) and trekking, or spend the night on Ko Panyi (1750B).

Sleeping & Eating

Several food stalls along Th Phetkasem sell delicious *kà·nŏm jeen* (thin wheat noodles) with chicken curry, *nám yah* (spicy groundfish curry) or *nám prík* (spicy sauce). There's a small **night market** (Th Phetkasem; mains from 30B; ⊙4-9pm) on Th Phetkasem, beside the 7-Eleven.

Thaweesuk Hotel GUESTHOUSE $
(☎076 412100; www.thaweesukhotel.com; 79 Th Phetkasem; r incl breakfast with fan/air-con 450/800B; ⊖❄🛜) A friendly family-run place in a historic building with a colourful mosaic-floor lobby, on north Th Phetkasem. Ground-floor cold-water fan/air-con rooms are simple, compact and clean. Hot-water air-con pads on the first floor are rather more stylish with varnished-wood floors. There's also a four-bed family room. Breakfast is downstairs in the lounge-like lobby.

The Sleep HOTEL $$
(☎076 411828; 144 Th Phetkasem; r 600-1000B; ❄🛜) This brand new hotel offers the most modern rooms in Phang-Nga, decked out in white and dark wood with comfortable beds, TVs and fridges, although the bathrooms are very tight. There's a terrace for free morning coffee.

Getting There & Away

The nearest airport to Phang-Nga is in Phuket, a 1½-hour drive away.

Phang-Nga's **bus terminal** (Th Phetkasem) is 4km south of the town centre. Motorcycle taxis charge a flat 50B to/from the station.

Minivans run to Khao Sok National Park (250B, two hours) at 8.30am, 10.30am, noon, 2pm, 3.30pm and 5.30pm. They'll drop you at your accommodation.

Buses for Takua Pa (150B, 1½ hours), where you can connect for Khao Lak, as well as Ranong and Khao Sok National Park, leave at 8am, 10am, 11am, noon, 2pm and 5.20pm.

Ao Phang-Nga Marine National Park อุทยานแห่งชาติอ่าวพังงา

The classic karst scenery of the 400-sq-km Ao Phang-Nga National Park (076 481188; www.dnp.go.th; adult/child 300/100B; 8am-4pm) was famously featured in the James Bond movie *The Man with the Golden Gun*. Huge vertical cliffs frame 42 islands, some with caves accessible only at low tide. The bay is composed of large and small tidal channels, which run north to south through Thailand's largest remaining primary mangrove forests.

Ao Phang-Nga's marine limestone environment conceals reptiles like Bengal monitor lizards, two-banded monitors, flying lizards, banded sea snakes, shore pit vipers and Malayan pit vipers. Mammals include serows, crab-eating macaques, white-handed gibbons and dusky langurs.

In high season (November to April) the bay becomes a clogged day-tripper superhighway. But if you visit in the early morning (ideally from the Ko Yao islands) or stay out later, you might just find a slice of beach, sea and limestone karst of your own. The best way to explore is by kayak.

Sights & Activities

You can charter boats to explore Ao Phang-Nga's half-submerged caves and oddly shaped islands from Tha Dan, 9km south of central Phang-Nga. Expect to pay 1500B to 2000B for a half-day tour.

Two- to three-hour tours (1000B per person) head to well-trodden Ko Phing Kan (เกาะเขาพิงกัน, James Bond Island), Ko Panyi (เกาะปันหยี) and elsewhere in the park. Tha Surakul, 13km southwest of Phang-Nga in Takua Thung, has private boats for hire at similar prices to tours. From the national park headquarters, you can hire boats (1400B, maximum four passengers) for three-hour islands tours. From Phuket, John Gray's Seacanoe (p295) is the top choice for Ao Phang-Nga kayakers.

Sleeping & Eating

Most people visit on day tours from either the Ko Yao islands, Phuket or Phang-Nga.

Ao Phang-Nga National Park Accommodation BUNGALOW **$$**
(076 481188, in Bangkok 02 562 0760; www.dnp.go.th; Rte 4144; bungalows 800-1000B) Simple air-con bungalows sleep two to three, in quiet shady grounds 8.5km south of central Phang-Nga. There's a basic waterside Thai restaurant.

Getting There & Away

From central Phang-Nga, drive 7km south on Hwy 4, turn left onto Rte 4144 and travel 2.6km to the park headquarters in Tha Dan. Opposite the headquarters is the jetty where you can hire boats to explore the park. Otherwise take a *sŏrng·tăa·ou* to Tha Dan (30B).

BUSES FROM PHANG-NGA

DESTINATION	FARE (B)	DURATION (HR)	FREQUENCY
Bangkok (VIP)	829	12	4pm, 5pm, 7pm, 8pm
Bangkok (1st class)	533-622	12	8.40am, 3pm, 4.30pm, 5.30pm, 6.30pm, 7.30pm
Hat Yai	265	6	8.50am, 9.50am, 10.50am, 12.50pm, 1.50pm
Krabi	80	1½	hourly 7.30am-6pm
Phuket	80	1½	hourly 5.30am-5.30pm
Ranong	170	5	10.15am
Surat Thani	150	4	9.30am, 11.30am, 1.30pm, 3.30pm
Trang	175	3½	hourly 8am-4.20pm

LOCAL KNOWLEDGE

ANCIENT ROCK ART

Many of Ao Phang-Nga's limestone islands have prehistoric rock art painted on or carved into cave walls and ceilings, rock shelters, cliffs and rock massifs. You can see rock art at Khao Khian, Ko Panyi, Ko Raya, Tham Nak and Ko Phra At Thao. Images at **Khao Khian** (the most visited cave-art site) contain human figures, fish, crabs, prawns, bats, birds and elephants, as well as boats, weapons and fishing equipment, seemingly referencing some communal effort tied to the all-important sea harvest. Most rock paintings are monochrome, though some have been traced in orange-yellow, blue, grey and black.

Ko Yao เกาะยาว

With mountainous backbones, unspoilt shorelines, hugely varied birdlife and a population of friendly Muslim fisherfolk, Ko Yao Yai and Ko Yao Noi are relaxed vantage points for soaking up Ao Phang-Nga's beautiful karst scenery. The islands are part of Ao Phang-Nga National Park (p285), but can be accessed from Phuket and elsewhere easily.

Ko Yao Noi is the main population centre, despite being smaller than its neighbour, with fishing, coconut farming and tourism sustaining its small, year-round population. It's not a classic beach destination: bays on the east coast, where most resorts are, recede to mudflats at low tides. Nevertheless, **Hat Pasai** (Ko Yao Noi), on the southeast coast, and **Hat Paradise** (Ko Yao Noi), on the northeast coast, are both gorgeous.

Ko Yao Yai is twice the size of its sibling and wilder. The most accessible beaches are **Hat Lo Pared** (Ko Yao Yai), on the southwest coast, and powder-white **Hat Chonglard** (Ko Yao Yai) on the northeast coast.

Activities

One-day three-island snorkelling tours (2000B) of Ao Phang-Nga are easily arranged through guesthouses or at the piers.

Kayaks (500B per day) are widely available on Ko Yao Noi, including at Sabai Corner.

Amazing Bike Tours (p295) runs popular small-group day trips to Ko Yao Noi from Phuket. If you're keen to explore the numerous dirt trails on Ko Yao Noi or Ko Yao Yai independently, most guesthouses rent bikes (250B per day), though they're more readily available on Ko Yao Noi.

Elixir Divers DIVING
(087 897 0076; www.elixirdivers.com; 2/3 Mu 3, Ko Yao Yai; 2 dives 2900-3900B; Oct-Apr) Ko Yao Yai's only dive school is an on-the-ball operator covering a range of PADI courses, two-dive day trips locally and to Ko Phi-Phi, and liveaboards to Hin Daeng, Hin Muang and the Similans (22,900B), plus snorkelling excursions to Ao Phang-Nga, Krabi and Ko Phi-Phi.

If you're staying on Ko Yao Noi, they'll help with transfers.

Mountain Shop Adventures CLIMBING
(083 969 2023; www.facebook.com/mountainshopadventures; Tha Khao, Ko Yao Noi; half-day 3200B; 9am-7pm) There are over 150 climbs on Ko Yao Noi; Mountain Shop owner Mark has routed most of them himself. Trips range from beginner to advanced and many involve boat travel to remote limestone cliffs. His ramshackle office is just down the road from the Tha Kao pier. It's best to contact him in advance.

Island Yoga YOGA
(087 387 9475; www.thailandyogaretreats.com; 4/10 Mu 4, Hat Tha Khao, Ko Yao Noi; classes 600B) This popular yoga school hosts daily drop-in classes at 10am, as well as scheduled classes at 7.30am and 4.30pm. Also does multiday yoga and tai chi retreats.

Sleeping & Eating

Almost all accommodation on Ko Yao Noi is on the east coast. The farther north you go, the wilder the roads get and shops and restaurants are very thin on the ground. Ko Yao Yai has fewer sleeping and eating choices.

Ko Yao Noi

Hill House BUNGALOW $$
(089 593 9523; www.hillhouse-kohyaonoi.com; Hat Tha Khao, Ko Yao Noi; r 1100-1300B;) A friendly, simple hillside spot where well-kept, dark-wood, hot-water, fan-cooled bungalows are swathed in mosquito nets and have beautiful views through trees to Ao Phang-Nga's limestone karsts from hammock-loaded terraces.

Sabai Corner Bungalows GUESTHOUSE $$
(☎076 597497; www.sabaicornerbungalows.com; Hat Khlong Jark, Ko Yao Noi; bungalows 1000-1900B;) Pocketed into a rocky headland, these no-fuss bungalows with whizzing fans, mosquito nets and hammocks on terraces are blessed with gorgeous sea views. One oddity is that there are no connecting doors to the bathrooms; you have to go outside to reach them. The good, chilled-out waterside **restaurant** (mains 95-300B; 8am-10pm;) is a bubbly place to hang out; kayaks for rent.

Ko Yao Island Resort RESORT $$$
(☎076 597474; www.koyao.com; 24/2 Mu 5, Hat Khlong Jark, Ko Yao Noi; villas 7400-19,900B; @) Open-concept thatched bungalows offer serene views across a palm-shaded garden and beach-facing infinity pool to a white strip of sand. We love the graceful, airy, safari-like feel of the villas, with their fan-cooled patios and indoor/outdoor bathrooms. There's a snazzy bar-restaurant area and service is stellar.

Suntisook BUNGALOW $$$
(☎075 582750, 089 781 6456; www.facebook.com/suntisookkoyaonoi; 11/1 Mu 4, Hat Tha Khao, Ko Yao Noi; r 2000-2200B;) Suntisook's comfy and fresh varnished-wood bungalows are sprinkled across an attractive garden just metres from a quiet beach. They're not huge, but all have spacious hammock-laden verandahs, fridges and pot plants. It's run efficiently by a helpful English-speaking Thai family, who offer a good authentic **restaurant** (mains 60-150B; 7.30am-9pm;) and kayak hire. It sometimes closes for parts of the low season (May to October).

Chaba Café INTERNATIONAL $
(☎087 887 0625; Hat Khlong Jark, Ko Yao Noi; mains 80-220B; 9am-5pm Mon-Sat;) Rustic-cute Chaba is a haven of pastel-painted prettiness, with driftwood walls, mellow music and a small gallery. Organic-oriented offerings include honey-sweetened juices, coconut-milk-and-avocado shakes, chrysanthemum tea and home-baked paninis, cookies and cakes, plus soups, pastas and Thai dishes. It's just beyond northern Hat Khlong Jark.

Pizzeria La Luna ITALIAN $$
(☎085 0689 4326; btwn Hat Khlong Jark & Hat Tha Khao, Ko Yao Noi; mains 170-320B; 3pm-10pm;) There's a big range of wood-fired pizzas, including veggie choices, at this laid-back, semi-open-air roadside eatery, as well as homemade pasta, salads, cakes and antipasto in high season (October to May). It's an equally good place to sip a cocktail, with a proper wooden bar to sit at.

★**Rice Paddy** INTERNATIONAL, THAI $$$
(☎076 454255, 082 331 6581; Hat Pasai, Ko Yao Noi; mains 180-890B; noon-10pm & 6-10pm May-Oct;) On the roadside corner at the southwest end of Hat Pasai, this sweet, all-wood, German-owned Thai-international kitchen is very special. Flash-fried *sôm·đam* (spicy green papaya salad), fantastic falafel and hummus, spicy, fruit enhanced curries served in clay pots and fresh salads are all delicious. They do excellent veggie dishes too, as well as decent cocktails.

At the time of research, there were rumours the restaurant would move to a new location on the island.

Ko Yao Yai

Thiwson Beach Resort BUNGALOW $$$
(☎081 956 7582; www.thiwsonbeach.com; 58/2 Mu 4, Hat Chonglard, Ko Yao Yai; r incl breakfast 2000-3600B;) Easily the sweetest of the island's humbler bungalow properties. Here are proper wooden thatch- or tin-topped huts with polished floors, outdoor bathrooms and wide patios overlooking the

SUSTAINABLE SPA

Need to get the rock climbing, kayaking and biking thoroughly massaged out of your system? Look no further than the back-to-nature elegance of **Six Senses Spa** (☎076 418500; www.sixsenses.com; 56 Mu 5, btwn Hat Khlong Jark & Hat Tha Khao, Ko Yao Noi; treatments 4200-25,000B; 8am-9pm). Therapists at the stilted 'spa village' are trained in massage and organic-fuelled treatments from China, India and Thailand. Prolong the pampering with an overnight stay in one of the five-star property's 56 hillside **pool villas** (☎076 418500; www.sixsenses.com; 56 Mu 5, btwn Hat Khlong Jark & Hat Tha Khao, Ko Yao Noi; villa incl breakfast 35,000-66,000B;) . Bonus: the resort has impressive commitment to sustainability.

island's prettiest, northeast-coast beach, fronted by an aqua pool. Beachfront bungalows are biggest, but fan rooms are excellent low-season value.

Glow Elixir RESORT **$$$**
(☎087 808 3838; www.glowhotels.com/elixir; 99 Mu 3, Prunai, Ko Yao Yai; bungalows incl breakfast 9100-23,200B;) Beside its own silky beach in the southwest corner of the island, the oldest of Yao Yai's four-star resorts offers tasteful beachfront and hillside peaked-roof villas steeped in classic Thai style: dark-wood floors, outdoor showers and fish-patterned ceramic-bowl sinks. Some have private pools. You'll also enjoy a high-season dive centre (p286), massage pagodas and spectacular sunsets over Phuket.

Koh Yao Yai Village RESORT **$$$**
(☎076 363700; www.kohyaovillage.com; 78 Mu 4, Ko Yao Yai; r 4300-10,200B;) This eco-friendly resort is upmarket without being over the top price-wise. It offers very big, light, elegantly furnished villas with outdoor bathrooms set high in the trees for spectacular sea views towards Phuket. There's also a tremendous infinity pool, spa, on-site restaurant and you're handily placed to access Hat Chonglard, the best beach on the island.

Information

There are ATMs in Ta Khao, Ko Yao Noi's largest settlement, and a few more dotted along the east coast. There's also an ATM at Tha Bang Rong (p293) pier on Phuket, where boats to Ko Yao depart from.

On Ko Yao Yai, there are a handful of ATMs. It's wise to take money with you; otherwise you'll have to head back to Tha Bang Rong to cash up.

Getting There & Away

TO/FROM AO NANG

From November to April, there's an 11am speedboat from the pier at Hat Noppharat Thara to Ko Yao Noi and Ko Yao Yai (both 650B, 45 minutes). It continues to Phuket's Tha Bang Rong, returning at 3pm.

TO/FROM KO PHI-PHI

Three weekly speedboats run to/from Ko Phi-Phi (500B) and Ko Lanta (500B) from October to April.

TO/FROM KRABI

From 9am to 5.30pm daily, there are frequent long-tails (150B) between Ko Yao Noi's Tha Khao and Krabi's Tha Len (33km northwest of Krabi Town). *Sŏrng·tăa·ou* (100B) run between Tha Len and Krabi's Th Maharat via Krabi's bus terminal.

TO/FROM PHANG-NGA

From Tha Dan in Phang-Nga there's a 1pm ferry to Ko Yao Noi (200B, 1½ hours), returning at 7.30am.

TO/FROM PHUKET

From Phuket's Tha Bang Rong, there are daily speedboats (200B, 30 minutes) to Ko Yao Noi at 7.50am, 8.40am, 9.15am, 9.50am, 10.30am, 11.30am, 1.30pm, 2.30pm, 5pm and 5.40pm, plus long-tails (120B, one hour) at 9.15am, 12.30pm and 5pm. Some stop en route at Tha Klong Hia on Ko Yao Yai (200B, 25 minutes). Boats return to Phuket between 6.30am and 4.40pm.

Taxis run from Tha Bang Rong to Phuket's resort areas for 600B to 800B, and *sŏrng·tăa·ou* (40B) leave for Phuket Town at 7am, 8.30am, 11am and 2.30pm daily.

Getting Around

Frequent shuttle boats run from Ko Yao Noi's Tha Manok to Ko Yao Yai's Tha Klong Hia (50B). On the islands, *túk-túk* rides cost about 150B, and most guesthouses rent motorbikes (250B to 300B per day). It's 100B for *sŏrng·tăa·ou* transport to the resorts.

PHUKET PROVINCE

First, let's get the pronunciation right. The 'h' in Phuket (ภูเก็ต) is silent. And then remember that this is the largest Thai island, so you rarely feel surrounded by water. But that means there is space for everyone.

Phuket offers such a rich variety of experiences – beach-bumming, culture, diving, fabulous food, hedonistic or holistic pleasures – that visitors are spoilt for choice. Each beach is different, from the upmarket resorts of Surin and Ao Bang Thao to family-oriented Rawai, or the sin city of Patong, home of hangovers and go-go girls.

ECOFRIENDLY TOURS

We recommend opting for a bike tour (p295) instead of supporting the questionable animal-welfare and environmental standards of Phuket's elephant ride and 4WD tour operators.

But there's also the culturally rich east-coast capital Phuket Town, as well as wildlife sanctuaries and national parks in the north.

Activities

There's no shortage of adrenaline-fuelled activities on Phuket, from bungee jumps to zip lines. Equipment quality and safety levels vary, and there have been serious, even fatal, accidents. Ask for recommendations and don't proceed if you have any doubts.

Diving & Snorkelling

Phuket enjoys an enviable central location relative to the Andaman Sea's top diving destinations. The much-talked-about Similan Islands lie 100km northwest, while dozens of dive sites orbit Ko Phi-Phi and Ko Lanta, 40km and 72km southeast. Trips from Phuket to these awesome destinations cost slightly more than from places closer to the sites, as you'll be forking out extra baht for transport costs.

Most Phuket operators take divers to the nine decent sites orbiting the island, including **Ko Raya Noi** and **Ko Raya Yai** (Ko Racha Noi and Ko Racha Yai), but these spots rank lower on the wow-o-meter. The reef off the southern tip of Raya Noi is the best among them, with soft corals and pelagic fish species aplenty, though it's usually reserved for experienced divers. Manta and marble rays are frequently glimpsed here and, if you're lucky, you might spot a whale shark.

One-day, two-dive trips to nearby sites start at 3000B. Non-divers and snorkellers can usually tag along for a significant discount. Open Water Diver certification costs 11,480B to 18,400B for three days' instruction. Some schools charge 500B extra for equipment.

From Phuket, you can join a huge range of liveaboard diving expeditions to the Similan Islands (p281) and Myanmar's Mergui Archipelago.

Snorkelling isn't wonderful off Phuket proper, though mask, snorkel and fins (200B per day) are available for rent in most resort areas. As with diving, you'll find better snorkelling (with greater visibility and variety of marine life) along the shores of small outlying islands, such as Ko Raya Yai and Ko Raya Noi.

Like elsewhere in the Andaman Sea, the best diving months are November to April, when weather is good and seas smooth and clear, though most dive shops power on (weather permitting) through the low season, with good discounts.

Recommended dive schools have branches across Phuket, including in Patong (p305), Kata (p311) and Karon (p313).

Surfing

Phuket is an under-the-radar surf destination. With the monsoon's midyear swell, glassy seas fold into barrels. The best waves arrive between June and September, when annual competitions are held on Hat Kata Yai (p310), Phuket's most popular surf spot, and Hat Kalim, just north of Patong. Phuket Surf (p311) is based at the south end of Kata Yai near the best break, which tops out at 2m. **Hat Nai Han** (หาดในหาน; Map p303) gets bigger waves (up to 3m), in front of the yacht club. Both Kata and Nai Han have vicious undertows that can claim lives.

Hat Kalim is sheltered and has a consistent break that gets up to 3m. This is a hollow wave, and is considered the best break on the island. The northernmost stretch of Hat Kamala (p314) has a nice 3m beach break. **Laem Singh** (แหลมสิงห์), 1km north, gets very big and fast waves, plus it's sheltered from wind by a massive headland. Hat Surin (p315) gets some of Phuket's most challenging waves.

Hat Nai Yang (p319) has a consistent (if soft) wave that breaks more than 200m offshore. **Hat Nai Thon** gets better-shaped

BIG BUDDHA

High atop the Nakkerd Hills, northwest of Chalong circle, and visible from half the island, the 45m-high **Big Buddha** (พระใหญ่; Map p290; www.mingmongkolphuket.com; off Rte 4021; ⏲6am-7pm) **FREE** sits grandly on Phuket's finest viewpoint. It's a tad touristy, but tinkling bells and flapping flags mean there's an energetic pulse. Pay your respects at the tented golden shrine, then step up to the glorious plateau, where you can peer into Kata's perfect bay, glimpse the shimmering Karon strand and, to the southeast, survey the pebble-sized channel islands of Chalong Bay.

From Rte 4021, follow signs 1km north of Chalong circle to wind 6km west up a steep country road, passing terraces of banana groves and tangles of jungle.

Phuket Province

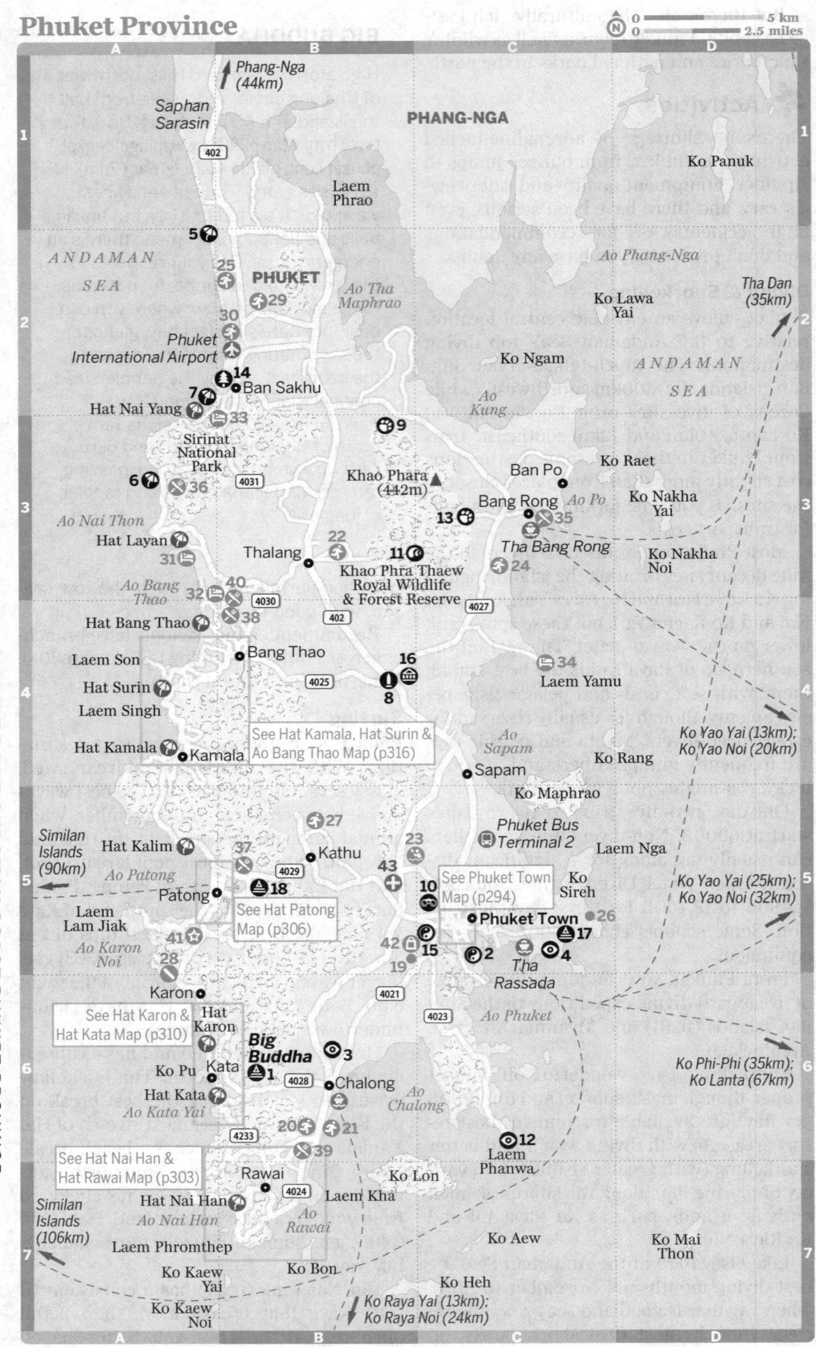

Phuket Province

Top Sights
1 Big Buddha ... B6

Sights
2 Bang Niew Shrine ... C5
3 Chalong Bay Rum ... B6
4 Chow Lair Village ... C5
5 Hat Mai Khao ... A2
6 Hat Nai Thon ... A3
7 Hat Nai Yang ... A2
8 Heroines Monument ... B4
9 Khao Phra Thaew Royal Wildlife & Forest Reserve ... B3
10 Khao Rang ... C5
Nam Tok Bang Pae ... (see 13)
11 Nam Tok Ton Sai ... B3
12 Phuket Aquarium ... C6
13 Phuket Gibbon Rehabilitation Project ... C3
14 Sirinat National Park ... B2
15 Sui Boon Tong Shrine ... C5
16 Thalang National Museum ... B4
17 Wat Sireh ... C5
18 Wat Suwan Khiri Wong ... B5

Activities, Courses & Tours
19 Amazing Bike Tours ... B5
20 Atsumi ... B6
Banyan Tree Spa ... (see 32)
21 Bob's Kite School ... B6
22 Cable Jungle Adventure Phuket ... B3
Cool Spa ... (see 12)
Coqoon Spa ... (see 7)
23 John Gray's Seacanoe ... B5
Kiteboarding Asia ... (see 7)
24 Phuket Elephant Sanctuary ... C3
25 Phuket Riding Club ... B2
26 Phuket Thai Cookery School ... C5
27 Phuket Wake Park ... B5
28 Sea Fun Divers ... A5
29 Soi Dog ... B2
30 Splash Jungle ... B2

Sleeping
31 Anantara Phuket Layan ... A3
32 Banyan Tree ... A3
Discovery Beach Resort ... (see 7)
Panwa Boutique Beach Resort ... (see 12)
33 Pensiri House ... B3
34 Point Yamu by Como ... C4
Pullman ... (see 6)
Sirinat National Park Accommodation ... (see 14)
Slate ... (see 7)
Sri Panwa ... (see 12)

Eating
35 Bang Rong Seafood ... C3
Breeze Restaurant ... (see 34)
36 Coconut Tree ... A3
Elements ... (see 6)
37 Kaab Gluay ... B5
Mr Kobi ... (see 7)
38 Night Market ... B4
39 Som Tum Lanna ... B6
40 Taste Bar & Grill ... B3

Entertainment
41 Phuket Simon Cabaret ... A5

Shopping
42 Weekend Market ... B5

Information
43 Phuket International Hospital ... B5

waves, with swells up to 3m high a few times per year.

In the low season, you can rent surfboards (150B to 300B per hour) on most of these beaches.

Sea Kayaking

Several Phuket-based companies offer canoe tours of spectacular Ao Phang-Nga, a collection of towering karst outcrops rising from the sea northeast of Phuket and close to the mainland. Kayaks can enter semi-submerged caves inaccessible to longtail boats. A day paddle (around 4000B per person) includes meals, equipment and boat transfer. Some outfits run all-inclusive, three-day (from 13,500B) or six-day (from 23,500B) kayaking and camping trips, covering Ao Phang-Nga and Khao Sok National Park. John Gray's Seacanoe (p295) is the island's star operator.

Kitesurfing

One of the world's fastest-growing sports is also among Phuket's latest addictions. The best kitesurfing spots are Hat Nai Yang (p319) from April to October and Rawai (p302) from mid-October to March. All listed kitesurfing outfitters are affiliated with the International Kiteboarding Organisation (www.ikointl.com).

Yachting

Phuket is one of Southeast Asia's main yachting destinations. You'll find all manner of craft anchored along its shores, from 80-year-old wooden sloops to the latest in high-tech motor cruisers.

Marina-style facilities with year-round anchorage are available at several locations. Marinas can advise in advance on the latest port-clearance procedures. Expect to pay from 11,300B per day for a high-season, bareboat charter.

Water Parks

Splash Jungle WATER PARK
(Map p290; ☎076 372111; www.splashjunglewaterpark.com; 65 Mu 4, Soi 4, Mai Khao; adult/child 1450/700B; ⊙10am-6pm) Within eyeshot of Phuket airport, this massive water park has a wave pool, a kids pool with water cannons, 12 multicoloured twisting water slides for all ages, a 'super-bowl' slide and...a bar for anyone craving a break. For an extra 400B per person you'll get picked up and returned to your hotel. Children under five get in free.

Phuket Wake Park WATER SPORTS
(Map p290; ☎076 510151; www.phuketwakepark.com; 86/3 Mu 6, Th Vichitsongkram, Kathu; adult/child 2hr visit 750/350B, day pass 1250/650B; ⊙9am-6pm;) Buzz Kathu's marvellous hill-backed lake on a wakeboard. This outfit, mostly aimed at teenagers and older kids, offers rides in two-hour blocks, by the day or as lessons (1000B per hour). Board rental is available (500B), as are hotel transfers.

Courses

Popular Thai cooking classes are held in Kata (p311), Phuket Town (p295), Ko Sireh (p301) and Patong (p305).

Information

DANGERS & ANNOYANCES

- Thousands of people are injured or killed every year on Phuket's highways. If you must rent a motorbike, make sure you at least know the basics and wear a helmet. Rental rarely includes insurance.
- Take special care on the roads from Patong to Karon and from Kata to the Rawai–Hat Nai Han area, where we've had reports of late-night motorbike muggings and stabbings.
- Women should think twice before sunbathing topless (a big no-no in Thailand anyway) or alone, especially on isolated beaches, as random sexual assaults can also happen.
- Avoid running alone at night or early in the morning.

MEDICAL SERVICES

Local medical care is generally good. Hospitals are equipped with modern facilities, emergency rooms and outpatient clinics.

Most diving emergencies are taken to **Phuket International Hospital** (p281), which has a hyperbaric chamber.

TOURIST INFORMATION

You can find **tourist information** (Map p294; Th Thalang; ⊙9am-4.30pm) offices in Phuket Town. There are police stations at all the major beaches.

WEBSITES

Local English-language newspapers include the following:

FLIGHTS TO/FROM PHUKET

DESTINATION	FREQUENCY	FARE (B)	AIRLINE
Bangkok (Don Muang)	14 daily	1600	Air Asia
Bangkok (Don Muang)	8 daily	1680	Nok Air
Bangkok (Suvarnabhumi)	7-9 daily	1700	Bangkok Airways
Bangkok (Suvarnabhumi)	9-10 daily	2500	THAI
Chiang Mai	3 daily	2100	Air Asia
Dubai	1-2 daily	16,370	Emirates
Hat Yai	daily	1600	Bangkok Airways
Hong Kong	daily	3800	Air Asia
Ko Samui	4-5 daily	3300	Bangkok Airways
Kuala Lumpur	5 daily	2200	Air Asia
Seoul	daily	12,800	Korean Air
Shanghai	2 daily	7350	China Eastern
Singapore	daily	2000	Air Asia

PHUKET TAXIS

Taxis remain seriously overpriced on Phuket. A 15-minute journey from, say, Hat Karon to Hat Patong will set you back 400B. Price boards outline *maximum* journey rates and drivers rarely budge from them.

Jot down the phone number of a metered taxi and use the same driver throughout your stay. The best way to do this is to take a metered taxi from the airport (the easiest place to find them) when you arrive. Metered taxis are 50m to the right as you exit airport arrivals. Set rates are 50B for the first 2km, 12B per kilometre for the next 15km and 10B per kilometre thereafter, plus a 100B 'airport tax'. That's no more than 700B to anywhere on the island from the airport.

For cheaper taxi options, the Grab app (www.grab.com/th) is increasingly popular in Thailand. Taxis booked via Grab use their meters and add a small pick-up charge on top, making them much cheaper than taxis hailed on the street. Your accommodation can also help book taxis (many hotel staff have Grab and are used to booking taxis for tourists with it).

Phuket Gazette (www.phuketgazette.net) Weekly information on island-wide activities, dining and entertainment, plus the latest scandals.

Phuket News (www.thephuketnews.com) Another source for up-to-date island news and local life.

Getting There & Away

AIR

Phuket International Airport (☎076 632 7230; www.phuketairportthai.com; Phuket Airport) is 30km northwest of Phuket Town. It takes 45 minutes to an hour to reach the southern beaches from here. A number of carriers serve domestic destinations.

BUS & MINIVAN

Interstate buses depart from **Phuket Bus Terminal 2** (p300), 4km north of Phuket Town.

Phuket travel agencies sell tickets (including ferry fare) for air-con minivans to destinations across southern Thailand, including Krabi, Ranong, Trang, Surat Thani, Ko Samui and Ko Pha-Ngan. Prices are usually slightly higher than for buses.

FERRY & SPEEDBOAT

Phuket's **Tha Rassada** (Map p290; Tha Rassada), 3km southeast of Phuket Town, is the main pier for boats to Ko Phi-Phi, Krabi, Ao Nang, Ko Lanta, the Trang Islands, Ko Lipe and even as far as Pulau Langkawi in Malaysia (which has ferry connections to Penang). Additional services to Krabi and Ao Nang via Ko Yao leave from **Tha Bang Rong** (Map p290; Tha Bang Rong), 26km north of Tha Rassada.

Getting Around

Local Phuket transport is terrible. The systems in place make tourists either stay on their chosen beach, rent a car or motorbike or take a heavily overpriced taxi or túk-túk. *Sŏrng·tăa·ou* run from Phuket Town to the beaches, but often you'll have to go via Phuket Town to get from one beach to another (say Hat Surin to Hat Patong), which takes hours.

Phuket Town เมืองภูเก็ต

☎076 / POP 78,900

Long before flip-flops and selfie sticks, Phuket was an island of rubber trees, tin mines and cash-hungry merchants. Attracting entrepreneurs from the Arabian Peninsula, China, India and Portugal, Phuket Town was a colourful blend of cultural influences. Today, it stands as a testament to the island's history. Wander down streets lined with Sino-Portuguese architecture housing arty coffee shops, eccentric galleries, bright textiles stores and fantastic restaurants, and peek down alleyways to incense-cloaked Chinese Taoist shrines.

The Old Town is Phuket's hipster heart, attracting artists and musicians in particular. That has led to some startling gentrification. Century-old shophouses and homes are being restored and it can feel like every other building is now a trendy polished-concrete cafe or a quirky guesthouse. But Phuket Town is still a wonderfully refreshing cultural break from the island's beaches, all of which it is connected to via a network of *sŏrng·tăa·ou*.

Sights

Phuket Thaihua Museum MUSEUM

(พิพิธภัณฑ์ภูเก็ตไทยหัว; Map p294; ☎076 211224; 28 Th Krabi; 200B; 9am-5pm) Formerly a Chinese language school, this flashy museum

Phuket Town

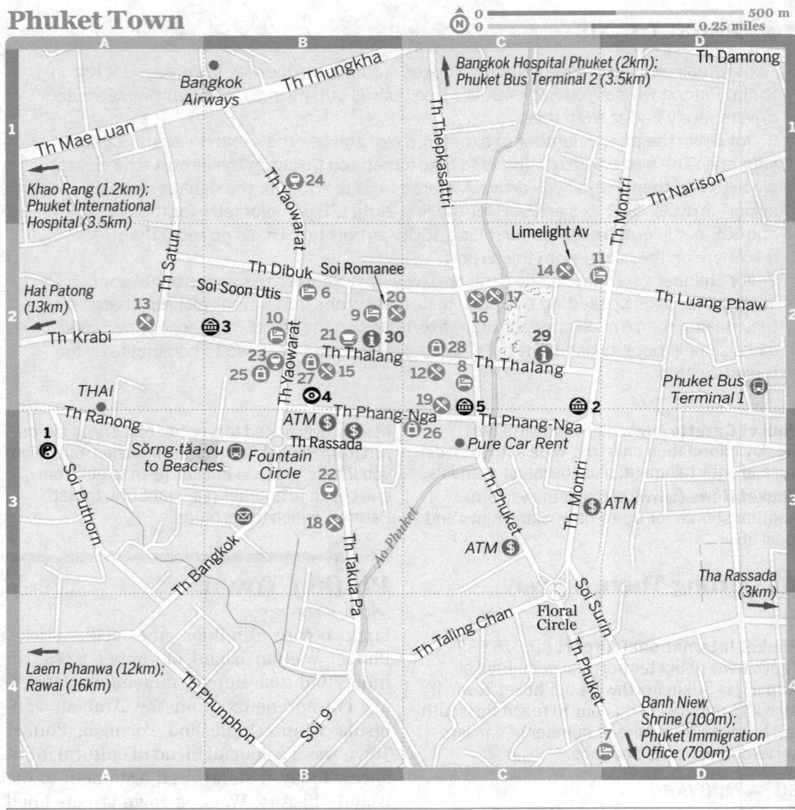

Phuket Town

Sights

1 Jui Tui Shrine A3
2 Phuket Philatelic Museum C2
3 Phuket Thaihua Museum B2
4 Shrine of the Serene Light B2
5 Standard Chartered Bank C2

Activities, Courses & Tours

Blue Elephant Cooking School .... (see 13)
Suay Cooking School .... (see 18)

Sleeping

6 Ai Phuket Hostel B2
7 Art-C House D4
8 Casa Blanca C2
9 RomManee B2
10 RomManee Classic B2
11 Tint @ Phuket Town C2

Eating

12 Abdul's Roti Shop C2
13 Blue Elephant A2
14 Indy Market C2
15 Kopitiam by Wilai B2
16 One Chun C2
17 Raya C2
18 Suay B3
19 Surf & Turf by Soul Kitchen C2
20 Torry's Ice Cream Boutique B2

Drinking & Nightlife

21 Bookhemian B2
22 Ka Jok See B3
23 Rockin' Angels B2
24 Timber Hut B1

Shopping

25 Ban Boran Textiles B2
26 Drawing Room C3
27 Oldest Herbs Shop B2
28 Ranida C2

Information

29 Tourism Authority of Thailand C2
30 Tourist Information Centre B2

is filled with photos and English-language exhibits on Phuket's history, from the Chinese migration (many influential Phuketian families are of Chinese origin) and the tin-mining era to local cuisine, fashion and literature. There's an overview of the building's history, which is a stunning combination of Chinese and European architectural styles, including art deco, Palladianism and a Chinese gable roof and stucco.

Shrine of the Serene Light SHRINE
(ศาลเจ้าแสงธรรม, Saan Jao Sang Tham; Map p294; Th Phang-Nga; ⏲8.30am-noon & 1.30-5.30pm) FREE A handful of Chinese temples pump colour into Phuket Town, but this restored shrine, tucked away up a 50m alley, is particularly atmospheric, with its Taoist etchings on the walls and the vaulted ceiling stained from incense plumes. The altar is always fresh with flowers and burning candles. The shrine is said to have been built by a local family in the 1890s.

Khao Rang VIEWPOINT
(เขารัง, Phuket Hill; Map p290) For a bird's-eye view of the city, climb (or drive) up Khao Rang, 3km northwest of the town centre. A new viewing platform has opened up the commanding panoramas across Phuket Town and all the way to Chalong Bay, Laem Phanwa and Big Buddha. It's at its best during the week, when the summit is relatively peaceful. There are a few restaurants up here. It's about an hour's walk, but don't try it at night. A taxi up costs 700B.

Activities

★ **John Gray's Seacanoe** KAYAKING
(Map p290; ☎076 254505; www.johngray-seacanoe.com; 86 Soi 2/3, Th Yaowarat; adult/child from 3950/1975B) The original, the most reputable and by far the most ecologically sensitive kayaking company on Phuket. The 'Hong by Starlight' trip dodges the crowds, involves sunset paddling and will introduce you to Ao Phang-Nga's famed after-dark bioluminescence. Like any good brand in Thailand, John Gray's 'Seacanoe' name and itineraries have been frequently copied. Located 3.5km north of Phuket Town.

Amazing Bike Tours CYCLING
(Map p290; ☎087 263 2031, 076 283436; www.amazingbiketoursthailand.asia; 32/4 Th Chaofa; half/full-day trip 1900/3200B) This highly popular adventure outfitter leads small groups on half-day bicycle tours through the villages of northeast Phuket, as well as on terrific full-day trips around Ko Yao Noi and more challenging three-day adventure rides around Khao Sok National Park (14,900B) and Krabi Province (15,900B). Prices include bikes, helmets, meals, water and national-park entry fees.

Courses

★ **Suay Cooking School** COOKING
(Map p294; ☎081 797 4135; www.suayrestaurant.com; 50/2 Th Takua Pa; classes per person 2500B) Learn from one of Phuket's top chefs at the most laid-back, soulful and fun cooking school around. Noy Tammasak leads visitors through the local market and teaches how to make three dishes, before cracking open a bottle of wine to enjoy with your culinary creations. Highly recommended; minimum three people.

Blue Elephant Cooking School COOKING
(Map p294; ☎076 354355; www.blueelephantcookingschool.com; 96 Th Krabi; half-day classes 3296B; ⏲Mon-Sun) Master the intricate art of royal Thai cooking in a stunningly restored Sino-Portuguese mansion. Options range from half-day (morning or afternoon) group lessons to private eight-dish vegetarian classes (7000B). Morning sessions visit the market. Book ahead.

Sleeping

Phuket Town is a treasure trove of affordable lodging, with hip hostels, guesthouses and boutique hotels spread across the Old Town.

Ai Phuket Hostel HOSTEL $
(Map p294; ☎076 212881; www.aiphukethostel.com; 88 Th Yaowarat; dm 299B, d 700-900B; ❄@☎) Popular, well-organised hostel in the heart of town. Doubles are tight but come with wood floors, black-and-white photos and, for two rooms, private bathrooms. Not all have windows, something of an Old Town trait. Dorms lack windows also but are colourful and clean, sleeping six

TO MARKET, TO MARKET

A wonderful way to embrace Phuket Town's local flavour is by getting lost in its markets. The **Weekend Market** (Map p290; off Th Chao Fa West; ⏲4-10pm Sat & Sun) is the pick of the bunch.

DON'T MISS

SINO-PORTUGUESE ARCHITECTURE

Stroll along Ths Thalang, Dibuk, Yaowarat, Ranong, Phang-Nga, Rassada and Krabi for a glimpse of Phuket Town's Sino-Portuguese architectural treasures. The most magnificent examples are the **Standard Chartered Bank** (ธนาคารสแตนดาร์ดชาร์เตอร์ด; Map p294; Th Phang-Nga), Thailand's oldest foreign bank; the **THAI office** (Map p294; ☎076 360444; www.thaiairways.com; 78/1 Th Ranong, Phuket Town; ⏰8am-4.30pm); and the **old post office building**, which now houses the **Phuket Philatelic Museum** (พิพิธภัณฑ์ตราไปรษณียากรภูเก็ต; Map p294; ☎076 211020; Th Montri; ⏰9am-4.30pm Mon-Fri, to noon Sat) FREE. Some of the most colourfully revamped buildings line Soi Romanee, off Th Thalang, once home to brothels, gambling and opium dens.

The best-restored residential properties lie along Ths Thalang, Dibuk and Krabi. The fabulous 1903 **Phra Phitak Chyn Pracha Mansion** has been refurbished into the upscale **Blue Elephant restaurant** (Map p294; ☎076 354355; www.blueelephant.com; 96 Th Krabi; mains 420-980B, set menus 1150-2050B; ⏰11.30am-2pm & 6.30-10pm; 📶✍) and **cooking school** (p295).

(women-only) to eight. All share polished-concrete hot-water bathrooms and a small downstairs hang-out lounge.

Art-C House GUESTHOUSE $
(Map p294; ☎082 420 3911; ArtCphuket@hotmail.com; 288 Th Phuket; d 800B; 📶) Not many guesthouses have their own climbing wall and a (smaller) bouldering wall inside. Art-C does, along with 10 tidy private rooms that are a good deal for pricey Phuket. There's a downstairs cafe and friendly staff; non-guests can access the climbing wall for 350B per day. There's no lift: you climb to your room (ropes provided free).

★**Casa Blanca** BOUTIQUE HOTEL $$
(Map p294; ☎076 219019; www.casablancaphuket.com; 26 Th Phuket; d 2300-2800B; ❄📶🏊) All whites and pastels, this elegantly revamped Sino-Portuguese beauty gets extra boutique spark from Moorish-themed touches such as patterned tiles and a plant-lined patio. Modern art adorns smart rooms, in soft greens and pale blues. Deluxe rooms have balconies with city panoramas; superior ones overlook the little pool. A teensy cafe doles out fresh-from-the-oven pastries in the bright lobby.

Tint @ Phuket Town BOUTIQUE HOTEL $$
(Map p294; ☎076 217099; www.thetintphuket.com; 2/11 Th Dibuk; r 1600-3100B; ❄📶) The different floors at this newish, reasonably priced boutique place are colour-themed, with the compact, comfortable and modern rooms decked out in bright pastel colours, ranging from orange and pink to blue and sea green. All have TVs, fridges, desks and small balconies. Staff are efficient and welcoming. It's down a small lane off Th Dibuk.

RomManee BOUTIQUE HOTEL $$
(Map p294; ☎089 728 9871; www.therommanee.com; Soi Romanee; d 1200B; ❄📶) On Phuket Town's prettiest street, this 'boutique guesthouse' has some style with its turquoise-toned exterior, varnished-concrete floors and wood-block reception bar. The four spacious rooms are competitively priced and have an arty modern feel: wood floors, flat-screen TVs, colour accent walls, neon-washed chairs and tasteful lighting. Stairs are steep and there's no lift. There's a less-stylish **branch** (Map p294; ☎076 214488; 4-6 Th Krabi; d 1200-1500B; ❄📶) a block away.

Eating

★**Abdul's Roti Shop** BREAKFAST $
(Map p294; Th Thalang; mains from 40B; ⏰7am-4pm Mon-Sat, to noon Sun) Time to try Abdul's legendary, delicious *roti*. At 75-years-plus, Abdul has been cooking flaky *roti* at the front of his shop for years. Whether you're a fan of sweet or savoury, this place has it covered, with sticky banana *roti* or plain served with spicy chicken, beef or fish massaman (curry).

Kopitiam by Wilai THAI $
(Map p294; ☎083 606 9776; www.facebook.com/kopitiambywilai; 18 Th Thalang; mains 95-180B; ⏰11am-10pm Mon-Sat; 📶) Kopitiam serves Phuket soul food in an atmospheric old shophouse setting. It does Phuketian *pàt tai* (thin rice noodles with egg, tofu and/or shrimp) with a kick, and a fantastic *mee sua*:

noodles sautéed with egg, greens, prawns, chunks of sea bass and squid. Wash it all down with fresh chrysanthemum or passionfruit juice.

Indy Market MARKET $
(Map p294; Limelight Av; mains 30-100B; ⏲4-10.30pm Wed-Fri) Local families, schoolkids and students flock to this smallish central market for the excellent array of food stalls, ranging from barbecue and dumplings to sushi and sweet snacks. There's also a couple of outdoor bars, live music and clothes and jewellery stalls.

★ **One Chun** THAI $$
(Map p294; ☎076 355909; 48/1 Th Thepkasattri; mains 90-350B; ⏲10am-10pm; 📶) A sister restaurant to **Raya** (Map p294; ☎076 218155; rayarestaurant@gmail.com; 48/1 Th Dibuk; mains 180-650B; ⏲10am-10pm), only the dishes here are cheaper and that's why the locals crowd it out every night. Superb seafood – the crabmeat curry in coconut milk is the best in Phuket Town – but also a great roasted-duck red curry. The atmospheric shophouse setting, with 1950s decor and tiled floors, adds to the experience.

★ **Torry's Ice Cream Boutique** ICE CREAM $$
(Map p294; ☎076 510888; www.torrysicecream.com; Soi Romanee; ice creams & desserts 60-200B; ⏲11am-9.30pm Tue-Sun) You'll find gourmet ice cream, sorbets and Phuket-style desserts at this very popular cafe-style place on Phuket Town's most photogenic street. It's a swish setting – a chandelier dangles over the ice-cream counter – in a cool conversion of an old shophouse. Also does coffee, tea and juices.

Surf & Turf by Soul Kitchen FUSION $$
(Map p294; ☎089 104 7432; 115 Th Phang-Nga; mains 240-420B; ⏲5.30-10.30pm; 📶) This relaxed, stylish restaurant scores with its twist on European-Thai fusion food, such as homemade ravioli with a yellow curry sauce and thinly sliced Australian beef on a delicate bed of white risotto. The portions aren't huge, but they are full of flavour and nicely presented. Small but proper wine list.

★ **Suay** INTERNATIONAL, THAI $$$
(Map p294; ☎081 797 4135; www.suayrestaurant.com; 50/2 Th Takua Pa; mains 300-1000B; ⏲5pm-midnight) Fabulous fusion at this converted house, just south of the Old Town proper. Prices have gone up, as the chef's fame has increased, but the food remains excellent. The grilled lemongrass lamb chops with a papaya salsa, the braised beef cheek massaman (curry) and sea bass steak in green curry rock, as do the many flavoursome salads.

Drinking & Nightlife

Phuket Town is where you can party like a local. Bars buzz until late, patronised almost exclusively by Thais and local expats.

★ **Bookhemian** CAFE
(Map p294; ☎098 090 0657; www.bookhemian.com; 61 Th Thalang; ⏲9am-7pm Mon-Fri, to 8.30pm Sat & Sun; 📶) Every town should have a coffee house this cool, with a split-level design that enables it to be both a cafe and an art exhibition space. Used books (for sale) line the front room, bicycles hang from the wall, and the offerings include gourmet coffee, tea and cakes, as well as all-day breakfasts, salads, sandwiches and pasta.

PHUKET BEACH CLEAN-UP

Since 2014, there has been a crackdown on illegal construction and commercial activity on the island's overcrowded beaches. Initially, all rental sunbeds, deckchairs and umbrellas were banned, with thousands removed under the watch of armed soldiers. Illegally encroaching buildings were bulldozed, including well-established beach clubs and restaurants, and others dramatically reduced in size.

The positive side of the crackdown is the beaches are cleaner and less cluttered than before. Beach mats and umbrellas are still available to rent, in limited numbers and in allocated areas; sunbeds remain banned. Tourists may pitch their own umbrellas and chairs within the designated areas too. Jet skis, which were suspended to begin with, are still very much operating in Patong. Some businesses have simply moved to new locations.

It's a confusing, fluid and typically Thai situation, so things may change again.

LOCAL KNOWLEDGE

VEGETARIAN FESTIVAL: BODY-PIERCING, FIRECRACKERS & FLAGELLATION

Deafening machine-gun-like popping sounds fill the streets, the air is thick with grey-brown smoke and men and women traipse along blocked-off city roads, their cheeks pierced with skewers and knives or, more surprisingly, lamps and tree branches. Some have blood streaming down their fronts or open lashes across their backs. No, this isn't a war zone, this is the **Vegetarian Festival** (www.phuketvegetarian.com; ⏲ late Sep-Oct), one of Phuket's most important celebrations and centred on Phuket Town.

The festival, which takes place during the first nine days of the ninth lunar month of the Chinese calendar, celebrates the beginning of 'Taoist Lent', when devout Chinese abstain from meat, dairy and alcohol. Most obvious to outsiders are the fast-paced daily processions winding through town with floats of ornately dressed children and *gà·teu·i* (also spelt *kàthoey;* Thai transgender and cross-dressers), armies of flag-bearing, colour-coordinated young people and, most noticeably, men and women engaged in outrageous acts of stomach-churning self-mortification. Shop owners along Phuket Town's central streets set up altars in front of their shopfronts offering nine tiny cups of tea, incense, fruit, firecrackers, candles and flowers to the nine emperor gods invoked by the festival.

Those participating as mediums bring the nine deities to earth by entering a trance state, piercing their cheeks with an impressive variety of objects, sawing their tongues or flagellating themselves with spiky metal balls. The temporarily possessed mediums (primarily men) stop at shopfront altars to pick up the offered fruit and tea and bless the house. The shop owners and their families stand by making a *wâi* (palms-together Thai greeting) gesture out of respect. Frenzied, surreal and overwhelming barely describe it.

Phuket Town's festival focuses on five Chinese temples. **Jui Tui Shrine** (ศาลเจ้าจุ้ยตุ่ยเต้าโบ้เก้ง; Map p294; Soi Puthorn; ⏲ 8am-8pm) FREE, off Th Ranong, is the most important, followed by **Bang Niew** (ศาลเจ้าบางเหนียว; Map p290; Th Ong Sim Phai; ⏲ 6am-6pm) FREE and **Sui Boon Tong** (ศาลเจ้าซุ่ยบุ่นต๋อง; Map p290; Soi Lorong; ⏲ hours vary) FREE shrines. There are also events in nearby Kathu (where the festival originated) and Ban Tha Reua. If you stop by any procession's starting point early enough (around 6am), you may spot a surprisingly professional, latex-glove-clad crew piercing the devotees' cheeks (not for the faint-hearted). Other ceremonies include firewalking and knife-ladder climbing. At the temples, everyone wears white. Beyond the headlining gore, fabulous cheap vegetarian food stalls line the side streets; many restaurants turn veg-only for the festival.

Oddly enough, there is no record of these acts of devotion associated with Taoist Lent in China. Local Chinese claim the festival was started in 1825 in Kathu, by a theatre troupe from China which performed a nine-day penance of self-piercing, meditation and vegetarianism after becoming seriously ill for failing to propitiate the nine emperor gods of Taoism.

Phuket's **Tourism Authority of Thailand** (TAT; Map p294; ☎ 076 211036; www.tourismthailand.org/Phuket; 191 Th Thalang; ⏲ 8.30am-4.30pm) prints festival schedules. The festival also takes place in Trang, Krabi, Phang-Nga and other southern towns.

Timber Hut CLUB
(Map p294; ☎ 076 211839; 118/1 Th Yaowarat; ⏲ 6pm-2am) Locals, expats and visitors have been packing out this two-floor pub-club nightly for 27 years, downing beers and whisky while swaying to live bands that swing from hard rock to pure pop to hip-hop. No cover charge.

Ka Jok See CLUB
(Map p294; ☎ 076 217903; kajoksee@hotmail.com; 26 Th Takua Pa; ⏲ 8pm-1am Nov-Apr, reduced hours May-Oct) Dripping with Old Phuket charm and the owner's fabulous trinket collection, this intimate, century-old house has two identities: half glamorous eatery, half crazy party venue. There's good Thai food (buffet 2500B per person), but once the tables are cleared it becomes a bohemian madhouse with top-notch music and – if you're lucky – some sensationally extravagant cabaret. Book a month or two ahead. There's no sign.

Rockin' Angels BAR

(Map p294; ☎089 654 9654; 55 Th Yaowarat; ⏲6pm-1am Tue-Sun) This intimate Old Town bar is packed with biker paraphernalia and framed LPs. It gets loud when Patrick, the Singaporean-born owner, jams with his house blues band from around 9.30pm most nights. Beers are cold and you'll be surrounded by a good mix of Thais and local expats.

Shopping

There are bohemian-chic boutiques scattered throughout the Old Town selling jewellery, women's fashions, fabrics and souvenirs, as well as many whimsical art galleries and antique shops.

★**Ranida** ANTIQUES, FASHION

(Map p294; ☎076 214801; 119 Th Thalang; ⏲10am-8pm Mon-Sat) An elegant antique gallery and boutique featuring antiquated Buddha statues and sculptures, organic textiles, and ambitious, exquisite high-fashion women's clothing inspired by vintage Thai garments and fabrics.

Drawing Room ART

(Map p294; ☎086 899 4888; isara380@hotmail.com; 56 Th Phang-Nga; ⏲9am-6pm) With a street-art vibe reminiscent of pre-boom Brooklyn or East London, this wide-open cooperative is by far the stand-out gallery in a town full of them. Canvases might be vibrant abstract squiggles or comical pen-and-ink cartoons. Metallic furniture and bicycles line concrete floors. House music thumps at low levels.

Ban Boran Textiles TEXTILES

(Map p294; ☎076 211563; 51 Th Yaowarat; ⏲10.30am-6pm) Shelves at this hole-in-the-wall shop are stocked high with quality silk scarves, Burmese lacquerware, sarongs, linen shirts, cute colourful bags and cotton textiles from Chiang Mai.

Oldest Herbs Shop FOOD & DRINKS

(Map p294; ☎099 359 9564; Th Thalang; ⏲7.30am-6pm Mon-Sat, to 11.30am Sun) Craving ginseng or perhaps dried insects? You can't miss the wafting aromas of Phuket's oldest herbs shop as you stroll along Th Thalang. Stop here to stock up on Chinese herbal remedies or to simply watch portions of herbs being weighed on antique scales and mixed together ready for sale at this generations-old family business.

Information

There are numerous ATMs on Ths Phuket, Ranong, Montri and Phang-Nga. Wi-fi is everywhere.

Getting There & Around

TO/FROM THE AIRPORT

Despite what airport touts say, an hourly bright-orange government airport bus (www.airportbusphuket.com) runs between the airport and Phuket Town (100B, one hour) via the Heroines Monument (p322) from 8am to

BUSES FROM PHUKET BUS TERMINAL 2

DESTINATION	FARE (B)	DURATION (HR)	FREQUENCY	BUS TYPE
Bangkok	913	13	5pm, 6.30pm	VIP
	587	13-14	6.30am, 7am, 1.30pm, 3.30pm, 5.30pm, 6pm, 6.30pm	air-con
Chiang Mai	1646	22	12.30pm	VIP
Hat Yai	507	7	9.45pm	VIP
	326	7	hourly 7.30am-12.30pm, 7.30pm & 9.30pm	air-con
Ko Samui	450	8 (bus/boat)	9am	air-con
Ko Pha-Ngan	550	9½ (bus/boat)	9am	air-con
Krabi	140	3½	hourly 4.50am-7pm	air-con
Phang-Nga	80	2½	hourly 4.50am-7pm	air-con
Ranong	225	6	hourly 5.30am-6.10pm	air-con
Satun	329	7	8.15am, 10.15am, 12.15pm, 8.15pm	air-con
Surat Thani	195	5	8am, 10am, noon, 2pm	air-con
Trang	230	5	hourly 4.50am-7pm	air-con

8.30pm. Taxis from the airport to Phuket Town cost 650B.

CAR & MOTORCYCLE

Th Rassada has cheap car-rental agencies near **Pure Car Rent** (Map p294; ☎076 211002; www.purecarrent.com; 75 Th Rassada; ⊙8am-7pm), a good central choice. Cars cost around 1200B per day (including insurance), although you'll get them for more or less the same price through the big car-hire chains at Phuket airport.

You can rent motorcycles on Th Rassada, including at Pure Car Rent, or from many other places around town, for 200B to 250B per day.

BUS

Phuket Bus Terminal 1 is mostly used by minivans. A local bus (30B) and minivans (50B) head to Patong 7am to 5pm from here too.

Interstate buses depart from **Phuket Bus Terminal 2** (Map p290; Th Thepkrasattri), 4km north of Phuket Town and 100B by motorcycle taxi, or 300B in a taxi.

MINIVAN

From **Phuket Bus Terminal 1** (Map p294; Th Phang-Nga), 500m east of Phuket Town centre, minivans run to destinations across southern Thailand, including the following:

DESTINATION	FARE (B)	DURATION (HR)
Hat Yai	360	7
Ko Lanta	280	5
Krabi	140	3
Phang-Nga	100	2
Surat Thani	200	4

BEACH SAFETY

During the May–October monsoon, large waves and fierce undertows can make swimming dangerous. Dozens of drownings occur every year on Phuket's beaches, especially Laem Singh, Kamala, Karon and Patong. Heed the red flags signalling serious rips.

At any time of year, keep an eye out for jet skis when you're swimming. Although the Phuket governor declared jet skis illegal in 1997 and they were re-banned again in 2014, enforcement of the rule is another issue. Long-tail boats can also be hazardous as they come in close to shore. Do not expect the boatman to see you!

SŎRNG·TĂA OU & TÚK-TÚK

Large bus-sized *sŏrng·tăa·ou* run regularly from Th Ranong near the day market to Phuket's beaches (20B to 40B per person, 30 minutes to 1½ hours), from 7am to 5pm; otherwise you'll have to charter a túk-túk to the beaches, which costs 400B (Rawai, Kata and Ao Bang Thao), 500B (Patong, Karon and Surin) or 600B (Kamala). Beware of tales that the only way to reach beaches is by taxi.

For a ride around town, túk-túk drivers charge 100B to 200B and motorcycle taxis 50B.

Laem Phanwa แหลมพันวา

An elongated jungle-covered cape jutting into the sea just south of Phuket Town, Laem Phanwa is an all-natural throwback. Some say this is the last vestige of Phuket as it once was. The biggest bloom of development is near the harbour at the cape's tip, 12km south of Phuket Town, where there are a number of high-end resorts and the Phuket Aquarium.

On either side of the harbour, the beaches and coves remain rustic, protected by rocky headlands and mangroves and reached by a dreamy, sinuous coastal road. This is very much a place for peace and quiet, with little or no nightlife.

Sights & Activities

Phuket Aquarium AQUARIUM
(สถานแสดงพันธุ์สัตว์น้ำภูเก็ต; Map p290; ☎076 391126; www.phuketaquarium.org; 51 Th Sakdidej; adult/child 180/100B; ⊙8.30am-4.30pm) Get a glimpse of Thailand's wondrous underwater world at Phuket's popular aquarium, by the harbour on the tip of Laem Phanwa. It's not the largest collection of marine life, but there are useful English-language displays and captions.

Check out the blacktip reef shark, the tiger-striped catfish resembling a marine zebra, and the electric eel with a shock of up to 600V.

★**Cool Spa** SPA
(Map p290; ☎076 371000; www.coolspaphuket.com; Sri Panwa, 88 Mu 8, Th Sakdidej; treatments from 4500B; ⊙10am-9pm) One of the best spas on Phuket, this is an elegant wonderland of fruit-infused wraps, facials and scrubs, and hilltop ocean-view pools. Oh, and then there's the dreamy setting, on the southernmost tip of Phuket's Laem Phanwa.

DON'T MISS

CHALONG BAY RUM

When Marine Lucchini and Thibault Spithakis, each born into a prestigious French wine family, met and fell in love, they bonded over booze – fine rum, in particular. Which is why they became master distillers and launched their own distillery, **Chalong Bay Rum** (ฉลองเบย์รัม ดิสทิลเลอรี่; Map p290; ☎093 575 1119; www.chalongbayrum.com; 14/2 Mu 2, Soi Palai 2; tour 300B; ⊙tours hourly 2-6pm).

They knew they wanted to make natural rum in the French style, the kind made in Martinique, which meant distilling sugar-cane juice, rather than molasses (as is used for most rum). Thailand is the world's fourth-largest sugar cane producer with over 200 varieties currently in cultivation and so, in 2012, the couple imported 40-year-old copper Armagnac stills and incorporated one of the world's great islands into their brand.

Chalong Bay Rum is white, has great flavour, took a gold medal at the 2015 San Francisco World Spirits Competition, and makes a mean mojito – which you'll be sipping as you tour the facility, learning way more about rum than you could ever imagine.

Book ahead, because you'll need directions. About 3km north of Chalong Circle, turn east at the signs to the zoo; it's signposted shortly after.

Sleeping & Eating

This is four- and five-star resort territory.

There are seafood restaurants along the harbour waterfront, where you can watch the fishing boats bobbing by.

★**Sri Panwa** RESORT $$$

(Map p290; ☎076 371000; www.sripanwa.com; 88 Mu 8, Th Sakdidej; d incl breakfast 29,700-279,000B; P ❄ 🛜 ≋) A genuine candidate for best hotel on Phuket, Sri Panwa is poised idyllically on the island's jungle-cloaked southernmost tip. Multi-room villas feature hot tubs, outdoor showers, private pools, personal sound systems and awesome sea views. More affordable digs are still wonderfully comfortable, with the solicitous staff claiming that when the guests see their rooms, 'they don't want to leave them'.

Panwa Boutique Beach Resort RESORT $$$

(Map p290; ☎076 393300; www.panwaboutiquebeachresort.com; 5/3 Mu 8, Ao Yon; d incl breakfast 4300-15,600B; P ❄ 🛜 ≋) With its own exclusive stretch of beachfront and views of Chalong, Rawai and Big Buddha, this slightly dated resort on the cape's west coast offers seclusion, sizeable rooms, a fantastic pool, three restaurants and four-star service without breaking the bank.

Getting There & Away

From Th Ranong in Phuket Town, *sŏrng·tăa·ou* travel here from 7am to 5pm (30B); the last stop is the Phuket Aquarium. A taxi here will cost 400B.

Ko Sireh เกาะสิเหร่

The tiny island of Ko Sireh, 4km east of Phuket Town and connected to Phuket by a bridge, is known for its hilltop reclining Buddha at **Wat Sireh** (วัดบ้านเกาะสิเหร่; Map p290; Th Sireh; ⊙daylight hours) FREE and its *chow lair* **village** (หมู่บ้านชาวเล; Map p290).

Thailand's largest settlement of *chow lair* is little more than a cluster of stilted, metal-roofed shacks. The Urak Lawoi, the most sedentary of the three *chow lair* groups, live only between here and the Tarutao-Langkawi archipelago, and speak a mixture of Malay and Mon-Khmer.

A single road loops the island, passing a few villas, prawn farms, rubber plantations, a bit of untouched forest and east-coast **Hat Teum Suk** (หาดเติมสุข). Just south on a quiet seafront plot, **Phuket Thai Cookery School** (Map p290; ☎082 474 6592; www.phuketthaicookery.com; Ko Sireh; 1-day course 2900B; ⊙8am-3pm, closed Wed) can get you acquainted with Thai spices on a market tour and cooking class (up to six hours). Round-trip transport is provided to most places in Phuket.

There are a few hotels and restaurants but most people visit on a day trip. *Sŏrng·tăa·ou* run here from Th Ranong in Phuket Town from 7am to 5pm (20B). A taxi here from Phuket Town is 300B.

Rawai ราไวย์

Rawai is a delightful place to stay or live, which is why this stretch of Phuket's south coast is teeming with retirees, artists, Thai and expat entrepreneurs, as well as a booming service sector.

The region is defined not just by its beaches but also by its lush coastal hills that rise steeply and tumble into the Andaman Sea, forming **Laem Phromthep** (แหลมพรหมเทพ; Map p303; Rte 4233). Phuket's beautiful southernmost point (for a more secluded sunset spot, seek out the **secret viewpoint** (มุมมอง; Map p303; Rte 4233) 1.5km north). These hills are home to pocket neighbourhoods and cul-de-sacs knitted together by just a few roads – although more are being carved into the hills each year and you can almost envision real-estate money chasing away all the seafood grills and tiki bars. Let's hope that's several decades off. Or at least one. Even with the growth you can still feel nature, especially when you hit the beach.

Activities

Rawai is the epicentre of Phuket's ever-growing *moo·ay tai* (Thai boxing, also spelt *muay Thai*) mania, home to half a dozen schools where students (of both sexes) live and train traditional-style in camps with professional *moo·ay tai* fighters.

Hat Rawai is an excellent place to arrange **boat charters** (Map p303; Hat Rawai) to neighbouring islands. Destinations include quiet Ko Bon (long-tail/speedboat 1200/2400B) and Coral Island (1800/3500B, maximum eight people) for snorkelling.

Kingka Supa Muay Thai HEALTH & FITNESS
(Map p303; ☎076 226495; www.supamuaythaiphuket.com; 43/42 Mu 7, Th Viset; per session/week 600/3000B; ⏲7am-7pm Mon-Sat, 9am-6pm Sun) Strap up those wrists and get fired up at this Thai boxing gym opened by a former *moo·ay tai* champion (he doesn't teach here). People come from around the world to learn how to fight alongside seasoned professionals. A mix of Thais and foreigners live in on-site dorms, but tourists can join drop-in classes or try a taekwondo session (200B).

Sinbi Muay Thai HEALTH & FITNESS
(Map p303; ☎083 391 5535; www.sinbi-muaythai.com; 100/15 Mu 7, Th Sai Yuan; per session/week 400/3000B; ⏲7.30am-7pm Mon-Sat) A well-respected boxing training camp for both men and women.

Bob's Kite School KITESURFING
(Map p290; ☎092 459 4191; www.kiteschoolphuket.com; Rte 4024; 1hr lesson 1500B, 3-day course 11,000B; ⏲Nov-Apr) Phuket's very first, German-run kite school is still going strong with keen, friendly staff. From May to mid-October it operates on the northwest side of the island at Hat Nai Yang (p319). Equipment hire costs 1000B per hour.

Atsumi SPA
(Map p290; ☎081 272 0571; www.atsumihealing.com; 34/18 Soi Pattana, Th Sai Yuan; massage 600-1000B, treatment 1200-1600B, detox package 5500-9100B; ⏲9am-5pm) Phuket isn't all about boozing and gorging on cream-loaded curries. In fact, there's a flourishing wellness scene. At this earthy fasting-detox retreat, guests check in for days-long water, juice and/or herb fasts with massages. But non-dieters are also welcome for spa sessions, taking in traditional Thai, oil and deep-tissue treatments, plus signature Thaiatsu (Thai meets shiatsu) massages and yoga (300B).

Sleeping

Good 9 at Home GUESTHOUSE $
(Map p303; ☎088 457 6969; www.facebook.com/good9athome; 62 Mu 6, Soi Wassana, Hat Rawai; d 900B; ❄📶) Set beside a cute patio, these seven fresh, gleaming contemporary-style rooms spiced up with colour accent walls, tiled bathrooms and the odd bit of artwork make for good-value digs, 300m up the street from **Hat Rawai** (หาดราไวย์; Map p303). The lime-green-and-grey house is kept clean, cosy and friendly, with a thoughtful little coffee corner thrown into the mix.

Phu Na Na BOUTIQUE HOTEL $$
(Map p303; ☎076 226673; www.phunana-phuket.com; 43/234 Mu 7, Th Viset; d 1500-3900B; ❄📶🏊) Set around a pool, the smart rooms here are like mini-apartments with comfortable beds, fridges, microwaves, decent bathrooms and terraces, making them a reasonable deal for the price. All are well-maintained and you're walking distance from **Hat Friendship** (Hat Mittraphap, หาดมิตรภาพ; Map p303), or a short motorbike or túk-túk ride to Hat Rawai's restaurants.

Vijitt RESORT $$$
(Map p303; ☎076 363600; www.vijittresort.com; 16 Mu 2, Th Viset; villas incl breakfast 6700-26,000B;

Hat Nai Han & Hat Rawai

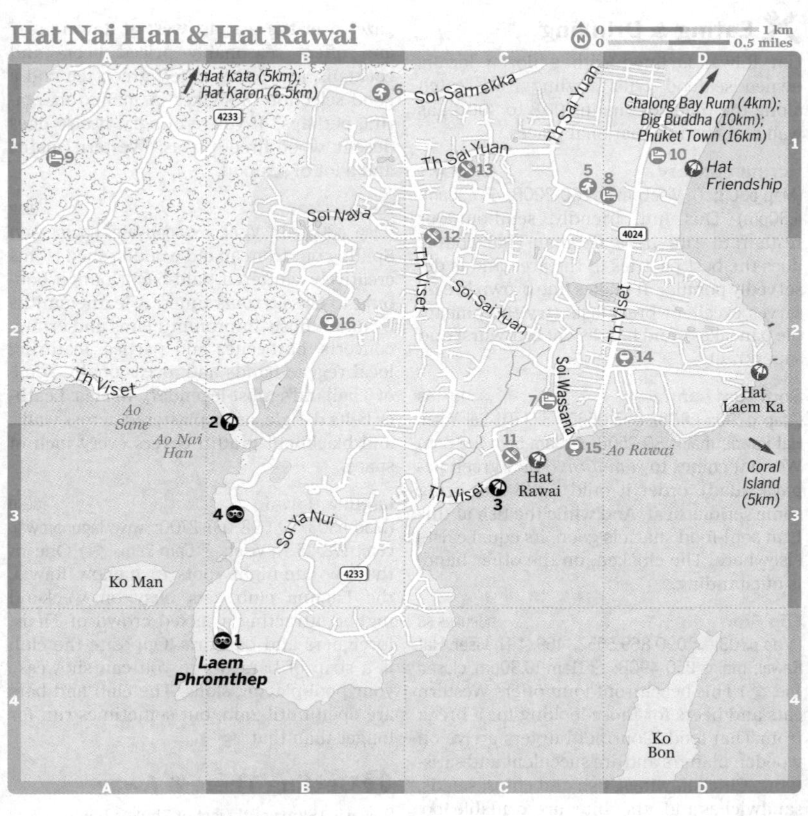

Hat Nai Han & Hat Rawai

Top Sights
1 Laem Phromthep B4

Sights
2 Hat Nai Han B2
3 Hat Rawai C3
4 Secret Viewpoint B3

Activities, Courses & Tours
Boat Charters .... (see 3)
5 Kingka Supa Muay Thai C1
6 Sinbi Muay Thai B1

Sleeping
7 Good 9 at Home C2
8 Phu Na Na D1
9 Sabai Corner A1
10 Vijitt D1

Eating
11 Flip Side C3
12 German Bakery C1
13 Rum Jungle C1

Drinking & Nightlife
14 Laguna Rawai D2
15 Nikita's C3
16 Reggae Bar B2

P ❄ ≈ ≋) Arguably the area's most elegant property, peaceful Vijitt is set around a garden sprinkled with frangipani trees. Deluxe villas boast limestone floors, large bathtubs, outdoor showers and gorgeous sea views from private terraces (some with their own pools). The stunning, multilevel, black-bottom infinity pool overlooks Hat Friendship.

Eating & Drinking

Hat Rawai is lined with a dozen locally owned seafood grills sizzling fresh catch along the roadside (mains 90B to 300B), as well as a few international places.

German Bakery EUROPEAN $

(Map p303; Th Viset; mains 80-200B; ⏲7.30am-4.30pm) This fun, friendly, semi-outdoor restaurant run by a German-Thai couple does the best pastries in the area and is deservedly popular. It makes fine brown bread, serves excellent breakfasts (try the pineapple pancakes), and has decent bratwurst and sauerkraut.

Som Tum Lanna THAI $$

(Map p290; ☎081 597 0569; 3/7 Th Sai Yuan, Hat Rawai; mains 80-250B; ⏲9am-5pm Tue-Sun) When it comes to *sôm·đam* (spicy green papaya salad), order it mild – it'll still bring some serious heat. And while the fish at this Isan soul-food shack is good, its equal exists elsewhere. The chicken, on the other hand, is outstanding.

Flip Side BURGERS $$

(Map p303; ☎090 869 5552; 469/4 Th Viset, Hat Rawai; mains 250-490B; ⏲11am-10.30pm, closed Tue; 📶) This beachfront joint offers Western eats and beers for those looking for a break from Thai food. Gourmet burgers arrive on wooden platters and are succulent and satisfying. Chicken wings, fish and chips, salads, sandwiches and other bites are available too, and there's a big menu of Belgian, German and US craft beers. Service can be slack.

★**Rum Jungle** INTERNATIONAL $$$

(Map p303; ☎076 388153; www.facebook.com/Rum-Jungle-Cafe-Rawai-Phuket-173738946050909; 69/8 Mu 1, Th Sai Yuan; mains 280-620B; ⏲3-11pm Mon-Sat; 🌿) Perhaps Rawai's finest restaurant, this semi-open thatched-roof place with an exceptional world-beat soundtrack serves up classy Italian and international dishes in a laid-back, intimate setting. The New Zealand lamb shank is divine, as are the steamed clams, and the pasta sauces are all made from scratch. Tempting veggie choices include aubergine parmigiana and pasta Gorgonzola. Book ahead.

Nikita's BAR

(Map p303; ☎076 288703; www.nikitas-phuket.com; Hat Rawai; mains 220-800B; ⏲10am-midnight; 📶) This popular open-air hang-out gazes over the sea just west of Rawai's pier and offers reasonably priced beers and cocktails, as well as coffee, green tea and a good selection of shakes. A mango margarita, perhaps? If you're hungry, it also does decent wood-fired pizzas, Western mains and a lot of seafood.

Reggae Bar BAR

(Map p303; Th Viset; ⏲noon-late, hours vary) Spilling out from an old wooden shed is this creatively cluttered, laid-back lounge bobbing to classic roots tunes. A leathersmiths by day, it hosts impromptu jams and erratic concerts, barbecues and parties, featuring local reggae bands and, occasionally, some of Thailand's most legendary Rastas. Leather belts dangle, art is plastered across walls, and blacklight graffiti covers every inch of space.

Laguna Rawai CLUB

(Map p303; ☎098 031 2700; www.lagunarawai.com; 178/15 Th Viset; ⏲5pm-2am; 📶) One of the few late-night spots in mellow Rawai, the Laguna club gets busy on weekend nights, attracting a mixed crowd of Thais, foreigners and bar girls. Opposite the club is a strip of bars where you can showcase your pool-playing skills. The club and bars are open until 2am, but sometimes run for longer than that.

Getting There & Away

Rawai is 18km southwest of Phuket Town. *Sŏrng·tăa·ou* run to Rawai (30B) from Phuket Town's Th Ranong between 7am and 5pm. Some continue to Hat Nai Han (40B), but not all, so ask first. Taxis from Rawai to Nai Han cost 200B.

Taxis go from Rawai and Hat Nai Han to Phuket airport (750B), Patong (700B) and Phuket Town (500B).

Hat Patong หาดป่าตอง

☎07620,600 / POP 20,600

Patong (ป่าตอง) is a free-for-all and by far Phuket's most notorious and divisive destination. Almost anything is available for the right price and while that's true of other places in Thailand, Patong doesn't try to hide it. That doesn't mean you're going to like it. But despite the concrete, silicone and moral turpitude, there's something honest about the place.

Gaze out at the wide, white-sand beach and its magnificent crescent bay, and you'll understand how the whole thing started. Diving and spa options abound, along with upscale dining, street-side fish grills, extravagant cabaret, Thai boxing, dusty antique shops and, of course, the opportunity to party from dusk till dawn.

The sun-scorched Russians in bad knock-off T-shirts, the Chinese tour groups, the Western men turning the midlife crisis into a full-scale industry, and the overwhelming disregard for managed development meanwhile make Patong ripe with unintentional comedy.

Sights & Activities

Wat Suwan Khiri Wong (วัดสุวรรณคีรีวงศ์; Map p290; cnr Th Phra Barami & Th Phisit Karani; daylight hours) FREE, just off Th Phra Barami at the northeast end of Patong, is a welcome respite from the chaos outside. Less tranquil but worth a look is the **Good Luck Shrine** (ศาลเจ้าโชคดี; cnr Th Tawiwong & Th Phra Barami), a beautiful, golden Bodhisattva statue in the middle of a traffic circle, adorned with rainbow-coloured ribbons and guarded by carved elephants festooned with flowers, incense and candles.

★ **Sea Fun Divers** DIVING
(Map p290; 076 340480; www.seafundivers.com; 29 Soi Karon Nui; 2/3-dive trip 3900/4400B, Open Water Diver certification 18,400B; 9am-6pm) An outstanding, very professional diving operation, with high standards, impeccable service and keen, knowledgeable instructors (though more expensive than other dive operators). Sea Fun is based at Le Meridien resort at the southern end of Patong; there's a second location (p311) in Kata Noi.

Nicky's Handlebar ADVENTURE
(076 343211; www.nickyhandlebars.com; 41 Th Rat Uthit; half/full-day tour incl bike hire from 7000/9000B) The big-beast bikes here are begging to be taken for a spin, but they aren't for amateurs. Nicky has been leading Harley tours around Phuket for over a decade. Full-day itineraries tour Phang-Nga Province; there are half-day options too, plus Harley rentals for independent explorations (from 4800B). You'll need a big-bike license from home. Hit the bar (p309) for post-drive refreshments.

Pum Thai Cooking School COOKING
(076 346269; www.pumthaifoodchain.com; 204/32 Th Rat Uthit; 3/5hr class 1700/3700B; 11am-9pm) This restaurant/cookery school (with other branches in Thailand, as well as France and the UK) holds daily classes. Popular, five-hour 'Little Wok' classes include a market tour and a take-home cookbook.

Sleeping

If you can't score a bed in a hostel – be sure to book ahead – you'll struggle to find a room for under 1000B between November and April. Outside this time period rates drop by 40% to 60%.

★ **Wire Hostel** HOSTEL $
(076 604066; 66/10 Th Bangla; dm 340-550B;) Patong's hostel of the moment is right in the belly of the beast: a minute's walk from the Bangla nightlife. There's some stylish design on display, three floors of dorms (none with doors but you can get a double bed if you fancy getting intimate in public). Downstairs bar, clean shared bathrooms but, unsurprisingly, it can get noisy. Book ahead.

TIGER KINGDOM

At some point during your stay, you'll likely be handed a brochure flaunting Phuket's controversial Tiger Kingdom. Launched in 2013, Tiger Kingdom Phuket (like its original in Chiang Mai) offers hundreds of daily visitors the chance to stroke, feed and pose over-enthusiastically with its 'domesticated' tigers.

Concerns about animal welfare and human safety abound, and there are constant reports about animals being maltreated, confined to small cages and sedated to keep them docile. Like the infamous Tiger Temple in Kanchanaburi, Tiger Kingdom denies all allegations that its tigers are mistreated.

In 2014, an Australian tourist was seriously mauled while visiting Tiger Kingdom. The tiger in question was 'retired'.

Given the significant animal-welfare issues involved, Lonely Planet does not recommend visiting Tiger Kingdom.

Hat Patong

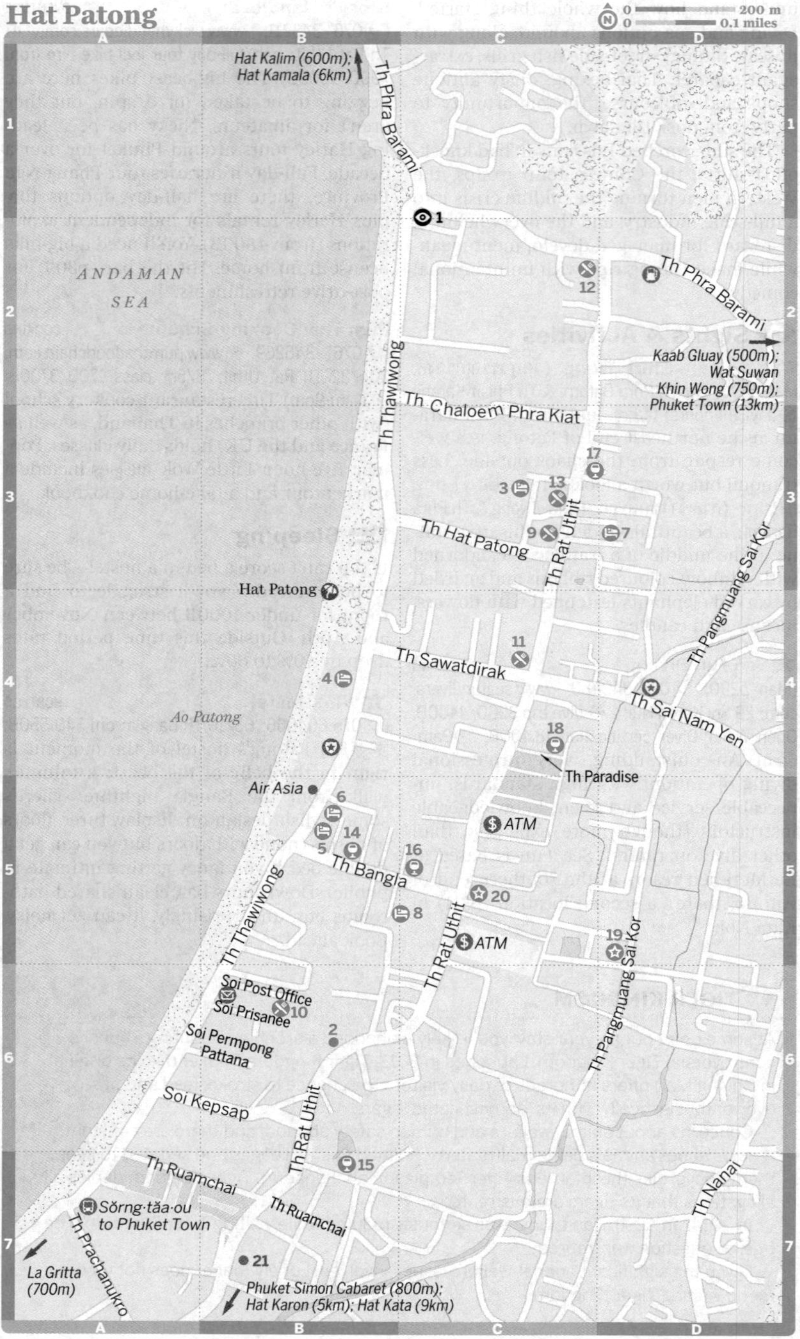

0 — 200 m
0 — 0.1 miles

Hat Kalim (600m); Hat Kamala (6km)
Th Phra Barami
1
12
Th Phra Barami
ANDAMAN SEA
Kaab Gluay (500m); Wat Suwan Khin Wong (750m); Phuket Town (13km)
Th Thawiwong
Th Chaloem Phra Kiat
17
3
13
Th Hat Patong
9
7
Th Rat Uthit
Th Pangmuang Sai Kor
Hat Patong
11
Th Sawatdirak
4
Th Sai Nam Yen
Ao Patong
18
Th Paradise
Air Asia
6
ATM
14
5
16
Th Bangla
20
8
Th Thawiwong
ATM
Th Rat Uthit
19
Soi Post Office
Soi Prisanee
10
2
Soi Permpong Pattana
Th Pangmuang Sai Kor
Soi Kepsap
Th Rat Uthit
15
Th Ruamchai
Th Ruamchai
Th Nanai
Sŏrng·tăa·ou to Phuket Town
Th Prachanukro
21
La Gritta (700m)
Phuket Simon Cabaret (800m); Hat Karon (5km); Hat Kata (9km)

Hat Patong

Sights

1	Good Luck Shrine	C1

Activities, Courses & Tours

	Nicky's Handlebar	(see 17)
2	Pum Thai Cooking School	B6
	Swasana Spa	(see 4)

Sleeping

3	BYD Lofts	C3
	Ella	(see 10)
4	Impiana Phuket Cabana	B4
5	Lupta Hostel	B5
6	Patong Backpacker Hostel	B5
7	Priew Wan Guesthouse	D3
8	Wire Hostel	C5

Eating

9	Chicken Rice Briley	C3
10	Ella	B6
11	Georgia Restaurant	C4
12	No.9 2nd Restaurant	C2
13	Patong Food Park	C3
	Sala Bua	(see 4)

Drinking & Nightlife

14	Aussie Bar	B5
15	Craft Beer Lounge	B7
16	Illuzion	C5
17	Nicky's Handlebar	C3
18	Zag Club	C4

Entertainment

19	Bangla Boxing Stadium	D5
20	Rock City	C5

Transport

21	Avis Rent A Car	B7

Patong Backpacker Hostel HOSTEL $
(☎076 341196; 140 Th Thawiwong; dm 300-550B; ❄📶) This busy budget spot has a great location across the road from the beach, a communal lounge and eccentric but welcoming staff. Colourful dorms sleep three to 10 and come with good mattresses and small lockers. The top floor is brightest, but dorms on the lower floors each have their own attached bathrooms.

Lupta Hostel HOSTEL $
(☎076 602462, 092 934 6453; www.luptahostel.com; 138 Th Tawiwong; dm/d 690/1390B; ❄@📶) Just 100m from Th Bangla, this well-kept place offers compact and comfortable four- to eight-bed dorms in light woods and whites, although not all have windows. Each bed gets its own locker, plug socket and tiny shelf. There's a women-only dorm, a sole private room and a social lobby loaded with cushions, high stools and rattan lamps.

Priew Wan Guesthouse GUESTHOUSE $$
(☎076 344441; info@priewwanguesthouse.com; 83/9 Th Rat Uthit; d 1600B; 📶) This long-running and reliable family-run guesthouse is hidden down a mostly residential soi, but is still only a 10-minute walk to the northern end of Hat Patong. Clean, sizeable rooms come with balconies, safes, fridges and TVs and are a good deal. Friendly staff and great low-season (April to October) discounts.

★**BYD Lofts** APARTMENT $$$
(☎076 343024; www.bydlofts.com; 5/28 Th Hat Patong; apt 3600-9900B; ❄📶🏊) Spread over four buildings, BYD feels like it's been torn straight out of an upmarket interior design magazine. Stylish and comfortable (and only a couple of minutes' walk from the beach), the apartments are coated in white and come with sharp lines and colourful art. Some rooms have private pools. For everyone else there's a turquoise rooftop pool.

Impiana Phuket Cabana HOTEL $$$
(☎076 340138; www.impiana.com; 41 Th Thawiwong; d 12,000-27,000B; P❄📶🏊) Cabana-style and bang on the best (north) part of the beach, Impiana's rooms are laden with sophisticated creature comforts and still close to all the action. There's good Asian-Mediterranean fusion food at poolside Sala Bua (p308), while indulgent treatments at the on-site **Swasana Spa** (massage or treatment 1500-5900B; ⏲10am-7pm) see you nestled in a cool glass cube with ocean views.

Eating

Bargain seafood and noodle stalls pop up at night. Try the sois around Th Bangla, and **Patong Food Park** (Th Rat Uthit; mains 50-200B; ⏲4.30pm-midnight) once the sun drops. The swishest restaurants sit above the cliffs on the north edge of town.

Chicken Rice Briley THAI $
(081 597 8380; Th Rat Uthit, Patong Food Park; mains 50-200B; 6am-9pm) One of few places in Patong Food Park (p307) to offer sustenance while the sun shines. Steamed chicken breast is served on rice with a bowl of chicken broth with crumbled bits of meat; the chili sauce is fantastic for dipping. The stewed pork on rice, plus mango with sticky rice, is popular too. There's a reason it's perennially packed here.

★ **Ella** INTERNATIONAL $$
(076 344253; 100/19-20 Soi Post Office; mains 150-400B; 9am-midnight;) This moulded-concrete, industrial-feel bistro-cafe is a lovely surprise. Inventive all-day breakfasts feature spicy Rajasthani scrambled eggs, massaman (curry) chicken tacos, omelettes stuffed with chicken and veg, and baguette French toast with caramelised banana. At night, it's also a bar and a cool spot for a cocktail.

There are similarly styled **rooms** (d 2200-4000B;) for rent upstairs.

★ **No.9 2nd Restaurant** ASIAN $$
(076 624445; 143 Th Phra Barami; mains 165-800B; 11.30am-11.30pm, closed 5th & 20th of every month) Deceptively simple, with wooden tables and photo-strewn walls, this is one of the best, busiest restaurants in Patong, thanks to the inventive and delicious mix of Thai, Japanese and Western dishes. It's a rare feat for a kitchen to be able to turn out authentic sushi, vegetarian versions of Thai curries and a lamb shank without any dip in quality.

★ **Georgia Restaurant** GEORGIAN $$
(076 390595; 19 Th Sawatdirak; mains 200-390B; noon-10pm, closed Sun) The influx of Russian visitors to Patong has seen a corresponding rise in eateries catering to them. Georgia is the pick of the bunch, offering Russian salads and dumplings alongside delicious *khachapuri*, a cheese-filled bread; *ajapsandali*, a rich, vegetarian stew; and classic eastern European dishes such as *solyanka*, a spicy, sour meat soup served in a clay pot.

Kaab Gluay THAI $$
(Map p290; 076 346832; 58/3 Th Phra Barami; mains 135-250B; 11am-2am;) Remodelled since our last visit, this busy, semi-open-air roadside eatery is a hit for its authentic, affordable Thai food, with switched-on staff and well-spelt (!) menus to match. Unpretentious dining under a huge roof with ceiling fans. Expect red-curry prawns, chicken satay, sweet-and-sour fish, deep-fried honeyed chicken, classic noodles and stir-fries, and 30-plus takes on spicy Thai salads.

Sala Bua FUSION $$$
(076 340138; www.impiana.com; 41 Th Thawiwong; mains 220-610B; 11am-11pm) Asian-Mediterranean fusion cuisine in a classy seaside four-star resort setting. Start with smoked-salmon Caesar salad or rock lobster, avocado and roasted veg salad, then move on to wood-fired pizzas, seafood-packed spaghetti or *pá·naang* curry osso buco.

GAY PRIDE IN PHUKET

Although Bangkok and Pattaya host big gay-pride celebrations, the **Phuket Gay Pride Festival** (www.phuket-pride.org; April) is widely considered the best in Thailand, possibly even in all of Southeast Asia. Though the date has changed several times since the festival's inception in 1999, it usually lands in late April. Whenever it blooms, (mostly male) revellers from all over the world flock to the island – to Patong, specifically, for a four-day weekend party.

For updates on future festivals and the local gay scene, check out Gay Patong (www.gaypatong.com).

At any other time of year, you'll find Phuket's gay pulse in the network of streets that link the Royal Paradise Hotel with Th Rat Uthit in Patong. It's a predominantly male scene.

Drinking & Nightlife

Some visitors may find that Patong's bar scene puts them off their *pàt tai*, but if you're in the mood for plenty of banging bass, winking neon and short skirts, it's certainly an experience.

Illuzion CLUB
(www.illuzionphuket.com; 31 Th Bangla; 9pm-late) Still the most popular of Patong's megaclubs, Illuzion is a multilevel mishmash of dance and gymnastics shows, international DJs, regular ladies' nights, all-night electronic beats, LED screens and more bars than you could ever count.

Craft Beer Lounge BAR
(www.grandmercurephuketpatong.com; Soi 1, Th Rat Uthit, Grand Mercure Phuket Patong; ⌚10am-11pm) Tapping into one of the world's booze crazes, this sleekly contemporary boutique beer bar stocks more than 100 international draught and craft labels, mostly from the US, plus local brands. For 500B you get free-flowing Singha beer for an hour, but the bartenders also make proper cocktails. The lounge is tucked into the back of the Grand Mercure's lobby.

Nicky's Handlebar BAR
(☎076 343211; www.nickyhandlebars.com; 41 Th Rat Uthit; ⌚7am-1am; 📶) This fun biker bar welcomes all, wheels or no wheels. Once a bit of a dive, Nicky's has never looked better. There's a good selection of beers and the menu encompasses Western and Thai, including what the bar claims is Thailand's spiciest burger. You can get your own wheels here by asking about Harley tours (p305) and hire (from 4800B).

Zag Club GAY, BAR
(123/8-9 Royal Paradise Complex; ⌚9pm-3am) Packed-out gay-scene favourite Zag Club hosts no less than three shimmering cabarets at 10.40pm, 11.40pm and 1.20am. In between, everyone drinks and dances to booming chart-toppers.

Aussie Bar PUB
(www.phuketaussiebar.com; Th Bangla; ⌚9am-late; 📶) Does what it says on the tin: Aussie sport on the many screens, Aussie food on the menu and lots of visiting Australians clutching beers. Also has pool tables and tabletop football, and it does provide an antidote to the surrounding go-go bars.

☆ Entertainment

Cross-dressing cabarets and Thai boxing are Patong's specialities.

Bangla Boxing Stadium SPECTATOR SPORT
(☎076 273416; www.banglaboxingstadiumpatong.com; Th Pangmuang Sai Kor; stadium/ringside 1700/2500B; ⌚9pm Wed, Fri & Sun) A packed line-up of competitive *moo·ay tai* (Thai boxing) bouts featuring Thai and foreign fighters.

Phuket Simon Cabaret CABARET
(Map p290; ☎076 342114; www.phuket-simoncabaret.com; 8 Th Sirirach; adult 800-1000B, child 600-800B; ⌚shows 6pm, 7.30pm & 9pm) About 500m south of town, Simon puts on fun, colourful trans cabarets that are wildly popular with Asian tourists. The 600-seat theatre is grand, the costumes are glittery, feathery extravaganzas, and the ladyboys are convincing. The house is usually full – book ahead.

Rock City LIVE MUSIC
(www.rockcitypatong.com; 169 Th Rat Uthit; ⌚8pm-2am) On the corner of Th Bangla and Th Rat Uthit, this suitably dark and sweaty den of rock lives on the glory of AC/DC, Metallica and Guns N' Roses tribute bands and attracts a headbanging crowd of tourists and locals. The live music gets going around 9pm.

ℹ Information

There are ATMs, currency-exchange facilities and wi-fi across town.

ℹ Getting There & Away

Sŏrng·tăa·ou from Th Ranong in Phuket Town go to the south end of Hat Patong (40B) from 7am to 6pm. From here you can walk or hop on motorbike taxis (30B per ride) or túk-túk. After-hours túk-túk charters from Phuket Town cost 500B. A 'local bus' runs between Phuket Town's Bus Terminal 1 and Patong (30B) from 7am to 5pm, or you can catch minivans that leave when full from the same place (50B).

Taxis to/from the airport cost 800B. There's a shared minibus from the airport to Patong (180B per person, minimum 10 people).

ℹ Getting Around

A túk-túk will circle Patong for around 200B per ride. Numerous places rent motorbikes (250B); Nicky's Handlebar rents Harleys (from 4800B). The mandatory helmet law is strictly enforced in Patong, where roadblocks/checkpoints can spring up suddenly. **Avis** (☎062 604 0361; www.avisthailand.com; 239/1 Th Rat Uthit; ⌚7.30am-7pm) hires cars at the south end of town.

Hat Kata หาดกะตะ

Classier than Karon and without Patong's seedy hustle, Kata (กะตะ) attracts travellers of all ages to its lively beach. While you won't bag a secluded strip of sand, you'll still find lots to do. A prime spot for surfing in the shoulder and wet seasons, Kata also has some terrific day spas, top-notch food and a highly rated yoga studio.

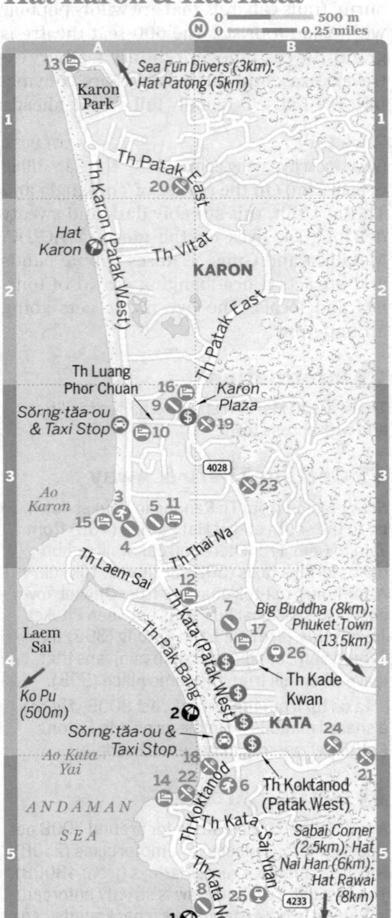

The golden-sand beach is carved in two by a rocky headland: **Hat Kata Yai** (หาดกะตะใหญ่; Map p310) lies on the north side; more secluded **Hat Kata Noi** (หาดกะตะน้อย; Map p310) unfurls to the south. The road between them is home to Phuket's original millionaire's row.

The main street, Th Kata, runs parallel to the beach. There are cheaper restaurants, bars and guesthouses on Th Thai Na, which branches inland just south of where Th Kata heads up over the hill into Karon.

Hat Karon & Hat Kata

Sights
1 Hat Kata Noi A5
2 Hat Kata Yai A4

Activities, Courses & Tours
Baray Spa .... (see 17)
Boathouse Cooking Class .... (see 18)
3 Dino Park A3
4 Dive Asia A3
5 Dive Asia A3
Infinite Luxury Spa .... (see 14)
6 Kata Hot Yoga B5
Phuket Surf .... (see 22)
7 Rumblefish Adventure B4
8 Sea Fun Divers B5
9 Sunrise Divers A3

Sleeping
10 Doolay Hostel A3
11 Fantasy Hill Bungalow A3
12 Fin Hostel A4
13 In On The Beach A1
14 Kata Rocks A5
15 Marina Phuket A3
16 Pineapple Guesthouse A3
Rumblefish Adventure .... (see 7)
17 Sawasdee Village B4

Eating
18 Boathouse Wine & Grill B5
19 Eat Bar & Grill B3
20 Elephant Cafe A1
21 Istanbul Restaurant B5
22 Kata Mama A5
23 Pad Thai Shop B3
24 Red Duck B4

Drinking & Nightlife
25 After Beach Bar B5
26 Art Space Cafe & Gallery B4
Ska Bar .... (see 22)

Sights & Activities

The small island of **Ko Pu** is just offshore, but be careful of rip currents, heed the red flags and don't go past the breakers in the rainy season unless you're a strong, experienced ocean swimmer.

Both of Kata's beaches offer decent surfing from April to November. Hiring stand-up paddle kit or kayaks costs 300/900B per hour/day. There's a branch of the highly rated Sea Fun Divers on Kata Noi.

Rumblefish Adventure DIVING
(Map p310; ☎095 441 8665; www.rumblefishadventure.com; 98/79 Beach Centre, Th Kata, Hat

Kata; 2/3-dive day trip 3500/3900B; ⏲10am-7pm) A terrific boutique dive shop offering all the standard courses, day trips and liveaboards from its Beach Centre location in Kata. The PADI Open Water Diver certification course costs 12,500B. There's a small **hostel** (Map p310; ☎076 330315; 98/79 Th Kata, Hat Kata; dm 300B, d 400-950B; ❄📶) attached: divers get a free dorm bed if there's room. Book ahead.

Phuket Surf SURFING
(Map p310; ☎063 870280; www.phuketsurfing.com; Hat Kata Yai; lessons 1500B, board rental per hour/day 150/500B; ⏲8am-7pm Apr-late Oct) Offers private 1½-hour surf lessons plus board rentals. Check the website for info on local surf breaks.

Sea Fun Divers DIVING
(Map p310; ☎076 330124; www.seafundivers.com; 14 Th Kata Noi, Katathani; 2/3-dive day trip 3900/4400B; ⏲9am-6pm) An outstanding and very professional diving operation, albeit rather more expensive than the competition. Standards are extremely high, service is impeccable and instructors are keen and knowledgeable. Open Water Diver certification costs 18,400B. Sea Fun also has a branch (p305) at Le Meridien resort at the southern end of Patong.

Dive Asia DIVING
(Map p310; ☎076 330598; www.diveasia.com; 24 Th Karon, Hat Kata; 2/3-dive day trip 3400/4900B; ⏲10am-9pm) This outfit runs an extensive range of PADI certification courses (Open Water Diver 11,480B) plus day-trip dives to Ko Phi-Phi and liveaboards to the Similan and Surin Islands (from 21,000B). There's another branch (p313) in Karon.

Courses

Kata Hot Yoga YOGA
(Map p310; ☎076 605950; www.katahotyoga.com; 217 Th Koktanod, Hat Kata; 550B per class; ⏲9-10.30am, 5.15-6.45pm, 7.15-8.45pm) Craving more heat? At Kata Hot Yoga, Bikram's famous asana series is taught over 90 minutes in a sweltering room by the expert owner and an international roster of visiting instructors. All levels welcome; no bookings needed. Multi-class packages offer good deals.

Boathouse Cooking Class COOKING
(Map p310; ☎076 330015; www.boathouse-phuket.com; 182 Th Koktanod, Hat Kata; classes 2570-4095B; ⏲classes 10am Wed, Sat & Sun) Kata's top fine-dining **restaurant** (Map p310; ☎076 330015; www.boathouse-phuket.com; 182 Th Koktanod, Hat Kata; mains 470-1750B, tasting menus 1800-2200B; ⏲11am-10.30pm) offers fantastic one-day and two-day Thai cooking classes with its renowned chef.

Sleeping

Hostels and guesthouses cluster near the north of Hat Kata Yai: posher hotels and resorts can be found further south.

If you're stuck without shelter, you'll probably find a room at the Beach Centre, a complex of new-build townhouses packed with way too many guesthouses to list. From Th Kata, turn inland just south of the intersection with Th Thai Na; it's signposted.

★**Fin Hostel** HOSTEL $
(Map p310; ☎088 753 1162; www.finhostelphuket.com; 100/20 Th Kata/Patak West; dm/capsules/d 400/600/2000B; ❄📶🏊) This well-kept, efficient hostel, set back from the road, spreads across two buildings. Dorms are spotless with comfy mattresses. The capsules are a step up – curtained spaces with either single or double mattresses – while private rooms have some quirky decoration, beanbags, TVs and fridges.

There's a decent communal area, a small rooftop pool and you're walking distance to Kata beach.

Fantasy Hill Bungalow BUNGALOW $
(Map p310; ☎076 330106; fantasyhill@hotmail.com; 8/1 Th Kata, Hat Kata; d 600-1200B; P❄📶) Tucked into a lush garden on a low-rise hill, long-standing Fantasy Hill is peaceful and central. The ageing but well-maintained bungalows and rooms are great value for the location (the cheapest are fan-only and compact) and staff are pleasant. Go for a corner air-con room with views across Kata and beyond.

Sabai Corner BUNGALOW $$
(Map p303; ☎089 875 5525; www.facebook.com/Sabai-Corner-150517525037992; Hat Kata, off Rte 4233; chalets 2000B; P📶) No other rooms on the island offer the fabulous 270-degree ocean views available from these isolated hillside chalets. Each is a spacious independent studio with pebbled bathroom, canopied four-poster bed, wall-mounted TV, fridge, sofa and safe, as well as a large outdoor terrace with lounge chairs. Book ahead.

★ **Kata Rocks** DESIGN HOTEL $$$
(Map p310; ☎076 370777; www.katarocks.com; 186/22 Th Koktanod, Hat Kata; d 35,000-84,800B; P❄📶🏊) A contemporary all-white beauty, poised on cliffs between Kata's two beaches. Villas are minimalist-chic apartments with iPad-controlled sound systems, full kitchens, Nespresso machines, private pools, hip contemporary artwork on the walls and electric blinds. Semi-submerged sunbeds dot the pale-turquoise sea-view infinity pool.

The innovative **Infinite Luxury Spa** (treatment 3600-9500B; ⏲10am-10pm) blends traditional therapies with bang-up-to-date technology such as anti-jetlag pods.

★ **Sawasdee Village** BOUTIQUE HOTEL $$$
(Map p310; ☎076 330979; www.phuketsawasdee.com; 38 Th Kade Kwan, Hat Kata; d 4800-15,000B; ❄@📶🏊) This opulent boutique resort mixes classic Thai style with Moroccan-esque flourishes, immersed in a lush tropical landscape laced with canals, waterfalls, Buddhist art installations and a stunning **spa** (treatment 1100-5000B; ⏲10am-10pm). Ornate, peaked-roof bungalows aren't huge but have super-comfy beds, wooden floors, beamed ceilings and lots of character. The villas are two-floor homes with direct access to one of two romantic pools.

Eating

Kata Mama THAI $
(Map p310; ☎076 284006; Hat Kata Yai; mains 100-200B; ⏲8am-10pm) Our pick of several cheapie seafood places at the southern end of Hat Kata Yai, long-standing Kata Mama keeps busy thanks to its charming management, reliably tasty Thai standards and low-key beachside setting.

★ **Red Duck** THAI $$
(Map p310; ☎084 850 2929; 88/3 Th Koktanod, Hat Kata; mains 240-380B; ⏲noon-11pm Tue-Sun; 📶🌱) Dishes here are more expensive than at other Thai restaurants, but they're delicious, MSG-free and prepared with the freshest of ingredients. The seafood curries and soups are especially fine. There's also a big vegan selection of Thai classics, such as pineapple or coconut curry and a vegetable *larb*.

Eat inside or on the small outdoor terrace. Service is excellent.

★ **Istanbul Restaurant** TURKISH $$
(Map p310; ☎091 820 7173; www.istanbulrestaurantphuket.com; 100/87 Th Koktanod, Hat Kata; mains 210-320B; ⏲8am-10pm) This delightful, family-run place is the most popular foreign restaurant in Kata and for good reason. The food is simply splendid, ranging from big Western- or Turkish-style breakfasts to completely authentic and super-tasty mains such as *hünkar beğendi* (beef stew on a bed of eggplant puree), kebabs and Turkish-style pizza. Then there are the superb soups, salads and delectable desserts.

Drinking & Nightlife

★ **Art Space Cafe & Gallery** BAR
(Map p310; ☎090 156 0677; Th Kade Kwan, Hat Kata; ⏲11am-1am) Hands down the most fabulously quirky bar in Phuket, this trippy, multi-use space bursts with colour and is smothered in uniquely brushed canvases and sculptures celebrating, especially, the feminine form. It's the work of an eccentric creative and his tattoo-artist wife, who whip up both decent cocktails and veggie meals (160B to 400B). There's normally live music around 8pm.

★ **Ska Bar** BAR
(Map p310; www.skabar-phuket.com; 186/12 Th Koktanod; ⏲1pm-2am) Tucked into the rocks on the southernmost curl of Hat Kata Yai and seemingly intertwined with the trunk of a grand old banyan tree, Ska is our choice for seaside sundowners. The Thai bartenders add to the laid-back Rasta vibe, and buoys, paper lanterns and flags dangle from the canopy. There's normally a fire show on Friday nights.

After Beach Bar BAR
(Map p310; ☎081 894 3750; Rte 4233; ⏲9am-11pm) It's impossible to overstate how glorious the 180-degree views are from this stilted, thatched reggae bar clinging to a cliff above Kata: rippling sea, rocky peninsulas and palm-dappled hills. Now put on the Bob Marley and you've got the perfect sunset-watching spot. When the fireball finally drops, lights from fishing boats blanket the horizon. Try the bursting-with-flavour *pàt tai*.

Information

There are plenty of ATMs and wi-fi is available everywhere.

Getting There & Around

Sŏrng·tăa·ou run from Th Ranong in Phuket Town to Kata (40B) from 7.30am to 6pm, stopping on Th Pak Bang (opposite Kata Beach Resort).

Taxis from Kata go to Phuket airport (1200B), Phuket Town (600B), Patong (500B) and Karon (300B). There's a minibus service from the airport to Kata (200B per person, minimum 10 people).

Motorbike rentals (250B per day) are widely available.

Hat Karon

หาดกะรน

Hat Karon is like the love child of Hat Patong and Hat Kata: chilled-out and starry-eyed but a tad sleazy. Despite the mega-resorts, there's still more sand space per capita here than at Patong or Kata. The further north you go the more beautiful the broad golden beach gets, culminating at the northernmost edge (accessible from a rutted road past the roundabout) where the water is like turquoise glass.

Within the inland network of streets and plazas you'll find a harmless jumble of good local food, more Russian signage than seems reasonable, low-key girly bars, T-shirt vendors and pretty Karon Park, with its artificial lake and mountain backdrop. The northern end of town, near the roundabout, is more package-touristy, while southern Karon blends into more sophisticated Kata.

Activities

During the April–October low season, you can take surf lessons (one hour 1200B) and rent surfboards/bodyboards (300/150B per hour) at the south end of **Hat Karon** (หาดกะรน; Map p310).

Kata-based Dive Asia has an office in south Karon.

Sunrise Divers DIVING

(Map p310; ☎084 626 4646, 076 398040; www.sunrise-divers.com; 269/24 Th Patak East; 3-dive trip 3700-3900B, liveaboard from 12,900B; ⏰9am-5pm) Managed by a long-time local blogger, Phuket's biggest liveaboard agent organises a range of budget to luxury multiday dives to the Similan and Surin Islands, Myanmar's Mergui Archipelago and Ko Phi-Phi. Also arranges day-trip dives, including to Ko Phi-Phi annad the Similans.

Dive Asia DIVING

(Map p310; ☎076 396199; www.diveasia.com; Th Karon/Patak West; day trip 2950B) Runs a big range of PADI certification courses (Open Water Diver 14,900B) plus day-trip dives to Ko Phi-Phi and liveaboards to the Similan and Surin Islands (from 21,000B). The main branch (p311) is in Kata.

Dino Park MINIGOLF

(Map p310; ☎076 330625; www.dinopark.com; Th Karon/Patak West; adult/child 240/180B; ⏰10am-11pm) *Jurassic Park* meets minigolf at this bizarre fun park on the southern edge of Hat Karon. It's a maze of caves, waterfalls, lagoons, leafy gardens and dinosaur statues, all spread across 18 holes of putting greens. Kids will have a blast, but really it's for everyone. Adults also have the option of retreating to the *Flintstones*-esque bar at the entrance.

Sleeping

★**Doolay Hostel** HOSTEL $

(Map p310; ☎062 451 9546; www.doolayhostel.com; 164 Th Karon/Patak West; dm 450-600B; ❄📶) There are 40 beds spread across six compact, four- and eight-bed dorms at this newish place that's a mere stroll across the road to the sand. Mattresses are good and the bathrooms are clean. There's a nice communal area and, best of all, a long 2nd-floor seafront terrace strewn with bean bags that's fine for lounging. Helpful staff. Book ahead.

Pineapple Guesthouse GUESTHOUSE $

(Map p310; ☎076 396223; www.pineapplephuket.com; 291/4 Karon Plaza; dm/d 300/1100B; ❄@📶) Pocketed away 400m inland from Hat Karon, Pineapple is a decent budget choice under warm Thai-English management. Rooms are old-fashioned, but clean and comfortable enough with colourful feature walls, fridges and, in some cases, small balconies. There's a simple 10-bed dorm (closed low season April to October) with its own bathroom and big lockers.

In On The Beach HOTEL $$

(Map p310; ☎076 398220; www.karon-inonthebeach.com; 695-697 Mu 1, Th Patak West; d incl breakfast 3500-4800B; P❄📶🏊) Steps from the northern end of Hat Karon, this hotel's slightly dated but comfortable cream-walled rooms set around a deep-blue pool were waiting for an upgrade at the time of research. Many have sea views, the staff are friendly and breakfast is served on the rooftop terrace. With substantial low-season discounts, it's an ideal surf lair.

Marina Phuket RESORT $$$
(Map p310; ☎076 330625; www.marinaphuket.com; 47 Th Karon; d incl breakfast 6600-18,600B; P❄📶🏊) Stilted boardwalks lead through lush, hushed gardens to comfy, secluded sea- and jungle-facing rooms decked out in classic Thai style. All enjoy breezy terraces, warm-wood decor, teak furniture and silk throws. Villas have hot tubs. There's a big pool, a spa and no fewer than four restaurants.

Eating

There are reliable Thai and seafood places at the north end of Hat Karon and on the main road near south Hat Karon.

★ **Pad Thai Shop** THAI $
(Map p310; Th Patak East; mains 50-80B; ⏲8am-7pm, closed Fri) This glorified roadside food shack makes rich, savoury chicken stew and absurdly good *kôw pàt poo* (fried rice with crab), *pàt see·éw* (fried noodles) and noodle soup. It also serves up some of the best *pàt tai* we've ever tasted: spicy and sweet, packed with tofu, egg and peanuts, and plated with spring onions, bean sprouts and lime.

Elephant Cafe THAI, INTERNATIONAL $$
(Map p310; ☎076 398129; 489 Th Patak East; mains 80-390B; ⏲10am-11pm; 🌶) Reliable and popular spot for both Thai and Western food. Dine on curries and spicy salads, or steaks, chops and pizza, in the enclosed, garden-like interior. Plenty of vegetarian choices too, as well as cakes and cocktails.

★ **Eat Bar & Grill** GRILL $$$
(Map p310; ☎085 292 5652; www.eatbargrill.com; 250/1 Th Patak East; mains 200-800B; ⏲11am-10pm; 📶) There's awesome burgers and superb steaks, a contender for the best on Phuket, at this laid-back place with a wooden bar and limited space (make sure to book ahead). The menu includes other dishes, including a great lamb shank, but beef is the thing here: prepared to your taste, stylishly presented and reasonably priced, given the quality. Proper cocktails too.

Getting There & Around

Sŏrng·tăa·ou run frequently from Th Ranong in Phuket Town to Hat Karon (30B) from 7.30am to 6pm.

Taxis from Karon go to Phuket airport (1000B), Phuket Town (550B), Patong (400B) and Kata (200B). A minibus runs from the airport to Karon (200B, minimum 10 people).

Motorbike rental costs 250B per day.

Hat Kamala หาดกมลา

A chilled-out hybrid of Hat Karon and Hat Surin, Kamala lures in a mix of longer-term, low-key visitors, including families and young couples. The bay is magnificent and serene, with palms and pines mingling on its leafy, rocky northern end, where the water is a rich emerald green and the snorkelling around the rock reef is halfway decent. The entire beach is backed by a paved path and lush rolling hills, which one can only hope are left alone...forever. Flashy new resorts are carved into the southern bluffs and jet skis make an appearance, but the nightlife is serene and Kamala is quietish and laid-back by Phuket standards.

Sights & Activities

During the May–October monsoon, you can hire surfboards (300B per hour) and take surf classes (1500B) on south Hat Kamala.

Tsunami Memorial MEMORIAL
(อนุสรณ์สถานสึนามิ; Map p316) Kamala was one of Phuket's worst-hit areas during the 2004 Boxing Day tsunami. The Heart of the Universe Memorial pays tribute to lost loved ones with a moving, wave-inspired metallic oval created by prominent Thai artist Udon Jiraksa.

Sleeping

Baan Kamala GUESTHOUSE $
(Map p316; ☎076 279053; www.baankamalaphuket.com; 74/42 Mu 3; dm 450-550B, d 2000B; ❄📶) A cross between a guesthouse and a hostel, welcoming Baan Kamala offers big and light six-bed dorms for backpackers and a collection of individually designed private rooms for flashpackers. The concrete walls of the spacious rooms are livened up with paintings and beds are comfortable, although bathrooms are a little poky. The communal area features its very own long-tail boat.

Papa Crab BOUTIQUE HOTEL $$
(Map p316; ☎076 385315; www.phuketpapacrab.com; 93/5 Mu 3; d 2300B; ❄📶) This elegant boutique guesthouse combines homey lodgings, a peaceful location and discreet, friendly service. A wooden bridge trails over the lobby's lily pond to tastefully styled terracotta-floor rooms with dark-wood beds and soothing lime-green-and-white colour schemes. It's better than many more-expensive nearby options. The hotel usually closes for August.

Cape Sienna HOTEL $$$
(Map p316; ☎076 337300; www.capesienna.com; 18/40 Mu 6, Th Nakalay; d 4600-16,650B; ❄📶🏊) This flashy, romantic hotel sprawls up the southern headland offering magnificent azure bay views from the lobby, pool and every room. Rooms are bright, smart and modern, with all amenities and splashes of orange and turquoise. Deluxe rooms have balcony hot tubs. Up above is Kamala's breeziest cocktail bar, **Vanilla Sky** (Map p316; 18/40 Mu 6, Th Nakalay, Cape Sienna; ⏲5pm-midnight), and there's fine steaks at the on-site Plum steakhouse.

Eating

Meena Restaurant THAI $
(Map p316; Hat Kamala; mains 80-150B; ⏲9am-5pm, closed May-Oct) This family-run beachside shack with rainbow-striped and leopard-print sarongs for tablecloths is a real find. The owners couldn't be more welcoming. The tasty authentic Thai food is exceptional and so are the fresh fruit shakes. The rustic setting is exactly what you likely came to Kamala for. It's at the north end of the beach.

Isaan Popeye Thai Food THAI $
(Map p316; ☎089 056 9605; 74/43 Mu 3; mains 100-200B; ⏲9.30am-10pm) One of the few restaurants in Kamala where you'll find locals dining, thanks to the winning combination of authentic and spicy northeastern dishes, fresh seafood and classic stir-fries and noodles. It also does Western breakfasts. It's a five-minute walk inland from the beach.

★ **Blue Manao** THAI $$
(Map p316; ☎076 385783; 93/13 Mu 3, Th Hat Kamala; mains 130-530B; ⏲noon-11pm; 📶) This relaxed, French-run eatery decked out in marine blue has rather more atmosphere than its nearby competitors, as well as a more individual menu. The seafood – barracuda, yellow curry squid – is an obvious draw, but the traditional Thai curries (whether meat, fish or vegetarian) are also excellent, as are the European desserts. It has a proper bar too.

Plum INTERNATIONAL $$$
(Map p316; ☎076 337300; 18/40 Mu 6, Th Nakalay, Cape Sienna; mains 500-5000B; ⏲6-11pm, closed Mon; 🖉) Part steakhouse, part European-style seafood emporium, Plum is dominated by its charcoal grill on which imported, melt-in-the-mouth cuts of beef are laid lovingly. But there's also a big seafood selection, pastas, risottos and salads, all generously served with beautiful beach and bay panoramas from up high. Book ahead to dine at an in-pool cabana table.

PHUKET FANTASEA

It's impossible to ignore the brochures and touts flogging Phuket Fantasea, the US$60 million 'cultural theme park' located just east of Hat Kamala and relentlessly promoted as one of the island's top 'family-friendly' attractions. While it is very popular with Asian tourists, and some Westerners, we recommend reading up on the numerous animal-welfare issues associated with this Vegas-style spectacle, at which animals are forced to 'perform' daily, before choosing to support it.

Getting There & Away

Sŏrng·tăa·ou run between Phuket Town's Th Ranong and Kamala (40B) from 7am to 5pm. *Sŏrng·tăa·ou* also go from Kamala to Hat Surin (20B). Taxis to/from the airport cost 700B.

Hat Surin หาดสุรินทร์

With a wide, golden beach, water that blends from pale turquoise in the shallows to a deep blue on the horizon, and lush, boulder-strewn headlands, Surin (สุรินทร์) is as attractive a spot as anywhere in Phuket. It's also home to five-star spa resorts, stunning galleries and fabulous boutiques. These days, Surin is very much an upmarket destination, attracting cashed-up foreigners and Thais.

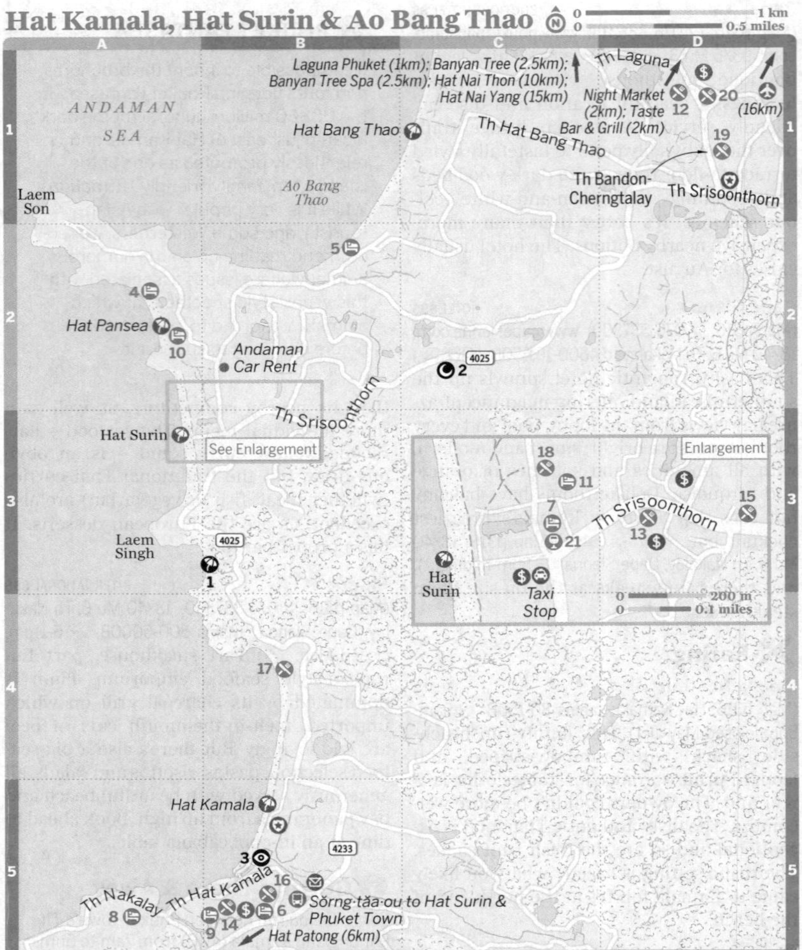

Phuket's crackdown on unlicensed beachfront restaurants and bars hit Surin particularly hard. All establishments on the sand have been cleared away, with some moving up the road to Ao Bang Thao (p318) and others just closing. As a consequence, there are rather fewer eateries and bars here than elsewhere on Phuket's west coast.

Despite this, Hat Surin remains welcoming and beautiful. North of here is small, secluded **Hat Pansea** (หาดพันซี), home to exclusive resorts.

Busy mosque **Masjid Mukaram Bang Thao** (มัสยิดมุการ์ร่ม บางเทา; Map p316; Rte 4025; ⏲daylight hours) FREE provides a good insight into Phuket village life and makes an interesting change of scene from the beach.

Sleeping

Hat Surin hosts some of Phuket's classiest resorts, but little for those on a budget.

Benyada Lodge HOTEL **$$**
(Map p316; ☎076 271777; www.benyadalodge-phuket.com; 106/52 Mu 3, Hat Surin; d incl

Hat Kamala, Hat Surin & Ao Bang Thao

Sights
1 Laem Singh B3
2 Masjid Mukaram Bang Thao C2
3 Tsunami Memorial B5

Sleeping
4 Amanpuri Resort A2
5 Andaman Bangtao Bay Resort B2
6 Baan Kamala B5
7 Benyada Lodge C3
8 Cape Sienna A5
9 Papa Crab B5
10 Surin Phuket A2
11 Twin Palms C3

Eating
Andaman Restaurant .... (see 5)
12 Bampot D1
13 Blue Lagoon D3
14 Blue Manao B5
15 Bocconcino D3
16 Isaan Popeye Thai Food B5
17 Meena Restaurant B4
18 Oriental Spoon C3
19 Pesto D1
Plum .... (see 8)
20 Tatonka D1

Drinking & Nightlife
21 9th Glass Wine Bar & Bistro C3
Vanilla Sky .... (see 8)

breakfast 1500-3000B;) A reasonably priced option in a neigbourhood dominated by upmarket resorts and just a couple of minutes from the beach, Benyada has big, slightly old-fashioned but comfortable rooms. The best come with small balconies. Smiley service, and you can catch the sunset from the rooftop bar.

★ Surin Phuket RESORT $$$
(Map p316; 076 621580; www.thesurinphuket.com; 118 Mu 3, Hat Pansea; bungalows incl breakfast 14,600-34,400B;) Almost any establishment on a secluded beach this quiet and stunning would be a top pick. But the bungalows here, hidden beneath hillside foliage and overlooking Hat Pansea, up the ante with homey, earthy, luxurious interiors, and the six-sided sea-view pool is gorgeously abstract. It's quite a walk up hills and over wooden walkways to many of the 'cottages'.

★ Amanpuri Resort RESORT $$$
(Map p316; 076 324333; www.amanresorts.com; Hat Pansea; villas US$1000-3100;) Understated, luxurious and immensely peaceful, celebrity-magnet Amanpuri is one of Phuket's finest, most exclusive hotels. Graceful traditional-design bungalows are all about the location on quiet Hat Pansea, with sea-facing cabanas, warm-wood decor and enormous bathrooms; many have their own private pools. There's a huge array of activities on offer (yoga, kayaking, surfing), plus a jet-black pool and supreme service.

Eating & Drinking

Surin's dining scene is now rather forlorn, with all the beachfront places ejected from the area. Most restaurants can be found along Th Srisoonthorn or on the soi just back from the beach.

Blue Lagoon THAI $
(Map p316; 087 923 8235; Th Srisoonthorn; mains 80-180B; 7.30am-11pm) One of a dwindling number of restaurants in Surin, following the crackdown on beachfront establishments, this family-run, semi-open-air joint serves up tasty versions of all your classic Thai dishes, as well as seafood and Western breakfasts. It's rather more down-to-earth than most Surin eateries.

Bocconcino DELI, ITALIAN $$$
(Map p316; 076 386531; www.bocconcinophuket.com; 8/71 Mu 3, Th Srisoonthorn; mains 320-520B; 9am-10pm;) An Italian deli may not be what you came to Phuket for, but Bocconcino's homemade gelato is classic Surin: refined and refreshing. This elegant, expat-frequented eatery houses an Italophile's dream of wines, coffee, cakes, cheeses, cured meats, homemade pastas, pizzas and changing specials. For something lighter, try traditional salads such as tomato and mozzarella. It's 600m east of Hat Surin.

Oriental Spoon THAI, INTERNATIONAL $$$
(Map p316; 076 316500; 106/46 Mu 3, Hat Surin; mains 350-1300B; 11am-11pm;) This big restaurant inside **Twin Palms** (Map p316; 076 316500; www.twinpalms-phuket.com; 106/46 Mu 3, Hat Surin; d incl breakfast 8900-26,100B;) resort gets busy for its popular Sunday brunch (1990B), but it's also worth checking out its unusual selection of dishes that show a Peranakan flavour: a mix of Thai, Chinese and Malay influences.

Expect spicy and sour, with lots of tamarind and lemongrass. It also does Western mains and has a comprehensive wine list.

9th Glass Wine Bar & Bistro WINE BAR
(Map p316; ☎076 068 0068; www.the9thglass.com; 106/16 Mu 3, Hat Surin; ⏰4pm-midnight Mon-Sat) The widest choice of wine in Surin, with labels spanning Europe, Australia, New Zealand and South Africa, as well as properly mixed cocktails and a big liquor selection. This refined, intimate bar also offers tapas to nibble while you imbibe, or Western-style mains. It's as close to the beach as is now possible for a bar in Surin.

Information

There are ATMs along Th Srisoonthorn. All hotels have wi-fi.

Getting There & Away

Sŏrng·tăa·ou go from Phuket Town's Th Ranong to Hat Surin (40B) from 7am to 5pm, continuing to Hat Kamala; túk-túk charters and taxis cost 500B. Taxis to/from the airport cost 700B.

Ao Bang Thao หาดบางเทา

Stunning **Hat Bang Thao**, 8km of white-sand beach, is the glue that binds this area's disparate elements together. The southern half of the region is dotted with three- and four-star resorts, and a swanky beach club. Further inland you'll find an old fishing village laced with canals, a number of upstart villa subdivisions, stellar restaurants and signs of more development. More than anywhere else on Phuket, Ao Bang Thao is still being remodelled.

Smack in the centre of it all is the somewhat bizarre Laguna Phuket complex, a network of four- and five-star resorts tied together by an artificial lake (patrolled by tourist shuttle boats) and a paved nature trail. At the northern end of the region, mother nature reasserts itself, and a lonely stretch of powder-white sand and tropical blue sea extends past the bustle into the peaceful bliss you originally had in mind.

Sleeping

The Laguna Phuket complex includes seven luxury resorts. There are cheaper beachfront resorts in southern Ao Bang Thao.

★**Anantara Phuket Layan** RESORT $$$
(Map p290; ☎076 317200; www.anantara.com; 168 Mu 6, Soi 4, Hat Layan; d 14,000B, villas 16,500-81,500B; P❄📶🏊) On its own secluded, wild-feel bay just north of Hat Bang Thao, this is an exquisite top-end choice. Chic, contemporary-Thai rooms come decked out with dark woods, marble floors, ceramic-bowl sinks and Apple gadgets. Villas have dark-tiled pools and 24-hour butlers. A laid-back lounge-bar overlooks the beachside pool. Dine at three excellent on-site restaurants or in a private beach cabana.

Banyan Tree RESORT $$$
(Map p290; ☎076 372400; www.banyantree.com; 33 Mu 4, Th Srisoonthorn, Laguna Phuket; d incl breakfast 17,900-31,500B; P❄@📶🏊) One of Phuket's finest hotels, and the first to introduce bungalows with their own personal pools, the sprawling Banyan Tree is a lushly shaded oasis of sedate, understated luxury. Accommodation is in sophisticated villas, with free-standing, open-air baths and private pools, and there's also an adults-only pool.

Don't miss the on-site **spa** (Map p290; www.banyantreespa.com; massage or treatment 3500-9500B; ⏰10am-10pm).

Eating

Some of Phuket's best international restaurants cluster in Ao Bang Thao. For cheap eats, head to the new **night market** (Map p290; Laguna Phuket, Ao Bang Thao; mains from 40B; ⏰5-10pm).

★**Pesto** THAI, INTERNATIONAL $$
(Map p316; ☎082 423 0184; Th Bandon-Cherngtalay; mains 135-530B; ⏰noon-11pm; 🖉) Mix a Paris-trained Thai chef with a simple streetside, semi-open-air location and you get delicious, wallet-friendly Thai and international food. Light pesto pasta and lobster lasagne whizz you to the Mediterranean. Otherwise, stay local with grilled tuna on Andaman seaweed, *đôm yam gûng* (spicy-sour prawn soup), deep-fried turmeric-spiced fish of the day and all your favourite curries.

Andaman Restaurant THAI $$
(Map p316; 82/9 Mu 3, Hat Bang Thao; mains 195-325B; ⏰8am-10pm; 📶) Part of the **Andaman Bangtao Bay Resort** (Map p316; ☎076 314290; www.andamanresort.com; d incl breakfast 1900-5900B; P❄📶🏊), this simple seaside

restaurant has a laid-back castaway paradise feel with rustic bamboo lanterns and driftwood furniture. Dine on decent-enough BBQ seafood and Thai curries on a multi-level platform trickling down to the sand.

★ Bampot INTERNATIONAL $$$

(Map p316; ☎ 093 586 9828; www.bampot.co; 19/1 Mu 1, Th Laguna; mains 500-1200B; ⏲ 6pm-midnight) Cool-blue booths, dangling pans, black-topped tables and white brick walls hung with art set the scene for ambitious European-inspired meals (lobster mac and cheese, sea bass ceviche with pomelo) straight from the open-plan kitchen. Creatively concocted cocktails and international wines round things off.

★ Taste Bar & Grill FUSION $$$

(Map p290; ☎ 087 886 6401; www.tastebargrill.com; 3/2 Mu 5, Th Srisoonthorn, Ao Bang Thao; mains 390-990B; ⏲ noon-11pm Tue-Sun; 📶) Minimalist modern lines, top-notch service, a sophisticated but chilled-out vibe and delicious fusion food make this eatery an outstanding choice. The menu features Thai and Mediterranean influences, but the steaks are great too. You can't go wrong with the seafood, and there are excellent salads and a huge array of starters.

Tatonka INTERNATIONAL $$$

(Map p316; ☎ 076 324349; 382/19 Mu 1, Th Laguna; mains 350-790B; ⏲ 6-10pm Mon-Sat; ✎) Tatonka bills itself as the home of 'globetrotter cuisine', which owner-chef Harold Schwarz has developed by combining local products with cooking techniques learned in Europe, Colorado and Hawaii. The eclectic, tapas-style selection includes inventive vegetarian and seafood dishes and such delights as Peking duck pizza, green-curry pasta and eggplant 'cookies' with goat's cheese. Book ahead in high season.

ℹ Getting There & Away

Sŏrng·tăa·ou run between Phuket Town's Th Ranong and Ao Bang Thao (30B) from 7am to 5pm. Túk-túk charters are 400B. Taxis to/from the airport cost 700B.

Sirinat National Park อุทยานแห่งชาติสิรินาถ

Comprising the exceptional beaches of Nai Thon, Nai Yang and Mai Khao, along with the former Nai Yang National Park and Mai Khao wildlife reserve, **Sirinat National Park** (Map p290; ☎ 076 328226, 076 327152; www.dnp.go.th; 89/1 Mu 1, Hat Nai Yang; adult/child 200/100B; ⏲ 6am-6pm) encompasses 22 sq km of coastline and 68 sq km of sea, stretching from the north end of Ao Bang Thao to Phuket's northernmost tip. This is one of the sweetest slices of the island, with slightly less tourist traffic than elsewhere, especially on **Hat Mai Khao** (หาดไม้ขาว; Map p290), and a generally chilled vibe. Kitesurfers flock to **Hat Nai Yang** (หาดในยาง; Map p290) from May to October, which gives you something to look at while you laze on the sand, but this part of Phuket is pretty quiet in low season.

The whole area is 15 minutes or less from Phuket International Airport.

Activities

During the May to October monsoon, Hat Nai Yang is great for kitesurfing. A number of schools, including **Kiteboarding Asia** (Map p290; ☎ 081 591 4594; www.kiteboardingasia.com; 116 Mu 1, Hat Nai Yang; 1hr lesson 2000B, 3-day course 11,000B; ⏲ Apr-Oct), **Kite Zone** (☎ 083 395 2005; www.kitesurfthailand.com; Hat Nai Yang; 1hr lesson 1100B, 3-day course 10,000B; ⏲ May–late-Oct) and Rawai-based Bob's Kite School (p302), teach budding kitesurfers.

Phuket's longest beach, Hat Mai Khao is a beautiful, secluded 10km stretch of sand extending from just south of the airport to the island's northernmost point. Sea turtles lay eggs here between November and February. Take care with the strong year-round undertow. Hat Nai Yang, 3km south of the airport, is sheltered by a reef that slopes 20m below the surface – which means good snorkelling in high season and fantastic kitesurfing during the monsoon. West-coast **Hat Nai Thon** (หาดในทอน; Map p290), 7km south of the airport, is a lovely arc of fine golden sand away from Phuket's busy buzz and good swimming (except at the height of the monsoon).

Phuket Riding Club HORSE RIDING

(Map p290; ☎ 081 787 2455; www.phuketriding club.com; 60/9 Th Thepkasattri, Mu 3, Mai Khao; 1/2hr rides 1200/2200B; ⏲ 7.30am-6.30pm) The perfect opportunity to live out that horse-riding-through-the-tropics dream. Phuket Riding Club offers fun one- or two-hour

VOLUNTEER WITH ANIMALS

About 2km from Hat Mai Khao, **Soi Dog** (Map p290; ☎081 788 4222; www.soidog.org; 167/9 Mu 4, Soi Mai Khao 10; admission by donation; ⌚9am-noon & 1-3.30pm Mon-Fri, tours 9.30am, 11am, 1.30pm & 2.30pm) is a nonprofit foundation that protects hundreds of cats and dogs (some rescued from the illegal dog-meat trade), focusing on sterilisation, castration, re-homing and animal-welfare awareness. Visits are by in-depth tour. The 'old dogs' enclosure can be upsetting, but they're in a happy home. Visitors can play with the animals, or become a dog-walking or long-term volunteer.

rides on the beaches and interior of northern Phuket. Book a day ahead.

Sleeping

There's a mix of accommodation here, with top resorts mingling with more affordable digs. If you want one of the cheaper places, reserve well in advance.

Pensiri House GUESTHOUSE $
(Map p290; ☎076 327683; www.pensirihouse.com; 112 Mu 5, Hat Nai Yang; d 800-1200B; ❄📶) 300m inland from Hat Nai Yang, this friendly place is the best budget option in the area. Rooms are spread across two buildings. The nicest are in the new block: sizeable, light, modern and with balconies. All come with TVs, fridges and safes.

Sirinat National Park Accommodation CAMPGROUND, BUNGALOW $
(Map p290; ☎076 327152, in Bangkok 02 562 0760; www.dnp.go.th; 89/1 Mu 1, Hat Nai Yang; camping per person 30B, bungalows 700-1000B) At the park headquarters at the north end of Hat Nai Yang you'll find campsites (bring your own tent) and large, concrete, air-con bungalows just back from the beach on a gorgeous, shady, white-sand bluff. Book ahead online or by phone.

Discovery Beach Resort GUESTHOUSE $$
(Map p290; ☎082 497 7500; discovery-phuket@hotmail.com; 90/34 Mu 5, Hat Nai Yang; d 1800-3200B; ❄📶) Rooms at this amenable place are a little old-fashioned, but they're spotless and come with sofas, TVs and fridges, while the beds are fine. It's nothing fancy, but the location – right on the beach – makes it great value.

★ **Slate** RESORT $$$
(Map p290; ☎076 327006; www.theslatephuket.com; 116 Mu 1, Hat Nai Yang; d 7700-22,000B, villas 45,400-61,500B; P❄📶🏊) One of Phuket's most unique mega-resorts takes its design cues from the island's tin-mining history. Hardware (vices, scales and other mining tools) features in the delicate decor, while the doors to the swish, stylish, luxurious rooms and villas are distressed metal. The best rooms have their own plunge pools. There are three restaurants on-site, and the fantastic **Coqoon Spa** (Map p290; massage or treatment 2000-8000B; ⌚10am-8pm).

Pullman RESORT $$$
(Map p290; ☎076 303299; www.pullmanphuketarcadia.com; 22/2 Mu 4, Hat Nai Thon; d 6500B, villas 24,400-32,400B; P❄@📶🏊) With a spectacular setting high on cliffs above northern Hat Nai Thon, this big resort offers stunning sea views almost from the moment you cross the arched bridge to the lobby. A dreamy network of reflection pools extends out above the sea. Service is divine. All rooms and the villas are spacious, supercomfortable and come with balconies.

Eating

Mr Kobi THAI $$
(Map p290; Hat Nai Yang; mains 150-350B; ⌚10am-11pm) The sign says 'Broken English spoken here perfect', but the ever-popular Mr Kobi speaks English very well. He handles the drinks, while Malee deals with the seafood and Thai faves served up in refreshingly unpretentious surroundings. One wall is dedicated to telling the story of the 2004 tsunami.

Coconut Tree THAI $$
(Map p290; ☎098 364 6366; Th Hat Nai Thon, Hat Nai Thon; mains 100-300B; ⌚10am-10pm; 📶) This friendly, relaxed spot towards the south end of the beach rustles up quality seafood dishes such as stir-fried crab with black pepper, and tiger prawns cooked in everything from yellow curry to bitter ginger, on a rustic semi-open verandah with a few pot-plants. Also does Western classics. The Andaman sparkles beyond soaring palms and casuarinas.

Elements THAI $$$
(Map p290; ☎076 303299; www.pullmanphuket arcadia.com; 22/2 Mu 4, Pullman, Hat Nai Thon; mains 270-1320B; ⊙noon-10.30pm) Perched high on the cliffs at the northern end of the beach, Nai Thon's sleekest resort (p320) offers sophisticated Thai food in a swish, spacious indoor-outdoor dining room with huge pillars, abstract modern art and beautiful views across the bay. Lunch sees burgers and sandwiches thrown into the mix, and on Fridays the restaurant fires up a seafood BBQ.

Getting There & Away

Sŏrng·tăa·ou from Phuket Town to Hat Nai Yang run between 7am and 5pm (40B). Taxis to/from the airport cost 400B to 500B, depending which beach you're on.

Thalang District อำเภอถลาง

Far from the beaches, untouristed Thalang (ถลาง) is an area that people tend to pass through while on their way somewhere else. That's a shame, because there are some intriguing cultural attractions here, including the **Thalang National Museum** (พิพิธภัณฑสถานแห่งชาติ ถลาง; Map p290; ☎076 379895; Th Srisoonthorn/Rte 4027; adult/child 200/100B; ⊙9am-4pm). Most people visit en route to the worthwhile and justifiably popular Phuket Elephant Sanctuary (p322).

WORTH A TRIP

KHAO PHRA THAEW ROYAL WILDLIFE & FOREST RESERVE อุทยานสัตว์ป่าเขาพระแทว

The **Khao Phra Thaew Royal Wildlife & Forest Reserve** (Map p290; off Rte 4027 & Hwy 402; adult/child 200/100B) protects 23 sq km of virgin island rainforest (evergreen monsoon forest) in north Phuket. Its royal status means it's better-maintained than the average Thai national park, although the staff have a reputation for being unhelpful towards visitors. The highest point is Khao Phra (442m).

Tigers, Malayan sun bears, rhinos and elephants once roamed here, but nowadays residents are limited to humans, wild boar, monkeys, slow loris, langurs, gibbons, deer, civets, flying foxes, cobras, pythons, squirrels and other smaller creatures.

Gibbon poaching is a big problem on Phuket, fuelled in no small part by tourism: captive gibbons are paraded around tourist bars. Financed by donations, the tiny **Phuket Gibbon Rehabilitation Project** (โครงการคืนชะนีสู่ป่า; Map p290; ☎076 260492; www.gibbonproject.org; off Rte 4027; admission by donation; ⊙9am-4.30pm, to 3pm Sat) adopts gibbons that were kept in captivity in the hope of reintroducing them to the wild. Swing by around 9am to hear the gibbons' morning song. You can't get too close to the animals, which may disappoint kids, but the volunteer work done here is outstanding.

Elsewhere, there are pleasant hill hikes and some photogenic waterfalls, including **Nam Tok Ton Sai** (น้ำตกโตนไทร; Map p290; ☎076 311998; off Hwy 402; adult/child 200/100B) and **Nam Tok Bang Pae** (น้ำตกบางแป; Map p290; off Rte 4027; adult/child 200/100B), 300m along a jungle-fringed path from the Gibbon Project. The falls are most impressive during the June–November monsoon. Park rangers may guide hikers in the park on request: expect to pay around 1500B. Tucked into the hills behind a quilt of pineapple fields, rubber plantations and mango groves is **Cable Jungle Adventure Phuket** (Map p290; ☎081 977 4904; www.cablejunglephuket.com; 232/17 Mu 8, Th Bansuanneramit; without/with hotel pickup 2150/2300B; ⊙9am-5pm), a maze of zip lines linking ancient ficus trees. The zips range from 6m to 50m above the ground and the longest run is 300m long. Closed-toe shoes are a must. Hotel pick up is available.

There is neither accommodation nor restaurants inside the park, but you're a taxi or motorcycle ride away from the rest of Phuket.

To get to Khao Phra Thaew from Phuket Town, take Th Thepkasattri 13km north to Thalang District. At the Heroines Monument (p322), drive 9km northeast on Rte 4027, turn left (west) towards Nam Tok Bang Pae and after 1km you're at the Phuket Gibbon Rehabilitation Project. A taxi will cost 800B. The reserve is also accessible off Hwy 402, 6km northwest of the Heroines Monument.

The district unfolds around the **Heroines Monument** (อนุสาวรีย์ท้าวเทพกษัตรีท้าวศรีสุนทร; Map p290; Hwy 402), 13km north of Phuket Town, which while not exactly in the centre of Phuket, acts as the island's central roundabout where roads heading in all directions intersect.

Sleeping & Eating

★ **Point Yamu by Como** RESORT $$$
(Map p290; ☎076 360100; www.comohotels.com/pointyamu; 225 Mu 7, Pa Klok, Laem Yamu; d incl breakfast 10,200-51,000B; P ❄ ☜ ≋) Breeze into the soaring lobby, where white-mosaic pillars frame ponds reflecting encircling palms, and fall in love. This five-star stunner blends Thai influences (monk-robe orange, lobster traps as lamps) into a coolly contemporary, Italian-designed creation. An array of huge rooms, some with private pools, come in royal-blue or turquoise, intensifying the endless sea and Ao Phang-Nga panoramas from the property.

Bang Rong Seafood THAI, SEAFOOD $$
(Map p290; ☎081 370 3401, 093 737 9264; Tha Bang Rong, off Rte 4027; mains 120-350B; ⊙10am-6pm) This rustic fish-farm-turned-restaurant sits on a floating pier amid the mangroves, accessed via a wooden boardwalk 750m east of Rte 4027. Your catch – red and white snapper, crab or mussels – is plucked after you order, so you know it's fresh. You can have everything steamed, fried, grilled, boiled or baked, but this is a Muslim enterprise so there's no beer.

★ **Breeze Restaurant** INTERNATIONAL $$$
(Map p290; ☎081 271 2320; www.breezecapeyamu.com; Laem Yamu; mains from 700B, tasting menus 2000-2150B; ⊙noon-10pm Wed-Sun; ☜ ✎) Classy yet understated, one of Phuket's finest restaurants sits in glorious hilltop, sea-surrounded seclusion, 20km northeast of Phuket Town. Blue beanbags overlook pool and sea from the pillared open-walled dining hall. Menus that change weekly triumph with divine, inventive European-style dishes infused with local produce. Pair with classic cocktails given a Thai twist. Book ahead.

Getting There & Away

Sŏrng·tăa·ou heading to Hat Surin and Ao Bang Thao from Phuket Town between 7am and 5pm pass by the Heroines Monument (30B), which is walking distance from the Thalang National Museum. To head anywhere else in the district you'll need private wheels or a taxi. A taxi from Phuket Town to the Phuket Elephant Sanctuary will cost 700B.

DON'T MISS

ELEPHANT REFUGE

The **Phuket Elephant Sanctuary** (Map p290; ☎094 990 3649; www.phuketelephantsanctuary.org; 100 Mu 2, Pa Klok, on 4027 Highway; adult/child 3000/1500B; ⊙9.30am-1pm & 2-5.30pm; ⓜ) is the island's only genuine refuge (beware of imitators) for pachyderms who have spent their lives being mistreated while working in the tourist and logging industries. It's a rare opportunity to get up close to these magnificent animals. Sadly, elephants are still being used to give tourists rides, or to perform for them, in Phuket and elsewhere in Thailand.

All tours here must be booked in advance. If you want to see more of the animals, the sanctuary accepts up to six volunteers at a time for week-long stays. The 16,000B fee goes directly to the care of the elephants and includes accommodation and three vegetarian meals a day.

KRABI PROVINCE

When travellers talk dreamily about the amazing Andaman, they usually mean Krabi, with its trademark karst formations curving along the coast like a giant limestone fortress of adventure, or rising out of the islands and hanging over idyllic white-sand beaches. Rock climbers will find their nirvana in Railay, while castaway wannabes should head to Ko Lanta, Ko Phi-Phi or any of the other 150-plus islands swimming off this 120km-long shoreline.

Krabi Town กระบี่

☎075 / POP 31,475

Bustling Krabi Town is majestically situated among impossibly angular limestone karst formations jutting from the mangroves, but mid-city you're more likely to be awestruck by the sheer volume of guesthouses and travel agencies packed into this compact

Krabi Town

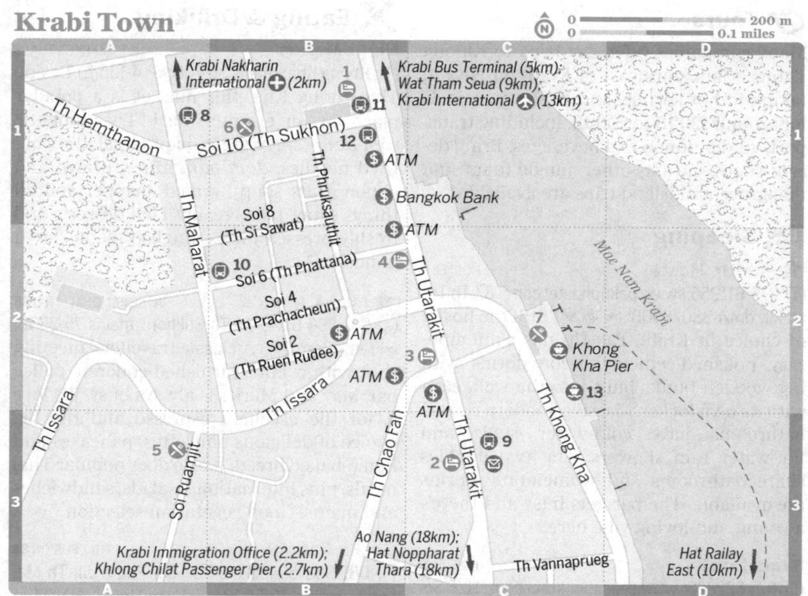

town. It's a key transport hub, around which a busy traveller scene continues to evolve. There's no shortage of restaurants, or gift shops selling the usual trinkets.

But hang around a while and you'll see that there's also a very real provincial scene going on beneath the tourist industry.

Sights & Activities

★Wat Tham Seua BUDDHIST TEMPLE

(วัดถ้ำเสือ, Tiger Cave Temple; dawn-dusk) This sprawling hill and cave temple complex 9km northwest of Krabi Town is an easy, worthwhile day trip. At the park entrance you'll come to a gruellingly steep 1260-step staircase leading to a 600m karst peak. After a 30- to 40-minute climb, the fit and fearless are rewarded with golden Buddha statues, a gilded stupa and spectacular views out to sea beyond Ao Nang. Start early and bring water; there are drinking taps at the top.

Sea Kayak Krabi KAYAKING

(089 724 8579, 075 630270; www.seakayakkrabi.com) A wide variety of recommended sea-kayaking tours, including to Ao Tha Len (half/full day 900/1500B), which has looming sea cliffs; Ko Hong (full day 2200B), famed for its emerald lagoon; and Ban Bho Tho (full day 2200B), which has karsts and sea caves with 2000- to 3000-year-old cave paintings. Rates include guides, transfers, lunch and water.

Krabi Town

Sleeping

1 Apo B1
2 Chan Cha Lay C3
3 Pak-Up Hostel C2
4 Seacation B2

Eating

5 Gecko Cabane A3
6 May & Mark's B1
7 Night Market C2

Drinking & Nightlife

Playground ..... (see 3)

Transport

8 Sŏrng·tăa·ou to Ao Luk A1
9 Sŏrng·tăa·ou to Ao Nang & Hat Noppharat Thara C3
10 Sŏrng·tăa·ou to Ao Nang & Hat Noppharat Thara B2
11 Sŏrng·tăa·ou to Ban Laem Kruat B1
12 Sŏrng·tăa·ou to Krabi Bus Terminal B1
13 Tha Khong Kha C2

Tours

Many companies offer day trips to Khlong Thom, 45km southeast of Krabi on Hwy 4, taking in hot springs and freshwater pools for around 1200B to 2000B, including transport, guides, lunch and beverages. Bring decent shoes. Various other 'jungle tours' and mangrove and island trips are available.

Sleeping

★Pak-Up Hostel HOSTEL $
(075 611955; www.pakuphostel.com; 87 Th Utarakit; dm/r 380/850B;) Still the hostel of choice in Krabi, Pak-Up has contemporary, polished-cement air-con dorms with big wooden bunks built into the wall, each with its own locker. Massive, modern shared bathrooms have cold-water stalls and hot-water rain showers. The two doubles share bathrooms and women-only dorms are available. The bar gets busy and there's a young, fun-loving vibe here.

Seacation HOSTEL $
(075 622828; www.seacationkrabi.com; 11/5 Soi 6 Th Maharat; dm/r 450/1200B;) Brand-new and smart hostel, even if the design and long corridors make it feel a little institutional. Dorms are comfortable with decent beds and big lockers, while there's an impressive communal area with a pool table. Private rooms are compact. Affable staff and an ideal location.

Apo HOTEL $$
(093 709 1811; www.apohotel.com; 189 Th Utarakit; r 1000-1700B;) The best-value of several fresh, modern guesthouses in this otherwise unremarkable block, Apo has big and bright, gleaming, minimalist-smart rooms decorated with a single colourful swirl and wall-mounted TVs, spread across two buildings. Some have river views from little balconies. The only drawback is that there's no lift.

Chan Cha Lay GUESTHOUSE $$
(075 620952; www.lovechanchalay.com; 55 Th Utarakit; r fan 400-1400B;) The en-suite, air-con rooms at long-standing Chan Cha Lay, done up in Mediterranean blues and whites with white-pebble and polished-concrete open-air bathrooms, are among Krabi's most comfortable and charming for the price. There's a range of cheaper rooms with shared-bathroom, and fan or A/C, which are plain and compact but spotless.

Eating & Drinking

Night Market MARKET, THAI $
(Th Khong Kha; mains 30-70B; 4-10pm) Beside Tha Khong Kha, this market is a popular place for an evening meal. Try authentic *sôm·đam* (spicy green papaya salad), wok-fried noodles, *đôm yam gûng* (prawn and lemon grass soup), grilled snapper and all things satay, plus creamy Thai desserts and freshly pressed juices. English menus are a bonus.

★May & Mark's INTERNATIONAL, THAI $$
(081 396 6114; 34 Th Sukhon; mains 75-250B; 7am-10pm;) A classic travellers' meeting spot with a bold varnished-concrete coffee bar, May and Mark's is always busy. We love it for the excellent espresso and the big choice of delicious omelettes, pancakes and home-baked bread. It also does popular Thai meals, plus international salads, sandwiches and mains. Good vegetarian selection.

Gecko Cabane THAI, FUSION $$
(081 958 5945; 1/36-37 Soi Ruam Jit, Th Maharat; mains 70-550B; 11am-11pm;) Thai dishes with a twist and Western food served up with style in an eye-catching conversion of two traditional shophouses. Dine on the dark-wood terrace, or in the living-room-like interior. The slow-cooked massaman curry is especially fine, as is the lamb shanks with mash potato, but all the dishes here are decent and good value.

Playground BAR
(www.facebook.com/krabiplaygroundbar; 87 Th Utarakit; 7pm-2am;) This bar with a large outside area at Pak-Up Hostel keeps the island bar tradition alive on the mainland, with beer pong, open-mic nights and occasional live music. Happy hour runs until 9.30pm.

Information

All guesthouses and many restaurants offer free wi-fi.

Bangkok Bank (Th Utarakit; 8.30am-3.30pm) Exchanges cash and travellers cheques and has ATMs.

Krabi Immigration Office (075 611097; 382 Mu 7, Saithai; 8.30am-4.30pm Mon-Fri) Handles visa extensions. Around 4km south-west of Krabi.

Krabi Nakharin International Hospital (075 626555; www.krabinakharin.co.th; 1 Th Pisanpob) Located 2km northwest of town.

Post Office (Th Utarakit; ⌚8.30am-4.30pm Mon-Fri, 9am-noon Sat & Sun) You can send mail overseas from here.

Getting There & Away

AIR

The airport is 14km northeast of Krabi on Hwy 4. Most domestic carriers fly between Bangkok and Krabi. Bangkok Air (www.bangkokair.com) flies daily to Ko Samui and Air Asia (www.airasia.com) to Chiang Mai.

BOAT

Ferries to Ko Phi-Phi and Ko Lanta leave from the **Khlong Chilat Passenger Pier** (Tha Khlong Chilat), 4km southwest of Krabi. Travel agencies selling boat tickets include free transfers.

Hat Railay East Long-tail boats (150B, 45 minutes) leave from Krabi's **Tha Khong Kha** between 7.45am and 6pm. Boatmen wait until they have eight passengers before leaving; otherwise, you can charter the whole boat (1200B). Boats to Hat Railay West leave from Ao Nang.

Ko Jum From November to late April, Ko Lanta boats stop at Ko Jum (400B, one hour), where long-tails shuttle you to shore.

Ko Lanta From November to late April, one daily boat (400B, two hours) leaves at 11.30am. During the rainy season, you can only get to Ko Lanta by frequent air-con minivans (250B to 300B, 2½ hours), which also run in high season.

Ko Phi-Phi Year-round boats (300B to 350B, 1½ to two hours) leave at 9am, 10.30am, 1.30pm and 3pm, returning at 9am, 10am, 1.30pm and 3.30pm. Ferries don't always run every day between May and October.

Phuket & Ko Yao Islands The quickest route is with direct boats from the pier at Hat Noppharat Thara (p333), 19km southwest of Krabi. *Sŏrng·tăa·ou* (50B) run between Krabi's Tha Khong Kha and the pier at Hat Noppharat Thara; taxis cost 600B. Boats also run several times daily to Ko Yao Noi from Tha Len (150B), 33km northwest of Krabi Town.

BUS

Krabi Bus Terminal (☎075 663503; cnr Th Utarakit & Hwy 4) is 4km north of central Krabi at Talat Kao, near theTh Utarakit and Hwy 4 junction.

MINIVAN

Travel agencies run air-con minivans and VIP buses to popular southern tourist centres, but you'll end up crammed cheek-to-jowl with other backpackers. Most offer combined minivan and boat tickets to Ko Samui (700B, five hours) and Ko Pha-Ngan (850B, seven hours). More (usually cheaper) minivans depart from the **bus terminal**. Departures from Krabi include the following:

DESTINATION	FARE (B)	DURATION (HR)
Hat Yai	230	4
Ko Lanta	250-300	2½
Phuket	140	2-3
Satun	200	4
Surat Thani	180	2½
Trang	100	2

SŎRNG·TĂA·OU

Sŏrng·tăa·ou run from the bus station to the centre of Krabi Town (30B) and on to Hat Noppharat

BUSES TO/FROM KRABI

DESTINATION	FARE (B)	DURATION (HR)	FREQUENCY
Bangkok (VIP)	862	12	5pm
Bangkok (air-con)	587	12	8am, 8.20am, 4pm, 5pm, 6pm
Hat Yai	255	4½	hourly 8.30am-7.20pm
Phuket	140	3	every 30min 8.30am-7.20pm
Ranong	210	5	8.30am & noon
Satun	212	5	11am, 1pm, 2pm, 3pm
Surat Thani	150	2½	hourly 4.30am-4.30pm
Trang	110	2	every 30min 7.30am-5pm

Thara (50B), Ao Nang (60B) and the Shell Cemetery at Ao Nam Mao (70B) between 6am and 7pm, picking up passengers along the way.

The most convenient places to catch them in Krabi's town centre are Th Utarakit and Th Maharat. From Th Maharat, you can catch *sŏrng·tăa·ou* to **Ao Luk** (80B, one hour, 6am to 3pm), Ao Nang and **Hat Noppharat Thara**. From Th Utarakit, there is also a service to **Ao Nang** and **Hat Noppharat Thara**, as well as to **Ban Laem Kruat**. In the opposite direction, Th Utarakit is the best place to pick up a *sŏrng·tăa·ou* to the **bus station**.

In high season services run until 10pm, but less frequently and for a small surcharge.

Getting Around

You can explore central Krabi on foot. *Sŏrng·tăa·ou* between the bus terminal and Krabi (30B) stop on Th Utarakit, outside the River View Hotel. Most travel agencies and guesthouses, including Pak-Up Hostel, rent motorbikes (200B per day).

TO/FROM THE AIRPORT

Taxis between the airport and Krabi Town cost 350B; motorcycle taxis cost 200B. Agencies and Pak-Up Hostel (p324) can arrange seats on the airport bus (130B). Several international car-rental companies have offices at the airport (vehicle hire from 1100B).

Railay ไร่เล

Krabi's fairytale limestone formations come to a dramatic climax at Railay (also spelt Rai Leh), the ultimate Andaman gym for rock-climbing fanatics. Monkeys frolic alongside climbers on the gorgeous crags, while down below some of the prettiest beaches in all Thailand are backed by proper jungle.

Accessible only by boat, but just a 15-minute ride from Ao Nang, the busiest parts of Railay are sandwiched between the scrappy, not good for swimming, beach of Hat Railay East and the high-end resorts and beautiful white sand of Hat Railay West and Hat Tham Phra Nang.

Railay is more crowded than it once was and sees many day trippers. Thankfully, though, it remains much less-developed than Ko Phi-Phi and if you head away from Hat Railay West and Hat Railay East the resorts disappear and the atmosphere is one of delightfully laid-back Thai-Rasta bliss.

Sights

Tham Phra Nang CAVE

(ถ้ำพระนาง, Princess Cave; Hat Tham Phra Nang) At the eastern end of Hat Tham Phra Nang is this important shrine for local fishermen (Muslim and Buddhist), who make offerings of carved wooden phalluses in the hope that the inhabiting spirit of a drowned Indian princess will provide a good catch. According to legend, a royal barge carrying the princess foundered here in a storm during the 3rd century BC. Her spirit took over the cave, granting favours to all who paid their respects.

Sa Phra Nang LAGOON

(Holy Princess Pool) Halfway along the trail linking Hat Railay East to Hat Tham Phra Nang, a sharp 'path' leads up the jungle-cloaked cliff wall to this hidden lagoon. The first section is a steep 10-minute uphill climb (with ropes for assistance). Fork right for the lagoon, reached by sheer downhill climbing. If you fork left, you'll quickly reach a dramatic cliff-side **viewpoint**; this is a strenuous but generally manageable, brief hike.

Activities

Rock Climbing

With more than 1000 routes in 51 areas, ranging from beginner to challenging advanced climbs, all with unparalleled cliff-top vistas, it's no surprise that Railay is among the world's top climbing spots. You could spend months climbing and exploring – many people do. Deep-water soloing, where free-climbers scramble up ledges over deep water, is incredibly popular. If you fall you'll probably just get wet, so even daring beginners can try.

Most climbers start off at **Muay Thai Wall** and **One, Two, Three Wall**, at the southern end of Hat Railay East, which have at least 40 routes graded from 4b to 8b on the French system. The mighty **Thaiwand Wall** sits at the southern end of Hat Railay West, offering a sheer limestone cliff with some of the most challenging climbing routes, graded from 6a to 7c+.

Other top climbs include **Hidden World**, with its classic intermediate routes, **Wee's Present Wall** (Hat Railay West), an overlooked 7c+ winner, and **Diamond Cave** and **Ao**

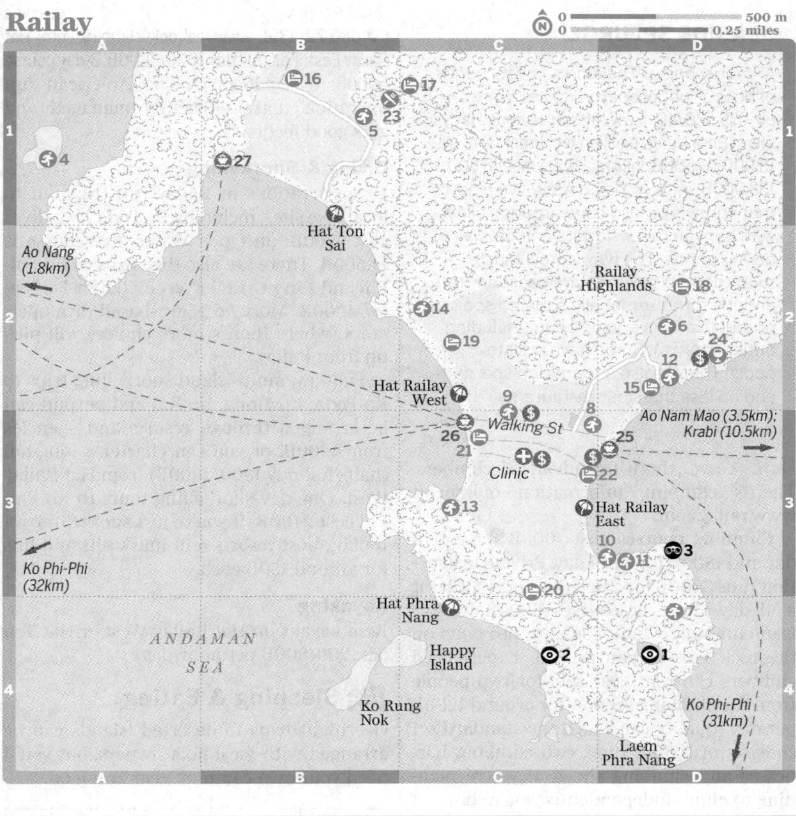

Railay

Sights
1 Sa Phra Nang ... D4
2 Tham Phra Nang ... C4
3 Viewpoint ... D3

Activities, Courses & Tours
4 Ao Nang Tower ... A1
5 Basecamp Tonsai ... B1
6 Diamond Cave ... D2
7 Hidden World ... D4
8 Hot Rock ... C3
9 King Climbers ... C3
10 Muay Thai Wall ... D3
11 One, Two, Three Wall ... D3
12 Real Rocks ... D2
13 Thaiwand Wall ... C3
14 Wee's Present Wall ... C2

Sleeping
15 Anyavee Railay Resort ... D2
16 Chill Out ... B1
17 Forest Resort ... C1
18 Railay Cabana ... D2
19 Railei Beach Club ... C2
20 Rayavadee ... C3
21 Sand Sea Resort ... C3
22 Sunrise Tropical Resort ... C3

Eating
23 Mama's Chicken ... B1
Sunset Restaurant ... (see 21)

Drinking & Nightlife
Chill Out ... (see 16)
24 Last Bar ... D2

Transport
25 Ferry Jetty ... D3
Long-Tail Boats to Ao Nam Mao ... (see 25)
26 Long-Tail Boats to Ao Nang ... C3
27 Long-Tail Boats to Ao Nang ... B1
Long-Tail Boats to Krabi ... (see 25)

SEASIDE SPLURGE

Arguably one of Thailand's finest chunks of beachfront property, **Rayavadee** (☎075 620740; www.rayavadee.com; Hat Tham Phra Nang; pavilion incl breakfast 15,900-51,500B, villa incl breakfast 58,500-138,000B; ❄📶🏊) is an exclusive resort that sprawls across huge grounds filled with banyan trees, flowers and meandering ponds. The two-storey, mushroom-domed pavilions are packed with antique furniture, locally sourced spa products and every mod con (including butler service). Some have private pools. There's also a top-notch spa, gym and no less than four restaurants.

Nang Tower, both for advanced climbers. There's climbing information online at www.railay.com.

Climbing courses cost 1000B for a half day and 1800B for a full day. Private instruction runs 3000B for a half day and 4500B for a full day. Three-day courses (6000B) involve lead climbing, where you clip into bolts on the rock face as you ascend. Experienced climbers can rent gear sets for two people from the climbing schools for around 1200B per day (quality can vary); the standard set consists of a 60m rope, two climbing harnesses and climbing shoes. If you're planning to climb independently, you're best off bringing your own gear.

Basecamp Tonsai CLIMBING
(☎081 149 9745; www.tonsaibasecamp.com; Hat Ton Sai; half/full day 800/1500B, 3-day course 6000B; ⏲8am-5pm & 7-9pm) Long-established, laid-back climbing outfit. Big on deep-water soloing (700B).

King Climbers CLIMBING
(☎081 797 8923; www.railay.com; Walking St; half/full day 1000/1800B, 3-day course 6000B; ⏲8.30am-9pm Mon-Fri, to 6pm Sat & Sun) One of the biggest, oldest and most reputable climbing schools.

Hot Rock CLIMBING
(☎085 641 9842; www.railayadventure.com; Hat Railay East; half/full day 1000/1800B, 3-day course 6000B; ⏲9am-8pm) Owned by one of the granddaddies of Railay climbing, Hot Rock has a good reputation.

Real Rocks CLIMBING
(☎080 718 1351; www.realrocksclimbing.com; Hat Railay East; half/full day 1000/1800B, 3-day course 6000B; ⏲8am-10pm) A Thai-American–run operation that's efficiently managed and gets good feedback.

Diving & Snorkelling

Dive operations in Railay run trips out to local dive sites, including Ko Poda. Two dives cost 3700B; an Open Water dive course is 14,500B. There are also dive trips to Ko Phi-Phi and **King Cruiser Wreck** (Ko Phi-Phi Don) for 4900B. Most Ao Nang–based dive operators (where there's more choice) will pick up from Railay.

Full-day, multi-island snorkelling trips to Ko Poda, Ko Hong, Ko Kai and beyond can be arranged through resorts and agencies from 1200B, or you can charter a long-tail (half-/full-day 1800/2800B) from Hat Railay West. One-day snorkelling tours to Ko Phi-Phi cost 2400B. If you're just snorkelling off Railay, most resorts rent mask sets and fins for around 150B each.

Kayaking

Rent kayaks on Hat Railay West or Hat Ton Sai (200/800B per hour/day).

Sleeping & Eating

Overnight trips to deserted islands can be arranged with local boat owners, but you'll need your own camping gear and food.

Hat Railay East หาดไร่เลย์ทิศตะวันออก

There are many midrange options around Hat Railay East and a fair few bars inland.

Anyavee Railay Resort RESORT $$
(☎075 819437; www.anyaveerailay.com; Hat Railay East; r 3050-3600B; ❄📶🏊) This place is consistently one of the best midrange options on what is a pricey island. The rooms aren't the newest, but they are spacious and clean with large balconies, TVs, fridges and safety boxes. All are set around a real jungle garden – expect to see white-faced monkeys passing through – with an attractive pool and overlooked by karst cliffs.

Sunrise Tropical Resort RESORT $$$
(☎075 819418; www.sunrisetropical.com; Hat Railay East; bungalows incl breakfast 3900-6300B; ❄@📶🏊) Swish 'chalets' and 'villas' here

rival some of the finest on Hat Railay West but are priced for Hat Railay East – so we reckon this is one of the best deals in Railay. Expect soothing smart decor, hardwood floors, four-poster beds or wooden mattress-platforms, lush bathrooms with aqua-tiled floors and private balconies or patios.

Hat Railay West หาดไร่เลย์ทิศตะวัน

Hat Railay West is home to upmarket resorts and the best beachfront restaurants.

★ **Railei Beach Club** VILLA $$$
(☎086 685 9359; www.raileibeachclub.com; Hat Railay West; house 2900-28,800B; ❄📶) At the northern end of the beach, hidden in forested grounds that stretch back to luscious limestone cliffs, is this collection of Thai-style homes for six to eight people, rented out on behalf of absent owners. They come with patios, kitchens and amenities, and there are also a few smaller but impeccably stylish dark-wood doubles. Only a few have air-con.

Sand Sea Resort RESORT $$$
(☎075 819463; www.krabisandsea.com; Hat Railay West; bungalows incl breakfast 3000-6500B; ❄@📶🏊) The cheapest resort on this sublime beach offers everything from ageing 'superior' bungalows to newly remodelled cottages and smart, sparkly, contemporary rooms with every amenity. The grounds aren't as swanky as the neighbours', but rooms are comfy and there are two peaceful, foliage-enclosed pools, one with karst views, making this a reasonable deal for the location.

At the recommended beachfront **Sunset Restaurant** (Hat Railay West; mains 180-400B; ⊙11am-9pm; 📶), red-shirted waiters take seafood-grill and Thai-curry orders on iPads.

Railay Highlands

There are many midrange accommodation options around the Railay Highlands.

Railay Cabana BUNGALOW $
(☎084 534 1928, 075 621733; Railay Highlands; bungalows 800B) Superbly located in a bowl of karst cliffs, this is your tropical mountain hideaway. The creaky yet clean thatched-bamboo bungalows with 24-hour electricity were undergoing renovation at the time of research, so expect prices to rise, and are surrounded by mango, mangosteen, banana and guava groves. It's just north of Tham Phra Nang Nai, inland from Hat Railay East.

Hat Ton Sai หาดต้นไทร

Hat Ton Sai, the most isolated beach, is where you'll find the best budget choices and a buzzing backpacker/climber scene. Cheap eats abound here, too. Note that on Hat Ton Sai, electricity runs only in the evening.

Forest Resort BUNGALOW $
(☎081 149 9745; www.basecamptonsai.com; Hat Ton Sai; dm 200B, r & bungalows 400-800B) The bamboo bungalows are slightly less scruffy than the sparse three-person, concrete-floor cells which pass for dorms here. The best bet are the wood-and-brick bungalows with tiled floors, red-brick bathrooms, private porches and tin roofs. All are fan cooled when the electricity is running (6pm to 1am). If there's no one around, ask at Basecamp Tonsa, which manages the place.

Chill Out BUNGALOW $$
(☎087 699 4527, 084 186 8138; www.chilloutkrabi.com; Hat Ton Sai; dm 300B, bungalows 600-1200B; 📶) While no more luxurious than Ton Sai's other offerings, Chill Out's bungalows bring a sociable, laid-back atmosphere and a pinch more style. Vibrantly painted international flags are plastered across the doors of basic tin-topped, wood-floored huts, which have terraces, cold-water bathrooms and mosquito nets. The dorm is functional with bunk beds. The bar (p330) gets busy. Electricity and wi-fi in evenings only.

Mama's Chicken THAI $
(Hat Ton Sai; mains 70-100B; ⊙7am-10pm; 🌿) Relocated to the jungle path leading inland to Hat Railay East and West, Mama's remains one of Ton Sai's favourite food stops for its international breakfasts, fruit smoothies and extensive range of cheap Thai dishes, including a rare massaman tofu and other vegetarian-friendly adaptations.

Drinking & Nightlife

There are a fair few bars inland from Hat Railay West and along Hat Railay East. Hat Ton Sai is reggae bar heaven.

★ **Last Bar** BAR
(Hat Railay East; ⏰11am-late) A reliably packed-out multilevel tiki bar that rambles to the edge of the mangroves, with bunting, balloons and cushioned seats on one deck, candlelit dining tables on another, live music at the back and waterside fire shows.

Chill Out BAR
(Hat Ton Sai; ⏰11am-late; 📶) Kick back over cold beers, live music, DJ beats and frenzied fire shows at Ton Sai's top jungle reggae bar.

ℹ Information

There's lots of local information on www.railay.com. There are many ATMs along Hat Railay East and on the paths leading to Hat Railay West. Bigger resorts change cash. Wi-fi is widely available.

The **clinic** (☎084 378 3057; Railay Bay Resort, Hat Railay West; ⏰8am-10pm) treats minor injuries. For anything serious, head to Krabi or Phuket.

ℹ Getting There & Away

Long-tails run to Railay from Krabi's Tha Khong Kha and from the seafront at Ao Nang and Ao Nam Mao. To Krabi, **long-tails** (⏰7.45am-6pm) leave from Hat Railay East. Boats in both directions leave between 7.45am and 6pm when they have eight people (150B, 45 minutes). Chartering the boat costs 1200B.

Boats to Hat Railay West or Hat Ton Sai from the southeastern end of Ao Nang (15 minutes) cost 100B from 8am to 6pm or 150B from 6pm to midnight. Boats don't leave until eight people show up. Private charters cost 800B. Services stop as early as 5pm May to October. **Long-tails** (⏰8am-6pm) return to Ao Nang from Hat Railay West on the same schedule. **Boats** (⏰8am-6pm) from Hat Ton Sai are less frequent, as fewer people travel from there. It's often quicker to head to Hat Railay West for a ride.

During exceptionally high seas, boats from Ao Nang and Krabi stop running; you may still be able to get a **long-tail** (⏰8am-6pm) from Hat Railay East to Ao Nam Mao (100B, 15 minutes), where you can take a *sŏrng·tăa·ou* (50B) to Krabi or Ao Nang.

A year-round ferry runs to Ko Phi-Phi (400B, 1¼ hours) from the **ferry jetty** at Hat Railay East at 9.45am; long-tails motor over to meet it. Boats to Ko Lanta (500B, two hours, 10.45am daily) operate only during the October–April high season. For Phuket (650B, 2¼ hours), there's a year-round ferry at 3.15pm. Some ferries pick up off Hat Railay West.

Ao Nang อ่าวนาง

First the hard truths. Thanks to its unchecked development huddled in the shadows of stunning karst scenery, Ao Nang is ugly-pretty. There's a slightly seedy undercurrent, too.

So, yes, it's a little trashy, but if you forgive that and focus on the beaches, framed by limestone headlands tied together by narrow strips of golden sand, there's plenty to like. In the dry season the sea glows a turquoise hue; during the monsoon, currents stir up the mocha shallows. If you're hankering for a snorkel in clearer waters, it's easy to get to the little islands that dot the horizon, which generally enjoy less murky water, at any time of the year. Divers too, are close to some prime spots for getting underwater. Above all, Ao Nang is a straightforward and compact, if blandly touristy, destination to visit and that's why people head here.

👁 Sights

Shell Cemetery NATURE RESERVE
(สุสานหอย, Gastropod Fossil, Su-San Hoi; adult/child 200/100B; ⏰8am-6pm) About 8km east of Ao Nang at the eastern end of Ao Nam Mao is the Shell Cemetery: giant slabs formed from millions of tiny 75-million-year-old fossil shells. There's a dusty **visitors centre** (⏰8am-4.30pm), with mildly interesting geological displays, plus stalls selling snacks. *Sŏrng·tăa·ou* from Krabi/Ao Nang cost 70/50B.

🏃 Activities

Diving & Snorkelling

Ao Nang has numerous dive schools offering trips to 15 local islands, including Ko Si, Ko Ha, Ko Poda, Yava Bon and Yava Son. Ko Mae Urai is one of the more unique local dives, with two submarine tunnels lined with soft and hard corals. Expect to pay 3200B for two dives.

Other trips run further afield to King Cruiser Wreck (p328) or Ko Phi-Phi, for 3500B to 3900B, and Hin Daeng, Hin Muang and **Ko Haa** south of Ko Lanta for 5700B to 6600B. An Open Water course costs 14,900B. Most dive companies also arrange snorkelling trips (from 1800B).

The Dive DIVING
(☎082 282 2537; www.thediveaonang.com; 249/2 Mu 2; 2 dives 3500B; ⏰11am-8pm) This keen

diving team with an excellent reputation runs trips to Ko Phi-Phi (3500B), which snorkellers can join (2500B), and to Ko Haa (6200B). Open Water certification costs 14,900B.

Aqua Vision DIVING
(☎086 944 4068; www.diving-krabi.com; 76/12 Mu 2; 2/3 dives 3600/4500B; ⏲9am-7pm) A reliable, well-informed dive school offering local dives, two-dive trips to Ko Phi-Phi, Open Water Diving courses (14,900B) and 'safaris' to Hin Daeng, Hin Muang and Ko Haa (5700B to 6600B), plus local snorkelling trips (1800B).

Kon-Tiki DIVING
(☎075 637826; www.kontiki-krabi.com; 161/1 Mu 2; 2/3 dives 3200/4000B; ⏲9am-9pm) A well regarded, large-scale operation, Kon-Tiki does fun dives to Ko Phi-Phi (3900B) and Ko Haa (6300B), local after-dark dives (4800B), snorkelling 'safaris' (2700B) and Open Water courses (15,500B).

Cycling

Take a Tour de Krabi by hooking up with **Krabi Eco Cycle** (☎081 607 4162, 075 637250; www.krabiecocycle.com; 309/5 Mu 5; half-/full-day tour 1500/3000B). The recommended full-day 15.5km pedal takes you through rubber plantations, small villages, hot springs and, finally, a cooler dip at the aptly named Emerald Pool. Lunch is included on all tours except the half-day bike-only tour.

Kayaking

Several companies offer kayaking tours to surrounding mangroves and islands from 1000B to 2500B, depending on the itinerary and whether you're travelling by speedboat. Popular destinations include the hidden lagoon at Ko Hong to view collection points for sea swallow nests (spurred by the ecologically dubious demand for bird's-nest soup). There are also trips to the lofty sea cliffs at Ao Tha Len and to the sea caves and 2000- to 3000-year-old paintings at Ban Bho Tho. Rates always include lunch, water, kayaks and guides.

Tours

All agencies can book you on popular four- or five-island tours from 1400B to 2000B, depending on whether you choose long-tail or speedboat. **Ao Nang Long-Tail Boat Service** (Hat Ao Nang, northwestern end; ⏲8am-4pm, to 2pm May-Oct) and **Ao Nang Long-Tail Boat Service Club** (Hat Ao Nang, southeastern end; ⏲8am-midnight, to 8pm May-Oct) offer private charters to Hong Island (2400B) and Bamboo Island (3800B), and half-day trips to Ko Kai (Chicken Island) and Ko Poda (1700B); maximum six people.

Tour agencies offer half-day tours to Khlong Thom (adult/child 1200/800B), including visits to freshwater pools and hot springs.

A speedboat tour to Ko Phi-Phi, including a stop at Bamboo Island is 2800B.

Sleeping

Ao Nang has a good mix of hostels, guesthouses, hotels and resorts, but the popular places fill up quickly in high season. Always book ahead. Prices drop by 50% during low season.

★ **Glur** HOSTEL $
(☎075 695297, 089 001 3343; www.krabiglurhostel.com; 22/2 Mu 2, Soi Ao Nang; dm 600B, d 1300-1500B; P❄@📶🏊) A fabulous retreat of a hostel, designed, built, owned and operated by a talented Thai architect and his wife. The complex incorporates shipping containers, glass, and moulded and polished concrete to create sumptuous dorms, with curtained-off turquoise bunk beds, as well as private rooms (also equipped with bunk beds), all set in a lovely garden with a small pool.

It's a walkable 1.5km northeast of Ao Nang proper.

Anawin BUNGALOW $$
(☎075 637664, 081 677 9632; www.anawinbungalows.com; 263/1 Mu 2; bungalows 1000-1600B; ❄📶) Zingy-yellow collection of 10 clean concrete cabins with TVs and fronted by little verandahs, all tucked into a quiet flowery corner just 400m northeast of Ao Nang beach. Rooms are a little old-fashioned, but they're decent-sized and the owner is friendly.

Phra Nang Inn HOTEL $$$
(☎075 637130; www.vacationvillage.co.th; Th Ao Nang; r incl breakfast 4000-8500B; ❄📶🏊) A thatched explosion of rustic coconut wood, shell curtains, bright orange and purple paint and elaborate Thai tiles with Mexico-inspired flair. Divided into two wings – there are also two pools – rooms aren't huge and some

could use a refresh (renovations were under way at the time of research), but the location is great and there's a beachfront bar.

Red Ginger Chic HOTEL $$$

(☎075 637999; www.redgingerchicresort.com; 168 Mu 3; r 5500-12,350B; ❄📶🏊) On a hotel-filled boulevard at the far western end of Ao Nang, Red Ginger is fashionable and colourful with detailed tiles, red paper lanterns, draped fabrics and a frosted glass bar in the lobby.

Spacious, smart rooms feature elegant wallpaper, modern furnishings and big balconies overlooking an expansive pool. Efficient staff.

Eating & Drinking

Ao Nang has many mediocre restaurants serving Thai, Indian, Italian and Scandinavian food. By far the best restaurants are the seafood joints. For budget meals, stalls pop up in the evening on the road to Krabi (near McDonald's).

You'll find *roti* (pancakes), *gài tôrt* (fried chicken), hamburgers and the like, and around lunchtime street stalls set up just north of Krabi Resort.

Krua Ao Nang Cuisine SEAFOOD $$

(☎075 695260; Soi Sunset; mains 150-400B; ⏲10am-10pm) One of the best (and most popular) of several seafood restaurants with gorgeous sea vistas in this pedestrian-only alley at the western end of the beach. A model ice boat at the entrance shows off the day's catch (you pay by the kilo for seafood). It's a little more pricey than other options around Ao Nang; you're paying for the view.

Myeong Dong KOREAN $$

(☎075 813164; 345 Mu 2; mains 150-700B; ⏲11am-10pm; 📶) If you want a change from seafood and mediocre Western cuisine, try this Korean barbecue place popular with Ao Nang's many Asian visitors. It offers classic Korean soups and stews, but the barbecue is the draw.

The grill is on your table, order your choice of meat; the veggies and side dishes come free.

Last Fisherman BAR

(☎081 267 5338; 266 Mu 2; ⏲10am-midnight) Sit at one of the breezy tables overlooking the beach, or perch at the long-tail boat-shaped bar, to enjoy your sundowner at this mellow but popular place at the southern end of Ao Nang.

Information

All so-called 'tourist information' offices on the main drag through Ao Nang are private tour agencies.

There are many ATMs and foreign-exchange windows (open approximately 10am to 8pm).

Getting There & Away

TO/FROM THE AIRPORT

White airport buses (150B) run hourly from 9am to 5pm, stopping outside McDonald's on the Krabi road. Private taxis (500B) and minivans (150B) go to/from the airport.

BOAT

Boats to Hat Railay West (15 minutes) are run by Ao Nang Long-Tail Boat Service (p331) and Ao Nang Long-Tail Boat Service Club (p331). Rates per person are 100B to 150B. Boats leave with eight passengers; you can charter the whole boat for the eight-person price.

CAR & MOTORCYCLE

Dozens of agencies along the main strip rent out motorcycles (200B to 250B). A number of places offer car hire from 1100B per day. Budget Car Hire (www.budget.co.th) has a desk at Krabi airport (vehicle rental per day from 1200B).

MINIVAN

Daily minivans (often combined boat-minivan tickets) go to destinations across southern Thailand.

DESTINATION	FARE (B)	DURATION (HR)
Khao Sok	400	3
Ko Lanta	400	3
Ko Lipe	1000	6
Ko Samui	700	4
Ko Tao	1100	7
Ko Pha-Ngan	850	5
Phuket	450	3

SŎRNG·TĂA·OU

Sŏrng·tăa·ou run to/from Krabi (60B, 30 minutes). The route goes from Krabi's bus terminal via Th Maharat to Krabi's Tha Khong Kha and on to Hat Noppharat Thara, Ao Nang and the Shell Cemetery. From Ao Nang to Hat Noppharat Thara or the Shell Cemetery costs 30B.

Hat Noppharat Thara หาดนพรัตน์ธารา

North of Ao Nang, the golden beach turns more natural as it curves 4km around a less developed headland, until the sea eventually spills into a busy natural lagoon at **Hat Noppharat Thara-Mu Ko Phi-Phi National Park** (อุทยานแห่งชาติหาดนพรัตน์ธารา-หมู่เกาะพีพี; ☎075 661145; www.dnp.go.th; adult/child Ko Phi-Phi 400/200B, other islands 200/100B) headquarters. Its visitors centre has displays on coral reefs and mangrove ecology in Thai and English.

Hat Noppharat Thara is quieter and less built-up than Ao Nang. Several resorts here deceptively advertise a 'central Ao Nang' location, though you may well prefer ending up here anyway.

Sleeping & Eating

Several restaurants serving typical Thai snacks (fried chicken, papaya salad, noodles and stir fries) cluster near the national park headquarters and in a little enclave near the Sabai Resort. There are some decent seafood restaurants along the beachfront road.

Sabai Resort HOTEL $$
(☎075 637791; www.sabairesort.com; 79/2 Mu 3; bungalows 1300-3500B;) The most professionally run of the area's bungalow properties. Tiled-roofed, mint-green, well-kept bungalows come in fan-cooled or air-con editions, with pebbled concrete patios overlooking a palm-shaded pool and flower-filled gardens. There are four-person family-sized rooms as well.

Hat Noppharat Thara-Mu Ko Phi-Phi National Park Accommodation BUNGALOW, CAMPGROUND $$
(☎075 661145; www.dnp.go.th; camping per person 30B, bungalows 1000B;) Rustic but well-maintained concrete, air-con, 24-hour-electricity bungalows, just over the road from the beach. No wi-fi. Note that while you can still camp here, just behind the park HQ, you will need your own tent as they're no longer available for rent. Book ahead online or at the visitors centre.

★**Krua Thara** SEAFOOD $$
(☎075 661166; 82 Mu 5; mains 150-250B; 11am-10pm) This cavernous, tin-roofed delight is one of the best restaurants in southern Andaman and one of the finest seafood kitchens in southern Thailand. There's no pretension here, just the freshest fish, crab, clams, oysters, lobster, squid and prawns done dozens of ways. The steamed yellow conch (a local delicacy) and the crab stir-fried in yellow curry are especially memorable.

Information

Hat Noppharat Thara-Mu Ko Phi-Phi National Park Visitors Centre (☎075 661145; www.dnp.go.th; 8am-4.30pm) Offers information about the national park. You can also book the park accommodation here.

Getting There & Away

BOAT

Boats leave from Hat Noppharat Thara's pier for the following destinations:

Ko Phi-Phi The *Ao Nang Princess* runs daily (450B, two hours) from around November to April, and on Wednesday, Friday and Sunday from May to October. Boats leave at 9.30am, returning from Ko Phi-Phi at 3.30pm, via Railay.

Ko Lanta A 10.30am *Ao Nang Princess* boat runs to Ko Lanta (550B, 2¾ hours).

Phuket From November to April, the fastest option to Phuket is the **Green Planet** (☎075 637488; www.krabigreenplanet.com) speedboat to Tha Bang Rong (1200B, 1¼ hours), via Ko Yao Noi and Ko Yao Yai (both 650B, 45 minutes). The boat leaves Hat Noppharat Thara's pier at 11am, returning from Phuket at 3pm; transport to your Phuket accommodation is included. There's also a 4pm *Ao Nang Princess* boat to Phuket (700B, three hours; reduced services May to October).

SŎRNG·TĂA·OU

Sŏrng·tăa·ou between Krabi (60B) and Ao Nang (30B) stop in Hat Noppharat Thara.

Ko Phi-Phi เกาะพีพีดอน

With their curvy, bleached beaches and stunning jungle interiors, Phi-Phi Don and Phi-Phi Leh – collectively known as Ko Phi-Phi – are the darlings of the Andaman Coast. Phi-Phi Don is a hedonistic paradise where visitors cavort by day in azure seas and party all night on soft sand. In contrast, smaller Ko Phi-Phi Leh is undeveloped and hotel-free, its coral reefs and crystal-clear waters overseen by soaring, jagged cliffs, and visited only on day or sunset cruises.

Ko Phi-Phi Don

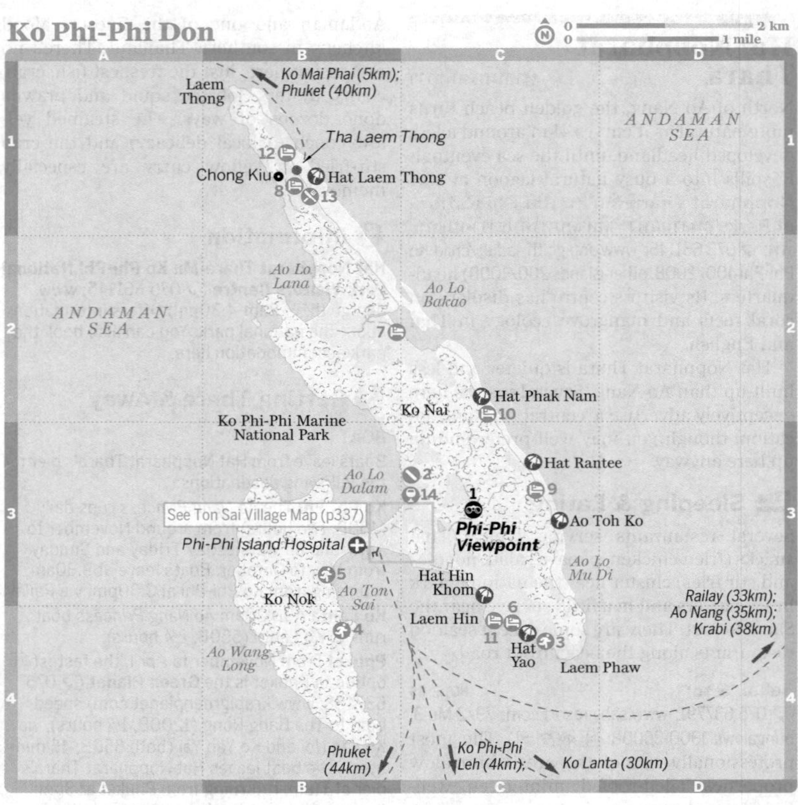

Ko Phi-Phi Don

Top Sights
1 Phi-Phi Viewpoint C3

Activities, Courses & Tours
2 Blue View Divers C3
3 Hat Yao C4
4 Hin Taak Climbing Area B4
5 Ton Sai Tower Climbing Area B3

Sleeping
6 Paradise Pearl Bungalow C4
7 Phi-Phi Island Village B2
8 PP Erawan Palms Resort B1
9 Rantee View C3
10 Relax Beach Resort C2
11 Viking Natures Resort C4
12 Zeavola B1

Eating
13 Jasmin B1
Paradise Pearl Bungalow .... (see 6)
Relax Beach Resort .... (see 10)

Drinking & Nightlife
14 Sunflower Bar C3

Rampant development has rendered the centre of Ko Phi-Phi Don, as well as the two bays that flank it, a chaotic, noisy mess of hotels, restaurants, bars and shops. If you want tranquillity, head to the stunning white coves of the east coast, or less-developed Hat Yao in the south. Tread lightly, manage your expectations and Ko Phi-Phi may seduce you as it has so many other travellers. You might, equally, find you can't wait to leave.

Sights

★ Phi-Phi Viewpoint VIEWPOINT
(จุดชมวิวเกาะพีพีดอน; Map p334; Ko Phi-Phi Don; 30B) The strenuous Phi-Phi-viewpoint climb is a steep, rewarding 20- to 30-minute hike up hundreds of steps and narrow twisting paths. Follow the signs on the road heading northeast from Ton Sai Village; most people will need to stop for a break (don't forget your water bottle). The views from the top are exquisite: Phi-Phi's lush mountain butterfly brilliance in full bloom.

Activities

Watersports Experience WATER SPORTS
(096 924 4043; www.watersportsexperience.com; Ko Phi-Phi Don; per person without/with sports 1500/2500B; tour 10am-6pm) Zip around in a speedboat and stand-up paddle board (SUP), wakeboard, water-ski, cliff-jump and snorkel the waters around Phi-Phi Don and Phi-Phi Leh. Anyone who doesn't fancy getting sporty is welcome to a discount. Book at any Ton Sai Village agency. Beers are included in the price.

Diving

Crystalline water and abundant marine life make the perfect recipe for top-notch scuba diving. Phi-Phi dive prices are fixed across the board. Open Water certification costs 13,800B, while standard two-dive trips cost 2500B to 3500B and Discover Scuba costs 3400B. Hin Daeng and Hin Muang, 60km south, are expensive ventures from Ko Phi-Phi (5500B); it's slightly cheaper to link up with a dive crew in Ko Lanta.

Blue View Divers DIVING
(Map p334; 094 592 0184; www.blueviewdivers.com; Phi Phi Viewpoint Resort, Ao Lo Dalam, Ko Phi-Phi Don; 2 dives 2500B; 10am-8pm) Professional, well-organised outfit that focuses on community involvement, beach clean-ups and environmental conservation, with two-dive trips (2500B), night dives (1900B), Open Water courses (13,800B) and Discover Scuba (3400B).

Princess Divers DIVING
(Map p337; 088 768 0984; www.princessdivers.com; Ton Sai Village, Ko Phi-Phi Don; 9.30am-10pm) Recommended dive outfit that speaks multiple languages and uses big boats, rather than long-tails or speedboats. Offers Discover Scuba (3400B) and SSI/PADI Open Water courses (12,900/13,800B).

Snorkelling

Ko Mai Phai (Bamboo Island; Ko Phi-Phi Don), 6km north of Phi-Phi Don, is a popular shallow snorkelling spot where you may see small sharks. There's good snorkelling along the eastern coast of **Ko Nok** (near Ao Ton Sai), along the eastern coast of **Ko Nai**, and off **Hat Yao**. Most resorts rent out snorkel, mask and fins sets (200B per day).

BEST KO PHI-PHI DIVE SITES

Leopard sharks and hawksbill turtles are common on Ko Phi-Phi's dive sites. Whale sharks sometimes make cameo appearances around Hin Daeng, Hin Bida and Ko Bida Nok in February and March. November to February boasts the best visibility. Top dives around Ko Phi-Phi include the following:

DIVE SITE	DEPTH (M)	FEATURES
Anemone Reef	17-26	Hard coral reef with plentiful anemones and clownfish
Hin Bida Phi-Phi (Ko Phi-Phi Don)	5-30	Submerged pinnacle with hard coral, turtles, leopard sharks and occasional mantas and whale sharks
King Cruiser Wreck	12-30	Sunken passenger ferry (1997) with snappers, leopard sharks, barracudas, scorpionfish, lionfish and turtles
Kledkaeo Wreck (Ko Phi-Phi Don)	14-26	Deliberately sunk decommissioned Thai navy ship (2014) with lionfish, snappers, groupers and barracudas
Ko Bida Nok (Ko Phi-Phi Don)	18-22	Karst massif with gorgonians, leopard sharks, barracudas and occasional whale sharks and mantas
Phi-Phi Leh	5-18	Island rim covered in coral and oysters, with moray eels, octopuses, seahorses and swim-throughs

Snorkelling trips go from 600B to 1500B, not including national park fees, depending on whether you travel by long-tail or speedboat. Snorkellers can tag along with dive trips.

Rock Climbing

Yes, there are good limestone cliffs to climb on Phi-Phi, and the views are spectacular. The main climbing areas are **Ton Sai Tower** (Map p334; Ko Phi-Phi Don), at the western edge of Ao Ton Sai, and **Hin Taak** (Map p334; Ko Phi-Phi Don), a short long-tail boat ride around the bay. Climbing operators, though, are in short supply, mostly congregating on nearby Railay. Ask the **Adventure Club** (Map p337; 081 895 1334; www.diving-in-thailand.net; 125/19 Mu 7, Ton Sai Village, Ko Phi-Phi Don; 2 dives 2500B; 7am-10pm) for a recommendation.

Courses

Pum Restaurant & Cooking School COOKING
(Map p337; 081 521 8904; www.pumthaifoodchain.com; 125/40 Mu 7, Ton Sai Village, Ko Phi-Phi Don; classes 11am, 4pm & 6pm) Thai food fans can take highly recommended cooking courses ranging from two-hour sessions (1500B) to five-hour 'healthy lifestyle' extravaganzas and, the most expensive, a whole day class with Pum herself (7500B). You'll learn the secrets behind some of the excellent dishes served in Pum's Ton Sai Village restaurant and go home with a cookbook.

Tours

Ever since Leo (DiCaprio) smoked a spliff in the film rendition of Alex Garland's *The Beach*, Phi-Phi Leh has become a pilgrimage site. Aside from long-tail boat trips to Phi-Phi Leh and Ko Mai Phai on Phi-Phi Don, tour agencies organise sunset tours around Phi-Phi Leh that include Monkey Bay and the beach at Wang Long.

PP Original Sunset Tour BOATING
(Map p337; Ton Sai Village, Ko Phi-Phi Don; per person 900B; tours 1pm) A sensational sunset cruise that sees you bobbing around Phi-Phi Leh aboard a double-decker boat to mellow beats, snorkelling and kayaking between Ao Pi Leh's sheer-sided cliffs and dining on fried rice off Maya Beach, led by an enthusiastic, organised team. Bliss.

Maya Bay Sleepaboard BOATING
(Map p337; www.mayabaytours.com; Ton Sai Village, Ko Phi-Phi Don; per person 3500B) You can no longer camp on Phi-Phi Leh's Maya Beach, but Maya Bay Sleepaboard can arrange for you to spend the night just offshore. Prices include food, sleeping bags and national park entry fees; tours depart at 3pm, returning at 10am the following morning. The same team runs the popular **Plankton Sunset Cruise** (www.mayabaytours.com; Ko Phi-Phi Leh; per person 1700B; 3-8pm) to Phi-Phi Leh.

Captain Bob's Booze Cruise BOATING
(Map p337; 094 464 9146; www.phiphiboozecruise.com; Ko Phi-Phi Don; women/men 2500/3000B; tours 1-7pm) One of Phi-Phi's most popular excursions: we can't think why. Cruise the waters around Phi-Phi Don and Phi-Phi Leh, beverage in hand. There are rumours that the days of the booze cruises are numbered, with locals ticked off with smashed *fa·ràng* (Westerners) returning to town just at the time more sober tourists are going out for dinner.

Sleeping

On Ko Phi-Phi Don, expect serious room shortages and extortionate rates, especially at peak holiday times. Book ahead. Life is much easier in low season (May to October), when prices drop dramatically.

There is no accommodation on Ko Phi-Phi Leh. Nor can you camp here anymore. Your only option is to sleep on a boat offshore, which can be arranged with Maya Bay Sleepaboard.

Ton Sai Village & Ao Lo Dalam บ้านต้นไทร/อ่าวโละดาลัม

The flat, packed-out, hourglass-shaped land between Ao Ton Sai and Ao Lo Dalam is crammed with lodging options. Central Ton Sai is called the 'Tourist Village'.

Ao Lo Dalam is the traditional backpacker beach and there are many functional hostels here. Framed by stunning karst cliffs, it's arguably Phi-Phi's prettiest stretch of sand. But it's clogged with people, long-tail boats, many beach bars and day trippers. After 9pm, it turns into a vast open-air nightclub.

Rock Backpacker HOSTEL $
(Map p337; 081 607 3897; Ton Sai Village, Ko Phi-Phi Don; dm 300B, r fan/air-con 900/2000B;) A proper hostel on the village hill, with clean, big dorms lined with bunk beds, small private rooms, an inviting restaurant-bar and

Ton Sai Village

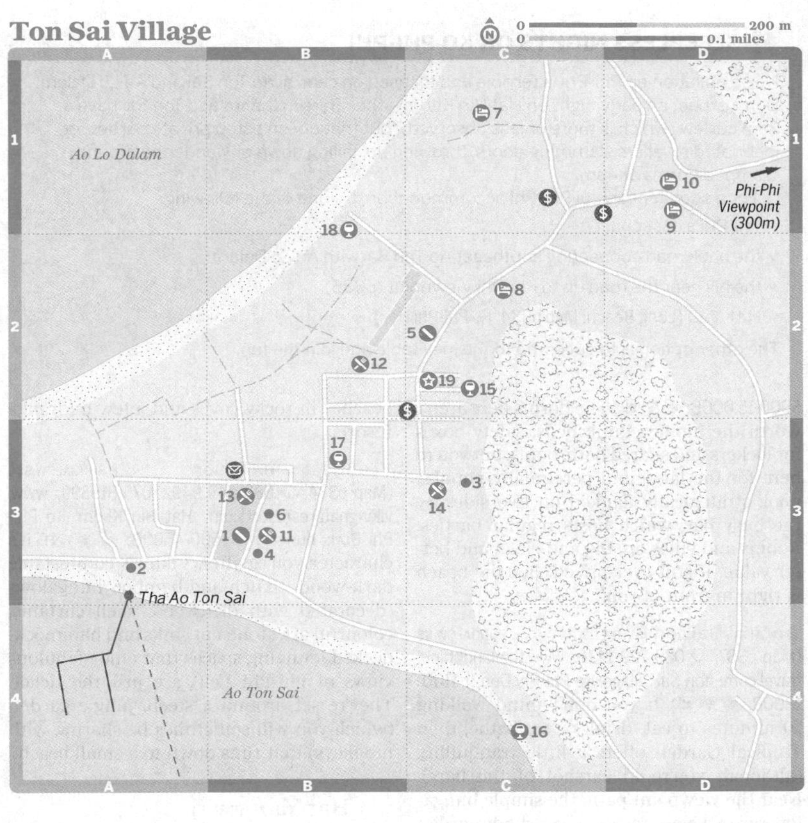

Ton Sai Village

Activities, Courses & Tours

1 Adventure Club B3
2 Captain Bob's Booze Cruise A3
3 Maya Bay Sleepaboard C3
4 PP Original Sunset Tour B3
5 Princess Divers C2
6 Pum Restaurant & Cooking School B3

Sleeping

7 Ibiza House C1
8 Rock Backpacker C2
9 Tropical Garden Bungalows D1
10 Up Hill Cottage D1

Eating

11 Efe B3
12 Esan Ganeang B2
13 Local Food Market B3
14 Papaya Restaurant C3
Unni's .... (see 11)

Drinking & Nightlife

15 Banana Bar C2
16 Carlito's C4
17 Relax Bar B3
18 Slinky B1

Entertainment

19 Kong Siam C2

a rugged, graffiti-scrawled exterior. It's still one of Ton Sai's cheaper pads and there's a buzzing backpacker scene – just don't expect an effusive welcome. Walk-ins only.

Ibiza House HOSTEL, HOTEL **$$**
(Map p337; ☎080 537 1868, 075 601274; ibizahouseppth@gmail.com; Ao Lo Dalam, Ko Phi-Phi Don; dm 1000-1500B, r incl breakfast 3500B, villas

SLEEPLESS NIGHTS ON KO PHI-PHI

Noise pollution on Phi-Phi is terrible and focused on central Ao Ton Sai and Ao Lo Dalam. Don't expect an early night on Hat Hin Khom either. Bars in Dalam and Ton Sai have a 2am curfew (which is more or less observed), but that doesn't stop private parties, or inebriated revellers slamming doors, throwing up, falling down or wandering around cramped dorms at 4am.

For a shot at peaceful Phi-Phi accommodation, try one of the following:

- Phi-Phi's east coast
- the back road connecting southeast Ao Ton Sai with Ao Lo Dalam
- the hill near the road up to Phi-Phi Viewpoint (p335)
- **Hat Yao** (Long Beach; Map p334; Ko Phi-Phi Don)

The other option is to succumb to the inevitable and join the fun.

5000-15,000B;) The dorms here aren't worth the money: bunk beds, safety boxes for lockers and shared bathrooms, but you're here for the large and perennially popular pool, strategically flanked on two sides by the busy bar, which hosts regular parties. Rooms and villas are big and clean and better value, if still over-priced. But the beach is right in front of you.

Tropical Garden Bungalows BUNGALOW **$$**
(Map p337; 089 729 1436; www.thailandphiphitravel.com; Ton Sai Village, Ko Phi-Phi Don; r 1100-1800B;) If you don't mind walking 10 minutes to eat, drink or sunbathe, then Tropical Garden offers a little tranquillity (although you're in earshot of the bars). Near the viewpoint path, the simple bungalows are set close together in a shady garden and come with balconies and hammocks. The cheapest are fan-only. There's a small flower-fringed pool with a swim-up bar.

Up Hill Cottage BUNGALOW **$$$**
(Map p337; 075 601124; www.phiphiuphillcottage.com; 140 Mu 7, Ton Sai Village, Ko Phi-Phi Don; r 2000-2500B;) These cream-painted, wood-panelled bungalows come in cute pastels offset by colourful bed runners and snazzily tiled bathrooms. Most enjoy island views (of varying beauty) from private balconies. It's *slightly* beyond the madness, at the eastern end of the main street heading north from Ton Sai Village. Small pool. Beware the hundreds of stairs.

Hat Hin Khom หาดหินคม

A 15-minute beach or jungle walk east of Ao Ton Sai, this area has a few small white-sand beaches in rocky coves and a few midrange resorts.

Viking Natures Resort BUNGALOW **$$$**
(Map p334; 083 649 9492, 075 819399; www.vikingnaturesresort.com; Hat Hin Khom, Ko Phi-Phi Don; bungalows 1500-4500B;) If it's character you're after, Viking's comfortable dark-wood, thatch-and-bamboo bungalows (decorated with driftwood, shell curtains, colourful art, stone-cut sinks and hammock-decked lounging spaces that enjoy fabulous views of Phi-Phi Leh) are just the ticket. They're set around a steep, jungle garden (which you will sometimes be sharing with monkeys) that runs down to a small beach.

Hat Yao หาดยาว

This lively stretch of pure-white south-coast beach is perfect for swimming, but don't expect it to yourself. There are also midrange resorts here. You can walk here in 30 minutes from Ton Sai via Hat Hin Khom or take long-tails (100B to 150B) from Ton Sai pier.

Paradise Pearl Bungalow RESORT **$$$**
(Map p334; 075 601248; www.phiphiparadisepearl.com; Hat Yao, Ko Phi-Phi Don; r incl breakfast 3000-5000B;) A sprawling complex of dark-wood Thai chalets, decked out with art, tucked into the rocky headland on the northern curl of Hat Yao. Delightfully old-fashioned beach-facing wooden 'houses' have four-poster beds, lace curtains and tea/coffee stands. The loungey **restaurant** (Map p334; Hat Yao, Ko Phi-Phi Don; mains 120-400B; 7.30am-10pm;), typically packed with young couples, rambles to the edge of the sand.

Hat Rantee หาดรันตี

This small, low-key, remote, grey-gold eastern bay has midrange family bungalows and good snorkelling. Arrive by long-tail from Ton Sai's pier (700B; return 200B per person, minimum four people; resorts provide free pick up if you've booked) or via the strenuous 45-minute hike over the viewpoint.

Rantee View BUNGALOW $$
(Map p334; ☎092 124 0599; Hat Rantee, Ko Phi-Phi Don; bungalows fan 1500B, air-con 2500-4500B;) Basic, acceptable-enough woven bamboo bungalows and newer, clean, tiled concrete bungalows with air-con and wide porches overlooking a trim garden path that leads to the sand. No restaurant. Closes low season.

Hat Phak Nam หาดผักน้ำ

This gorgeous white-sand beach shares its bay with a small fishing hamlet, is quiet and has a few midrange places to stay. Charter a long-tail from Ao Ton Sai (1000B; 200B by shared taxi boat to return) or make the sweaty one-hour hike over the viewpoint.

Relax Beach Resort BUNGALOW $$$
(Map p334; ☎089 475 6536; www.phiphirelaxresort.com; Hat Phak Nam, Ko Phi-Phi Don; bungalows 2100-4600B;) These 47 lacquered Thai-style bungalows, with wood floors, thatched roofs, two-tiered terraces with lounging cushions and mosaic bathrooms (in the best rooms), are rimmed by lush jungle. There's a good seafood-focused Thai/international **restaurant** (Map p334; mains 120-350B; 7.30am-9pm;) and breezy bar, and it's run by charming staff who treat guests like family.

Ao Lo Bakao อ่าวโละบาเกา

Ao Lo Bakao's fine stretch of northeastern palm-backed sand, ringed by dramatic hills, is one of Phi-Phi's loveliest, with offshore views over aqua bliss to Bamboo and Mosquito Islands. A long-tail charter from Ao Ton Sai costs 1000B.

Phi-Phi Island Village BUNGALOW $$$
(Map p334; ☎075 628900; www.phiphiislandvillage.com; Ao Lo Bakao, Ko Phi-Phi Don; r incl breakfast 7300-26,400B;) This whopping resort – 201 wood-and-concrete bungalows mostly set just back from the beach with palms swaying between them – is its own self-contained world with everything you'd need on site, including two pools, restaurant, coffee shop, spa, dive shop and tennis courts (as well as its own tsunami shelter). The resort arranges long-tail transfers to/from Ton Sai. Discounts if you book online.

Hat Laem Thong หาดแหลมทอง

Despite the upmarket resorts here, this northeastern white-sand beach is busy (it's a stop on day tours from Phuket) and has a small, rubbish-strewn *chow lair* settlement at its northern end. Long-tail charters from Ao Ton Sai cost 1200B; hotels arrange transfers.

★**Zeavola** HOTEL $$$
(Map p334; ☎075 627000; www.zeavola.com; Hat Laem Thong, Ko Phi-Phi Don; bungalows incl breakfast 11,100-22,100B;) Hibiscus-lined pathways lead to shady teak bungalows with sleek, distinctly Asian indoor-outdoor floorplans. Each comes with floor-to-ceiling windows on three sides, beautiful 1940s fixtures and antique furniture, huge ceramic sinks, indoor/outdoor showers, tea/coffee pods on a private terrace and impeccable service. The finest villas enjoy their own infinity pools and there's a fabulous couples-oriented spa.

PP Erawan Palms Resort HOTEL $$$
(Map p334; ☎075 627500; www.pperawanpalms.com; Hat Laem Thong, Ko Phi-Phi Don; r incl breakfast 4500-9000B;) Step onto the grounds and let the stress fall away as you follow a meandering path through gardens to bright, spacious, modern yet traditional-feel 'cottages' and smaller rooms decorated with Thai art and handicrafts. Beds could be bigger and better, but there's an inviting pool bar plus friendly service.

Eating

★**Esan Ganeang** THAI $
(Map p337; Ton Sai Village, Ko Phi-Phi Don; mains 70-150B; 10am-midnight) On an alley jammed with hole-in-the-wall places favoured by the locals, family-run Esan Ganeang has fantastic and authentic dishes from the Isan region in northeast Thailand. Come here for fiery salads and soups, as well as more mild curries and noodle dishes packed with

flavour. Make sure to order sticky rice to accompany your meal.

Local Food Market MARKET, THAI $

(Map p337; Ton Sai Village, Ko Phi-Phi Don; mains 60-80B; ⏲7am-10pm) Phi-Phi's cheapest, most authentic eats are at this market close to the pier. A handful of enthusiastic local stalls serve up scrumptious *pàt tai*, fried rice, *sôm·đam* (spicy green papaya salad) and smoked catfish.

★**Unni's** INTERNATIONAL $$

(Map p337; ☎091 837 5931; Ton Sai Village, Ko Phi-Phi Don; mains 140-600B; ⏲8am-11pm; 📶) Swing by this local expat fave for homemade breakfast bagels topped with everything from smoked salmon to meatballs. or specials like avocado-and-feta toast, served in a bright and pleasant cafe-style atmosphere. Other excellent global treats include massive Greek salads, pastas, burritos, nachos, burgers, tapas, cocktails and more.

★**Efe** TURKISH $$

(Map p337; ☎095 150 4434; Ton Sai Village, Ko Phi-Phi Don; mains 170-640B; ⏲noon-10.30pm; 📶) This Mediterranean newcomer has swiftly become the restaurant of choice for discerning travellers and expats, thanks to its super selection of kebabs served on sizzling plates, salads and wraps. Also does fine burgers and pizzas. It's a cosy place, with a few tables inside and a tiny patio, so expect to wait for a table during the dinner rush.

★**Jasmin** SEAFOOD $$

(Map p334; Hat Laem Thong, Ko Phi-Phi Don; mains 150-500B; ⏲10am-10pm) Break out of your posh resort to eat at this fine and relaxed, semi-open-air seafood place right in the middle of idyllic Laem Thong beach. The fresh fish (pay by the weight), lovingly grilled, is the draw, but it also whips up all your Thai classics, Western standards, sandwiches and breakfasts. Also does a reasonable cocktail.

Papaya Restaurant THAI $$

(Map p337; ☎087 280 1719; Ton Sai Village, Ko Phi-Phi Don; mains 70-450B; ⏲8.30am-10pm) Cheap, tasty and spicy. Here's some real-deal Thai food served in heaping portions. It has your basil and chilli, all the curries, *sôm·đam* (spicy green papaya salad) and *đôm yam*, too.

THEFT WARNING

Thefts can be a problem on Ko Phi-Phi Don. Watch your possessions and close windows and lock doors.

Drinking & Nightlife

Buckets of cheap whisky and Red Bull and sickly sweet cocktails make this the domain of gap-year craziness and really bad hangovers. Be wary of anyone offering you drugs on the beaches: they may be setting you up for a visit from the local coppers.

Banana Bar BAR

(Map p337; Ton Sai Village, Ko Phi-Phi Don; ⏲11am-2pm; 📶) The 'alt' bar destination in Ton Sai Village, inland for those seeking to escape the house and techno barrage on the beach, Banana is spread over multiple levels. Climb to the rooftop, or lounge on cushions on the raised decks around the bar. Solid sounds and popular with people who like to roll their own cigarettes. Also does Mexican food.

Slinky CLUB

(Map p337; Ao Lo Dalam, Ko Phi-Phi Don; ⏲9pm-2am) Still the best fire show on Ao Lo Dalam and still the beach dancefloor of the moment. Expect throbbing bass, buckets of liquor (from 350B) and throngs of tourists mingling, flirting and flailing to the music.

Relax Bar BAR

(Map p337; Ton Sai Village, Ko Phi-Phi Don; ⏲noon-1am) The coldest beer on Phi-Phi, with a fridge chilled to Arctic temperatures, this intimate, mellow bar lives up to its name and is unusual for the island in attracting locals, as well as travellers and expats. Reasonably priced drinks and no wi-fi: you have to talk to each other here.

Sunflower Bar BAR

(Map p334; Ao Lo Dalam, Ko Phi-Phi Don; ⏲11am-2am; 📶) This ramshackle driftwood gem is one of Phi-Phi's most chilled-out bars and excellent for nursing a beer while the sun dips into the sea. Destroyed in the 2004 tsunami, it was rebuilt with reclaimed wood. The long-tail booths are named for the four loved ones the owner lost in the deluge.

Carlito's BAR

(Map p337; Ao Ton Sai, Ko Phi-Phi Don; ⏲11am-1am; 📶) For a more toned-down take on the fire-twirling madness that dominates Ao Lo Dalam, sit at one of the candlelit tables, or pull up a plastic chair on the sand, at this fairy-light-lit joint on Ao Ton Sai. There's a nightly fire show and live music, but it's a rather more refined and romantic venue than most of Phi-Phi's beach bars.

★ Entertainment

Kong Siam LIVE MUSIC

(Map p337; Ton Sai Village, Ko Phi-Phi Don; ⏲6pm-2am) Live music nightly at this popular place that draws Thais and *fa·ràng* (Westerners). The owner is a talented guitarist, and his mates and the other acts who play here aren't too shabby either.

ℹ Information

ATMs are spread thickly throughout the Tourist Village on Ko Phi-Phi Don, but are non-existent on the eastern beaches and there are none on Ko Phi-Phi Leh. Wi-fi is everywhere.

Phi-Phi Island Hospital (Map p334; ☎075 622151) Emergency care at the west end of Ao Ton Sai. For anything truly serious, get on the first boat to Krabi or, better still, Phuket.

Post Office (Map p337; Ton Sai Village, Ko Phi-Phi Don; ⏲9am-5pm Mon-Fri & 9am-1pm Sat) You can send mail overseas from here.

ℹ Getting There & Away

Ko Phi-Phi Don can be reached from Ao Nang, Krabi, Phuket, Railay and Ko Lanta. Most boats moor at **Ao Ton Sai** (Map p337; Ton Sai Village, Ko Phi-Phi Don), though a few from Phuket use isolated, northern **Tha Laem Thong** (Map p334). Ferries operate year-round, although not always every day.

There are also combined boat and minivan tickets to destinations across Thailand, including Bangkok (850B, 11 hours, 3.30pm), Ko Samui (500B, 6½ hours, 10.30am) and Ko Pha-Ngan (600B, seven hours, 10.30am).

You can travel to Ko Phi-Phi Leh on tours, or by long-tail boat (600B to 800B) and speedboat (2500B).

ℹ Getting Around

There are no real roads on Ko Phi-Phi Don and while some locals do use motorbikes, foreigners can't hire them. Transport is by foot, or long-tails can be chartered at Ao Ton Sai for short hops around both islands.

Long-tails leave Ao Ton Sai pier for Hat Yao (100B to 150B), Hat Rantee (700B), Hat Phak Nam and Ao Lo Bakao (1000B), Laem Thong (1200B) and Viking Cave (on Ko Phi-Phi Leh; 600B).

Chartering a long-tail for three/six hours costs 1500/3000B; a half-day speedboat charter costs 5000B.

Ko Lanta เกาะลันตา

☎075 / POP 26,800

Once the domain of sea gypsies, Lanta has morphed from a luscious Thai backwater into a getaway for both Asian and European, especially Scandinavian, visitors who come for the divine miles-long beaches (though the northern coast is alarmingly eroded) and nearby dive spots of Hin Daeng, Hin Muang and Ko Haa.

Charming Lanta remains more calm and real than its brash neighbour Ko Phi-Phi, although – whisper it quietly – the backpacker party scene is growing. Flatter than surrounding islands and with reasonable roads that run 22km from north to south, Lanta is easily toured on a motorbike, revealing a colourful crucible of cultures – fried-chicken stalls sit below slender minarets, stilted villages of *chow lair* cling to the island's east side, and small Thai wát hide within tangles of curling mangroves.

Ko Lanta is technically called Ko Lanta Yai. Boats pull into dusty Ban Sala Dan, on the northern tip of the island.

TRANSPORT TO/FROM KO PHI-PHI DON

DESTINATION	FARE (B)	DURATION (HR)	TO KO PHI-PHI	FROM KO PHI-PHI
Ao Nang	450	1¾	9.30am	3.30pm
Ko Lanta	350-600	1½	8am, 11.30pm, 1pm, 4pm	11.30am, 3pm & 3.30pm
Krabi	350	1½-2	9am, 10.30am, 1.30pm, 3.30pm	9am, 10.30am, 1.30pm & 3.30pm
Phuket	350	1¼-2	9am, 11am, 1pm, 1.30pm, 3pm	9am,11am, 2pm, 2.30pm & 3.30pm
Railay	450	1¼	9.45am	3.30pm

Sights

★Ban Si Raya

VILLAGE

(บ้านศรีรายา, Lanta Old Town; Map p346) Halfway down Lanta's eastern coast, Ban Si Raya was the island's original port and commercial centre, providing a safe harbour for Arab and Chinese trading vessels sailing between Phuket, Penang and Singapore. Known to the locals as Lanta Old Town, the vibe here is very different from the rest of the island, with wooden century-old stilt houses and shopfronts transformed into charming, characterful guesthouses. Pier restaurants offer fresh catch overlooking the sea, and there are some cute bohemian shops dotted around.

Tham Khao Maikaeo

CAVE

(ถ้ำเขาไม้แก้ว; Map p346; ☎089 288 8954; tours 300B) Monsoon rains pounding away at limestone crevices for millions of years have created this complex of caverns and tunnels. There are cathedral-size chambers, dripping with stalactites and stalagmites, tiny passages you have to squeeze through on hands and knees, and even a subterranean pool. A local family runs hourly treks to the caves (with headlamps). The full trip takes two hours; sensible shoes essential. It's signposted off the main road from Hat Khlong Tob to the east coast. Phone ahead for timings.

Lanta Animal Welfare

ANIMAL SANCTUARY, VOLUNTEERING

(Map p344; ☎084 304 4331; www.lantaanimalwelfare.com; 629 Mu 2, Ban Phra Ae; tours by donation; ⊙10am-4pm) This long-standing animal rescue centre cares for around 30 dogs and 60 cats through feeding, sterilising and re-homing, and vaccination and local awareness campaigns. Visitors can join hourly 40-minute facilities tours and play with kittens. The centre also welcomes casual dog-walking visitors and volunteers for longer placements.

Activities

Diving & Snorkelling

Some of Thailand's top diving spots are within arm's reach of Lanta. The best diving can be found at the undersea pinnacles of Hin Muang and Hin Daeng, two hours away by boat. These lone mid-sea coral outcrops act as important feeding stations for large pelagic fish such as sharks, tuna, barracudas and occasionally whale sharks and manta rays. Hin Daeng is commonly considered to be Thailand's second-best dive site after Richelieu Rock (p274), near the Myanmar border.

The sites around Ko Haa have consistently good visibility, with depths of 18m to 34m, plenty of marine life (including turtles) and a three-chamber cave known as 'the Cathedral'. Lanta dive outfitters run trips up to King Cruiser Wreck (p328), Anemone Reef (Ko Phi-Phi Don) and several other Ko Phi-Phi dive sites.

Lanta's dive season is November to April, though some operators run weather-dependent dives during low season. Trips to Hin Daeng and Hin Muang cost 3600B to 4500B; Ko Haa dives are 3100B to 4000B. PADI Open Water courses cost 13,700B to 15,900B. Rates usually exclude national park fees.

From mid-October to April, agencies across Lanta offer four-island snorkelling and kayaking tours (1200B to 1900B) to Ko Rok Nok, the Trang Islands and other nearby isles.

Scubafish

DIVING

(Map p346; ☎075 665095; www.scubafish.com; Ao Kantiang; 2 dives 3500B; ⊙8am-8pm) A long-running outfit based in the south of Lanta (closer to the dive sites) with a stellar reputation, Scubafish offers personable programs, including the Liquid Lense underwater photography courses, although it's pricier than other outfits. The three-day dive packages (9975B) are popular. One-day Discover Scuba is 5200B; Open Water certification costs 15,900B.

Lanta Diver DIVING
(Map p344; ☎075 668058; www.lantadiver.com; 197/3 Mu 1, Ban Sala Dan; 2 dives 3600B; ⏱10am-6pm) A very professional Scandinavian-run operator, based near the pier and with smaller resort concessions. Two-dive day trips to Hin Daeng and Hin Muang run 3600B to 4100B; two-dive Discover Scuba is 4500B. Open Water certification is 14,400B.

Blue Planet Divers DIVING
(Map p344; ☎075 668165; www.divinglanta.com; 3 Mu 1, Ban Sala Dan; 2 dives 3100B; ⏱8.30am-9pm) The first Lanta school to specialise in free-diving instruction (from 2700B). Also does Open Water certification (13,700B), Discover Scuba (4300B) and snorkelling tours (1500B).

Go Dive DIVING
(Map p344; ☎075 668320; www.godive-lanta.com; 6 Mu 1, Ban Sala Dan; 2 dives 3300B; ⏱Oct-Apr) One of Lanta's newer outfitters. Fun dives (two for 4200B at Hin Daeng/Hin Muang), two-dive Discover Scuba (4400B) and Open Water certification (PADI/SSI 13,900/12,900B).

Yoga

Drop-in classes (250B to 400B) are offered during high season (November to April) at **Oasis Yoga** (Map p344; ☎085 115 4067; www.oasisyoga-lanta.com; Hat Khlong Dao) and **Relax Bay** (Map p344; ☎075 684194; www.relaxbay.com; Ao Phra Ae; r 1800-4900B; ❄📶🏊). Sri Lanta (p345) has classes year-round for 550B.

Courses

Time for Lime COOKING
(Map p344; ☎075 684590; www.timeforlime.net; Hat Khlong Dao; ⏱class 4pm) On south Hat Khlong Dao, this popular beachfront school-restaurant offers excellent cooking courses (2000B) in the high season with a slightly more exciting recipe selection than most Thai cookery schools. The five-hour courses can be adapted for vegetarians and there are multiple-class discounts. Profits finance Lanta Animal Welfare. Book ahead. The on-site restaurant offers a tasting menu from Monday to Saturday (540B).

Sleeping

Some resorts close for the May–October low season; others drop rates by 50%. Reservations are essential in high season.

Hat Khlong Dao หาดคลองดาว

Costa Lanta HOTEL $$$
(Map p344; ☎075 668186; www.costalanta.com; Hat Khlong Dao; r incl breakfast 7100-9700B; ❄📶🏊) These Zen-like standalone abodes are nestled in a coconut-palm garden laced with tidal canals at the north end of Hat Khlong Dao. Everything from the floors to the walls to the washbasins is polished concrete, and the barn doors of each minimalist-chic cabana open on two sides to maximise space and breezes. Big bathrooms.

Lanta Island Resort BUNGALOW $$$
(Map p344; ☎075 684124; www.lantaislandresort.com; 10 Mu 3, Hat Khlong Dao; bungalows 1800-5300B; ❄📶🏊) Oldish concrete bungalows with white tiled floors, but they are sizeable and well-kept, dotted around a leafy garden and pool a few metres from the beach. The bungalows have some space between them, allowing for privacy. The resort's **Island Bar** (Map p344; 10 Mu 3, Hat Khlong Dao; ⏱noon-late; 📶) is an amenable spot for a sundowner and has live music in high season.

Hat Phra Ae หาดพระแอ

Chill Out House HOSTEL $
(Map p344; ☎082 183 2258; www.chillouthouselanta.com; Hat Phra Ae; dm 220B, d 280-320B; ⏱Sep-Apr; 📶🏊) This buzzing backpacker 'treehouse community' set back from the beach has three different and simple dorms, shared bathrooms, chalkboard doors and rickety doubles with bathrooms. It's basic, but you can't beat the laid-back vibe (or the price): swings at the bar, a communal iPod dock, and a wonderful (yes) chill-out lounge heavy on hammocks.

Lanta Baan Nok Resort BUNGALOW $$
(Map p344; ☎075 684459; lantabaannokresort@gmail.com; Hat Phra Ae; bungalows 1500B; ❄📶) New resort with eight spotless, comfortable bungalows with modern bathrooms, beds raised up off the floor on platforms, balconies with hammocks and an agreeably

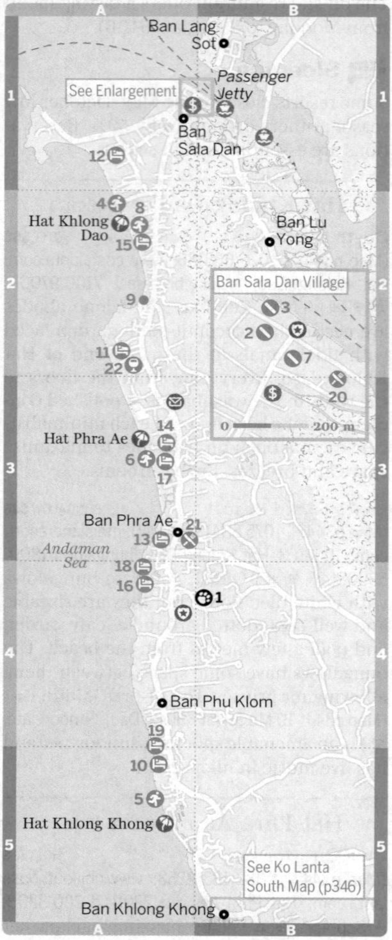

Ko Lanta North

Ko Lanta North

Sights
1 Lanta Animal Welfare.........B4

Activities, Courses & Tours
2 Blue Planet Divers.........B2
3 Go Dive.........B2
4 Hat Khlong Dao.........A2
5 Hat Khlong Khong.........A5
6 Hat Phra Ae.........A3
7 Lanta Diver.........B2
8 Oasis Yoga.........A2
9 Time for Lime.........A2

Sleeping
10 Bee Bee Bungalows.........A5
11 Chill Out House.........A2
12 Costa Lanta.........A1
13 Hutyee Boat.........A3
14 Lanta Baan Nok Resort.........A3
15 Lanta Island Resort.........A2
16 Lazy Days.........A4
17 Long Beach Chalet.........A3
18 Relax Bay.........A4
19 Where Else!.........A4

Eating
20 Kung Restaurant.........B3
21 Patty's Secret Garden.........A3

Drinking & Nightlife
Feeling Bar.........(see 19)
22 Irie.........A2
Island Bar.........(see 15)

laid-back vibe. A decent deal for the price. It's a short walk to the beach.

Hutyee Boat BUNGALOW $$
(Map p344; ☎083 633 9723; Hat Phra Ae; bungalows 600-1200B; 📶) A hidden, hippie paradise of big, basic, fan-only bungalows on stilts with tiled bathrooms, mini fridges and swinging hammocks in a forest of palms and bamboo. It's just back from the beach (behind Nautilus Resort) and run by a friendly Muslim family.

Long Beach Chalet BUNGALOW $$$
(Map p344; ☎075 695668; www.longbeachchalet.net; Hat Phra Ae; bungalows 3000-9000B; 📶🏊) Large wooden bungalows with balconies raised up on concrete stilts surround a cool pool and manicured garden a 200m walk from the beach. The gimmick here is that the bungalows are divided into two halves: one houses the bedroom, the other the bathroom. Efficient staff.

Lazy Days BUNGALOW $$$
(Map p344; ☎075 656291; www.lantalazydays.com; Hat Phra Ae; bungalows 4200-5000B; ❄📶) Lazy days indeed if you can score one of the fine nine bungalows tucked away here in a secluded spot at the end of Phra Ae beach. The bungalows are bamboo with thatched roofs and balconies; inside they are very comfortable with great beds, decent bathrooms, hot water, TVs, fridges and safety boxes. There's a restaurant too.

Hat Khlong Khong หาดคลองโขง

★Bee Bee Bungalows BUNGALOW $$
(Map p344; ☎081 537 9932; Hat Khlong Khong; bungalows 700-1000B; ⊙Oct-Apr; 📶) Bee Bee's is comprised of a dozen creative bamboo cabins managed by super-friendly staff. Each bungalow is unique; a few are stilted in the trees. The on-site restaurant has a library of tattered paperbacks to keep you occupied while you wait for your delicious Thai staples.

Where Else! BUNGALOW $$
(Map p344; ☎092 942 6554, 093 293 6545; where-else-lanta@hotmail.com; Hat Khlong Khong; bungalows 600-1500B; 📶) One of Lanta's hippie outposts – think thatched bungalows with semi-outdoor cold-water bathrooms. If you're trying to avoid late-night parties and tropical critters look elsewhere. Still, the place buzzes with backpackers, the owner is cool and there's a fun barefoot-beach vibe centred on the popular Feeling Bar (p349). Pricier bungalows are multilevel abodes sleeping up to four.

Hat Khlong Nin หาดคลองนิน

Round House GUESTHOUSE $$
(Map p346; ☎086 950 9424; www.lantaroundhouse.com; Hat Khlong Nin; bungalows without/with bathroom 800/1500B, house 3000B; ❄📶) A cute multi-option find on the north end of the beach. Stilted bamboo-and-wood fan bungalows are simply styled (the cheapest share hot-water bathrooms) and sit just behind the breezy beachfront restaurant. Also available is a cool two-person adobe round house, concrete rooms fronted by porches and an air-con beach house perfect for families. There's morning yoga classes, too (300B).

Sri Lanta BOUTIQUE HOTEL $$$
(Map p346; ☎075 662688; www.srilanta.com; Hat Khlong Nin; r 3400-7400B; ❄📶🏊) 🍃 At the southern end of the beach, this ecospot popular with Asian tourists consists of comfortable wooden villas with lots of light in gardens stretching from the beach to the hillside behind. There's a flower-fringed beachside area with two pools, restaurant and massage pavilions. The resort strives

ⓘ WHERE TO STAY IN KO LANTA

Ban Sala Dan There's decent budget accommodation in characterful Ban Sala Dan. It's also handy for local-flavoured seafood restaurants and boat arrivals/departures, but not on the beach.

Hat Khlong Dao (Map p344) Once an outstanding 2km white-sand stretch perfect for swimming, this beach has become so eroded that at high tide there's no sand at all.

Hat Phra Ae (Long Beach; Map p344) A large travellers' village has grown up along sandy Hat Phra Ae, 3km south of Ban Sala Dan. The beach has suffered erosion recently, but there's a nice stretch on its northern flank.

Hat Khlong Khong (Map p344) This is thatched-roof, Rasta-bar bliss and backpacker central with beach volleyball, moon parties and the occasional well-advertised mushroom shake, 9km south of Ban Sala Dan.

Hat Khlong Nin (Map p346) The main road heading south forks 13km south of Ban Sala Dan (after Hat Khlong Tob). The right-hand road hugs the coastline for 14km to Ko Lanta's southernmost tip. The first beach is lovely white-sand Hat Khlong Nin, which has lots of small, flashpacker-type guesthouses at its north end. Shop around.

Ao Kantiang (Map p346) This superb southwestern sweep of sand backed by mountains is also its own self-contained village with mini-marts, motorbike rental and restaurants.

Ao Mai Pai (Map p346) A lush nearly forgotten cove at the southwestern curve just before the cape, Ao Mai Pai is one of Lanta's finest beaches.

Laem Tanod (Map p346) The wild, jungled, mountainous southern tip of the island has sheer drops and massive views.

Ban Si Raya (p342) There are a handful of guesthouses in Lanta's oft-ignored, wonderfully dated and culturally rich east-coast Old Town, which has its own bohemian groove.

Ko Lanta South

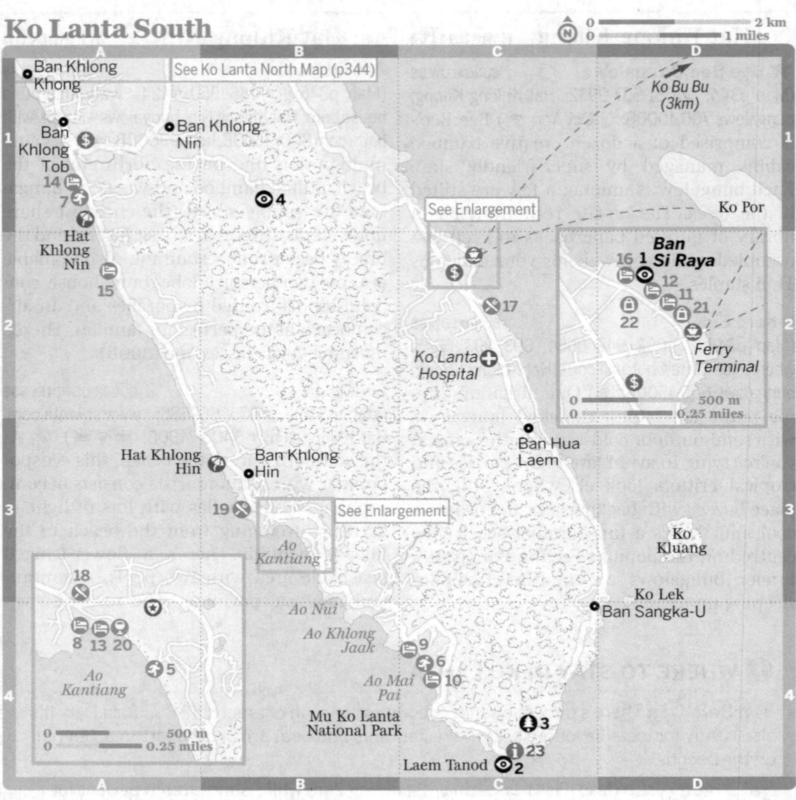

Ko Lanta South

Top Sights
1 Ban Si Raya D2

Sights
2 Laem Tanod C4
3 Mu Ko Lanta National Park C4
4 Tham Khao Maikaeo B1

Activities, Courses & Tours
5 Ao Kantiang A4
6 Ao Mai Pai C4
7 Hat Khlong Nin A1
Scubafish .... (see 8)

Sleeping
8 Baan Laanta Resort & Spa A4
9 Baan Phu Lae C4
10 La Laanta C4
11 Mango House D2
Mu Ko Lanta National Park Accommodation .... (see 23)
12 Old Times D2
13 Phra Nang Lanta A4
14 Round House A1
15 Sri Lanta A2
16 Sriraya D2

Eating
17 Caoutchouc C2
18 Drunken Sailors A3
La Laanta .... (see 10)
19 Phad Thai Rock'n'Roll B3

Drinking & Nightlife
20 Why Not Bar A4

Shopping
21 Hammock House D2
22 Malee Malee D2

Information
23 Mu Ko Lanta National Park Headquarters C4
Mu Ko Lanta National Park Visitors Centre .... (see 23)

for low environmental impact by using biodegradable products and minimising energy use and waste.

Ao Kantiang อ่าวกันเตียง

Baan Laanta Resort & Spa HOTEL $$$
(Map p346; ☎075 665091; www.baanlaanta.com; Ao Kantiang; bungalows incl breakfast 4500-5500B; ❄📶🏊) Landscaped grounds wind around comfortable wooden bungalows with terraces and a sultry dark infinity pool refreshed by elephant fountains and surrounded by frangipani trees, all overlooking an idyllic white sandy beach. Fixtures are a little old-fashioned, but the bungalows are sizeable, with sofas and futon-style beds raised off the floor. The Scubafish (p342) dive school is on-site.

Phra Nang Lanta HOTEL $$$
(Map p346; ☎075 665025; www.vacationvillage.co.th; Ao Kantiang; r 4250-5252B; ❄📶🏊) These 15 gorgeous, Mexican-style, adobe-looking concrete studios are straight off the pages of an interiors magazine. Think: clean lines, hardwood and whites accented with vibrant colours, lounge cushions and ceramic sinks. Outside, flowers and foliage climb over bamboo lattice sunshades, and the pool and restaurant-bar look over the beautiful beach. Excellent low-season deals.

Ao Mai Pai อ่าวไม้ไผ่

★**La Laanta** BOUTIQUE HOTEL $$$
(Map p346; ☎087 883 9966, 087 883 9977; www.lalaanta.com; Ao Mai Pai; bungalows incl breakfast 2800-6200B; ❄📶🏊) Operated by a young English-speaking Thai-Vietnamese couple, this is one of the grooviest spots on Lanta. Thatched bungalows have polished-concrete floors, platform beds, floral-design murals and decks overlooking a sandy volleyball pitch, which blends into a rocky beach. The laid-back **restaurant** (Map p346; Ao Mai Pai; mains 120-350B; ⌚8am-9pm; 📶) does a tasty Thai menu with lots of veggie-friendly choices. It's the last turn before the national park, far from everything else.

Baan Phu Lae BUNGALOW $$$
(Map p346; ☎085 474 0265, 075 665100; www.baanphulaeresort.com; Ao Mai Pai; bungalows fan 1800B, air-con 2000-2400B; ⌚Oct-Apr; ❄📶) Set on secluded rocks at the northern end of the final beach before Lanta's southern cape, this collection of cute, canary-yellow concrete fan and air-con bungalows have thatched roofs, colourful art, bamboo beds and private porches. Just behind stand stilted, wooden, air-con bungalows. They also arrange diving and snorkelling trips, cooking classes, massages and transport.

Laem Tanod แหลมโตนด

Mu Ko Lanta National Park Accommodation BUNGALOW, CAMPGROUND $
(Map p346; ☎075 660711, in Bangkok 02 561 4292; www.dnp.go.th; Laem Tanod; bungalows 1500-3000B, campsite per person 40B, with tent hire 300B) Engulfed by craggy outcrops and the sound of crashing waves, the secluded national park headquarters grounds are a gloriously serene place to stay, in simple four- to eight-person bungalows or tents. There are toilets and running water, and there's also a shop but you'll need to bring your own food. You can also get permission for camping on Ko Rok here.

Ban Si Raya บ้านศรีราชา

Sriraya GUESTHOUSE $
(Map p346; ☎075 697045; punpun_3377@hotmail.com; Ban Si Raya; r with shared bathroom 600B; 📶) Sleep in a simple but beautifully restored, thick-beamed Chinese shophouse with plenty of style and a friendly welcome. Walls are brushed in earth tones and sheets are bright. Go for the street-front balcony room overlooking the old town's characterful centre. The restaurant does great food.

★**Old Times** GUESTHOUSE $$
(Map p346; ☎075 697255, 075 697288; www.theoldtimeslanta.com; Ban Si Raya; r 500-1700B; ❄📶) Tucked into two artfully revamped 100-year-old teak houses facing each other across the street, this is an excellent choice. Impeccably-styled rooms grace various sizes and budgets, under music-inspired names such as 'Yellow Submarine'. The best – bright and decked with black-and-white photos – jut out over the sea on the jetty, where there's a cushioned communal chill-out area. Fun, fresh and friendly.

★**Mango House** GUESTHOUSE $$$
(Map p346; ☎095 014 0658; www.mangohouses.com; Ban Si Raya; ste 2500-3000B, villas 4000-7000B; 📶) These century-old Chinese teak pole houses and former opium dens are stilted over the harbour. The original time-worn wood floors are intact, ceilings soar and the

three, house-sized suites are kitted out with kitchenettes, satellite TVs, DVD players and ceiling fans. There are also new-build Old Town–style seafront villas sleeping two to six people. Rates drop by 50% in low season.

Eating

The best-value places for seafood are along the northern edge of Ban Sala Dan, which offer fresh fish sold by weight (including cooking costs) on verandahs over the water.

Phad Thai Rock'n'Roll THAI **$**
(Map p346; ☎080 784 8729; www.facebook.com/phadthairock77; Ao Kantiang; mains 90-150B; ⏲11am-9pm) It's not every day you get your spiced-to-taste *pàt tai* whipped up streetside by a guitarist. Choose from just six options ('jazz' fried rice, 'blues' fried noodles, veg, chicken, pork or seafood), swiftly and artfully prepared in simple contemporary surrounds. With about as many tables as dishes, it's deservedly popular, so you may have to wait.

★Drunken Sailors INTERNATIONAL, THAI **$$**
(Map p346; ☎075 665076; www.facebook.com/drunkensailors; Ao Kantiang; mains 130-200B; ⏲9am-3pm & 6-10pm;) This super-relaxed place features beanbags, hammocks and low-lying tables spilling out onto a terrace. The global, want-to-eat-it-all menu employs quality ingredients and roams from handmade pasta, baguettes and burgers to top-notch Thai, including perfectly spiced ginger stir-fries and red curries cooked to personal taste. Coffees, cakes and juices are also excellent. It closes for a couple of months in the low season.

★Kung Restaurant SEAFOOD **$$**
(Map p344; ☎075 656086; 413 Mu 1, Ban Sala Dan; mains 90-220B; ⏲5-11pm) Highly rated by both visiting Thais and locals, this Thai-Chinese place offers a delectable range of fresh fish (pay by the weight) in a simple setting close to the pier in Sala Dan. The sea bass, snapper and barracuda go quick, so get here early in the evening. There's also a large menu of Thai standards and some Chinese-style dishes.

Patty's Secret Garden THAI **$$**
(Map p344; ☎098 978 8909; 278 Mu 2, Hat Phra Ae; mains 120-320B; ⏲9am-11pm;) Not so secret now that more and more travellers are discovering this casual, family-friendly place set in a pleasant, plant- and flower-filled shaded garden. The menu mixes Thai favourites with Western standards, including a kids selection, and it's also good for breakfast.

Caoutchouc INTERNATIONAL, THAI **$$**
(Map p346; ☎075 697060; Ban Si Raya; mains 150-300B; ⏲10am-9pm) For Thai-international flavours blended into delectable creative concoctions, hunt down this rustic-chic restaurant 800m south of the Old Town pier. The menu changes at the whim of the eccentric but friendly French owner. Normally,

WORTH A TRIP

MU KO LANTA NATIONAL PARK

Established in 1990, **Mu Ko Lanta National Park** (อุทยานแห่งชาติหมู่เกาะลันตา; Map p346; ☎075 660711, in Bangkok 02 561 4292; www.dnp.go.th; adult/child/motorbike 200/100/20B; ⏲8am-6pm) protects 16 islands in the Ko Lanta group, including the southern tip of Ko Lanta Yai. The park is increasingly threatened by the runaway development on west-coast Ko Lanta Yai, though other islands in the group have fared slightly better.

Ko Rok Nai (Ko Rok Nai) is still very beautiful, with a crescent-shaped bay backed by cliffs, fine coral reefs and a sparkling white-sand beach. Camping is permitted on adjacent **Ko Rok Nok** with permission from the park headquarters. On the eastern side of Ko Lanta Yai, **Ko Talabeng** (Map p342) has some dramatic limestone caves that you can visit on sea-kayaking tours (1300B). National park fees apply if you visit any of the islands. Ko Rok Nai, Ko Rok Nok and Ko Haa (p331) are off limits to visitors from 16 May to 31 October.

The national park headquarters and visitors centre are at Laem Tanod, on the southern tip of Ko Lanta Yai, reached by a steep paved road. There are some basic hiking trails, two twin beaches and a gorgeously scenic lighthouse, plus camping facilities and bungalows amid wild, natural surroundings.

though, you should be able to enjoy a deliciously fresh feta-and-rice or shrimp curry salad, served alongside mango or pineapple lassi.

Drinking & Nightlife

If you fancy a low-key bar scene with music wafting well into the night, Lanta has options on most beaches, and particularly around Hat Phra Ae. Things move around depending on the day, so check out posters island-wide for upcoming events. Low season (May to October) is very mellow.

★Why Not Bar BAR
(Map p346; Ao Kantiang; ⌚11am-2am;) Tap into Ao Kantiang's laid-back scene at this driftwood-clad beachfront hang-out. It keeps things simple but fun with a killer mix of fire twirlers, sturdy cocktails, bubbly bar-staff and fantastic nightly live music jams, best enjoyed at low-slung wooden tables on a raised deck.

Feeling Bar BAR
(Map p344; Hat Khlong Khong; ⌚11am-late;) Joined to the rickety but much-loved Where Else! (p345) bungalows, Feeling keeps that original Lanta hippie-backpacker vibe alive with its 'Friday Feeling' beach parties. Three different bar counters and palm-thatched raised platforms to imbibe on.

Irie BAR
(Map p344; ☎084 170 6673; ⌚11am-late) The Monday-night live reggae session (in high season) at this ramshackle joint has become famous across Lanta (they put on rock bands sometimes too), but Irie is a relaxed place for a drink at any time. Also does OK Thai food.

Shopping

★Hammock House HOMEWARES
(Map p346; ☎084 847 2012; www.jumbohammock.com; Ban Si Raya; ⌚10am-6pm) For unique, quality, colour-bursting hammocks, crafted by rural villagers and threatened Mlabri tribespeople in northern Thailand, don't miss Hammock House. They sometimes close for part of low season (May to October).

★Malee Malee FASHION & ACCESSORIES
(Map p346; ☎075 697235; 55/3 Mu 2, Ban Si Raya; ⌚9am-9pm) A bohemian wonderland of quirky homemade goods, from silk-screened and hand-painted T-shirts and silk scarves to journals, toys, baby clothes, paintings, jewellery and handbags. Prices are low, it's super fun to browse and a sweet cafe (coffees around 80B) sits on the doorstep.

Information

There are ATMs all along the western coast. ATMs that take foreign cards can be found at **Ban Sala Dan** (Map p344; Ban Sala Dan), **Ban Si Raya** (Map p346; Ban Si Raya) and **Hat Khlong Nin** (Map p346; Hat Khlong Nin).

There are police stations at **Hat Phra Ae** (Map p344; Hat Phra Ae) and **Ban Sala Dan** (Map p344; ☎075 668192; Ban Sala Dan) and a **police outpost** (Map p346; Ao Kantiang) in the south of Lanta.

Ko Lanta Hospital (Map p346; ☎075 697017; Ban Si Raya) About 1km south of the Ban Si Raya Old Town.

Mu Ko Lanta National Park Headquarters (Map p346; ☎075 660711, in Bangkok 02 561 4292; Laem Tanod; ⌚8am-4pm) The national park HQ is in the far south of Lanta.

Mu Ko Lanta National Park Visitors Centre (Map p346; Laem Tanod; ⌚8am-6pm) The national park visitors centre is in the far south of Lanta.

The Lanta Pocket Guide (www.lantapocketguide.com) is a useful resource

Post Office (Map p344; Hat Phra Ae)

Getting There & Away

Transport to Ko Lanta is by boat or air-con minivan. If arriving independently, you'll need to use the frequent **vehicle ferries** (motorcycle/pedestrian/car 20/20/200B; ⌚6am-10pm) between Ban Hua Hin and Ban Khlong Mak (Ko Lanta Noi) and on to Ko Lanta Yai.

BOAT

Ban Sala Dan has two piers. The **passenger jetty** (Map p344; Ban Sala Dan) is 300m from the main strip of shops; vehicle ferries leave from a **jetty** (Map p344; Ban Sala Dan) 2km east.

From mid-October to mid-April, the high-speed **Tigerline** (☎075 590490, 081 358 8989; www.tigerlinetravel.com) ferry runs between Phuket (1500B, two hours) and Ban Sala Dan (Ko Lanta) and on to Ko Lipe (1700B, five hours), via Ko Ngai (750B, one hour), Ko Kradan (850B, 1½ hours) and Ko Muk (850B, two hours). The service heads south at 10am, returning from Lipe at 10am the following day and stopping on Ko Lanta around 3pm before continuing north.

Ko Phi-Phi Ferries between Ko Lanta and Ko Phi-Phi run year-round. Boats leave Ko Lanta at 8am and 1pm (300B, 1½ hours), returning from Ko Phi-Phi at 11.30am and 3pm. There are also high-season speedboats between Lanta and Phi-Phi (700B to 800B, one hour).

Krabi From November to late April, boats leave Ko Lanta for Krabi's Khlong Chilat pier at 8.30am and 11.30pm (400B, two hours) and return from Krabi at 11.30am. During high season, they stop at Ko Jum (400B, one hour).

Phuket There are year-round ferries to Phuket at 8am and 1pm (500B), although you normally have to transfer boats at Ko Phi-Phi.

Trang Islands From November to early April, speedboats buzz from Ko Lanta to the Trang Islands, including the **Satun Pak Bara Speedboat Club** (Map p364; ☎099 404 0409, 099 414 4994; www.spcthailand.com) and **Bundhaya Speedboat** (☎075 668043; www.bundhayaspeedboat.com). Stops include Ko Ngai (650B, 30 minutes), Ko Muk (900B, one hour), Ko Kradan (1150B, 1¼ hours), Ko Bulon Leh (1600B, two hours) and Ko Lipe (1900B, three hours).

Ko Lanta Noi A **vehicle ferry** (Map p342; Ko Lanta Noi) and a **passenger ferry** (Map p342; Ko Lanta Noi) link Ko Lanta Noi to Ko Lanta Yai.

MINIVAN

Minivans are your easiest option from the mainland and they run year-round, but they're particularly packed in this region and traffic jams for vehicle ferries can cause delays. Most minivans offer pick ups from resorts. Frequency is reduced in low season.

Minivans to Krabi airport (300B, 2½ hours) and Krabi Town (300B, three hours) run hourly between 7am and 4pm in both directions. You can connect in Krabi for further destinations, including Khao Lak and Bangkok. Departures from Lanta include the following:

DESTINATION	FARE (B)	DURATION (HR)	FREQUENCY
Ko Pha-Ngan	750	8½	8am
Ko Samui	550	6½	8am
Phuket	500	6	8am & noon.
Trang	450	3	8am, 9am, 10.30am & 1pm

Getting Around

Most resorts send vehicles to meet the ferries – a free ride to your resort. In the opposite direction expect to pay 100B to 400B. Alternatively, take a motorcycle taxi from outside 7-Eleven in Ban Sala Dan; fares run from 50B to 400B, depending on distance.

Motorbikes (250B per day) can be rented everywhere (without insurance), as can bicycles (150B per day). Agencies in Ban Sala Dan rent out small 4WDs (1300B per day).

Ko Jum & Ko Si Boya เกาะจำ/เกาะศรีบอยา

Just north of Ko Lanta, Ko Jum and its low-lying neighbour Ko Si Boya are surprisingly undeveloped; what's there is tucked away in the trees. There's little more to do than wander the long beaches on Ko Jum (Ko Si Boya's beach is less impressive) and soak up the rustic beauty.

Ko Jum was once the exclusive domain of Lanta's *chow lair*, but ethnic Chinese began arriving after communist takeover of China in 1949. At the time there were no Thai people living here at all, but eventually the three cultures merged into one, a mix best sampled early in the morning amid the ramshackle poetry of Ban Ko Jum, the fishing village on the southeast side of the island.

Although technically one island, local people consider only the flatter southern part of Ko Jum to be Ko Jum. The northern hilly bit is Ko Pu.

Sleeping & Eating

Ko Jum

Accommodation is strung out along Ko Jum's west coast. Most resorts have on-site restaurants; some close for the May–October low season.

Bodaeng BUNGALOW $

(☎081 494 8760; Hat Yao, Ko Jum; bungalows 200-400B) An old-fashioned hippie vortex with very basic bamboo bungalows and a couple of newer wood huts with their own bathrooms, set in the trees behind Hat Yao. No fans – sea breezes only – no wi-fi and squat toilets in the shared bathrooms. Limited electricity sometimes. But the grinning matriarch owner is a charmer and you are right by the beach.

★ **Woodland Lodge** BUNGALOW $$

(☎081 893 5330; www.woodland-koh-jum.com; Hat Yao, Ko Jum; bungalows 1300-1700B;) Tasteful, clean, fan-cooled bamboo huts with proper thatched roofs, polished wood floors and verandahs, spaciously laid out across shady grounds, make this our favourite spot on Ko Jum. Concrete-and-wood family bungalows sleep three. The friendly British-Thai owners organise boat trips and run the excellent on-site **Fighting Fish Restaurant** (Hat Yao; mains 100-30B; ⏲8am-4pm & 6-10pm; 📶).

★ Koh Jum Beach Villas VILLA $$$
(☎086 184 0505; www.kohjumbeachvillas.com; Hat Yao, Ko Jum; villas incl breakfast 12,000-32,000B; 📶❄) 🌿 The poshest digs on Ko Jum. Huge and elegant wooden homes with their own living rooms and kitchens and sea views sprawl back among frangipani- and bougainvillea-filled gardens from a luscious golden beach. Some have romantic private infinity pools. The resort keeps things as environmentally and socially responsible as possible. Staff are delightful, the **restaurant** (Hat Yao; mains 250-900B; ⏲7.30am-10pm; 📶) and bar scrumptious.

Koh Jum Lodge RESORT $$$
(☎089 921 1621; www.kohjumlodge.com; Hat Yao, Ko Jum; bungalows incl breakfast 4500-7000B; ⏲Nov-Apr; 📶❄) An ecolodge with style: 19 spacious cottages with lots of hardwood and bamboo, gauzy mosquito netting, coconut palms, Thai carvings and silk throws. Then there are the manicured grounds, massage pavilions and a hammock-strewn curve of white sand out front. It strikes that hard-to-get balance of authenticity and comfort.

Hong Yong Restaurant THAI $
(Ban Ting Rai, Ko Jum; mains 70-100B; ⏲7.30am-9pm) Local food talk sends you inland to this makeshift village restaurant, where bubbly Rosa sizzles up delicious Thai curries, stir-fries and international breakfasts at bargain prices. Try the fragrant massaman curry or the seasonal seafood specials. Also known as Rosa's.

Ko Si Boya

Low-lying, rural Ko Si Boya has yet to garner more than a trickle of the annual tourism stream, and that's just fine with repeat visitors.

Siboya Bungalows BUNGALOW $$
(☎081 979 3344; www.siboyabungalows.com; Ko Si Boya; bungalows 350B, house 500-1800B; 📶) Ko Si Boya's beach isn't spectacular, but the mangrove setting is wild and full of life, the bungalows and private homes are large, stylish and affordable, and the excellent restaurant is wired with high-speed internet. No wonder ever-smiling, secretive 50-somethings flock here like it's a retiree's version of Alex Garland's *The Beach*. There are family-friendly homes that sleep four people.

Getting There & Away

From November to May, the boat from Krabi to Ko Lanta will drop you at Ko Jum, for the full fare (400B, one hour, 11.30am); boats return from Lanta at 8.30am. In high season, daily boats run from Ko Jum to Ko Phi-Phi (600B, 1½ hours) at 8.30am, collecting guests from the Hat Yao resorts; boats return from Phi-Phi at 2pm.

There are year-round long-tails to Ko Jum from Ban Laem Kruat, 38km southeast of Krabi at the end of Rte 4036, off Hwy 4. Boats (100B, 30 minutes) leave at 9am, 10am, 11.30am, noon, 1pm, 2.30pm, 4pm, 5.30pm and 6.15pm, and return at 6.30am, 7.15am, 7.40am, 8am, 8.30am, 10.30pm, 1.30pm, 2.30pm and 4pm.

If you're arriving on Ko Jum via Laem Kruat, note that boats run to three different piers; Ban Ko Jum and Mu Tu piers are the most convenient. Guesthouses will arrange transfers from the piers if you call in advance, otherwise you're relying on the kindness of strangers.

Daily boats to Ko Si Boya (50B, 15 minutes) run from Laem Kruat every hour between 8am and 5.30pm, returning hourly from 6.15am to 5pm. Call Siboya Bungalows to arrange transfer from the pier.

Sŏrng·tăa·ou meet boats at Laem Kruat and go to Krabi (100B), via Krabi airport and Nua Khlong (where you can connect for Ko Lanta).

Getting Around

Several places in Ban Ko Jum and some Ko Jum guesthouses rent bicycles (100B) and motorbikes (250B).

TRANG PROVINCE

South of Krabi, Trang Province has an impressive limestone-covered Andaman Coast with several sublime islands that see marginally fewer visitors than their nearby and better-known counterparts. For the adventurous, there's plenty of big nature to explore in the lush interior, including dozens of scenic waterfalls and limestone caves. And it's nowhere near as popular as Krabi, which means you're more likely to see working rubber plantations here than rows of T-shirt vendors. Transport links are good and during the high season (November to April) you can easily island-hop all the way to Malaysia.

Trang ตรัง

075 / POP 60,000

Most visitors to Trang are in transit to nearby islands, but if you're an aficionado of culture, Thai food or markets, stay a day or more. Here is an easy-to-manage, old-school Thai town where you can get lost in wet markets, hawker markets and Chinese coffee shops. At nearly any time of year, there will be some minor festival that oozes local colour.

Most tourist facilities lie along Th Praram VI, between the clock tower and the train station.

Sights & Activities

The lively, colourful **wet and dry markets** on Th Ratchadamnoen and Th Sathani are worth exploring.

Tour agencies around the train station and Th Praram VI offer boat trips to Hat Chao Mai National Park and the Trang Islands (850B, plus park fees), snorkelling trips to Ko Rok (per person 1700B) and private car trips to local caves and waterfalls (2000B, maximum four people).

Wat Tantayaphirom BUDDHIST TEMPLE
(วัดตันตยาภิรม; Th Tha Klang) FREE Wat Tantayaphirom has a huge white-and-gold *chedi* (stupa) enshrining a footprint of the Buddha that's mildly interesting.

Festivals & Events

★ **Vegetarian Festival** CULTURAL
(Oct) As much a Buddhist festival as it is food heaven for veggies – by not eating meat participants gain merit for themselves – Trang celebrates this wonderful nine-day festival all over town to coincide with Phuket's Vegetarian Festival (p298) in the first two weeks of October.

Sleeping & Eating

The town is famous for its *mŏo yâhng* (crispy barbecued pork), spongy cakes, early-morning dim sum breakfasts and *ráhn go·þíi* (coffee shops) that serve real filtered coffee. You can find *mŏo yâhng* in the mornings at some coffee shops or by weight at the wet market on Th Ratchadamnoen.

Yamawa Guesthouse GUESTHOUSE $
(099 402 0349, 075 290477; www.yamawaguesthouse.blog.com; 94 Th Visetkul; r fan/air-con 350/450B;) Simple, spotless, old-fashioned fan or air-con rooms equipped with fridges that are decent value for the price. The sweet local owners hand out detailed Trang maps, sound advice and rent motorbikes (250B per day). Often full in high season (November to April), so book ahead.

Mitree House GUESTHOUSE $$
(075 212292; mitreehouse.trang@gmail.com; 6-8 Th Sathani; r 750-1050B;) New-ish, well-located guesthouse that has immaculate, modern rooms with comfy beds and reasonably sized bathrooms. The cheapest lack windows; the more expensive ones upstairs are big and bright. Communal areas on both floors, helpful staff and the price includes a simple breakfast. Motorbikes can be rented for 250B per day. Good wi-fi.

Rua Rasada Hotel HOTEL $$$
(075 214230; www.ruarasadahotel.com; 188 Th Phattalung; r incl breakfast 6000-60,000B;) Trang's slickest choice is this hulking monolith handily located opposite the bus station, a 10-minute (40B) motorbike ride northeast from the train station. From the outside it looks its age a bit, and inside it feels a little 1980s, too. But rooms are huge and comfortable, while the pool is massive. You can normally score 40% to 50% discounts in low season.

★ **Night Market** MARKET $
(btwn Th Praram VI & Th Ratchadamnoen; mains from 40B; 4-9pm) The finest night market on the Andaman Coast will have you salivating over bubbling curries, fried chicken and fish, deep-fried tofu, *pàt tai* and an array of Thai desserts. Go with an empty stomach and a sense of adventure. There's a second, equally glorious weekend **night market** (Train Station; mains from 40B; 6-10pm Thu-Sun) opposite the train station.

Asia Ocha THAI $
(Th Kantang; mains 25-200B; 7am-5pm) Open for 60-plus years, this cool, old school Sino-Thai coffee shop has vintage marble-topped tables, helicopter fans and a menu that includes excellent soups, as well as delicious roast duck and crispy pork. It serves a few Western-style dishes too.

Khao Tom Kim THAI $$
(50 Th Kantang; mains 60-200B; 3.30pm-midnight) A popular spot with the locals and always lively, thanks to a solid selection of

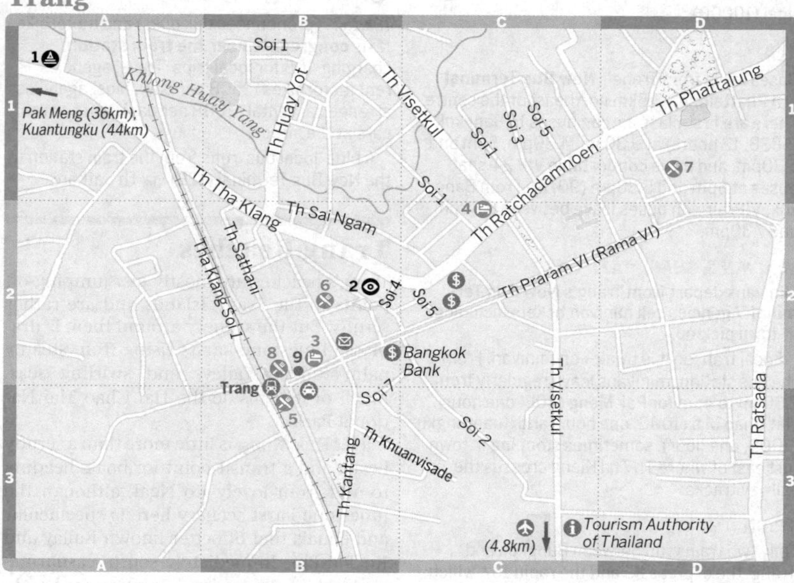

Trang

Sights
1 Wat Tantayaphirom....A1
2 Wet & Dry Market....B2

Sleeping
3 Mitree House....B2
4 Yamawa Guesthouse....C2

Eating
5 Asia Ocha....B3
6 Khao Tom Kim....B2
7 Night Market....D1
8 Night Market....B2

Information
9 Trang Happy Trip & Tour....B2

curries and seafood dishes. It stays open later than most Trang restaurants. Not much English spoken, but there is an English menu.

Information

ATMs and foreign-exchange booths line Th Praram VI. The following take foreign cards:

ATM (Th Praram VI)

Bangkok Bank (Th Praram VI)

There is also an **ATM on Th Ratchadamnoen** (Th Ratchadamnoen) that accepts foreign cards.

Post Office (cnr Th Praram VI & Th Kantang; 8.30am-4.30pm Mon-Fri, 9am-noon Sat) You can send mail overseas from here.

Tourism Authority of Thailand (TAT; 075 211580, 075 215867; www.tourismthailand.org; 199/2 Th Visetkul; 8.30am-4.30pm) Tourist information, although you're better off speaking to one of the many travel agencies that cluster close to the train station.

Trang Happy Trip & Tour (075 219757; www.facebook.com/tranghappytrip&tour; 22 Th Sathani; 6.30am-10pm) Knowledgeable and reliable Sai and Jip run this travel agency close to the train station. They can arrange private cars, rent motorbikes, book minivan and boat tickets/transfers and run one-day tours around the Trang Islands.

Getting There & Away

AIR

The airport is 5km south of Trang. Air Asia (www.airasia.com) and Nok Air (www.nokair.com) fly here daily from Bangkok (Don Mueang).

Minivans to town (90B) meet flights. In the reverse direction, taxis, motorbike taxis or *túk-túks* (pronounced *đúk đúks*) cost 100B to 120B. Agencies at airport arrivals sell combined taxi-boat tickets to Trang's islands, including Ko Ngai (1000B).

BUS

Buses leave from Trang's **New Bus Terminal** (Th Phattalung), 3.5km northeast of the centre. There are first-class air-con buses to Bangkok (583B, 12 hours) at 9.30am, 4.30pm, 5pm and 5.30pm, and more comfortable VIP 24-seat buses at 5pm and 5.30pm (907B). From Bangkok, VIP/air-con buses leave between 6.30pm and 7.30pm.

MINIVAN & SHARE TAXI

Minivans depart from Trang's **New Bus Terminal**. Agencies sell minivan tickets including in-town pick-up.

Local transport is by air-con minivan. From the bus station, minivans leave regularly from 7.30am to 4pm for Pak Meng (80B, one hour), Hat Chao Mai (100B, one hour) and Kuantungku (100B, one hour), sometimes stopping in town just east of where Th Tha Klang crosses the railway tracks.

TRAIN

Only two trains run between Bangkok and Trang: the express 83 and the rapid 167, which leave from Bangkok's Hualamphong station at 5.05pm and 6.30pm and arrive in Trang the next morning at 8.05am and 10.30am respectively.

From Trang, trains leave at 1.30pm and 5.25pm, arriving in Bangkok at 5.35am and 8.35am the following morning. Fares are range from 245B for 3rd class to 1480B for 1st-class air-con sleeper.

Getting Around

Túk-túks (pronounced *đúk đúks*) and motorbike taxis **congregate near the train station**, charging 40B for local trips. Travel agencies rent motorbikes (250B per day). Most agencies arrange car rental (200B per day). You can rent cars at the airport.

A blue 'local bus' runs from the train station to the New Bus Terminal (12B) via Th Sathani.

Trang Beaches

Trang's beaches are mostly just jumping-off points to the Trang Islands and are rather scruffy. But the scenery around them is dramatic: limestone karsts rising from steamy palm-studded valleys and swirling seas. Much of it is inside the Hat Chao Mai National Park.

Hat Pak Meng is little more than a scruffy beach and a transit point for boats heading to and from lovely Ko Ngai, although the limestone karst scenery here is spectacular and equals that of better-known Railay and Ko Phi-Phi. Immediately south, casuarina-backed **Hat Chang Lang** is a prettier beach, but still can't compare to the ones on the nearby islands. The Hat Chao Mai National Park headquarters is at the southern end of the beach.

Sights & Activities

Pak Meng tour agencies organise one-day boat tours to Ko Muk, Ko Cheuk, Ko Ma

TRANSPORT FROM TRANG

Buses from Trang

DESTINATION	FARE (B)	DURATION (HR)	FREQUENCY
Hat Yai	120	3	every 30min 5.30am-5.30pm
Krabi	110	2	hourly 5.30am-6.30pm
Phang-Nga	170	4	hourly 5.30am-6.30pm
Phuket	230	5	hourly 5.30am-6.30pm

Minivan & Share Taxi from Trang

DESTINATION	FARE (B)	DURATION (HR)	FREQUENCY
Hat Yai	120	2	hourly 6am-6pm
Ko Lanta	250	2½	five daily 9.50am-4.30pm
Krabi	100	2	hourly 7am-5pm
Satun	120	2	every 40min 6am-6pm
Surat Thani	160	3	hourly 7am-5pm

Trang Province

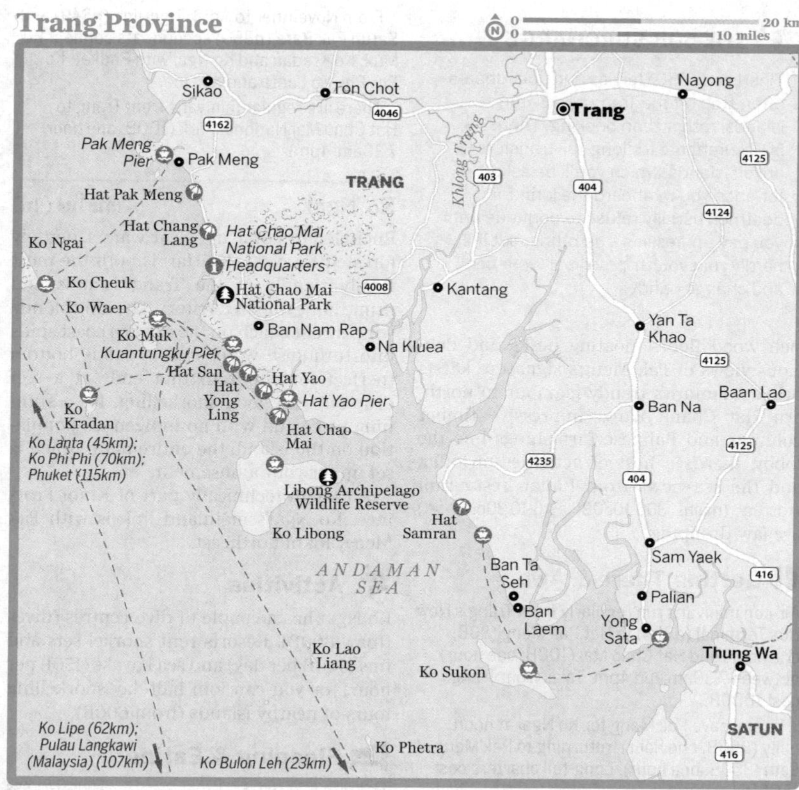

and Ko Kradan, and snorkelling day tours, all including lunch (per person 750B, plus Hat Chao Mai National Park fees). Mask and snorkel sets and fins can be rented by the pier (50B each).

Hat Chao Mai National Park NATIONAL PARK
(อุทยานแห่งชาติหาดเจ้าไหม; ☎075 203308; www.dnp.go.th; adult/child 200/100B; ⊙9am-4pm) This 231-sq-km park covers the shoreline from Hat Pak Meng to Laem Chao Mai, and encompasses the islands of Ko Muk, Ko Kradan and Ko Cheuk (plus a host of small islets). While touring the coast and islands, you may spot endangered dugongs and rare black-necked storks, as well as more common species like barking deer, sea otters, macaques, langurs, wild pigs, pangolins, little herons, Pacific reef egrets, white-bellied sea eagles and monitor lizards.

Park headquarters (☎075 210 099; www.dnp.go.th; Hat Chang Lang; ⊙8am-4pm) are at the southern end of Hat Chang Lang, just south of where the beachfront road turns inland.

Sleeping & Eating

Several seafood restaurants, popular with Thais on day trips or weekend getaways, can be found in Pak Meng, where Rte 4162 meets the coast.

Hat Chao Mai National Park Accommodation CAMPGROUND, BUNGALOW $
(☎075 203308; www.dnp.go.th; Hat Chang Lang; bungalows 800B, campsites per person 30B, with tent hire 225B) Simple fan-cooled cabins sleep two to six people or you can camp under the casuarinas. There's also a restaurant.

Anantara Si Kao HOTEL $$$
(☎075 205888; www.sikao.anantara.com; Hat Chang Lang; r incl breakfast 4080-13,680B; P❄📶🏊) Deluxe oceanfront rooms with

THE 50B SURCHARGE

Tigerline (p350) ferries and speedboats often stop off the Trang and Satun islands, rather than docking. There's a 50B surcharge for long-tail transfers on/off islands, which you'll be asked for once you're aboard the long-tail; boatmen usually refuse to continue until you pay up. Yes, it's frustrating, but it'll hardly ruin your trip, so keep your cool and change handy.

rich wood floors, floating desks and delicious views of Pak Meng's signature karsts bring Anantara's trendy glamour to northern Hat Chang Lang. Impressive timber columns and Balinese furnishings line the lobby, there's a host of activities on offer, and the sea-views from Italian restaurant **Acqua** (mains 300-1050B; 6-10.30pm;) are jaw-dropping.

Getting There & Away

Air-con minivans run regularly from Trang's New Bus Terminal (p354) to Hat Pak Meng (80B, one hour) and Hat Chao Mai (100B, one hour) between 7.30am and 4pm. Taxis from Trang cost 1000B.

Boats leave Pak Meng for Ko Ngai at noon daily (350B, one hour), returning to Pak Meng at 9am (350B, one hour). Long-tail charters cost 1500B.

The Hat Chao Mai National Park headquarters is 1km off the main road, down a clearly signposted track.

Trang Islands

Covered in verdant jungle and lined with pure white-sand beaches, the Trang Islands are less developed than other Andaman islands and have far smaller populations. This is real honeymooners territory – there's very little nightlife – so don't come here if you want to party all night long.

Getting There & Away

Boats to the Trang Islands run from three different piers: Hat Yao, Kuantungku and Pak Meng, all an hour south of Trang. Regular minivans run to the piers (80B to 100B, one hour, 7.30am to 4pm). If you book your boat ticket with a travel agency in Trang, they will arrange the transfer to the boat.

From November to April, Tigerline (p349) and Satun Pak Bara (p350) speedboats connect Ko Muk, Ko Kradan and Ko Ngai with Phuket, Ko Phi-Phi, Ko Lanta and Ko Lipe.

There are regular minivans from Trang to Hat Chao Mai National Park (100B, one hour, 7.30am-4pm).

Ko Ngai เกาะไหง (ไห)

Encircled by coral and clear waters, densely forested Ko Ngai (Ko Hai) is both the most family-friendly of the Trang Islands and prime honeymoon territory. The long blonde wind-swept beach on the eastern coast spills into turquoise water with a sandy bottom (perfect for children) that ends at a reef drop-off with good snorkelling. It's a stunning place and with no indigenous population on the island, the entire main beach is set up for your amusement.

Although technically part of Krabi Province, Ko Ngai's mainland link is with Pak Meng, 16km northeast.

Activities

Ko Ngai has a couple of dive centres (dives from 1300B). Resorts rent snorkel sets and fins (300B per day) and sea kayaks (150B per hour), or you can join half-day snorkelling tours of nearby islands (from 600B).

Sleeping & Eating

Thanya Resort BUNGALOW $$$
(075 206 967, 086 950 7355; www.kohngaithanyaresort.com; r incl breakfast 3700-6900B;) Ko Ngai's Bali-chic choice has dark but stylish, spacious teak bungalow with indoor hot showers and outdoor country-style bucket showers (don't knock it until you've tried it). Laze in the gorgeous beachside pool and gaze across the frangipani-filled lawn rolling out towards the sand from your terrace. There's an on-site **dive centre** (085 056 3455; 1 dive 1300-1500B) plus a reasonably priced Thai **restaurant** (mains 150-300B; 7am-8pm;). It's at the south end of main beach.

Coco Cottage BUNGALOW $$$
(089 724 9225; www.coco-cottage.com; bungalows 3300-7900B; Oct-May;) These cottages are coconut thatched-roof extravaganzas with coconut-wood walls and coconut-shell lanterns, set in a jungle garden just back from the north end of the main beach. Wake up to twinkling Andaman

vistas through floor-to-ceiling windows in sea-view bungalows. Other perks include bamboo loungers, massage pavilions and a decent Thai/fusion beachfront **restaurant-bar** (mains 170-260B; ⏲7-10am, 11am-4pm & 6-9.30pm). It's at the north end of main beach.

Ko Hai Fantasy Resort & Spa RESORT **$$$**
(☎075 210 317; www.kohhai.com; r 3300-17,200B; ❄📶🏊) Well-kept, comfortable, modern, decent-sized rooms meander back from the southern end of the main beach and straggle around a neat garden and up the surrounding hillside. The seafront restaurant is reasonable, there's a mini-mart, and snorkelling and island trips can be arranged.

Talay Lounge Restaurant THAI, INTERNATIONAL **$$**
(Thapwarin Resort; mains 170-300B; ⏲7am-10pm mid-Jun–mid-May; 📶) Catch evening fire shows beneath rubber trees at this beach-facing lounge bar and restaurant, which tackles everything from grilled snapper to pizza and pasta. It's part of **Thapwarin Resort** (☎081 894 3585; www.thapwarin.com; north end of main beach; garden/sea-view bungalow incl breakfast 4500/5500B; ⏲mid-Jun–mid-May; ❄📶), at the northern end of Ko Ngai's main beach.

ℹ Getting There & Away

There's a daily boat from Ko Ngai to Pak Meng (350B, one hour) at 9am, returning to Ko Ngai at noon. You can also charter long-tails to and from Pak Meng (1500B), Ko Muk (1500B), Ko Kradan (1500B) and Ko Lanta (2000B); enquire at **Ko Ngai Seafood Bungalows** (☎095 014 1853; kob_1829@hotmail.com; middle of the main beach; bungalow 1500-1800B; ⏲year-round; 📶). Most resorts arrange transfers to the mainland.

From mid-October to mid-April, Tigerline (p349) ferries stops just off Ko Ngai en route between Phuket and Ko Lipe. From November to early April, Satun Pak Bara Speedboat Club (p350) and **Bundhaya Speedboat** (☎074 750389, 074 750388; www.bundhayaspeedboat.com) offer faster and comfier island-hopping transport.

The pier is at Koh Ngai Resort, but long-tails usually drop you at your resort.

Ko Muk เกาะมุก

Motoring toward jungle-clad Ko Muk is unforgettable, whether you land on sugary white eastern sand bar **Hat Sivalai**, on humble, local-flavoured **Hat Lodung** or on southwest **Hat Farang** (Hat Sai Yao, Charlie Beach), where jade water kisses a perfect beach.

The accommodation options here are improving all the time, the west-coast sunsets are glorious, it's an easy hop to most islands in the province, the principal village by the main pier remains more real than those on many tourist islands, and you'll be mixing with travellers who are more likely to relish the calm than party all night. The only drawback is that there's a steady stream of package tourists tramping Hat Sivalai and day-tripping over to Tham Morakot from Ko Lanta.

BOATS TO/FROM KO NGAI

DESTINATION	BOAT COMPANY	FARE (B)	DURATION
Ko Lanta	Tigerline	750	1hr
	Speedboat	650	30min
Ko Lipe	Tigerline	1600	4hr
	Speedboat	1300	2½hr
Ko Kradan	Tigerline	750	30min
	Satun Pak Bara Speedboat Club	400	25min
Ko Muk	Tigerline	750	1hr
	Speedboat	350	30min
Ko Phi-Phi	Tigerline	1350	2½hr
	Satun Pak Bara Speedboat Club	1350	2hr
Phuket	Tigerline	1800	3½hr
	Satun Pak Bara Speedboat Club	2150	3hr

Sights & Activities

Between Ko Muk and Ko Ngai are two small karst islets, **Ko Cheuk** and **Ko Waen**, both with small sandy beaches and good snorkelling (though there's some coral damage).

Koh Mook Garden Beach Resort rents out bikes (150B per day) with self-guided maps, several resorts rent kayaks (100B to 300B per hour) and motorbikes (250B per day), and you can spend hours walking through rubber plantations and the island's devout Muslim sea shanty villages (remember to cover up).

Tham Morakot CAVE
(ถ้ำมรกต, Emerald Cave) This beautiful limestone tunnel leads 80m into a cave on Ko Muk's west coast. No wonder pirates buried treasure here. You have to swim through the tunnel, part of the way in darkness, before exiting at a small white-sand beach surrounded by lofty limestone walls. A piercing shaft of light illuminates it around midday. National park fees (adult/child 200/100B) apply.

Sleeping & Eating

Hat Sivalai, a short walk from the main pier on the eastern side, has the poshest digs. Hat Lodung, west of the pier beyond a stilt village and mangroves, has cheaper options, but the beach isn't nearly as nice.

The sea is cleaner on crescent-shaped Hat Farang, where more budget-friendly resorts lie inland from the beach. It's a 10-minute motorbike taxi to/from the pier (50B).

Koh Mook Hostel HOSTEL $
(☎089 724 4456; www.kohmookhostel.com; dm 380B; ❄📶) The only hostel in the Trang Islands, this place is run by a friendly Muslim family and consists of two decent-sized and clean dorm rooms (one female-only). They're painted in breezy pastel colours, as is the communal area, while the attached bakery cafe serves up homemade bread, cakes and pizza. It's a 10-minute walk from lovely Hat Sivalai.

Koh Mook Garden Beach Resort GUESTHOUSE $$
(☎081 748 3849; DaDakohmook@gmail.com; Hat Lodung; r 1000-1500B; ❄📶) Endearingly ramshackle and very laid-back, Garden Beach Resort stands out from the more anonymous (and professional) resort crowd thanks to its family feel. Bungalows, both the older and basic bamboo ones and the newer, more comfortable concrete ones, are scattered around a garden leading to your own small section of Hat Lodung. The attached restaurant serves up tasty Thai food.

Phusambig Resort HOTEL $$$
(☎09 1706 7727; cee210919@hotmail.com; r incl breakfast 1200-2700B; ❄📶) Chilled-out and welcoming, Phusambig's bungalows lie in a garden 10 minutes' walk from Hat Farang. They come in a variety of guises and sizes – the cheapest are fan-only – but all are modern with OK bathrooms and are a step up from similarly priced digs elsewhere. During low season you'll be serenaded at night by the local bullfrogs.

Sivalai HOTEL $$$
(☎089 723 3355; www.komooksivalai.com; Hat Sivalai; bungalows incl breakfast 5500-8500B; ❄📶🏊) Straddling an arrow-shaped white-sand peninsula framed by views of karst islands and the mainland, Sivalai wins the award for Ko Muk's most fabulous location. The elegant dark-wood bungalows are sizeable and tasteful; some have wraparound verandahs. There are two pools, a handy spa (massages from 700B) and the restaurant sits right at the tip of the peninsula.

★ **Hilltop Restaurant** THAI $$
(mains 100-300B; ⏲9am-10pm) Still the most atmospheric place to eat on Ko Muk – a jungle-cloaked, garden setting – this welcoming, family-run operation serves up all your Thai favourites. The seafood curries are superb (spice levels are adjusted on request) and will have you returning for seconds, but all the dishes are prepared with love and care. It's about 800m inland from Hat Farang.

Getting There & Away

Boats and long-tails to Ko Muk (120B to 250B, 30 minutes) leave daily from the pier at Kuantungku at noon, 1pm and 5pm November to April, returning to the mainland at 8am, 9am and 2pm. Services peter out in November and April, but the cheapest long-tail runs year-round at 1pm. Minibus-and-boat combo tickets take you to/from Trang (350B, 1½ hours) and Trang airport (500B, 1½ hours). You can also charter long-tails to/from Kuantungku (800B, 30 minutes).

From November to early April, Ko Muk is a stop on the Tigerline (p349) and Satun Pak Bara (p350) speedboats connecting Ko Lanta (950B, one hour), Ko Ngai (350B to 750B, 30 minutes) and Ko Lipe (1400B to 1600B, two hours).

Long-tail charters from Ko Muk to Ko Kradan (800B, 30 minutes), Ko Ngai (1000B, one hour) and Pak Meng (1500B, 45 minutes to one hour) are easily arranged on the pier or by asking at your accommodation.

Ko Kradan เกาะกระดาน

Beautiful Ko Kradan is dotted with slender, silky, white-sand beaches, bathtub-warm shallows and dreamy views across the twinkling turquoise sea to Ko Muk, Ko Libong and limestone karsts from its main, east-coast beach. The water is clean, clear and inviting, and there's a small but lush tangle of jungle inland.

LOCAL KNOWLEDGE

WET WEDDING

Every Valentine's Day, Ko Kradan hosts an unusual wedding ceremony. Around 40 couples don scuba gear and descend to an underwater altar amid the coral reefs, exchanging vows in front of the Trang District Officer. How the couples manage to say 'I do' underwater remains a mystery, but the ceremony made it into the *Guinness World Records* in 2000 as the world's largest underwater wedding. Fancy scuba goggles instead of a veil for your special day? Check out www.underwaterwedding.com.

Activities

Hat South SNORKELLING

Although some of Kradan's coral structure has been decimated, there's good snorkelling when the wind is calm off the island's south beach, which you can reach in a 10-minute walk along a jungly path from Paradise Lost guesthouse, signposted at the south end of the main beach.

Hat Sunset BEACH

A short signposted track at the south end of the main beach leads past Paradise Lost guesthouse and over the ridge to sunset beach, a mostly wet and rocky patch of sand facing open seas – and a fun place to get a little beachside privacy over a flaming pink sunset.

Sleeping & Eating

Kalume HOTEL $$

(☎080 932 0029; www.kalumekradan.com; r 1200-1800B; 📶) The cheapest beachfront resort, Kalume has a collection of bamboo and wooden bungalows set around a garden. None are very special or spacious, with minimal facilities inside, but you're steps away from Kradan's best beach, the staff are amenable and the laid-back bar and restaurant is a good place to while away the night.

Paradise Lost GUESTHOUSE $$

(☎081 894 2874; www.kokradan.wordpress.com; dm 300B, bungalows 700-1200B) One of Kradan's first lodgings, this inland property is in walking distance of all three of Kradan's main beaches. There's an airy five-bed, fan-cooled dorm, but the bungalows are basic with the cheapest sharing bathrooms. The bigger and more expensive bungalows have their own bathrooms but are still only functional. Closed low season.

The open-plan **kitchen** (mains 140-350B; ⌚8am-9pm) dishes up tasty food in big portions.

Seven Seas Resort HOTEL $$$

(☎075 2033 8990; www.sevenseasresorts.com; r incl breakfast 6000-12,000B; ❄📶🏊) This

BOATS TO/FROM KO KRADAN

DESTINATION	BOAT COMPANY	FARE (B)	DURATION
Hat Yao (for Trang)	Tigerline	1050	1hr
Ko Lanta	Tigerline	950	1½hr
	Satun Pak Bara Speedboat Club	1150	1¼hr
Ko Lipe	Tigerline	1600	3½hr
	Satun Pak Bara Speedboat Club	1400	2hr
Ko Muk	Satun Pak Bara Speedboat Club	300	15min
Ko Ngai	Tigerline	750	30min
	Satun Pak Bara Speedboat Club	400	45min

OFF THE BEATEN TRACK

KO SUKORN เกาะสุกร

Little-visited Ko Sukorn is a natural paradise of tawny beaches, light-green sea, jungle-shrouded black-rock headlands, and stilted shack neighbourhoods home to 2600-odd mainly Muslim residents whose rice fields, watermelon plots and rubber plantations unfurl along narrow concrete roads.

With few hills, expansive panoramas, plenty of shade and lots of opportunities to meet islanders, Sukorn is best explored by rented bike (200B). The main beach, dotted with a few low-key resorts, extends along the island's southwestern coast. Cover up away from the beach.

Enjoy fiery pink sunsets over outlying islands from the gorgeous long beach at the front of **Yataa Island Resort** (☎089 647 5550; www.yataaresort.com; Ao Lo Yai Beach; bungalow incl breakfast 1400-6500B; ❄📶🏊), whose green-roofed concrete air-con bungalows frame a cool blue pool. The restaurant is excellent, too. Alternatively, **Sukorn Cabana** (☎089 724 2326; www.sukorncabana.com; bungalow incl breakfast 900-1500B; ⏲closed May; ❄📶) has clean, if a little old, bungalows sporting thatched roofs, fridges, polished-wood interiors and plush verandahs.

The easiest way to get to Sukorn is by private transfers from Trang, arranged through your resort (per person 1900B). The cheapest way is to take a *sŏrng·tăa·ou* (pick-up minibus) from Trang to Yan Ta Khao (80B, 40 minutes), then transfer to Ban Ta Seh (50B, 45 minutes), from where long-tails to Ban Saimai (50B), Sukorn's main village, leave when full. Trang guesthouses and travel agents arrange *sŏrng·tăa·ou*-and-boat transfers (250B to 350B) to Ban Saimai via Ban Ta Seh, departing Trang at 11am daily.

Otherwise, book a taxi from Trang to Ban Ta Seh (900B). The resorts are a 3km walk or 100B motorcycle-taxi ride from Ban Saimai. You can charter long-tails directly to the beach resorts (400B).

boutique resort is by far the swishest and best option on Kradan. Super-sleek rooms draw many Scandinavian visitors with their terrazzo floors, indoor/outdoor bathrooms blending into tropical gardens, enormous low-slung beds and, for some, private cabanas. Hugging the jet-black infinity pool, the breezy **restaurant** (mains 200-1000B; ⏲7am-10pm; 📶) serves pricey Thai/international dishes. Prime location halfway up Kradan's main beach.

Getting There & Away

From November to April, daily boats to Kuantungku on the mainland leave at 8.30am and 1pm; tickets include connecting minibuses to Trang (450B) or Trang airport (550B). From Trang, combined minibus-and-boat services depart for Ko Kradan at 11am and 4pm. You can charter long-tails to/from Kuantungku (1500B, 45 minutes to one hour), Ko Muk (800B, 30 minutes) and Ko Ngai (1500B, 45 minutes).

The Phuket–Ko Lipe Tigerline (p349) stops off Ko Kradan from mid-October to mid-May. November to early April, Satun Pak Bara Speedboat Club (p350) offers faster and cheaper links.

Ko Libong เกาะลิบง

Trang's largest island is just 30 minutes by long-tail from mainland Hat Yao. Less visited than neighbouring islands, it's a gorgeous, lush mountainous pearl, wrapped in rubber trees, thick with mangroves and known for its captivating flora and fauna (especially the resident dugongs and migrating birds) more than its thin gold-brown beaches. The island is home to a small Muslim fishing community and has a few west-coast resorts. With its scruffy sweetness and untouristy backwater charm, Libong has a way of drawing you in, if you let it.

Sights

Libong Archipelago Wildlife Reserve NATURE RESERVE

This large mangrove area on Ko Libong's east coast at Laem Ju Hoi is protected by the Botanical Department. The sea channels are one of the last habitats of the endangered dugong: over 100 graze on the sea grass that flourishes in the bay. Most of Ko Libong's resorts offer dugong-spotting boat tours, led by trained naturalists, for 1000B to 1500B.

Sleeping & Eating

Almost all of Ko Libong's lodgings are on the west coast, which has the nicest beaches.

Libong Beach Resort BUNGALOW $$
(084 849 0899; www.libongbeach-resort.com; bungalows 1000-2500B;) Cute spot with everything from bland slap-up shacks behind a murky stream to more upmarket varnished wood-and-thatch beachfront chalets with semi-outdoor bathrooms. It also offers wildlife-spotting trips, transport info and motorbike rental (250B per day). We love the restaurant; try the *pàt see·éw* (fried noodles) or the *đôm yam kà-mîn* (turmeric fish soup).

Libong Relax Beach Resort BUNGALOW $$$
(094 582 5113, 091 825 4886; www.libongrelax.com; r incl breakfast 1600-3700B;) Top choice at this friendly, laid-back resort are stylish wood bungalows with terracotta sinks, shiny floors and shuttered doors that open up to the sea. Fan-cooled bamboo cottages are more rustic, simple and compact but well-kept. The resort offers bird and dugong-spotting and snorkelling trips, plus kayak rental (200B per hour). The beachside **restaurant** (mains 120-350B; 7.30am-3pm & 5-9pm;) does a good line in Thai staples.

Getting There & Away

During daylight hours, long-tail boats to Ban Ma Phrao on Ko Libong's east coast leave when full from Hat Yao (per person 100B, 30 minutes). On Ko Libong, motorcycle taxis run across to the west-coast resorts (per person 100B). Chartered long-tails from Hat Yao to the resorts cost 900B. You can charter boats to Ko Kradan (1500B), Ko Muk (1500B) and Ko Ngai (2300B).

SATUN PROVINCE

Satun was until recently mostly overlooked, but that's all changed thanks to the dynamic white sands of Ko Lipe – a one-time backpacker secret turned mainstream beach getaway. The rest of the province passes by in the blink of an eye, as visitors rush north to Ko Lanta or south to Pulau Langkawi (Malaysia). Which means that they miss the untrammelled beaches and sea caves of Ko Tarutao, the rugged trails and ribbon waterfalls of Ko Adang, the rustic beauty of Ko Bulon Leh and easygoing Satun itself.

Largely Muslim in make-up, Satun has seen little of the political turmoil that plagues the fellow Muslim majority provinces of neighbouring Yala, Pattani and Narathiwat.

Satun สตูล

074 / POP 23,800

Lying in a steamy jungle valley surrounded by limestone cliffs and a murky river, isolated Satun is a surprisingly bustling little city: the focal point of a province that's home to over 300,000 people. Few foreign visitors pass through, and most of them are heading to and from Malaysia, or are yachties dropping in for cheap repairs in Satun's acclaimed boat yard. If you do stick around you'll discover that Satun has some intriguing Sino-Portuguese and religious architecture, delicious food, lots of friendly smiles and plenty of authentic charm. The surrounding countryside is lovely and ripe for exploration.

Sights & Activities

Housed in a restored 1902 Sino-Portuguese mansion, Satun's excellent little **museum** (พิพิธภัณฑ์สถานแห่งชาติสตูล, Kuden Mansion; Soi 5, Th Satun Thanee; 50B; 9am-4pm Wed-Sun) was originally constructed as a temporary home for King Rama V during a royal visit. Now, it features informative displays on local history, customs and Muslim life in southern Thailand.

Soak up Satun's beauty by hiking **Monkey Mountain**, a jungle mound of limestone teeming with macaques.

Sleeping & Eating

Quick, cheap Chinese and Muslim restaurants are on Th Burivanich and Th Samanta Prasit. Chinese food stalls specialise in *kôw mŏo daang* (red pork with rice); Muslim restaurants offer *roti* with southern-style chicken curry and the local version of biryani. There's a decent night market too.

Satun Tanee Hotel GUESTHOUSE $
(074 711010, 074 712309; www.satuntaneehotel.com; 90 Th Satun Thanee; r 300-570B;) Behind the lime-green-and-orange exterior lie reasonably sized, modern rooms with comfortable beds and wood-panelled floors, plus dingier, cheaper, unrenovated fan-only rooms on the top floor (no lift). It's a bit

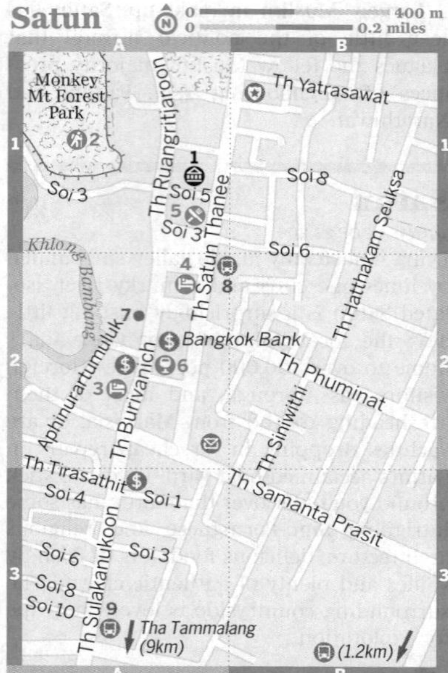

Satun

Sights

1 Satun National Museum A1

Activities, Courses & Tours

2 Monkey Mountain A1

Sleeping

3 On's Guesthouse A2

4 Satun Tanee Hotel A2

Eating

5 Night Market A1

Drinking & Nightlife

6 On's Living Room A2

Information

7 Immigration Office A2

Transport

8 Buses to Trang and Hat Yai A2

9 Sŏrng·tăa·ou to Tha Tammalang A3

institutional, but the updated rooms are good value and you get a warm welcome.

★ **Night Market** MARKET $
(off Th Satun Thanee; mains from 40B; ⌚5-9pm) Satun's small but busy night market springs to life with flavour-packed *pàt tai*, fried fish, chicken satay and excellent, spicy, southern-style curries. There's a larger Saturday night market on Th Burivanich.

Drinking & Nightlife

★ **On's Living Room** BAR
(☎074 724133; 36 Th Burivanich; ⌚5pm-2am; 📶) Satun's only Western-style bar takes up the ground floor of an atmospheric, tastefully converted Sino-Portuguese-style shophouse. There's a fine long wooden bar, a pool table and plenty of space to lounge around. This is where you will find Satun's tiny foreign community, and any *fa·ràng* passing through town. Upstairs houses part of On's Guesthouse.

Information

Bangkok Bank (Th Burivanich; ⌚8.30am-3.30pm Mon-Fri) has a foreign-exchange desk and an ATM. ATMs line Th Burivanich.

Immigration Office (☎074 711080; Th Burivanich; ⌚8.30am-4.30pm Mon-Fri) Opposite the clocktower, this office handles visa issues and extensions. It's easier for tourists to exit and re-enter Thailand via the border checkpoint at Tha Tammalang.

Police Station Satun's main police station.

Post Office (cnr Th Satun Thanee & Th Samanta Prasit; ⌚8.30am-4.30pm Mon-Fri, 9am-noon Sat) Satun's main post office.

Getting There & Away

The nearest airport to Satun is at Hat Yai, a two-hour drive away.

BOAT

From Tha Tammalang (10km south of Satun), there are two ferries daily to Pulau Langkawi (10am and 3pm, 300B) in Malaysia. In the reverse direction, ferries leave Pulau Langkawi daily for Satun at 10.30am and 5.15pm (RM36).

BUS

Buses leave from **Satun Bus Terminal**, 2km south of town. **Buses to Trang** (100B, two hours, hourly 5am to 4.30pm) also pick up passengers on Th Satun Thanee by the 7-Eleven. Trang buses go via La-Ngu (50B), where you can hop a *sŏrng·tăa·ou* to Pak Bara (20B) for boats to Ko Lipe and other islands.

Departures include the following:

Bangkok – VIP (1042B, 14 hours, 4pm)

Bangkok – air-con (679B, 14 hours, 7am, 2.30pm, 3pm, 4.30pm)

Krabi (215B, five hours, 8.15am, 10.15am, 12.15pm, 8pm)

Phuket (329B, eight hours, 8.15am, 10.15am, 12.15pm, 8pm)

MINIVAN & SHARE TAXI

Minivans run from Satun Bus Terminal to Krabi (200B, five hours, 7am and 2pm), Trang (120B, two hours, hourly 5am to 5pm), Hat Yai (100B, two hours, 6am to 5pm) and Hat Yai airport (300B 2½ hours, 6am to 5pm). **Minivans to Hat Yai** also pick up passengers on Th Satun Thanee by the 7-Eleven. There are also minivans to Kuala Perlis in Malaysia (400B). They don't run every day and pick you up from your accommodation. **On's Guesthouse** (☎074 724133; onmarch13@hotmail.com; 36 Th Burivanich; dm 250B, r 350-600B; ❄ 📶) can organise tickets.

Getting Around

The centre of Satun is easily walkable, but you can rent bicycles (150B per day) and motorbikes (250B per day) from On's Guesthouse.

Sŏrng·tăa·ou to the bus station cost 40B per person. Orange *sŏrng·tăa·ou* to **Tha Tammalang** pick up passengers at the 7-Eleven on Th Sulakanukoon. Motorcycle taxis run around town for 50B.

Pak Bara ปากบารา

☎074 / POP 3000

Pak Bara, 60km northwest of Satun, is the main jumping-off point for the dazzling islands of the Ko Tarutao Marine National Park (p366). Facilities are slowly improving as Pak Bara becomes increasingly packed with tourists, although almost all are in transit to the islands.

The main road from La-Ngu (Rte 4052) terminates at the pier, which is basically a massive passenger terminal for Lipe- and Tarutao-bound speedboats. The Ko Tarutao Marine National Park **visitors centre** (Map p364; ☎074 783485; Pak Bara Pier; ⏲8am-5pm) is by the pier. Local travel agents arrange one-day tours (2000B) to the parks' islands.

Getting There & Away

BUS

From Satun, take an ordinary Trang bus and get off at La-Ngu (50B, 30 minutes), continuing by *sŏrng·tăa·ou* to Pak Bara (20B, 20 minutes). A few minivans also make the run daily (60B). Pick up the bus and minivans outside the 7-Eleven on Th Satun Thanee.

BOAT

From mid-October to mid-May **speedboats** (p350) run from **Pak Bara's Ferry Terminal** (Map p364) to Ao Pante Malacca on Ko Tarutao (450B, 30 minutes), and on to Ko Lipe (650B, 1½ hours) at 11.30am. There are speedboats to Ko Tarutao (450B) only at 11am and 2.30pm October to May. Further speedboats run directly to Ko Lipe at 9.30am, 12.30pm, 1.30pm and 3.30pm. Boats return from Ko Lipe at 9.30am, 11.30am, 12.30pm, 1pm and 1.30pm.

For Ko Bulon Leh (450B, 30 minutes), boats depart at 12.30pm and buzz on to Ko Lipe. If you miss the Bulon boat, you can charter long-tails from local fishermen (2000B, 1½ hours). During low season, services to Ko Lipe are less frequent, but you can always count on the 11.30am boat from Pak Bara (weather permitting), returning at 9.30am.

MINIVANS TO/FROM PAK BARA

Air-con minivans run every 45 minutes between 7.30am and 6.30pm from Hat Yai to Pak Bara pier (120B, two hours). Minivan services may be reduced mid-May to mid-October.

Ko Tarutao Marine National Park อุทยานแห่งชาติหมู่เกาะตะรุเตา

One of Thailand's most exquisite, unspoilt regions, **Ko Tarutao Marine National Park** (Map p364; ☎074 783485; www.dnp.go.th; adult/child 200/100B; ⏲mid-Oct–mid-May) encompasses 51 islands blanketed by well-preserved

MINIVANS TO/FROM PAK BARA

DESTINATION	FARE (B)	DURATION (HR)	FREQUENCY
Hat Yai	120	2	11.30am, 1.30pm, 3.30pm
Hat Yai Airport	200	2	11.30am, 1.30pm, 3.30pm
Ko Lanta	400	3	11.30am
Krabi	350	4	11.30am
Phuket	500	6	1.30am, 1pm
Trang	200	2	11.30am, 1pm, 2pm, 3pm

Ko Tarutao Marine National Park & Around

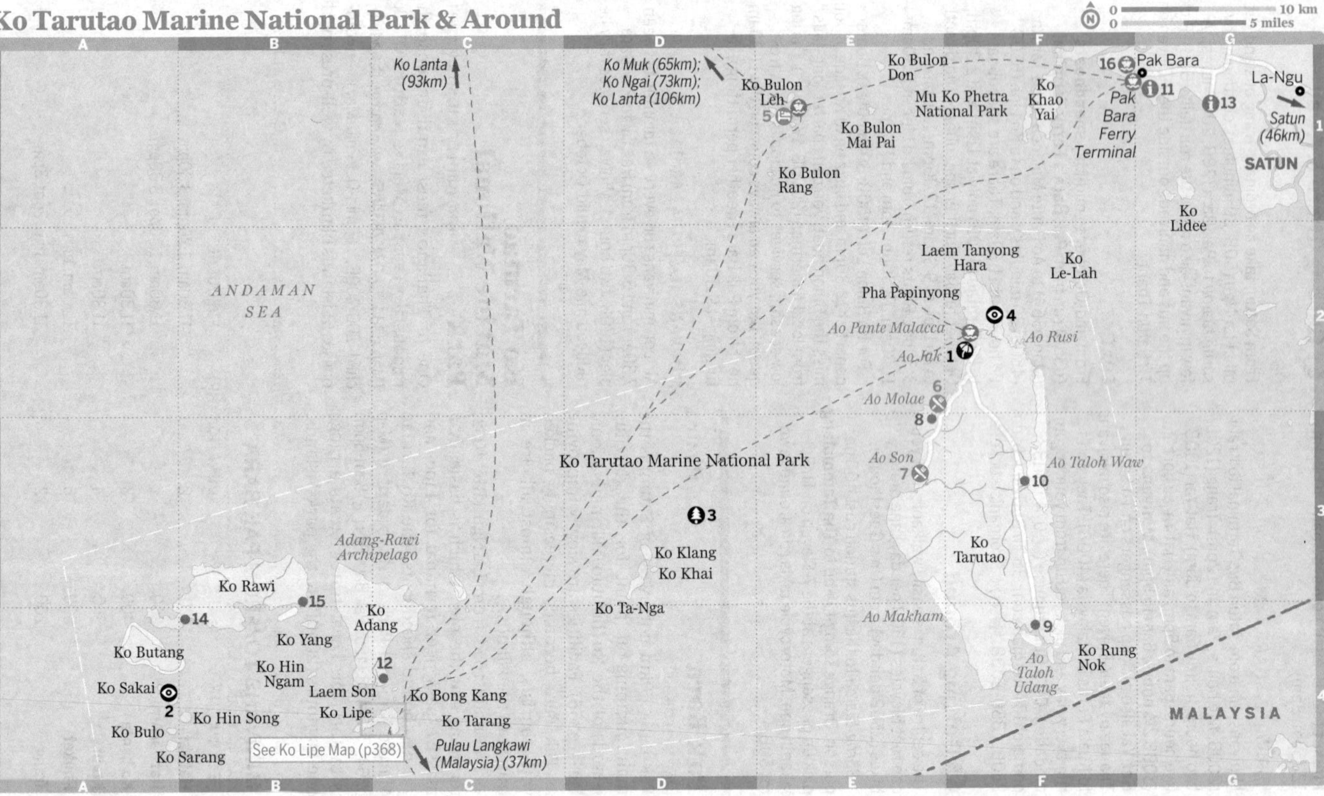

Ko Tarutao Marine National Park & Around

Sights
1 Ao Pante Malacca....F2
2 Ko Sarang....A4
3 Ko Tarutao Marine National Park....D3
4 Tham Jara-Khe....F2
Toe-Boo Cliff....(see 1)

Sleeping
Ao Molae National Park Accommodation....(see 6)
Ao Pante Malacca National Park Accommodation....(see 1)
Ao Son National Park Accommodation....(see 7)
5 Bulone Resort....E1
Chaolae Homestay....(see 5)
Ko Tarutao Marine National Park Accommodation....(see 12)

Eating
6 Ao Molae Canteen....E2
Ao Pante Malacca Canteen....(see 1)
7 Ao Son Canteen....E3
Bulone Resort....(see 5)
Su's Corner....(see 5)

Information
8 Ao Molae Ranger Station....E3
Ao Son Ranger Station....(see 7)
9 Ao Taloh Udang Ranger Station....F4
10 Ao Taloh Waw Ranger Station....F3
Ko Tarutao Marine National Park Headquarters....(see 1)
11 Ko Tarutao Marine National Park Visitors Centre....G1
Ko Tarutao Visitors Centre....(see 1)
12 Laem Son Ranger Station....C4
13 Mu Ko Phetra National Park Headquarters....G1
14 Ranger Station....B4
15 Ranger Station....B3

Transport
16 Satun Pak Bara Speedboat Club....F1

rainforest teeming with fauna, surrounded by healthy coral reefs and radiant white beaches. Within, you might spot dusky langurs, crab-eating macaques, mouse deer, wild pigs, sea otters, fishing cats, tree pythons, water monitors, Brahminy kites, sea eagles, hornbills, reef egrets and kingfishers.

Ko Lipe has become a high-profile tourist destination and it's where most travellers stay. It's exempt from national park rules governing development because it is home to communities of *chow lair*.

The only other islands you can stay on are Ko Tarutao, the biggest island and home to the park headquarters (p366), and Ko Adang.

Rubbish on the islands is a problem. Do your part and tread lightly. Apart from Ko Lipe, the park officially shuts from mid-October to mid-May.

Ko Tarutao เกาะตะรุเตา

Most of Ko Tarutao's whopping 152 sq km is covered in jungle, rising sharply to the park's 713m peak, making this one of Thailand's wildest islands. Mangrove swamps and limestone cliffs circle much of it, while steep trails and rough roads lead through the interior, making this a great place for fit hikers and mountain bikers. Tarutao's beaches are less inviting, thanks to tidal garbage and cloudy water. If you're after idyllic strips of sand and snorkelling, head to Ko Adang or Ko Rawi instead.

Ko Tarutao has a squalid past as a prison island: one of the reasons why it has never been developed.

The island closes officially from mid-May to mid-October.

Sights & Activities

With a navigable river and long paved roads, Tarutao is perfect for independent exploration. Hire kayaks (200/500B per hour/day) or mountain bikes (50/250B) from park headquarters.

Toe-Boo Cliff VIEWPOINT
(จุดชมวิวผาโต๊ะบู; Map p364) Behind park headquarters at Ao Pante Malacca, on the northwest side of the island, a steep 500m (20-minute) trail winds through the jungle below a limestone karst dripping with precipitation, then climbs a series of stone-cut steps to this dramatic rocky outcrop with fabulous views across Ko Tarutao towards Ko Adang and other surrounding isles.

Tham Jara-Khe CAVE
(ถ้ำจระเข้, Crocodile Cave; Map p364) The large stream flowing inland from **Ao Pante Malacca** (อ่าวพันเตมะละกา; Map p364; Ko Tarutao), on northwest Ko Tarutao, leads to Tham Jara-Khe, once home to deadly saltwater crocodiles. The cave is navigable for 1km at

POLITICAL PRISONERS

Between 1938 and 1948, more than 3000 Thai criminals, including 70 political rebels, were incarcerated on Ko Tarutao. Among them were So Setabutra, who compiled the first Thai–English dictionary while imprisoned on Tarutao, and Sittiporn Gridagon, son of Rama VII.

During WWII, food and medical supplies from the mainland were severely depleted and hundreds of prisoners died from malaria, starvation and maltreatment. Prisoners and guards allied and mutinied, taking to piracy in the nearby Strait of Malacca until they were suppressed by British troops in 1946.

The ruins of the political prisoners camp can be seen at Ao Taloh Udang. You can also visit Ao Taloh Waw, the east coast site of the camp for ordinary criminals, although there are no buildings left. The Ko Tarutao Visitors Centre has some displays about the island's prison past.

low tide and can be visited on long-tail tours (500B) from Ao Pante Malacca's jetty.

Sleeping & Eating

There are basic government-run bungalows at **Ao Pante Malacca** (Map p364; www.dnp.go.th; Ao Pante Malacca; r 600-1200B; ⏲mid-Oct–mid-May), **Ao Molae** (Map p364; www.dnp.go.th; Ao Molae; r 600B; ⏲mid-Oct–mid-May) and **Ao Son** (Map p364; www.dnp.go.th; Ao Son; r 350-550B; ⏲Nov–mid-May). Water is rationed, electricity runs from 6.30pm to 6am. You can also camp at Ao Molae, Ao Son, Ao Makham, Ao Taloh Waw and Ao Taloh Udang. Facilities are very basic and monkeys often wander into tents. Shut them tight.

Accommodation can be booked online or, more easily, at the park's visitors centre (p363) in Pak Bara.

There are simple canteens offering Thai food at **Ao Pante Malacca** (Map p364; Ao Pante Malacca; mains 80-180B; ⏲7.45am-2.30pm & 5.30-8.30pm), **Ao Molae** (Map p364; Ao Molae; mains 70-140B; ⏲7am-2pm & 5-9pm) and **Ao Son** (Map p364; Ao Son; mains 60-140B; ⏲7am-8pm).

Information

Ko Tarutao Marine National Park Headquarters (Map p364; Ao Pante Malacca, Ko Tarutao; ⏲8am-5pm)

Ko Tarutao Visitors Centre (Map p364; Ao Pante Malacca, Ko Tarutao; ⏲8am-5pm) Maps and local information.

There are ranger stations across the island, at **Ao Molae** in the northwest, **Ao Son** on the west coast, **Ao Taloh Udang** in the south and **Ao Taloh Waw** on the east of the island.

Getting There & Away

From mid-October to mid-May, there are three speedboats daily from Pak Bara to the **ferry terminal** (Map p364; Ao Pante Malacca, Ko Tarutao) at Ao Pante Malacca on Ko Tarutao (450B, 30 minutes). They leave at 11am, 11.30am and 2.30pm. During high season, you can also visit on speedboat day tours from Pak Bara (including park fees, lunch, drinks and snorkelling around 2000B).

If you're staying at Ao Molae, take a shared van from Ao Pante Malacca at 11am or 1pm daily (per person 50B; demand-dependent).

Ko Lipe เกาะหลีเป๊ะ

Once a serene tropical paradise, Ko Lipe is now a poster child for untamed development on Thailand's islands. Blessed with two beautiful wide white-sand beaches separated by jungle-covered hills and close to protected coral reefs, the centre of Ko Lipe has been transformed into an ever-expanding maze of hotels, restaurants, cafes, travel agencies and shops. The biggest losers have been the 700-strong community of *chow lair,* whose ancestors were gifted Lipe as a home by King Rama V in 1909, but who sold it in the 1970s.

Despite all the development, there is still an awful lot to love about Lipe: those gorgeous, salt-white sand crescents for a start, sensational dive sites, a jungle interior, chilled-out reggae bars, a contagiously friendly vibe and a good few inhabitants keen to minimise their environmental impact. Just don't expect to have it to yourself.

Activities

Diving

Diving is outstanding when the visibility clarifies, somewhat counter-intuitively, in the early part of the wet season (mid-April to mid-June). There are some fun drift dives and two rock-star dive sites.

Eight Mile Rock is a deep pinnacle that attracts devil rays and (very) rare whale sharks. **Stonehenge** is popular because of its resident seahorses, rare leopard sharks and reef-top boulders. **Ko Sarang** (Map p364) has gorgeous soft corals, a ripping current and solar flares of fish that make it many people's favourite Lipe dive spot.

Ko Lipe Diving DIVING
(Map p368; ☎088 397 7749, 087 622 6204; www.kolipediving.com; Walking St; 1/2 dives 1700/2800B; ⏰8am-10pm) Well-organised, professional dive operator with consistently glowing reviews for its selection of specialist courses and fun dives focused on diving education. Two-dive Discover Scuba costs 2800B; PADI certification is 14,500B.

Forra Dive DIVING
(Map p368; ☎084 407 5691; www.forradiving.com; Hat Sunrise; 1/2 dives 1500/2800B) French-owned Forra is one of Lipe's longest running outfitters. It offers Discover Scuba (from 1500B) and Open Water Diver courses (14,500B), as well as more advanced qualifications.

Has another office on **Walking St** (Map p368; ☎084 407 5691; www.forradiving.com; Walking St; 1/2 dives 1500/2800B).

Davy Jones' Locker DIVING
(Map p368; ☎085 361 7923; www.scubadivekohlipe.com; Hat Pattaya; dives from 2500B) One-dive Discover Scuba sessions cost 2500B; PADI Open Water certification is 14,000B (including free accommodation at Ko Lipe Backpackers).

Snorkelling

There's good coral along the southern coast and around **Ko Kra** (Map p368) and **Ko Usen** (Map p368), the islets opposite Hat Sunrise (be careful with oncoming long-tails). Most resorts rent out mask-and-snorkel sets and fins (200B). Travel agents and some dive operators arrange four-point snorkel trips to Ko Adang, Ko Rawi and other coral-fringed islands from 450B per person.

Kitesurfing

It is possible to kitesurf on Lipe, but winds are variable. Forra Dive can rent you the requisite gear.

Yoga

Swing by Castaway Resort for beachfront yoga (400B; 7am, 9am and 4.30pm).

Sleeping

More and more Ko Lipe resorts are staying open year-round. A few humble bamboo bungalows still stand strong, but resorts are colonising, particularly on Hat Pattaya. If

GETTING TO MALAYSIA

Keep in mind that Malaysia is one hour ahead of Thai time.

Ko Lipe to Pulau Langkawi

From mid-October to mid-April, Tigerline (p350), Bundhaya Speedboat (p357) and Satun Pak Bara Speedboat Club (p350) run daily from Ko Lipe to Pulau Langkawi in Malaysia (1000B to 1200B, 2½ hours). Departures are at 9.30am, 10.30am, 11am and 4pm. Head to the **immigration office** (Map p368; ⏰8am-6pm) in the centre of Hat Pattaya 1½ hours ahead to get stamped out. In reverse, boats leave Pulau Langkawi for Ko Lipe at 9.30am and 2.30pm Malaysian time.

Satun to Kuala Perlis or Pulau Langkawi

There are currently no speedboats or long-tail boats running from Satun to Pulau Langkawi in Malaysia.

It's possible to take a minivan from Satun to Kuala Perlis (400B) in Malaysia via the Wang Prajan/Wang Kelian border crossing, but they don't run every day. On's Guesthouse (p363) sells tickets.

At The Border

Citizens of the US, EU, Australia, Canada and several other countries may enter Malaysia for up to 90 days without prior visa arrangements. If you have questions about your eligibility, check with the nearest Malaysian embassy or consulate and apply for a visa in advance.

Ko Lipe

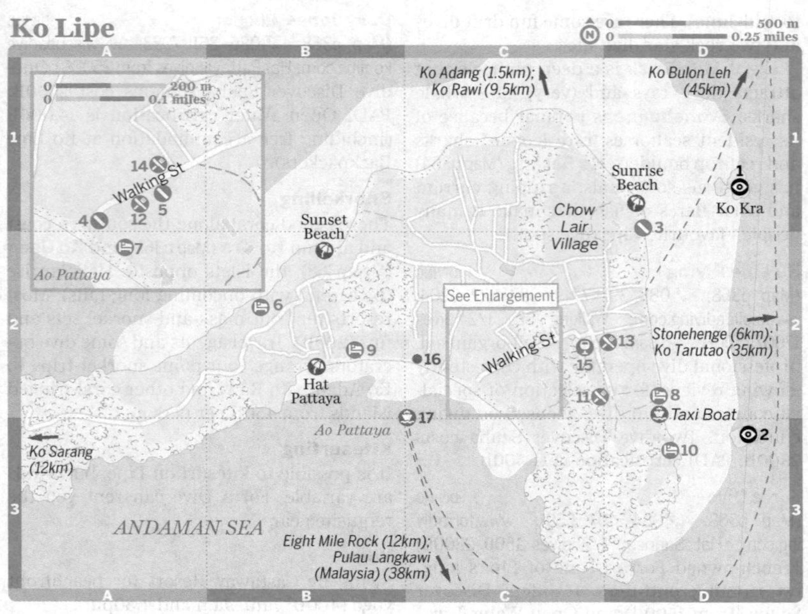

Ko Lipe

Sights
1 Ko Kra D1
2 Ko Usen D3

Activities, Courses & Tours
Castaway Divers .... (see 8)
Davy Jones' Locker .... (see 9)
3 Forra Dive D1
4 Forra Dive A1
5 Ko Lipe Diving A1

Sleeping
6 Bila Beach B2
7 Blue Tribes A2
8 Castaway Resort D2
9 Koh Lipe Backpackers Hostel B2
10 Serendipity D3

Eating
11 Barracuda C2
12 Elephant Coffee House A1
13 Nee Papaya D2
14 Papaya Mom A1

Drinking & Nightlife
15 Pooh's Bar C2

Information
16 Immigration Office C2

Transport
17 Ferry Jetty C2

you want tranquillity, head to less busy Hat Sunset. Book well ahead during high season and holidays, when prices skyrocket.

Koh Lipe Backpackers Hostel HOSTEL **$$**
(Map p368; ☎085 361 7923; www.kohlipebackpackers.com; Hat Pattaya; dm 500B, r 2500-3000B; ❄📶) There's a slightly random, spacey feel to Lipe's only hostel. Rooms and dorm are housed in a contemporary-style concrete block on west Hat Pattaya. Showers are shared, but you get private lockers, wi-fi, the on-site Davy Jones' Locker dive school (p367; divers get a discount) and the beach location is ace. Upstairs are simple but comfortable enough air-con private rooms.

Bila Beach BUNGALOW **$$**
(Map p368; ☎087 570 3684; www.bilabeachresort.com; Hat Sunset; bungalows 1500B) A killer bamboo reggae bar and beachfront restaurant lurk below stylish shaggy-haired cliffside bungalows set above a tiny, secluded white-sand cove, which is strewn with

boulders and adjacent to Hat Sunset. It's the perfect setting for your hippie honeymoon and a short sweaty walk over the hill from Hat Pattaya.

Blue Tribes BUNGALOW **$$$**
(Map p368; ☎080 546 9464, 083 654 0316; www.bluetribeslipe.com; Hat Pattaya; bungalows 1800-3000B; 📶) Tucked into flower-filled gardens, Blue Tribes is one of Hat Pattaya's more laid-back resorts. The best choices are two-storey thatched wooden bungalows with downstairs living rooms and top-floor bedrooms that offer sea views. Other bungalows are simple and no frills, but they come with balconies and you're just steps from the beach. The attached restaurant is pretty good.

★ **Castaway Resort** HOTEL **$$$**
(Map p368; ☎083 138 7472, 081 170 7605; www.castaway-resorts.com; Hat Sunrise; bungalows 2700-4750B; 📶) Roomy dark-wood bungalows with hammock-laden terraces, cushions everywhere, overhead fans and fabulous, modern-meets-natural bathrooms embody Lipe at its barefoot-beach-chic best. This welcoming resort is also one of Lipe's most environmentally friendly, run on solar water heaters and lights (there's no AC). There's a super-chilled beachside cafe, plus high-season yoga classes (450B) and a good **dive school** (Map p368; ☎087 478 1516; www.kohlipedivers.com; Castaway Resort, Hat Sunrise; 1/2 dives 2500/3800B; ⏲10am-8pm).

★ **Serendipity** BUNGALOW **$$$**
(Map p368; ☎088 395 5158; www.serendipityresort-kohlipe.com; Hat Sunrise; r 6720-14,400B; ❄📶🏊) An exquisitely designed spot, delightfully isolated by draping itself up above the boulder-strewn southern point of Hat Sunrise and accessed via a wooden boardwalk. Spacious dark-wood thatched bungalows feature private patios offering super views, great beds and stylish bathrooms, while the most expensive have plunge pools. If you're feeling flush, go for the lavish 200 sq metre Big Lebowski suite.

Eating

There's some great seafood: the best places are mostly inland. Find cheap eats at the *roti* stands and small Thai cafes along Walking St. Please take advantage of the waste-reducing water refill points at many resorts and eateries.

★ **Nee Papaya** THAI **$**
(Map p368; mains 80-150B; ⏲9am-11pm) Delightful Nee offers an affordable fish grill nightly, all the standard curries (including a dynamite beef *pá·naang*), noodles and stir-fries (beef, chicken, seafood or veggie), along with an array of fiery Isan dishes. She'll tone down the chillis on request, but her food is best when spiced for the local palate, which is why she attracts many Thai tourists.

★ **Barracuda** SEAFOOD **$$**
(Map p368; mains 80-250B; ⏲9am-10pm) Every second restaurant on Lipe offers fresh seafood barbecue, but this is the one the locals patronise the most. The other dishes on the menu are also great, especially the salads. The ramshackle, slightly tucked away setting adds to the sense that you're eating at a place designed for Thais rather than foreigners.

Elephant Coffee House INTERNATIONAL **$$**
(Map p368; ☎089 657 2178; www.facebook.com/ElephantKohLipe; Walking St; mains 120-420B; ⏲8am-1am) The bar is a long-tail, second-hand books are for sale and black-and-white local-life photos are plastered across varnished-concrete walls. Pop into this coolly contemporary cafe for fabulous all-day breakfasts of thick French toast, excellent coffee and homemade muesli loaded with tropical fruit. Otherwise choose from fresh

BEACH VOLUNTEERS

The pioneering, increasingly successful brainchild of a Thai-Swiss duo, **Trash Hero** (www.trashhero.org) organises regular Monday volunteer clean-ups to preserve Lipe's beloved white-sand beaches and others in Ko Tarutao Marine National Park. The program launched in December 2013 with the straightforward aim of protecting the islands' beaches using only materials and people-power to hand. Local businesses quickly pledged support, supplying long-tails, food, drinks and rubbish bags.

Over 1000 volunteers (locals and tourists) have since removed 21,000kg of rubbish from local beaches. Trash Hero now runs weekly clean-ups at 11 official points across Thailand and Indonesia.

> **BEACH SAFETY**
>
> Keep your eyes open for long-tail boats while swimming, especially in low season. People have been run down before. Don't expect boats to see you.
>
> Do not try to swim the narrow strait between Lipe and Adang at any time of year; currents are swift and can be deadly.

salads, sandwiches, burgers and pizzas. Also hosts live music most evenings.

Papaya Mom THAI $$

(Map p368; Walking St; mains 90-500B; ⊙8am-10pm;) The big menu at this friendly place crosses regional Thai food boundaries, and offers some Western dishes, but it is the fiery and authentic Isan dishes from the north-east that draw in Thai travellers and many locals. Vegetarians can raid the luscious fruit stand, or order from the thoughtful veggie menu featuring a delicious bean-curd-and-bean-sprouts stir-fry.

Drinking & Nightlife

Coffee shops are sprinkled all over the island, especially on Walking St.

A few driftwood-clad Rasta bars can still be found on the beaches, especially Hat Pattaya and Hat Sunset.

Pooh's Bar BAR

(Map p368; 089 463 5099, 074 750345; www.poohlipe.com; Walking St; ⊙1pm-1am;) This sprawling complex (which includes bungalows, a dive shop and several restaurants) was built by a Lipe pioneer and remains a popular local expat hang-out. Nightly films and sports are projected onto the big screen and there's often live music.

Information

Immigration Office (p367) Immigration now has its own official kiosk on the beach next to Bundaya Resort.

Getting There & Away

From mid-October to mid-May, speedboats run from Pak Bara to Ko Lipe via Ko Tarutao or Ko Bulon Leh at 9.30am, 11.30am, 12.30pm, 1.30pm and 3.30pm (650B, 1½ hours). Boats return to Pak Bara at 9.30am, 11.30am, 12.30pm, 1pm and 1.30pm. Low-season transport is weather dependent, but there's usually a direct daily boat from Pak Bara to Lipe at 11.30am, returning at 9.30am.

From November to late April, the high-speed Tigerline (p349) ferry departs Ko Lipe at 10am for Phuket (2100B, eight hours), via Ko Phi-Phi (1750B, seven hours), Ko Lanta (1500B, five hours), Ko Muk (1400B, 3½ hours), Ko Kradan (1600B, 3½ hours) and Ko Ngai (1400B, 4½ hours).

From mid-November to late March, Bundhaya Speedboat (p357) and Satun Pak Bara Speedboat Club (p350) leave Ko Lipe at 9am for Ko Lanta (1900B, three hours), via Ko Bulon Leh (600B, one hour), Ko Kradan (1400B, two hours), Ko Muk (1400B, two hours) and Ko Ngai (1600B, 2½ hours). Speedboats return from Lanta at 10.30am.

Boats also run from Ko Lipe to Pulau Langkawi (1000B to 1200B, 2½ hours) in Malaysia, mid-October to mid-April.

No matter which boat you end up using, you'll have to take a 50B long-tail shuttle to/from the **floating ferry jetty** (Map p368) off Hat Pattaya, and pay a 20B 'entrance fee'. It's part of a local agreement to share the flow. Speedboats *may* drop you directly on Hat Pattaya. During low season (May–October), boats mostly dock at Hat Sunrise and there's no long-tail shuttle fee.

Getting Around

There are few experiences as relaxing as pottering between the jungle gems of Ko Rawi, Ko Adang and surrounding islets. The best way to see the archipelago is to hire a *chow lair* captain from the **Taxi Boat** (Map p368; Hat Sunrise) stand on Hat Sunrise. You can rent kayaks (250B per hour) across the island, including at Daya's.

Ko Adang & Ko Rawi เกาะอาดัง/เกาะราวี

Ko Adang, the 30-sq-km island immediately north of Ko Lipe, is a former pirate haunt and has brooding, densely forested hills, white-sand beaches and healthy coral reefs. There's a *chow lair* village on the east coast, as well as an illegally built resort that has yet to open. It's possible to stay in national park accommodation, and to camp.

Ko Rawi, a rocky, 29-sq-km jungle-covered ellipse 1km west of Ko Adang, is almost completely uninhabited. There are fantastic beaches on both the north and south of the island and large coral reefs offshore, which make for excellent snorkelling.

Both islands are popular stops on day snorkelling tours from Ko Lipe.

Sights & Activities

There are a few short jungle trails on Ko Adang that lead to small waterfalls. Great views can be had from Chado Cliff, a half-hour hike above the main beach. Ko Rawi has a few trails too.

There's fine snorkelling off both Ko Adang and Ko Rawi. Top spots include north Ko Yang, 1km south of Ko Rawi's southeastern end, and tiny Ko Hin Ngam, 3km further south, which has underwater fields of giant clams, vibrant anemones and striped pebble beaches.

Sleeping & Eating

You can stay in simple bungalows on Ko Adang or camp. Camping (per person 30B, tent hire 200B) at Ao Lik on Ko Rawi, close to the Ranger Station, is allowed, with park permission, but facilities are very basic.

There's a restaurant at the accommodation on Ko Adang, and a very simple one on Ko Rawi at the Ranger Station on the southeast coast.

Ko Tarutao Marine National Park Accommodation BUNGALOW **$**
(Map p364; ✆089 736 9328; www.dnp.go.th; Ko Adang; d 600B, campsite per person 30B, with tent hire 280B; ⌚mid-Oct–mid-May) Ko Adang's park accommodation is near Laem Son ranger station in the island's southeast, set back from the beach. There are attractive but simple, fan-cooled doubles, as well as six-person family bungalows (1800B), all with attached cold-water bathrooms, plus camping facilities. Book ahead, online or at the Pak Bara park visitors centre (p363). A small restaurant provides good Thai meals.

Information

There are no ATMs or shops on Ko Adang or Ko Rawi. Bring cash and everything you might need.

There are ranger stations near the accommodation on **Ko Adang** (Map p364), and on Ko Rawi's **southeast coast** (Map p364; Ko Rawi) and **southwest coasts** (Map p364; Ko Rawi).

Getting There & Away

Long-tail boats from Ko Lipe take you to Ko Adang for around 400B or Ko Rawi for 600B, depending on your bargaining skills. Even a short stop on the islands will cost you the park entrance fee.

Ko Bulon Leh เกาะบุโหลนเล

Gracious and peaceful Ko Bulon Leh, 23km west of Pak Bara, is surrounded by the Andaman's signature clear waters and has its share of faultless alabaster beaches with swaying casuarinas. This gorgeous island is in that perfect phase of being developed enough to offer some facilities, yet it's not so popular that you have to book weeks in advance (though bungalow numbers are on the rise).

The exceptional, main white-sand beach extends along the east coast from Bulone Resort, on the northeast cape, to Pansand Resort. In places it narrows, especially where buffered by gnarled mangroves and strewn with thick sun-bleached logs, making it easy to find a secret shady spot with dreamy views.

Sights & Activities

The island's wild beauty is accessible on the northern coast at blue, coral-gravel-laden **Ao Panka Yai**, which has decent snorkelling. This bay is linked by a small paved path to **Ao Panka Noi**, a fishing village with a clutch of good, simple restaurants, on the eastern half of the northern coast. Follow a signposted trail nearby west through remnant jungle and rubber plantations to wind your way south to **Ao Muang** (Mango Bay), where there's an authentic *chow lair* squid-fishing camp.

There's good coral off **Laem Son** on the northeastern edge of the island and down the eastern coast. You can rent masks, snorkels and fin sets (200B) and kayaks (200B per hour) at Bulone Resort and Pansand Resort. Snorkelling is best at low tide.

Resorts can arrange guided snorkelling trips (1700B, four hours, maximum six people) to other islands. Tours usually take in the glassy emerald waters of **Ko Gai** and **Ko Ma**. But the most stunning sight is **White Rock**: bird-blessed spires shooting out of the open sea. Beneath the surface is a mussel-crusted rock reef teeming with colourful fish.

Sleeping & Eating

Most places close from mid-April to November. It's worth wandering over to Ao Panka Noi for food. There are a few local restaurants and shops in the Muslim village between Ao Panka Noi and Ao Panka Yai. All the resorts have their own restaurants.

Chaolae Homestay BUNGALOW $
(Map p364; ☎086 290 2519, 086 967 0716; www.facebook.com/chaolae.homestay; Ao Panka Yai, Ko Bulon Leh; bungalows 600B; ⏲Dec-Apr) Simple bamboo-and-wood bungalows with cold water showers and squat toilets. It's a blissfully quiet, shady spot, close to the village and run by a welcoming *chow lair* family, and steps away from decent snorkelling at Ao Panka Yai.

The restaurant is OK too. No wi-fi.

Bulone Resort HOTEL $$$
(Map p364; ☎081 897 9084; www.bulone-resort.com; Main Beach; bungalows incl breakfast 3000-4500B; ⏲Nov-Apr; ❄📶) Perched on Bulon's northeast cape with access to two exquisite white-sand stretches, Bulone Resort steals the island's top location. Cute whitewashed-wood bungalows (some fan, some air-con) come with queen-sized beds, iron frames and ocean breezes. Huge alpine chalet-style air-con rooms tower behind on stilts, with glorious views.

Enjoy 24-hour electricity, a Thai-international **restaurant** (mains 180-350B; ⏲7.30-10am & 6-10pm; 📶) and a coffee corner.

Su's Corner THAI, BREAKFAST $
(Map p364; ☎081 189 7183; Ao Panka Noi, Ko Bulon Leh; mains 80-140B; ⏲7am-8pm) Anyone who can transform veggie fried rice into something magical deserves high praise. This simple open-air cafe, with only a few tables scattered under palms just inland from Ao Panka Noi, is deservedly popular for its baguettes, shakes, cakes and Thai staples done with flair.

ℹ Information

There are no ATMs on Ko Bulon Leh; the nearest are at Pak Bara. Bring cash. Wi-fi is available but signals are not always great.

ℹ Getting There & Away

From November to April, speedboats to Ko Bulon Leh (450B, 30 minutes) leave from Pak Bara at 12.30pm daily. Long-tail ship-to-shore transfers cost 50B; ask to be dropped off on the beach closest to your resort. In the reverse direction, **the boat** (Map p364) moors in the bay in front of Pansand Resort at 9am. You can charter long-tails to/from Pak Bara (2000B, 1½ hours).

From November to April, daily speedboats (600B, one hour) run from Ko Bulon Leh to Ko Lipe at 2pm, stopping in front of Pansand Resort. Boats originate in Ko Lanta (1600B, two hours) and make stops at Ko Ngai (1050B, 1½ hours), Ko Muk (900B, one hour) and Ko Kradan (900B, one hour), returning from Lipe at 9am.

Understand Thailand's Islands & Beaches

Thailand's Islands & Beaches Today

Thailand continues to maintain the artificial calm that has been in place since a 2014 coup ousted the last democratically elected civilian government. On the surface, military rule has stabilised Thailand, but with elections delayed once more until at least 2018, the country remains politically divided between the rural poor and the traditional elite and urban middle classes. The death of the beloved King Rama IX in 2016 means that Thailand has its first new king in 70 years.

Best in Print

The Lioness in Bloom: Modern Thai Fiction about Women (translated by Susan Fulop Kepner; 1996) A collection of short stories detailing the experiences of Thai women across the 20th century.

Four Reigns (Kukrit Pramoj; originally published 1953) A woman's life inside and outside the royal palace during the reign of four Thai kings from the 1890s to the end of WWII.

Bangkok 8 (John Burdett; 2003) Southeast Asian noir as a Thai detective and an FBI agent track down a murderer in the Bangkok underworld.

The Sad Part Was (Prabda Yoon; 2017) Satirical short stories about the lives of middle-class Thais in present-day Bangkok.

Best on Film

Last Life in the Universe (2003) A dreamlike, beautifully shot, absorbing story of the relationship between a Thai woman and a Japanese man.

Tom-Yum-Goong (2005) A successful martial arts movie starring Tony Jaa, the Jackie Chan of Thailand.

Paradoxocracy (2013) The country's political history is traced from the 1932 revolution onwards.

By the Time it Gets Dark (2016) The 1976 massacre of student protesters at Thammasat University in Bangkok is relived by a group of film-makers.

The Post-Coup Years

In late August 2017, Yingluck Shinawatra, the last democratically elected prime minister of Thailand, fled into exile in Dubai to avoid appearing in court to hear a judgment on corruption charges that she and her supporters claim are politically motivated. For the military government that ousted Yingluck from power in May 2014, her flight was undoubtedly a relief. Had she been found guilty and imprisoned, the legions of Shinawatra supporters may have taken to the streets in protest, perhaps leading to a replay of the political violence that plagued Thailand between 2010 and 2014.

But no one in Thailand thinks this is the end of the Shinawatras and their Pheu Thai political party, which has won every general election since 2001. Thailand remains fundamentally divided between the many people who regard the Shinawatras as the only politicians to have ever done anything for them, and a coalition of the traditional elite, the urban middle classes and voters in the south of the country who accuse the Shinawatras of massive corruption.

Since the 2014 military takeover, Thailand has stayed in a political holding pattern, with elections repeatedly postponed. In October 2017, Thailand's leader, former general Prayuth Chan-o cha, announced that a general election will be held in November 2018, although he said also that the actual date wouldn't be confirmed until mid-2018.

The military has named its government the National Council for Peace and Order (NCPO). While blaming the failure to hold elections on the lack of stability in the country, the NCPO has spent the last three years crafting a new constitution, the country's 20th in the last 80-odd years. Like all Thailand's previous constitutions, the latest version is designed to restrict the power of whoever wins the next election.

As everyone waits for the next elections, the NCPO has been accused of trying to muzzle the media, and detaining and imprisoning critical academics and political opponents. The NCPO has also had to deal with a number of human-trafficking scandals that have received worldwide attention. The death of the much-loved King Bhumibol Adulyadej in October 2016, Thailand's longest-serving monarch, has only added to the uncertainty in the country.

Southern Separatism

Thailand's south is mostly synonymous with golden beaches and swaying palm trees, but in the Deep South, abutting the Malaysian border, a long-running insurgency pits the Thai security forces against ethnic Malay Muslim separatists. Thailand's three southernmost provinces, Yala, Pattani and Narathiwat, and parts of neighbouring Songkhla Province were once part of the sultanate of Pattani, which ruled the region from the 15th century until the turn of the 20th century when Buddhist Siam claimed the land. These areas have retained their culture and Muslim religion and speak their own language: Yawi, a Malay dialect. After 100-plus years of Thai rule, many of the area's 1.8 million residents want their own independent state or, at the very least, autonomy from Bangkok.

Resentment of the Thai authorities' rule of the region, which includes making the mostly Muslim, Yawi-speaking school population study in Thai and learn about Buddhism, has long festered. But the insurgency really began in 2004, after security forces crushed a demonstration in Tak Bai in Narathiwat Province, resulting in the deaths of 85 protesters. Now an estimated 12,500 to 15,000 insurgents launch sporadic attacks. Since 2004 over 6500 people have been killed in the insurgency, making this Southeast Asia's most violent conflict, but foreigners have never been targeted.

Lacklustre peace talks continue to take place, but have foundered on the inability of either side to compromise or trust each other. After well over a decade of sometimes extreme violence, there is no end in sight to the insurgency and many Thais are only dimly aware that it is happening.

AREA: **198,115 SQ MILES**

GDP: **US$406.8 BILLION**

INFLATION: **1.35%**

GDP PER CAPITA: **US$5901**

POPULATION BELOW THE POVERTY LINE: **10.5%**

UNEMPLOYMENT: **0.8%**

if Thailand were 100 people

94 would be Buddhist
5 would be Muslim
1 would be Christian

land use (%)

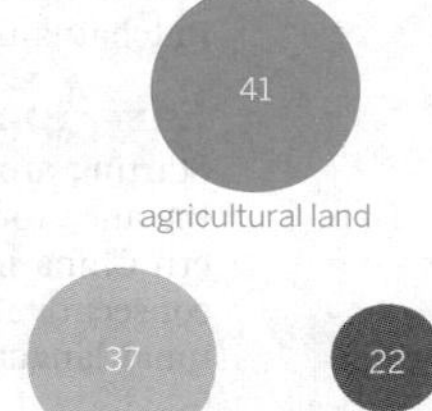

population per sq km

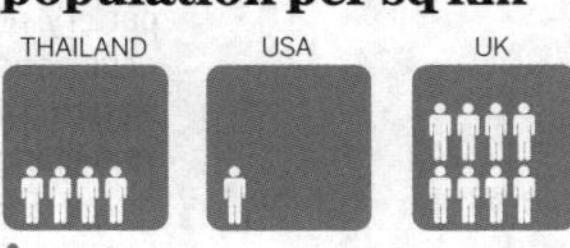

History

Thailand's history begins in neolithic times, moves through the dawn of Hindu and Buddhist civilisations and morphs into a time of great immigration, wars and various kingdoms. From 1932, the country has been nominally a democracy, but frequent coups mean that in reality there have only been a few truly democratic governments since then.

The Beginning

Immigrants from all directions have competed for power and dominance over the land that would become Siam and then Thailand. Eventually the country fused a national identity around language, religion and monarchy. While the kings resisted colonisation from the expansionist West, they ceded their absolute grip on the country when challenged by forces within. Since the transition to a constitutional monarchy in 1932, the military has predominantly ruled the country with a few democratic hiccups in between. Ongoing political tensions continue to fester.

Sacred Landmarks

Tham Phraya Nakhon, Khao Sam Roi Yot National Park

Sanctuary of Truth, Pattaya

Wat Phra Mahathat Woramahawihaan, Nakhon Si Thammarat

Khmer temples, Phetchaburi

Big Buddha, Phuket

Ancient History

Little evidence remains of the cultures that existed in Thailand before the middle of the 1st millennium AD. *Homo erectus* fossils in Thailand's northern province of Lampang date back at least 500,000 years, and the country's most important archaeological site is Ban Chiang, outside Udon Thani, which provides evidence of one of the world's oldest agrarian societies. It is believed that the Mekong River Valley and Khorat Plateau were inhabited as far back as 10,000 years ago by farmers and bronze-workers. Cave paintings in Pha Taem National Park near Ubon Ratchathani date back some 3000 years.

Early Empires

Starting around the 10th century, the 'Tai' people, who are considered the ancestors of the contemporary Thais, began emigrating from southern China into present-day Southeast Asia. These immigrants came in consecutive waves and spoke Tai-Kadai, a family of monosyllabic and tonal languages said to be the most significant ethno-linguistic group

TIMELINE

4000–2500 BC

Prehistoric neolithic people develop pottery, rice and cereal cultivation, cattle and pig farming, and bronze metallurgy in northern Thailand.

6th–11th centuries AD

The Buddhist and Hindu, Indian-influenced Dvaravati, thought to be predominantly of the Mon ethnicity, establish city-states in central Thailand.

9th–13th centuries

Angkor extends control across parts of Thailand. The region is still influenced by the extravagant architectural and sculptural style of this once-dominant Southeast Asian kingdom.

in Southeast Asia. Some settled in the river valleys of modern-day Thailand, while others chose parts of modern-day Laos and the Shan state of Myanmar.

They settled in villages as farmers, hunters and traders and organised themselves into administrative units known as *meu·ang*, under the rule of a lord, which became the building block of the Tai state. Over time, the Tai expanded from the northern mountain valleys into the central plains and northeastern plateau, where there existed several important trading centres ruled by various indigenous and 'foreign' empires, including the Mon-Dvaravati, Khmer (Cambodia) and Srivijaya (Malay).

Dvaravati

The Mon dominated parts of Burma (present-day Myanmar), western Thailand and the central plains. From the 6th to 9th centuries, the Dvaravati emerged as a distinct Buddhist and Hindu culture associated with the Mon people. Little is known about this period, but it is believed that Nakhon Pathom might have been the centre, and that overland trade routes and trading outposts extended west to Burma, east to Cambodia, north to Chiang Mai and Laos, and towards the northeast, as evidenced by findings of distinctive Dvaravati Buddha images, temples and stone inscriptions in Mon language.

The Dvaravati was one of many Indian-influenced cultures that established themselves in Southeast Asia at the time, but scholars single out the Dvaravati because of its artistic legacy and the trade routes that might have provided an early framework for what would become the core of the modern-day Thai state.

Khmer

While the Dvaravati are a historical mystery, the Khmers were Southeast Asia's equivalent of the Roman Empire. This kingdom became famous for its extravagant sculpture and architecture and had a profound effect on the art and religion of the region. Established in the 9th century, the Khmer kingdom built its capital in Angkor (modern-day Cambodia) and expanded westward across present-day central and northeastern Thailand. Administrative centres anchored by Angkor-style temples were built in Lopburi (then known as Lavo), Sukhothai and Phimai (near Nakhon Ratchasima) and linked by road to the capital.

The Khmer's large-scale construction projects were a symbol of imperial power in its frontier regions and examples of the period's most advanced technologies. Khmer elements – Hinduism, Brahmanism, Theravada Buddhism and Mahayana Buddhism – mark the cultural products of this period in Thailand.

Relief carvings at Angkor Wat depict Tai mercenaries serving in Khmer armies. The Khmer called them 'Syam'. The name was transliterated to 'Siam' by the English trader James Lancaster in 1592.

10th century	1240–1438	1283	1292
Tai peoples arrive in Thailand from Southern China in several waves. Settlements expand from the northern mountain valleys to the central plains and northeast plateau.	Approximate dates of Sukhothai kingdom, which the Thais consider the first real Thai kingdom. The period is marked by flourishing arts and culture.	Early Thai script is invented by King Ramkhamhaeng of Sukhothai. The script is based on Indian, Mon and Khmer scripts. Buddhism is established as the official religion.	Chiang Mai becomes the capital of Lanna. King Mengrai, a skilled diplomat, creates ties that dispel outside threats and allow the culture to grow.

Srivijaya

While mainland Thailand was influenced by forces from the north and west, the Malay peninsula was economically and culturally fused to cultures further south. Between the 8th and 13th centuries, the Malay peninsula was under the sway of the confederation of the Srivijaya, which controlled maritime trade between the South China Sea and Indian Ocean. The Srivijaya capital is believed to have been in Palembang on Sumatra.

Of the series of Srivijaya city-states that grew to prominence along the Malay peninsula, Tambralinga established its capital near present-day Nakhon Si Thammarat and adopted Buddhism in the 13th century, while the states further south fell under the influence of Islam, creating a religious boundary that persists to this day. Remains of Srivijaya culture can be seen around Chaiya and Nakhon Si Thammarat. Many art forms of the Srivijaya kingdom, such as *năng đà·lung* (shadow theatre) and *lá·kon* (classical dance-drama), persist today.

Emerging Tai Kingdoms

In the 13th century, the regional empires started to decline and prosperous Tai city-states emerged with localised power and military might. The competing city-states were ultimately united into various kingdoms that began to establish a Thai identity. Scholars recognise Lanna, Sukhothai and Ayuthaya as the unifying kingdoms of the period.

Lanna

King Naresuan is portrayed as a national hero and became a cult figure, especially worshipped by the Thai army. His story inspired a high-budget, blockbuster film series, *King Naresuan*, by film-maker Chatrichalerm Yukol, funded in part by the Thai government.

The Lanna kingdom, based in northern Thailand, dates its formation to the upper Mekong River town of Chiang Saen in the middle of the 12th century by King Mengrai, who settled the bickering between neighbouring towns by conquering them. He then migrated south to Chiang Mai (meaning 'new city') in 1292 to establish his capital. The king was a skilled diplomat and forged important alliances with potential rivals, notably King Ngam Muang of Phayao and King Ramkhamhaeng of Sukhothai; a bronze statue commemorating this confederation stands in Chiang Mai today. King Mengrai is also credited for successfully repulsing Mongol invasions in the early 14th century and building diplomatic ties in lieu of future attacks.

The Lanna kingdom is also recognised for its royal patronage of the Sinhalese tradition of Theravada Buddhism, now widely practised in Thailand, and of the distinctive northern Thai culture that persists in the region. The Lanna kingdom never went through an extensive expansion period as it was plagued by dynastic intrigues and wars, especially against Sukhothai and Ayuthaya.

1351–1767

The Ayuthaya kingdom reigns; at its height in the 1600s it controls parts of Burma, Laos and Cambodia, making it the predominant power in Southeast Asia at the time.

1511

Portuguese Duarte Fernandes becomes the first European to establish diplomatic relations with Thailand when he founds a foreign mission in Ayuthaya; other European nations follow.

1688

The death of pro-foreign King Narai is followed by the Palace Revolution and the expulsion of the French. As a result, Thailand's ties with the West are near-severed until the 1800s.

1700

Ayuthaya's population is estimated to be one million, making it probably the largest city in the world at the time.

Sukhothai

During the 13th century, several principalities in the central plains united and wrested control from the dying Khmer empire, making their new capital at Sukhothai (meaning 'Rising of Happiness'). Thais consider Sukhothai the first true Thai kingdom and the period is recognised as an artistic and cultural awakening.

The most revered of the Sukhothai kings was Ramkhamhaeng, who is credited with developing the modern Thai writing system, which is based on Indian, Mon and Khmer scripts. He also established Theravada Buddhism as the official religion.

In its prime, the Sukhothai kingdom extended as far as Nakhon Si Thammarat in the south, to the upper Mekong River Valley in Laos and to Bago (Pegu) in southern Myanmar. For a short time (1448–86) the Sukhothai capital was moved to Phitsanulok, but by that time another star was rising in Thailand, the kingdom of Ayuthaya.

Ayuthaya

In the mid-14th century, the Ayuthaya kingdom began to dominate the Chao Phraya River basin during the twilight of the Khmer period. It survived for 416 years, defining itself as Siam's most important early kingdom. It had an expansive sphere of influence (including much of the former Khmer empire) and played a fundamental role in organising the modern Thai state and social structure.

With a strategic island location formed by encircling rivers, Ayuthaya grew wealthy through international trade during the 17th century's age of commerce and fortified itself with superior Portuguese-supplied firearms and mercenaries. The river system connected to the Gulf of Thailand and to the hinterlands as well.

During this period Western traders 'discovered' Southeast Asia, and Ayuthaya hosted many foreign settlements. Accounts by foreign visitors mention Ayuthaya's cosmopolitan markets and court. In 1690 Londoner Engelbert Campfer proclaimed, 'Among the Asian nations, the kingdom of Siam is the greatest.'

Ayuthaya adopted Khmer court customs, honorific language and ideas of kingship. The monarch styled himself as a Khmer *devaraja* (divine king) rather than Sukhothai's *dhammaraja* (righteous king); Ayuthaya continued to pay tribute to the Chinese emperor, who rewarded this ritualistic submission with generous gifts and commercial privileges.

The glories of Ayuthaya were interrupted by the expansionist Burmese. In 1569 the city had fallen to the great Burmese king, Bayinnaung, but regained independence under the leadership of King Naresuan. Then, in 1765, Burma's ambitious and newly established Kongbaung dynasty pushed eastward to eliminate Ayuthaya as a political and commercial

Top History Reads

Thailand: A Short History (David K Wyatt; 2003)

A History of Thailand (Chris Baker and Pasuk Phongpaichit; 2009)

Chronicle of Thailand: Headlines Since 1946 (edited by Nicholas Grossman; 2010)

1767

After a 14-month siege, the capital city of Ayuthaya is sacked by the Burmese, bringing an end to the kingdom.

1768

Thai Chinese King Taksin founds a new capital in Thonburi and re-establishes Thai supremacy following the sack of Ayuthaya.

1782

The Chakri dynasty is founded with Bangkok as the new capital. King Rama I is ruler and his lineage continues to hold the throne to this day.

1826

King Rama III signs a treaty with Britain to fight with it against the Burmese.

rival. Burmese troops laid siege to the capital for a year before destroying it in 1767. The city was devastated, its buildings and people wiped out. The surrounding areas were deserted. So chilling was this historic sacking and razing of Ayuthaya that the perception of the Burmese as ruthless foes and aggressors still persists in the minds of many Thais to this day.

In 1868 King Mongkut (Rama IV) abolished a husband's right to sell his wife or her children without her permission. The older provision, it was said, treated the woman 'as if she were a water buffalo'.

The Bangkok Era

With Ayuthaya in ruins, the royal line of succession was broken and chaos ensued. A former general, Taksin, claimed his right to rule, handily defeating potential rivals, and established his new capital in Thonburi, a settlement downriver from Ayuthaya with better access to trade. Consolidating his power, King Taksin, the son of a Chinese father and Thai mother, strongly promoted trade with China.

The king was deposed in 1782 by the military. One of the coup organisers, Chao Phraya Chakri, assumed the throne as Phraphutthayotfa Chulalok (r 1782–1809; posthumously known as Rama I) and established the Chakri dynasty, which still rules today. The new monarch moved the capital across the Chao Phraya River to modern-day Bangkok.

The first century of Bangkok rule focused on rebuilding what had been lost when Ayuthaya was sacked. Surviving knowledge and practices were preserved or incorporated into new laws, manuals of government practice, religious and historical texts, and literature. At the same time, the new rulers transformed their defence activities into expansion by means of war, extending their influence in every direction. Destroying the capital cities of both Laos and Cambodia, Siam contained Burmese aggression and made a vassal of Chiang Mai. Defeated populations were resettled and played an important role in increasing the rice production of Siam, much of which was exported to China.

Unlike the Ayuthaya rulers, who identified with the Hindu god Vishnu, the Chakri kings positioned themselves as defenders of Buddhism.

FRIENDS OF THE KING

In the 1680s many foreign emissaries were invited to Ayuthaya by King Narai, who was keen to acquire and adopt foreign goods, culture and ideas. His court placed orders for spyglasses, hourglasses, paper, walnut trees, cheese, wine and marble fountains. He joined the French Jesuits to observe the eclipse at his palace in Lopburi and received a gift of a globe from France's King Louis XIV.

In the 1680s, Narai recruited the services of the Greek adventurer Constantine Phaulkon, who was later accused of conspiring to overthrow the ailing king. Instead, the accusers led a coup and executed Constantine.

1851–68

The reign of King Mongkut (Rama IV) ushers in a period of Western influence. The king moves to modernise the country and integrates it into the world market of the day.

1855

The Bowring Treaty between Siam and Britain stimulates the Thai economy by granting extraterritorial rights to British subjects in Siam and liberalising trade rules and regulations.

1868–1910

King Chulalongkorn (Rama V) reigns and continues replacing the old political order with the model of the nation state. European imperialism increases in neighbouring countries.

1874

Slavery and the state labour system that had been in place since the Ayuthaya period is abolished. A salaried bureaucracy, police force and army are created.

They undertook compilations and Thai translations of essential Buddhist texts and constructed many royal temples.

By the mid-19th century, a new social order and market economy was taking shape. Siam turned to the West for modern scientific and technological ideas and reforms in education, infrastructure and legal systems. One of the great modernisers, King Mongkut (Rama IV) never expected to be king. Before his ascension he had spent 27 years in a monastery, founding the Thammayut sect based on the strict disciplines of the Mon monks he had followed. During his monastic career, he became proficient in Pali, Sanskrit, Latin and English and studied Western sciences.

During Mongkut's reign, from 1851 to 1868, Siam concluded treaties with Western powers that integrated the kingdom into the world market system, ceded royal monopolies and granted extraterritorial rights to British subjects.

Mongkut's son, King Chulalongkorn (Rama V), who ruled between 1868 and 1910, was to take much greater steps in replacing the old political order with the model of the nation-state. He abolished slavery and the corvée system (state labour), which had lingered on ineffectively since the Ayuthaya period. Chulalongkorn's reign oversaw the creation of a salaried bureaucracy, a police force and a standing army. His reforms brought uniformity to the legal code, law courts and revenue offices. Siam's agricultural output was improved by advances in irrigation techniques and increasing peasant populations. Schools were established along European lines. Universal conscription and poll taxes made all men the king's men.

In 'civilising' his country, Chulalongkorn relied greatly on foreign advisers, mostly British. Within the royal court, much of the centuries-old protocol was abandoned and replaced by Western forms. The architecture and visual art of state, like the new throne halls, were designed by Italian artists.

Like his father, Chulalongkorn was regarded as a skilful diplomat and is credited with successfully playing European powers off one another to avoid colonisation. In exchange for independence, Thailand ceded territory to French Indochina (Laos in 1893 and Cambodia in 1907) and British Burma (three Malayan states in 1909). In 1902 the former Pattani kingdom was ceded to the British, who were then in control of Malaysia, but control reverted to Thailand seven years later. Many residents of the Deep South continue to regard Thailand as a colonial power occupying their land.

Siam was becoming a geographically defined country in a modern sense. By 1902 the country no longer called itself Siam but Prathet Thai (the country of the Thai) or Ratcha-anachak Thai (the kingdom of the Thai). By 1913 all those living within its borders were defined as 'Thai'.

Chulalongkorn (Rama V) enjoys a cult-like devotion due in part to the endearing photographs of him in European dress, ordinary farmer garb or military pomp. He defied tradition by allowing himself to be seen in public by his subjects and having his image widely disseminated.

Landmarks of the Bangkok Era

Wat Arun

Wat Phra Kaew and Grand Palace

Dusit Palace Park

1893

The French blockade the Chao Phraya River over disputed Indochina territory. Bangkok is forced to cede the territory to France, strengthening French influence in the region.

1909

The Anglo–Siamese Treaty sets Siam's southern border, giving it Yala, Pattani and Narathiwat from the former Pattani sultanate. Lands further south later become part of the Unfederated Malay States.

1913

King Vajiravudh requires all citizens to adopt surnames unique to their family. Before this time most Thais used only a first name.

1916

The first Thai university, Chulalongkorn University, is established by King Vajiravudh. Even today diplomas are handed out by members of the royal family.

Democracy vs Military

In 1932 a group of young military officers and bureaucrats calling themselves Khana Ratsadon (People's Party) mounted a successful, bloodless coup that marked the end of absolute monarchy and introduced a constitutional monarchy. The leaders of the group were inspired by the democratic ideology they had encountered during their studies in Europe.

In the years after the coup, rival factions (royalist, military and civilian) struggled for the upper hand in the new regime. Even the People's Party was not unified in its vision of a democratic Thailand, and before general elections were held the military wing of the party seized control of the government. The leader of the civilian wing of the People's Party, Pridi Phanomyong, a French-educated lawyer, was forced into exile in 1933 after introducing a socialist-leaning economic plan that angered the military generals. King Prajadhipok (Rama VII) abdicated in 1935 and retired to Britain. Thailand's first general election was held in 1937 for half of the seats in the People's Assembly, the newly instated legislative body. General Phibul Songkhram, one of the leaders of the military faction of the People's Party, became prime minister, a position he held from 1938 to 1944 and again from 1948 to 1957.

Phibul's regime coincided with WWII and was characterised by strong nationalistic tendencies centring on 'nation' and 'Thai-ness'. He collaborated with the Japanese and allowed them to use Thailand as a staging ground for its invasion of other Southeast Asian nations. By siding with the Japanese, the Phibul government hoped to gain international

Prime Minister Phibul Songkhram changed the name of the country in 1939 from 'Siam' to 'Prathet Thai' (or 'Thailand' in English); it was considered an overt nationalistic gesture intended to unite all the Tai-speaking people.

LIBERAL COUNTERWEIGHT

Pridi Phanomyong (1900–83) was a French-educated lawyer and a civilian leader in the 1932 revolution and the People's Party. His work on democratic reforms in Thailand was based on constitutional measures and attempts to restrict by law military involvement in Thai politics. He supported nationalisation of land and labour, state-led industrialisation and labour protection. In 1934 he founded Thammasat University. He also served as the figurehead of Seri Thai (the resistance movement against WWII Japanese occupation of Thailand) and was Thailand's prime minister (1946).

Though acknowledged as a senior statesman, Pridi Phanomyong was a controversial figure and a major foe of Phibul and the military regimes. He was accused of being a communist by his critics and forced out of the country under suspicion of regicide following the mysterious death of King Ananda Mahidol. Since the thawing of the Cold War, his legacy has been re-examined and recognised for its democratic efforts and the counterbalancing effects it had on military interests. He was named one of Unesco's great personalities of the 20th century in 2000.

1917

Siam sends troops to join the Allies in WWI in hopes of gaining favour with the French and British, thus protecting the country's sovereignty.

1924

Don Mueang International Airport (opened as a military base in 1914) welcomes its first commercial flight, opening the country to nonmilitary air travel.

1932

A bloodless coup ends absolute monarchy and puts in place a constitutional monarchy. Leaders of the coup are inspired by democratic ideology learned from studies in Europe.

1935

King Prajadhipok abdicates. The government chooses Prince Mahidol as his successor.

leverage and reclaim historical territory lost during France's expansion of Indochina. Thailand intended to declare war on the USA and Britain during WWII. But Seni Pramoj, the Thai ambassador in Washington and a member of Seri Thai (the Thai Liberation Movement), refused to deliver the formal declaration of war, and thus saved Thailand from bearing the consequences of defeated-nation status. Phibul was forced to resign in 1944 and was tried for war crimes.

In an effort to suppress pro-royalist sentiments, Ananda Mahidol, the nephew of the abdicated king, was crowned Rama VIII in 1935, though he was only 10 years old and spent much of his childhood studying abroad. After returning to Thailand, he was shot dead under mysterious circumstances in his bedroom in 1946. In the same year, his brother, His Majesty Bhumibol Adulyadej (pronounced *poomípon adunyádèt*) was appointed the ninth king of the Chakri dynasty, going on to become the longest-reigning monarch in Thai history until his death in October 2016.

For a brief period after the war, democracy flourished: full elections for the National People's Assembly were held, and the 1946 Constitution sought to reduce the role of the military and provide more democratic rights. It lasted until the death of King Ananda, the pretext the military used to return to power with Phibul at the helm.

Military Dictatorships

In 1957 Phibul's successor, General Sarit Thanarat, subjected the country to a military dictatorship: abolishing the constitution, dissolving the parliament and banning political parties. From the 1950s, the US directly involved itself in Southeast Asia to contain communist expansion in the region. During the Cold War, the USA government gave economic and military support to the Sarit government and continued that relationship with subsequent military dictators, Thanom Kittikachorn and Praphat Charusathien, who ruled from 1964 to 1973. They negotiated a package of economic deals with the USA in exchange for allowing the US military to establish bases in Thailand to support the Vietnam War.

By 1973 an opposition group of left-wing activists, mainly intellectuals and students, along with peasants, workers and portions of the middle class, organised political rallies demanding a constitution from the military government. On 14 October that year, the military suppressed a large demonstration in Bangkok, killing 77 people and wounding more than 800. The event is commemorated by a monument on Th Ratchadamnoen Klang in Bangkok, near the Democracy Monument. King Bhumibol stepped in and refused to support further bloodshed, forcing Thanom and Praphat to leave Thailand.

A brief period of unstable democracy followed the events of 1973, with the increasingly radical student movement creating fears of home-grown

The Democrat Party (Phak Prachathipat), founded in 1946, is now the longest-surviving political party in Thailand.

1939

The country's English name is officially changed from Siam to Thailand to align the name more closely with the majority ethnic group.

1941

Japanese forces enter Thailand during WWII, using the country for access to invade British Malaya and Burma. Japanese pressure leads to Thailand signing an alliance with Japan.

1945

WWII ends; Thailand cedes seized territory from Laos, Cambodia and Malaysia that it gained from the French and British during the war.

1946

King Bhumibol Adulyadej (Rama IX) ascends the throne and will become the longest reigning monarch in Thai history. Thailand joins the UN.

communism among many Thais. In 1976 Thanom returned to Thailand (ostensibly to become a monk) and was received warmly by the royal family. In response, protestors organised demonstrations at Thammasat University against the perceived perpetrator of the 14 October massacre. Right-wing, anti-communist civilian groups clashed violently with students. In the aftermath, many students and intellectuals were forced underground, and joined armed communist insurgents – known as the People's Liberation Army of Thailand (PLAT) – based in the jungles of northern and southern Thailand.

Military control of the country continued through the 1980s. The government of the 'political soldier', General Prem Tinsulanonda, enjoyed a period of political and economic stability. Prem dismantled the communist insurgency through military action and amnesty programs. But the country's new economic success created challenging rivals: prominent business leaders who criticised the military's role in government and their now-dated Cold War mentality. Communists, they maintained, should be business partners, not enemies.

It's Just Business

In 1988 Prem was replaced in fair elections by Chatichai Choonhavan, leader of the Chat Thai Party, who created a government dominated by well-connected provincial business people. His government shifted power away from the bureaucrats and set about transforming Thailand into an 'Asian Tiger' economy. But the business of politics was often bought and sold like a commodity and in February 1991 Chatichai was overthrown by the military on grounds of extreme corruption. This coup marked an emerging trend in Thai politics: the Bangkok business community and educated classes siding with the military against Chatichai, his provincial business-politicians and their money politics approach to governance.

In 1992, after reinstating elections, Suchinda Kraprayoon, the head of the Royal Thai Army, inserted himself as prime minister. This was met with popular resistance and the ensuing civilian–military clash was dubbed 'Black May'. Led by former Bangkok governor and major general, Chamlong Srimuang, around 200,000 protestors (called the 'mobile phone mob', representing their rising urban affluence) launched a mass demonstration against the military rulers in Bangkok that resulted in three nights of violence with armed soldiers. On the night of 20 May, King Bhumibol called an end to the violence.

After Black May, a new wave of democracy activists advocated for constitutional reforms. For most of the 1990s, the parliament was dominated by the Democrat Party, which represented the urban middle class and business interests. Its major base of support came from the southern Thai population centres. Formerly port towns, these were now

1957

Sarit Thanarat leads a coup that introduces military rule, which lasts until 1973. The constitution is abolished, parliament is dissolved and political parties are banned.

1959

Thailand's first tourism authority is created. The first overseas office opens in New York in 1965 and a regional office opens in Chiang Mai in 1968.

1965

Thailand hosts US military bases during the Vietnam War under a 'gentlemen's agreement'. Around 80% of US air strikes in North Vietnam will originate from Thailand.

1968

Thailand is a founding member of the Association of Southeast Asian Nations (ASEAN), designed to promote regional economic growth, social progress, peace and stability.

dominated by tourism and exports (rubber, tin and fishing). On the other side of the spectrum were the former pro-military politicians based in the central plains and the people of the agrarian northeast in new provincial towns who focused on state-budget distribution to their provinces. These political lines exist today.

In 1997 the boom years went bust and the Asian economic crisis unfolded. The country's economy was plagued by foreign-debt burdens, an over-extension in the real-estate sector and a devalued currency. Within months of the crisis, the Thai currency plunged from 25B to 56B per US$1. The International Monetary Fund stepped in to impose financial and legal reforms and economic liberalisation programs in exchange for more than US$17 billion to stabilise the Thai currency.

In the aftermath of the crisis, the Democrats returned to power uncontested, but were viewed as ineffective as the economy worsened.

Thaksinocracy

The economic slump began to ease in 2000 and business interests eclipsed the military as the dominant political force in Thai politics. Telecommunications billionaire and former police officer Thaksin Shinawatra, through his Thai Rak Thai (TRT or 'Thai Loving Thai') party, capitalised on this rising nationalism and won a majority in the elections of 2001. Self-styled as a CEO-politician, Thaksin swiftly delivered on his campaign promises for rural development, including agrarian debt relief, village capital funds and cheap health care.

Thanks to the 1997 constitutional reforms designed to strengthen the prime minister's position, Thaksin's government was one of the most stable in Thai history. The surging economy and his bold, if strong-arm, leadership won an outright majority in 2005, effectively introducing one-party rule. His popularity among the working class and rural voters was immense.

In 2006 Thaksin was accused of abusing his powers and of conflicts of interest, most notably in his family's sale of their Shin Corporation to the Singaporean government for 73 billion baht (US$1.88 billion), a tax-free gain thanks to telecommunications legislation that he had helped craft. Demonstrations in Bangkok called for him to be ousted, and on 19 September 2006 the military staged a bloodless coup that forced Thaksin into exile. The TRT party was dissolved by court order and party executives were barred from politics for five years. As promised, the interim government held general elections in December, returning the country to civilian rule, but the outcome was unsatisfactory to the military and the Bangkok upper and middle classes when Thaksin's political allies won a majority and formed a government led by Samak Sundaravej.

Demonstrations against the Thaksin-aligned government were led by Chamlong Srimuang (a Black May activist and former Bangkok governor)

Thaksin was the first prime minister in Thai history to complete a four-year term of office. His sister Yingluck managed three years before being deposed in a coup.

1973

Thai students, workers and farmers force the military government led by Thanom Kittikachorn to step down.

1976

The violent suppression of a student movement by the military ends a brief period of unstable democracy.

1979

After three years of military rule, elections and parliament are restored. Thai authorities give safe haven to Khmer Rouge fleeing the North Vietnamese invasion of Cambodia.

1980

Prem Tinsulanonda's government works to undermine the communist insurgency movement with military action and amnesty programs, and eventually ends it with a political solution.

and Sondhi Limthongkul (a long-time business and political rival of Thaksin). Their group, the People's Alliance for Democracy (PAD), earned the nickname 'Yellow Shirts' because they wore yellow (the king's birthday colour) to express their royalist allegiances; it was believed that Thaksin was so successfully consolidating power during his tenure that he had designs on the throne or at least planned to interrupt the royal succession.

Samak Sundaravej was unseated by the Constitutional Court in September 2008 on a technicality: while in office, he hosted a TV cooking show that the court found to be a conflict of interest. Still not politically satisfied, the Yellow Shirts seized control of Thailand's main airports, Suvarnabhumi and Don Mueang, for a week in November 2008 until the military engineered a silent coup and another favourable court ruling that further weakened Thaksin's political proxies. Through last-minute coalition building, Democrat Abhisit Vejjajiva was elected in a parliamentary vote, becoming Thailand's 27th prime minister.

Thaksin supporters organised their own counter-movement, the United Front for Democracy Against Dictatorship, better known as the 'Red Shirts'. Supporters hail mostly from the north and northeast, and include anti-coup, pro-democracy activists as well as die-hard Thaksin fans. There is a degree of class struggle, with some Red Shirts expressing animosity towards the aristocrats. The Red Shirts' most provocative demonstration came in 2010 when Thailand's Supreme Court ordered the seizure of US$46 billion of Thaksin's assets after finding him guilty of abusing his powers as prime minister. Red Shirts occupied Bangkok's central shopping district for two months and demanded the dissolution of the government and reinstatement of elections. Protest leaders and the government were unable to reach a compromise and in May 2010 the military used force to evict the protesters, resulting in bloody clashes (91 people were killed) and a smouldering central city, with damage estimated at US$15 billion.

A general election was held in 2011, and Thaksin's politically allied Pheu Thai party won a parliamentary majority. Thaksin's sister, Yingluck Shinawatra, became Thailand's first female prime minister and the country's youngest-ever premier. Widely seen as a proxy for her brother, demonstrations against the government began to intensify, until by late 2013 parts of central Bangkok were occupied by protesters demanding that Yingluck step down.

In May 2014, following a series of violent clashes that left 28 people dead, Yingluck was forced to stand down. A caretaker government was appointed, only for the Thai military to declare martial law on 20 May. Two days later, the military seized control of the country in Thailand's 13th coup since 1932. General Prayuth Chan-o-cha became the leader of the National Council for Peace and Order (NCPO), the name the junta

1988

Chatichai Choonhavan becomes the first elected PM since 1976 and creates a government dominated by well-connected provincial business people.

1991–92

General Suchinda attempts to seize power due to the extreme corruption of Chatichai's government; King Bhumibol intervenes to halt civil turmoil surrounding 'Black May' protests.

1997

The Asian economic crisis hits and a historic 'people's constitution' is passed. The International Monetary Fund steps in to reform and stabilise the Thai currency.

2001

Self-styled CEO-politician Thaksin Shinawatra is elected prime minister. Campaign promises of rural development, agrarian debt and cheaper health care are quickly delivered.

has given its government, and immediately ordered a new constitution – Thailand's 20th in the last 80-odd years – to be drafted.

Since then, elections have been delayed repeatedly – the latest date is scheduled for November 2018 – while the new constitution has been finalised. On the surface, Thailand has remained calm, even when Yingluck fled into exile in August 2017 to avoid appearing in court to hear a judgement on corruption charges she claimed were politically motivated. Whoever wins the next election – Pheu Thai is expected to be the largest party in the lower house of parliament – will have to deal with an upper house appointed entirely by the military and a 20-year, NCPO-drafted reform plan that any government is legally obliged to follow. Those restrictions will severely limit the power of the next administration and ensure that the army will continue to be a major player in Thai politics.

On 26 December 2004, the deadliest tsunami in recorded history rolled across the Indian Ocean, killing an estimated 5000 people and injuring a further 9000 in Southern Thailand alone. The region is now back to normal, with tsunami evacuation signs at beaches one of the few reminders of the tragedy that occurred here.

Troubles in the Deep South

Since 2001 ethnic Malay Muslim separatists have been waging a low-level insurgency in Thailand's southernmost provinces of Pattani, Narathiwat and Yala. These three provinces once comprised the historic sultanate of Pattani until it was conquered by the Chakri kings. Under King Chulalongkorn, the traditional ruling elite was replaced with central government officials and bureaucrats from Bangkok. During WWII a policy of nation-building set out to transform the multi-ethnic society into a unified and homogenous Thai Buddhist nation. This policy was resisted in the Deep South and gave birth to a strong separatist movement fighting for the independence of Pattani. In the 1980s and '90s, the assimilation policy was abandoned and then-prime minister Prem promised support for Muslim cultural rights and religious freedoms. He also offered amnesty to the armed insurgents and implemented an economic development plan for the historically impoverished region.

The Thaksin regime took another approach to the region. Greater central control was exerted; this was viewed as a thinly disguised attempt to break up the traditional stronghold of the Democrat Party. But the policy did not take into consideration the sensitive and tenacious Muslim culture of the Deep South. In 2002, the government dissolved the long-standing joint civilian-police-military border security office – a unit often lauded for maintaining peace and stability and providing a communication link between the Thai government and the southern Muslims. In its place the Thai provincial police assumed control of security. In 2004, the government responded harshly to demonstrations and at least 180 Muslims, many of them unarmed civilians, were killed. In 2005, martial law was declared in the area.

After more than a decade of violence, there is no end in sight to the conflict. Peace talks continue to be held sporadically, but with neither

2003

The Government stages a huge, controversial crackdown on drugs, during which some 2500 people are killed. Human-rights groups blame the government; the government blames gangs.

2004

The Indian Ocean tsunami kills 5000 people and damages tourism and fishing industries; a Muslim insurgency reignites in the Deep South after brewing steadily since 2001.

2006

King Bhumibol celebrates his 60th year on the throne; the Thaksin government is overthrown in a coup and prime minister forced into exile. Thaksin's allies win the following elections.

2008

Yellow Shirt, anti-Thaksin, pro-royalist activists seize Bangkok's international airports, causing a weeklong shutdown.

side apparently willing to compromise and a deep-seated lack of trust between them, few observers are optimistic. Some form of autonomy for the Deep South is probably the only realistic way forward, but successive Thai governments have been unwilling to contemplate the prospect of loosening their grip over the region.

One of the junta's first actions after seizing power in the 2014 coup was to announce a crackdown on crime and vice. In Phuket, that resulted in deploying the army to evict unlicensed food stands, massage joints and hawkers from the beaches. These days there is less commercial activity on Phuket's beaches, but many vendors have simply moved locations.

Contemporary Politics

Government

Much of the political drama that has unfolded over the last decade involves a long-standing debate about how to structure Thailand's legislative body and, ultimately, who gets greater control. The National Assembly (or parliament of Thailand) currently has 650 members divided into two chambers (House of Representatives and the Senate). Seats for the House of Representatives are directly elected, but under Thailand's latest constitution the 250-seat Senate will be entirely appointed by the military. The idea is to restrict the power of any government, while maintaining the army's influence, so there is no repeat of the situation of the late 1990s, when direct elections to both the House of Representatives and the Senate enabled Thaksin Shinawatra and his Thai Rak Thai party to gain near complete control of the National Assembly.

When Thai voters go to the polls they cast a ballot for the constituency MP (member of parliament) and for their preferred party, the results of which are used to determine individual winners and proportional representation outcomes for the positions assigned by party vote.

The prime minister is the head of the government and is elected via legislative vote by the majority party. The NCPO, which took power in the 2014 coup, has suggested that in the future, an unelected prime minister can be installed.

Voting in Thailand is compulsory for all eligible citizens (over the age of 18), but members of the clergy are not allowed to vote. Voter turnout for national elections has steadily increased since the new millennium, a reflection of the way the various Thaksin governments have succeeded

SIGNS OF ELECTION

Preceding an election, Thai candidates paper the roadways and electricity poles with political billboards and signs. Traditional posters show the candidate posing seriously in an official uniform, but recent trends include ad-like approaches with catchy slogans and evocative imagery.

Residents complain about the signs' obstruction of traffic, but signmakers like the boost in business. All candidate posters are vulnerable to vandalism or theft, but the plastic ones are particularly desired as makeshift sunshades or roof patches.

2008

Cambodia successfully petitions Unesco to list Phra Wihan (known as Phrea Vihear in Cambodia) as a World Heritage Site, reigniting border tensions with Thailand.

2010

Red Shirt, pro-Thaksin activists occupy central Bangkok for two months demanding the dissolution of the government and reinstatement of elections; a military crackdown results in 91 deaths.

2011

The Puea Thai party wins the general election; Yingluck Shinawatra (Thaksin's younger sister) becomes Thailand's first female prime minister on a platform of reconciliation.

2012

More Yellow Shirt protests take place, culminating in a 10,000-strong march against Prime Minister Yingluck, whom protestors see as a puppet of ousted Prime Minister Thaksin.

in politicising the rural poor. Charges of vote-buying typically accompany every election. Anecdotally, local party leaders make their rounds through the villages handing out money for the promise of a vote. In some cases, villagers will accept money from competing parties and report that they have no loyalty at the ballot box.

The ballots include a 'no' vote if the voter wishes to choose 'none of the above'. It is also common to 'spoil' the ballot, or disqualify it, by writing on it or defacing it.

Media

Southeast Asian governments are not usually fond of uncensored media, but Thailand often bucked this trend during the 1990s, even ensuring press freedoms in its 1997 constitution, albeit with fairly broad loopholes. This ended with the ascension of Thaksin Shinawatra, a telecommunications billionaire, at the start of the 21st century. With Thaksin as prime minister and his party holding a controlling majority, the press encountered the kind of censorship and legal intimidation not seen since the 1970s era of military dictatorships. The government filed a litany of defamation lawsuits against individuals, publications and media groups who printed embarrassing revelations about the Thaksin regime.

After the 2006 ousting of Thaksin, the media managed to retain its guarantees of press freedoms in the new constitution, but this was a 'paper promise' that did little to rescue the press from intimidation, lawsuits and physical attacks. Sweeping powers to ensure national security, often invoked against the press, were added to the emergency powers laws that went into effect after the coup.

Following the 2014 coup, there has been a widespread crackdown on both the media and freedom of expression. In its immediate aftermath, 15 TV and radio stations were closed and 100 websites were blocked, while around 1000 people – academics, bloggers, journalists, students and opposition politicians – have been detained for various periods. The domestic media now self-censors its stories to avoid getting into trouble, and some websites, like the Thailand section of the Human Rights Watch website, remain blocked in Thailand.

There has also been a sharp rise in the number of people being prosecuted under the country's lèse-majesté laws – causing offence against the dignity of the monarchy – which are some of the strictest in the world. Critics accuse the army of using the laws to silence their political opponents. Recent cases have seen people receiving long prison sentences for posting comments on their Facebook pages and being jailed for appearing in a play said to have defamed the monarchy.

Thailand has had 20 constitutions, all rewritten following various military coups. The latest was signed by the king in April 2017, but has yet to become law. Each reincarnation seeks to allocate power within the branches of government with a bias for the ruling interest (military, royalist or civilian) and against its political foes.

2013

The International Court of Justice rules that Phra Wihan is part of Cambodia, although the area surrounding it and another 100km of border are still disputed.

2014

In May, the military launches its 13th coup since 1932, ousting Yingluck Shinawatra's Puea Thai government.

2016

King Bhumibol Adulyadej (Rama IX) dies on 13 October after 70 years on the throne. His son King Vajiralongkorn succeeds him as Rama X.

2017

Yingluck Shinawatra, the last democratically elected prime minister of Thailand, flees into exile in August to avoid appearing in court to hear a judgement on corruption charges.

People & Society

Thailand's cohesive national identity provides a unifying patina for ethnic and regional differences that evolved through historical migrations and geographic kinships with ethnically diverse neighbours.

Ethnic Makeup

Some 75% of the citizens of Thailand are ethnic Thais, providing a superficial appearance of sameness, but subtle regional differences do exist. In the central plains (Chao Phraya delta), Siamese Thais united the country through historic kingdoms and promulgated its culture and language. Today the central Thai dialect is the national standard and Bangkok exports unified culture through media and standardised education.

Southern (*pàk đâi;* often spelt *pàk tâi*) Thais define the characteristics of the south. The dialect is a little faster than standard Thai, the curries are spicier, and there is more mixing of Muslim folk beliefs into the regional culture thanks to the geographic proximity to Malaysia and the historic Muslim population.

Ethnic Malays make up around 3% of the Thai population, with most residing in the provinces of the Deep South. The remaining minority groups in the south include a smaller percentage of non-Thai-speaking Moken *(chow lair)*. A growing number of Europeans and other non-Asians reside in Thailand too.

Thai Chinese

People of Chinese ancestry – second- or third-generation Hakka, Teochew, Hainanese or Cantonese – make up 14% of the population, the world's largest overseas Chinese population. Bangkok and the nearby coastal areas have a large population of immigrants from China who came for economic opportunities in the early to mid-20th century. Historically wealthy Chinese introduced their daughters to the royal court as consorts, developing royal connections and adding a Chinese bloodline that extends to the current king.

INVISIBLE MIGRANTS

The people of Myanmar fled to Thailand in enormous numbers during the most oppressive years of the Myanmar state. Approximately 150,000 people have entered the kingdom as political and ethnic refugees, but the vast majority are economic migrants (estimated at around two to three million). They fill the low-level jobs – fish-processing, construction, and domestic and factory work – that used to employ unskilled northeastern Thai labourers.

In the south, most of the hotel and restaurant staff you meet day to day will likely be from Myanmar. Many Thais believe Thailand needs this imported workforce as the population is ageing faster than it is reproducing; others resent the influx. For their part, the people of Myanmar in southern Thailand complain of exploitative working conditions, especially in the fishing industry, and of being scapegoated for crimes.

The mercantile centres of most Thai towns are run by Thai-Chinese families and many places in the country celebrate Chinese festivals such as the annual Vegetarian Festival.

Chinese Buddhist temples, often highly colourful and displaying an allegiance to southern Chinese folklore and belief, are widespread, especially in the south. Temples to Mazu (Tianhou; Tienhau) – the Queen of Heaven and goddess of fisherfolk and those who make their living from the sea – are common and typical of the southern seaboard provinces of China, from where many Thai Chinese can trace their ancestors. You will also encounter temples to Guandi, colloquially known as the God of War and frequently red-faced, as well as a host of other Taoist deities, some deeply obscure. Guanyin – the Buddhist Chinese Goddess of Mercy – is also widely venerated by the Thai Chinese, as are other bodhisattvas who enjoy similar adoration throughout China. Chinese guildhalls and ancestral halls are also plentiful.

Thai Muslims

At around 5% of the population, Muslims make up Thailand's largest religious minority, living side by side with the Buddhist majority. Many of Thailand's Muslims reside in the south, but an ever greater number is scattered through the nation. Most of Thailand's southern Muslims are ethnically Malay and speak Malay or Yawi (a dialect of Malay written in the Arabic script) in addition to Thai. In northern Thailand there are also a substantial number of Chinese Muslims who emigrated from Yúnnán in the late 19th century.

Regional Identity

Religion, royalty and tradition are the defining characteristics of Thai society. Thailand is the only country in Southeast Asia never colonised by a foreign power and this has led to a profound sense of pride. However, the country is not homogenous, and in the south a strong cultural identity prevails that is more in tune with the Islamic culture of Malaysia across the border.

Before modern political boundaries divided the Malay peninsula into two countries, the city-states, sultanates and villages were part of an Indonesian-based Srivijaya empire – with intermingled customs and language – all vying for local control over shipping routes. Many southern Thai towns and geographic names bear the hallmark of the Bahasa language, and some village traditions would be instantly recognised by a Sumatran but not by a northern Thai. Chinese culture is also prominent in southern Thailand, as seen in the numerous temples and clan houses along with the often widespread appearance of Chinese writing on shopfronts. It is this intermingling of domestic and 'foreign' culture that defines the south.

Lifestyle

The ordinary life of southern Thais can be divided into two categories: country and city.

Those in rural coastal areas are typically employed in rubber farming or fishing, though rice and livestock farming are also evident. Rubber farmers live in small, typically inland settlements identified by straight rows of trees and pale sheets of drying latex; many islands on the Andaman Coast are dotted with these shady rubber forests. Traditional Muslim villages are built directly over the water in a series of connected stilt houses. Because the Andaman Sea had a history of tranquil behaviour, there was no fear of the ocean's wrath, a preconception painfully destroyed by the 2004 tsunami.

Within the cities, life looks a lot like the rest of the country (busy and modern), but the presence of Chinese and Indian merchants marks the

Lifestyle Statistics

Average age of marriage for a Thai man/woman: 27/24 years

Minimum daily wage in Bangkok: 300B

Entry-level professional salary: 12,000B per month

Instead of a handshake, the traditional Thai greeting is the *wâi* – a prayerlike gesture with the palms placed together.

SAVING FACE

Thais believe strongly in the concept of saving face, ie avoiding confrontation and endeavouring not to embarrass themselves or other people (except when it's *sà·nùk* – or 'fun' – to do so). The ideal face-saver doesn't bring up negative topics in conversation, doesn't express firm convictions or opinions, and doesn't claim to have an expertise. Agreement and harmony are considered to be the most important social graces.

While Westerners might find a heated discussion to be good sport, Thais avoid such confrontations and regard any instance where voices are raised as rude and potentially volatile. Losing your temper causes a loss of face for everyone present, and Thais who have been crossed often react in extreme ways.

Minor embarrassments, such as tripping or falling, might elicit giggles from a crowd of Thais. In this case they aren't taking delight in your mishap, but helping you save face by laughing it off.

uniqueness of southern Thai cities. The commercial centres are also the market towns, where the brightly coloured fishing boats ease into the harbour, unloading the catch and filling the marina with the aroma of fish.

Family Values

There is no universally accepted method of transliterating from Thai to English, so some words and place names are spelt a variety of ways.

The importance of the family unit in Thai society is immediately apparent to a visitor in the many family-owned and -operated businesses. It is still common to see three generations employed in a family-run guesthouse, or sharing the same house. The elderly are involved in day-to-day life, selling sweets to neighbourhood kids or renting motorcycles to tourists, for example. Although tourism has significantly altered the islanders' traditional way of life, these jobs help to keep many ambitious children from seeking employment on the mainland, resulting in a secure family unit.

Religion

Buddhism

Approximately 93% of Thais follow Theravada Buddhism, also known as Hinayana or 'Lesser Vehicle' Buddhism to distinguish it from the Mahayana or 'Great Vehicle' school of Buddhism. The primary difference between the faiths is that Theravada Buddhists believe individuals are responsible for their own enlightenment, while Mahayana Buddhists believe in putting the salvation of others over one's own.

The ultimate end of all forms of Buddhism is to reach *nibbana* (from Sanskrit, nirvana), which literally means the 'blowing out' or extinction of all desire and thus of all *dukkha* (suffering). Having achieved *nibbana*, an individual is freed from the cycle of rebirths and enters the spiritual plane. In reality, most Thai Buddhists aim for rebirth in a 'better' existence in the next life, rather than striving to attain *nibbana*. To work towards this goal, Buddhists carry out meritorious actions *(tam bun)* such as feeding monks, giving donations to temples and performing regular worship at the local wát (temple). The Buddhist theory of karma is well expressed in the Thai proverb *'tam dee, dâi dee; tam chôo·a, dâi chôo·a'* (do good and receive good; do evil and receive evil).

There is no specific day of worship in Thai Buddhism; instead the faithful go to temple on certain religious holidays, when it is convenient or to commemorate a special family event. Most temple visits occur on *wan prá* (holy days), which occur four times a month, according to phases of the moon. Other activities include offering food to the temple *sangha* (community of monks and nuns), meditating, listening to monks chanting *suttas* (discourses of the Buddha) and attending talks on *dhamma* (right behaviour).

Islam

Thailand is home to 3.3 million Muslims (just under 5% of Thailand's population), the majority of whom are concentrated in the south of the country. Many Thai Muslims are of Malay origin and generally follow a moderate version of the Sunni sect mixed with pre-Islamic animism.

A decade-long revival movement has cultivated stricter Islamic practices and suspicions of outside influences. Under this stricter interpretation of Islam, many folk practices have been squeezed out of daily devotions and local people see the mainly Buddhist government and education system as intolerant of their way of life. Schools and infrastructure in the Muslim-majority south are typically underfunded and stick to the same curriculum as elsewhere (which means compulsory lessons about Buddhism), and frustration with the Bangkok government is sometimes defined as a religious rather than political struggle.

There are mosques throughout southern Thailand, but few are architecturally interesting and most are closed to women. If you do visit a mosque, remember to cover your head and remove your shoes.

Other Religions

About 1.2% of the population – primarily hill tribes converted by missionaries and Vietnamese immigrants – is Christian, while another half a per cent is made up of Confucians, Taoists, Mahayana Buddhists and Hindus. There is also a community of around 70,000 Sikhs. More primordial animist beliefs, which long predate Buddhism and Hinduism, survive most noticeably in 'spirit houses' – shrines that provide a residence for a plot of land's *prá poom* (guardian spirits) – but also in festivals such Loi Krathong, the origins of which reside in animist belief, honouring the spirit of the water.

Arts

Much of Thailand's creative energy has traditionally gone into the production of religious and ceremonial art. Painting, sculpture, music and theatre still play a huge role in the ceremonial life of Thais, and religious art is very much a living art form.

Architecture

The most striking aspect of Thailand's architectural heritage is its frequently magnificent Buddhist temples (wát). As with many Chinese Buddhist temple pagodas, one of the most distinctive features of Buddhist temple architecture is the *chedi* (stupa), a mountain-shaped monument that pays tribute to the enduring stability of Buddhism. Many contain relics of important kings or the historical Buddha, or the remains of notable monks or nuns. Thai temples freely mix different foreign influences, from the corn-shaped stupa inherited from the Khmer empire to the bell-shaped stupa of Sri Lanka.

Thai temples are replete with Hindu-Buddhist iconography. *Naga*, a mythical serpent-like creature who guarded Buddha during meditation, is often depicted in entrance railings and outlining roof gables. On the

THE NICKNAME GAME

At birth Thai babies are given auspicious first names, often bestowed by the family patriarch or matriarch. These poetic names are then relegated to bureaucratic forms and name cards, while the child is introduced to everyone else by a one-syllable nickname. Thai nicknames are usually playful and can be inspired by the child's appearance (Moo, meaning 'pig', if he/she is chubby) or a favourite pastime (Toon, short for 'cartoon', for avid TV-watchers). Girls are often named Lek or Noi (both of which mean 'small').

CHOW LAIR

Southern Thailand is home to one of Thailand's smallest ethnic groups, the *chow lair* (also spelt *chao leh;* literally, 'people of the sea' or 'sea gypsies'). Also known as Moken *(mor·gaan),* the *chow lair* are an ethnic group of Malay origin who are found along coasts as far north as Myanmar and as far south as Borneo. The remaining traditional bands of *chow lair* are hunter-gatherers who are recognised as one of the few groups of humans that live primarily at sea, although in recent years many have turned to shanty-like settlements on various islands. Perhaps as a result of generations of this marine lifestyle, many *chow lair* can hold their breath for long periods of time and also have an uncanny ability to see underwater. Life at sea has also helped them in other ways; during the 2004 tsunami, virtually no *chow lair* were killed, as oral history handed down from generation to generation alerted them to the dangers of the quickly receding tide, and they were able to escape to higher ground.

The *chow lair* were mostly ignored until the 1980s when their islands became valuable for tourism. Entrepreneurs bought up large tracts of beachfront land and the *chow lair* moved on to smaller, less valuable islands. With these pressures, it was perhaps inevitable that the *chow lair* culture would slowly be diminished. Many sea gypsies now make a living ferrying tourists around the islands or harvesting fish for seafood buffets at tourist resorts. One vestige of traditional *chow lair* life you may see is the biannual 'boat floating' ceremony in May and November, in which an elaborate model boat is set adrift, carrying away bad luck.

tip of the temple hall roof is the *chôr fáh:* a golden bird-shaped silhouette suggesting flight.

A venerated Buddhist symbol, the lotus bud is another sacred motif that often decorates the tops of temple gates, verandah columns and the spires of Sukhothai-era *chedi.* Images of the Buddha often depict him meditating on a lotus pedestal. It carries with it a reminder of the tenets of Buddhism: the lotus can bloom even from the mud of a rancid pond, illustrating the capacity for religious perfection in a defiled environment.

Thais began mixing traditional architecture with European forms in the late 19th and early 20th centuries. Maritime cities, including Bangkok and Phuket Town, acquired fine examples of Sino-Portuguese architecture – buildings of stuccoed brick decorated with an ornate facade – a style that followed the Portuguese sea traders during the colonial era. It is locally known as 'old Bangkok' or 'Ratanakosin'.

Top Non-fiction

Very Thai (Philip Cornwel-Smith; 2004) Colourful photos and essays on Thailand's quirks.

A Kingdom in Crisis: Thailand's Struggle for Democracy in the Twenty-First Century (Andrew MacGregor Marshall; 2014) Banned in Thailand, so read it before you go.

Bangkok Days (Lawrence Osborne; 2009) An amusing, well-written, Englishman's take on life in Bangkok.

Literature

The most pervasive and influential work of classical Thai literature is the *Ramakian,* based on the Hindu holy book, the *Ramayana,* which was brought to Southeast Asia by Indian traders and introduced to Thailand by the Khmer about 900 years ago. Although the main theme remains the same, the Thais embroidered the *Ramayana* by providing much more biographical detail on arch-villain Ravana (Thotsakan in the *Ramakian*) and his wife Montho. The monkey-god, Hanuman, is also transformed into something of a playboy.

The epic poem *Phra Aphai Mani* was composed by poet Sunthorn Phu (1786–1855) and is set on the island of Ko Samet. *Phra Aphai Mani* is Thailand's most famous classical literary work, and tells a typically epic story of an exiled prince.

The leading contemporary writer is Prabda Yoon, whose short-story collection *Probability* won the 2002 SEA Write award. Only one of his books is available in English, but he also works as a film-maker: he wrote the screenplay for the Pen-ek Ratanaruang–directed movies *Last Life in the Universe* and *Invisible Waves* and has directed one film himself. In 2004 Prabda was commissioned by Thailand's Ministry of Culture to write a piece on the 2004 tsunami. The result, *Where We Feel: A Tsunami Memoir by an Outsider,* was distributed free along the Andaman Coast.

Music

Traditional Thai music may sound a little strange to visitors, as the eight-note Thai octave is broken in different places to the European octave. Thai scales were first transcribed by Thai-German composer Phra Chen Duriyanga (Peter Feit), who also composed Thailand's national anthem in 1932.

The classical Thai orchestra is called the *pèe·pâht* and can include anything from five to 20 musicians. The most popular stringed instrument is the *ja·kêh,* a slender guitarlike instrument played horizontally on the ground. Woodwind instruments include the *klòo·i,* a simple wooden flute, and the *pèe,* a recorderlike instrument with a reed mouthpiece. You'll hear the *pèe* being played if you go to a Thai boxing match. Perhaps the most familiar Thai instrument is the *kĭm* (hammered dulcimer), responsible for the plinking, plunking music you'll hear in Thai restaurants across the world.

The contemporary Thai music scene is strong and diverse. The most popular genre is undoubtedly *lôok tûng* (a style analogous to country and western in the USA), which tends to appeal most to working-class Thais. The 1970s ushered in a new style dubbed *pleng pêu·a chee·wít* (literally 'music for life'), inspired by the politically conscious folk rock of the USA and Europe. The biggest modern Thai music icons are rock staple Carabao, pop star Thongchai 'Bird' McIntyre, sometimes controversial singer Tata Young and *lôok tûng* queen Pumpuang Duangchan, who died tragically young in 1992.

Today there are hundreds of youth-oriented Thai bands, from chirpy boy and girl bands to metal rockers, making music that is easy to sing along with and maddeningly hard to get out of your head.

Painting

Except for the prehistoric and historic cave paintings found in the south of the country, not much ancient formal painting exists in Thailand,

TRANSLATED THAI FICTION

Thai literature isn't often translated. Some modern works you may find in English include the following:

The Sad Part Was (Prabda Yoon; 2017) A playful short-story collection that satirises urban Thai life.

Pisat (Evil Spirits) (Seni Saowaphong; 1957) Deals with conflicts between the old and new generations.

Lai Chiwit (Many Lives; Kukrit Pramoj; translation 1996) A collection of short stories featuring the lives of 11 different Thais.

Monsoon Country (Pira Sudham; 1988) Brilliantly captures the northeast's struggles against nature and nurture.

The Judgement (Chart Korbjitti; 1981) A drama about a young village man wrongly accused of a crime.

Jasmine Nights (SP Somtow; 1994) An upbeat coming-of-age novel that fuses traditional ideas with modern Thai pop culture.

Married to the Demon King (Sri Doruang; 2004) Adapts the *Ramakian,* the Thai version of the Indian epic *Ramayana,* into modern Bangkok.

Several Thai novels and short stories translated by Marcel Barang, including stories by Chart Korbjitti and two-time SEA Write winner Win Lyovarin, can be downloaded as e-books at www.thaifiction.com.

partly due to the devastating Burmese invasion of 1767. The vast majority of what exists is religious in nature, and typically takes the form of temple paintings illustrating the various lives of the Buddha.

Since the 1980s boom years, Thai secular sculpture and painting have enjoyed increased international recognition, with a handful of Impressionism-inspired artists among the initial few to have reached this vaunted status. Succeeding this was the 'Fireball' school of artists, such as Manit Sriwanichpoom, who specialise in politically motivated, mixed-media art installations. In recent years Thai artists have again moved away from both traditional influences and political commentary and towards contemporary art, focusing on more personal themes, such as those seen in the gender-exploring works of Pinaree Sanpitak, or Maitree Siriboon's identity-driven work.

Arts Reading

The Thai House: History and Evolution (2002; Ruethai Chaichongrak)

The Arts of Thailand (1998; Steve Van Beek)

Flavours: Thai Contemporary Art (2005; Steven Pettifor)

Bangkok Design: Thai Ideas in Textiles & Furniture (2006; Brian Mertens)

Buddhist Temples of Thailand: A Visual Journey Through Thailand's 40 Most Historic Wats (2010; Joe Cummings)

The Roots of Thai Art (2012; Piriya Krairiksh)

Cinema

When it comes to Thai cinema, there are usually two concurrent streams: movies that are financially successful and films that are considered cinematically meritorious. Only rarely do the two successfully overlap.

Popular Thai cinema ballooned in the 1960s and '70s, especially when the government levied a tax on Hollywood imports, which kick-started a home-grown industry. The majority of films were cheap action flicks that were typically dubbed *nám nôw* (stinking water), but the fantastic (even nonsensical) plots and rich colours left a lasting impression on modern-day Thai film-makers.

Thai cinema graduated into international film circles in the late 1990s and early 2000s, thanks in part to the output of Pratt Institute–educated arthouse director and screenwriter Pen-Ek Ratanaruang and his gritty and engrossing oeuvre. His most recent film is *Samui Song* (2017), which follows a soap opera actress and her foreigner husband who has joined a cult. Apichatpong Weerasethakul is another critically acclaimed director; he has garnered three Cannes accolades, including the Palme d'Or (the festival's highest prize) for his *Uncle Boonmee Who Can Recall His Past Lives* (2010). His subsequent work, such as the horror-tinged *Cemetery of Splendour* (2015), is rather more mainstream.

International film festivals today play host to a new crop of experimental directors from Thailand. Nawapol Thamrongrattanarit gained acclaim for his modern-girl-in-the-city screenplay *Bangkok Traffic Love Story* (2009) and followed up with his directorial debut *36* (2012), which uses 36 static camera shots to explore lost love and lost memories. *Mary Is Happy, Mary Is Happy* (2013) is a film festival hit that adapted the Twitter feed of a Thai teen into a movie. His latest films include *Heart Attack* (2015) and the documentary *The Master* (2014).

Film-fest fare has been bolstered by independent film clubs and self-promotion through social media. This is how low-budget film-makers bypass the big studios, the ever-vigilant cinema censors and the skittish, controversy-averse movie theatres. In 2009 the film board introduced a rating system with seven classifications (including banned). Being censored may seem like the kiss of death, but it often guarantees indie success and cult status. Two political documentaries of 2013 challenged the board's sensitivities: Pen-ek's historical *Paradoxocracy* had to mute objectionable dialogue while Nontawat Numbenchapol's *Boundary* was initially banned, though that was lifted after an appeal. The Thai horror *Arbat* was banned in 2015 because it depicted 'misconduct' by Thai monks, which was considered a slur against Buddhism.

The big studios like ghost stories, horror flicks, historic epics, soppy love stories and camp comedies. Elaborate historical movies and epics serve a dual purpose: they can be lucrative and they promote national identity. Criticised as a propaganda tool, the *Legend of King Naresuan* epic focuses on the Ayuthaya-era king who repelled an attempted Burmese invasion. Each chapter (six have been released so far) has been a box-office winner.

Theatre & Dance

Traditional Thai theatre consists of four main dramatic forms: *kŏhn* is a formal masked dance-drama, traditionally reserved for royalty, depicting scenes from the *Ramakian; lá·kon* is dance-drama performed for common people; *lí·gair* is a partly improvised, often bawdy, folk play featuring dancing, comedy, melodrama and music; and *hùn lŏo·ang (lá·kon lék)* is traditional puppet theatre enacting religious legends or folk tales.

Most of these forms can be enjoyed in Bangkok, both at dinner shows for tourists and at formal theatrical performances. There are also some distinctively southern theatrical styles, predating the arrival of Islam on the Malay peninsula. The most famous is *má·noh·rah,* the oldest surviving Thai dance-drama, which tells the story of Prince Suthon, who sets off to rescue the kidnapped Manohraa, a *gin·ná·ree* (woman-bird) princess. As in *lí·gair,* performers add extemporaneous, comic rhymed commentary. Trang also has a distinctive form of *lí·gair,* with a storyline depicting Indian merchants taking their Thai wives back to India for a visit.

Another ancient theatrical style in the south is shadow-puppet theatre (also found in Indonesia and Malaysia), in which two-dimensional figures carved from buffalo hide are manipulated against an illuminated cloth screen. The capital of shadow puppetry today is Nakhon Si Thammarat, which has regular performances at its festivals. While sadly a dying art, puppets are popular souvenirs for tourists.

Economy

Thanks to tourism, fishing, prawn farming and rubber, the south is Thailand's wealthiest region. Most rubber tappers are born into the industry, inheriting the profession of their parents. Prawn and fish farming, on the other hand, are relatively new industries, introduced as an economic development program for rural communities losing ground to commercial fishing operations. The venture proved profitable and Thailand is now one of the leading exporters of farm-raised prawns. However, fish farms have been largely unregulated until recently, leading to a host of environmental problems, such as water pollution and the destruction of mangrove forests (p405).

Tourism has undoubtedly had the most tangible impact on the economy of the area, transforming many small villages into bilingual enterprises. Women who would otherwise sell products at market have studied Thai traditional massage. Other DIY franchises, so prolific in Thai communities, have been tailored to tourists: shops along beach thoroughfares sell sunscreen and postcards instead of rice whisky and grilled fish, itinerant vendors hawk sarongs and henna tattoos instead of feather dusters and straw brooms, while fishermen sometimes abandon their nets for bigger catches – tourists on snorkelling trips.

Across Thailand, the size of the middle class is growing, bridging the gap between rich and poor. The number of people living under the poverty line has been reduced from 67% in 1986 to just over 10% in 2017, and the average annual Thai income has risen to US$4900. Many people in rural areas, though, earn far less. Thailand doesn't suffer from poverty of sustenance; even the most destitute Thai citizens can have shelter and food. Rather, the lower rung of Thai society suffers from poverty of material: money isn't available for further education, material goods or health care.

Thailand Demographics

Population: 68.4 million

Fertility rate: 1.5 per woman

Percentage of people over 65: 11%

Urbanisation rate: 3%

Life expectancy: 74.7 years

The Sex Industry in Thailand

Thailand has had a long and complex relationship with prostitution that persists today. It is also an international sex tourism destination, a designation that began around the time of the Vietnam War. The industry targeted to foreigners is very visible, with multiple red-light districts in Bangkok alone, but there is also a more clandestine domestic sex industry and myriad informal channels of sex-for-hire.

Help stop child-sex tourism by reporting suspicious behaviour on a dedicated hotline (☎1300) or by reporting perpetrators directly to the embassy of their home country.

History & Cultural Attitudes

Prostitution has been widespread in Thailand since long before the country gained a reputation among international sex tourists. Throughout Thai history the practice was accepted and common among many sectors of society, though it has not always been respected by society as a whole.

Due to international pressure from the UN, prostitution was declared illegal in 1960, though venues (go-go bars, beer bars, massage parlours, karaoke bars and bathhouses) are governed by a separate law passed in 1966. These establishments are licensed and can legally provide non-sexual services (such as dancing, massage or a drinking buddy); sexual services occur through these venues but they are not technically the businesses' primary purpose.

With the arrival of the US military in Southeast Asia during the Vietnam War era, enterprising forces adapted the existing framework to suit foreigners, in turn creating an international sex tourism industry that persists today. Indeed, this foreigner-oriented sex industry is still a prominent part of Thailand's tourist economy.

In 1998 the International Labour Organization, a UN agency, advised Southeast Asian countries, including Thailand, to recognise prostitution as an economic sector and income generator. It is estimated that one third of the entertainment establishments are registered with the government and the majority pay an informal tax in the form of police bribes.

PROS & CONS

Women's rights groups take oppositional approaches to the issue of prostitution. Abolitionists see prostitution as exploitation and an infraction of basic human rights. Meanwhile, mitigators recognise that there is demand and supply, and try to reduce the risks associated with the activity through HIV/AIDS prevention and education programs (especially for economic migrants). Sex-worker organisations argue that prostitution is a legitimate job and the best way to help women is to treat the issue from a workers' rights perspective, demanding fair pay and compensation, legal redress and mandatory sick and holiday time. Also, according to pro-sex-worker unions, the country's quasi-legal commercial sex establishments provide service-industry jobs (dishwashers, cooks, cleaners) to non-sex-worker staff, who would otherwise qualify for employment protection if the employer were a restaurant or a hotel.

Economic Motivations

Regardless of their background, most women in the sex industry are there for financial reasons: for many sex work is one of the highest-paying jobs for their level of education particularly if they have financial obligations (be it dependants or debts).

The International Labour Organization estimates a Thai sex workers' salary at 270B (US$9) a day, the average wage of a Thai service-industry worker. These economic factors provide a strong incentive for rural, unskilled women (and, to a lesser extent, men) to engage in sex work.

As with many workers in Thai society, a large percentage of sex workers' wages are remitted back to their home villages to support their families (parents, siblings and children).

Organisations working across borders to stop child prostitution include Ecpat (End Child Prostitution & Trafficking; www.ecpat.org) and its Australian affiliate Child Wise (www.childwise.org.au).

An Illegal (and Vast) Industry

Prostitution is technically illegal in Thailand. However, anti-prostitution laws are often ambiguous and unenforced. Some analysts have argued that the high demand for sexual services in Thailand limits the likelihood of the industry being curtailed; however, limiting abusive practices within the industry is the goal of many activists and government agencies.

It is difficult to determine the number of sex workers in Thailand, the demographics of the industry or its economic significance. This is because there are many indirect forms of prostitution, the illegality of the industry makes research difficult and different organisations use varying approaches to collect data. In 2003 measures to legalise prostitution cited the Thai sex industry as being worth US$4.3 billion (about 3% of GDP) and employing roughly 200,000 sex workers. A study conducted in 2003 by Thailand's Chulalongkorn University estimated 2.8 million sex workers, of which 1.98 million were adult women, 20,000 were adult men and 800,000 were children, defined as any person under the age of 18.

The Coalition Against Trafficking in Women (CATW; www.catwinternational.org) is an NGO that works internationally to combat prostitution and trafficking in women and children.

Child Prostitution & Human Trafficking

Urban job centres such as Bangkok have large populations of displaced and marginalised people (immigrants from Myanmar, ethnic hill-tribe members and impoverished rural Thais). Children of these fractured families often turn to street begging, which is a pathway to prostitution, often through low-level criminal gangs. According to a number of reports conducted by different research bodies, there are an estimated 60,000 to 800,000 children involved in prostitution in Thailand.

In 1996 Thailand passed a reform law to address the issue of child prostitution (defined by two tiers: 15 to 18 years old and under 15 years old). Fines and jail time are imposed on customers, establishment owners and even parents involved in child prostitution (under the old law only prostitutes were culpable). Many countries also have extraterritorial legislation that allows nationals to be prosecuted in their own country for such crimes committed in Thailand.

Thailand is also a conduit and destination for people-trafficking (including child-trafficking) from Myanmar, Laos, Cambodia and China. As stated by the UN, human trafficking is a crime against humanity and involves recruiting, transporting, harbouring and receiving a person through force, fraud or coercion for purposes of exploitation. In 2015 the US State Department labelled Thailand as a Tier 3 country, meaning that it does not comply with the minimum standards for prevention of human-trafficking and is not making significant efforts to do so.

Created by a sex workers' advocacy group, **This Is Us** (☎02 526 1294; www.empowerfoundation.org/index_en.html) is a museum that leads visitors through the history and working conditions of sex workers in Thailand.

Environment

Bound to the east by the Gulf of Thailand and to the west by the Andaman Sea, an extension of the Indian Ocean, Thailand possesses one of the most alluring coastlines in the world, with exquisitely carved limestone formations above water and tremendously rich coral reefs below. Hundreds of tropical islands of all shapes and sizes adorn the coast, from flat sandbars covered in mangroves to looming karst massifs licked by azure waters and ringed by white-sand beaches.

The Land

Thailand's odd shape – bulky and wide up north, with a long pendulous arm draping to the south – has often been compared to the head of an elephant. With an area of 517,000 sq km, which makes it slightly larger than Spain, Thailand stretches an astounding 1650km along a north–south axis and experiences an extremely diverse climate, including two distinct monsoons from both the southwest and northwest. The north of the country rises into high forested mountains, while the south consists of a long ridge of limestone hills, covered in tropical rainforest.

Both the Andaman and the Gulf coasts have extensive coral reefs, particularly around the granitic Surin and Similan islands in the Andaman Sea. More reefs and Thailand's most dramatic limestone islands sit in Ao Phang-Nga near Phuket. The west coast is of particular interest to divers because the waters are stunningly clear and extremely rich in marine life.

Wildlife

With its diverse climate and topography, it should come as no surprise that Thailand is home to a remarkable diversity of flora and fauna. What is more surprising is that Thailand's environment is still in relatively good shape, particularly considering the relentless development going on all over the country. That said, there are certainly problems for some endangered species and marine environmental issues.

Thailand has cracked down on the illegal ivory trade with splendid results. In 2014 more than 7000 ivory products were found on sale in Bangkok markets. By June 2016 that number had declined to under 300.

Animals

Animals that live on the coasts and islands of Thailand must adapt to shifting tides and the ever-changing mix of salt water and freshwater. Beyond larger animals, keep your eyes open for smaller creatures, such as the odd little mudskipper, a fish that leaves the water and walks around on the mudflats when the tide goes out; or the giant water monitor, a fearsome 350cm-long lizard that climbs and swims effortlessly in its hunt for small animals.

Without a doubt you will see some of the region's fabulous bird life – Thailand is home to 10% of the world's bird species – especially sandpipers and plovers on the mudflats, and herons and egrets in the swamps. Look overhead for the sharply attired, chocolate-and-white Brahminy kite, or scan low-lying branches for one of the region's many colourful kingfishers. You are likely to spot a troop of gregarious and noisy crab-eating macaques, and don't be surprised to see these monkeys swimming from shore. With luck you may glimpse a palm civet, a complexly marbled catlike creature, or a serow, the reclusive 'goat-antelope', which bounds fearlessly among inaccessible limestone crags.

The oceans on either side of the Thai peninsula are home to hundreds of species of coral, and the reefs created by these tiny creatures provide the perfect living conditions for countless species of fish, crustaceans and tiny invertebrates. You can find one of the world's smallest fish (the 1cm-long dwarf pygmy goby) and the largest cartilaginous fish (the 12m-long whale shark), plus reef denizens such as clownfish, parrotfish, wrasse, angelfish, triggerfish and lionfish. Deeper waters are home to larger species such as groupers, barracudas, sharks, manta rays, marlin and tunas. You might also encounter turtles, whales and dolphins.

Endangered Species

Thailand is a signatory to the UN Convention on International Trade in Endangered Species of Wild Fauna and Flora (Cites), but the enforcement of these trade bans is often lax. Due to habitat loss, pollution and poaching, a depressing number of Thailand's mammals, reptiles, fish and birds are endangered, and even populations of formerly common species are diminishing at an alarming rate. Rare mammals, birds, reptiles, insects, shells and tropical aquarium fish are routinely smuggled out to collectors around the world or slaughtered to make souvenirs for tourists.

Many of Thailand's marine animals are under threat, including whale sharks, although they have been seen more frequently in Thai waters recently, and sea turtles, which are being wiped out by hunting for their eggs, meat and shells. Many other species of shark are being hunted to extinction for their fins, which are used to make shark-fin soup. Thailand is the world's largest exporter of shark fins, with almost all exports going to Hong Kong, but shark-fin soup is also a popular dish in Thailand.

The rare dugong (similar to the manatee and sometimes called a sea cow), once thought extinct in Thailand, is now known to survive in a few small pockets, mostly around Trang in southern Thailand, but it is increasingly threatened by habitat loss and the lethal propellers of tourist boats.

The Thai government is slowly recognising the importance of conservation, and many of the kingdom's zoos now have active breeding and conservation programs. Wildlife organisations such as the Phuket Elephant Sanctuary and the Phuket Gibbon Rehabilitation Centre are working to educate the public about native wildlife and have initiated a number of wildlife rescue and rehabilitation projects.

If anyone in Thailand comes across a white elephant, it must be reported to the Bureau of the Royal Household (www.brh.thaigov.net) and the king will decide whether it meets the criteria to be a royal white elephant.

Plants

Southern Thailand is chock-full of luxuriant vegetation, thanks to its two monsoon seasons. The majority of forests away from the coast are evergreen rainforests, while trees at the ocean edge and on limestone formations are stunted due to lack of freshwater and exposure to harsh minerals.

The most beautiful shoreline trees are the many species of palm trees occurring in Thailand, including some found nowhere else in the world. All have small tough leaves with characteristic fanlike or featherlike shapes that help dissipate heat and conserve water. Look for the elegant cycad palm on limestone cliffs, where it grows in cracks despite the complete absence of soil. Collected for its beauty, this common ornamental plant is disappearing from its wild habitat.

Thailand is also home to nearly 75 species of salt-tolerant mangroves – small trees highly adapted to living at the edge of salt water. Standing tiptoe-like on clumps of tall roots, mangroves perform a vital ecological function by trapping sediments and nutrients, and by buffering the coast from the fierce, erosive power of monsoons. This habitat serves as a secure nursery for the eggs and young of countless marine organisms, yet Thailand has destroyed at least 50% of its mangrove swamps to make way for prawn farms and big hotels. Mangrove restoration projects across Thailand are attempting to reverse these massive losses.

National Parks

National parks in Thailand are a huge draw. The popular island getaways of Ko Chang and Ko Samet sit just off the mainland along the eastern gulf coast. Ko Tarutao Marine National Park is remote and undeveloped for real back-to-nature holidays. Ao Phang-Nga, north of Phuket, is endlessly photogenic with its limestone cliffs jutting out of the aquamarine water while knotted mangrove roots cling to thick mudflats. Meanwhile the Similan Islands and Surin Islands Marine National Parks, in the waters of the Andaman Sea, have some of the world's best diving.

Approximately 13% of Thailand is covered by 127 national parks (including marine national parks) and 44 wildlife sanctuaries. Of Thailand's protected areas, 18 parks protect islands and mangrove environments. Thailand's parks and sanctuaries contain more than 850 resident and migratory species of birds and dwindling numbers of tigers, clouded leopards, koupreys, elephants, tapirs, gibbons and Asiatic black bears, among other species.

Despite promises, official designation as a national park or sanctuary does not always guarantee protection for habitats and wildlife. Local farmers, wealthy developers and other business interests will often prevail, either legally or illegally, over environmental protection in Thailand's national parks. Islands that are technically exempt from development may not adhere to the law and government doesn't always sufficiently enforce regulations.

Environmental Issues

Thailand is wealthier, more developed and better educated than its regional neighbours, so there is an awareness of environmental issues that barely exists in countries such as Cambodia and Myanmar. But that awareness is often limited in scope, and while this is slowly changing, it rarely develops into the sort of high-profile, widespread movements seen in Europe, North America or Australia.

As such most issues have a low profile, with only the most visible problems, such as pollution, over-development and a lack of adequate planning, registering with visitors. Look a little deeper, however, and it's evident that the environment has often been the victim in Thailand's rapid modernisation drive. Many Thais don't see a problem with cutting down mangroves to make space for prawn farms, or powering their development with energy from dams in Laos and natural gas from Myanmar (exported to Thailand under deals made with that country's former military rulers).

A raft of well-intentioned environmental laws suggest Thailand is turning the corner towards greater ecological consciousness, but corruption and lack of political resolve have severely hampered efforts to enforce such laws, and the deep split within Thai politics means that this situation is unlikely to change in the short term. Ironically, however, this same lack of political stability has also scared off investment in environmentally damaging sectors.

THAILAND'S MAIN NATIONAL PARKS

PARK	FEATURES	ACTIVITIES
Mu Ko Chang National Marine Park	archipelago marine park with virgin rainforests, waterfalls, beaches & coral reefs	snorkelling, diving, elephant interactions, hiking
Khao Laem Ya/Mu Ko Samet National Park	marine park with beaches, near-shore coral reefs	snorkelling, diving, boat trips, sailboarding
Kaeng Krachan National Park	mainland park with waterfalls & forests; plentiful bird life & jungle mammals	birdwatching
Khao Sam Roi Yot National Park	coastal park with caves, mountains, cliffs & beaches; serow, Irrawaddy dolphins & 300 bird species	cave tours, birdwatching, kayaking
Ang Thong Marine National Park	40 scenic tropical islands with coral reefs, lagoons & limestone cliffs	sea kayaking, hiking, snorkelling
Khao Luang National Park	mainland park with forested mountain peaks, streams & waterfalls; jungle mammals, birds & orchids	hiking
Ao Phang-Nga National Marine Park	coastal bay with limestone cliffs, islands & caves; coral reefs & mangroves	sea kayaking, snorkelling, diving
Khao Lak/Lam Ru National Park	coastal park with cliffs & beaches; hornbills, monkeys & bears	hiking, boat trips
Khao Sok National Park	mainland park with thick rainforest, waterfalls & rivers; tigers, monkeys, *Rafflesia kerrii* & 180 bird species	hiking, elephant interactions, tubing
Laem Son National Park	coastal & marine park with 100km of mangroves; jungle & migratory birds	birdwatching, boat trips
Similan Islands Marine National Park	marine park with granite islands; coral reefs & seabirds; underwater caves	snorkelling, diving
Sirinat National Park	coastal park with casuarina-backed beaches; turtles & coral reefs	walking, snorkelling, diving
Surin Islands Marine National Park	granite islands; coral reefs, whale sharks & manta rays	snorkelling, diving
Hat Chao Mai National Park	coastal park with sandy beaches, mangroves, lagoons & coral islands; dugong & mangrove birds	sea kayaking, snorkelling, diving
Khao Phanom Bencha National Park	mainland mountain jungle with tumbling waterfalls; monkeys	hiking
Ko Phi-Phi Marine National Park	archipelago marine park with beaches, lagoons & sea cliffs; coral reefs & whale sharks	sea kayaking, snorkelling, diving
Ko Tarutao Marine National Park	archipelago marine park with remote jungle islands & tropical beaches; monkeys, jungle mammals & birds	snorkelling, hiking, diving
Mu Ko Lanta Marine National Park	archipelago marine park with scenic beaches; coral reefs & reef sharks	sea kayaking, hiking, snorkelling, diving
Mu Ko Phetra Marine National Park	rarely visited archipelago marine park; dugong, birds & coral reefs	sea kayaking, snorkelling
Tharnbok Korannee National Park	coastal park with mangrove forests & limestone caves; monkeys, orchids & seabirds	sea kayaking

The Land Environment

The main area in which Asia exceeds the West in terms of environmental damage is deforestation, though current estimates indicate Thailand still has about 25% of its forests remaining, which stands up favourably against the UK's more modest 13%. The government's National Forest Policy, introduced in 1985, recommended that 40% of the country should be forested, and a complete logging ban in 1989 was a big step in the right direction. By law Thailand must maintain 25% of its land area as 'conservation forests'. But the logging ban has simply shifted the need for natural resources elsewhere. While illegal logging persists in Thailand on a relatively small scale, in neighbouring Cambodia, Laos and particularly Myanmar the scale has been huge since the ban. A large number of logs are illegally slipped over the border from these countries.

Despite Thailand being a signatory to Cites, all sorts of land species are still smuggled out of Thailand, either alive or as body parts for traditional Chinese medicines. Tigers may be protected by Thai law, but the kingdom remains one of the largest exporters of tiger parts to China (tiger penis and bone are believed to have medicinal effects and to increase libido). Other animal species are hunted (often illegally) to make souvenirs for tourists, including elephants, jungle spiders, giant insects and butterflies; and along the coast clams, shells and pufferfish.

The government has cracked down on restaurants serving *ah·hăhn bàh* (jungle food), which includes endangered wildlife species such as barking deer, bears, pangolins, gibbons, civets and gaurs. A big problem is that national park officials are underpaid and undertrained, yet are expected to confront armed poachers and mercenary armies funded by rich and powerful godfathers.

The widely touted idea that ecotourism can act as a positive force for change has been extensively put to the test in Thailand. In some instances tourism has definitely had positive effects. The expansion of Thailand's national parks has largely been driven by tourism. In Khao Yai National Park, all hotel and golf-course facilities were removed to reduce damage to the park environment. As a result of government and private-sector pressure on the fishing industry, coral dynamiting has been all but eliminated in the Similan and Surin Islands, to preserve the area for tourists.

However, tourism can be a poisoned chalice. Massive developments near, and often within, national parks have ridden roughshod over the local environment in their rush to provide bungalows, luxury hotels, beach bars and boat services for tourists. Ko Phi-Phi and Ko Samet are two national parks where business interests have definitely won out over the environment. In both cases, the development began in areas set aside for *chow lair* (also spelt *chao leh;* 'sea gypsies', the semi-nomadic people who migrate up and down the coast). Ko Lipe in Ko Tarutao Marine National Park and Ko Muk in Hat Chao Mai National Park now seem to be heading the same way.

Rubbish and sewage are growing problems in all populated areas, even more so in heavily visited areas where an influx of tourists overtaxes the local infrastructure. One encouraging development was the passing of the 1992 Environmental Act, which set environmental quality standards, designated conservation and pollution-control areas, and doled out government clean-up funds. Pattaya built its first public wastewater treatment plant in 2000 and conditions have improved ever since.

The famous white sands of Thailand's beaches are actually tiny bits of coral that have been defecated by coral-eating fish.

While Thais generally remain reluctant to engage in broader environmental campaigns, people are increasingly aware of the issues, particularly when they will be affected. Local people have campaigned for years against the building of dams, though usually without success. With Thailand aiming to boost its production of renewable energy by a quarter by 2021, the Energy Generating Authority of Thailand (EGAT) is set to buy 95% of the US$3.5 billion Thai-built Xayaburi Dam's electrical output in northern Laos (one of 11 dams along the lower Mekong), when it becomes operational. Damming the Mekong for hydroelectric power may generate 'clean' electricity, but comes at great environmental cost, including contributing to the extinction of the endangered Mekong giant catfish and the disappearance of the Irrawaddy dolphin from Mekong waters.

The Marine Environment

Thailand's coral reef system, including the Andaman Coast from Ranong to northern Phuket and the Surin and Similan Islands, is one of the world's most diverse. Some 600 species of coral reef fish, endangered marine turtles and other rare creatures call this coastline home.

The 2004 tsunami caused high-impact damage to about 13% of the Andaman coral reefs. However, damage from the tsunami was much less than first thought and relatively minor compared to the ongoing environmental degradation that accompanies an industrialised society. Coral reefs naturally recover, and this restoration process among the Andaman reefs was rapid, with corals showing regrowth just two to three years after the tsunami. It is estimated, however, that about 25% of Thailand's coral reefs have died as a result of industrial pollution and that the annual loss of healthy reefs will continue at a rapid rate. Even around the dive centre of Phuket, dead coral reefs are visible on the northern coast. The biggest threat to corals is sedimentation from coastal development: new condos, hotels, roads and houses. High levels of sediment in the water stunts coral growth. Other common problems include pollution from anchored tour boats or other marine activities, rubbish and sewage dumped directly into the sea, and agricultural and industrial run-off. Even people urinating in the water as they swim creates by-products that can kill sensitive coral reefs.

Thailand's fish farms harvested a staggering 300,000-odd tonnes of shrimp in 2016, two-thirds of it for the export market.

The environmental wake-up call from the tsunami emphasised the importance of mangrove forests, which provide a buffer from storm surges. Previously mangroves were considered wastelands and were indiscriminately cut down. It is estimated that about 80% of the mangrove forests lining the gulf coast and 20% of those on the Andaman Coast have been destroyed for conversion into fish and prawn farms, tourist development or to supply the charcoal industry. Prawn farms constitute the biggest threat because Thailand is the world's leading producer of black tiger prawns, and the short-lived, heavily polluting farms are built in pristine mangrove swamps at a terrific environmental and social cost. Prawn farms are huge business (Thailand produces around 300,000 tonnes of prawns annually), and the large prawn-farming businesses are often able to operate in spite of environmental protection laws. Protesting voices rarely get heard in the media.

Contributing to the deterioration of the overall health of the ocean are Thailand and its neighbours' large-scale fishing industries, frequently called the 'strip-miners of the sea'. Fish catches have declined by up to 33% in the Asia-Pacific region in the past 25 years and the upper portion of the Gulf of Thailand has almost been fished to death. Most of the commercial catches are sent to overseas markets and rarely see a Thai dinner table. The seafood sold in Thailand is typically from fish farms.

Making a Difference

A group of ecologically engaged Buddhist monks, popularly known as Thai Ecology Monks, uses peaceful activism to empower local communities in their fight against deforestation and other environmental exploitation.

It may seem that the range of environmental issues in Thailand is overwhelming, but there is actually much that travellers can do to minimise the impact of their visit, or to even make a positive impact. The way you spend your money (and what you spend it on) has a profound influence on the kingdom's economy and on the profitability of individual businesses. Ask questions up front and take your money elsewhere if you don't like the answers. For instance, a number of large-scale resorts that lack road access transport clients across fragile mudflats on tractors (a wantonly destructive practice), so when booking a room inquire about transport to the hotel.

Of the region's countless dive shops, some are diligent about minimising the impact their clients have on the reefs; however, if a dive shop trains and certifies inexperienced divers over living reefs, then it may be damaging the local ecosystem. Ask up front if a dive operation is engaged in any projects to protect the environment. As a rule, do not touch or walk on coral, monitor your movements so that you avoid accidentally sweeping into coral, and do not harass marine life (responsible dive shops should make you aware of this).

With more evidence available than ever to support claims by animal welfare experts that elephant rides and shows are harmful to these gentle giants, who are often abused to force them to perform for humans, a small but growing number of sanctuaries offer more sustainable interactions, such as walking with and bathing retired and rescued elephants. Lonely Planet does not recommend riding on elephants or viewing elephant performances. We also urge visitors to be wary of organisations that advertise as being a conservation centre but actually offer rides and performances.

Make a positive impact by checking out one of the many environmental and social groups working in the kingdom. If you do some research and make arrangements before arriving, you may connect with an organisation that matches your values.

Thai Massage

For many visitors, Thai massage is just another way to relax, or relieve aching muscles following a long bus or train ride. But this complex art is a major part of traditional Thai medicine and is the fruit of spiritual and medicinal roots that reach back to the time of the historical Buddha.

Spiritual & Philisophical Origins

The Thai form of massage can be traced to Tantric Buddhist Vajrayana teachings that originated in India and Tibet. Translated from the Sanskrit, Vajrayana means 'Diamond Vehicle' or 'Thunderbolt Vehicle', and marks a transition in Mahayana Buddhism when practices became more ritualised as opposed to primarily using abstract meditations to reach nirvana. Among other things, Vajrayana introduced the ideas of mantra (a symbol, word or group of words that can help spiritual transformation) and mandala (a symbol, often artistically depicted, that represents the universe). The school of thought flourished in India and Tibet between the 6th and 11th centuries, but its main influence on Thailand was its healing arts.

Like Thai culture itself, influences on medicine came from many directions, including China, India and other Southeast Asian regions. Both Ayurvedic and traditional Chinese medicine are at the roots of Thai massage. Practitioners generally follow the 10 Sen lines, or channels, through the body with specific pressure points along them, which are similar to the Chinese meridians and Indian *nadis*. In Thai theory, these lines carry several types of 'wind' (depending on the Sen line), from air that is inhaled through the lungs. When a line is blocked or unbalanced, illness or symptoms will ensue. At the same time, yoga *asana* stretches are used to open joints, aided by the loosening power of rocking, thumb pressure and rhythmic compression.

TRADITIONAL THAI MEDICINE

Much like other schools of Asian medicine, traditional Thai medicine (TTM) takes a holistic approach to health to include the physical body, heart, mind, spirit and flow of energy through the Sen. Much is based on the four elements fire, water, air and earth, with each element ruling body parts and functions – earth rules the organs, air rules the 'wind' (generally meaning respiration and digestion), water rules bodily fluid and fire rules four types of bodily heat (including circulation). Living in harmony with nature, eating well and being in tune with one's own natural cycles (from night and day to ageing) are the keys to health by TTM standards.

Tastes are important to Thais in a culinary sense, and this extends into the realm of medicine. How a herbal remedy tastes determines how it balances the elements and what ailment it can treat. For example, sweet treats fatigue, salty is good for constipation, and bitter helps fight infection. TTM treatments generally include herbal remedies, massage and lifestyle changes.

Thai massage is often called the 'expression of loving kindness' because at the the heart of the practice is the compassionate intent of the healer. In its true form, the masseur will bond with the client in a meditative state and both parties will experience a deeper sense of awareness through humility and concentration.

King Rama V commissioned a textbook, completed in 1900, of traditional Thai medicine that included massage.

History

Jivaka Komarabhacca, the physician to the historical Buddha himself, is said to be the father of Thai massage and traditional Thai medicine. Although he wasn't mentioned at length in Buddhist scriptures, Dr Jivaka holds extremely high status in Thai lore; there's a statue of him at the Grand Palace in Bangkok, and you'll often see his likeness next to statues of the Buddha, like a protector. It's said that the doctor spread the practice of massage to monasteries to help ease the monks' pain after long hours of meditation. Today's massage practitioners still practise *wâi kroo* (the Thai tradition of giving prayers and offerings to a teacher) devoted to the revered physician with chants that include his name.

Massage techniques and knowledge were passed down through the generations by masters to their disciples within the monasteries. With the support of royalty and the devotion of the practitioners, techniques evolved for healing the sick and injured of the community. Everything was passed down orally until the 1830s when Wat Pho was built and included stone engravings and statues explaining and depicting Thai massage arts. It wasn't until the 1920s that Thai massage became a profession.

THE TEN SEN

Thai massage is based on these 10 energy pathways, and the goal of a good practitioner will be to balance and/or unblock these channels.

SEN	LOCATION	MAIN INDICATIONS
Sen Sumana	Tip of the tongue to the solar plexus region	Digestive system, asthma, heart disease, bronchitis
Sen Ittha	Left nostril, over the head, down the back to the left knee	Headache, sinus problems, urinary tract, back pain
Sen Pingkhala	Same as Sen Ittha but on right side	Same as Sen Ittha plus gallbladder and liver disease
Sen Kalathari	Two lines make an X across body from tips of toes to shoulders and down to fingertips	Digestive system, hernia, arthritis, mental disorder
Sen Sahatsarangsi	Left eye, down left side around to back of left leg, under foot, up front of left leg to navel	Toothache, eye function, depression, gastrointestinal disease
Sen Thawari	Same as Sen Sahatsarangsi but on the right side	Same as Sen Sahatsarangsi plus appendicitis and jaundice
Sen Lawusang	Left ear to left nipple to mid solar plexus region	Ear disorders, cough, toothache, gastrointestinal disorders
Sen Ulangwa	Same as Sen Lawusang but on the right side	Same as Sen Lawusang plus itchy skin and insomnia
Sen Nanthakrawat	Two lines, each from the navel: one to urine passageway and other to the anus	Infertility, impotence, diarrhoea, irregular menstruation
Sen Kitchanna	Navel to penis in men, navel to uterus in women	Same as Sen Nanthakrawat plus balances libido

Getting a Massage

Where & How Much

Any tourist area in southern Thailand will have many massage options. Most places are air-conditioned shops with big reclining chairs for foot massages and manicures/pedicures, and another area for a row or two of mattresses with curtained partitions for full-body massages. Some shops also offer body scrubs and other spa services. Along busy beaches you'll find sheltered, elevated platforms with rows of mattresses where you can be pummelled in your swimsuit as you gaze at the sea. There may only be a massage therapist or two in more remote areas, but these independent practitioners tend to be more skilled than those working in the big shops.

Massages are generally most expensive near posh resorts, but this isn't always the case. Sometimes just walking a minute or two off the main drag or further down the beach will yield lower prices. Expect to pay 200B to 500B for a one-hour Thai massage or foot massage. Prices go up for additions like oil, aloe for sunburn, aromatherapy or hot herbal compresses.

A more upmarket option is to get a deluxe massage at an independent or resort spa. Practitioners here tend to have more credentials than the street shop or beach therapists, although that doesn't always mean that they're better. The real advantage here is the more luxurious surroundings, which may include beautiful views, trickling water and teak furniture, a relaxing soundtrack, lots of pleasant smells and more privacy. At a spa you'll also have a bevy of other services on offer from body wraps to flower baths and foot scrubs. Massage prices at spas tend to start at around 500B.

Check-in

On busier, sleazier beaches there may be a tout outside the salon hustling tourists by crooning 'meestaa, want massage?' In classier parts of town, services are announced by a spa menu outside the door, or perhaps a group of giggling masseuses hanging out on the front step. Most massage therapists are women, although a few are male. If the practitioners are dressed professionally, usually in matching uniforms, the place will probably be a straightforward massage parlour. If the women are very young, scantily dressed or heavily made up, this is a red flag that other services may be on offer. Private massage rooms at the back of the salon in lieu of the more common curtained-off massage areas can be another clue that the salon may be geared towards less savoury practices. A man asking for an 'oil massage' may also sometimes lead to techniques not on the advertised menu, even at what appear to be classy establishments. If the massage seems to be going that way, get up and leave.

A foot massage begins with a foot bath and moisturising treatment before the practitioner strongly works pressure points.

Once you're inside, take off your shoes and follow your practitioner. Sometimes you'll be asked to leave your clothes on while at other places you'll be given a pair of Thai-style pyjamas or a sarong. In the case of the latter, strip down to your underwear, either behind your curtain or in a changing area, and put on the supplied garments. On the beach you'll usually be massaged in your swimsuit; a sarong is sometimes offered to women who wish to take off their bikini tops.

The Massage

Thai massage is not for wimps. The session usually begins with relaxing kneading of the back, arms and legs and the practitioner will often ask you if the pressure is light or strong enough. Then it gets gnarly. First there's the chiropractic-like popping of joints – mostly fingers and toes but sometimes whole legs and arms as well as the back and neck. Then,

WAT PHO

Wat Pho next to the Royal Palace in Bangkok is the ground zero of Thai massage. Before the royal wát was built on this site by Rama I in the late 1800s, a centre for traditional Thai medicine was here. The future wát incorporated this history into its curriculum and eventually became home to the first official school of Thai massage; inscribed tablets of the Sen pathways grace the temple's interior walls. Today the school is still considered the best in the country and visitors can attend training programs or simply come in and have a massage. In 2008 Wat Pho was recognised by Unesco in its Memory of the World Program. The manager of the school, Khun Serat, is the founder's grandson and many of the instructors are descendants of the original faculty.

Check the website www.watphomassage.com for details on everything from 30-hour Thai massage or foot massage courses, to several month-long training programs. A five-day course starts at 9500B, or you can get a half hour or hour-long traditional massage at the wát for 260B to 420B.

even the tiniest masseuses will muscle you into yoga contortions that arch the back, extend the legs and arms and so much more that it feels like you're being turned into a human pretzel. You'll start the session on your back, get moved to a prone position about midway and then end with your head in the practitioner's lap for a final head massage and a popping back stretch. Overall the treatment itself isn't very relaxing, but you'll feel incredible afterwards. Let your massage therapist know in advance if you have any injuries and don't be afraid to tell them to ease up on a stretch or joint pop. As with any good workout, know your limits.

Practitioners recommend drinking lots of water or green tea after a massage to flush out any dislodged toxins.

That said, Thai massage in many tourist areas has become very watered down and you may end up without being contorted or popped in the slightest. Older women tend to give the most violent yet rewarding massages, but even with younger ones, you won't know until your nose is hitting your knee what kind of torturous therapy they're capable of.

If this sounds too scary, Swedish and other types of massage are often available, but you'll be missing out on a big cultural and maybe even spiritual experience. A more simple reflexology foot massage (available at almost all salons) may be a good place to start if you've never had a professional massage or are wary of the practice in any way.

Survival Guide

Directory A–Z

Accommodation

It doesn't hurt to book ahead, especially popular places, even outside high season. But during the low season of May to October, prices drop dramatically and sometimes walk-in prices can be cheaper than those you will find online.

Guesthouses

Guesthouses are generally the cheapest accommodation in Thailand and can be found all along the backpacker trail. In more remote areas like the eastern seaboard, guesthouses (as well as tourists) are not as widespread.

Rates vary according to facilities and location. In provincial towns, the cheapest rooms range from 250B to 400B, and usually have shared bathrooms and rickety fans. Private facilities, air-con and sometimes a TV can be had for 400B to 800B. But prices are much higher in the beach resorts, where a basic fan room can start at 600B to 800B. Many guesthouses make their bread and butter from on-site restaurants that serve classic backpacker fare (banana pancakes and fruit shakes). Although these restaurants are convenient and a good way to meet other travellers, don't judge Thai food based on these dishes.

Most guesthouses cultivate a travellers' ambience with friendly, knowledgeable staff and book exchanges. But there are also plenty of guesthouses with grumpy, disgruntled clerks.

Many guesthouses can be booked online, but due to inconsistent cleanliness and quality, it is advisable to look at a room in person before committing. In tourist centres, there are usually alternatives nearby if your preferred place is full. Guesthouses normally require payment in cash.

COMMISSION HASSLES

In many popular tourist spots you'll be approached, and sometimes surrounded, by touts or drivers who get a commission from the guesthouse for bringing in potential guests. While it's annoying for the traveller, this is an acceptable form of advertising among small-scale businesses in Thailand. As long as you know the drill, everything should work out in your favour. Touts get paid for delivering you to a guesthouse or hotel (whether you check in or not).

Some places refuse to pay commissions, so in return the touts will steer customers away from those places (by saying they are closed). In less scrupulous instances, they'll tell you that the commission-paying hotel is the one you requested. If you meet with resistance, call the guesthouse for a pick-up, as they are often aware of these aggressive business tactics.

BOOK YOUR STAY ONLINE

For more accommodation reviews by Lonely Planet authors, check out http://lonelyplanet.com/thailand/hotels. You'll find independent reviews, as well as recommendations on the best places to stay. Best of all, you can book online.

Hostels

Hostels are less common in Thailand than elsewhere in Asia, mostly because guesthouses are so cheap, but there are still plenty scattered around, especially in the destinations where backpackers cluster. All offer a mix of dorms and private

SLEEPING PRICE RANGES

The following price ranges refer to a double room with bathroom in high season. Unless otherwise stated, tax is not included in the price, which only applies to larger hotels and high-end options.

$ less than 1000B

$$ 1000–4000B

$$$ more than 4000B

rooms, as well as the usual traveller services. You can find dorm beds for around 300B plus a night. Almost all can be booked online.

Hotels

In provincial capitals and small towns, the older Thai-Chinese hotels, once the standard in Thailand, are the cheapest options. Most cater to Thai guests and English is usually limited. These hotels are multistorey buildings and might offer a range of rooms from midrange options with private bathrooms, air-con and TVs to cheaper ones with shared bathroom facilities and a fan.

In a few of the really old places the toilets are squats and the 'shower' is a *klong* (large terracotta basin from which you scoop out water for bathing). Although these Thai-Chinese hotels have some accidental retro charm, we've found that, unless they've been recently refurbished, they are too old and worn to represent good value compared to guesthouses.

In recent years, there has been a push to fill the budget gap for older backpackers and young affluent travellers who want the ambience of a guesthouse with the comforts of a hotel. 'Flashpacker' hotels in major tourist towns have dressed up the utilitarian options of the past with stylish decor and more creature comforts.

International chain hotels can be found in Bangkok, Phuket and other high-end beach resorts. Many of these upmarket resorts combine traditional Thai architecture and modern minimalism.

Most top-end hotels and some midrange hotels add a 7% government tax (VAT) and an additional 10% service charge. The additional charges are often referred to as 'plus plus'. A buffet breakfast will often be included in the room rate. If the hotel offers Western breakfast, it is usually referred to as 'ABF', meaning 'American breakfast'.

Midrange and chain hotels, especially in major tourist destinations, can be booked in advance and many offer internet discounts through their websites or online agents. They also accept most credit cards, but fewer places accept American Express.

National Parks Accommodation

Most national parks have bungalows or campsites available for overnight stays. Bungalows typically sleep as many as 10 people and rates range from 800B to 2000B, depending on the park and the size of the bungalow. These are popular with extended Thai families, who bring enough provisions to survive the Apocalypse. A few parks also have *reu·an tăa·ou* (longhouses).

Camping is available at many parks for 30B to 90B per night if you have your own tent. Some parks rent tents and other sleeping gear, but the condition of the equipment can be poor.

Reservations for all park accommodation must be made in advance through the online system of the **National Park Office** (☎02 562 0760; http://nps.dnp.go.th; 61 Th Phahonyothin).

USEFUL PHRASES

While it's very easy to score walk-in bookings at many midrange and budget spots, we recommend booking your first few nights in advance. The following phrases will help you when booking accommodation.

Hello. สวัสดี sà-wàt-dee

I would like to book a room. ขอจองห้องหน่อย kŏr jorng hôrng nòy

a single room ห้องเดี่ยว hôrng dèe·o

a double room ห้องเตียงคู่ hôrng đee·ang kôo

My name is... ผม/ดิฉันชื่อ... pŏm/dì-chăn chêu ... (m/f)

from... to... (date) จากวันที่... ถึงวันที่... jàhk wan têe ... tĕung wan têe ...

How much is it...? ... ละเท่าไร ... lá tôw-rai

per night คืน keun

for two people สำหรับสองคน săm·ràp sŏrng kon

Thank you. ขอบคุณ kòrp kun

Activities

Rock Climbing

Thailand has a range of climbing options, ranging in skill from total beginner to those who rival Spiderman. Most climbs are in the south, but the north has several challenging peaks.

Meditation & Spiritual Retreats

Thais often go on spiritual retreats to rejuvenate themselves. You can join them at temples or meditation centres.

Muay Thai

Ever dreamed of becoming a Thai boxing champ? *Moo·ay tai* (also spelt muay thai) training camps put you through your paces with packages that involve general fitness and ring work.

Thai Cooking

Learning how to cook authentic Thai food is high on many visitors' to-do list. Many Thai chefs are happy to share their secrets and take foodies on trips to local markets to teach them about specific ingredients.

Surfing & Kiteboarding

The monsoon's mid-year swell creates surfable barrels off Phuket, while almost year-round gusty winds lure kiteboarders to the east coast.

PRACTICALITIES

Newspapers English-language newspapers include the *Bangkok Post* (www.bangkokpost.com), the business-heavy *Nation* (www.nationmultimedia.com) and *KhaoSod English* (www.khaosodenglish.com), the English-language service of a mainstream Thai newspaper. Weeklies such as the *Economist* and *Time* are sold at news stands.

Radio There are more than 400 AM and FM radio stations. Many smaller radio stations and international services are available to stream over the internet.

TV Six VHF TV networks carry Thai programming, plus TrueVision cable has international programming.

Weights & Measures The metric system is used. Gold and silver are weighed in *bàat* (15g).

Climate

Bangkok

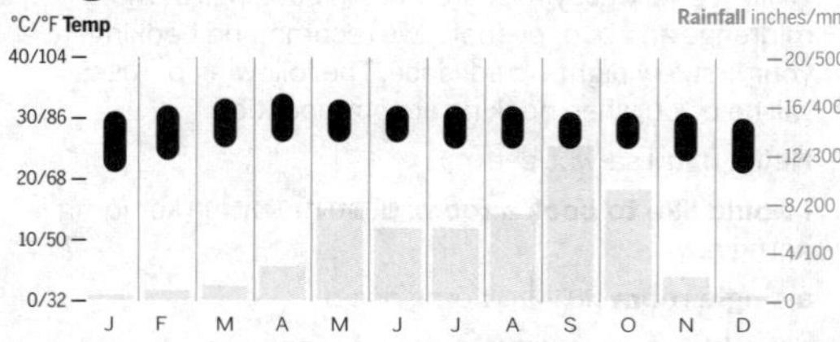

Phuket

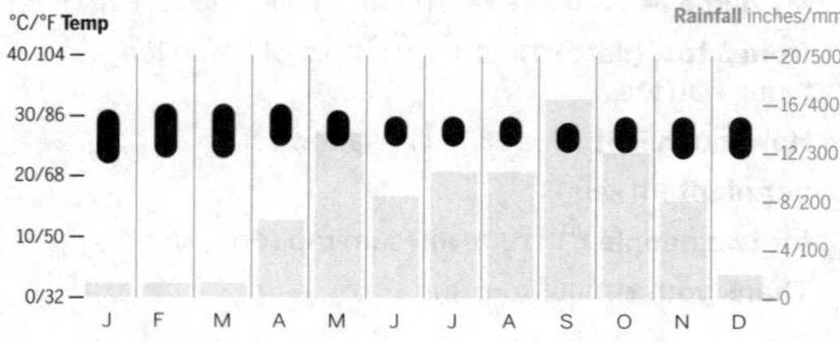

Customs Regulations

The Customs Department (www.customs.go.th) maintains a helpful website with specific information about customs regulations. Thailand has the usual list of prohibited imports, such as illegal drugs, firearms and ammunition (unless registered in advance) and pornographic media. Items allowed include the following:

- a reasonable amount of personal effects (clothing and toiletries)
- professional instruments
- 200 cigarettes
- 1L of wine or spirits

When leaving Thailand, you must obtain an export licence for any antique reproductions or newly cast Buddha images. Submit two front-view photos of the object(s), a photocopy of your passport, the purchase receipt and the object(s) in question to the **Office of the National Museum** (Map p70; ☎02 224 1370; National Museum, 4 Th Na Phra That, Bangkok; ⊙9am-4pm Tue-Fri; ⛴Chang Pier, Maharaj Pier, Phra Chan Tai Pier). Allow four days for the application and inspection process to be completed.

Electricity

Thailand uses 220V AC electricity; power outlets most commonly feature two-prong round or flat sockets.

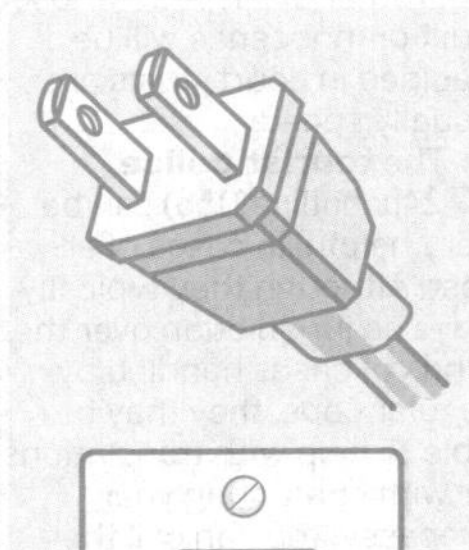

Type A
220V/50Hz

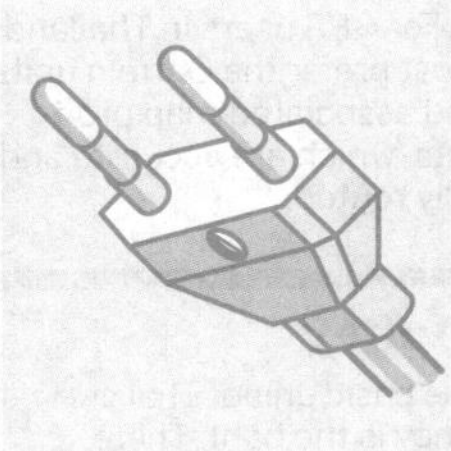

Type C
220V/50Hz

Embassies & Consulates

Foreign embassies are located in Bangkok; some nations also have consulates in Chiang Mai, Pattaya, Phuket and Songkhla.

Australian Embassy (Map p88; ☎02 344 6300; www.thailand.embassy.gov.au; 181 Th Witthayu/Wireless Rd, Bangkok; ⊙8.30am-4.30pm Mon-Fri; Ⓜ Lumphini exit 2) Consulates in Chiang Mai, Ko Samui and Phuket.

Cambodian Embassy (Map p94; ☎02 957 5851; 518/4 Soi Ramkhamhaeng 39, Th Pracha Uthit, Bangkok; ⊙8.30am-noon & 2-5pm Mon-Fri; Ⓜ Phra Ram 9 exit 3 & taxi) Consulate in Sa Kaew.

Canadian Embassy (Map p88; ☎02 646 4300; www.thailand.gc.ca; 15th fl, Abdulrahim Pl, 990 Rama IV, Bangkok; ⊙9am-noon Mon-Fri; Ⓜ Si Lom exit 2, Ⓢ Sala Daeng exit 4) Consulate in **Chiang Mai** (☎05 3850147; 151 Superhighway, Tambon Tahsala; ⊙9am-noon Mon-Fri).

French Embassy (Map p92; ☎02 657 5100; www.ambafrance-th.org; 35 Soi 36/Rue de Brest, Th Charoen Krung, Bangkok; ⊙8.30am-noon Mon-Fri; Oriental Pier) Consulates in **Chiang Mai** (☎053 281466; 138 Th Charoen Prathet, Chiang Mai; ⊙10am-noon Mon-Fri), Chiang Rai and Pattaya.

German Embassy (Map p88; ☎02 287 9000; www.bangkok.diplo.de; 9 Th Sathon Tai/South, Bangkok; ⊙7.30-11.30am Mon-Fri; Ⓜ Lumphini exit 2)

Irish Embassy (Map p80; ☎02 016 1360; www.dfa.ie/irish-embassy/thailand; 12th fl, 208 Th Witthayu/Wireless Rd, Bangkok; ⊙9.30am-12.30pm & 2.30-3.30pm Mon-Thu, 9.30am-noon Fri; Ⓢ Phloen Chit exit 1)

Laotian Embassy (Map p94; ☎02 539 6667; 502/1-3 Soi Sahakarnpramoon, Th Pracha Uthit/Soi Ramkhamhaeng 39, Bangkok; ⊙8am-noon & 1-4pm Mon-Fri; Ⓜ Phra Ram 9 exit 3 & taxi)

Malaysian Embassy (Map p88; ☎02 629 6800; www.kln.gov.my/web/tha_bangkok/home; 33-35 Th Sathon Tai/South, Bangkok; ⊙8am-4pm Mon-Fri; Ⓜ Lumphini exit 2) Consulate in Songkhla.

Myanmar Embassy (Map p88; ☎02 233 7250; www.myanmarembassybkk.com; 132 Th Sathon Neua/North, Bangkok; ⊙9am-noon & 1-3pm Mon-Fri; Ⓢ Surasak exit 3)

Netherlands Embassy (Map p80; ☎02 309 5200; www.netherlandsworldwide.nl/countries/thailand; 15 Soi Ton Son; ⊙8.30am-noon & 1.30-4.30pm Mon-Thu, 8.30-11.30am Fri; Ⓢ Chit Lom exit 4)

New Zealand Embassy (Map p80; ☎02 254 2530; www.nzembassy.com/thailand; 14th fl, M Thai Tower, All Seasons Pl, 87 Th Witthayu/Wireless Rd, Bangkok; ⊙8am-noon & 1-2.30pm Mon-Fri; Ⓢ Phloen Chit exit 5)

UK Embassy (Map p80; ☎02 305 8333; www.gov.uk/government/world/organisations/british-embassy-bangkok; 14 Th Witthayu/Wireless Rd, Bangkok; ⊙8am-4.30pm Mon-Thu, to 1pm Fri; Ⓢ Phloen Chit exit 5)

US Embassy (Map p80; ☎02 205 4000; https://th.usembassy.gov; 95 Th Witthayu/Wireless Rd, Bangkok; ⊙8am-4pm Mon-Fri; Ⓢ Phloen Chit exit 5) Consulate in **Chiang Mai** (☎05 3107700; https://th.usembassy.gov; 387 Th Wichayanon; ⊙8am-3.30pm Tue & Thu).

LGBT Travellers

Thai culture is relatively tolerant of both male and female homosexuality. There is a fairly prominent LGBT scene in Bangkok, Pattaya and Phuket. With regard to dress or mannerisms, the LGBT community is generally accepted without comment. However, public displays of affection – whether hetero-sexual or homosexual – are frowned upon.

It's worth noting that, perhaps because Thailand is

EATING PRICE RANGES

The following price ranges refer to a standard main-course meal.

$ less than 150B

$$ 150–350B

$$$ more than 350B

still a relatively conservative place, lesbians generally adhere to rather strict gender roles. Overtly 'butch' lesbians, called tom (from 'tomboy'), typically have short hair, bind their breasts and wear men's clothing. Femme lesbians refer to themselves as *dêe* (from 'lady'). Visiting lesbians who don't fit into one of these categories may find themselves met with confusion.

Utopia (www.utopia-asia.com) posts lots of Thailand information for LGBT travellers and publishes a gay guidebook to the kingdom.

Insurance

A travel-insurance policy to cover theft, loss and medical problems is a sound idea. Be sure that the policy covers ambulances or an emergency flight home.

Some policies specifically exclude 'dangerous activities', which can include diving, motorcycling or even trekking. A locally acquired motorcycle licence is not valid under some policies. Do not dive without diver's insurance.

You may prefer a policy that pays doctors or hospitals directly rather than you having to pay on the spot and claim later. If you have to claim later, make sure you keep all documentation.

Worldwide travel insurance is available at www.lonelyplanet.com/bookings. You can buy, extend and claim online any time – even if you're already on the road.

Internet Access

Wi-fi is available in almost all hotels and guesthouses, as well as in many cafes, restaurants and bars. Internet cafes are a dying breed in the big cities, but can still be found (in much smaller numbers) in tourist destinations.

Legal Matters

In general, Thai police don't hassle foreigners, especially tourists. In fact, they often go out of their way to avoid having to speak English with a foreigner, especially regarding minor traffic issues. However, on-the-spot fines for foreigners riding motorbikes without wearing a helmet do happen, particularly on Phuket.

One major exception is drugs, which most Thai police view as either a social scourge against which it's their duty to enforce the letter of the law, or occasionally an opportunity to make untaxed income via bribes.

If you are arrested for any offence, the police will allow you the opportunity to make a phone call to your embassy or consulate in Thailand, if you have one, or to a friend or relative, if you don't.

There's a whole set of legal codes governing the length of time and manner in which you can be detained before being charged or put on trial, but a lot of discretion is left to the police. In the case of foreigners the police are more likely to bend these codes in your favour. However, as with police worldwide, if you don't show respect, you will make matters worse.

Thai law does not presume an indicted detainee to be either 'guilty' or 'innocent', but rather a 'suspect' whose guilt or innocence will be decided in court. Trials are usually speedy.

The **tourist police** (☎24hr hotline 1155) can be very helpful in cases of arrest. Although they typically have no jurisdiction over the kinds of cases handled by regular cops, they may be able to help with translations or with contacting your embassy. You can call the hotline to lodge complaints or request assistance with regard to personal safety.

Maps

ThinkNet (www.thinknet.co.th) produces high-quality, bilingual city and country maps, including interactive-map CDs.

For GPS users in Thailand, most prefer the Garmin units and associated map products, which are accurate and fully routed.

Money

The basic unit of Thai currency is the baht. There are 100 satang in one baht; coins include 25-satang and 50-satang pieces and baht in 1B, 2B, 5B and 10B coins. Older coins have Thai numerals only, while newer coins have Thai and Arabic numerals. The 2B coin is similar in size to the 1B coin but is gold in colour. The two-satang coins are typically only issued at supermarkets where prices aren't rounded up to the nearest baht.

Paper currency is issued in the following denominations: 20B (green), 50B (blue), 100B (red), 500B (purple) and 1000B (beige).

ATMs & Credit and Debit Cards

ATMs dispensing Thai baht are widespread throughout the country. You can also buy baht at foreign-exchange booths at some banks.

Thai ATMs charge a 200B foreign transaction fee on top of whatever currency conversion and out-of-network fees your home bank charges. Before leaving home, shop around for a bank account that has free international ATM usage and reimburses fees incurred at other institutions' ATMs.

Aeon is the one Thai bank that charges a lower fee, 150B, but its ATM distribution is somewhat limited – most Aeon ATMs are located in Big C or Tesco Lotus stores.

Credit cards, as well as debit cards, can be used for purchases at some shops, hotels and restaurants. The most commonly accepted cards are Visa and MasterCard. American Express is typically only accepted at high-end hotels and restaurants.

To report a lost or stolen credit/debit card, call your bank's hotline in Bangkok.

Changing Money

Banks or the rarer private moneychangers offer the best foreign-exchange rates. When buying baht, US dollars are the most accepted currency, followed by British pounds and euros. Most banks charge a commission and duty for each traveller's cheque cashed.

Current exchange rates are printed in the *Bangkok Post* and the *Nation* every day, or you can walk into any Thai bank to see a daily rate chart.

Foreign Exchange

Visitors must declare cash over US$20,000 when arriving or departing. There are also certain monetary requirements for foreigners entering Thailand; demonstration of adequate funds varies per visa type but typically does not exceed a traveller's estimated trip budget. It's rare that you'll be asked to produce such financial evidence, but be aware that these laws do exist. The **Ministry of Foreign Affairs** (☎02 203 5000; www.mfa.go.th) can provide more detailed information.

It's legal to open a foreign-currency account at any commercial bank in Thailand. As long as the funds originate from out of the country, there aren't any restrictions on maintenance or withdrawal.

Opening Hours

Banks and government offices close for national holidays. Some bars and clubs close during elections and certain holidays when alcohol sales are banned; closing times may also vary due to local enforcement of curfew laws. Shopping centres have banks that open late.

Photography

Be considerate when taking photographs of the locals. Indicate that you want to take a picture and wait for an embarrassed nod. In some of the regularly visited hill-people areas, be prepared for the photographed subject to ask for money in exchange for a picture. Some hill peoples will not allow you to point a camera at them.

Post

Thailand has a very efficient postal service and local postage is inexpensive. Typical provincial post offices are open between 8.30am and 4.30pm on weekdays and 9am and noon on Saturdays. Larger main post offices in provincial capitals may also be open for a half-day on Sunday.

Most provincial post offices sell DIY packing boxes. Don't send cash or other valuables through the mail.

Thailand's poste restante service is generally very reliable. When you receive mail, you must show your passport and fill out some paperwork.

Public Holidays

1 January New Year's Day

February (date varies) Makha Bucha, Buddhist holy day

6 April Chakri Day

13–15 April Songkran Festival

1 May Labour Day

5 May Coronation Day; commemorates the 1946 coronation of HM the King and HM the Queen

May/June (date varies) Visakha Bucha, Buddhist holy day

July (date varies) Asanha Bucha, Buddhist holy day

28 July King's Birthday

12 August Queen's Birthday

23 October Chulalongkorn Day

October/November (date varies) Ork Phansaa, the end of Buddhist Lent

5 December The late King's Birthday

10 December Constitution Day

31 December New Year's Eve

Safe Travel

Thailand is generally a safe country to visit, but it's smart to exercise caution, especially when it comes to dealing with strangers (both Thai and foreigners) and travelling alone.

➡ Avoid being ripped off, scammed or having personal possessions surreptitiously stolen by keeping your wits about you.

➡ Be aware that an innocent flirtation might convey firmer intentions to a recipient who does not share your culture's sexual norms.

Assault

Assault of travellers is rare in Thailand, but it does happen. Causing a Thai to 'lose face' (feel public embarrassment or humiliation) can sometimes elicit an inexplicably strong and violent reaction. Drunk travellers are also a potential risk. Often alcohol is the number-one factor.

Border Issues & Hot Spots

Thailand enjoys generally amicable relations with its neighbours, and most land borders are fully functional for both people and goods. However, the ongoing violence in the Deep South means Lonely Planet does not recommend the crossings at Sungai Kolok and Padang Besar to Malaysia, while the entire Muslim-majority provinces (Yala, Pattani and Narathiwat) should be avoided by casual visitors.

Drug Possession

Belying Thailand's anything-goes atmosphere are strict punishments for possession and trafficking of drugs, which are not relaxed for foreigners. It is illegal to buy, sell or possess opium, heroin, amphetamines, hallucinogenic mushrooms and marijuana. Possession of drugs can result in at least one year or more of prison time. Drug smuggling – defined as attempting to cross a border with drugs in your possession – carries considerably higher sanctions, including the death penalty.

Scams

Thais can be so friendly and laid-back that some visitors are lulled into a false sense of security, making them vulnerable to scams of all kinds. Bangkok is especially good at long, involved frauds that dupe travellers into thinking they've made a friend and are getting a bargain on highly valuable gemstones (which are actually pretty, sparkling glass).

All offers of free shopping or sightseeing help from strangers should be ignored. They will invariably take a commission from your purchases.

Theft & Fraud

Exercise diligence when it comes to your personal belongings. Ensure that your room is securely locked and carry your most important effects (passport, money, credit cards) on your person. Take care when leaving valuables in hotel safes.

Follow the same practice when you're travelling. A locked bag will not prevent theft on a long-haul bus.

When using a credit card, don't let vendors take your credit card out of your sight to run it through the machine. Unscrupulous merchants have been known to rub off three or four or more receipts with one purchase. Sometimes they wait several weeks – even months – between submitting each charge receipt to the bank so that you can't remember whether you've been billed by the same vendor more than once.

To avoid losing all of your travel money in an instant, use a credit card that is not directly linked to your bank account back home so that the operator doesn't have access to immediate funds.

Contact the **tourist police** (☎24hr hotline 1155) if you have any problems with consumer fraud.

Touts & Commissions

Touting is a longtime tradition in Asia, and while Thailand doesn't have as many touts as, say, India, it has its share. In Bangkok, túk-túk drivers, hotel employees and bar girls often take new arrivals on city tours; these almost always end up in high-pressure sales situations at silk, jewellery or handicraft shops.

Touts also steer customers to certain guesthouses that pay a commission (p412). Travel agencies are notorious for talking newly arrived tourists into staying at badly located, overpriced hotels.

Some travel agencies often masquerade as TAT, the government-funded tourist information office. They might put up agents wearing fake TAT badges or have signs that read TAT in big letters to entice travellers into their offices where they can sell them bus and train tickets for a commission. Be aware that the official TAT offices do not make hotel or transport bookings. If such a place offers to do this for you, then it is a travel agency not a tourist information office.

When making transport arrangements, talk to several travel agencies to look for the best price, as the commission percentage can vary greatly between agents. And resist high-intensity sales tactics from an agent trying to sign you up for everything: plane tickets, hotel, tours etc.

Government Travel Advice

The following government websites offer travel advisories and information on current hot spots.

Australian Department of Foreign Affairs (www.smarttraveller.gov.au)

British Foreign Office (www.gov.uk/foreign-travel-advice)

Canadian Department of Foreign Affairs (www.dfait-maeci.gc.ca)

New Zealand Foreign Affairs & Trade (www.safetravel.govt.nz)

US State Department (www.travel.state.gov/traveladvisories)

Telephone

The country code for Thailand is 66 and is used when calling the country from abroad. All Thai telephone numbers are preceded by a '0' if you're dialling domestically (the '0' is omitted when calling from overseas). After the initial '0', the next three numbers represent the provincial area code, which is now integral to the telephone number. If the initial '0' is followed by an '8' or a '9', then you're dialling a mobile phone.

International Calls

If you want to call an international number from a telephone in Thailand, you must first dial an international access code plus the country code followed by the subscriber number.

The standard international direct-dial prefix is 001. It is operated by the Communications Authority of Thailand (CAT) and is considered to have the best sound quality; it connects to the largest number of countries but is also the most expensive. The next best is 007, a prefix operated by the telecommunications company TOT, with reliable quality and slightly cheaper rates. If you have a Thai SIM card, the carrier will have its own direct-dial prefix, often with very cheap rates.

Dial 100 for operator-assisted international calls or reverse-charges (or collect) calls. Alternatively, contact your long-distance carrier for its overseas operator number, a toll-free call, or try 001 9991 2001 from a CAT phone and 1 800 000 120 from a TOT phone.

Mobile Phones

The easiest phone option in Thailand is to acquire a mobile phone equipped with a local SIM card. Mobile-phone providers include AIS, DTAC and True Move.

You have two phone options. You can buy a mobile phone in Thailand at one of the urban shopping malls or phone stores near the markets in provincial towns. Or you can use an imported phone that isn't SIM-locked (and supports the GSM network). To get started buy a SIM card from one of the carriers (AIS and DTAC are most popular), which includes an assigned telephone number. You will need to show your passport when you buy a SIM card, under a new regulation that means all phone numbers must be registered. Once your phone is SIM-enabled you can buy minutes with prepaid phonecards. SIM cards and refill cards (usually sold in 50B to 500B denominations) can be bought from 7-Elevens throughout the country.

Thailand has a 3G network and DTAC and True Move offer 4G LTE coverage in Bangkok, although it's not as fast as 4G should be. Coverage and quality of the different carriers varies from year to year based on network upgrades and capacity. True is regarded as having the highest data connectivity. Carriers usually sell talk-data packages based on usage amounts.

There are various promotions, but rates typically hover at around 1B to 2B per minute anywhere in Thailand and between 5B and 9B for international calls. SMS is usually 3B per message, making it the cheapest 'talk' option. All the companies offer unlimited data deals, usually for a week or a month, so shop around.

Overseas calls made in most hotel rooms usually incur additional surcharges (sometimes as much as 50% over and above the CAT rate); however, sometimes local calls are free or at standard rates. Some guesthouses will have a mobile phone or landline that customers can use for a per minute fee for overseas calls.

Time

Thailand is seven hours ahead of GMT/UTC (London). Times are often expressed according to the 24-hour clock.

Toilets

The Asian-style squat toilet is becoming less common in Thailand. There are still specimens in rural places, provincial bus stations, older homes and modest restaurants, but the Western-style toilet is becoming more prevalent and appears wherever foreign tourists can be found.

If you encounter a squat, here's what you should know. You should straddle the two footpads and face the door. To flush, use the plastic bowl to scoop water out of the adjacent basin and pour into the toilet bowl. Some places supply a small pack of toilet paper at the entrance (5B); otherwise bring your own stash or use water to clean yourself.

Even in places where sit-down toilets are installed, the septic system may not be designed to take toilet paper. In such cases there will be a waste basket where you should place used toilet paper and feminine hygiene products. Most modern toilets also come with a small spray hose – Thailand's version of the bidet.

Tourist Information

The government-operated tourist information and promotion service, **Tourism Authority of Thailand** (TAT; ☎nationwide call centre 1672; www.tourismthailand.org), produces excellent pamphlets on sightseeing, accommodation and transport. TAT's head office is in Bangkok and there are 22 regional offices throughout the country. TAT also has a number of overseas information offices; check its website for contact information.

Travellers with Disabilities

Thailand presents one large, ongoing obstacle course for the mobility impaired. With its high curbs, uneven footpaths and nonstop traffic, Bangkok can be particularly difficult. Many streets must be crossed via pedestrian bridges flanked by steep stairways, while buses and boats don't stop long enough even for the fully mobile. Rarely are there any ramps or other access points for wheelchairs.

A number of more expensive top-end hotels make consistent design efforts to provide disabled access to their properties. Other deluxe hotels with high employee-to-guest ratios are usually good about accommodating the mobility impaired by providing staff help where building design fails. For the rest, you're pretty much left to your own resources.

Some organisations and publications that offer tips on international travel include Accessible Journeys (www.disabilitytravel.com), Mobility International USA (www.miusa.org) and Society for Accessible Travel & Hospitality (www.sath.org).

Visas

Tourist Visas & Exemptions

The Thai government allows tourist-visa exemptions for 61 different nations – including Australia, New Zealand, the USA and most of Europe – allowing entry to the country without a pre-arranged visa for 30 days. A further 19 countries, including China, can get a visa on arrival valid for 15 days.

For those arriving in the kingdom by air, a 30-day visa is issued without a fee. For those arriving via a land border, the visa is valid for 15 days unless you hold a G7 passport, in which case you'll get 30 days. Some countries (including Brazil, South Korea, Argentina, Chile and Peru) receive a 90-day free visa at all borders.

Without proof of an onward ticket and sufficient funds for the projected stay any visitor can be denied entry, but in practice this is a formality that is rarely enforced.

If you plan to stay in Thailand longer than 30 days (or 15 days for land arrivals), you should apply for a 60-day tourist visa or, better still, a six-month multiple entry tourist visa from a Thai consulate or embassy before your trip. The six-month multiple-entry visa does require you to leave the country every 60 days (even if you only walk across a border, or fly out, and then come straight back). Contact the nearest Thai embassy or consulate to obtain application procedures and determine fees for tourist visas.

The **Ministry of Foreign Affairs** (☑02 203 5000; www.mfa.go.th) oversees immigration and visa issues.

Visa Extensions & Renewals

If you decide you want to stay longer than the allotted time, you can extend your visa by applying at any immigration office in Thailand. The usual fee for a visa extension is 1900B. Those issued with a standard stay of 15 or 30 days can extend their stay for seven to 10 days (depending on the immigration office) if the extension is handled before the visa expires. The 60-day tourist visa can be extended by up to 30 days at the discretion of Thai immigration authorities.

Another visa-renewal option is to cross a land border. A new 15-day visa (or 30 days if you hold a passport from a G7 country) will be issued upon your return and some short-term visitors make a day trip out of the 'visa run'.

If you overstay your visa, the usual penalty is a fine of 500B per day, with a 20,000B limit. Fines can be paid at the airport or in advance at an immigration office. If you've overstayed only one day, you don't have to pay. Children under 14 travelling with a parent do not have to pay the penalty.

Foreign residents in Thailand should arrange visa extensions at the immigration office closest to their in-country address.

Non-Immigrant Visas

The Non-Immigrant Visa is good for 90 days and is intended for foreigners entering the country for business, study, retirement and extended family visits. There are multiple-entry visas available in this visa class; you're more likely to be granted multiple entries if you apply at a Thai embassy in Europe, the USA or Australia than elsewhere. If you plan to apply for a Thai work permit, you'll need to possess a Non-Immigrant Visa first.

Volunteering

There are many wonderful volunteering organisations in Thailand that provide meaningful work and cultural engagement. Volunteer Work Thailand (www.volunteerworkthailand.org) maintains a database of opportunities. See p36 for more information.

Women Travellers

Women travellers face relatively few problems in Thailand. With the great amount of respect afforded to women, an equal measure should be returned.

➡ Thai women, especially the younger generation, are showing more skin than in the recent past. You can wear spaghetti-strap tops and navel-bearing shirts without offending Thais' sense of modesty. But it is respectful to cover up if you're going deep into rural communities, entering temples or going to/from the beach.

➡ Attacks and rapes are not common in Thailand, but do occur, especially when an attacker observes a vulnerable target. If you return home from a bar alone, be sure to have your wits about you. Avoid accepting rides from strangers late at night or travelling around in isolated areas by yourself.

➡ Be aware that frivolous flirting could unintentionally cause a Thai man to feel a loss of face, especially when the involved parties have different intentions.

Work

Thailand is a huge destination for temporary work stints, especially those involving English teaching. To work legally in the country, you need a non-immigrant visa (p420) and a work permit – which legitimate institutions should be able to provide. An excellent resource for background on teaching in Thailand, as well as a resource for jobs, is Ajarn.com (www.ajarn.com).

Transport

GETTING THERE & AWAY

Flights, tours and rail tickets can be booked online at lonelyplanet.com/bookings.

Entering Thailand

Entry procedures for Thailand, by air or by land, are straightforward: you'll have to show your passport and you'll need to present completed arrival and departure cards. Blank arrival and departure cards are usually distributed on the incoming flight or, if you're arriving by land, can be picked up at the immigration counter.

Air

Airports & Airlines

Bangkok is Thailand's primary international and domestic gateway and one of the world's busiest air hubs. Most major airlines, and many smaller ones, fly to Bangkok. Chiang Mai, Ko Samui and Phuket also have international flights. There are smaller airports throughout the country serving domestic and sometimes inter-regional routes.

SUVARNABHUMI INTERNATIONAL AIRPORT

Located 30km east of central Bangkok, **Suvarnabhumi International Airport** (☎02 132 1888; www.suvarnabhumiairport.com) began commercial international and domestic service in 2006 and is today the country's principal international airport. The airport's name is pronounced *sù·wan·ná·poom*. The airport website has real-time details of arrivals and departures.

DON MUEANG INTERNATIONAL AIRPORT

Bangkok's other airport, **Don Mueang International Airport** (☎02 535 2111; www.donmueangairportthai.com), 25km north of central Bangkok, was retired from service in 2006 only to reopen later as Bangkok's de facto budget airline hub. Many short-haul international flights, principally to Asian destinations, arrive and depart from here. Terminal 1 handles international flights while Terminal 2 handles domestic destinations.

PHUKET INTERNATIONAL AIRPORT

Phuket International Airport (☎076 632 7230; www.phuketairportthai.com) serves several domestic and international destinations.

SAMUI INTERNATIONAL AIRPORT

Samui International Airport (www.samuiairportonline.com) serves overseas destinations including Singapore.

Tickets

In some cases – such as when travelling to neigh-

CLIMATE CHANGE & TRAVEL

Every form of transport that relies on carbon-based fuel generates CO_2, the main cause of human-induced climate change. Modern travel is dependent on aeroplanes, which might use less fuel per kilometre per person than most cars but travel much greater distances. The altitude at which aircraft emit gases (including CO_2) and particles also contributes to their climate change impact. Many websites offer 'carbon calculators' that allow people to estimate the carbon emissions generated by their journey and, for those who wish to do so, to offset the impact of the greenhouse gases emitted with contributions to portfolios of climate-friendly initiatives throughout the world. Lonely Planet offsets the carbon footprint of all staff and author travel.

bouring countries or to domestic destinations – it is still convenient to use a travel agent in Thailand. The amount of commission an agent will charge varies, so shop around to gauge the discrepancy in prices. Paying by credit card generally offers purchasing protection, because most card issuers provide refunds if you can prove you didn't get what you paid for. Agents who accept only cash should hand over the tickets straightaway and not tell you to 'come back tomorrow'. After you've made a booking or paid your deposit, call the airline and confirm that the booking was made.

Air fares during the high season (December to March) can be expensive and seats book up quickly.

Land

Thailand shares land borders with Laos, Malaysia, Cambodia and Myanmar. Travel between all of these countries can be done by land via sanctioned border crossings. With improved highways, it is also becoming easier to travel from Thailand to China.

Bus, Car & Motorcyle

Road connections exist between Thailand and all of its neighbours, and these routes can be travelled by bus, shared taxi and private car. In some cases, you'll take a bus to the border point, pass through immigration and then pick up another bus or shared taxi on the other side. In other cases, especially when crossing the Cambodian and Malaysian borders, the bus will stop for immigration formalities and then continue to its destination across the border.

Train

There are several border crossings for which you can take a train to the border and then switch to automobile transport on the other side. The Thai–Cambodian border crossing of Aranya Prathet to Poipet and the Thai–Laos crossing of Nong Khai to Vientiane are two examples.

There are also trains to Sungai Kolok and Padang Besar, where you can cross the border to Malaysia, but because of ongoing violence in Thailand's Deep South we don't recommend these routes for travellers.

Border Crossings

Make sure you familiarise yourself with all relevant visa information (p420).

CAMBODIA

Cambodian tourist visas are available at the border for US$30, though some borders charge 1200B. Bring a passport photo and avoid the runner boys who want to issue a health certificate or other 'medical' paperwork for additional fees.

Aranya Prathet to Poipet The most direct land route between Bangkok and Angkor Wat.

Chong Sa to Ngam Choam Remote border crossing, where you'll have to hire private transport (instead of a shared taxi) on the Cambodian side of the border.

Hat Lek to Krong Koh Kong The coastal crossing for travellers heading to/from Ko Chang/Sihanoukville.

O Smach to Chong Chom Periodically closed due to fighting at Khao Phra Wihan. You'll have to hire private transport on the Cambodian side.

Pong Nam Ron to Pailin A backdoor route from Ko Chang (via Chanthaburi) to Battambang and Angkor Wat.

CHINA

Yúnnán province in southwest China is accessible via Laos. You'll need to arrange your Chinese visa prior to departure, ideally in Bangkok or Chiang Mai.

The main crossing in Laos is Boten to Mengla. You can reach Boten in five to six hours from Chiang Khong via Huay Xai.

LAOS

It is hassle-free to cross into Laos from northern and northeastern Thailand. Lao visas (US$35 to US$50) can be obtained on arrival, and applications require a passport photo.

Chiang Khong to Huay Xai Increasingly popular now that you can cross via the fourth Thai–Lao Friendship Bridge. From Huay Xai, there are boats to Luang Prabang.

Chong Mek to Vangtao Land crossing to southern Laos. From Vangato, there are buses to Pakse.

Nakhon Phanom to Tha Khaek Cross the third Thai–Lao Friendship Bridge to central Laos.

Nong Khai to Vientiane The main transport gateway to Laos via the first Thai–Lao Friendship Bridge.

Mukdahan to Savannakhet Mainly used by locals. The site of the second Thai–Lao Friendship Bridge.

MALAYSIA

Malaysia, especially the west coast, is easy to reach via bus, train and even boat.

As well as the crossings listed here, other crossings include Hat Yai to Padang Besar and Sungai Kolok to Kota Bharu, but we don't recommend taking these routes due to the violence in the Deep South.

Ko Lipe to Pulau Langkawi Boats provide a convenient high-season link between these two Andaman islands.

Satun to Kuala Perlis Minivans run between Satun and the Malaysian town of Kuala Perlis.

To and from Langkawi by boat You can cross into and out of Thailand via public boat from the Andaman coast to the Malaysian island of Langkawi. All foreign-registered private vessels, skippers and crew must check in with the relevant Thai authorities within 24 hours of entering Thai waters. Although major ports throughout Thailand offer port check-ins, most leisure-boating visitors check in at Phuket, Krabi,

Ko Samui, Pranburi or Pattaya. Before departing from Thailand by boat, you must also check out with immigration, customs and the harbourmaster.

MYANMAR

It is possible to cross to/from Myanmar at four different places. The Singkhon Pass crossing close to Prachuap Khiri Khan is expected to open to foreigners in the future. You must obtain a visa in advance from a Myanmar embassy or consulate.

Ban Phu Nam Ron to Htee-Khee The most isolated and least-used crossing. Ban Phu Nam Ron is accessed from Kanchanburi. From Htee-Khee, there is transport to Dawei in southern Myanmar.

Mae Sai to Tachileik This crossing is popular with travellers looking to renew their Thai visas, as it is close to Chiang Mai and Chiang Rai.

Mae Sot to Myawaddy Remote and mostly used by locals. From Myawaddy, there is onward transport to Hpa-an, Mawlamyine and Yangon in Myanmar.

Ranong to Kawthoung Crossing in southern Thailand. It's convenient if you've been travelling the Andaman Coast.

Sea

Bangkok and the big islands are frequent ports of call for cruise ships.

In high season, ferries link Ko Lipe to Pulau Langkawi in Malaysia.

GETTING AROUND

Air

Hopping around the country by air continues to be affordable. Most routes originate from Bangkok, but Ko Samui and Phuket all have a few routes to other Thai towns.

Thai Airways International operates many domestic air routes from Bangkok to provincial capitals. Bangkok Air is another established domestic carrier. Air Asia and Nok Air are the domestic budget carriers.

Bicycle

For travelling just about anywhere outside Bangkok, bicycles are an ideal form of local transport – cheap, nonpolluting and slow-moving enough to allow travellers to see everything. Bicycles can be hired in many locations, especially guesthouses, for as little as 100B per day, though they aren't always high quality. A security deposit isn't usually required.

Bicycle touring is also a popular way to see the country; most roads are sealed and have roomy shoulders. With duties high on imported bikes, in most cases you'll do better to bring your own bike to Thailand rather than purchasing one there.

No special permits are needed for bringing a bicycle into the country, although it may be registered by customs – which means if you don't leave the country with your bicycle, you'll have to pay a customs duty. It's advisable to bring a well-stocked repair kit.

Boat

Long-tail boats are a staple of transport on rivers and canals in Bangkok and in the south.

Between the mainland and islands in the Gulf of Thailand or the Andaman Sea, you may also see 8m- to 10m-long wooden boats, with an inboard engine and a simple roof to shelter passengers and cargo. Faster, more expensive hovercraft or jetfoils are available in tourist areas.

Bus & Minivan

The bus network in Thailand is prolific and reliable, and is a great way to see the countryside and sit among the locals. The Thai government subsidises the Transport Company (*bò·rí·sàt kŏn sòng*), usually abbreviated to Baw Khaw Saw (BKS). Every city and town in Thailand linked by bus has a BKS station, even if it's just a patch of dirt by the side of the road.

By far the most reliable bus companies in Thailand are the ones that operate out of the government-run BKS stations. In some cases the companies are entirely state-owned; in others they are private concessions.

Be aware of bus scams. We do not recommend using bus companies that operate directly out of tourist centres, such as Bangkok's Th Khao San, because of repeated instances of theft and commission-seeking stops.

Increasingly minivans are the middle-class option. They are run by private companies and because their vehicles are smaller they can depart from the market (instead of the out-of-town bus stations) and will deliver guests directly to their hotel.

Classes

The cheapest and slowest are the *rót tam·má·dah* (ordinary fan buses), which stop in every little town and for every waving hand along the highway. Only a few of these ordinary buses, in rural locations or for local destinations, still exist since most have been replaced by air-con buses.

The bulk of the bus service consists of faster, more comfortable air-con buses, called *rót aa* (air bus). Longer routes offer at least two classes of air-con buses: 2nd class and 1st class. The latter have toilets. 'VIP' and 'Super VIP' buses have fewer seats so that each seat reclines further; sometimes these are called *rót norn* (sleeper bus).

It is handy to bring along a jacket, especially for long-distance trips, as the air-con can put the cabin into a deep freeze.

The service on these buses is usually quite good and normally includes a beverage service and video.

On overnight journeys the buses usually stop somewhere en route for 'midnight *kôw đôm*' (rice soup), when passengers are awakened to get off the bus for a meal.

Reservations

➡ You can book air-con BKS buses at any BKS terminal.

➡ Ordinary (fan) buses cannot be booked in advance.

➡ Privately run buses can be booked through most hotels or any travel agency, but it's best to book directly through a bus office to be sure that you get what you pay for.

Car & Motorcycle

Renting a motorbike or car to get around makes things convenient, but be wary. Driving on Thai roads can be a hazardous affair: jumping red lights, undertaking (passing on the kerb side of the slower vehicle) and driving on the wrong side of the road are just some of the dangers to watch out for. Make sure you have insurance to cover any medical bills.

Driving Licence

Short-term visitors who wish to drive vehicles (including motorcycles) in Thailand need an International Driving Permit (IDP), though this requirement is rarely enforced when renting motorbikes.

Fuel

Modern petrol (gasoline) stations are in plentiful supply all over Thailand wherever there are paved roads. In more remote, off-road areas *ben·sin/nám·man rót yon* (petrol containing benzene) is usually available at small roadside or village stands. All fuel in Thailand is unleaded, and diesel is used by trucks and some passenger cars. Several alternative fuels, including gasohol (a blend of petrol and ethanol that comes in different octane levels, either 91% or 95%) and compressed natural gas, are used by taxis with bifuel capabilities. For news and updates about fuel options, and other car talk, see the website of BKK Auto (www.bkkautos.com).

Hire

Cars, 4WDs and vans can be rented in most major cities and at airports from local companies as well as international chains. Local companies are sometimes cheaper than the international chains, but their fleets of cars tend to be older and not as well maintained.

Motorcycles can be rented in major towns and many smaller tourist centres from guesthouses and small family businesses for 200B a day and up. Renting a motorcycle in Thailand is easy and a great way to tour the countryside.

➡ Many tourists are injured riding motorcycles in Thailand because they don't know how to handle the vehicle and are unfamiliar with the road rules and conditions.

➡ Before renting a motorcycle, check the vehicle's condition and ask for a helmet (which is required by law).

➡ Drive slowly, especially when roads are slick, to avoid damage to yourself and to the vehicle, and be sure you have adequate health insurance.

➡ If you've never ridden a motorcycle before, stick to the smaller 100cc step-through bikes with automatic clutches.

➡ Remember to distribute weight as evenly as possible across the frame of the bike to improve handling.

➡ If you fall off, you will be paying both medical bills and for any damage to the bike.

Insurance

Thailand requires a minimum of liability insurance for all registered vehicles on the road. The better hire companies include comprehensive coverage for their vehicles.

➡ Always verify that a vehicle is insured for liability before signing a rental contract; you should also ask to see the dated insurance documents.

➡ If you have an accident while driving an uninsured vehicle, you're in for some major hassles.

Road Rules & Hazards

Thais drive on the left-hand side of the road (most of the time!). Other than that, just about anything goes, in spite of road signs and speed limits.

The main rule to be aware of is that right of way goes to the bigger vehicle; this is not what it says in the Thai traffic law, but it's the reality. Maximum speed limits are 50km/h on urban roads and 80km/h to 100km/h on most highways – but on any given stretch of highway you'll see various vehicles travelling as slowly as 30km/h and as fast as 150km/h.

In Bangkok traffic is chaotic, roads are poorly signposted, and motorcycles and random contraflows mean you can suddenly find yourself facing a wall of cars coming the other way. Outside the capital, the principal hazard when driving in Thailand, besides the general disregard for traffic laws, is having to contend with so many different types of vehicles on the same road – trucks, bicycles, túk-túks and motorcycles. This danger is often compounded by the lack of working lights. In village areas the vehicular traffic is lighter, but you have to deal with stray chickens, dogs and water buffaloes.

- Indicators are often used to warn passing drivers about oncoming traffic.
- A flashing left indicator means it's OK to pass, while a right indicator means that someone's approaching from the other direction.
- Horns are used to tell other vehicles that the driver plans to pass. When drivers flash their lights, they're telling you not to pass.

SĂHM·LÓR & TÚK-TÚK

Săhm·lór (also spelt '*săamláw*') are three-wheeled pedicabs and are now all but extinct.

The modern era's version of the human-powered săhm·lór is the motorised túk-túk (pronounced *đúk đúk*). They're small utility vehicles, powered by screaming engines (usually LPG-powered) and a lot of flash and sparkle.

With either form of transport the fare must be established by bargaining before departure. In tourist centres, túk-túk drivers often grossly overcharge foreigners, so it's useful to have a sense of how much the fare should be before soliciting a ride. Hotel staff are helpful in providing reasonable fare suggestions.

Readers interested in pedicab lore and design may want to have a look at Lonely Planet's hardcover pictorial book *Chasing Rickshaws*, by Lonely Planet founder Tony Wheeler.

Hitching

Hitching is never entirely safe, and we don't recommend it. Travellers who hitch should understand that they are taking a small but potentially serious risk.

Hitching is rare in Thailand these days, so most passing motorists might not realise the intentions of the foreigner standing on the side of the road with a thumb out. When Thais want a ride they wave their hand with the palm facing the ground. This is the same gesture used to flag a taxi or bus, which is why some drivers might stop and point to a bus stop if one is nearby.

In some of the national parks without public transport, Thais are often willing to pick up a passenger standing by the side of the road.

Local Transport

City Bus & Sŏrng·tăa·ou

Bangkok has the largest city-bus system in the country. The etiquette for riding public buses is to wait at a bus stop and hail the vehicle by waving your hand palm-side downward. You typically pay the fare once you've taken a seat or, in some cases, when you disembark.

Elsewhere, public transport is provided by *sŏrng·tăa·ou* (a small pick-up truck outfitted with two facing rows of benches for passengers). They sometimes operate on fixed routes, just like buses, but they may also run a shared taxi service where they pick up passengers going in the same general direction. In tourist centres, *sŏrng·tăa·ou* can be chartered just like a regular taxi, but you'll need to negotiate the fare beforehand. You can usually hail a *sŏrng·tăa·ou* anywhere along its route and pay the fare when you disembark.

Depending on the region, *sŏrng·tăa·ou* might also run a fixed route from the centre of town to outlying areas or even points within the provinces. Sometimes these vehicles are larger six-wheeled vehicles (sometimes called *rót hòk lór*).

Mass Transit

Bangkok is the only city in Thailand to have an above-ground and an underground light-rail public-transport system. Known as the Skytrain and the Metro respectively, both systems have helped to alleviate the capital's notorious traffic jams, but are restricted to just three routes.

Motorcycle Taxi

Many cities in Thailand have *mor·deu·sai ráp jâhng* (100cc to 125cc motorcycles) that can be hired, with a driver, for short distances. If you're empty-handed or travelling with a small bag, they can't be beaten for transport in a pinch.

In most cities, you'll find motorcycle taxis clustered near street intersections. Usually they wear numbered vest-like jackets. Fares start at 15B for very short hops. Establish the price before you jump on the back.

Taxi

Bangkok has the most formal system of metered taxis. In other cities, a taxi can be a private vehicle with negotiable rates. You can also travel between cities by taxi, but you'll need to negotiate a price as few taxi drivers will run a meter for intercity travel.

Train

Thailand's train system is most convenient as an alternative to buses for the long journey south or from Bangkok to Chiang Mai. However, delays are common on many routes.

The 4500km rail network is operated by the **State Railway of Thailand** (SRT; www.railway.co.th) and covers four main lines: the northern, southern, northeastern and eastern lines. All long-distance trains originate from Bangkok's Hualamphong station.

Classes

The SRT operates passenger trains in three classes – 1st, 2nd and 3rd – but each class varies considerably depending on whether you're on an ordinary, rapid or special-express train.

First class In 1st class, passengers have private cabins, which are available only on rapid, express and special-express trains.

Second class The seating arrangements in a 2nd-class, non-sleeper carriage are similar to those on a bus, with padded seats facing towards the front of the train. On 2nd-class sleeper cars, pairs of seats face one another and convert into two fold-down berths. The lower berth has more headroom than the upper berth and this is reflected in a higher fare. Children are always assigned a lower berth. There are air-con and fan 2nd-class carriages; 2nd-class carriages are only found on rapid and express trains.

Third class A typical 3rd-class carriage consists of two rows of bench seats divided into facing pairs. Each bench seat is designed to seat two or three passengers, but on a crowded rural line nobody seems to care.

Costs

Fares are determined by a base price with surcharges added for distance, class and train type (special-express, express, rapid or ordinary). Extra charges are added if the carriage has air-con and for sleeping berths (either upper or lower).

Reservations

Advance bookings can be made from one to 60 days before your intended date of departure. You can make bookings in person at any train station. Train tickets can also be purchased at travel agencies, which usually add a service charge to the ticket price. If you are planning long-distance train travel from outside the country, you should email the State Railway of Thailand (via the Contact Us page on its website) at least two weeks before your journey. You will receive an email confirming the booking. Pick up and pay for tickets an hour before leaving at the scheduled departure train station.

It is advisable to make advanced bookings for long-distance sleeper trains from Bangkok, especially around Songkran in April and the peak tourist-season months of December and January.

For short-distance trips you should purchase your ticket at least a day in advance for seats (rather than sleepers).

Partial refunds on tickets are available depending on the number of days prior to your departure you arrange for a cancellation. These arrangements can be handled at the train station booking office.

Station Services

You'll find that all train stations in Thailand have baggage-storage services (or cloak rooms). Most stations have a ticket window that will open between 15 and 30 minutes before train arrivals. There are also newsagents and small snack vendors and cafes.

Most train stations have printed timetables in English, although this isn't always the case for smaller stations. Bangkok's Hualamphong station is a good spot to load up on timetables.

Health

Health risks and the quality of medical facilities vary depending on where and how you travel in Thailand. The majority of major cities and popular tourist areas are well developed with adequate and even excellent medical care. This is not the case in remote rural areas.

Travellers tend to worry about contracting exotic infectious diseases when visiting the tropics, but such infections are far less common than problems with pre-existing medical conditions and accidental injury (especially as a result of traffic accidents).

Becoming ill in some way is common, however. Respiratory infections, diarrhoea and dengue fever are particular hazards in Thailand. Fortunately, most common illnesses can be prevented or are easily treated.

BEFORE YOU GO

Insurance

Don't travel without health insurance – accidents *do* happen. You may require extra cover for adventure activities such as rock climbing or diving, as well as scooter/motorcycle riding. If your health insurance doesn't cover you for medical expenses abroad, ensure you get specific travel insurance that does. Most hospitals require an upfront guarantee of payment (from yourself or your insurer) prior to admission.

Enquire before your trip about payment of medical charges and retain all documentation (medical reports, invoices etc) for claim purposes.

Medication

Pack medications in clearly labelled original containers and obtain a signed and dated letter from your physician describing your medical conditions, medications and syringes or needles. If you have a heart condition, bring a copy of your electrocardiography (ECG) taken just prior to travelling.

If you take any regular medication bring double your needs. In Thailand you can buy many medications over the counter without a doctor's prescription, but it can be difficult to find the exact medication you are taking.

Websites

International Travel & Health (www.who.int/ith) Published by the World Health Organization.

Centers for Disease Control & Prevention (www.cdc.gov) Has country-specific advice.

Travelling Well (www.travellingwell.com.au) A health guidebook and website by Dr Deborah Mills.

IN THAILAND

Availability & Cost of Health Care

Bangkok is considered the nearest centre of medical excellence for many countries in Southeast Asia. Private hospitals are more expensive than other medical facilities but offer a superior standard of care and English-speaking staff. The cost of health care is relatively cheap in Thailand compared to most Western countries.

Self-treatment may be appropriate if your problem is minor (eg traveller's diarrhoea), you are carrying the appropriate medication and you are unable to attend a recommended clinic or hospital.

Be careful buying medication over the counter as there are still cases of fake medications and poorly stored or out-of-date drugs, especially outside major cities.

Infectious Diseases

Cutaneous Larva Migrans

This disease, caused by dog or cat hookworm, is particularly common on the beaches of Thailand. The rash starts as a small lump, and then slowly spreads like a winding line. It is intensely itchy, especially at

MOSQUITO AVOIDANCE TIPS

Travellers are advised to prevent mosquito bites by taking these steps:

- use a DEET-containing insect repellent on exposed skin
- sleep under a mosquito net, ideally impregnated with permethrin
- choose accommodation with screens and fans
- impregnate clothing with permethrin in high-risk areas
- wear long sleeves and trousers in light colours
- use mosquito coils
- spray your room with insect repellent before going out

night. It is easily treated with medications and should not be cut out or frozen.

Dengue Fever

This mosquito-borne disease is increasingly problematic throughout Southeast Asia, especially in cities. The southern islands of Thailand are particularly high-risk areas. As there is no vaccine, it can only be prevented by avoiding mosquito bites. The mosquito that carries dengue is a daytime biter, so use insect-avoidance measures at all times.

Symptoms include high fever, severe headache (especially behind the eyes), nausea and body aches (dengue was previously known as 'breakbone fever'). Some people develop a rash (which can be very itchy) and experience diarrhoea. There is no specific treatment, just rest and paracetamol – do not take aspirin or ibuprofen as they increase the risk of haemorrhaging. See a doctor to be diagnosed and monitored.

Dengue can progress to the more severe and life-threatening dengue haemorrhagic fever; however, this is very uncommon in tourists. The risk of this increases substantially if you have previously been infected with dengue and are then infected with a different serotype.

Hepatitis A

The risk in Bangkok is decreasing but there is still significant risk in most of the country. This food- and water-borne virus infects the liver, causing jaundice (yellow skin and eyes), nausea and lethargy. There is no specific treatment for hepatitis A. In rare instances, it can be fatal for those over the age of 40. All travellers to Thailand should be vaccinated against hepatitis A.

Hepatitis B

The only sexually transmitted disease (STD) that can be prevented by vaccination, hepatitis B is spread by body fluids, including sexual contact. In some parts of Thailand up to 20% of the population are carriers of hepatitis B, and usually are unaware of this. The long-term consequences can include liver cancer, cirrhosis and death.

HIV/AIDS

HIV/AIDS is now one of the most common causes of death for people under the age of 50 in Thailand. Always practise safe sex and be careful if getting tattooed. Never use unclean or used syringes.

Influenza

Present year-round in the tropics, flu is the most common vaccine-preventable disease contracted by travellers, so everyone should consider vaccination. There is no specific treatment, just rest and paracetamol.

Leptospirosis

Leptospirosis is contracted from exposure to infected surface water – most commonly after river rafting or canyoning. Early symptoms are very similar to the flu and include headache and fever. It can vary from a very mild ailment to a fatal disease. Diagnosis is made through blood tests and it is easily treated with Doxycycline.

Malaria

Most parts of Thailand visited by tourists, particularly city and resort areas, have minimal to no risk of malaria, and the risk of side effects from taking antimalarial tablets is likely to outweigh the risk of getting the disease itself. If you are travelling to high-risk rural areas (unlikely for most visitors), seek medical advice on the right medication and dosage for you.

Malaria is caused by a parasite transmitted by the bite of an infected mosquito. The most significant symptom of malaria is fever, but general symptoms such as headache, diarrhoea, cough or chills may also occur – the same symptoms as many

RECOMMENDED VACCINATIONS

The only vaccine required in Thailand by international regulations is yellow fever. Proof of vaccination will only be required if you have visited a country in the yellow-fever zone (in Africa and South America only) within the six days prior to entering Thailand.

Specialised travel-medicine clinics are your best source of information on which vaccinations you should consider taking. The Centers for Disease Control (www.cdc.gov) has a travellers' health section that contains recommendations for vaccinations.

RARE, BUT BE AWARE

Avian Influenza Most of those infected have had close contact with sick or dead birds.

Filariasis A mosquito-borne disease that is common in the local population; practise mosquito-avoidance measures.

Hepatitis E Transmitted through contaminated food and water and has similar symptoms to hepatitis A; can be a severe problem in pregnant women. Follow safe eating and drinking guidelines.

Japanese B Encephalitis Viral disease transmitted by mosquitoes, typically occurring in rural areas; vaccination is recommended for travellers spending more than one month outside cities.

Meliodosis Contracted by skin contact with soil. The symptoms are very similar to tuberculosis (TB). There is no vaccine, but it can be treated with medications.

Strongyloides A parasite transmitted by skin contact with soil; common in local populations. It is characterised by an unusual skin rash – a linear rash on the trunk that comes and goes. An overwhelming infection can follow. It can be treated with medications.

Tuberculosis The main symptoms are fever, cough, weight loss, night sweats and tiredness. Treatment is available with long-term multidrug regimens.

Typhus Murine typhus is spread by the bite of a flea; scrub typhus is spread via a mite. Symptoms include fever, muscle pains and a rash. Following general insect-avoidance measures and taking Doxycycline will also prevent them.

other infections. A diagnosis can only be made by taking a blood sample.

Measles

This highly contagious viral infection is spread through coughing and sneezing and remains prevalent in Thailand. Measles starts with a high fever and rash and can be complicated by pneumonia and brain disease. There is no specific treatment. Ensure you are fully vaccinated.

Rabies

This uniformly fatal disease is spread by the bite or lick of an infected animal – most commonly a dog or monkey. You should seek medical advice immediately after any animal bite and commence post-exposure treatment. Having a pre-travel vaccination means the post-bite treatment is greatly simplified.

If an animal bites you, gently wash the wound with soap and water, and apply iodine-based antiseptic. If you are not pre-vaccinated, you will need to receive rabies immunoglobulin as soon as possible, followed by five shots of vaccine over 28 days. If pre-vaccinated, you need just two shots of vaccine given three days apart.

STDs

The sexually transmitted diseases most common in Thailand include herpes, warts, syphilis, gonorrhoea and chlamydia. People carrying these diseases often have no signs of infection. Condoms will prevent gonorrhoea and chlamydia but not warts or herpes. If after a sexual encounter you develop any rash, lumps, discharge or pain when passing urine, seek immediate medical attention. If you have been sexually active during your travels, have an STD check on your return home.

Typhoid

This serious bacterial infection is spread through food and water. It gives a high and slowly progressive fever and severe headache, and may be accompanied by a dry cough and stomach pain. It is diagnosed by blood tests and treated with antibiotics. Vaccination is recommended for all travellers spending more than a week in Thailand, or travelling outside the major cities. Be aware that vaccination is not 100% effective, so you must still be careful with what you eat and drink.

Traveller's Diarrhoea

Traveller's diarrhoea is by far the most common problem affecting travellers – up to 50% of people will suffer from some form of it within two weeks of starting their trip. In over 80% of cases, traveller's diarrhoea is caused by a bacteria (there are numerous potential culprits), and responds promptly to treatment with antibiotics.

Here we define traveller's diarrhoea as the passage of more than three watery bowel movements within 24 hours, plus at least one other symptom such as vomiting, fever, cramps, nausea or feeling generally unwell.

Treatment consists of staying well hydrated; rehydration solutions such as Gastrolyte are the best for this. Antibiotics such as Norfloxacin, Ciprofloxacin or Azithromycin will kill the bacteria quickly.

Loperamide is just a 'stopper' and doesn't get to the cause of the problem. It can be helpful, for example, if you have to go on a long bus ride. Don't take Loperamide if you have a fever or blood in your stools. Seek medical attention quickly if you do not respond to an appropriate antibiotic.

Giardia lamblia is a parasite that is relatively common in travellers. Symptoms include nausea, bloating, excess gas, fatigue and intermittent diarrhoea. 'Eggy' burps are often attributed solely to giardiasis. The treatment of choice is Tinidazole, with Metronidazole being a second-line option.

Amoebic dysentery is very rare in travellers but may be misdiagnosed by poor-quality labs. Symptoms are similar to bacterial diarrhoea. You should always seek reliable medical care if you have blood in your diarrhoea. Treatment involves two drugs: Tinidazole or Metronidazole to kill the parasite in your gut and then a second drug to kill the cysts. If left untreated, complications such as liver abscesses can occur.

Environmental Hazards

Food

Eating in restaurants is the biggest risk factor for contracting traveller's diarrhoea. Ways to avoid it include eating only freshly cooked food and avoiding food that has been sitting around in buffets. Peel all fruit and cook vegetables. Eat in busy restaurants with a high turnover of customers.

Heat

For most people it takes at least two weeks to adapt to the hot climate. Prevent swelling of the feet and ankles as well as muscle cramps caused by excessive sweating by avoiding dehydration and excessive activity in the heat of the day.

Heatstroke requires immediate medical treatment. Symptoms come on suddenly and include weakness, nausea, a hot dry body with a body temperature of more than 41°C (105.8°F), dizziness, confusion, loss of coordination, fits and eventually collapse and loss of consciousness.

Insect Bites & Stings

Bedbugs live in the cracks of furniture and walls and then migrate to the bed at night to feed on humans. You can treat the itch with an antihistamine.

Ticks are contracted when walking in rural areas. They are commonly found behind the ears, on the belly and in armpits. If you've been bitten by a tick and a rash develops at the site of the bite or elsewhere, along with fever or muscle aches, see a doctor. Doxycycline prevents tick-borne diseases.

Leeches are found in humid rainforests. They do not

MEDICAL CHECKLIST

Recommended items for a personal medical kit include the following:

- antifungal cream, eg Clotrimazole
- antibacterial cream, eg Muciprocin
- antibiotic for skin infections, eg Amoxicillin/Clavulanate or Cephalexin
- antibiotics for diarrhoea include Norfloxacin, Ciprofloxacin or Azithromycin for bacterial diarrhoea; for giardiasis or amoebic dysentery take Tinidazole
- antihistamine – there are many options, eg Cetrizine for daytime and Promethazine for night
- antiseptic, eg Betadine
- contraceptives
- decongestant
- DEET-based insect repellent
- oral rehydration solution for diarrhoea (eg Gastrolyte), diarrhoea 'stopper' (eg Loperamide) and antinausea medication (eg Prochlorperazine)
- first-aid items such as scissors, Elastoplasts, bandages, gauze, thermometer (but not one with mercury), sterile needles and syringes (with a doctor's letter), safety pins and tweezers
- hand gel or hand wipes (both alcohol based)
- ibuprofen or another anti-inflammatory
- laxative, eg Coloxyl
- paracetamol
- steroid cream for allergic or itchy rashes, eg 1% to 2% hydrocortisone
- thrush (vaginal yeast infection) treatment, eg Clotrimazole pessaries or Diflucan tablet
- Ural or equivalent if you are prone to urine infections

transmit disease, but their bites are often itchy for weeks afterwards and can easily become infected. Apply an iodine-based antiseptic to the bite to help prevent infection.

Bee and wasp stings mainly cause problems for people who are allergic to them. Anyone with a serious allergy should carry an injection of adrenalin (eg an EpiPen) for emergencies. For others, pain is the main problem – apply ice to the sting and take painkillers.

Parasites

Numerous parasites are common in local populations in Thailand, but most of these are rare in travellers. To avoid parasitic infections, wear shoes and avoid eating raw food, especially fish, pork and vegetables.

Skin Problems

Prickly heat is a common skin rash in the tropics, caused by sweat being trapped under the skin. Treat by taking cool showers and using powders.

Two fungal rashes commonly affect travellers. The first occurs in the groin, armpits and between the toes. It starts as a red patch that slowly spreads and is usually itchy. Treatment involves keeping the skin dry, avoiding chafing and using an antifungal cream such as Clotrimazole or Lamisil. The fungus *Tinea versicolor* causes small and light-coloured patches, most commonly on the back, chest and shoulders. Consult a doctor.

Cuts and scratches become easily infected in humid climates. Immediately wash all wounds in clean water and apply antiseptic. If you develop signs of infection, see a doctor. Coral cuts can easily become infected.

Snakes

Though snake bites are rare for travellers, there are more than 85 species of venomous snakes in Thailand. Wear boots and long pants if walking in an area that may have snakes.

The Thai Red Cross produces antivenin for many of the poisonous snakes in Thailand.

Sunburn

Even on a cloudy day, sunburn can occur rapidly. Use a strong sunscreen (at least factor 30+), making sure to reapply after a swim, and always wear a wide-brimmed hat and sunglasses outdoors. If you become sunburnt stay out of the sun until you have recovered, apply cool compresses and take painkillers for the discomfort. 1% hydrocortisone cream applied twice daily is also helpful.

JELLYFISH STINGS

Box jellyfish stings are extremely painful and can even be fatal. There are two main types of box jellyfish – multi-tentacled and single-tentacled.

Multi-tentacled box jellyfish are present in Thai waters – these are the most dangerous and a severe envenomation can kill an adult within two minutes. They are generally found along sandy beaches near river mouths and mangroves during the warmer months.

There are many types of single-tentacled box jellyfish, some of which can cause severe symptoms known as the Irukandji syndrome. The initial sting can seem minor; however, severe symptoms such as back pain, nausea, vomiting, sweating, difficulty breathing and a feeling of impending doom can develop between five and 40 minutes later. There are many other jellyfish in Thailand that cause irritating stings but no serious effects. The only way to prevent these stings is to wear protective clothing.

For severe, life-threatening envenomations, experts say the first priority is keeping the person alive. Send someone to call for medical help and start immediate CPR if they are unconscious. If the victim is conscious, douse the stung area liberally with vinegar for 30 seconds.

Vinegar can also reduce irritation from minor stings. It is best to seek medical care quickly in case any other symptoms develop over the next 40 minutes.

TAP WATER

Although it's deemed potable by the authorities, the Thais don't drink the tap water, and neither should you. Stick to bottled or filtered water during your stay.

Women's Health

- In 2016, the Zika virus was confirmed in Thailand, and two cases of birth defects related to the virus were reported. Check the International Association for Medical Assistance for Travellers (www.iamat.org) website for updates on the situation.
- Sanitary products are readily available in Thailand's urban areas.
- Certain brands or types of birth control may not be available – bring adequate supplies.
- Urinary-tract infections can be precipitated by dehydration or long bus journeys without toilet stops; bring suitable antibiotics for treatment.

Language

Thailand's official language is effectively the dialect spoken and written in central Thailand, which has successfully become the lingua franca of all Thai and non-Thai ethnic groups in the kingdom.

In Thai the meaning of a single syllable may be altered by means of different tones. In standard Thai there are five: low tone, mid tone, falling tone, high tone and rising tone. The range of all five tones is relative to each speaker's vocal range, so there is no fixed 'pitch' intrinsic to the language.

➡ **low tone** – 'Flat' like the mid tone, but pronounced at the relative bottom of one's vocal range. It is low, level and has no inflection, eg bàht (baht – the Thai currency).

➡ **mid tone** – Pronounced 'flat', at the relative middle of the speaker's vocal range, eg dee (good). No tone mark is used.

➡ **falling tone** – Starting high and falling sharply, this tone is similar to the change in pitch in English when you are emphasising a word, or calling someone's name from afar, eg mâi (no/not).

➡ **high tone** – Usually the most difficult for non-Thai speakers. It's pronounced near the relative top of the vocal range, as level as possible, eg máh (horse).

➡ **rising tone** – Starting low and gradually rising, sounds like the inflection used by English speakers to imply a question – 'Yes?', eg săhm (three).

WANT MORE?

For in-depth language information and handy phrases, check out Lonely Planet's *Thai Phrasebook*. You'll find it at **shop.lonelyplanet.com**, or you can buy Lonely Planet's iPhone phrasebooks at the Apple App Store.

The Thai government has instituted the Royal Thai General Transcription System (RTGS) as a standard method of writing Thai using the Roman alphabet. It's used in official documents, road signs and on maps. However, local variations crop up on signs, menus etc. Generally, names in this book follow the most common practice.

In our coloured pronunciation guides, the hyphens indicate syllable breaks within words, and some syllables are further divided with a dot to help you pronounce compound vowels, eg mêu·a-rai (when).

The vowel a is pronounced as in 'about', aa as the 'a' in 'bad', ah as the 'a' in 'father', ai as in 'aisle', air as in 'flair' (without the 'r'), eu as the 'er' in 'her' (without the 'r'), ew as in 'new' (with rounded lips), oh as the 'o' in 'toe', or as in 'torn' (without the 'r') and ow as in 'now'.

Most consonants correspond to their English counterparts. The exceptions are b̶ (a hard 'p' sound, almost like a 'b', eg in 'hip-bag'); đ (a hard 't' sound, like a sharp 'd', eg in 'mid-tone'); ng (as in 'singing'; in Thai it can occur at the start of a word) and r (as in 'run' but flapped; in everyday speech it's often pronounced like 'l').

BASICS

The social structure of Thai society demands different registers of speech depending on who you're talking to. To make things simple we've chosen the correct form of speech appropriate to the context of each phrase.

When being polite, the speaker ends his or her sentence with kráp (for men) or kâ (for women). It is the gender of the speaker that is being expressed here; it is also the common way to answer 'yes' to a question or show agreement.

The masculine and feminine forms of phrases in this chapter are indicated where relevant with 'm/f'.

Hello.	สวัสดี	sà-wàt-dee
Goodbye.	ลาก่อน	lah gòrn
Yes./No.	ใช่/ไม่	châi/mâi
Please.	ขอ	kŏr
Thank you.	ขอบคุณ	kòrp kun
You're welcome.	ยินดี	yin dee
Excuse me.	ขออภัย	kŏr à-pai
Sorry.	ขอโทษ	kŏr tôht

How are you?
สบายดีไหม — sà-bai dee măi

Fine. And you?
สบายดีครับ/ค่า แล้วคุณล่ะ — sà-bai dee kráp/kâ láa·ou kun lâ (m/f)

What's your name?
คุณชื่ออะไร — kun chêu à-rai

My name is ...
ผม/ดิฉันชื่อ... — pŏm/dì-chăn chêu ... (m/f)

Do you speak English?
คุณพูดภาษาอังกฤษได้ไหม — kun pôot pah-săh ang-grìt dâi măi

I don't understand.
ผม/ดิฉันไม่เข้าใจ — pŏm/dì-chăn mâi kôw jai (m/f)

ACCOMMODATION

Where's a ...?	... อยู่ที่ไหน	... yòo têe năi
campsite	ค่ายพักแรม	kâi pák raam
guesthouse	บ้านพัก	bâhn pák
hotel	โรงแรม	rohng raam
youth hostel	บ้านเยาวชน	bâhn yow-wá-chon

Do you have a ... room?	มีห้อง ... ไหม	mee hôrng ... măi
single	เดี่ยว	dèe·o
double	เตียงคู่	đee·ang kôo
twin	สองเตียง	sŏrng đee·ang

air-con	แอร์	aa
bathroom	ห้องน้ำ	hôrng nám
laundry	ห้องซักผ้า	hôrng sák pâh
mosquito net	มุ้ง	múng
window	หน้าต่าง	nâh đàhng

QUESTION WORDS

What?	อะไร	à-rai
When?	เมื่อไร	mêu·a-rai
Where?	ที่ไหน	têe năi
Who?	ใคร	krai
Why?	ทำไม	tam-mai

DIRECTIONS

Where's ...?
... อยู่ที่ไหน — ... yòo têe năi

What's the address?
ที่อยู่คืออะไร — têe yòo keu à-rai

Could you please write it down?
เขียนลงให้ได้ไหม — kĕe·an long hâi dâi măi

Can you show me (on the map)?
ให้ดู (ในแผนที่) ได้ไหม — hâi doo (nai păan têe) dâi măi

Turn left/right.
เลี้ยวซ้าย/ขวา — lée·o sái/kwăh

It's ...	อยู่ ...	yòo ...
behind	ที่หลัง	têe lăng
in front of	ตรงหน้า	đrong nâh
next to	ข้างๆ	kâhng kâhng
straight ahead	ตรงไป	đrong bai

EATING & DRINKING

I'd like (the menu), please.
ขอ (รายการอาหาร) หน่อย — kŏr (rai gahn ah-hăhn) nòy

What would you recommend?
คุณแนะนำอะไรบ้าง — kun náa-nam à-rai bâhng

That was delicious!
อร่อยมาก — à-ròy mâhk

Cheers!
ไชโย — chai-yoh

Please bring the bill.
ขอบิลหน่อย — kŏr bin nòy

I don't eat ...	ผม/ดิฉันไม่กิน ...	pŏm/dì-chăn mâi gin ... (m/f)
eggs	ไข่	kài
fish	ปลา	Ƀlah
red meat	เนื้อแดง	néu·a daang
nuts	ถั่ว	tòo·a

Key Words

bar	บาร์	bah
bottle	ขวด	kòo·at
bowl	ชาม	chahm
breakfast	อาหารเช้า	ah-hăhn chów
cafe	ร้านกาแฟ	ráhn gah-faa
chopsticks	ไม้ตะเกียบ	mái đà-gèe·ap
cold	เย็น	yen
cup	ถ้วย	tôo·ay
dessert	ของหวาน	kŏrng wăhn
dinner	อาหารเย็น	ah-hăhn yen
drink list	รายการ เครื่องดื่ม	rai gahn krêu·ang dèum
fork	ส้อม	sôrm
glass	แก้ว	gâa·ou
hot	ร้อน	rórn
knife	มีด	mêet
lunch	อาหาร กลางวัน	ah-hăhn glahng wan
market	ตลาด	đà-làht
menu	รายการ อาหาร	rai gahn ah-hăhn
plate	จาน	jahn
restaurant	ร้านอาหาร	ráhn ah-hăhn
spicy	เผ็ด	pèt
spoon	ช้อน	chórn
vegetarian (person)	คนกินเจ	kon gin jair

SIGNS

ทางเข้า	Entrance
ทางออก	Exit
เปิด	Open
ปิด	Closed
ที่ติดต่อสอบถาม	Information
ห้าม	Prohibited
ห้องสุขา	Toilets
ชาย	Men
หญิง	Women

with	มี	mee
without	ไม่มี	mâi mee

Meat & Fish

beef	เนื้อ	néu·a
chicken	ไก่	gài
crab	ปู	Ƀoo
duck	เป็ด	Ƀèt
fish	ปลา	Ƀlah
meat	เนื้อ	néu·a
pork	หมู	mŏo
seafood	อาหารทะเล	ah-hăhn tá-lair
squid	ปลาหมึก	Ƀlah mèuk

Fruit & Vegetables

banana	กล้วย	glôo·ay
beans	ถั่ว	tòo·a
coconut	มะพร้าว	má-prów
eggplant	มะเขือ	má-kĕu·a
fruit	ผลไม้	pŏn-lá-mái
guava	ฝรั่ง	fa-ràng
lime	มะนาว	má-now
mango	มะม่วง	má-môo·ang
mangosteen	มังคุด	mang-kút
mushrooms	เห็ด	hèt
nuts	ถั่ว	tòo·a
papaya	มะละกอ	má-lá-gor
potatoes	มันฝรั่ง	man fa-ràng
rambutan	เงาะ	ngó
tamarind	มะขาม	má-kăhm
tomatoes	มะเขือเทศ	má-kĕu·a têt
vegetables	ผัก	pàk
watermelon	แตงโม	đaang moh

Other

chilli	พริก	prík
egg	ไข่	kài
fish sauce	น้ำปลา	nám Ƀlah
ice	น้ำแข็ง	nám kăang

noodles	เส้น	sên
oil	น้ำมัน	nám man
pepper	พริกไทย	prík tai
rice	ข้าว	kôw
salad	ผักสด	pàk sòt
salt	เกลือ	gleu·a
soup	น้ำซุป	nám súp
soy sauce	น้ำซีอิ๊ว	nám see-éw
sugar	น้ำตาล	nám đahn
tofu	เต้าหู้	đôw hôo

Drinks

beer	เบียร์	bee·a
coffee	กาแฟ	gah-faa
milk	นมจืด	nom jèut
orange juice	น้ำส้ม	nám sôm
soy milk	น้ำเต้าหู้	nám đôw hôo
sugarcane juice	น้ำอ้อย	nám ôy
tea	ชา	chah
water	น้ำดื่ม	nám dèum

EMERGENCIES

Help!	ช่วยด้วย	chôo·ay dôo·ay
Go away!	ไปให้พ้น	ɓai hâi pón

Call a doctor!
เรียกหมอหน่อย　rêe·ak mŏr nòy

Call the police!
เรียกตำรวจหน่อย　rêe·ak đam·ròo·at nòy

I'm ill.
ผม/ดิฉันป่วย　pŏm/dì-chăn ɓòo·ay (m/f)

I'm lost.
ผม/ดิฉัน หลงทาง　pŏm/dì-chăn lŏng tahng (m/f)

Where are the toilets?
ห้องน้ำอยู่ที่ไหน　hôrng nám yòo têe năi

SHOPPING & SERVICES

I'd like to buy ...
อยากจะซื้อ ...　yàhk jà séu ...

I'm just looking.
ดูเฉย ๆ　doo chĕu·i chĕu·i

Can I look at it?
ขอดูได้ไหม　kŏr doo dâi măi

How much is it?
เท่าไร　tôw-rai

That's too expensive.
แพงไป　paang ɓai

Can you lower the price?
ลดราคาได้ไหม　lót rah-kah dâi măi

There's a mistake in the bill.
บิลใบนี้ผิด นะครับ/ค่ะ　bin bai née pìt ná kráp/kâ (m/f)

TIME & DATES

What time is it?
กี่โมงแล้ว　gèe mohng láa·ou

morning	เช้า	chów
afternoon	บ่าย	bài
evening	เย็น	yen
yesterday	เมื่อวาน	mêu·a wahn
today	วันนี้	wan née
tomorrow	พรุ่งนี้	prûng née

Monday	วันจันทร์	wan jan
Tuesday	วันอังคาร	wan ang-kahn
Wednesday	วันพุธ	wan pút
Thursday	วันพฤหัสฯ	wan pá-réu-hàt
Friday	วันศุกร	wan sùk
Saturday	วันเสาร์	wan sŏw
Sunday	วันอาทิตย์	wan ah-tít

TRANSPORT

Public Transport

bicycle rickshaw	สามล้อ	săhm lór
boat	เรือ	reu·a
bus	รถเมล์	rót mair
car	รถเก๋ง	rót gĕng
motorcycle	มอร์เตอร์ไซค์	mor-đeu-sai
taxi	รับจ้าง	ráp jâhng
plane	เครื่องบิน	krêu·ang bin
train	รถไฟ	rót fai
túk-túk	ตุ๊ก ๆ	đúk đúk

NUMBERS

1	หนึ่ง	nèung
2	สอง	sŏrng
3	สาม	săhm
4	สี่	sèe
5	ห้า	hâh
6	หก	hòk
7	เจ็ด	jèt
8	แปด	ɓàat
9	เก้า	gôw
10	สิบ	sìp
11	สิบเอ็ด	sìp-èt
20	ยี่สิบ	yêe-sìp
21	ยี่สิบเอ็ด	yêe-sìp-èt
30	สามสิบ	săhm-sìp
40	สี่สิบ	sèe-sìp
50	ห้าสิบ	hâh-sìp
60	หกสิบ	hòk-sìp
70	เจ็ดสิบ	jèt-sìp
80	แปดสิบ	ɓàat-sìp
90	เก้าสิบ	gôw-sìp
100	หนึ่งร้อย	nèung róy
1000	หนึ่งพัน	nèung pan
10,000	หนึ่งหมื่น	nèung mèun
100,000	หนึ่งแสน	nèung săan
1,000,000	หนึ่งล้าน	nèung láhn

When's the ... bus? รถเมล์คัน ... มาเมื่อไร rót mair kan ... mah mêu·a rai

first แรก râak

last สุดท้าย sùt tái

next ต่อไป đòr ɓai

A ... ticket, please. ขอตั๋ว ... kŏr đŏo·a ...

one-way เที่ยวเดียว têe·o dee·o

return ไปกลับ ɓai glàp

I'd like a/an ... seat. ต้องการที่นั่ง ... đôrng gahn têe nâng ...

aisle ติดทางเดิน đìt tahng deun

window ติดหน้าต่าง đìt nâh đàhng

platform ชานชาลา chan-chah-lah

ticket window ช่องขายตั๋ว chôrng kăi đŏo·a

timetable ตารางเวลา đah-rahng wair-lah

What time does it get to (Chiang Mai)?
ถึง (เชียงใหม่) กี่โมง tĕung (chee·ang mài) gèe mohng

Does it stop at (Saraburi)?
รถจอดที่ (สระบุรี) ไหม rót jòrt têe (sà-rà-bù-ree) măi

Please tell me when we get to (Chiang Mai).
เมื่อถึง (เชียงใหม่) กรุณาบอกด้วย mêu·a tĕung (chee·ang mài) gà-rú-nah bòrk dôo·ay

I'd like to get off at (Saraburi).
ขอลงที่(สระบุรี) kŏr long têe (sà-rà-bù-ree)

Driving & Cycling

I'd like to hire a ... อยากจะเช่า ... yàhk jà chôw ...

car รถเก๋ง rót gĕng

motorbike รถมอร์เตอร์ไซค์ rót mor-đeu-sai

I'd like ... ต้องการ ... đôrng gahn ...

my bicycle repaired ซ่อมรถจักรยาน sôrm rót jàk-gà-yahn

to hire a bicycle เช่ารถจักรยาน chôw rót jàk-gà-yahn

Is this the road to (Ban Bung Wai)?
ทางนี้ไป (บ้านบุ่งหวาย) ไหม tahng née ɓai (bâhn bùng wăi) măi

Where's a petrol station?
ปั๊มน้ำมันอยู่ที่ไหน ɓâm nám man yòo têe năi

Can I park here?
จอดที่นี่ได้ไหม jòrt têe née dâi măi

How long can I park here?
จอดที่นี่ได้นานเท่าไร jòrt têe née dâi nahn tôw-rai

I need a mechanic.
ต้องการช่างรถ đôrng gahn châhng rót

I have a flat tyre.
ยางแบน yahng baan

I've run out of petrol.
หมดน้ำมัน mòt nám man

Do I need a helmet?
ต้องใช้หมวกกันน็อกไหม đôrng chái mòo·ak gan nórk măi

GLOSSARY

ah·hăhn – food
ao/ow – bay or gulf

bâhn/ban – house or village
bòht – central sanctuary or chapel in a Thai temple
BTS – Bangkok Mass Transit System (Skytrain)

chedi – stupa; monument erected to house a Buddha relic
chow lair/chao leh/chow nám – sea gypsies

dhamma – right behaviour and truth according to Buddhist doctrine

fa·ràng – foreigner of European descent; guava

ga·teu·i/kathoey – 'ladyboy'; transvestites and transsexuals
gò – see *ko*

hàht/hat – beach
hôrng/hong – room or chamber; island caves semisubmerged in the sea

Isan/ìsăhn – general term for northeastern Thailand

jataka – stories of the Buddha's previous lives
jeen – Chinese

kathoey – see *ga·teu·i*
khao/kŏw – hill or mountain
klorng/klong/khlong – canal
ko/koh/gò – island
Khun – honorific used before first name

laem/lăam – geographical cape

masjid/mátsàyít – mosque
meu·ang/muang – city
moo·ay tai/muay·thai – Thai boxing
MRT – Metropolitan Rapid Transit (Metro); the underground railway in Bangkok

nám – water or juice
nám đòk – waterfall
nibbana – nirvana; the 'blowing out' or extinction of all desire and thus of all suffering
nóy/noi – small

ow – see *ao*

pak tai/Ѣàk đâi – southern Thailand
Pali – language derived from Sanskrit, in which the Buddhist scriptures are written
prá/phra – monk or Buddha image
prang/Ѣrang – Khmer-style tower on temples

Ѣàk đâi – southern Thailand
Ѣèe·pâht/pìi-phâat – classical Thai orchestra
Ѣrang – see *prang*

ráhn goh·Ѣêe – coffee shops (southern Thailand)
Ramakian – Thai version of India's epic literary piece, the Ramayana
reu·an tăa·ou – a longhouse
rót aa – blue-and-white air-conditioned bus
rót tam·má·dah – ordinary bus (no air-con) or ordinary train (not rapid or express)

săh·lah/sala – open-sided, covered meeting hall or resting place
săhm·lór – three-wheeled pedicab
sangha – brotherhood of Buddhist monks; temple inhabitants (monks and nuns)
sà·nùk – fun
soi – lane or small street
Songkran – Thai New Year, held in mid-April
sŏrng·tăa·ou – small pickup truck with two benches in the back, used as bus/taxi
SRT – State Railway of Thailand
stupa/chedi – domed edifice housing Buddhist relics
suttas – discourses of the Buddha

talat – see *đa·làht*
TAT – Tourism Authority of Thailand
tha/tâh – pier, landing
tâm/tham – cave
thànŏn – street, road, avenue (we use the abbreviation 'Th' in this book)
túk-túk – motorised *săhm·lór*

vipassana – Buddhist insight meditation

wâi – palms-together Thai greeting
wan prá – Buddhist holy days which coincide with the main phases of the moon (full, new and half) each month
wang – palace
wát – temple, monastery
wí·hăhn/wihan – counterpart to *bòht* in Thai temples, containing Buddha images but not circumscribed by sema stones

yài – big

Behind the Scenes

SEND US YOUR FEEDBACK

We love to hear from travellers – your comments keep us on our toes and help make our books better. Our well-travelled team reads every word on what you loved or loathed about this book. Although we cannot reply individually to your submissions, we always guarantee that your feedback goes straight to the appropriate authors, in time for the next edition. Each person who sends us information is thanked in the next edition – the most useful submissions are rewarded with a selection of digital PDF chapters.

Visit **lonelyplanet.com/contact** to submit your updates and suggestions or to ask for help. Our award-winning website also features inspirational travel stories, news and discussions.

Note: We may edit, reproduce and incorporate your comments in Lonely Planet products such as guidebooks, websites and digital products, so let us know if you don't want your comments reproduced or your name acknowledged. For a copy of our privacy policy visit lonelyplanet.com/privacy.

WRITER THANKS

Damian Harper

Huge thanks to the late Neil Bambridge, much gratitude for everything, may you rest in peace. Also thanks to Neil's wife Ratchi, to Maurice Senseit, the jolly staff at Nira's in Thong Sala, Piotr, Gemma, James Horton, George W, Celeste Brash and everyone else who helped along the way, in whatever fashion.

Tim Bewer

A hearty *kòrp jai lăi lăi dêu* to the perpetually friendly people of Isan who rarely failed to live up to their reputation for friendliness and hospitality when faced with my incessant questions, in particular Prapaporn Sompakdee (especially for her crispy pork expertise) and Julian Wright. Special thanks to my wife Suttawan for everything.

Austin Bush

A big thanks to Destination Editors Dora Ball and Clifton Wilkinson, as well as to all the people on the ground in Bangkok and northern Thailand.

David Eimer

Thanks to my fellow island writers and all the Lonely Planet crew in London. Thanks also to Alex and co for the nights out on Phuket. As ever, much gratitude to everyone I met on the road who passed on tips, whether knowingly or unwittingly.

Andy Symington

A great number of people, from taxi drivers to information officers, gave me excellent advice and help along the way; I'm very grateful to all of them. Specific thanks go to Siriporn Chiangpoon, Ian on Ko Chang, Maitri in Si Racha, Chayanan in Chanthaburi and the friendly Ang Sila volunteers.

ACKNOWLEDGEMENTS

Climate map data adapted from Peel MC, Finlayson BL & McMahon TA (2007) 'Updated World Map of the Köppen-Geiger Climate Classification', Hydrology and Earth System Sciences, 11, 163–344.

Illustrations pp68–9, pp74–5 by Michael Weldon.

Cover photograph: Railay, Krabi, IakovKalinin/Getty Images ©

THIS BOOK

This 11th edition of Lonely Planet's *Thailand's Islands & Beaches* guidebook was researched and written by Damian Harper, Tim Bewer, Austin Bush, David Eimer and Andy Symington. The previous edition was written by Mark Beales, Austin Bush, David Eimer, Damian Harper and Isabella Noble. This guidebook was produced by the following:

Destination Editors Dora Ball, Tanya Parker, Clifton Wilkinson

Product Editor Grace Dobell

Senior Product Editor Kate Chapman

Senior Cartographer Diana Von Holdt

Book Designer Wibowo Rusli

Assisting Editors Judith Bamber, Imogen Bannister, Peter Cruttenden, Melanie Dankel, Andrea Dobbin, Bruce Evans, Victoria Harrison, Jennifer Hattam, Gabrielle Innes, Lou McGregor, Rosie Nicholson, Susan Paterson, Tamara Sheward

Assisting Cartographers Anita Banh, Alison Lyall

Cover Researcher Naomi Parker

Thanks to Ross Taylor, Rachel Rawling, Kirsten Rawlings, Victoria Smith, Tracy Whitmey

Index

Map Pages **000**
Photo Pages 000

Map Pages **000**
Photo Pages **000**

Map Pages **000**
Photo Pages **000**

Map Legend

Sights

- Beach
- Bird Sanctuary
- Buddhist
- Castle/Palace
- Christian
- Confucian
- Hindu
- Islamic
- Jain
- Jewish
- Monument
- Museum/Gallery/Historic Building
- Ruin
- Shinto
- Sikh
- Taoist
- Winery/Vineyard
- Zoo/Wildlife Sanctuary
- Other Sight

Activities, Courses & Tours

- Bodysurfing
- Diving
- Canoeing/Kayaking
- Course/Tour
- Sento Hot Baths/Onsen
- Skiing
- Snorkelling
- Surfing
- Swimming/Pool
- Walking
- Windsurfing
- Other Activity

Sleeping

- Sleeping
- Camping
- Hut/Shelter

Eating

- Eating

Drinking & Nightlife

- Drinking & Nightlife
- Cafe

Entertainment

- Entertainment

Shopping

- Shopping

Information

- Bank
- Embassy/Consulate
- Hospital/Medical
- Internet
- Police
- Post Office
- Telephone
- Toilet
- Tourist Information
- Other Information

Geographic

- Beach
- Gate
- Hut/Shelter
- Lighthouse
- Lookout
- Mountain/Volcano
- Oasis
- Park
- Pass
- Picnic Area
- Waterfall

Population

- Capital (National)
- Capital (State/Province)
- City/Large Town
- Town/Village

Transport

- Airport
- Border crossing
- Bus
- Cable car/Funicular
- Cycling
- Ferry
- Metro/MRT/MTR station
- Monorail
- Parking
- Petrol station
- Skytrain/Subway station
- Taxi
- Train station/Railway
- Tram
- Underground station
- Other Transport

Routes

- Tollway
- Freeway
- Primary
- Secondary
- Tertiary
- Lane
- Unsealed road
- Road under construction
- Plaza/Mall
- Steps
- Tunnel
- Pedestrian overpass
- Walking Tour
- Walking Tour detour
- Path/Walking Trail

Boundaries

- International
- State/Province
- Disputed
- Regional/Suburb
- Marine Park
- Cliff
- Wall

Hydrography

- River, Creek
- Intermittent River
- Canal
- Water
- Dry/Salt/Intermittent Lake
- Reef

Areas

- Airport/Runway
- Beach/Desert
- Cemetery (Christian)
- Cemetery (Other)
- Glacier
- Mudflat
- Park/Forest
- Sight (Building)
- Sportsground
- Swamp/Mangrove

Note: Not all symbols displayed above appear on the maps in this book

OUR STORY

A beat-up old car, a few dollars in the pocket and a sense of adventure. In 1972 that's all Tony and Maureen Wheeler needed for the trip of a lifetime – across Europe and Asia overland to Australia. It took several months, and at the end – broke but inspired – they sat at their kitchen table writing and stapling together their first travel guide, *Across Asia on the Cheap*. Within a week they'd sold 1500 copies. Lonely Planet was born.

Today, Lonely Planet has offices in Franklin, London, Melbourne, Oakland, Dublin, Beijing and Delhi, with more than 600 staff and writers. We share Tony's belief that 'a great guidebook should do three things: inform, educate and amuse'.

OUR WRITERS

Damian Harper

Ko Samui & the Lower Gulf With two degrees (one in modern and classical Chinese from SOAS University of London), Damian has been writing for Lonely Planet for more than two decades, contributing to titles on places as diverse as China, Vietnam, Thailand, Ireland, London, Mallorca, Malaysia, Singapore, Brunei, Hong Kong and the UK. A seasoned guidebook writer, Damian has penned articles for numerous newspapers and magazines, including *The Guardian* and *The Daily Telegraph*.

Tim Bewer

Hua Hin & the Upper Gulf After briefly holding fort behind a desk as a legislative assistant, Tim decided he didn't have the ego to succeed in the political world (or the stomach to work around those who did). He quit his job at the capitol to backpack around West Africa, during which time he pondered what to do next. His answer was to write a travel guide to the parks, forests and wildlife areas of Wisconsin. He's been a freelance travel writer and photographer ever since.

Austin Bush

Bangkok Austin originally came to Thailand in 1999 as part of a language study program hosted by Chiang Mai University. The lure of city life, employment and spicy food eventually led him to Bangkok. City life, employment and spicy food have managed to keep him there ever since and he now works as a writer and photographer. Austin also contributed to the Plan, Understand and Survive sections of this book.

David Eimer

Phuket & the Andaman Coast David has been a journalist and writer ever since abandoning the idea of a law career in 1990. After spells working in his native London and in Los Angeles, he moved to Beijing in 2005, where he contributed to a variety of newspapers and magazines in the UK. Since then, he has travelled and lived across China and in numerous cities in Southeast Asia, including Bangkok, Phnom Penh and Yangon.

Andy Symington

Ko Chang & the Eastern Seaboard Andy has written or worked on more than a hundred books and other updates for Lonely Planet (especially in Europe and Latin America) and other publishing companies, and has published articles on numerous subjects for a variety of newspapers, magazines and websites. He part-owns and operates a rock bar, has written a novel and is currently working on several fiction and nonfiction writing projects.

Published by Lonely Planet Global Limited
CRN 554153
11th edition – Jul 2018
ISBN 978 1 78657 059 8

10 9 8 7 6 5 4 3 2 1
Printed in China